Risk Measures and Insurance Solvency Benchmarks

Chapman & Hall/CRC Financial Mathematics Series

Aims and scope:

The field of financial mathematics forms an ever-expanding slice of the financial sector. This series aims to capture new developments and summarize what is known over the whole spectrum of this field. It will include a broad range of textbooks, reference works and handbooks that are meant to appeal to both academics and practitioners. The inclusion of numerical code and concrete real-world examples is highly encouraged.

Series Editors
M.A.H. Dempster
Centre for Financial Research
Department of Pure Mathematics and Statistics
University of Cambridge

Dilip B. Madan
Robert H. Smith School of Business
University of Maryland

Rama Cont
Department of Mathematics
Imperial College

Handbook of Financial Risk Management
Thierry Roncalli

Optional Processes

Stochastic Calculus and Applications

Mohamed Abdelghani, Alexander Melnikov

Machine Learning for Factor Investing

Guillaume Coqueret and Tony Guida

Malliavin Calculus in Finance

Theory and Practice

Elisa Alos, David Garcia Lorite

Risk Measures and Insurance Solvency Benchmarks

Fixed-Probability Levels in Renewal Risk Models

Vsevolod K. Malinovskii

For more information about this series please visit: https://www.crcpress.com/Chapman-and-Hall CRC-Financial-Mathematics-Series/book-series/CHFINANCMTH

Risk Measures and Insurance Solvency Benchmarks

Fixed-Probability Levels in Renewal Risk Models

Vsevolod K. Malinovskii

CRC Press
Taylor & Francis Group
Boca Raton London New York

CRC Press is an imprint of the
Taylor & Francis Group, an **informa** business
A CHAPMAN & HALL BOOK

First edition published 2022
by CRC Press
6000 Broken Sound Parkway NW, Suite 300, Boca Raton, FL 33487-2742

and by CRC Press
2 Park Square, Milton Park, Abingdon, Oxon, OX14 4RN

CRC Press is an imprint of Taylor & Francis Group, LLC

Library of Congress Cataloging-in-Publication Data

Names: Malinovskii, Vsevolod K., author.
Title: Risk measures and insurance solvency benchmarks : fixed-probability levels in renewal risk models / Vsevolod K. Malinovskii.
Description: First edition. | Boca Raton : C&H\CRC Press, 2021. | Series: Chapman and Hall/CRC financial mathematics series | Includes bibliographical references and index.
Identifiers: LCCN 2021007695 (print) | LCCN 2021007696 (ebook) | ISBN 9780367740269 (hardback) | ISBN 9780367744021 (paperback) | ISBN 9781003157625 (ebook)
Subjects: LCSH: Risk (Insurance)--Mathematical models. | Risk assessment--Mathematical models.
Classification: LCC HG8054.5 .M36 2021 (print) | LCC HG8054.5 (ebook) | DDC 368/.01015118--dc23
LC record available at https://lccn.loc.gov/2021007695
LC ebook record available at https://lccn.loc.gov/2021007696

ISBN: 9780367740269 (hbk)
ISBN: 9780367744021 (pbk)
ISBN: 9781003157625 (ebk)

Typeset in CMR10 font
by KnowledgeWorks Global Ltd.

To my wife Larissa,
with love and respect.

Contents

Preface

There exists (or existed quite recently) a tendency to look at the insurance industry from an "options and derivatives" viewpoint (see, e.g., [28], [170]), treating an insurance policy as a financial instrument, thus embedding it into a financial environment. There exists also a tendency to use in insurance practice the Value-at-Risk[1] measure, which is simpler (and coarser) than many risk measures based on the probability of ruin. Nevertheless, it is believed by some academics (see, e.g., [9], p. ix) that the viewpoint of ruin theory, stemming from the desire to gain a deeper understanding of the insurance process, is not only important in itself, but can also be of a great benefit in the modern risk management.

First proposed in [13], in the early 1960s, for Markowitz's portfolio selection, Value-at-Risk has been recognized (see [142], [143], and particularly [14]) as an important method for measuring risk[2]. This technique (and its many modifications) has been pompously named (see, e.g., [92], p. 80) *fundamental principle* underlying risk measuring in finance and insurance, but essentially remained just finding a quantile of some properly chosen distribution.

This opposition of the Value-at-Risk and risk theory methods[3], accompanied by a sort of exaltation in favor of the former, and to the detriment of the latter, does not seem to be acceptable. Plainly, both of these methods are intended to answer the same question: how much capital does a company need to cover the risks in its portfolio, and in what time frame? These two methods are closely related to each other, which requires a detailed explanation based on advanced probabilistic analysis.

This book examines risk measures, showing their relationship with risk theory. From a practical point of view, we turn to a theoretical foundation of the capital requirements in Solvency II and Swiss Solvency Test regulatory systems. Referring to multi-year insurance business models introduced in [134],

[1]Throughout what follows, we use the term "Value-at-Risk" and the shorthand for it "VaR" introduced in [142] as a component of Risk-Metrics which is a set of tools that enable participants in the financial markets to estimate their exposure to market risk. In [56], the term "Capital-at-Risk" is used.

[2]In [39], it is argued that the Value-at-Risk (VaR) has become a mainstay of risk management in financial markets since its introduction by J.P. Morgan in [143].

[3]Quite a few papers on the links between ruin probabilities and risk measures exist, see, e.g., [32], [83], [185]. However, using the "Capital-at-Risk" has always been considered "a useful way to analyze the situation" regarding "the probability that the ultimate risk reserve will fall below a limit which can be described as the ruin barrier" (see [56], p. 16–17). The main impediment in using the concept of "ruin barrier" is technical complexity.

we focus on the annual solvency provisions of two kinds: non-loss and non-ruin capitals. Both of them can be seen as Value-at-Risk benchmarks, but with respect to different source risks. When selected as the initial capital in the annual risk reserve process, the former guarantees non-negativity of the capital at the end of the year, while the latter guarantees the absence of ruin during the year; in both cases this holds with a given confidence level.

Comparing these two benchmarks to each other, the non-loss capital is a lower bound to the non-ruin capital. The former is deficient to guarantee solvency, i.e., non-ruin, within a year: in most interesting cases, it severely underestimates the annual initial capital needed for this. But, looking at this issue from a different angle, the non-ruin capital is an implicit function[4], i.e., a solution to an equation, whose left-hand side is the finite-time probability of ruin and the right-hand side is a given risk tolerance level. Typically, this equation cannot be obtained in a closed form. At first glance, the search for non-ruin capital looks analytically insoluble and it seems impossible to use this theoretically adequate, but oversophisticated risk measure, whence its replacement with the non-loss capital, which is a handy, but pointless to guarantee non-ruin, benchmark.

Typically, risk measuring techniques, such as Value-at-Risk and its variants[5], while imperfect in the above sense, are viewed as a competitor (or even the opposite) of those coming from risk theory. This book aims to break this impasse. We argue the contrary: they are very similar to each other, with a key difference in choosing the source risks. Moreover, sophisticated risk measures, such as non-ruin capital, that naturally occur (see [134]) in dynamic insurance business models, can be viewed as quantile risk measures, conceptually not much different from the Value-at-Risk measure. We claim — rather unexpectedly — that the non-ruin capital, related to both risk theory and risk measuring in insurance and finance, is an issue well-balanced in terms of efficiency and simplicity; its structure is as handy as that of the apparently simpler non-loss capital. Seeking to demonstrate this, we examine the non-ruin capital as a solution to the mathematical inverse level-crossing problem for compound renewal processes, formulated in the book [135].

We will show that under very general conditions on the model there exist simple-looking analytical results for non-ruin capital; amazingly, they are as simple as the results for a seemingly less sophisticated non-loss capital. We will also show that the latter is naturally related to Gaussian distributions, while the former is naturally related to inverse Gaussian distributions.

In terms of practical implementation, which essentially boils down to using a fairly straightforward Monte Carlo simulation, calculating the non-ruin capital requires almost the same effort and resources as calculating non-loss capital and its variations. In essence, this fully agrees with the well-known

[4]Strictly speaking, much the same can be said for Value-at-Risk, but the equation by which it is determined is much simpler.

[5]Such as Tail Value-at-Risk or Expected shortfall methods.

idea that good simulation analysis differs from poor simulation analysis in that the former makes more correct choice about what to simulate.

This book consists of seven chapters and two appendices. Chapter 1 is an introduction to this book and a summary of the whole of its main results. The first two sections of Chapter 1 outline the economic background. This refers to the definition and main properties of quantile risk measures used in finance and portfolio management, to the concept of economic capital, and to the risk measures used in the Solvency II and Swiss Solvency Test insurance regulation systems. Since most analytical studies are often academic in nature, while the Monte Carlo simulation dominates in practice, we touch on the interdependence of these two methods in the first section of Chapter 1.

Regarding a right balance between the analytical methods and Monte Carlo simulation central in Chapters 6 and 7 of this book, it is worth noting the following. This issue was much discussed (see, e.g., [15], [56], [146]) since the beginning of the computer era in the 1980s, and the conclusion was that traditional analytical methods and simulation should under no circumstances be considered as competing techniques. The general rule (see [56], p. 154) is that one should strive for analytical solutions whenever possible, but resist the temptation to manipulate the premises of the model; a deliberate simplification (or even moronization) of the model in order to obtain analytical solutions is unacceptable. In fact, no simplifications are allowed if this leads to a violation of the applicability of the model in real-world conditions.

The third section of Chapter 1 is devoted to mathematical aspects of insurance risk theory and to its links to risk measurement techniques. It starts with the definition of a model of multi-year insurance business process introduced in [134], moves on to the annual probability mechanism of insurance, whose core is the risk reserve process in Lundberg's model, and proceeds with such concepts as the event of ruin, probability of ruin within finite time, and non-ruin capital. In this section, non-loss and non-ruin capitals are compared with each other in terms of their properties which are discovered through analytical study based on currently available methods of risk theory.

A description (in more detail than below in this Preface) of the readership for which this book is intended, as well as an outline of the rest of this book, conclude Chapter 1.

In the rest of the book, i.e., in Chapters 2–7, a rationale and more detailed presentation of what is stated in Chapter 1 are given. Chapters 2–6 differ from the final Chapter 7. These five chapters are an advanced mathematics of the same nature as [135], and we move from economic to mathematical terminology. This does not mislead the reader, who has mastered Chapter 1. Moreover, in a table we give a list of equivalent terms used for quantile risk measures, insurance solvency benchmarks, and solutions to the mathematical level-crossing problem. For example, non-ruin capital (a term used in insurance risk theory) is the same as Value-at-Risk based on sup-loss net of premium income taken as source risk (a term used in risk measuring), or fixed-probability level (a term used in inverse level-crossing problem).

In Chapter 2, addressing an auxiliary diffusion model, we trace a road map towards the goal of this book. We focus on a shifted diffusion process (which is a rough but handy model of the risk reserve process), on the time when it crosses for the first time a high horizontal level, and on the fixed-probability level (which is a mathematical counterpart of the non-ruin capital). In this auxiliary model, the equation that defines the fixed-probability level is available in a closed form. We examine the structure of the fixed-probability level and show that it differs when the shifted diffusion process is shifted so that it tends up and down. In the former case, we have quite satisfactory asymptotic results. In the latter case, we construct quite accurate upper bounds expressed in terms of elementary functions. They are suitable for numerical calculations.

In Chapter 3, we follow the road map of Chapter 2, dealing with a shifted renewal process with exponentially distributed intervals between renewals (which is a mathematical counterpart of inter-claim intervals) and exponentially distributed jump sizes at the moments of renewals (which is a mathematical counterpart of claim sizes). In this model, the non-linear equation that determines the fixed-probability level is available in closed form, as in Chapter 2, but is much more complicated. Its asymptotic analysis is possible, but requires much more analytical effort than in the diffusion model.

In Chapter 4, we turn to an auxiliary non-linear equation which comes from the inverse Gaussian approximation for the distribution of the first level-crossing time, studied in [135]. We focus on the implicit function defined by this equation and on its relation with the fixed-probability level. This analytical problem has an independent interest and is useful for constructing numerical procedures.

In Chapter 5, which is the core of this book, we deal with the shifted renewal process, when intervals between renewals and jump sizes at the moments of renewals are generally distributed. In this case, we follow the road map of Chapter 2 as much as possible in the situation when the equation that determines the fixed-probability level is not available in a closed form. In this situation, we rely on Kendall's identity and apply an extension of the analytical technique developed in [135]. Our study shows that the structure of the fixed-probability level differs when the shifted diffusion process tends up and down. In the former case, under very wide conditions on the model, we have quite satisfactory asymptotic results. In the latter case, we have to consider different classes of the model, which require different methods of analysis. We focus on simple-looking upper bounds and on some results suitable for constructing numerical procedures.

Chapter 6 contains a number of case studies and numerical illustrations for the fixed-probability level explored in Chapter 5. In this chapter, for the most typical distributions of intervals between renewals and jump sizes at the moments of renewals, we examine the accuracy of the analytical results of Chapters 3–5, comparing them with the Monte-Carlo simulation results.

The last Chapter 7 stands apart from Chapters 2–6, but is closely related to them. This is a re-visit (see [134], Chapters 4 and 5) of ERS-analysis[6] of an insurance risk model with migration. Returning to insurance risk terminology, we model the probability mechanism of insurance of a company operating in a competitive market, where a price competition generates migration of policyholders, and focus on the compound Poisson risk model with migration and with generally distributed claim sizes. Applying the new analytical results of Chapters 3–6, we carry out ERS-analysis in such a model.

In Appendices A and B, we collected some results from probability and analysis, which makes the exposition self-contained.

The bibliography contains 199 items.

Notations are assembled together in the "List of notations" section, given at the end of this book, but we bring a few matters now to the reader's attention. We always tried to avoid any, except minor, abuses of notation. We use the symbols, e.g., O-symbol, o-symbol, and $\sim$ asymptotic equivalence sign, standard (see, e.g., [30]) in the asymptotic analysis. In definitions and identities, as opposed to equations, we occasionally write $:=$ instead of $=$. We use the habitual symbols P and E for probability and expectation. We use the symbol D for variance; it may be less usual, at least for those who are accustomed to the symbol Var.

We assume that conventional notation such as "$T_i \overset{d}{=} T$" for "random variables T_i and T have the same distribution" is known to the reader; by $f(x)\,|_{x=a}^{b}$ we always denote $f(b) - f(a)$, whereas $f(x;z)\,|_{z=a}$ means $f(x;a)$. Throughout the text, K, K_1, K_2, etc., are always "sufficiently large" positive constants and ϵ, ϵ_1, ϵ_2, etc., are "sufficiently small" positive constants which may vary from formula to formula, but not in the same. We use abbreviations like "a.s." for "almost surely", "c.d.f." for "compound distribution function", "p.d.f." for "probability density function", "m.g.f." for "moment generating function", and "i.i.d." for "independent and identically distributed".

The formal prerequisite for this book is a good background in analysis. The desired prerequisite is a probability training, but a person with knowledge of the classical real-variable theory can freely read it. For those who find the proofs too complicated, it may be reassuring that most results of this book, summarized in Chapter 1, are formulated in rather elementary terms.

This book, at least some of its parts, can be a reading material for basic courses in risk measures, insurance mathematics, and applied probability. This was used by the author in his courses at several universities in Moscow, at the Copenhagen University, and at the University of Montréal.

This book is written for academics and practitioners who are concerned about potential weaknesses and flaws in the theoretical basis of acting regulatory systems. It is also addressed to those who are interested in pure and applied probability and, having a taste for classical and asymptotic analysis,

---

[6]This is an abbreviation for Expansion, Revenue, and Solvency analysis introduced in [125] and developed in [134].

are motivated to delve into rather intensive calculations. Readers who have both of these interests will benefit the most.

The author is grateful to many colleagues for their general advices or specific comments made with varying degrees of benevolence toward the author. Among the most valuable and most friendly are the comments by N.H. Bingham and M. Dacorogna, to whom particular thanks are due. The simulation reported in Chapters 6 and 7 was done by K.V. Malinovskii. The work on this book was partly supported by RFBR (grant No. 19-01-00045).

Vsevolod K. Malinovskii

Chapter 1

Risk Measures in Finance and Insurance

This chapter is an introduction to this book and a summary of its main results. We start with quantile risk measures in finance and portfolio management and proceed to the economic capital, which is a comprehensive concept put forth for predicting the strength of financial institutions. We touch on some aspects of the capital requirements of the Solvency II regulatory system, which are identified as Value-at-Risk at the 99.5% threshold. We argue that this can create confusions when choosing an adequate risk measure. To describe the essence of this concern, we turn to the non-ruin capital calculated on the basis of probability of ruin in Lundberg's collective risk model and focus on its difference from the non-loss capital calculated on the basis of year-end financial result, both of which are Value-at-Risk quantile measures.

1.1 Risk Measures in Finance and Portfolio Management

In insurance mathematics, the losses[1] of an insurer are modeled by the random variables with continuous distributions, with possibly a small number of jumps. In order to avoid inessential technical difficulties, in the further presentation we will consider only continuous[2] (without jumps) distributions of losses, denote by $0 < \alpha < 1$ a sufficiently small number, i.e., $\alpha = 0.05$ or $\alpha = 0.01$, and use the shorthand notation $A := 1 - \alpha$.

The following well-known definition (see, e.g., [99], § 32.2) is an integral part of the general theory of probability distributions (see, e.g., [94], [98], [103], [140], and [145]).

Definition 1.1 (Quantile of a continuous distribution) *Let ξ be a random variable with continuous distribution and $A \in (0, 1)$. A value of x, such*

[1]Incidentally, we note that by return (the opposite to loss), we always mean loss or expenditure with the opposite sign. In this book, to avoid confusion, we will always adhere to the loss basis.

[2]That is, we exclude discrete distributions of loss X and assume that X has a probability density function (p.d.f.) f_X, such that $F_X(x) = \int_{-\infty}^{x} f_X(z)\, dz$, $x \in \mathsf{R}$. Moreover, we often assume that p.d.f. f_X is bounded from above by a finite constant.

that

$$\mathsf{P}\{\xi \leqslant x\} = A, \tag{1.1}$$

denoted by x_A*, is called the* A*-quantile of the distribution of the random variable* ξ*, i.e., the value below which* $100\,A$ *per cent of the distribution lies.*

To put it in another way, the A-quantile x_A of the random variable ξ is the abscissa of the point where the graph of cumulative distribution function (c.d.f.) $F_\xi(x) := \mathsf{P}\{\xi \leqslant x\}$, $x \in \mathsf{R}$, crosses[3] the horizontal level A.

Definition 1.2 (A conditional average) *Let* ξ *be a random variable with continuous distribution, whose c.d.f. is* F_ξ *and probability density function (p.d.f.) is* f_ξ*, and* $A \in (0,1)$*. For* A*-quantile* x_A*, the average of the random variable* ξ *conditional on that* ξ *exceeds* x_A*, i.e.,*

$$\mathsf{E}(\xi \mid \xi \geqslant x_A) = \frac{1}{1-A} \int_{F_\xi^{-1}(A)}^{\infty} z\, f_\xi(z)\, dz, \tag{1.2}$$

is referred to as conditional average.

Both the A-quantile x_A defined as a solution to (1.1) and the conditional average (1.2) are numerical characteristics of the distribution of the random variable ξ. One can argue about the relative complexity of their calculating, noting that x_A is usually given by a non-linear equation. Anyway, to calculate (1.2), one has to start with x_A.

1.1.1 Value-at-Risk quantile method and related notions

Let us consider some fund, or portfolio of risky assets, and set a fixed time horizon t. By $\mathcal{X}_t$, we denote the random value of loss on this portfolio at time t. By $F_{\mathcal{X}_t}(x) := \mathsf{P}\{\mathcal{X}_t \leqslant x\}$, we denote c.d.f. of this random variable. We call the Value-at-Risk of this portfolio at the confidence level $A \in (0,1)$ the number $x_{A,t}$ which is a solution to the equation

$$\mathsf{P}\{\mathcal{X}_t \leqslant x\} = A \tag{1.3}$$

with respect to (w.r.t.) x.

In probabilistic terms, the Value-at-Risk at the confidence level A, when $\mathcal{X}_t$ is the random value of loss at time t, is A-quantile of the distribution $F_{\mathcal{X}_t}(x)$. Bearing in mind the simplicity of this definition, it seems unclear why it has become (see, e.g., [67], p. 26) "an overarching technique for measuring risks", but it has become. Typical values for the confidence level $A \in (0,1)$ in the right-hand side of (1.3) are 0.95, whence $\alpha = 0.05$, or 0.99, whence $\alpha = 0.01$. In the market risk management, the time[4] horizon t is usually 1 or 10 days,

[3]Since the distribution of ξ is continuous, the function $F_\xi(x)$ is strictly monotone increasing, as x increases.

[4]In finance, calendar time is usually considered. In insurance applications, it is common to move on to operational time, which will be defined below.

in credit risk management and operational risk management t is usually one year.

Components of the Value-at-Risk method. The Value-at-Risk method is often referred to as the quantile method of measuring risks. However, in comparison with finding a quantile in the theory of distributions, this method, due to its origin and field of application, has some peculiarities. In contrast to the problem of finding a quantile in the theory of distributions, which requires nothing more than the random variable ξ and the real number $A \in (0, 1)$, the components of the problem of finding Value-at-Risk are:

- the source risk $\mathcal{X}_t$, which is a t-time component of the random process $\mathcal{X}_s$, $s \geqslant 0$,
- the holding period, which starts at zero and ends at time t,
- the confidence level A.

From the standpoint of economics, the correct formulation of the risk measuring problem, using the Value-at-Risk method, looks like this[5]: calculate

the Value-at-Risk of a risky portfolio to a confidence level of 99.5% over a 1-year period.

Thus, in order to specify the random variable for which the quantile is calculated, it is necessary, first, to specify what is meant by the quantitative characteristic of a risky portfolio over time and, secondly, what is the holding period. Usually, the former is the random variable $\mathcal{X}_t$, where $\mathcal{X}_s$, $s \geqslant 0$, is a random process, and the latter is the time interval ranging from zero to $t > 0$. Besides, it is necessary to define the confidence level properly.

For setting the problem correctly, paramount is the choice of the source risk $\mathcal{X}_t$ which models the loss that may arise for a given portfolio over time, up to the time t. This time t is often selected as the end of a financial year, or other accounting period. Figuratively speaking, the losses over time, up to the time t, is an iceberg, whose visible top is the loss at time t, for which we are striving to calculate a quantile.

Considering the definition of Value-at-Risk of a portfolio formally, it relies (see (1.3)) on the single random variable $\mathcal{X}_t$ that describes the state of this portfolio at the fixed time point t. But for a portfolio which develops over time, this definition implies the dynamics of the portfolio during the time interval ranging from zero to t. This time interval is usually an accounting year or another similar time period.

[5]In [142], Value-at-Risk is defined as follows: this is a measure of the maximum potential change in value of a portfolio of financial instruments with a given probability over a pre-set horizon.

Four steps of the Value-at-Risk methodology. The Value-at-Risk methodology[6] has (see [39], p. 31) four steps, as follows:

- to specify the time horizon over which a potential loss is estimated by the decision-maker,
- to select the risk tolerance level, which is the confidence level set to calculate the Value-at-Risk benchmark,
- to devise a probability distribution of likely losses for the financial instrument or portfolio under consideration,
- to calculate the Value-at-Risk benchmark.

In the first step, depending on economic particulars, time horizons of 1 day to 1 year are used. For instance, bank front-office traders are often interested in calculating the amount which they might lose in a 1-day period or 10-days period. Regulators and participants in illiquid markets may want to estimate exposures to market risk over a longer period. Insurance companies are focussed on an accounting period; in normal situation, this is one year. The same period is usually chosen by supervisors and regulators.

In the second step, the risk tolerance level is selected depending on the risk appetite of the institution in question and the purpose of the study. In particular, for a bank, the 95% confidence level may be sufficient, which means focussing on the largest probable loss that will be suffered 95 times out of 100, or on 1 day out of 20. In certain regulatory requirements, a 99% confidence level is required. Shareholders are often interested in potential losses arising from catastrophic events, such as a stock market crash, so a 99% confidence level[7] is also appropriate for them.

In the third step, several methods can be used. The simplest of them is to highlight the latest historical losses for an asset or portfolio; this is often associated with a Gaussian (or normal) distribution. Besides this one, many other distributions can be selected by means of expert judgments, modeling, or even ad hoc. Just as in the general theory of probability distributions used in mathematical statistics, this is advisable to set an inventory of standard distributions, especially skewed ones. For a portfolio consisting of several assets, the correlation between them can be very important for a correct selection of their characteristics.

From the angle of mathematics, the fourth step, i.e., calculating the Value-at-Risk benchmark, inevitably involves solving a non-linear equation or, in other words, finding an implicitly defined function. This, depending on the requirements for the solution, can be done analytically or numerically.

The Gaussian distribution and Value-at-Risk. It may be seen (see, e.g., [39], p. 24) that, to evaluate losses over a specified time period for a

[6] According to [142], i.e., RiskMetrics, the Value-at-Risk method is merely a tool in "a set of methodologies and data for measuring market risk".

[7] In the case of Solvency II, the level is 99.5%.

portfolio of assets, the Gaussian curve is used in various Value-at-Risk techniques. Moreover, the natural assumption in various Value-at-Risk techniques is (see [67], p. 27) that the price changes over time follow a Gaussian probability distribution[8], or another distribution tightly related to the Gaussian distribution.

Here and in what follows, we denote p.d.f and c.d.f. of a standard Gaussian distribution by

$$\varphi_{(0,1)}(x) := \frac{1}{\sqrt{2\pi}} e^{-\frac{x^2}{2}}, \quad x \in \mathsf{R},$$
$$\Phi_{(0,1)}(x) := \int_{-\infty}^{x} \varphi_{(0,1)}(z)\, dz, \quad x \in \mathsf{R},$$

respectively, and by $\kappa_\gamma := \Phi^{-1}_{(0,1)}(1-\gamma)$ we denote the $(1-\gamma)$-quantile of a standard Gaussian distribution. Plainly, $0 < \kappa_\gamma < \kappa_{\gamma/2}$, when $0 < \gamma < 1/2$. If γ increases from 0 to 1/2, i.e., if $1-\gamma$ decreases from 1 to 1/2, then κ_γ monotone decreases from $+\infty$ to 0. For symmetry reasons, we have $\kappa_\gamma = -\kappa_{1-\gamma}$, whence $\kappa_{1/2} = 0$.

When the random value $\mathcal{X}_t$ of loss at time t has a Gaussian distribution with mean μ and variance σ^2, whose c.d.f. is

$$\Phi_{(\mu,\sigma^2)}(x) = \Phi_{(0,1)}\left(\frac{x-\mu}{\sigma}\right), \quad x \in \mathsf{R},$$

equation (1.3) can be rewritten as

$$\Phi_{(0,1)}\left(\frac{x-\mu}{\sigma}\right) = A.$$

This equation is easy to solve. Its solution, which is the Value-at-Risk of $\mathcal{X}_t$ over a holding period of length t with a confidence level A, is

$$\begin{aligned} x_{A,t} &= \mu + \sigma\, \Phi^{-1}_{(0,1)}(A) \\ &= \mu + \sigma\, \kappa_\alpha. \end{aligned} \tag{1.4}$$

Regarding this expression, everything is clear: c.d.f. of the standard Gaussian distribution is well-studied and the quantiles are tabulated.

When the choice of the Gaussian distribution for $\mathcal{X}_t$ agrees with the economic sense of the problem in question, (1.4) yields the Value-at-Risk in a closed form. When $\mathcal{X}_t$ is non-Gaussian, there are (see, e.g., [89]) great difficulties in analytical assessment of the Value-at-Risk. In practical applications, as a rule, it is difficult even to correctly select the distribution function of the considered risk, using a method other than Monte Carlo simulation.

---

[8]According to [39], p. 96, "the standard assumption made by most Value-at-Risk models is that returns (prices) are normally distributed". Plainly, the same holds for the losses.

Skewed and fat-tail distributions and Value-at-Risk. The normality assumption greatly simplifies Step 4, i.e., calculating the Value-at-Risk benchmark, of the Value-at-Risk methodology. But it often disagrees with the requirements of Step 3.

Despite the heuristic assumption that markets assume a Gaussian distribution of assets, equities, and bond prices, it is known (see, e.g., [39], p. 24) that the distributions of these prices are more skewed. Furthermore, in practice, the asset prices show the so-called "leptokurtosis", also known as[9] "fat tails" (or "heavy tails"), which makes the Gaussian distribution assumption groundless (see, e.g., [89]). A visible manifestation of this flaw is that extreme price movements, such as stock market corrections, occur more frequently than it would be in accordance with the Gaussian distribution.

As for skewed distributions, they arise in financial time series when negative values are noticeably less in the absolute value than positive values, or when negative values (see example below) do not appear at all. In this case, skewed distributions (see, e.g., [103]), such as Pareto or log-normal, come to the fore. In particular, the choice of a log-normal distribution is natural when the logarithm of the loss values is used instead of the loss values themselves; taking logarithm completely eliminates negative values.

Let us consider an example of a skewed fat-tail distribution concentrated on the positive half-line. This distribution may appear in modeling a risky portfolio of a reinsurance undertaking[10]. We assume that the holding period is of length t, the confidence level is A, and $\mathcal{X}_t$ has a Pareto distribution

$$\mathsf{P}\{\mathcal{X}_t \leqslant x\} = 1 - \frac{1}{1+x}, \qquad x \geqslant 0.$$

In this case, the Value-at-Risk has even a simpler form than in (1.4): equation (1.3) can be rewritten as $(1 + x_{A,t})^{-1} = 1 - A$, whence $x_{A,t} = A(1-A)^{-1}$. For more examples of Value-at-Risk expressions for fat-tail and skewed distributions, see, e.g., [103].

Value-at-Risk in a diffusion model. Let us consider a fund or portfolio of risky assets, whose loss net of premium income is modeled over time by the random process $V_s - cs$, $s \geqslant 0$. Here loss is modeled by the diffusion process[11] $V_s = \vartheta s + \sigma \mathsf{W}_s$, $s \geqslant 0$, premium income is modeled by cs, $s \geqslant 0$, and parameters c, ϑ, σ are positive.

The corresponding Value-at-Risk at time t with the confidence level A, commonly chosen sufficiently large, e.g., 0.95, or 0.99, is a solution to the equation (w.r.t. x)

$$\mathsf{P}\{(\vartheta t + \sigma \mathsf{W}_t) - ct \leqslant x\} = A. \tag{1.5}$$

[9] Recall that the right tail of c.d.f. $F(x)$, $x \in \mathsf{R}$, is $1 - F(x)$, $x > 0$, whereas the left tail is $F(-x)$, $x > 0$. In both cases, large x are focussed.

[10] Large claims in reinsurance arise more often than in direct insurance, whence the greater attention to distributions with a fat tail.

[11] By W_s, $s \geqslant 0$, we denote a standard Wiener process.

When looking at this fund or portfolio of risky assets from a different angle, the loss net of premium income can be modeled over time by means of another random process, or another performance measure, namely $\sup_{0\leqslant r\leqslant s}(V_r - cr) = \sup_{0\leqslant r\leqslant s}((\vartheta r + \sigma \mathsf{W}_r) - cr)$, $s \geqslant 0$, referred to as "sup-loss net of premium income". The corresponding Value-at-Risk at time t with the confidence level A is a solution to the equation (w.r.t. x)

$$\mathsf{P}\Big\{ \sup_{0\leqslant s\leqslant t} ((\vartheta\, s + \sigma\, \mathsf{W}_s) - c\, s) \leqslant x \Big\} = A. \tag{1.6}$$

Denoting the solution of (1.5) by $\underline{x}_{A,t}$ and the solution of (1.6) by $x_{A,t}$, we have measured the Value-at-Risk at time t, and with the confidence level A, but with two different source risks, in two different ways. It is easy to see from (1.5) and (1.6) that $\underline{x}_{A,t} \leqslant x_{A,t}$ for any c, ϑ, and σ positive.

This example, which will be analyzed in more detail in Chapter 2, shows that Value-at-Risk is a set of risk measures lumped together, rather than a unique risk measure; for the same portfolio of risky assets many Value-at-Risk measures, with different source risks, may be introduced. In Chapter 2, we will show that (1.5) is naturally associated with a Gaussian distribution, whereas (1.6) is naturally associated with an inverse Gaussian distribution.

Coherent and non-coherent risk measures. Coherence of a risk measure M means the following: when losses are altered or combined, which is often done when a portfolio of several assets is considered, the risk measure M behaves similarly.

To give a formal definition, by $\mathcal{X}_t$ and $\mathcal{Y}_t$ we denote source risks representing random losses at time t, related to two different portfolios, and set $\mathcal{S}_t = \mathcal{X}_t + \mathcal{Y}_t$. By $M(\mathcal{X}_t)$, $M(\mathcal{Y}_t)$, and $M(\mathcal{S}_t)$ we denote the respective Value-at-Risk expressions. The risk measure M is coherent, if for all $\mathcal{X}_t$, $\mathcal{Y}_t$ the following properties hold:

- monotonicity: if[12] $\mathcal{X}_t \preccurlyeq \mathcal{Y}_t$, then $M(\mathcal{X}_t) \leqslant M(\mathcal{Y}_t)$,
- sub-additivity: $M(\mathcal{X}_t + \mathcal{Y}_t) \leqslant M(\mathcal{X}_t) + M(\mathcal{Y}_t)$,
- positive homogeneity: $M(k\,\mathcal{X}_t) = kM(\mathcal{X}_t)$, where k is a constant,
- translational invariance: $M(\mathcal{X}_t + k) = M(\mathcal{X}_t) + k$, where k is a constant.

In words, monotonicity means that a risk measure should increase, if the potential losses increase. Sub-additivity means that a combining of two risks cannot create any additional risk; on the contrary, according to a coherent measure, the total amount of risk may decrease due to the effects of diversification. Positive homogeneity implies that, if a risk is scaled by some factor k, then the risk measure increases by the same factor. Finally, translational invariance means that, if the risk of loss is reduced by a fixed amount, then the risk measure decreases by the same amount.

[12]The notation $\mathcal{X}_t \preccurlyeq \mathcal{Y}_t$ for the random variables $\mathcal{X}_t$ and $\mathcal{Y}_t$ means that in a certain sense $\mathcal{X}_t$ is less than or equal to $\mathcal{Y}_t$. Typically, this means that $\mathsf{P}\{\mathcal{X}_t \leqslant \mathcal{Y}_t\} = 1$.

A theoretical problem with the Value-at-Risk method is (see, e.g., [6]) that it typically[13] does not constitute a coherent risk measure, for it is not sub-additive. This means that the Value-at-Risk corresponding to an aggregate of a number of portfolios is not necessarily less than or equal to the sum of the Value-at-Risk summands, each of them corresponding to the individual portfolio within this aggregate. As a result, it is not appropriate to determine the Value-at-Risk for an organization by aggregating the Values-at-Risk for the organization's constituent departments.

1.1.2 Tail Value-at-Risk and expected shortfall

Whereas the Value-at-Risk methodology is central[14] in the Solvency II regulatory system, the Swiss Solvency Test regulatory system deals with the Tail Value-at-Risk. This measure, in several versions, has been proposed (see, e.g., [2]) as a remedy for the shortcomings of Value-at-Risk, which, generally speaking, is not a coherent risk measure.

The risk measure called Tail Value-at-Risk, or Tail Conditional Expectation, is related to the conditional average defined in (1.2) in the same way as the Value-at-Risk is related to the quantile defined in (1.1). This coherent[15] risk measure was introduced in [6]. Given the random variable $\mathcal{X}_t$ of loss at time t, whose distribution is continuous, and the confidence level A, which yield the Value-at-Risk $x_{A,t}$, the Tail Value-at-Risk is defined as

$$\mathsf{E}(\mathcal{X}_t \mid \mathcal{X}_t \geqslant x_{A,t}).$$

Since $\mathsf{E}(\mathcal{X}_t \mid \mathcal{X}_t \geqslant x_{A,t}) \geqslant x_{A,t}$, this is a majorant of the Value-at-Risk $x_{A,t}$.

If the random value $\mathcal{X}_t$ of loss at time t has a Gaussian distribution with mean μ and variance σ^2, whence[16] (see (1.4)) $x_{A,t} = \mu + \sigma\,\kappa_\alpha$, the Tail Value-at-Risk is given as

$$\mu + \sigma\,\frac{\varphi_{(0,1)}(\kappa_\alpha)}{1-A}$$

by elementary calculations.

Other terms (see [67], p. 29) for the Tail Value-at-Risk are expected policyholder's deficit (EPD), or expected shortfall (ES). An alternative definition of expected shortfall, given in [182], is $(1-A)\,\mathsf{E}(\mathcal{X}_t \mid \mathcal{X}_t \geqslant x_{A,t})$. If the distribution of $\mathcal{X}_t$ is assumed to be Gaussian, then this is equal to $(1-A)\,\mu + \sigma\,\varphi_{(0,1)}(\kappa_\alpha)$.

As it has been already said, the Tail Value-at-Risk measure, unlike the Value-at-Risk measure, is coherent. This means that it has a number of properties, i.e., monotonicity, sub-additivity, positive homogeneity, and translational

---

[13] The case of a Gaussian distribution stands alone: Value-at-Risk is coherent for Gaussian distributions. This is not the case for fat-tail distributions.

[14] See Section 1.2.

[15] In [2], the coherence property of this risk measure is considered, including details in its definition when the underlying distribution of losses has discontinuities.

[16] Recall that κ_α equals $\Phi^{-1}_{(0,1)}(1-\alpha)$, or $\Phi^{-1}_{(0,1)}(A)$.

invariance, that are attractive and desirable. Foremost, if the Tail Value-at-Risk is calculated for a number of lines of business within a company, the results can be aggregated to give an overall Tail Value-at-Risk for the company. On the one hand, when Tail Value-at-Risk measure is used, skewed distributions do not cause any implausible results. On the other hand, the capital requirement evaluated on the base of the Tail Value-at-Risk, which is a majorant of the Value-at-Risk, is higher than the capital requirement evaluated on the base of the Values-at-Risk technique, for the same threshold[17].

There are following rationales for and against Tail Value-at-Risk. Although this is a coherent risk measure, whereas the Value-at-Risk is (typically) not, there are voices in favor of the latter and to the detriment of the former, as well as vice versa. For example, it is argued in [54] that the Value-at-Risk, yielding more accurate risk forecasts, is superior to the Tail Value-at-Risk. In [2], the contrary is stated. In [17], it is emphasized that the Value-at-Risk is intrinsically pro-cyclical. In [75], a comparison of standard risk measures from the angle of practice, in terms of risk management and model validation, is made with conclusions in favor of Tail Value-at-Risk.

In this book, we focus on the analytical study of risk measures, such as commonly used Value-at-Risk and Tail Value-at-Risk, as well as their further defined less commonly used competitors. Looking at them from a mathematical angle, we see their common drawback: for all of them, the analytical study is fraught with substantial difficulties in almost all cases named in [89] "non-Gaussian finance". For this reason, in the practical application of these measures, when it is difficult even to find the distribution function of the considered risk, analytical calculations are almost never used; they are replaced by numerical calculations, such as Monte Carlo simulation.

1.1.3 Value-at-Risk and its variants: boon or bane?

There are clear arguments in favor of the Value-at-Risk measure and its many variations, including Tail Value-at-Risk. They are as follows:

- such risk measures, operating with numbers, assume monetary units,
- such risk measures can be used to compare profitability and risk of different units, different types of assets (stocks, bonds, currencies, derivatives, or any other assets with price), and different portfolios;
- when a portfolio consists of several assets, such risk measures can be altered or combined with more or less success, depending on coherence or non-coherence,
- such risk measures are based on an easy-to-understand methodology,
- such risk measures are often available in financial software, and this is used by everybody.

[17]That is why Basel IV wants to use instead 97.5% for the Tail Value-at-Risk.

The following commonly pronounced arguments are against risk measures, such as Value-at-Risk and its variants:

- such risk measures do not measure the worst-case loss[18]; this creates a false sense of security,
- such risk measures may involve cumbersome calculations for large portfolios, when the correlations between individual assets matter,
- different methods lead to different results for the same portfolio,
- the measurement results are as good as the data and assumptions underlying the financial issue under consideration.

It might seem that the methods, such as Value-at-Risk and its variants, are a versatile tool that only needs to be supplemented with other methods to become ideal. However, many experts[19] disagree with that.

To begin with, the last of the above arguments against the Value-at-Risk measure and its variants seems to be crucial: within a perfectly designed model, this would be a wonderful tool, but there are no such models in practice. Therefore, the incorrectness of all models where the risk measures are used is larger than the incorrectness of these measures themselves. Furthermore, when numerical benchmarks, no matter which ones[20], are used instead of the risk in terms of probability distributions, this seems like a refusal of a probabilistic description in favor of a deterministic description[21], and this can do harm. Despite this philosophy[22], deterministic benchmarks are welcomed by practice and, therefore, inevitable. But the benefit or harm of their use depends on many particulars, e.g., on the relevance of risk measures.

There are objections rooted into the basics of management, e.g., that "banks have the ingrained habit of plunging headlong into mistakes together where blame-minimizing managers appear to feel comfortable making blunders so long as their competitors are making the same ones", or that "the Value-at-Risk is the alibi bankers will give shareholders (and the bailing-out taxpayer) to show documented due diligence and will express that their blow-up came from truly unforeseeable circumstances and events with low probability — not from taking large risks they did not understand", but we leave this aside from our analysis.

---

[18]The worst-case loss may be either slightly higher than the Value-at-Risk, or high enough to trigger bankruptcy.

[19]See, e.g., discussion of Philippe Jorion and Nassim Taleb; the radical conclusion of the latter is "to suspend the current version of the Value-at-Risk as potentially dangerous malpractice and unseasonned quantitative method."

[20]The simplest of them are mean and variance.

[21]To set an example, the probabilities of ruin in the risk theory is a kind of probabilistic description.

[22]Prudent scholars have consistently warned that the mathematical aspects of risk cannot be summarized into one number, e.g., by putting forth as the title the statements like (see [156]) "a single number can't hedge against economic catastrophes", or (see [16], Chapter 7) "it's dangerous to think of risk as a number".

We conclude that the Value-at-Risk calculations should be only a deliberate step in the risk management process; it must be complemented with using other tools, based on more comprehensive modeling, especially with taking care of the worst cases, which Value-at-Risk virtually ignores.

1.1.4 Economic capital: a comprehensive concept

Economic capital (see, e.g., [118], Section 1.4.3, or [182], Chapter 18) is the capital that a financial institution needs[23] to reduce the probability of insolvency to a given level, over a given time horizon. It is calculated using a dynamic internal capital model designed to predict the future financial position of the financial institution. Then, using the selected risk measure, calculated is the level of capital required to start a business in the year in question, as the risk tolerance level and time horizon are specified.

Dynamic internal capital model. Economic capital is so called because it measures risk in terms of economic realities, rather than accounting rules or regulatory requirements. To calculate it prudently for a long period, a multi-year model is needed that takes into account the interests of various participants in the insurance market and the dynamics of this market itself, where underwriting cycles are often observed. In [134], the structure and methods of building such a multi-year model, including modeling management strategies which take into account not only the strategic goals of the company, but also the basic market conditions, such as falling and raising soft market, falling and raising hard market, etc., are discussed.

The ultimate question that naturally arises is: how much capital the company needs to cover the risks in its portfolio, and within which time horizon. Therefore, rationally selected annual solvency provisions are a prerequisite for any acceptable control; they constitute an integral part of any prudent management. Maintaining solvency, especially in the long run, is more than just calculating the probability of ruin, Value-at-Risk, or using other measures of risk, although the latter may be important.

In practice, calculating economic capital is a comprehensive issue. Since financial institutions are made up of many departments and manage the capital that shareholders invest in these institutions to achieve institutional solvency and profitability, this involves a combination of different risks. Hence, this requires a careful selection of both internal capital model and risk measures.

Economic capital on a break-up basis. One approach to maintaining insurer's solvency (see, e.g., [15], p. 10) is to ensure that, at the end of each

[23]The economic capital, also called (see [52]) the available capital on the company's balance sheet, is the capital you need; the physical capital is the capital you have. Most corporate financial decisions are based on their comparison. The economic capital is often compared to the minimum capital required by the company to cover the risks in a portfolio, called "risk-adjusted capital".

accounting year, assets are at least equal to the total liabilities, possibly increased by some legally established margin. This requirement implies that insurance business ceases permanently at the end of the accounting year. Financial obligations, such as those due to outstanding claims, must be cleared up during a liquidation process at the end of the year in question, whence the term "break-up basis"[24].

In other words, the core of this annual economic capital model is the risk reserve process, selected as the internal capital model, which is the difference between incoming premiums and outgoing claims plus provisions at the beginning of the year; this process is viewed at time t, which is the end of the year in question.

With this approach, it is natural to use the Value-at-Risk measure, or similar risk measures: the source risk is generated by the internal capital model, the time horizon is t, and the confidence level is, e.g., 95%. The problem is to evaluate these issues and to find a minimum solvency margin; this adequately guarantees the fulfillment of the obligations of the insurer.

Economic capital on a going concern basis. An alternative approach to insurer's solvency (see, e.g., [15], p. 10) is to assume that the business will go on. Then, in addition to the risks involved with the break-up situation described above, it is necessary to counteract the risks throughout the year.

By definition, using "going concern" basis[25] entails more stringent requirements than using "break-up" basis. Consequently, using the former leads to demands for a greater solvency margin and safety loading, than does using the latter. This, of course, assumes that the fundamental principles are held on both going concern basis and break-up basis. It may be noted that, if something is calculated on the break-up basis, there may be incompatibility with the same on the going-concern basis.

With this approach, instead of the Value-at-Risk measure, it is natural to use the probability of ruin[26]: the source risk is generated by the annual economic capital model, the time horizon is $t > 0$, and the confidence level is clearly defined. The problem is to evaluate these issues and to find a minimum solvency margin in a way which still gives an adequate guarantee for the fulfilment of the commitments of the insurer throughout the whole year, rather than at the year-end t.

Minimum annual solvency requirements. The approach that is most justified and most comprehensive, is to consider the probability of ruin based

[24]In accounting, a valuation basis which assumes that the writing of new business ceases is known as break-up basis, or wind-up basis.

[25]In accounting, a valuation basis which assumes that a business will meet its financial obligations when they fall due and functions without the threat of liquidation for the foreseeable future which is usually regarded as an accounting year.

[26]Or redefine the Value-at-Risk, considering a more complicated annual economic capital model as the source risk.

on the market value of the assets and liabilities; recall that ruin occurs when the value of assets falls below the value of liabilities. If the risk tolerance level is specified, then this calculation returns the value of assets that must be held to achieve this level; we call this solvency reserve.

In this book, we focus on calculating the minimum annual solvency requirements in the models for economic capital of an insurance company. We will consider the choice of a risk measure, such as the Value-at-Risk, or the probability of ruin, when the risk tolerance level is selected and the time horizon is specified. We will show that using a simple risk measure, such as Value-at-Risk, instead of a more sophisticated risk measure, such as the probability of ruin, does not always lead to a significant simplification in terms of used mathematical apparatus.

As an internal capital model, we take Lundberg's collective risk model with, first, exponentially distributed inter-claim times and claim sizes and, second, generally distributed inter-claim times and claim amounts. Since we switch from the calendar time to the operational time, the annual time horizon t is proportional to the size of the portfolio; assuming that the company is large enough, we thus assume that t is large enough. This assumption allows us to delve into intensive analytical research, using asymptotic methods. The result will be illustrated by numerical calculations, based on the Monte Carlo simulation.

1.1.5 Simulation in finance and insurance

The simulation method is akin to coin tossing. This method consists in observing the actual values appearing in some experiment similar to sampling from a distribution, in order to draw conclusions about this distribution. The difference is that no physical experiment is actually performed, but is "played" or "simulated" by means of random numbers. Similar to coin tosses, the sample paths of the risk reserve process are simulated many times. The shape and position of a bundle thus obtained contains information about solvency: if this bundle lies safely over the ruin barrier, then the company is solvent.

The same as the coin tossing can be used to evaluate the probability of getting heads or tails (or fairness of the coin), the Monte Carlo method makes it possible to evaluate the probability of ruin within time t: it is approximately equal to a fraction, whose numerator is the number of sample paths that have fallen below the ruin barrier at least once before time t, and whose denominator is the total number of sample paths in the bundle.

Having information about the dynamics of the risk reserve process over time, with the randomness introduced by means of a random number generator (which is a computer program), one can trace the sample paths of the risk reserve process under very broad assumptions about the model, whence the main advantage of the Monte Carlo simulation. This approach easily incorporates various factors, in contrast to analytical methods where simplifying assumptions must be introduced. The main disadvantage of simulation is relatively low accuracy and only numerical results, in contrast to the comprehensive results of analytical studies.

The simulation technique yields valuable conclusions under very broad assumptions, both in the long-term analysis and in the scenario analysis. People in banks typically use simulated distributions to calculate risk measures. People in insurance, when calculate the Value-at-Risk and the expected shortfall, mostly use simulation. This approach is what most people need; in insurance solvency regulation, it was put forth in the 1980s by the Finnish Solvency Working Party and, particularly, by its head T. Pentikäinen[27].

1.1.6 Analytical methods and simulation

In general, even if the analytical method is based on very special assumptions, it can reveal most relationships between the variables in the model. Even if the values obtained by the analytical method are very different from the real values, it is likely that at least the basic interdependencies can be studied in this way. This analysis makes it easier to understand the structure of a sophisticated model and the relationship between its components[28].

A disadvantage of simulation method is that an attempt to take into account the relationships between variables in the model can lead to a significant increase in the amount of computations. For instance, this is relatively easy to find the initial capital which makes the probability of ruin equal to a predetermined (small) value, given that the premium intensity does not depend on the initial capital: it requires shifting the same bundle or, more precisely, a bundle of the same shape, up and down. But if the premium intensity depends on the initial capital, the bundle's shape varies (see Fig. 1.1), and a shift up and down would require a complete re-calculation of the entire bundle.

Another disadvantage of simulation method is that it gives only partial numerical results, i.e., related to the fixed set of model's parameters, with which the simulation is carried out. On the contrary, if we manage to find an analytical solution, it will provide a solution for the entire set of model's parameters, although under the conditions in which the analytical solution was obtained. Therefore, the analytical approach, in contrast to simulation, is better suited to the development of general recommendations. This drawback

[27]Teivo Pentikäinen (1917–12 June 2006), Finnish expert and manager of a number of insurance companies. In 1948–1962 he was Director of Insurance Department in the Ministry of Social Affairs and Health, a state regulation authority in the field of personal and social security. Since 1962 and before his retirement in 1977, he was President and CEO of the newly formed company *Ilmarinen*. Under his leadership, this company was engaged in pension insurance and has become the biggest on the Finnish market. In 1952 he chaired the committee that radically reformed the Finnish law on insurance companies; in the early 1960s he played a crucial role in the reform of legislation on motor insurance and workers' compensation. Throughout his life he taught at the University of Helsinki. In 1977 he received the title of Honorary Professor.

[28]Apparently, T. Pentikäinen came first to such conclusions; in the mid-1970s he was a pioneer in using simulation in the insurance modeling (see [147], pp. 30, 45).

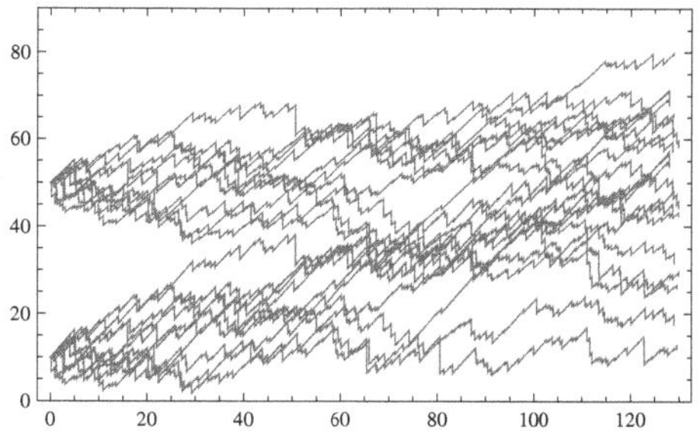

FIGURE 1.1: Two bundles of simulated trajectories for (see Section 1.3.2) Lundberg's risk model with generic inter-claim interval T and claim size Y exponentially distributed with parameters $\delta = 1$ and $\rho = 1$, respectively. *Lower bundle:* initial risk reserve is $u = 10$, premium intensity is $c = 1.26$. *Upper bundle*: initial risk reserve is $u = 50$, premium intensity is $c = 1.06$.

can be mitigated (subject to the presence of sufficient computing power), but not completely eliminated, by a reasonable choice of simulation strategy.

1.2 Risk Measures in Solvency II System

The Solvency II system (see Directives [63], [64]) of regulating a competitive insurance market, which applies to Europe, came into effect on January 1, 2016. This system embodies the risk-based approach to insurance regulation and management[29], which differs from the traditional accounting views on company's management.

The risk-based approach to regulation provides more incentives for insurance and reinsurance companies to properly measure and manage their risks. This means a focus on the probability mechanism of insurance, which embodies the laws of nature governing the large-scale phenomena, called also probability laws. They allow the insurer to manage risk in a predictable and controllable way. In particular, this implies that under certain circumstances the total number of claims and subsequent aggregate payments are susceptible to prediction, and that the premiums sufficient for insurance protection of the customers, whose risks are placed in the portfolio, may be forecasted.

[29]Changes in the insurance industry related to risk-based regulation, such as Solvency II and Swiss Solvency Test, are discussed in [52].

1.2.1 Capital requirements in Solvency II system

In the Solvency II system, insurer's strategy for capital management is largely focussed on the capital efficiency. Sound risk management means keeping the capital resources at an appropriate level related to the risks taken over insurer's business planning horizon.

Primary instructions for finding the capital which makes the insurer allowed to conduct its business without regulatory interventions, is the regulatory solvency capital requirement[30] (SCR), which describes the legal rules for calculating the mandatory solvency capital's level. The approach to calculating SCR is to use either a predefined standard formula within partial internal models, or a full internal model. Besides this, the regulatory minimum capital requirement[31] (MCR) sets the level of mandatory minimum solvency capital. This yields a minimum level below which the amount of financial resources should not fall. This level is calculated in accordance with a simple formula based on data that can be audited.

Insurance and reinsurance undertakings shall hold eligible own funds which cover the last reported SCR and MCR. These funds allow the company to absorb significant losses; this gives a reasonable guarantee to policyholders and beneficiaries that payments will be made as they fall due. To ensure, subject to any changes in the risk profile, that such funds are held on an on-going basis, insurers should calculate SCR at least annually, monitor it continuously, and recalculate it whenever the risk profile alters significantly.

In addition to this mandatory solvency capital, the economic capital is commonly used for internal risk management and decision-making. Economic capital is an internal measure. It is put forth to establish internal risk limits and manage the aggregated risk exposure. This requires an internal model used to calculate all major quantifiable risk's components, including their diversified aggregation, whereas the mandatory solvency capital results from simplified calculations based on using the standard formula. The internal model is central in calculating the economic capital, including validation of the model and forecasting risk and capital under normal and stressed circumstances.

1.2.2 Risk measuring in Solvency II system

The scope of Directives [63], [64] is very wide: they apply to all types of diversified insurance business and to all companies, from large to small. In the calculation of SCR a modular approach is adopted, which means that the individual exposure to risk from each risk category must be assessed and then aggregated. The modules, such as life, non-life and health underwriting risks are highlighted in Directive [63] and are deemed undertaking-specific.

---

[30] See Directive [63], Title I, Chapter VI, Section 4: Solvency capital requirement (Articles 100–135).

[31] See Directive [63], Title I, Chapter VI, Section 5: Minimum capital requirement (Articles 128–131).

In terms of the philosophy of the Solvency II system, it aims to create a range of incentives for different companies to improve their risk management practices. It is focussed on the cost of insurance insolvencies for the economy, rater than on avoiding any insurance insolvency[32]. This agrees with the proportionality principle and reflects the nature, scale, and complexity of the business.

Solvency requirements identified to Value-at-Risk. In light of practical recommendations and limitations, we are especially concerned about the narrower problem of choosing a risk measure for calculating both the minimum capital requirements and, especially, the solvency capital requirements. It seems to us that this choice is technically very limited.

We strive to see how reasonable (and acceptable) is the choice of the Value-at-Risk measure in these calculations, as required in Section 1.1, rather than, e.g., the probability of ruin or another risk measure derived from it, such as, e.g., the non-ruin capital. To provide a comprehensive answer, we must focus on what the real difference between these risk measures is, and approach this issue in terms of a rigorously defined mathematical model.

For the sake of curiosity, we draw attention to a point in the text of Directive [63] that may cause confusion or misunderstanding. To begin with, we note that the word "ruin", which is so common in the academic literature on risk theory, appears only once in Directive [63], in the preambular paragraph (64), where the objectives are formulated:

> in order to promote good risk management and align regulatory capital requirements with industry practices, the Solvency Capital Requirement should be determined as the economic capital to be held by insurance and reinsurance undertakings in order *to ensure that ruin occurs* no more often than once in every 200 cases or, alternatively, that those undertakings will still be in a position, with a probability of at least 99.5%, to meet their obligations to policy holders and beneficiaries over the following 12 months. That economic capital should be calculated on the basis of the true risk profile of those undertakings, taking account of the impact of possible risk-mitigation techniques, as well as diversification effects.

In this quote, the words in italics (this is our emphasis) are a terminological slip: in the main text, in the article devoted to the basic solvency capital requirement[33], we read (words in italics are also our emphasis):

---

[32]There is an asymmetry in approaches from the perspectives of supervision and of an individual company. From the first perspective, despite the fact that the probability or frequency of ruin of smaller companies is higher, the ruin of a larger company brings much more harm to the economy. From the perspective of individual insurer, the impact of its insolvency on the economic system may be irrelevant and the focus could be on its own financial strength only.

[33]See Directive [63], Title I, Chapter IV, Section 4: Solvency capital requirement, Article 104 (4).

each of the risk modules referred to in paragraph 1 shall be calibrated *using a Value-at-Risk measure*, with a 99.5% confidence level, over a one-year period.

Issues related to a mix-up of risk measures. The Value-at-Risk and the risk measure related to occurrence of ruin for the same holding period[34] differ from each other: the former, unlike the latter, is linked to the result at the end of the year and ignores what happens at the intermediate times throughout the year. In other words, the former is built on the break-up basis, whereas the latter is built on the going concern basis. A mix-up of these measures of risk has technical, but very important, consequences; they are related to the choice of fundamental distributions.

To clarify this idea, the Value-at-Risk (see [165], Section 14.3.2) is "just a percentile or quantile of a given distribution of aggregate risks". By the "given distribution of aggregate risks", the distribution of the risk reserve[35] at a specific time point, i.e., at the end of a given period, say one year, is commonly meant. Here lies a substantial difference between the probability of ruin over a certain time period, such as one year, and the Value-at-Risk at this same time period, both viewed as risk measures.

Looking at this matter in a slightly different way (this book is devoted to a detailed explanation of this point from the angle of mathematics), calculations involving the Value-at-Risk measures are carried out on the "Gaussian" basis, whereas calculations involving the probability of ruin are carried out on the "inverse Gaussian" basis. In a nutshell, this conclusion follows from [135], where the inverse Gaussian approximation is obtained for the probability of ruin within finite time under very mild technical conditions.

Whether risk measures may be mixed-up? It seems to us that the fears that the risk measure may be mixed-up, are substantial. These fears are twofold. First, there are dominating tendencies to use risk measures on the break-up basis (as they are actually often used), rather than on the going concern basis. Second, there is a strong temptation to calculate — at least analytically — the risk measures like Value-at-Risk or Tail Value-at-Risk under explicitly or implicitly imposed normality (or Gaussian) assumptions.

The latter observation does not apply to the use of numerical methods, such as Monte Carlo simulation, which became so widely used partly because the analytical methods failed in computing Value-at-Risk for general, non-normal distributions; in practice, this is exactly what is needed and is being done. Mathematically, while the definition of the quantile does not imply any restrictive assumption on the underlying distribution, its calculating in

[34]Note that we should compare the Value-at-Risk and the non-ruin capital (rather than the probability of ruin), both measured in monetary units; the latter is the capital which makes the probability of ruin equal to a prescribed small value. This issue, central in this book, will be discussed in detail in what follows.

[35]This is a commonly used academic term for the cumulative risks that arise over time.

most particular cases is very sophisticated: this inevitably leads to finding an implicit function, which is always difficult.

Regarding temptations to use risk measures on the break-up basis, note that most manuals and textbooks (see, e.g., [92], p. 79) discuss (and accentuate) quantitative procedures developed for finding the capital requirements on the basis of empirical capital distribution *at the end of the year*, for both Value-at-Risk and Tail Value-at-Risk measures. It is tacitly assumed that this is exactly the method that can and should be used, with mentioning the Solvency II security demands[36], but without mentioning theoretical advantages and disadvantages, and without mentioning alternative (though technically more cumbersome) methods. This may be misleading.

Regarding normality (or Gaussian) assumptions, this comes from (see, e.g., [89]) the fact that analytical evaluation of risk measures, like Value-at-Risk or Tail Value-at-Risk, is always technically difficult: the distribution function of the risk, except its simulated counterpart, remains largely unknown even when a stochastic model is developed and used for studying the future evolution. For this reason (see, e.g., [89]), the Value-at-Risk benchmarks are built in Basel I and II under the assumption that the risk in question *has a Gaussian distribution*, whence relatively simple formulas. Unfortunately, the values given by this technique are often too small to give the theoretical hedging of the risk in practical situations. Therefore, the regulators sometimes choose as final values the theoretically calculated values multiplied by three.

1.2.3 Criteria for selecting loss distributions

Modular approach to modeling. Directive [63] applies to a wide variety of companies, including life and non-life, insurance and reinsurance undertakings[37]. It prescribes to determine SCR using either the Standard Formula, or the internal model, or a combination of the two.

The Standard Formula has a modular structure, where the main risk modules are: non-life underwriting risk module, health underwriting risk module, market risk module, counterparty default risk module. The non-life underwriting risk module deals with premium and reserve risk sub-module and catastrophe risk sub-module. The capital requirements are first derived for each module and then aggregated to the overall SCR.

When constructing an internal model, a probabilistic analysis is needed in modules related to large-scale insurance. The dynamics of business in these modules is described by Lundberg's collective risk model (see [114], [115]). The

[36]For instance, see [92], p. 43: "The Solvency Capital Requirement (SCR) specifies the amount of capital needed for an insurance company to fulfil the Solvency II security demands. It is calibrated by the Value-at-Risk (VaR) of the own funds to a confidence level of 99.5% over a 1-year period such that insolvency within that period should be observed only once in 200 years on average".

[37]This is a significant difference from previous practice, when, e.g., separate Directives [61], [62] were for life and non-life insurance.

division of risk modules into groups[38] is a traditional practice in probabilistic and statistical analysis, e.g., time series[39] (see [29], [192], [90], [186]).

Risk measures for insurance and reinsurance undertakings. In reinsurance (see, e.g., [36]), the insureds are direct insurers. Reinsurance is designed to provide protection against one or more large individual losses, or accumulation of losses arising from a single event, or large deviation of the annual aggregate claim amount around the mean value. This produces a further spreading of losses and provides an insurer with additional underwriting capacities: it accepts a risk that it would never have accepted without it.

Many principles applicable to direct insurance are applicable to reinsurance. To be considered technically solvent, both insurance and reinsurance companies must comply with the solvency requirements established by the supervisory authority; otherwise they will be wound up. However, due to differences in the type of business, legislation for direct insurance and reinsurance has long been different. The innovation of Directive [63] is that it applies to both of them, although (see item (22) of preamble to Directive [63]) "the supervision of reinsurance activity should take account of the special characteristics of reinsurance business, notably its global nature and the fact that the policy holders are themselves insurance or reinsurance undertakings".

In terms of modeling, the main difference between insurance and reinsurance is that the loss distributions are light-tail in the former and fat-tail in the latter (see, e.g., [56], [73], [103], [158]). In the calculation of SCR, this can be coped by using a modular approach: the individual exposure to each risk category should be assessed and then aggregated.

1.2.4 Some concerns regarding Solvency II system

The Solvency II system's developers (unlike critics) believed that the Value-at-Risk is balanced in terms of efficiency and simplicity, but we argued that this risk measure is oversimplified. It may become inadequate, which may lead to deficiencies, e.g., understated legal capital requirements. In this section, we will focus on some other criticisms regarding the Solvency II system.

Concerns regarding SCR aggregation formula. Preamble to Directive [63], item (65), says:

> Provision should be made to lay down a standard formula for the calculation of the solvency capital requirement, to enable all insurance and reinsurance undertakings to assess their economic

---

[38] In some groups, the laws of large-scale phenomena are of a paramount importance. In other groups, other aspects (including non-random ones) come to the fore.

[39] The modular approach facilitates separation of deterministic and random components of risk; in time series analysis it roughly corresponds to elimination of trend and seasonal components.

capital. For the structure of the standard formula, a modular approach should be adopted, which means that the individual exposure to each risk category should be assessed in a first step and then aggregated in a second step.

The standard approach to calculating SCR is a formula that is applicable to all insurers, regardless of size, portfolio structure and geographical location. Insurers, however, are allowed to develop an internal model that better fits their risk profile, with the outcomes subject to supervisory approval.

The aggregation algorithm used in this formula raised (see [141], [150]) significant criticism, as follows. In the standard formula, the overall SCR is calculated via individual SCR, in a way that imitates the calculation of the standard deviation for a sum of normally distributed risks. However, in order to cope with the individual risk distributions' skewness, this formula must be calibrated accordingly, in order to maintain the prescribed level of confidence. According to [150], in the general setup these methods are subject to stability problems.

First, if the individual SCR based on the Value-at-Risk, which is chosen as underlying risk measure, are exactly known and the resulting aggregate risk distribution is symmetric (and hence no calibrations are necessary), the square root formula can severely underestimate the true SCR. Second, under a certain kind of dependence structure (so called grid type copulas), it is easy to construct examples of uncorrelated risks for which the square root formula fails in a similar manner.

The criticism in [141] is essentially similar to one in [150], with the conclusion that the standard formula with the currently proposed calibration settings may yield biased and inaccurate capital requirements.

Concerns regarding multi-year dynamics. The obsolete Directive [62], Article 16a, establishes solvency demands in terms of required solvency margin. It shall be calculated on the basis of the annual amount of premiums or contributions, or on the basis of average burden of claims for the past three (in some cases, seven) financial years. The algorithm of this calculation[40], clearly formulated in Directive [62], was critically examined in [134], Section 1.4.2. It was argued that, being designed for a business that runs smoothly, it will work poorly and even very poorly when there are certain adverse effects in a number of successive years. Such effects did take place in 2007 and 2008, during the financial crisis. This revealed serious weaknesses in the supervision system established in Directive [62]: it was not able to foresee adverse macro-prudential changes, or prevent the accumulation of excessive risks in the financial system.

Directive [63], just like Directive [62], does not establish strict restrictions

[40]This algorithm is no longer present in Directive [63], but the approach set for calculating the minimum level of security below which the amount of financial resources should not fall (i.e., MCR) is similar, being a recipe, or a set of tough prescribed actions.

on the strategic planning of insurers. However, it claims that supervisors, seeking to achieve the main goal of supervision, i.e., protection of policyholders and beneficiaries in times of exceptional movements in the financial markets, should take into account the potential pro-cyclical effects of their actions Moreover, insurers shall develop a regular cycle of model validation, which includes monitoring of the internal model's performance, reviewing of the ongoing appropriateness, and testing results against experience[41].

Concerns related to competition. Directive [63] is focussed on the annual solvency requirements, but in the matters of solvency the strategic approach is crucial: even a rapidly growing company in a profitable insurance market, which satisfied the solvency capital requirements over a series of past years, may suddenly become insolvent (see, e.g., [129]).

All market participants seek individual success, which generates competition. Insurance managers (by the very nature of their profession) compete for money of both investors and customers. One of the main tools of the competition is the rates cut. This is not illegal by itself. But this causes similar responses all over the market. For this reason, accumulated errors in assessing the long-term financial strength may occur. In the worst case, this leads to individual insolvencies and, even worse, clustered insolvencies (see, e.g., [134]).

Concerns related to diversification. The use of Value-at-Risk in regulation can create clear incentives for diversification. To show this, a model has been built in [80]. A very strong macro-systemic effect is induced by such regulation in a linear model, where it is likely that the majority (or a significant part) of insurers want to diversify the liability risk in order to raise the risk-reward profile. The more diversified is the company, i.e., the more it is exposed to systematic risk, the more it is exposed to market shortfalls. Therefore, in the event of a global crisis, it is more prone to bankruptcy. Thus, Solvency II system based on the Value-at-Risk measure can push the insurance market to fall in a crisis, thus contributing to the crisis itself.

This observation shows that modeling the dependence linearly is worse than modeling it via copula with tail dependence, since the diversification benefit assessment in the latter case is (see [34]) much more accurate.

1.3 Risk Measures in Risk Theory

It appears that a breakthrough regarding risk measures in insurance can come from a detailed examination of the relationship between quantile risk

[41] See Directive [63], Article 28: Financial stability and pro-cyclicality, and Article 124: Validation standards.

measures, like the Value-at-Risk, calculated on the break-up basis, and the risk measures used to define solvency provisions on the base of annual probabilities of ruin, i.e., on the going concern basis. Such a comparison of risk measures can be carried out only within the framework of a rigorously defined mathematical model of the dynamics of the insurance process, the most famous of which is Lundberg's model, i.e., in the framework of risk theory.

Of course, this is only true if the various risks are aggregated with the right dependence model[42]. Otherwise, it would not help. We start with fairly simple one-dimensional models, thus overlooking dependencies between components of multi-dimensional models. Further research could do better, and, to use a Chinese expression, why should the azure not be superior to the blue?

In this section, we will start with a brief description of the integral model of multi-year insurance process, proceed to determining the annual mechanisms of insurance, introduce the Value-at-Risk and the non-ruin capital, the latter being an implicit function given by an equation, when the annual probability of ruin equals to the risk tolerance level, and give an overview of the results of this book. The main observation, whose justification is not at all simple from the point of view of mathematics, is that the non-ruin capital, a risk measure seemingly much more sophisticated than the Value-at-Risk, has a structure that is quite similar in complexity to the structure of the Value-at-Risk.

1.3.1 Integral model of multi-year insurance process

The insurance process consists of consecutive insurance years; every year starts with taking a control decision valid throughout this whole year, and every year ends with submitting an account to supervision. Although some insurers may sometimes want to change their control decisions, which is largely related to prices, they have no right to change the terms of polices before the expiration date. This is the point that distinguishes the insurance market from many other financial markets.

Let us introduce (see [134]) a general long-term model of insurance business process. First, we choose the initial random vector $(W^{[0]}, U^{[0]})$ and the controlled random sequence $(W^{[k]}, U^{[k]})$, $k = 1, 2, \ldots$, defined on the elementary state space $(\Omega, \mathcal{F})$. Its trajectories develop over time according to the following diagram

$$\underbrace{\mathsf{w}^{[0]} \xrightarrow{\gamma^{[0]}} \mathsf{u}^{[0]} \xrightarrow{\pi^{[1]}} \mathsf{w}^{[1]}}_{\text{1-st year}} \;\cdots\; \xrightarrow{\pi^{[k-1]}} \underbrace{\mathsf{w}^{[k-1]} \xrightarrow{\gamma^{[k-1]}} \mathsf{u}^{[k-1]} \xrightarrow{\pi^{[k]}} \mathsf{w}^{[k]}}_{k\text{-th year}} \;\cdots. \tag{1.7}$$

Here $\mathsf{w}^{[k]}$, $k = 0, 1, \ldots$, are the outcomes of the random variables $W^{[k]}$,

[42]We can even say more: given that the various risks are aggregated with the right dependence model, that the annual models are duly aggregated in a properly selected multi-year model, that this model takes into account not only the strategic goals of the company, but also the basic market conditions, such as falling and raising soft market, falling and raising hard market, and so on.

$k = 0, 1, \dots$, and $\mathsf{u}^{[k]}$, $k = 0, 1, \dots$, are the outcomes of the random variables $U^{[k]}$, $k = 0, 1, \dots$. The former lie in the state space W endowed with the σ-algebra $\mathcal{W}$. The latter lie in the control space U endowed with the σ-algebra $\mathcal{U}$. By $\pi^{[k]}$, we denote the probability mechanism of insurance in the k-th year; its input is the control variable $\mathsf{u}^{[k-1]}$, and its output is the state variable $\mathsf{w}^{[k]}$. By $\gamma^{[k-1]}$, we denote the control in the k-th year. The infinite sequence of annual controls $\gamma = \{\gamma^{[k]}, k = 0, 1, \dots\}$ is referred to as strategy with infinite time horizon. The finite sequence of annual controls ${}^{\{n\}}\gamma = \{\gamma^{[k]}, k = 0, 1, \dots, n-1\}$ is referred to as strategy with time horizon of n years.

1.3.2 Annual models and the event of ruin

Collective risk and the probability mechanisms of insurance. The insurance protection relies on its collective nature: when more or less equivalent individual risks are transferred to the insurer from the policyholders in a large portfolio, the probability mechanism of insurance is actuated: the losses of insureds suffered damage are covered from the insurance premiums collected from all of them in this portfolio. This experience is often called "spreading of risks within a collective".

The concept of collective risk (see, e.g., [43]–[45], [56], [158]) implies that there exists a random mechanism generating successive claims; the company's portfolio is considered as a whole, rather than a collection of a certain number of individual policies. This mechanism is closely related to dynamic internal capital model discussed in Section 1.1.4.

To illustrate this concept, suppose that an insurance company receives online the information about the time and severity of each claim that has just occurred. This is aggregated in the form of the initial capital, plus the total amount of premiums, minus the aggregate claim payments. By ruin within time t, we call the event that this sum, evolving with time, falls below zero at least once within the time interval $(0, t]$. In this framework, besides calculation of the aggregate claim payout's distribution, the problem of finding the probability of ruin comes to the fore.

Fundamental risk in Lundberg's collective risk model. The basis of Lundberg's risk model is the fundamental risk, i.e., the sequences $T_i \stackrel{d}{=} T$, $i = 1, 2, \dots$, and $Y_i \stackrel{d}{=} Y$, $i = 1, 2, \dots$, both consisting of positive random variables. The former refers to the length of intervals between the successive claims, the latter refers to severities of these claims.

Traditionally, as the severity of imposed restrictions increases, considered are the following Lundberg's risk models[43]:

(a) a model when the sequences $T_i \stackrel{d}{=} T$, $i = 1, 2, \dots$, and $Y_i \stackrel{d}{=} Y$, $i = 1, 2, \dots$,

[43]The most general case is Sparre Andersen's model introduced in [3]: (T_i, Y_i), $i = 1, 2, \dots$, are independent and identically (but generally) distributed random vectors; their components may be dependent.

of independent and identically distributed (i.i.d.) random variables are mutually independent,

(b) a model when, additionally to assumptions in (a), $T_i \overset{d}{=} T$, $i = 1, 2, \ldots$, are exponentially distributed with a positive parameter δ, i.e., the claim arrival process is Poisson with intensity δ,

(c) a model when, additionally to assumptions in (b), i.i.d. claim amounts $Y_i \overset{d}{=} Y$, $i = 1, 2, \ldots$, are exponentially distributed with a positive parameter ρ. This model is often referred to as classical Lundberg's model.

Risk reserve processes. In the models (a)–(c), the risk reserve process, which is a difference of incoming premiums and outgoing claims, is defined as

$$R_s = u + cs - V_s, \quad s \geqslant 0, \tag{1.8}$$

where $u \geqslant 0$ is the initial capital, or the initial risk reserve, $c \geqslant 0$ is the premium intensity, called for brevity price,

$$V_s = \sum_{i=1}^{N_s} Y_i, \tag{1.9}$$

or 0, if $N_s = 0$ (or $T_1 > s$), is the aggregate claim payout process, and

$$N_s = \max\left\{n > 0 : \sum_{i=1}^{n} T_i \leqslant s\right\}, \tag{1.10}$$

or 0, if $T_1 > s$, is the claim arrival process.

The concept of risk reserve R_s, $s \geqslant 0$, is (see [15], p. 4) closely related to the concepts of solvency margin, or net worth, frequently used in insurance practice. Even though such definitions diverge in detail[44], they are referred to the difference between the values of assets and liabilities developing in time. The risk reserve can be understood as the content of a "reservoir" or a "pool", where the underwriting profit comes in, if positive, or goes away, if negative.

From the standpoint of multi-year model (1.7), the concept of risk reserve is key in the description of the probability mechanisms of insurance $\pi^{[k]}$, $k = 1, 2, \ldots$. To obtain a long-term, multi-year model (see [134]), such annual mechanisms are connected in a chain, when accounts are made annually and new control parameters are assigned at the beginning of each year, depending on the business goals of the company, market conditions, and regulatory requirements.

Operational time and the length of a year. The risk reserve process R_s, $s \geqslant 0$, introduced in (1.8), as well as its components introduced in (1.9) and (1.10), are homogeneous random processes with operational (see, e.g., [180] p. 219), rather than calendar time.

[44] For example, whether the assets are deemed book values or current market values.

The operational time, measured in monetary units, is proportional to the ball-park figure of the annual financial transactions of the company, whose portfolio's volume does not change during the insurance year. We face this situation in Chapters 2–6. Assuming additionally that $t \to \infty$, we are in the situation where the annual ball-park figure of financial transactions is large, or portfolio's volume is large.

In Chapter 7, modeling a company whose business is expanding or shrinking due to migration of policyholders, whence varying portfolio's volume, we turn to inhomogeneous risk models. When building a model, this entails a transition from the original operational time to a transformed operational time, which takes into account the changes in the portfolio's volume. A change of time which is proportional to the changes in portfolio's volume leads us again to a model with homogeneous random processes.

The event of ruin and probabilities of ruin. The event

$$\Big\{\inf_{0\leqslant s\leqslant t} R_s < 0\Big\} = \bigcup_{0\leqslant s\leqslant t} \{R_s < 0\}$$

is called ruin within time t, or (assuming that t is the year-length) annual ruin. The random variable $\Upsilon_{u,c} := \inf\{s \geqslant 0 : R_s < 0\}$, or $+\infty$, if $R_s \geqslant 0$ for all $s \geqslant 0$, which may be rewritten equivalently as

$$\Upsilon_{u,c} := \inf\{s \geqslant 0 : V_s - cs > u\}, \tag{1.11}$$

or $+\infty$, if $V_s - cs \leqslant u$ for all $s \geqslant 0$, is referred to as time of the first ruin.

Definition 1.3 (Probability of ruin within a finite time) *The probability*

$$\begin{aligned}\psi_t(u,c) &:= \mathsf{P}\Big\{\inf_{0\leqslant s\leqslant t} R_s < 0\Big\} = \mathsf{P}\Big\{\sup_{0\leqslant s\leqslant t} (V_s - cs) > u\Big\} \\ &= \mathsf{P}\{\Upsilon_{u,c} \leqslant t\}\end{aligned} \tag{1.12}$$

is called the probability of ruin within time t.

The following probabilities are related to $\psi_t(u,c)$. The probability of ultimate ruin is $\psi_\infty(u,c) := \lim_{t\to\infty} \psi_t(u,c)$. Plainly, $\psi_\infty(u,c) := \mathsf{P}\{\Upsilon_{u,c} < \infty\}$, or $\psi_\infty(u,c) := \mathsf{P}\{\inf_{s\geqslant 0} R_s < 0\}$. The probability of survival, or non-ruin within time t, is $\phi_t(u,c) := \mathsf{P}\{\inf_{0\leqslant s\leqslant t} R_s > 0\}$. The probability of ultimate survival, or ultimate non-ruin, is $\phi_\infty(u,c) := \mathsf{P}\{\inf_{s\geqslant 0} R_s > 0\}$. The probability of ultimate ruin after, but not before time t, is $\varphi_t(u,c) = \mathsf{P}\{\inf_{s\geqslant 0} R_s < 0, \inf_{0\leqslant s\leqslant t} R_s \geqslant 0\}$. Plainly, $\phi_t(u,c) := 1 - \psi_t(u,c)$, $\phi_\infty(u,c) := 1 - \psi_\infty(u,c)$, and $\varphi_t(u,c) := \psi_\infty(u,c) - \psi_t(u,c)$.

Equilibrium price c^*, profitable and unprofitable business. According to the model (1.8)–(1.10) of risk reserve processes, the whole insurance process consists of mutually independent inter-claim intervals of the same type. When $\mathsf{E}(Y - cT) < 0$, i.e., $c > c^* := \mathsf{E}\,Y/\mathsf{E}\,T$, the average premium income in an inter-claim interval exceeds the average claim loss in this interval, and vice versa when $\mathsf{E}(Y - cT) > 0$, i.e., $c < c^*$. In the former case, profitable intervals prevail. In the latter case, unprofitable intervals prevail. In this way, the price $c^* := \mathsf{E}\,Y/\mathsf{E}\,T$, called equilibrium price, is of critical importance in the model (1.8)–(1.10): it separates the prices when the risk reserve processes is profitable, i.e., $c > c^*$, from the prices when it is unprofitable, i.e., $0 \leqslant c < c^*$.

Remark 1.1 (Expected value principle) Equilibrium price $c^* := \mathsf{E}\,Y/\mathsf{E}\,T$ is tightly related to the expected value principle[45]: the average payout at time t is $\mathsf{E}V_t = (\mathsf{E}\,Y/\mathsf{E}\,T)\,t$, and c^* is a solution to the equation $\mathsf{E}V_t = c\,t$ w.r.t. c.

The concept of equilibrium price is useful for an intuitive, albeit crude, insight into the essence of the profitability and non-profitability, which is closely related to solvency. In particular, it follows that the choice of a price equal to c^* does not guarantee yet profitability (and solvency) of the insurance process, whence the need to use safety loading, which is an addendum to c^*.

The primary analysis of this issue is to resort to the random walks. Let us write $\mathcal{Z}_n := \sum_{i=1}^n T_i$, $\mathcal{V}_n := \sum_{i=1}^n Y_i$, and $\mathcal{S}_n := \sum_{i=1}^n (Y_i - c\,T_i)$, $i = 1, 2, \ldots$. We put $\mathcal{Z}_0 = \mathcal{V}_0 = \mathcal{S}_0 = 0$ and have

$$\begin{aligned}\psi_t(u,c) &:= \mathsf{P}\Big\{\sup_{n:\mathcal{Z}_n \leqslant t} \mathcal{S}_n > u\Big\} \\ &= \mathsf{P}\{\mathcal{Z}_{\nu(u)} \leqslant t\}\end{aligned} \tag{1.13}$$

and

$$\begin{aligned}\psi_\infty(u,c) &:= \mathsf{P}\Big\{\sup_n \mathcal{S}_n > u\Big\} \\ &= \mathsf{P}\{\mathcal{Z}_{\nu(u)} < \infty\},\end{aligned} \tag{1.14}$$

where $\nu(u) = \min\{n \geqslant 1 : \mathcal{S}_n > u\}$ or 0, if the random walk $\mathcal{S}_n$, $n = 0, 1, 2, \ldots$, never crosses the level $u > 0$.

To demonstrate (1.13) and (1.14), note the following. Since premiums are paid with a positive intensity, the ruin can only occur in the time of a claim payment; in the moments between claims a ruin is impossible. Therefore, considering the probability $\psi_t(u,c)$, we examine only the values of risk reserve R_s, $0 < s \leqslant t$, at the points $\mathcal{Z}_1 \leqslant \mathcal{Z}_2 \leqslant \cdots \leqslant \mathcal{Z}_{N_t} \leqslant t$, and ignore all other points in the interval $0 < s \leqslant t$. If ruin in the time interval $(0,t]$ occurs, then at least one of the values $R_{\mathcal{Z}_1} = u + cT_1 - Y_1 = u - X_1$, $R_{\mathcal{Z}_2} = u + (cT_1 - Y_1) + (cT_2 - Y_2) = u - X_1 - X_2$, $\ldots$, $R_{\mathcal{Z}_{N_t}} = u + (cT_1 - Y_1) + (cT_2 - Y_2) + \cdots + (cT_{N_t} - Y_{N_t}) = u - X_1 - X_2 - \cdots - X_{N_t}$ must be negative. The value of $\nu(u)$ is the number of the first claim when risk reserve of the

[45]Besides expected value principle, there exist (see, e.g., [31], Chapter 4: Premium Calculation) standard deviation principle, variance principle, principle of zero utility, and many others.

company drops below zero. The first time moment when it happens is $\mathcal{Z}_{\nu(u)}$. This yields equality (1.13). To have (1.14), put t equal to $+\infty$ in (1.13).

Since the increments of the random walk $\mathcal{S}_n = \mathcal{V}_n - c\,\mathcal{Z}_n$, $n \geqslant 0$, assume the values of any sign[46], it may drift either to $+\infty$, or to $-\infty$, depending on the sign of $\mathsf{E}(Y - cT)$. By Theorem B.8, if $\mathsf{E}(Y - cT) < 0$, i.e., $c > c^*$, then this random walk drifts to $-\infty$ with probability 1. If $\mathsf{E}(Y - cT) > 0$, i.e., $c < c^*$, then this random walk drifts to $+\infty$ with probability 1. Using formulas (1.14) and (1.13), the reader can easily draw conclusions about the ultimate ruin and survival of the insurance business in these cases.

Prices in the vicinity of the equilibrium price. In the classical risk theory, the equilibrium price c^* is called "fair price" because in this case the mean aggregate claim, or the mean total claim amount paid out up to time t, is equal to the aggregate premium collected during this time period. It was long believed that the case $c < c^*$, when the insurance business is ultimately ruinous, is of no interest. Since interesting was the case $c > c^*$, the focus was on $c = (1+\tau)\,\mathsf{E}Y/\mathsf{E}T$, where $\tau = c\,\mathsf{E}T/\mathsf{E}Y - 1 > 0$ is referred to as premium loading, or safety loading.

In the context of a long-term model (see [134]), rather than a separate annual model, this is not the case: in the model (1.7) of long-term insurance business, the main interest is the prices close to the equilibrium price c^*, either moderately higher or moderately lower than c^*. This is due to the following reasons: if (in one or in several consecutive years) the price c was either much higher or much less than c^*, then a price competition may start in the next year and migration of policyholders ensues; this can unfold underwriting cycles.

1.3.3 Annual solvency provisions of two kinds

In this section, we introduce annual solvency provisions of two kinds, called non-loss capital and non-ruin capital. Both of them are (see Section 1.1.1) Value-at-Risk measures associated with the same insurance portfolio, collective risk model, confidence level $A \in (0,1)$, and holding period of length t, i.e., the year-length. However, these two differently defined Value-at-Risk measures differ significantly from each other.

Non-loss capital: year-end provision. The non-loss capital[47] is tightly related to the economic capital on a break-up basis, discussed in Section 1.1.4. We recall that by $0 < \alpha < 1$ we denote a sufficiently small number, i.e., $\alpha = 0.05$ or $\alpha = 0.01$, and use the shorthand notation $A = 1 - \alpha$.

---

[46] Unlike the increments of the random walks $\mathcal{Z}_n$, $n \geqslant 0$, and $\mathcal{V}_n$, $n \geqslant 0$, which are positive.

[47] Also called year-end securing capital, profit provision, or annual non-loss capital.

Definition 1.4 (Non-loss capital) *The non-loss capital* $\underline{u}_{\alpha,t}(c)$, $c \geqslant 0$, *is a positive solution to the equation (w.r.t. u)*

$$\mathsf{P}\{V_t - ct \leqslant u\} = A. \tag{1.15}$$

We set $\underline{u}_{\alpha,t}(c)$ *equal to zero for those c, for which this solution is negative.*

In risk theory, common is to write (1.15) as

$$\mathsf{P}\{R_t < 0\} = \alpha, \tag{1.16}$$

in terms of the risk reserve process (1.8).

Using (1.16), the origin of the term "non-loss capital" is straightforward: if $\underline{u}_{\alpha,t}(c)$ is chosen to be the initial capital in the expression (1.8) for the risk reserve, then the probability of the negative total balance at the end of the year is equal to α.

Non-ruin capital: annual solvency provision. The non-ruin capital[48] is tightly related to the economic capital on a going concern basis, discussed in Section 1.1.4. Unlike the non-loss capital, this is a ruin-related functional[49].

Definition 1.5 (Non-ruin capital) *The non-ruin capital* $u_{\alpha,t}(c)$, $c \geqslant 0$, *is a positive solution to the equation (w.r.t. u)*

$$\mathsf{P}\Big\{\sup_{0\leqslant s\leqslant t}(V_s - cs) \leqslant u\Big\} = A. \tag{1.17}$$

We set $u_{\alpha,t}(c)$ *equal to zero for those c, for which this solution is negative.*

In risk theory, common is to write (1.17) as

$$\mathsf{P}\Big\{\inf_{0\leqslant s\leqslant t} R_s < 0\Big\} = \alpha, \tag{1.18}$$

in terms of the risk reserve process (1.8). Plainly (see (1.12)), the left-hand side of (1.18) is the probability of ruin within time t. Using (1.18), the origin of the term "non-ruin capital" is straightforward: if $u_{\alpha,t}(c)$ is chosen to be the initial capital in the expression (1.8) for the risk reserve, then the probability of ruin $\psi_t(u,c)$ is equal to α.

From the angle of economics, in the framework of Lundberg's collective risk model, (1.16) differs from (1.17) by how the risk underwritten by insurers is understood. In (1.17), one has to watch not only the year-end cash-flow position, but also its dynamics throughout the whole year.

---

[48] Also called the year-end solvency capital, solvency provision, or annual non-ruin capital.

[49] In the risk theory, many ruin-related functionals, e.g., the amount that can be lost immediately when ruin occurs, called deficit or severity of ruin, introduced in [84], are of paramount importance. The real practical importance of these concepts in the risk management is a stand-alone issue. A detailed overview of the current status of these studies can be found in [195].

TABLE 1.1: Terminology applicable to non-ruin capital $u_{\alpha,t}(c)$ and non-loss capital $\underline{u}_{\alpha,t}(c)$, $c \geqslant 0$, introduced in Definitions 1.4 and 1.5

	Value-at-Risk measure	Insurance solvency benchmark
$u_{\alpha,t}(c)$	Value-at-Risk based on sup-loss net of premium income, a solution to $\mathsf{P}\{\sup_{0\leqslant s\leqslant t}(V_s - cs) \leqslant u\} = A$	Non-ruin capital, a solution to $\psi_t(u,c) = \alpha$, i.e., to $\mathsf{P}\{\inf_{0\leqslant s\leqslant t} R_s < 0\} = \alpha$
$\underline{u}_{\alpha,t}(c)$	Value-at-Risk based on loss net of premium income, a solution to $\mathsf{P}\{V_t - ct \leqslant u\} = A$	Non-loss capital, a solution to $\mathsf{P}\{R_t < 0\} = \alpha$

Equivalent terminology applicable to non-ruin capital $u_{\alpha,t}(c)$ and non-loss capital $\underline{u}_{\alpha,t}(c)$, $c \geqslant 0$, in the risk measures theory and in the insurance risk theory, respectively, is shown in Table 1.1.

Difference in source risks. Having compared (1.15) and (1.3) (see also (1.5)), we see that $\underline{u}_{\alpha,t}(c)$ is a sort of Value-at-Risk measure on the loss basis, with the source risk $V_s - cs$, $s \geqslant 0$, the holding period of length t, and the confidence level $A = 1-\alpha$, where α is small. Having compared (1.17) and (1.3) (see also (1.6)), we see that $u_{\alpha,t}(c)$ is also a kind of Value-at-Risk measure on the loss basis: the source risk, called "sup-loss net of premium income", is $\sup_{0\leqslant r\leqslant s}(V_r - cr)$, $s \geqslant 0$, the holding period is of length t, and the confidence level is $A = 1 - \alpha$, where α is small.

The non-loss capital $\underline{u}_{\alpha,t}(c)$ and the non-ruin capital $u_{\alpha,t}(c)$ are the quantiles of the random variables $\mathcal{X}_t := V_t - ct$ and $\mathcal{Y}_t := \sup_{0\leqslant s\leqslant t}(V_s - cs)$, respectively. These source risks are generated by different processes modeling losses. A significant difference between the source risks $\mathcal{X}_t$ and $\mathcal{Y}_t$ is easily seen. In particular, $\mathcal{X}_t$ is concentrated on the whole real line, whereas $\mathcal{Y}_t$ is concentrated on the positive half-line. These random variables have quite different asymptotic behavior, as $t \to \infty$. The random variable $\mathcal{X}_t$ is asymptotically normal, whereas the random variable $\mathcal{Y}_t$ is related to the inverse Gaussian distribution; in the further presentation we will dwell on this in detail.

Non-loss capital versus non-ruin capital. For a number of reasons that will be discussed below, both non-loss capital $\underline{u}_{\alpha,t}(c)$ and non-ruin capital $u_{\alpha,t}(c)$ are often considered as the annual solvency provisions[50] in the probability mechanism of insurance modeled in (1.8)–(1.10). However, regarding solvency, which means avoiding a ruin, we should focus on $u_{\alpha,t}(c)$, rather than on $\underline{u}_{\alpha,t}(c)$. Since $\inf_{0\leqslant s\leqslant t} R_s$ is always less than or equal to R_t, we have

$$\underline{u}_{\alpha,t}(c) \leqslant u_{\alpha,t}(c), \quad c \geqslant 0,$$

and $\underline{u}_{\alpha,t}(c)$ is a lower bound on $u_{\alpha,t}(c)$.

[50]Recall that $\underline{u}_{\alpha,t}(c)$ and $u_{\alpha,t}(c)$ are Value-at-Risk measures, though defined differently.

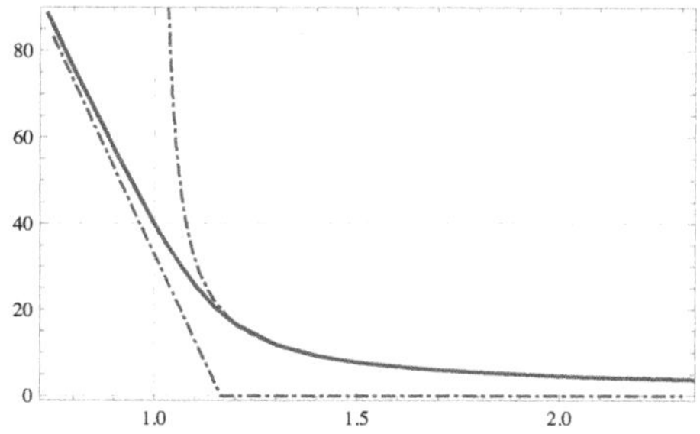

FIGURE 1.2: Graphs (X-axis is c) of $u_{\alpha,t}(c)$ (solid line) and $\underline{u}_{\alpha,t}(c)$, $\overline{u}_{\alpha}(c)$ (dash-dotted lines), when T and Y are exponentially distributed with parameters $\delta = 1$, $\rho = 1$, respectively, and $\alpha = 0.05$, $t = 200$. Horizontal grid line: $u_{\alpha,t}(\delta/\rho) = 40.08$. Vertical grid line: $\delta/\rho = 1$.

This is quite clear that the non-loss capital $\underline{u}_{\alpha,t}(c)$ always[51] understates the non-ruin capital $u_{\alpha,t}(c)$. But to deal with this observation quantitatively, rather than qualitatively, we must calculate both $\underline{u}_{\alpha,t}(c)$ and $u_{\alpha,t}(c)$ in the risk model (1.8)–(1.10), trying to keep the most general assumptions about T and Y. This is relatively easy to do for $\underline{u}_{\alpha,t}(c)$, but not for $u_{\alpha,t}(c)$; our aim in this book is address the later issue.

An upper bound on non-ruin capital. For the non-ruin capital, there are many upper bounds, but one of them seems to be the most natural.

Definition 1.6 (Upper bound for non-ruin capital) *A positive solution $\overline{u}_{\alpha}(c)$, $c \geqslant 0$, to the equation (w.r.t. u)*

$$\mathsf{P}\Big\{\sup_{s\geqslant 0}(V_s - cs) \leqslant u\Big\} = A \tag{1.19}$$

is called ultimate upper bound for the non-ruin capital $u_{\alpha,t}(c)$, $c \geqslant 0$. We set $\overline{u}_{\alpha}(c)$ equal to zero for those c, for which this solution is negative and equal to $+\infty$ for those c, for which this solution does not exist.

Although $u_{\alpha,t}(c)$ is defined as the quantile of $\sup_{s\geqslant 0}(V_s - cs)$, it is not a Value-at-Risk because there is no holding period in its definition. Equation (1.19) can be rewritten in terms of the risk reserve process (1.8) as[52]

$$\mathsf{P}\Big\{\inf_{s\geqslant 0} R_s < 0\Big\} = \alpha, \tag{1.20}$$

[51]The discrepancies can be both very significant and rather small (see illustration in Fig. 1.2), depending on c.

[52]An alternative is $\mathsf{P}\{\Upsilon_{u,c} < \infty\} = \alpha$, where (see (1.11)) $\Upsilon_{u,c}$ is the time of the first ruin.

where the left-hand side is the probability of ultimate ruin $\psi_\infty(u,c)$. This probability has been studied in detail (see, e.g., [158], Chapters 5 and 6). In this notation, it is easy to see why it is called "ultimate upper bound for non-ruin capital": the inequality $\psi_t(u,c) \leqslant \psi_\infty(u,c)$ which holds for all $c \geqslant 0$ yields $u_{\alpha,t}(c) \leqslant \overline{u}_\alpha(c)$ for all $c \geqslant 0$.

The functions

$$\underline{u}_{\alpha,t}(c) \leqslant u_{\alpha,t}(c) \leqslant \overline{u}_\alpha(c), \quad c \geqslant 0,$$

are illustrated in Fig. 1.2. When c is much larger than $c^* := \mathsf{E}Y/\mathsf{E}T$, the difference between $u_{\alpha,t}(c)$ and $\overline{u}_\alpha(c)$ is almost negligible. However, $u_{\alpha,t}(c)$ and $\overline{u}_\alpha(c)$ differ significantly, when c is not much larger than c^*. It is worth noting that $\overline{u}_\alpha(c)$ is tending to infinity, as $c \to c^*$, and is $+\infty$ for $0 \leqslant c \leqslant c^*$. When c is much smaller than c^*, the difference between $u_{\alpha,t}(c)$ and $\underline{u}_{\alpha,t}(c)$ is not very large, but for other c it is quite significant.

Do the bounds always make economic sense? In Section 1.3.2, we argued that in the integral model (1.7) of long-term insurance business the main interest is prices c around c^*. For such c (see illustration in Fig. 1.2), the lower and upper bounds $\underline{u}_{\alpha,t}(c)$ and $\overline{u}_\alpha(c)$ on the non-ruin capital $u_{\alpha,t}(c)$ give very little insight, bordering to uselessness. In particular, except for c much larger than c^*, where the proximity between $u_{\alpha,t}(c)$ and $\overline{u}_\alpha(c)$ is high, the latter bound obviously cannot serve as a sensible annual solvency benchmark in the probability mechanism of insurance modeled in (1.8)–(1.10).

In [95], Chapter 6, Section 2, the function $\overline{u}_\alpha(c)$, $c \geqslant 0$, is called "minimal admissible initial capital", with an emphasis on its economic meaning within the collective risk model (1.8)–(1.10). Specifically, assuming that[53] the "insurer wants to attract as many clients as possible keeping the relative safety loading at the lowest possible level", focussed in [95] is $\overline{u}_\alpha(c)$, as $c \to c^*$. Thus, addressed is the problem (see [95], p. 27) of finding "the initial capital securing a prescribed risk level when the relative safety loading tends to zero".

In our opinion, the focus on $\overline{u}_\alpha(c)$, as $c \to c^*$, is useless[54] "to attract as many clients as possible keeping the relative safety loading at the lowest possible level", given that "the insurer accepts at most α as an acceptable risk level". And even worse, it is hard to accept that (see [95], p. 175) it "can help the insurer to determine whether the initial capital suffices to start the business". Overall, we disagree with [95], which actually claims that when the insurer's price c decreases to the equilibrium price c^*, as often (quite normally) happens in some years of the real insurance business, "the initial capital securing a prescribed risk level" tends to infinity.

Methods for calculating non-loss and non-ruin capitals. Analytical investigation of both non-loss and non-ruin capitals crucially depends on

[53]We quote here from [95], pp. 172–173.
[54]We quote here from [95], pp. 172–173.

whether it is possible to represent the left-hand side of equations (1.15) and (1.17) in a closed form. If this can be done, then — no matter how complex this left-hand side may be — the problem reduces to finding a function that is implicitly defined by non-linear equations. This problem is usually extremely difficult; it can be approached from two sides: numerical calculations and analytical insight, including the attempts to find a closed-form expression.

When t is fixed, to find analytical expressions for $\underline{u}_{\alpha,t}(c)$ and $u_{\alpha,t}(c)$ is impossible even in exceptional cases; only an asymptotic analysis, as $t \to \infty$, seems possible. Since time in the collective risk model (1.8)–(1.10) is operational, the assumption that t is large is equivalent to the assumption that the company's portfolio is large, which is quite reasonable in this framework. The asymptotic analysis, as $t \to \infty$, is possible even when no closed-form expressions for the left-hand side of equations (1.15) and (1.17) is available. This will be discussed in detail in Chapters 3 and 5.

When the left-hand side of equations (1.15) and (1.17) is known in a closed form, we can apply standard numerical analysis. There are many algorithms for finding roots, e.g., the Newton method, also known as the Newton-Raphson method, which produces (see, e.g., [10]) increasingly accurate approximations to the root. If derivatives can be calculated, this method is easy to apply.

We will focus as well on a direct numerical method for finding $\underline{u}_{\alpha,t}(c)$ and $u_{\alpha,t}(c)$, which does not require expressing the left-hand side of equations (1.15) and (1.17) in terms of elementary or special functions; this method, called Monte Carlo simulation, will be discussed in detail in Chapter 6. According to this method, the probability of ruin, which is the left-hand side of equation (1.17), can be approached (see, e.g., [15], p. 228) as follows: each realization of business process up to time t is visualized by a sample path (see illustration in Fig. 1.1), and the whole process is visualized by a bundle of these paths. Some of the sample paths in the bundle fall below the ruin barrier and are earmarked as "ruined", the remainder as "survived". To evaluate the ruin probability, we resort to the ratio, whose numerator is the number of "ruins" and denominator is the number of sample paths. To evaluate the non-ruin capital $u_{\alpha,t}(c)$, we are looking for the starting point of the bundle for which this ratio equals α. The non-loss capital $\underline{u}_{\alpha,t}(c)$ is calculated analogously.

1.3.4 Non-loss and non-ruin capitals in an exceptional risk model

When T and Y in the model (1.8)–(1.10) are exponentially distributed with positive parameters δ and ρ, respectively[55], many items of our interest may be presented in a closed form. In this section, we present some of these results without proof. The interested reader will find them discussed in detail in Chapter 3.

[55] Recall that we deal with Lundberg's collective risk model of Section 1.3.2, case (c).

Aggregate claim amount distribution and non-loss capital. Since non-loss capital is defined by equation (1.16), whose left-hand side is the aggregate claim amount distribution, the study of the latter precedes the study of the former. We start with the aggregate claim amount distribution.

When T and Y are exponentially distributed with positive parameters δ and ρ, respectively, we have[56] the following closed-form results for the aggregate claim amount V_t:

$$\mathsf{E}(V_t) = (\delta/\rho)\,t, \quad \mathsf{D}(V_t) = 2\,(\delta/\rho^2)\,t, \tag{1.21}$$

and

$$\begin{aligned} \mathsf{P}\{V_t \leqslant x\} &= e^{-t\delta} + e^{-t\delta} \sum_{n=1}^{\infty} \frac{(t\delta)^n}{n!} \frac{\rho^n}{\Gamma(n)} \int_0^x e^{-\rho z}\, z^{n-1}\, dz \\ &= e^{-t\delta} + e^{-t\delta}(\delta\rho t)^{1/2} \\ &\quad \times \int_0^x z^{-1/2} I_1(2\sqrt{\delta\rho t z}\,)\, e^{-\rho z}\, dz, \quad x > 0. \end{aligned} \tag{1.22}$$

Let us proceed with the non-loss capital. Using equality (1.22), equation (1.15), which defines the implicit function $\underline{u}_{\alpha,t}(c)$, $s \geqslant 0$, can be written as

$$e^{-t\delta} + e^{-t\delta}(\delta\rho t)^{1/2} \int_0^{u+ct} z^{-1/2} I_1(2\sqrt{\delta\rho t z}\,)\, e^{-\rho z}\, dz = 1 - \alpha. \tag{1.23}$$

This implicit function cannot be found in a closed form, but it can be evaluated numerically; see illustration in Fig. 1.2.

The fact that the time in the collective risk model (1.8)–(1.10) is operational and the volume of portfolio is large, we can naturally turn to the asymptotic analysis of $\underline{u}_{\alpha,t}(c)$, as $t \to \infty$.

Note that V_t is (see (1.9)) the sum of N_t i.i.d. random variables, where $\mathsf{E}(N_t) = \delta t$ is large, as $t \to \infty$, which allows us to address the central limit theory. Hence, we have V_t asymptotically Gaussian, whose mean and variance are given in (1.21); equation (1.23) is closely related to the equation

$$\varPhi_{(0,1)}\left(\frac{u + ct - (\delta/\rho)\,t}{\sqrt{2\,(\delta/\rho^2)\,t}} \right) = 1 - \alpha, \tag{1.24}$$

whose solution $(\delta/\rho - c)\,t + (\sqrt{2\delta}/\rho)\,\kappa_\alpha \sqrt{t}$ is straightforward. Applying simple arguments based on the proximity of two implicit functions, for all $c \geqslant 0$ we conclude that

$$\underline{u}_{\alpha,t}(c) = \max\left\{0, (\delta/\rho - c)\,t + \frac{\sqrt{2\delta}}{\rho}\,\kappa_\alpha \sqrt{t}\,(1 + o(1))\right\}, \quad t \to \infty. \tag{1.25}$$

[56]These equalities are well known, see, e.g., [135], Theorems 4.1 and 4.2. Equality (1.22) will appear later, in Theorem 3.1 of Chapter 3.

Probability of ruin and non-ruin capital. Since non-ruin capital is defined by equation (1.18), whose left-hand side is the probability of ruin within time t, the study of the latter precedes the study of the former. We start with the probability of ruin within time t, i.e., with $\mathsf{P}\{\varUpsilon_{u,c} \leqslant t\}$.

When T and Y are exponentially distributed with positive parameters δ and ρ, respectively, we have the following closed-form result[57]:

$$\mathsf{P}\{\varUpsilon_{u,c} \leqslant t\} = \mathsf{P}\{\varUpsilon_{u,c} < \infty\} - \frac{1}{\pi}\int_0^{\pi} f(x)\,dx, \tag{1.26}$$

where

$$\mathsf{P}\{\varUpsilon_{u,c} < \infty\} = \begin{cases} 1, & \delta/(c\rho) \geqslant 1, \\ \dfrac{\delta}{c\rho}\exp\{-u\,(c\rho-\delta)/c\}, & \delta/(c\rho) < 1, \end{cases} \tag{1.27}$$

and

$$\begin{aligned} f(x) &= (\delta/(c\rho))(1+\delta/(c\rho) - 2\sqrt{\delta/(c\rho)}\cos x)^{-1} \\ &\quad \times \exp\Big\{u\rho\,(\sqrt{\delta/(c\rho)}\cos x - 1) - t\delta(c\rho/\delta) \\ &\quad \times \big(1+\delta/(c\rho) - 2\sqrt{\delta/(c\rho)}\cos x\big)\Big\} \\ &\quad \times \big(\cos(u\rho\sqrt{\delta/(c\rho)}\sin x) - \cos(u\rho\sqrt{\delta/(c\rho)}\sin x + 2x)\big). \end{aligned}$$

Let us proceed with the non-ruin capital. Using equality (1.26), we express the left-hand side of the equation

$$\mathsf{P}\{\varUpsilon_{u,c} \leqslant t\} = \alpha \tag{1.28}$$

in a closed form, whence $u_{\alpha,t}(c)$, $c \geqslant 0$, is an implicit function defined by (1.28). This implicit function, just like $\underline{u}_{\alpha,t}(c)$, $c \geqslant 0$, cannot be found in a closed form. But it can be evaluated numerically. The graph of $u_{\alpha,t}(c)$, $c \geqslant 0$, evaluated numerically, is drawn in Fig. 1.2.

The structure of the function $u_{\alpha,t}(c)$, $c \geqslant 0$, can be analyzed asymptotically; this analysis is based on the properties of Bessel functions. We have[58]

$$u_{\alpha,t}(c) = \begin{cases} (\delta/\rho - c)\,t + \dfrac{\sqrt{2\,\delta}}{\rho}\,\mathsf{z}_{\alpha,t}\Big(\dfrac{\rho\,(\delta/\rho - c)}{\sqrt{2\,\delta}}\sqrt{t}\Big)\sqrt{t}, & 0 \leqslant c \leqslant c^*, \\ \dfrac{\sqrt{2\,\delta}}{\rho}\,\mathsf{z}_{\alpha,t}\Big(\dfrac{\rho\,(\delta/\rho - c)}{\sqrt{2\,\delta}}\sqrt{t}\Big)\sqrt{t}, & c > c^*, \end{cases} \tag{1.29}$$

where $c^* = \delta/\rho$ and the function $\mathsf{z}_{\alpha,t}(x)$, $x \in \mathsf{R}$, is (see Fig. 1.3) continuous, monotone increasing, as x increases from $-\infty$ to 0, monotone decreasing, as x

[57]This result is examined in detail in Chapter 3; see Theorem 3.4.
[58]This is Theorem 3.8 in Chapter 3.

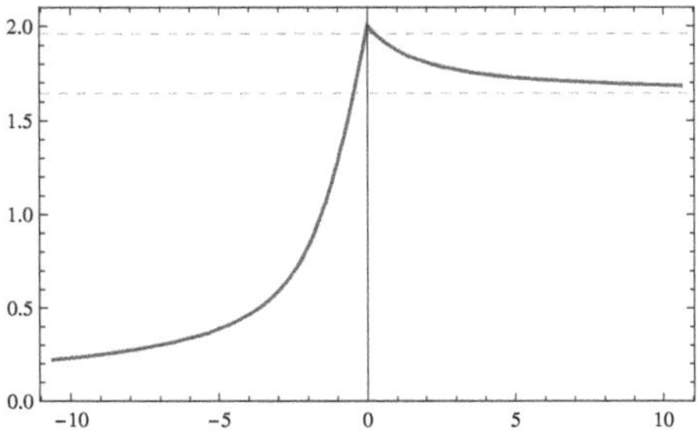

FIGURE 1.3: Graph (X-axis is x) of $\mathsf{z}_{\alpha,t}(x)$, when T and Y are exponentially distributed with parameters $\rho = 1$, $\delta = 1$, respectively, and $\alpha = 0.05$, $t = 200$. Horizontal grid lines: $\kappa_\alpha = 1.65$ and $\kappa_{\alpha/2} = 1.96$.

increases from 0 to ∞, and such that $\lim_{x\to-\infty} \mathsf{z}_{\alpha,t}(x) = 0$, $\lim_{x\to\infty} \mathsf{z}_{\alpha,t}(x) = \kappa_\alpha$, and $\mathsf{z}_{\alpha,t}(0) = \kappa_{\alpha/2}(1 + o(1))$, as $t \to \infty$. In particular, we have

$$\begin{aligned} u_{\alpha,t}(0) &= (\delta/\rho)\, t + \frac{\sqrt{2\delta}}{\rho}\, \kappa_\alpha \sqrt{t}\, (1 + o(1)), \quad t \to \infty, \\ u_{\alpha,t}(c^*) &= \frac{\sqrt{2\delta}}{\rho}\, \kappa_{\alpha/2} \sqrt{t}\, (1 + o(1)), \quad t \to \infty. \end{aligned} \tag{1.30}$$

The first equality in (1.30) is straightforward. The second equality in (1.30) and equality (1.29) are Theorems 3.6 and 3.7 in Chapter 3, respectively.

Upper bounds on the fixed-probability level $u_{\alpha,t}(c)$, $c \geqslant 0$, expressed in terms of elementary functions, are constructed (see Section 3.5), when $0 \leqslant c \leqslant c^*$ and (see Section 3.6) $c > c^*$. In the former case, for t sufficiently large, these bounds can be easily presented in a form that is quite satisfactory for subsequent applications. In the latter case, many bounds can be presented, the accuracy and simplicity of which varies depending on the information about the function $u_{\alpha,t}(c)$, $c \geqslant c^*$. In particular, simple but coarse bounds are based on (see Section 3.6.1) monotony, whereas more sophisticated, but more accurate bounds are based on (see Section 3.6.2) convexity of $u_{\alpha,t}(c)$, $c \geqslant c^*$.

1.3.5 Non-loss capital in the general risk model

In the general case, when T and Y are non-exponentially distributed, there is no hope of finding explicit expressions for the moments and distribution of the aggregate claim amount, such as (1.21) or (1.22), for all t. But since the asymptotic analysis, as $t \to \infty$, is based on fairly general central limit theory, it is easy to obtain analogues of (1.24) and (1.25).

To be specific, $\mathsf{P}\{V_t \leqslant x\}$ is approximated by $\Phi_{(M_V t, D_V t)}(x)$, as $t \to \infty$, where[59]

$$\begin{aligned} M_N &= 1/\mathsf{E}T, & M_V &= \mathsf{E}Y/\mathsf{E}T, \\ D_N^2 &= \mathsf{D}T/(\mathsf{E}T)^3, & D_V^2 &= \mathsf{E}(T\mathsf{E}Y - Y\mathsf{E}T)^2/(\mathsf{E}T)^3. \end{aligned} \tag{1.31}$$

This approximation, being a version of the central limit theorem, is valid under well-known mild technical conditions on T and Y. It can be applied to (1.15).

In more detail, though in the general case equation (1.15) cannot be written in terms of elementary or special functions, as it was done (see (1.23)) in the exponential case, for t sufficiently large equation (1.15) is close to the equation (cf. (1.24))

$$\Phi_{(0,1)}\left(\frac{u + ct - M_V t}{D_V\sqrt{t}}\right) = 1 - \alpha, \tag{1.32}$$

whose closed-form solution $(M_V - c)\,t + \kappa_\alpha\, D_V\sqrt{t}$ is straightforward. Applying simple arguments based on the proximity of two implicit functions, we conclude that (cf. (1.25)) for all $c \geqslant 0$

$$\underline{u}_{\alpha,t}(c) = \max\{0, (M_V - c)\,t + \kappa_\alpha\, D_V\sqrt{t}\,(1 + o(1))\}, \quad t \to \infty. \tag{1.33}$$

In conclusion, note that the analysis just done in the general case differs little, regarding both applied technique and results, from the analysis in the exponential case.

1.3.6 Probability of ruin in the general risk model

It is generally accepted that in the general risk model, where T and Y are non-exponentially distributed, the situation described in Section 1.3.4 deteriorates dramatically, and the non-ruin capital $u_{\alpha,t}(c)$, $c \geqslant 0$, becomes intractable. Let us first look closer at the reasons for this belief. We will then show that the situation is not so bad, and certain innovative approaches provide a way out of it. We present the corresponding results without proof. The interested reader will find them discussed in detail in [135], Chapter 9, and in Chapters 4–6.

The first noteworthy fact is that the results of asymptotic analysis, as $u \to \infty$, so much discussed in the literature, are unsatisfactory from the angle of their further application to asymptotical, as $t \to \infty$, analysis of the non-ruin capital $u_{\alpha,t}(c)$, $c \geqslant 0$. We will show this by referring to Cramér's (or normal) and diffusion approximations that are best known. We start with the former and point out its deficiencies.

Cramér's (or normal) approximation. Note first that everything that is said below about this approximation is the folklore of risk theory. This can be found in [135], Chapter 9, and in many textbooks, e.g., in [78], [158].

[59] It is noteworthy that $\mathsf{E}(N_t) = M_N\, t + \frac{\mathsf{D}T - (\mathsf{E}T)^2}{2\,(\mathsf{E}T)^2} + o(1)$, $\mathsf{D}(N_t) = D_N^2\, t + o(t)$, $\mathsf{E}(V_t) = M_V\, t + \frac{\mathsf{E}Y(\mathsf{D}T - (\mathsf{E}T)^2)}{2\,(\mathsf{E}T)^2} + o(1)$, $\mathsf{D}(V_t) = D_V^2\, t + o(t)$, $t \to \infty$.

Let us introduce $M_X(r) := \mathsf{E}(e^{rX})$, which is the moment generating function of $X \stackrel{d}{=} Y - cT$; plainly, $M_X(0) = 1$. The primary assumption is that there exists a positive solution $\varkappa$, called either adjustment coefficient, or Lundberg's exponent, to the equation (w.r.t. r)

$$M_X(r) = 1, \tag{1.34}$$

which is referred to as Lundberg's equation.

This assumption is a significant limitation of the model. It implies that $M_X(r)$ is finite in a neighborhood of 0 or, in other words, that the right tail of c.d.f. F_X is exponentially bounded above. The latter follows from the equality $\mathsf{E}(e^{\varkappa X}) = 1$ and Markov's inequality, as follows:

$$1 - F_X(x) \leqslant e^{-\varkappa x}\, \mathsf{E}\,(e^{\varkappa X}) = e^{-\varkappa x}, \quad x > 0. \tag{1.35}$$

Starting with c.d.f. $F_{XT}(x,t) = \mathsf{P}\{X \leqslant x, T \leqslant t\}$ and having $\varkappa > 0$ found, we introduce the associated joint distribution[60], whose c.d.f. $F_{\bar{X}\bar{T}}(x,t) = \mathsf{P}\{\bar{X} \leqslant x, \bar{T} \leqslant t\}$ is defined by the equality[61]

$$F_{\bar{X}\bar{T}}(x,t) = \int_{-ct}^{x} \int_{0}^{t} e^{\varkappa z}\, F_{XT}(dz, dw).$$

Plainly, this is a proper probability distribution.

Recall that $c^* := \mathsf{E}Y/\mathsf{E}T$. The Cramér's (or normal) approximation is formulated separately, when $0 \leqslant c < c^*$ and $c > c^*$, with the case $c = c^*$ excluded, as follows.

For $0 \leqslant c < c^*$, i.e., for $\mathsf{E}X = \mathsf{E}Y - c\,\mathsf{E}T > 0$, we write[62]

$$m_{\triangledown} = \mathsf{E}T/\mathsf{E}X, \quad D_{\triangledown}^2 = \mathsf{E}\,(X\mathsf{E}T - T\mathsf{E}X)^2/(\mathsf{E}X)^3.$$

Plainly, we have $m_{\triangledown} > 0$ and $D_{\triangledown}^2 > 0$.

Proposition 1.1 (Case $0 \leqslant c < c^*$**)** *Assume that p.d.f. of the random vector (T, Y) is bounded above by a finite constant and $0 < D_{\triangledown}^2 < \infty$. Then*

$$d_u = \sup_{t>0} \left| \mathsf{P}\{\Upsilon_{u,c} \leqslant t\} - \Phi_{(m_{\triangledown} u, D_{\triangledown}^2 u)}(t) \right| = o(1), \quad u \to \infty.$$

If, in addition, $\mathsf{E}(Y^3) < \infty$, $\mathsf{E}(T^3) < \infty$, then $d_u = O(u^{-1/2})$, as $u \to \infty$.

When $c > c^*$, i.e., when $\mathsf{E}X = \mathsf{E}Y - c\,\mathsf{E}T < 0$, we write

$$m_{\vartriangle} = \mathsf{E}\bar{T}/\mathsf{E}\bar{X}, \quad D_{\vartriangle}^2 = \mathsf{E}\,(\bar{X}\mathsf{E}\bar{T} - \bar{T}\mathsf{E}\bar{X})^2/(\mathsf{E}\bar{X})^3,$$

$$\mathbb{C} = \frac{1}{\varkappa\,\mathsf{E}\bar{X}} \exp\left\{ -\sum_{n=1}^{\infty} \frac{1}{n} \mathsf{P}\{S_n > 0\} - \sum_{n=1}^{\infty} \frac{1}{n} \mathsf{P}\{\bar{S}_n \leqslant 0\} \right\},$$

---

[60] See, e.g., Example (b) in [78], Chapter XII, Section 4.

[61] Commonly used shorthand notation for it is $F_{\bar{X}\bar{T}}(dx, dt) = e^{\varkappa z} F_{XT}(dx, dt)$.

[62] Note that $m_{\triangledown}$, $D_{\triangledown}^2$, as well as $m_{\vartriangle}$, $D_{\vartriangle}^2$, $\varkappa$, $\mathbb{C}$ introduced below depend on c.

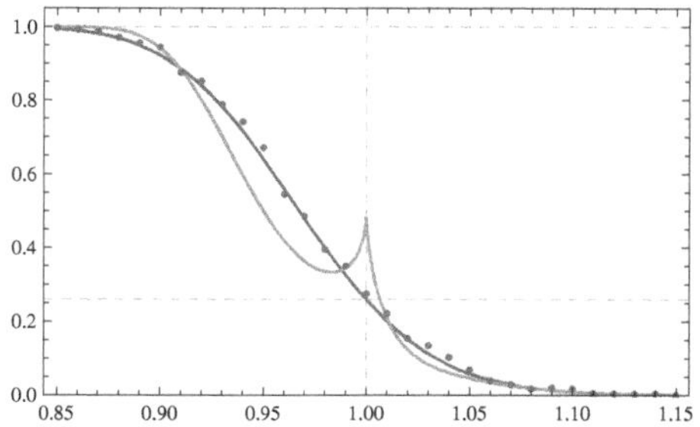

FIGURE 1.4: Graphs (X-axis is c) of numerically evaluated $\mathsf{P}\{\varUpsilon_{u,c} \leqslant t\}$ (smooth solid line), of the approximations of Proposition 1.3 (non-smooth solid line), and simulated values ($\Delta c = 0.05$, $N = 1000$) of $\mathsf{P}\{\varUpsilon_{u,c} \leqslant t\}$ (dots), when T and Y are exponentially distributed with parameters $\rho = 1$, $\delta = 1$, respectively, and $t = 1000$, $u = 50$. Horizontal grid line: $\mathsf{P}\{\varUpsilon_{u,c^*} \leqslant t\} = 0.26$.

where $\bar{X}_i \overset{d}{=} \bar{X}$, $i = 1, 2, \dots$, and $\bar{T}_i \overset{d}{=} \bar{T}$, $i = 1, 2, \dots$, are associated random variables, and $\bar{S}_n = \sum_{i=1}^n \bar{X}_i$, and $\bar{Z}_n = \sum_{i=1}^n \bar{T}_i$, $n = 1, 2, \dots$, are associated random walks.

Proposition 1.2 (Case $c > c^*$) *Assume that a positive solution $\varkappa > 0$ to equation (1.34) exists, p.d.f. of the random vector (T, Y) is bounded above by a finite constant, and $0 < D_{\vartriangle}^2 < \infty$. Then*

$$d_u = \sup_{t>0} \left| e^{\varkappa u} \mathsf{P}\{\varUpsilon_{u,c} \leqslant t\} - \mathbb{C}\,\varPhi_{(m_{\vartriangle} u, D_{\vartriangle}^2 u)}(t) \right| = o(1), \quad u \to \infty.$$

If, in addition, $\mathsf{E}(T^3) < \infty$, then $d_u = O(u^{-1/2})$, as $u \to \infty$.

When T and Y are exponentially distributed with positive parameters δ and ρ, respectively, elementary calculations (see [136], Proposition 2.3) yield $c^* = \delta/\rho$,

$$\begin{aligned} \mathbb{C} &= \delta/(c\rho), & \varkappa &= \rho\,(1 - \delta/(c\rho)), \\ m_{\triangledown} &= -\frac{1}{c\,(1 - \delta/(c\rho))}, & D_{\triangledown}^2 &= -\frac{2\,(\delta/(c\rho))}{c^2\rho\,(1 - \delta/(c\rho))^3}, \\ m_{\vartriangle} &= \frac{\delta/(c\rho)}{c\,(1 - \delta/(c\rho))}, & D_{\vartriangle}^2 &= \frac{2\,(\delta/(c\rho))}{c^2\rho\,(1 - \delta/(c\rho))^3}, \end{aligned} \tag{1.36}$$

and Propositions 1.1 and 1.2 are combined, as follows.

Proposition 1.3 *In the renewal model with T and Y exponentially distributed with positive parameters δ and ρ, respectively, when $0 \leqslant c < c^*$, we have*

$$\sup_{t>0} \left| \mathsf{P}\{\varUpsilon_{u,c} \leqslant t\} - \varPhi_{(m_{\triangledown} u, D_{\triangledown}^2 u)}(t) \right| = o(1), \quad u \to \infty, \tag{1.37}$$

where $m_{\triangledown} > 0$, $D^2_{\triangledown} > 0$ *are defined in* (1.36), *and, when* $c > c^*$, *we have*

$$\sup_{t>0} \left| e^{\varkappa u}\, \mathsf{P}\{\Upsilon_{u,c} \leqslant t\} - \mathbb{C}\,\Phi_{(m_{\vartriangle} u, D^2_{\vartriangle} u)}(t) \right| = o(1), \quad u \to \infty, \tag{1.38}$$

where $\varkappa > 0$, *and* $0 < \mathbb{C} < 1$, $m_{\vartriangle} > 0$, $D^2_{\vartriangle} > 0$ *are defined in* (1.36).

Diffusion approximation and heuristic procedures. The diffusion approximation is rigorously proved (see [86], [87]) in the scheme of series, which ties together a number of risk models, when $c_u = (1 + \tau_u)\,\mathsf{E}Y/\mathsf{E}T$ and $\tau_u\, u \to \kappa > 0$, as $u \to \infty$. This problem setting differs from the original one: having c_u related to u, we change the original risk reserve process, as u tends to infinity, which is illustrated (within the simulation framework) in Fig. 1.1: in the original setting, an increase of u would lead merely to a shift up of the entire bundle of simulated trajectories, without changing its shape, whereas in the setting with c_u dependent on u, as above, the shape changes.

By an awesome mix-up, the term "diffusion approximation" began to be used[63] for a certain kind of heuristic procedures proposed for numerical calculations (in the single risk model), rather than the original theoretically rationalized approximation (in the scheme of series, with many risk models).

The rigorous fundamentals of the diffusion approximation, as it is proved in [86], [87], are inevitably associated with "a family of claim surplus processes" (we quote from [9], last paragraph on p. 136), but its abstraction is given in [9], p. 136 as follows[64]:

> the idea behind the diffusion approximation is to first approximate the claim surplus process by a Brownian motion with drift by matching the two first moments, and next to note that such an approximation in particular implies that the first passage probabilities are close.

In [104], p. 246, it is formulated as follows:

> we take a limit of the process as the expected number of downward jumps becomes large and, simultaneously, the size of the jumps becomes small. Because the Brownian motion with drift

[63] In itself, replacing a rigorously proven result with a heuristic one is not a flaw, if it is not misleading. But if this substitution is disguised by the phrases like "for practical purposes", and by vague hints with mixed terminology, like "this is just the same as for the heavy traffic approximation for infinite horizon ruin probabilities" (see [9], p. 136), it may be misleading. Only an attentive reader, having encountered the phrase "these results can be used as approximations for the original surplus process based on the compound Poisson model" will pay attention to the disclaimer "all these are completely intuitive" (see [104], p. 253) placed a few paragraphs below.

[64] See also [9], p. 18, where it is even more straightforward: "the idea is simply to approximate the risk process by a Brownian motion (or a more general diffusion) by fitting the first and second moments, and to use the fact that first passage probabilities are more readily calculated for diffusions than for the risk process itself".

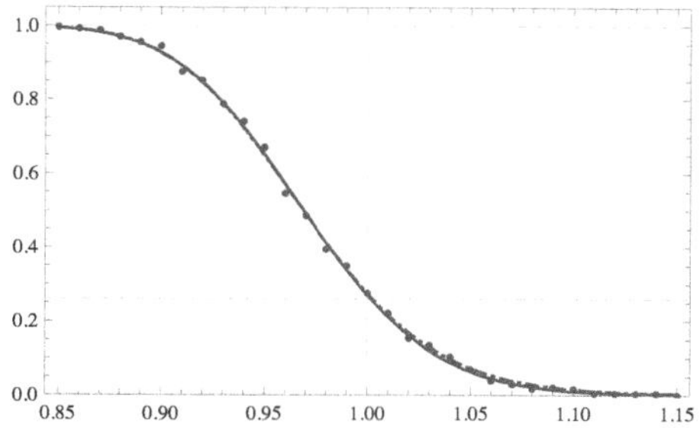

FIGURE 1.5: Graphs (X-axis is c) of numerically evaluated $\mathsf{P}\{\varUpsilon_{u,c} \leqslant t\}$ (solid line), of $\mathcal{M}_{u,c}(t)$ (dash-dotted line), and simulated values ($\Delta c = 0.05$, $N = 1000$) of $\mathsf{P}\{\varUpsilon_{u,c} \leqslant t\}$, when T and Y are exponentially distributed with parameters $\delta = 1$, $\rho = 1$, respectively, and $t = 1000$, $u = 50$. Horizontal grid line: $\mathsf{P}\{\varUpsilon_{u,c^*} \leqslant t\} = 0.26$.

> process is characterized by the infinitesimal mean and infinitesimal variance, we force the mean and variance functions to be the same for the two processes. In this way, the Brownian motion with drift can be thought of as an approximation to the compound Poisson-based surplus process. Similarly, the compound Poisson process can be used as an approximation for Brownian motion.

In both cases, this looks like an outline of a heuristic procedure, whose nub is a matching of the first two moments, rather than a summary of the proof of a mathematical result, referred to as the diffusion approximation, whose highlight is the weak convergence of probability measures (see, e.g., [20]) in the Skorohod space $D[0, \infty)$.

Since the diffusion process is skip-free, this idea ignores the presence of the overshoot. To account for this and other similar deficits, a so-called corrected diffusion approximation (see, e.g., [176]) was put forth.

Inverse Gaussian approximation. The inverse Gaussian approximation for $\mathsf{P}\{\varUpsilon_{u,c} \leqslant t\}$ is an innovative result, which we recall without proof. The interested reader will find it discussed in detail in [135], Chapter 6.

First, recall that the inverse Gaussian distribution with positive parameters μ and λ is (for more information, see Section B.1, or [135], Chapter 1) a distribution concentrated on the positive half-line, whose p.d.f. is

$$\begin{aligned} f(x; \mu, \lambda, -\tfrac{1}{2}) &:= \frac{\lambda^{1/2}}{\sqrt{2\pi}}\, x^{-3/2} \exp\left\{ -\frac{\lambda\,(x-\mu)^2}{2\,\mu^2 x} \right\} \\ &= \lambda^{1/2} x^{-3/2}\, \varphi_{(0,1)}\left(\sqrt{\frac{\lambda}{x}} \left(\frac{x}{\mu} - 1 \right) \right), \quad x > 0, \end{aligned}$$

TABLE 1.2: Models in Figs. 1.5–1.8

	Inter-claim interval T	Claim amount Y	M	D^2
Fig. 1.5:	Exponentially distributed; $\delta = 1$	Exponentially distributed; $\rho = 1$	1	2
Fig. 1.6:	2-mixture; $\delta_1 = 1$, $\delta_2 = 2$, $p = 2/3$	Pareto; $a_Y = 4.0$, $b_Y = 0.35$	0.88	2.30
Fig. 1.7:	Erlang; $\delta = 6.0$, $k = 4$	Pareto; $a_Y = 4.0$, $b_Y = 0.4$	0.8	1.2
Fig. 1.8:	Pareto; $a_T = 4.0$, $b_T = 0.4$	Pareto; $a_Y = 4.0$, $b_Y = 0.4$	1	1.33

and whose c.d.f. is

$$\begin{aligned} F(x;\mu,\lambda) := {} & \varPhi_{(0,1)}\Bigg(\sqrt{\frac{\lambda}{x}}\left(\frac{x}{\mu}-1\right)\Bigg) \\ & + \exp\left\{\frac{2\lambda}{\mu}\right\}\varPhi_{(0,1)}\Bigg(-\sqrt{\frac{\lambda}{x}}\left(\frac{x}{\mu}+1\right)\Bigg), \quad x > 0. \end{aligned} \tag{1.39}$$

This distribution is skewed[65]. Its mean, variance, and the third central moment are (see Section B.1) μ, μ^3/λ, and $3\,\mu^5/\lambda^2$, respectively.

Let us write (see [135], Section 3.2)

$$\mathcal{M}_{u,c}(t) := \int_0^{\frac{ct}{u}} \frac{1}{x+1}\,\varphi_{\left(cM(x+1),\frac{c^2D^2}{u}(x+1)\right)}(x)\,dx, \tag{1.40}$$

where

$$M := \mathsf{E}\,T/\mathsf{E}\,Y, \quad D^2 := ((\mathsf{E}\,T)^2\mathsf{D}\,Y + (\mathsf{E}\,Y)^2\mathsf{D}\,T)/(\mathsf{E}\,Y)^3. \tag{1.41}$$

Bearing in mind that $c^* := \mathsf{E}\,Y/\mathsf{E}\,T$, it can be rewritten as $c^* := M^{-1}$.

We can show (see [135], Section 3.2) by elementary calculations that

$$\mathcal{M}_{u,c}(t) = \begin{cases} \Bigg(F\Big(\dfrac{ct}{u}+1;\mu,\lambda\Big) \\ \qquad -F(1;\mu,\lambda)\Bigg)\Bigg|_{\mu=\frac{1}{1-cM},\lambda=\frac{u}{c^2D^2}}, & 0 < c \leqslant c^*, \\ \exp\left\{-\dfrac{2\lambda}{\hat\mu}\right\}\Bigg(F\Big(\dfrac{ct}{u}+1;\hat\mu,\lambda\Big) \\ \qquad -F(1;\hat\mu,\lambda)\Bigg)\Bigg|_{\hat\mu=\frac{1}{cM-1},\lambda=\frac{u}{c^2D^2}}, & c > c^*, \end{cases} \tag{1.42}$$

[65]The appearance of this skewed distribution in Proposition 1.4 below correlates with numerous claims by many practitioners that (see [150]) the "world of normal or, more generally, elliptically contoured risk distributions" is chosen wrongly when solvency problems are considered, whereas the "world of skewed distributions" is adequate in this framework.

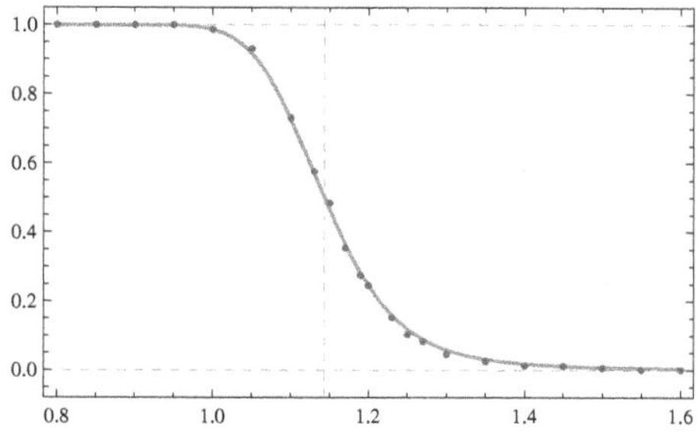

FIGURE 1.6: Graph (X-axis is c) of numerically evaluated $\mathcal{M}_{u,c}(t)$ (solid line) and simulated values ($\Delta c = 0.05$, $N = 1000$) of $\mathsf{P}\{\varUpsilon_{u,c} \leqslant t\}$ (dots), when T is 2-mixture and Y is Pareto (see details in Table 1.2) $t = 1000$, $u = 40$.

where, calculating the appropriate limits, $\mathcal{M}_{u,\infty}(t) = 0$,

$$\mathcal{M}_{u,0}(t) = \varPhi_{(0,1)}\left(\frac{M\sqrt{u}}{D}\right) - \varPhi_{(0,1)}\left(\frac{Mu - t}{D\sqrt{u}}\right),$$

$$\mathcal{M}_{u,c^*}(t) = 2\left(\varPhi_{(0,1)}\left(\frac{M\sqrt{u}}{D}\right) - \varPhi_{(0,1)}\left(\frac{Mu}{D\sqrt{u + c^*t}}\right)\right).$$

The following core proposition is Theorem 5.5 in Chapter 5.

Proposition 1.4 *Assume that p.d.f. $f_T(x)$ and $f_Y(x)$ are bounded above by a finite constant, $D^2 > 0$, $\mathsf{E}(T^3) < \infty$, $\mathsf{E}(Y^3) < \infty$. Then for any $c \geqslant 0$*

$$\sup_{t>0} \left| \mathsf{P}\{\varUpsilon_{u,c} \leqslant t\} - \mathcal{M}_{u,c}(t) \right| = o(1), \quad t, u \to \infty.$$

We repeat that the proof of Proposition 1.4, called inverse Gaussian approximation, is presented in detail in [135]. In a nutshell, it is based on (see Section 5.2.1) Kendall's identity, which represents the distribution of $\varUpsilon_{u,c}$ in terms of convolution powers of p.d.f. $f_T(x)$ and $f_Y(x)$. Then the central limit theory is applied to these convolution powers.

A collation of normal and inverse Gaussian approximations. Let us compare Cramér's (or normal) and inverse Gaussian approximations. We will focus on the generality and accuracy of these results.

First, the normal approximation is of a limited applicability: the moment condition on Y in Proposition 1.2, i.e., that the distribution of Y must be light-tail, is overly restrictive. Formally, this is shown in (1.35). On the contrary, the moment conditions of Proposition 1.4 are very general for both T and Y.

Second, the normal approximation fails near the point c^* which, from the angle of such approximation, looks like an irregular point. Not to mention that the case $c = c^*$ is formally excluded, the accuracy of the normal approximation

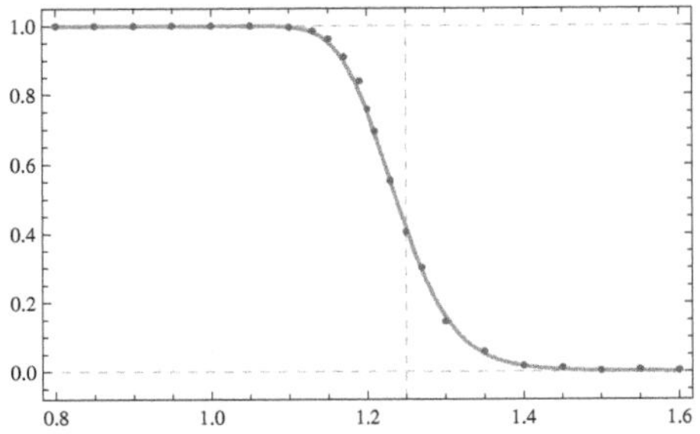

FIGURE 1.7: Graph (X-axis is c) of numerically evaluated $\mathcal{M}_{u,c}(t)$ (solid line) and simulated values ($\Delta c = 0.05$, $N = 1000$) of $\mathsf{P}\{\varUpsilon_{u,c} \leqslant t\}$ (dots), when T is Erlang and Y is Pareto (see details in Table 1.2), $t = 1000$, $u = 40$.

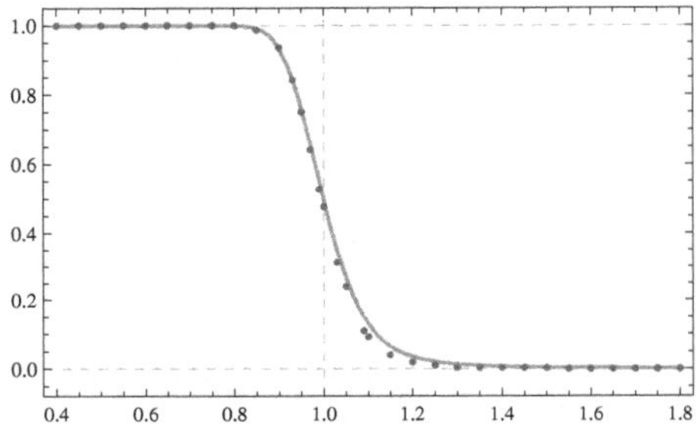

FIGURE 1.8: Graph (X-axis is c) of numerically evaluated $\mathcal{M}_{u,c}(t)$ (solid line) and simulated values ($\Delta c = 0.05$, $N = 1000$) of $\mathsf{P}\{\varUpsilon_{u,c} \leqslant t\}$ (dots), when T and Y are Pareto (see details in Table 1.2), $t = 1000$, $u = 40$.

near c^* is very poor. This is illustrated in Fig. 1.4. On the contrary, the point c^*, which is not at all any special point (if we look at our problem as at a level crossing problem for a compound renewal process, like in [135]), is a fairly regular point from the standpoint of inverse Gaussian approximation.

The accuracy of inverse Gaussian approximation of $\mathsf{P}\{\varUpsilon_{u,c} \leqslant t\}$ by $\mathcal{M}_{u,c}(t)$ is high for all c for which these values are not negligibly small. This is illustrated in Figs. 1.5–1.8. Note that Figs. 1.4 and 1.5 are drawn under the same conditions and their comparison is very instructive. We emphasize it that the advantages of the latter approximation are especially noticeable, when c (including the point c^* and its neighborhood) is such that the values of $\mathsf{P}\{\varUpsilon_{u,c} \leqslant t\}$ are not too small.

To demonstrate[66] that the inverse Gaussian approximation works well for fat-tail Y, we address Figs. 1.6–1.8, where $t = 1000$, $u = 40$. To get simulated values of $\mathsf{P}\{\varUpsilon_{u,c} \leqslant t\}$ according to the algorithm described in Section 6.2.1,

[66]The reader will find a more detailed discussion of these issues in Chapter 6.

we take $\Delta c = 0.05$ (and even less in the vicinity of c^*, where this function's curvature is considerable), and $N = 1000$.

In Fig. 1.6, we draw the graph of $\mathcal{M}_{u,c}(t)$ calculated by means of numerical integration in (1.40) for T, which is two-mixture of exponential with parameters $\delta_1 = 1$, $\delta_2 = 2$, $p = 2/3$ and Y, which is Pareto with parameters $a_Y = 4.0$, $b_Y = 0.35$, whence $c^* = 1.143$, $M = 0.8750$, and $D^2 = 2.3042$. In Fig. 1.7, we do this for T, which is Erlang with parameters $\delta = 6.0$, $k = 4$ and Y, which is Pareto with parameters $a_Y = 4.0$, $b_Y = 0.4$, whence $c^* = 1.25$, $M = 0.8$, and $D^2 = 1.2$. In Fig. 1.8, we do this for T, which is Pareto with parameters $a_T = 4.0$, $b_T = 0.4$ and Y, which is Pareto with parameters $a_Y = 4.0$, $b_Y = 0.4$, whence $c^* = 1$, $M = 1$, and $D^2 = 1.33$.

1.3.7 Non-ruin capital in the general risk model

In the general risk model (except for some very special one) to try to express $\mathsf{P}\{\varUpsilon_{u,c} \leqslant t\}$ for all $t \geqslant 0$ in terms of elementary or special functions is hopeless, which nobody can deny. A more challenging problem, i.e., to express the implicit function $u_{\alpha,t}(c)$, $c \geqslant 0$, for all $t \geqslant 0$ in terms of elementary or special functions, is even more hopeless. Moreover, it is hopeless, at least when c is around c^*, to try to approximate $u_{\alpha,t}(c)$, as $t \to \infty$, using the normal approximation, for its accuracy is very low. But even besides this, there is a structural obstacle that hinders us along this way.

A structural imbalance. Let us describe an issue that we have named a structural imbalance. Note first that the structure of the approximation in Propositions 1.1 and 1.2 is significantly different from the structure of the CLT-type approximation used to get (1.32) and (1.33). This is particularly evident when $c = 0$, i.e., when the left-hand sides of equations (1.16) and (1.28) are the same and can be written as $\mathsf{P}\{V_t > u\}$.

Plainly, being solutions to the same equation, $u_{\alpha,t}(0)$ and $\underline{u}_{\alpha,t}(0)$ coincide with each other. The CLT-type approximation is

$$\mathsf{P}\{V_t > u\} \approx \varPhi_{(0,1)}\left(\frac{u - M_V\, t}{D_V\,\sqrt{t}}\right), \quad t \to \infty, \tag{1.43}$$

whereas the approximation in Proposition 1.1 is

$$\mathsf{P}\{V_t > u\} \approx \varPhi_{(0,1)}\left(\frac{t - m_{\triangledown}|_{c=0}\, u}{D_{\triangledown}|_{c=0}\,\sqrt{u}}\right), \quad u \to \infty. \tag{1.44}$$

When T and Y are exponentially distributed with positive parameters δ and ρ, respectively, $m_{\triangledown}|_{c=0} = \rho/\delta$, $D^2_{\triangledown}|_{c=0} = 2\rho/\delta^2$ in (1.43), and $M_V = \delta/\rho$, $D_V^2 = 2\delta/\rho^2$ in (1.44).

It is worth noting that if $u_{\alpha,t}(0)$ did not tend to infinity, as $t \to \infty$, the approximation (1.44) (unlike (1.43)) would be useless to get information about

$u_{\alpha,t}(0)$, as $t \to \infty$. Fortunately, $u_{\alpha,t}(0) \sim M_V\, t$, which tends to infinity, as $t \to \infty$. Indeed, $u_{\alpha,t}(0)$ is equal to $\underline{u}_{\alpha,t}(0)$ and (see (1.33))

$$\underline{u}_{\alpha,t}(0) = M_V\, t + \kappa_\alpha\, D_V \sqrt{t}\,(1 + o(1)), \quad t \to \infty.$$

When c is sufficiently larger than c^*, i.e., when $c > Kc^*$ with $K > 1$ sufficiently large, $u_{\alpha,t}(c)$ is finite regardless of t. So, the structural difference between the approximations of Propositions 1.1 and 1.2 matters.

We make the following conclusion. In order to approximate $u_{\alpha,t}(c)$, $c \geqslant 0$, as $t \to \infty$, we can use Propositions 1.1–1.2, i.e., the normal approximation (provided that it is sufficiently accurate), and Proposition 1.4, i.e., the inverse Gaussian approximation, but only for those c, for which $u_{\alpha,t}(c)$ tends to infinity, as $t \to \infty$.

The structure of non-ruin capital. The analytical technique developed in [135], which, in particular, yields Proposition 1.4, is suitable for asymptotic analysis of the non-ruin capital in the general risk model.

The following proposition, which is Theorems 5.13 and 5.14 in Chapter 5 below, gives an asymptotic representation for $u_{\alpha,t}(c)$ at the points $c = 0$ and $c = c^*$, where (see (1.41)) $c^* := \mathsf{E}\,Y/\mathsf{E}\,T$ equals to $1/M$; this generalizes the asymptotic equalities (1.30).

Proposition 1.5 *Assume that p.d.f.* $f_T(x)$ *and* $f_Y(x)$ *are bounded above by a finite constant,* $D^2 > 0$, $\mathsf{E}(T^3) < \infty$, $\mathsf{E}(Y^3) < \infty$. *Then*

$$u_{\alpha,t}(0) = \frac{t}{M} + \frac{D}{M^{3/2}}\,\kappa_\alpha \sqrt{t}\,(1 + o(1)), \quad t \to \infty,$$

and

$$u_{\alpha,t}(c^*) = \frac{D}{M^{3/2}}\,\kappa_{\alpha/2} \sqrt{t}\,(1 + o(1)), \quad t \to \infty.$$

The following proposition is Theorem 5.15 in Chapter 5 below. It yields an asymptotic representation for $u_{\alpha,t}(c)$, $c \geqslant 0$, which generalizes the asymptotic equality (1.29).

Proposition 1.6 *Assume that differentiable p.d.f.* $f_T(x)$ *and* $f_Y(x)$ *are bounded above by a finite constant,* $D^2 > 0$, $\mathsf{E}(T^3) < \infty$, $\mathsf{E}(Y^3) < \infty$. *Then*

$$u_{\alpha,t}(c) = \begin{cases} (c^* - c)\,t + \dfrac{D}{M^{3/2}}\,\mathsf{z}_{\alpha,t}\!\left(\dfrac{M^{3/2}(c^* - c)}{D}\sqrt{t}\right)\sqrt{t}, & 0 \leqslant c \leqslant c^*, \\[2ex] \dfrac{D}{M^{3/2}}\,\mathsf{z}_{\alpha,t}\!\left(\dfrac{M^{3/2}(c^* - c)}{D}\sqrt{t}\right)\sqrt{t}, & c > c^*, \end{cases} \tag{1.45}$$

where for t sufficiently large the function $\mathsf{z}_{\alpha,t}(x)$, $x \in \mathsf{R}$, *is continuous, monotone increasing as* x *increases from* $-\infty$ *to* 0, *monotone decreasing as* x *increases from* 0 *to* ∞, *and such that*

$$\lim_{x \to -\infty} \mathsf{z}_{\alpha,t}(x) = 0, \ \lim_{x \to \infty} \mathsf{z}_{\alpha,t}(x) = \kappa_\alpha$$

and $\mathsf{z}_{\alpha,t}(0) = \kappa_{\alpha/2}(1 + o(1))$, $t \to \infty$.

Note that (1.45) (the same as (1.29)) does not give an explicit expression for $u_{\alpha,t}(c)$, $c \geqslant 0$. Indeed, the right-hand sides of (1.45) and (1.29) depend on the function $\mathsf{z}_{\alpha,t}(x)$, $x \in \mathsf{R}$, which is not explicitly specified.

Analytically, the form of the function $u_{\alpha,t}(c)$, $c \geqslant 0$, is described in Proposition 1.6 quite satisfactorily, which will be complemented in Chapters 3–5 by asymptotic analysis in specially selected areas for c. But practical applications require numerical calculations. We need sound numerical procedures and simple but accurate (upper) bounds on $u_{\alpha,t}(c)$, $c \geqslant 0$, in terms of elementary functions.

A procedure for calculating non-ruin capital, when $0 \leqslant c \leqslant c^*$. For (see (1.41)) $M := \mathsf{E}T/\mathsf{E}Y$, $D^2 := ((\mathsf{E}T)^2\mathsf{D}Y + (\mathsf{E}Y)^2\mathsf{D}T)/(\mathsf{E}Y)^3$, and $\mathcal{M}_{u,c}(t)$ introduced in (1.40) and written in a closed form in (1.42), a solution to (see (4.22)) the equation

$$\mathcal{M}_{u,c}(t) = \alpha, \tag{1.46}$$

denoted by $u^{[\mathcal{M}]}_{\alpha,t}(c)$, $c \geqslant 0$, and referred to as $\mathcal{M}$-level, is calculated using standard numeric procedures.

When $0 \leqslant c \leqslant c^* := \mathsf{E}Y/\mathsf{E}T$ (this interval may be slightly expanded by moving c^* a bit to the right, depending on t, see Chapter 5 for detail), the difference between $u_{\alpha,t}(c)$ and $u^{[\mathcal{M}]}_{\alpha,t}(c)$ tends to zero, as $t \to \infty$. Therefore, for t large, the numerical procedure that yields $u^{[\mathcal{M}]}_{\alpha,t}(c)$ for such values of c as a solution to (1.46) also yields $u_{\alpha,t}(c)$. For such values of c that $u_{\alpha,t}(c)$ and $u^{[\mathcal{M}]}_{\alpha,t}(c)$ do not have to be close to each other for t large, i.e., for $c > Kc^*$, $K > 1$, this is not true.

Bounds on non-ruin capital, when $0 \leqslant c \leqslant c^*$. We start with the following bilateral bounds, when $0 \leqslant c \leqslant c^*$. They are straightforward from Proposition 1.6:

$$\begin{aligned}(c^* - c)\,t + \frac{D}{M^{3/2}}\,\kappa_\alpha\sqrt{t}\,(1 + o(1)) &\leqslant u_{\alpha,t}(c)\\ &\leqslant (c^* - c)\,t + \frac{D}{M^{3/2}}\,\kappa_{\alpha/2}\sqrt{t}\,(1 + o(1)), \quad t \to \infty.\end{aligned} \tag{1.47}$$

Bounds on non-ruin capital, when $c > c^*$. We proceed with the upper bounds, when $c > c^*$. In this case, sensible is to start with $\overline{u}_\alpha(c)$, $c > c^*$, which yields an accurate upper bound, when c is much larger than c^*, and a very inaccurate upper bound, when c is a little less than c^*. We further correct this bound, balancing precision and complexity, and get a number of upper bounds for all $c > c^*$. Finally, we compare these bounds with the simulated values of $u_{\alpha,t}(c)$, $c > c^*$.

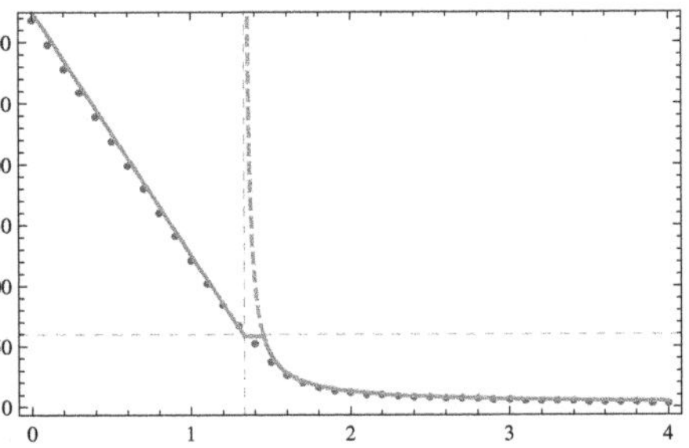

FIGURE 1.9: Graphs (X-axis is c) of upper bound (1.47), when $0 \leqslant c \leqslant c^*$, upper bound (1.49), when $c > c^*$, and simulated values of $u_{\alpha,t}(c)$ (dots) in Model (A), i.e., for T and Y exponentially distributed with parameters $\delta = 3/5$, $\rho = 4/5$, respectively, and $\alpha = 0.05$, $t = 200$. Vertical grid line: $c^* = 4/3$. Horizontal grid line: $u_{\alpha,t}(c^*) = 59.90$.

Seeking for more or less elementary, but accurate, upper bounds for $u_{\alpha,t}(c)$, $c > c^*$, we focus first on its natural upper bound $\overline{u}_\alpha(c)$, $c > c^*$. Recall that the latter is a solution to equation (1.20), which in terms of (see (1.11)) the time of the first ruin $\varUpsilon_{u,c} := \inf\{s \geqslant 0 : V_s - cs > u\}$ may be rewritten as

$$\mathsf{P}\{\varUpsilon_{u,c} < \infty\} = \alpha.$$

The left-hand side of this equation is the well-studied (see, e.g., [158]) probability of ultimate ruin[67]. Following the theory developed for $\mathsf{P}\{\varUpsilon_{u,c} < \infty\}$, when $c > c^*$, we focus on the following particular models.

- Model (A): compound Poisson model, when Y is exponentially distributed,
- Model (B): compound Poisson model, when distribution of Y is light-tailed (but not exponential),
- Model (C): compound Poisson model, when distribution of Y is fat-tailed,
- Model (D): renewal (but not compound Poisson) model, when Y is exponentially distributed,
- Model (E): renewal (but not compound Poisson) model, when distribution of Y is light-tailed (but not exponential),
- Model (F): renewal (but not compound Poisson) model, when the distribution of Y is fat-tailed.

Model (A). This model is verbally described as a model with generic interclaim interval T and claim size Y both exponentially distributed, with positive parameters δ and ρ, respectively. The assumption on T can be also formulated as that claims arrival process is Poisson, with intensity δ.

[67]We recall that $\psi_\infty(u, c) := \mathsf{P}\{\varUpsilon_{u,c} < \infty\}$, or $\psi_\infty(u, c) := \mathsf{P}\{\inf_{s\geqslant 0} R_s < 0\}$.

By elementary calculations, we have $c^* = \delta/\rho$, $M = \rho/\delta$, $D^2 = 2\,\rho/\delta^2$. The adjustment coefficient, or Lundberg's exponent, is $\varkappa = \rho - \delta/c$.

When $c > \delta/\rho$, we have (see Section 5.2.4)

$$\mathsf{P}\{\varUpsilon_{u,c} < \infty\} = (1 - \varkappa/\rho)\, e^{-\varkappa u}, \quad c > \delta/\rho,$$

for all $u \geqslant 0$. This can be rewritten as[68]

$$\mathsf{P}\{\varUpsilon_{u,c} < \infty\} = (\delta/(c\rho)) \exp\{-(\rho - \delta/c)\, u\}, \quad c > \delta/\rho, \tag{1.48}$$

for all $u \geqslant 0$, and by elementary calculations we have

$$u_{\alpha,t}(c) \leqslant \max\left\{0, -\frac{\ln(\alpha c\rho/\delta)}{\rho - \delta/c}\right\}, \quad c > \delta/\rho, \tag{1.49}$$

which is an upper bound that satisfies our needs.

In Fig. 1.9, the upper bounds (1.47) in the case $0 \leqslant c \leqslant \delta/\rho$, and (1.49) in the case $c > \delta/\rho$, are drawn for $t = 200$, $\alpha = 0.05$, $\delta = 4/5$, $\rho = 3/5$, whence $c^* = 1.3333$, $M = 0.75$, and $D^2 = 1.875$. By dots are shown the simulated values of $u_{\alpha,t}(c)$.

Note that in Fig. 1.9 a bound slightly to the right of the point $c^* = \delta/\rho$ is shown as a horizontal line at the level $u_{\alpha,t}(c^*) = 59.9033$, up to its intersection with $\overline{u}_\alpha(c)$, $c > \delta/\rho$. This is a justified upper bound on $u_{\alpha,t}(c)$, which is obviously monotone decreasing, as c increases. If we prove (which is uneasy) that $u_{\alpha,t}(c)$ is convex[69], then we would construct more accurate bounds. This issue will be addressed in Section 3.6.

Let us make a remark concerning (see Proposition 1.3) the normal approximation, which turns out to be useless for the above analysis. In Model (A), when $c > c^* = \delta/\rho$, we have (see (1.38))

$$\lim_{u\to\infty} \mathsf{P}\{\varUpsilon_{u,c} < \infty\}\, e^{\varkappa u} = \mathbb{C}, \tag{1.50}$$

where $0 < \mathbb{C} = \delta/(c\rho) < 1$ and $\varkappa = \rho - \delta/c > 0$.

Nobody can deny that (1.50) is one of the most famous and best known results of risk theory. This result holds not only in Model (A), but in much more general renewal risk models (see, e.g., [158], Theorems 5.4.2 and 6.5.7). But the information on the asymptotic behavior of $\mathsf{P}\{\varUpsilon_{u,c} < \infty\}$, as $u \to \infty$, is pointless in the study of $u_{\alpha,t}(c)$, when $c > Kc^*$, $K > 1$, as above, because in this case $u_{\alpha,t}(c)$ is finite.

Model (B). This model is verbally described as a model with generic interclaim interval T exponentially distributed with parameter δ, and claim size Y whose distribution is (see Section B.1) light-tail, but non-exponentially distributed, e.g.,

---

[68] Recall that $\overline{u}_\alpha(c)$ is a solution to equation $\mathsf{P}\{\varUpsilon_{u,c} < \infty\} = \alpha$. In this case, this equation can be rewritten as $(\delta/(c\rho)) \exp\{-(\rho - \delta/c)\, u\} = \alpha$.

[69] Convex functions are of the shape $\smile$.

Example (a): T is exponentially distributed and Y is 2-mixture,

Example (b): T is exponentially distributed and Y is Erlang.

The assumption on T can be also formulated as that claims arrival process is Poisson, with intensity δ.

Since $c^* = \delta\,\mathsf{E}\,Y$, equation (1.34) can be rewritten as the equation (w.r.t. r) $\mathsf{E}\exp\{r\,Y\} = 1+c\,r/\delta$, whose positive solution $\varkappa$ is the adjustment coefficient, or Lundberg's exponent. When $c > c^*$, we have (see Section 5.2.4)

$$\mathsf{P}\{\Upsilon_{u,c} < \infty\} \leqslant e^{-\varkappa u}, \quad c > \delta\,\mathsf{E}\,Y, \tag{1.51}$$

for all $u \geqslant 0$. Therefore, by simple calculations we have

$$u_{\alpha,t}(c) \leqslant -\frac{\ln\alpha}{\varkappa}, \quad c > \delta\,\mathsf{E}\,Y, \tag{1.52}$$

and the problem reduces to finding $\varkappa$ in a closed form.

Let us make a remark concerning the balance between efficiency and simplicity. In Model (A), to get the upper bound (1.49) for $u_{\alpha,t}(c)$, $c > \delta/\rho$, we used a closed-form expression (1.48) for $\mathsf{P}\{\Upsilon_{u,c} < \infty\}$. In Model (B), which includes Model (A) as a special case, we used inequality (1.51): in this case there are no such accurate and simple-looking results as (1.48). Consequently, the upper bound (1.52), which for Y exponentially distributed with parameter ρ takes the form

$$u_{\alpha,t}(c) \leqslant -\frac{\ln\alpha}{\rho - \delta/c}, \quad c > \delta/\rho, \tag{1.53}$$

is less accurate than (1.49). Thus, sacrificing accuracy for generality, we strive not to sacrifice simplicity.

Model (C). This model is verbally described as a model with generic inter-claim interval T exponentially distributed with parameter δ, and claim size Y whose distribution is (see Section B.1) fat-tail, e.g.,

Example (a): T is exponentially distributed and Y is Pareto,

Example (b): T is exponentially distributed and Y is Kummer.

The assumption on T can be also formulated as that claims arrival process is Poisson, with intensity δ.

In this case, we have no inequality like (1.51), but we have its substitutes of a rather complex structure. We will discuss this issue in detail (see Section 5.2.4, Theorem 5.9) in Chapter 5 below.

To set an example, let us focus on Model (C), Example (a): T is exponentially distributed with parameter $\delta > 0$ and Y is Pareto with parameters $a_Y > 0$, $b_Y > 0$, whose p.d.f. are

$$f_T(x) = \delta\,e^{-\delta\,x}, \quad f_Y(x) = \frac{a_Y b_Y}{(x\,b_Y + 1)^{a_Y+1}}, \quad x > 0,$$

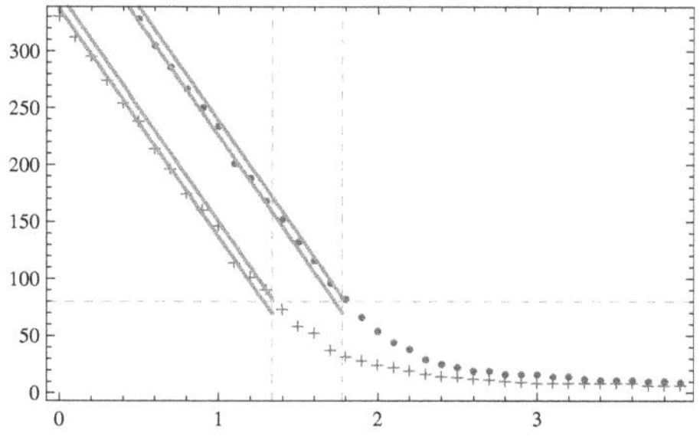

FIGURE 1.10: Graphs (X-axis is c) of two-sided bounds (1.47), when $0 \leqslant c \leqslant c^*$, and simulated values of $u_{\alpha,t}(c)$ in Model (C), Example (a), i.e., for T exponentially distributed with parameter $\delta = 4/5$ and Y Pareto with parameters $a_Y = 10$, $b_Y = 0.05$ (dots), $a_Y = 3$, $b_Y = 0.3$ (crosses), and $\alpha = 0.05$, $t = 200$. Vertical grid lines: $c^* = 1.78$ (dots) and $c^* = 1.33$ (crosses). Horizontal grid line: $u_{\alpha,t}(c^*) = 80$ (the same for dots and crosses).

respectively. We can show by elementary calculations that

$$\begin{aligned} \mathsf{E}\,T &= 1/\delta, & \mathsf{D}\,T &= 1/\delta^2, \\ \mathsf{E}\,Y &= 1/((a_Y-1)\,b_Y), & \mathsf{D}\,Y &= a_Y/((a_Y-1)^2\,(a_Y-2)\,b_Y^2). \end{aligned}$$

Plainly, $c^* = \delta/((a_Y-1)\,b_Y)$, the constants defined in (1.41) are

$$M = \frac{(a_Y-1)\,b_Y}{\delta}, \quad D^2 = \frac{2\,(a_Y-1)^2\,b_Y}{\delta^2\,(a_Y-2)},$$

and the adjustment coefficient does not exist.

In Fig. 1.10, the upper and lower bounds (1.47) in the case $0 \leqslant c \leqslant c^*$ are drawn. By dots, drawn are simulated values of $u_{\alpha,t}(c)$, $c \geqslant 0$. We note that for $a_Y = 3$, $b_Y = 0.3$ (crosses), the third moment $\mathsf{E}(Y^3)$ is infinite, and Fig. 1.10 suggests that the moment conditions in Propositions 1.5 and 1.6 may be relaxed.

To set another example, let us focus on Model (C), Example (b): T is exponentially distributed with parameter $\delta > 0$ and Y is Kummer with parameters $k_Y > 0$, $l_Y > 0$, whose p.d.f. are[70]

$$f_T(x) = \delta\,e^{-\delta\,x}, \quad f_Y(x) = \frac{k_Y}{2}\,\frac{\Gamma\big(\frac{k_Y+l_Y}{2}\big)}{\Gamma\big(\frac{k_Y}{2}\big)}\,U\Big(1+\frac{l_Y}{2}, 2-\frac{k_Y}{2}, \frac{k_Y}{l_Y}\,x\Big), \quad x>0,$$

with $U(a,b,z) = \Gamma(a)^{-1}\int_0^\infty e^{-zt}t^{a-1}(1+t)^{b-a-1}\,dt$, respectively. We can show by elementary calculations that

$$\mathsf{E}(T^k) = \frac{k!}{\delta^k}, \quad \mathsf{E}(Y^k) = \frac{\Gamma\big(\frac{k_Y}{2}+k\big)\Gamma\big(\frac{l_Y}{2}-k\big)}{\Gamma\big(\frac{k_Y}{2}\big)\Gamma\big(\frac{l_Y}{2}\big)}\,l_Y^k\,k_Y^{-k}, \quad 2k < l_Y, \quad k = 1,2,\ldots.$$

[70]For other equivalent formulas for $f_Y(x)$ see [119].

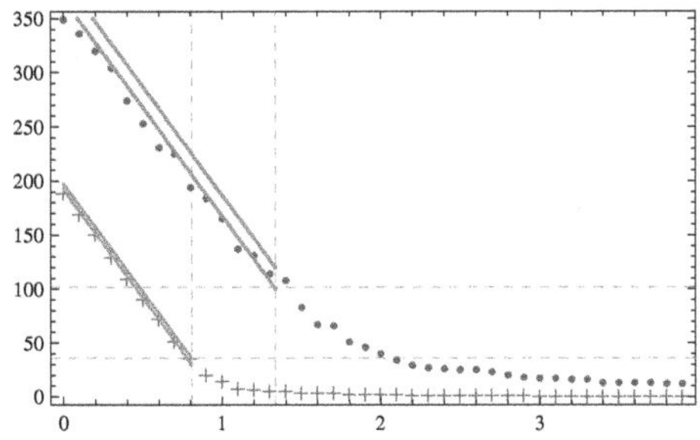

FIGURE 1.11: Graphs (X-axis is c) of two-sided bounds (1.47), when $0 \leqslant c \leqslant c^*$, and simulated values of $u_{\alpha,t}(c)$ in Model (C), Example (b), i.e., for T exponentially distributed with parameter $\delta = 4/5$ and Y Kummer with parameters $k_Y = 5$, $l_Y = 5$ (dots), $k_Y = 200$, $l_Y = 200$ (crosses), and $\alpha = 0.05$, $t = 200$. Vertical grid line: $c^* = 1.33$ (dots) and $c^* = 0.81$ (crosses). Horizontal grid lines: simulated $u_{\alpha,t}(c^*) = 102$ (dots) and $u_{\alpha,t}(c^*) = 36$ (crosses).

In particular,

$$\mathsf{E}T = 1/\delta, \qquad \mathsf{D}T = 1/\delta^2,$$
$$\mathsf{E}Y = \frac{l_Y}{l_Y - 2}, \quad \mathsf{D}Y = \frac{l_Y^2(4(l_Y - 2) + k_Y l_Y)}{k_Y(l_Y - 2)^2(l_Y - 4)}.$$

Plainly, $c^* = \delta\, l_Y/(l_Y - 2)$, the constants defined in (1.41) are

$$M = \frac{l_Y - 2}{\delta\, l_Y}, \quad D^2 = \frac{2\,(2 + k_Y)(l_Y - 2)^2}{\delta^2 k_Y(l_Y - 4)\, l_Y},$$

and the adjustment coefficient does not exist.

In Fig. 1.11, the upper and lower bounds (1.47) in the case $0 \leqslant c \leqslant c^*$ are drawn. Bounds, when $c > c^*$, are beyond the scope of this article and are not considered, although the essence of the complexity in their construction is clear. By dots, drawn are the simulated values of $u_{\alpha,t}(c)$, $c \geqslant 0$.

Let us make a final remark concerning analytical results in the case $c > c^*$, which will be studied in detail in Chapter 6 below. Although the analytical aspects of the problem of finding $\overline{u}_\alpha(c)$ in Model (C) are conceptually clear, the analytical solution is extremely difficult to present in an observable form, as it was done in Model (A). This entails a computational awkwardness, rather than complexity, which is easy to overcome by a sacrifice of elegance of the bound, e.g., its smoothness and even strict monotone decrease, as c increases[71].

Two approaches to numerical calculations are as follows: if an analytical expression for $\mathsf{P}\{\Upsilon_{u,c} < \infty\}$ is available, then $u_{\alpha,t}(c)$ is evaluated by numerically solving (see, e.g., [10] or [33]) the equation $\mathsf{P}\{\Upsilon_{u,c} < \infty\} = \alpha$ at every point c of interest. Otherwise, $u_{\alpha,t}(c)$ is obtained by Monte Carlo simulation.

[71]Simply speaking, the bound may be horizontal in some places.

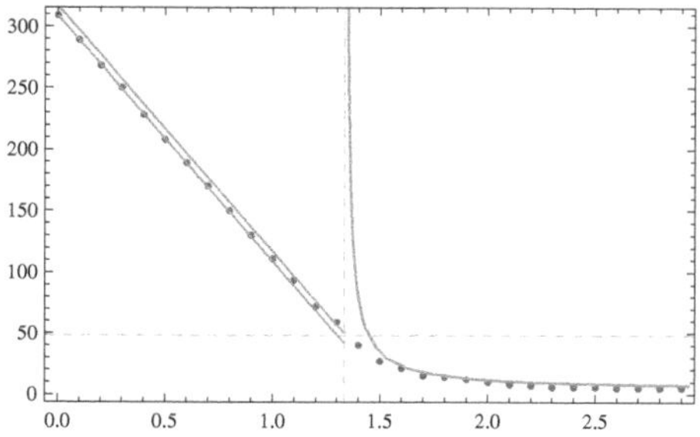

FIGURE 1.12: Graphs (X-axis is c) of two-sided bounds (1.47), when $0 \leqslant c \leqslant c^*$, upper bound, when $c > c^*$, and simulated values of $u_{\alpha,t}(c)$ (dots) in Model (D), Example (b), i.e., for T Erlang with parameters $\delta = 8/5$, $k = 2$, and Y exponentially distributed with parameter $\rho = 3/5$, $\alpha = 0.05$, $t = 200$. Vertical grid line: $c^* = 4/3$. Horizontal grid line: $u_{\alpha,t}(c^*) = 48$.

Model (D). This model is verbally described as a model with renewal claims arrival, i.e., the distribution of T is non-exponential, and with claim size Y exponentially distributed with parameter ρ, e.g.,

Example (a): T is 2-mixture and Y is exponentially distributed,
Example (b): T is Erlang and Y is exponentially distributed,
Example (c): T is Pareto and Y is exponentially distributed,
Example (d): T is Kummer and Y is exponentially distributed.

Plainly, we have $c^* = 1/(\rho\,\mathsf{E}\,T)$, equation (1.34) can be rewritten as the equation (w.r.t. r) $\mathsf{E}\exp\{-r\,c\,T\} = 1 - r/\rho$, and $\varkappa$ is its positive solution. When $c > c^*$, we have (see Section 5.2.4) $\mathsf{P}\{\Upsilon_{u,c} < \infty\} = (1 - \varkappa/\rho)\,e^{-\varkappa u}$ for all $u \geqslant 0$. Bearing in mind that $1 - \varkappa/\rho \leqslant 1$, we have

$$u_{\alpha,t}(c) \leqslant -\ln\alpha/\varkappa, \quad c > 1/(\rho\,\mathsf{E}\,T), \tag{1.54}$$

and the problem reduces to finding $\varkappa$ in a closed form.

To set an example, let us focus on[72] Model (D), Example (b): T is Erlang with parameters k integer and $\delta > 0$ and Y is exponentially distributed with parameter $\rho > 0$.

We can show by elementary calculations that $c^* = \delta/(k\rho)$, the constants defined in (1.41) are

$$M = k\rho/\delta, \quad D^2 = k\,(k+1)\,\rho/\delta^2,$$

and, when $c > \delta/(k\rho)$, the positive solution $\varkappa$ to Lundberg's equation (1.34), which can be rewritten as the equation (w.r.t. r)

$$(\rho - r)\,(\delta + c\,r)^k - \delta^k\,r = 0,$$

is easy to find numerically.

[72]Note that this model is a particular case of Model (E), where T is Erlang with parameters k integer and $\delta > 0$ and Y is Erlang with parameters m integer and $\rho > 0$.

In Fig. 1.12, the upper and lower bounds (1.47) in the case $0 \leqslant c \leqslant \delta/\rho$, and the upper bound (1.54) in the case $c > \delta/\rho$, are drawn for $t = 200$, $\alpha = 0.05$, $\delta = 8/5$, $k = 2$, $\rho = 3/5$, whence $c^* = 1.3333$, $M = 0.75$, and $D^2 = 1.40625$. In Fig. 1.12, by dots are drawn the simulated values of $u_{\alpha,t}(c)$.

Model (E). This model is verbally described as a model with renewal claims arrival, i.e., the distribution of T is non-exponential, and with claim size Y whose distribution is light-tail, but not exponential, e.g.,

Example (a): T is Erlang and Y is Erlang,
Example (b): T is Erlang and Y is 2-mixture.

We address $X \overset{d}{=} Y - cT$, whose c.d.f. is F_X, denote by $\overline{F}_X(x) = 1 - F_X(x)$ is tail function, and write $x_0 = \sup\{x : F_X(x) < 1\}$. When $c > c^* := \mathsf{E}\,Y/\mathsf{E}\,T$, we have (see Section 5.2.4, Theorem 5.10)

$$b_\ominus\, e^{-\varkappa u} \leqslant \mathsf{P}\{\varUpsilon_{u,c} < \infty\} \leqslant b_\oplus\, e^{-\varkappa u} \quad \text{for all} \quad u \geqslant 0, \tag{1.55}$$

where $\varkappa$ is a positive solution to (1.34) and

$$b_\oplus = \inf_{x\in[0,x_0]} \frac{e^{\varkappa x}\overline{F}_X(x)}{\int_x^\infty e^{\varkappa y}\, dF_X(y)}, \qquad b_\ominus = \sup_{x\in[0,x_0]} \frac{e^{\varkappa x}\overline{F}_X(x)}{\int_x^\infty e^{\varkappa y}\, dF_X(y)}.$$

Alternatively (see Section 5.2.4, Theorem 5.11), the inequalities (1.55) hold true with

$$b_\oplus^* = \inf_{x\in[0,x_0^*]} \frac{e^{\varkappa x}\overline{F}_Y(x)}{\int_x^\infty e^{\varkappa y}\, dF_Y(y)}, \qquad b_\ominus^* = \sup_{x\in[0,x_0^*]} \frac{e^{\varkappa x}\overline{F}_Y(x)}{\int_x^\infty e^{\varkappa y}\, dF_Y(y)},$$

where $x_0^* = \sup\{x : F_Y(x) < 1\}$; the inequalities $0 \leqslant b_\ominus^* \leqslant b_\ominus \leqslant b_\oplus \leqslant b_\oplus^* \leqslant 1$ hold.

Both upper and lower bounds for $\overline{u}_\alpha(c)$, $c > c^*$, which is a solution to equation $\mathsf{P}\{\varUpsilon_{u,c} < \infty\} = \alpha$, and therefore upper bounds for $u_{\alpha,t}(c)$, $c > c^*$, is easy to get from (1.55), at least numerically.

Model (F). This model is verbally described as a model with renewal claims arrival, i.e., the distribution of T is non-exponential, and with claim size Y, whose distribution is fat-tail, e.g.,

Example (a): T is 2-mixture and Y is Pareto,
Example (b): T is Erlang and Y is Pareto,
Example (c): T is Pareto and Y is Pareto.

Regarding this model, we repeat that any upper bound for $u_{\alpha,t}(c)$, $c > c^*$, which assumes *small, rather than large* values, is tightly related to the probability $\mathsf{P}\{\varUpsilon_{u,c} < \infty\}$ for *small, rather than large* values of u.

1.4 Aim and Structure of the Book

Aim of the book. The aim of this book is to get a series of simple-looking, but insightful analytical results for the non-ruin capital, aiming to contribute to its wider used in practice. At least, this will increase attention of practitioners to Value-at-Risk measures whose source risk is more complicated, but more adequate, than commonly selected.

This requires developing efficient mathematical methods, in particular, asymptotic analysis backed by direct numerical methods such as simulation, used to illustrate analytical results and demonstrate their practical applicability.

In a narrower sense, in relation to insurance, this contributes to a search for reliable insurance solvency benchmarks, which may be imbedded in the framework of the Value-at-Risk technique and its variants. This should be based on the solid fundament of risk theory, rather than chosen for reasons of simplicity or convenience. In particular, this refers to the Solvency II system, where the solvency capital requirement is (apparently, somewhat awry) formulated in terms of Value-at-Risk at the 99.5% threshold, with the source risk set as the loss net of premium income at the year-end time moment. Apparently, it would be more rational to set this Value-at-Risk with the source risk set as the sup-loss net of premium income, i.e., to address the non-ruin capital, rather than the non-loss capital.

Structure of the book. Chapter 1 has been announced as an introduction to this book, but also as a summary of its main results. In Section 1.1, we presented some facts about risk measures in finance and portfolio management. In Section 1.2, we discussed some details of risk measuring in the Solvency II system. In Section 1.3, we have presented the main technical results of this book. Those readers who are not interested in their proofs and further discussion, which requires uneasy mathematics, can stop reading this book now: the basic information has already been obtained.

The rest of the book consists of 6 chapters. Chapter 2 outlines the road map to the goal of this book. It deals with a diffusion risk model, which is a handy auxiliary tool. Chapters 3 and 5 are devoted to analytic investigations of the non-ruin capital in an exceptional and general models, respectively. Chapter 4 is technical. It connects the problem under consideration with the inverse Gaussian approximation straightforwardly. Chapter 6 contains a number of numerical illustrations. Chapter 7 deals with ERS-analysis[73] in a model with migration, where the non-ruin capital is the main tool.

In more detail, Chapter 2 deals with the non-ruin capital in a diffusion risk model. This is an implicit function, i.e., a solution to a non-linear equation

[73]The ERS-analysis, which is an abbreviation for Expansion, Revenue, and Solvency, was introduced in [125] and developed in [134].

available in a closed form. Even in relatively simple diffusion model a closed-form expression for the non-ruin capital cannot be found, but its structure can be elucidated, which is the first step in the road map. The next step is the analysis of monotony and convexity of the non-ruin capital, followed by its asymptotic analysis. The final step is getting closed-form bounds on the non-ruin capital, which greatly simplifies its use.

In Chapter 3, which is an extended presentation of the results outlined in Section 1.3.4, we follow the road map of Chapter 2 in an exceptional case of a risk reserve process with exponentially distributed inter-claim intervals and claim sizes[74]. All steps outlined in the road map of Chapter 2 can be made in a similar way, albeit with significantly greater analytical efforts: the probabilities of ruin expressed in terms of Bessel functions are much more complicated.

In Chapter 4, we introduce the auxiliary non-linear equation $\mathcal{M}_{u,c}(t) = \alpha$, called $\mathcal{M}$-equation, whose right-hand side is defined in (1.40). We are focussed on the function $u_{\alpha,t}^{[\mathcal{M}]}(c)$, $c \geqslant 0$, which is called $\mathcal{M}$-level and is a solution to the $\mathcal{M}$-equation. It is noteworthy that the right-hand side in this equation is given in an explicit form, which links Chapter 4 with Chapters 2 and 3. The connection of $\mathcal{M}$-level with the main topic of this book, especially when $0 \leqslant c \leqslant c^*$, is shown in the next chapter.

Chapter 5 is a rigorous presentation of the results outlined in Section 1.3.7, which is the main body of this book. Dealing with Lundberg's collective risk model with generally distributed inter-claim intervals and claim sizes, we follow the road map of Chapter 2. Despite the fact that the equation that defines the non-ruin capital cannot be written in a closed form, i.e., in terms of elementary or special functions, we can proceed, using Kendall's identity. This approach, which focusses on the asymptotic technique, as $t \to \infty$, is a development of the approach of [135]. We conduct a rigorous asymptotic analysis of the non-ruin capital, essentially following the road map of Chapter 2, but with no closed-form equation that defines this implicit function.

In Chapter 6, we deal with numerical illustrations of the results of Chapters 3 and 5. Unless the reader is an expert in Monte Carlo simulation, useful are the overview of the balance between analytical and numerical methods and the summary of basic simulation concepts, such as pseudo-random number generator and the inverse function method, presented in Appendix A.

In Chapter 7, we re-visit (see [134], Chapters 5–11) the expansion, revenue, and solvency analysis, called for brevity ERS-analysis, in the compound Poisson risk model with migration. We extend it from exponentially distributed claim sizes to generally distributed claim sizes.

To make exposition self-contained, some auxiliary results are collected in Appendices A, B. Most credits are put in Notes and comments section. The

[74]In application-neutral terms, this is compound renewal process with exponentially distributed jump sizes and inter-renewal intervals.

List of notation is given at the end of this book. The bibliography contains 199 items.

1.5 Readers, to Whom this Book is Addressed

The target audience of this book is academics working in risk measurement and practitioners interested in potential weaknesses of the Solvency II system. Readers who have both of these interests, will benefit the most. This book can be useful for students studying economics, finance and mathematical modeling.

This book is linked to the books [134] and [135] by this author: the former is devoted to price competition and regulation of financial stability in multi-year insurance models, the latter deals with the inverse Gaussian approximation in the level-crossing problem. Ideally, this book is addressed to the readers with interest in both these topics.

Those who have read the book [135], have all the necessary skills to master this book too; apparently, these are mathematicians of different degrees of professional training. It will not be difficult for them to get acquainted with modeling long-term insurance processes presented in the book [134], which will contribute to a better understanding of the objectives of this book.

Readers of the book [134] interested in practical aspects, rather than mathematical technique, can focus on the main results. These readers will be pleased to find that these results (if not proofs) are readily accessible to them, since they require merely basic mathematics. Thus, a certain level of mathematical maturity is assumed, but the prerequisites are rather low and boil down to the basics of probability theory and analysis, as well as to some basic programming skills.

Problems

Problem 1.1 By comparison of equations (1.16) and (1.12), check that the Value-at-Risk is a lower bound for the non-ruin capital; ponder numerical illustration set in Fig. 1.2. Relate this observation to the text of Directives [63] and [64].

Problem 1.2 Show that equation (1.23) is close to equation (1.24). Applying Theorem A.5 on proximity between two implicit functions, try to prove rigorously that solution to equation (1.23) is close to the solution to equation (1.24).

Problem 1.3 Show that equality (1.22) follows from Theorem 3.4.

Problem 1.4 Show that (1.26) follows from Theorem 3.4.

Problem 1.5 Show that equality (1.29) follows from Theorem 3.8.

Problem 1.6 Show that equalities (1.30) follow from Theorems 3.6 and 3.7.

Problem 1.7 Refine the arguments outlined in Section 1.3.7. In particular, note that M_V introduced in (1.31) is equal to c^*, that $(M_V - c)\,t + \kappa_\alpha\, D_V \sqrt{t}\,(1 + o(1))$ is of order $O(t)$ for $0 \leqslant c < K < c^*$, and give rigorous proof based on applying Theorem A.5 on proximity between two implicit functions.

Problem 1.8 Pondering the fact that in the approximation of Theorems 1.1 and 1.2 (or Theorem 1.3, when Y and T are exponentially distributed) the case $c = c^*$ is formally excluded, consider Fig. 1.4, where the approximation of Theorem 1.3 is used formally, as a tool of numerical calculations, for all $c \geqslant 0$.

Problem 1.9 Do numerical calculations, as in Fig. 1.4, with with different values of δ and ρ, and t and u. Pay attention to the behavior near $c^* = \delta/\rho$.

Problem 1.10 Bearing in mind that for Y and T exponentially distributed with parameters ρ and δ, we have (check it!) $m_{\triangledown}|_{c=0} = \rho/\delta$, $M_V = \delta/\rho$, $D^2_{\triangledown}|_{c=0} = 2\rho/\delta^2$, and $D^2_V = 2\delta/\rho^2$, ponder the difference between (1.43) and (1.44).

Problem 1.11 In the light of the standard concepts of asymptotic analysis set forth in Section A.1.6, ponder the difference between equalities (1.37) and (1.38).

Chapter 2

Fixed-probability Level in the Diffusion Model

This chapter deals with an auxiliary diffusion model. Focusing on two risk measures with different source risks, like non-loss and non-ruin capitals introduced in Definitions 1.4 and 1.5, we draw a road map to the goal of this book. Mathematically, we are focused on a solution to the inverse level-crossing problem for a diffusion process. This solution is called "fixed-probability level", i.e., the level which the diffusion process crosses before time t with a fixed probability α.

2.1 Diffusion Model: An Auxiliary Tool

This chapter explores the mathematical problems discussed in this book in a relatively simple diffusion framework. We use the generally accepted mathematical terminology. The reader will have no difficulty in establishing a correlation with the economic problem of measuring risk, discussed in Chapter 1.

2.1.1 Model and equivalent terminology

At time $s \geqslant 0$, the diffusion model (see Section 1.1.1) has the form

$$R_s = u + cs - V_s, \quad V_s = \vartheta s + \sigma \mathsf{W}_s, \tag{2.1}$$

where u denotes the initial capital, c is the premium intensity called for simplicity price, and W_s, $s \geqslant 0$, is a standard Wiener process. The claim payout process V_s, $s \geqslant 0$, is a diffusion process starting at zero and having positive drift and diffusion parameters ϑ and σ, whence $\mathsf{E}V_s = \vartheta s$ and $\mathsf{D}V_s = \sigma^2 s$.

Looking at the trajectory of risk reserve process (1.8) through an inverted telescope, i.e., moving away from it for a considerable distance, we would see something similar to the trajectory of a Brownian motion with trend. This suggests that the diffusion process can be used as a simplified model of the risk reserve process[1].

[1]This observation is the basis for the diffusion approximation, considered as a heuristic procedure for numerical calculations, see [135], Chapter 9.

TABLE 2.1: Equivalent terminology for $u^{[\mathrm{dif}]}_{\alpha,t\,|\,\vartheta}(c)$ and $\underline{u}^{[\mathrm{dif}]}_{\alpha,t\,|\,\vartheta}(c)$

	Value-at-Risk measure	Solvency benchmark	Solution to inverse level-crossing problem
$u^{[\mathrm{dif}]}_{\alpha,t\,|\,\vartheta}(c)$	Value-at-Risk based on sup-loss net of premium income, a solution to $\mathsf{P}\{\sup_{0\leqslant s\leqslant t}(V_s - cs) \leqslant u\} = A$	Non-ruin capital, a solution to $\mathsf{P}\{\inf_{0\leqslant s\leqslant t} R_s < 0\} = \alpha$	Fixed-probability level, a solution to $\mathsf{P}\{\varUpsilon^{[\mathrm{dif}]}_{u,c\,|\,\vartheta} \leqslant t\} = \alpha$, where $\varUpsilon^{[\mathrm{dif}]}_{u,c\,|\,\vartheta}$ is the time of the first level u crossing
$\underline{u}^{[\mathrm{dif}]}_{\alpha,t\,|\,\vartheta}(c)$	Value-at-Risk based on loss net of premium income, a solution to $\mathsf{P}\{V_t - ct \leqslant u\} = A$	Non-loss capital, a solution to $\mathsf{P}\{R_t < 0\} = \alpha$	A lower bound for $u^{[\mathrm{dif}]}_{\alpha,t\,|\,\vartheta}(c)$

Resorting to insurance terminology, according to the expected value principle (see, e.g., [31], p. 85) which requires that the aggregate claim payments and premiums collected be equal at any given time, the "fair" price c in (2.1) is set equal to ϑ. If $c = \vartheta(1+\tau)$, then τ is referred to as premium loading on the "fair" price.

For a standard Brownian motion W_s, $s \geqslant 0$, started at zero, (2.1) may be rewritten as

$$R_s = u + (c-\vartheta)s - \sigma\,\mathsf{W}_s, \quad s \geqslant 0,$$

whence $R_0 = u$, and we refer to

$$\begin{aligned}\varUpsilon^{[\mathrm{dif}]}_{u,c\,|\,\vartheta} &:= \inf\{s>0 : R_s < 0\}\\ &= \inf\{s>0 : (\vartheta s + \sigma\mathsf{W}_s) - c\,s > u\},\end{aligned} \tag{2.2}$$

or $+\infty$, if $(\vartheta s + \sigma \mathsf{W}_s) - cs \leqslant u$ for all $s \geqslant 0$, as the time of the first ruin, or the time of the first crossing of the level u.

This duality of terminology cannot cause confusion. The former term, i.e., the time of the first ruin, refers to insurance applications and is better suited to the first expression in (2.2). The latter term, i.e., the time of the first crossing of the level u, is application-neutral and is better suited to the second expression in (2.2).

When we focus on risk measures, insurance solvency, or mathematical level-crossing problem, we can switch to terminology (see Table 2.1) that is more appropriate for each of these fields. Since the mathematical aspects are the main challenge in the following presentation, we will adhere to the application-neutral terminology used in the level-crossing problem.

To begin with, recall (see [135]) that the direct level-crossing problem is to explore $\mathsf{P}\{\Upsilon^{[\mathrm{dif}]}_{u,c\,|\,\vartheta} \leqslant t\}$, whereas the inverse level-crossing problem is to investigate a solution with respect to u to the equation

$$\mathsf{P}\{\Upsilon^{[\mathrm{dif}]}_{u,c\,|\,\vartheta} \leqslant t\} = \alpha. \tag{2.3}$$

Denoted by $u^{[\mathrm{dif}]}_{\alpha,t\,|\,\vartheta}(c)$, $c \geqslant 0$, it is referred to as fixed-probability level.

Remark 2.1 In the theory of stochastic processes, there are problems that are similar in name, but not identical to ours (see, e.g., [149], [199]). One of them is as follows. Let the continuous function $g : (0,1) \to \mathsf{R}$ be such that $g(0+) \geqslant 0$, and let $\Upsilon_g = \inf\{s > 0 : \mathsf{W}_s \geqslant g(s)\}$ be the time of the first passage of a standard Brownian motion W_s, $s \geqslant 0$, that starts at zero, through the boundary g. Let F be the distribution function of Υ_g. The first-passage problem is to determine F, when g is given. The inverse first-passage problem is to determine g, when F is given.

2.1.2 Outline of road map

The main purpose of this chapter is to create a road map that will then be used to investigate the fixed-probability level in renewal models. Its first step is to explore the analytical structure of the fixed-probability level $u^{[\mathrm{dif}]}_{\alpha,t\,|\,\vartheta}(c)$, $c \geqslant 0$. Being an implicit function defined by equation (2.3), the left side of which is specified in (2.12) or (2.7), it cannot be written in a closed form, but we can get a fairly complete insight into its global structure.

The second step is the study of monotony and convexity of the fixed-probability level. The first of these properties is obvious, whereas the second is not. However, we start by studying the former, using analytical methods, which we then extend to study the latter. Both of these properties will then be used when constructing upper bounds for the fixed-probability level.

The third step is investigation of the asymptotic behavior of $u^{[\mathrm{dif}]}_{\alpha,t\,|\,\vartheta}(c)$, $c \geqslant 0$, as $t \to \infty$. We show that, when c is less than a value slightly larger than $c^* := \vartheta$, it tends to infinity, as $t \to \infty$. When c exceeds such a value, it is bounded by a finite constant.

Finally, accepting the fact that no relatively simple closed-form expression for the fixed-probability level $u^{[\mathrm{dif}]}_{\alpha,t\,|\,\vartheta}(c)$, $c \geqslant 0$, may be found, we construct for it several bounds, some of them fairly accurate, which are represented in terms of elementary functions.

2.2 Direct Level-crossing Problem

We recall that the probability density function (p.d.f.) and cumulative distribution function (c.d.f.) of a standard Gaussian distribution are denoted by

$$\varphi_{(0,1)}(x) := \frac{1}{\sqrt{2\pi}}\, e^{-\frac{x^2}{2}}, \quad x \in \mathsf{R}, \quad \varPhi_{(0,1)}(x) := \int_{-\infty}^{x} \varphi_{(0,1)}(z)\, dz, \quad x \in \mathsf{R}.$$

The Mills' ratio is

$$\begin{aligned} \mathcal{M}(x) &:= \frac{1 - \varPhi_{(0,1)}(x)}{\varphi_{(0,1)}(x)} \\ &= e^{x^2/2} \int_x^{\infty} e^{-t^2/2}\, dt, \quad x \in \mathsf{R}. \end{aligned}$$

Basic information about these three functions is collected in Section B.2. In particular, $\mathcal{M}(x) = x^{-1}(1 + o(1))$, $x \to \infty$, which is equivalent to

$$1 - \varPhi_{(0,1)}(x) = x^{-1} \varphi_{(0,1)}(x)\, (1 + o(1)), \quad x \to \infty.$$

It is easy to check that for $z + y > 0$ and $y > 0$, we have

$$y\, \mathcal{M}(z + 2y) - 1 < y/(z + 2y) - 1 < 0, \tag{2.4}$$

and (see (B.21)) for any $z, y \in \mathsf{R}$, we have

$$(z + 2y)\, \mathcal{M}(z + 2y) - 1 < 0. \tag{2.5}$$

The direct level-crossing problem focusses on the distribution of the first level-crossing time $\varUpsilon^{[\mathrm{dif}]}_{u,c\,|\,\vartheta}$. In our case, this problem has a complete solution.

Theorem 2.1 *For all $u \geqslant 0$, $t > 0$, and for $\sigma > 0$, we have*

$$\begin{aligned} \mathsf{P}\{\varUpsilon^{[\mathrm{dif}]}_{u,c\,|\,\vartheta} \leqslant t\} = &\big(1 - \varPhi_{(0,1)}(x - y) \\ &+ \varPhi_{(0,1)}(-x - y) \exp\{2xy\}\big)\Big|_{x=\frac{u}{\sigma\sqrt{t}},\, y=\frac{(\vartheta - c)\sqrt{t}}{\sigma}}. \end{aligned} \tag{2.6}$$

Theorem 2.1 follows straightforwardly from Theorem B.10, which is a well-known result in the theory of diffusion processes. We leave details to the reader.

In terms of inverse Gaussian distribution[2] with positive parameters μ and λ, whose c.d.f. is

$$\begin{aligned} F(x; \mu, \lambda, -\tfrac{1}{2}) = &\varPhi_{(0,1)}\left(\sqrt{\frac{\lambda}{x}}\left(\frac{x}{\mu} - 1\right)\right) \\ &+ \exp\left\{\frac{2\lambda}{\mu}\right\} \varPhi_{(0,1)}\left(-\sqrt{\frac{\lambda}{x}}\left(\frac{x}{\mu} + 1\right)\right), \quad x > 0, \end{aligned}$$

Theorem 2.1 may be rewritten as follows[3].

---

[2]We encountered (see (1.39)) this expression in Section 1.3.6. For more information, see Section B.1.

[3]We recall that $f(x)\,|_{x=a}^{b}$ means $f(b) - f(a)$, whereas $f(x; z)\,|_{z=a}$ means $f(x; a)$.

Theorem 2.2 *For all $u \geqslant 0$, $t > 0$, and for $\sigma > 0$, we have*

$$\mathsf{P}\{\Upsilon_{u,c\,|\,\vartheta}^{[\mathrm{dif}]} \leqslant t\} = \begin{cases} F(t;\mu,\lambda,-\tfrac{1}{2})\,\big|_{\mu=\frac{u}{\vartheta-c},\lambda=\frac{u^2}{\sigma^2}}, & 0 \leqslant c < \vartheta, \\ (e^{-\frac{2\lambda}{\hat\mu}}\,F(t;\hat\mu,\lambda,-\tfrac{1}{2}))\big|_{\hat\mu=-\frac{u}{\vartheta-c},\lambda=\frac{u^2}{\sigma^2}}, & c > \vartheta, \end{cases} \tag{2.7}$$

and, calculating the appropriate limit,

$$\begin{aligned} \mathsf{P}\{\Upsilon_{u,\vartheta\,|\,\vartheta}^{[\mathrm{dif}]} \leqslant t\} &= \lim_{\mu\to\infty} F(t;\mu,\lambda,-\tfrac{1}{2})\,\big|_{\lambda=\frac{u^2}{\sigma^2}} \\ &= 2\left(1-\Phi_{(0,1)}\left(\sqrt{\frac{\lambda}{t}}\right)\right)\bigg|_{\lambda=\frac{u^2}{\sigma^2}} \\ &= 2\left(1-\Phi_{(0,1)}\left(\frac{u}{\sigma\sqrt{t}}\right)\right). \end{aligned} \tag{2.8}$$

Let us introduce

$$\begin{aligned} \mathsf{F}(z,y\,|\,-\tfrac{1}{2}) := {} & 1-\Phi_{(0,1)}(z-y) \\ & +\Phi_{(0,1)}(-z-y)\exp\{2zy\}, \qquad z,y>0, \end{aligned} \tag{2.9}$$

which is referred to as auxiliary function of the first kind. The following theorem (see [135], Theorem 2.4) is straightforward.

Theorem 2.3 *For $\mu > 0$, $\lambda > 0$, we have*

$$F(t;\mu,\lambda,-\tfrac{1}{2}) = \mathsf{F}(z,y\,|\,-\tfrac{1}{2})\,\big|_{z=\frac{\sqrt{\lambda}}{\sqrt{t}},y=\frac{\sqrt{\lambda\,t}}{\mu}}, \qquad t>0, \tag{2.10}$$

and for $\hat\mu > 0$, $\lambda > 0$, we have

$$\begin{aligned} &\exp\left\{-\frac{2\lambda}{\hat\mu}\right\}F(t;\hat\mu,\lambda,-\tfrac{1}{2}) \\ &\quad = \left(\exp\{-2\,zy\}\,\mathsf{F}(z,y\,|\,-\tfrac{1}{2})\right)\big|_{z=\frac{\sqrt{\lambda}}{\sqrt{t}},y=\frac{\sqrt{\lambda\,t}}{\hat\mu}}, \qquad t>0. \end{aligned} \tag{2.11}$$

Using Theorem 2.3 allows us to reformulate Theorem 2.2 as follows.

Theorem 2.4 *For all $u \geqslant 0$, $t > 0$, and for $\sigma > 0$, we have*

$$\mathsf{P}\{\Upsilon_{u,c\,|\,\vartheta}^{[\mathrm{dif}]} \leqslant t\} = \begin{cases} \mathsf{F}(z,y\,|\,-\tfrac{1}{2})\,\big|_{z=\frac{u}{\sigma\sqrt{t}},y=\frac{(\vartheta-c)\sqrt{t}}{\sigma}}, & 0 \leqslant c < \vartheta, \\ (\exp\{-2\,zy\} \\ \quad\times\mathsf{F}(z,y\,|\,-\tfrac{1}{2}))\,\big|_{z=\frac{u}{\sigma\sqrt{t}},y=\frac{(c-\vartheta)\sqrt{t}}{\sigma}}, & c > \vartheta, \end{cases} \tag{2.12}$$

and $\mathsf{P}\{\Upsilon_{u,\vartheta\,|\,\vartheta}^{[\mathrm{dif}]} \leqslant t\}$ is given in (2.8).

2.3 Inverse Level-crossing Problem

The inverse level-crossing problem focusses on the analytical structure and the shape of the fixed-probability level. Unfortunately, unlike the direct level-crossing problem, it usually does not have a closed-form solution.

2.3.1 Analytical structure of fixed-probability level

Before moving on to core Theorem 2.7, we start with two simple theorems.

Theorem 2.5 *When $c = 0$, the fixed-probability level, i.e., the solution to equation* (2.3) *is*

$$u^{[\mathrm{dif}]}_{\alpha,t\,|\,\vartheta}(0) = \vartheta\, t + \sigma\, \kappa_{\alpha,t}\sqrt{t}, \tag{2.13}$$

where $\kappa_{\alpha,t} \geqslant \kappa_\alpha$ for all $t > 0$ and $\lim_{t\to\infty} \kappa_{\alpha,t} = \kappa_\alpha$.

Proof. Using equality (2.7) with $c = 0$, we set in (2.3) $u = \vartheta\, t + \sigma\, x\sqrt{t}$ and rewrite (2.3), which is an equation with respect to (w.r.t.) x, as follows:

$$1 - \Phi_{(0,1)}(x) + \exp\left\{\frac{2u\,\vartheta}{\sigma^2}\right\}\Phi_{(0,1)}\left(-\frac{2\vartheta t + \sigma x\sqrt{t}}{\sigma\sqrt{t}}\right) = \alpha. \tag{2.14}$$

Using the shorthand notation

$$\varepsilon_t := \exp\left\{\frac{2u\,\vartheta}{\sigma^2}\right\}\Phi_{(0,1)}\left(-\frac{2\vartheta t + \sigma x\sqrt{t}}{\sigma\sqrt{t}}\right),$$

we note that $\varepsilon_t \geqslant 0$ for all $t > 0$, and that $\lim_{t\to\infty} \varepsilon_{\alpha,t} = 0$ for all x. Consequently, the solution to (2.14) for all $t > 0$ exceeds the solution to the equation $1 - \Phi_{(0,1)}(x) = \alpha$, which is κ_α, and tends to it, as $t \to \infty$. □

Theorem 2.6 *When $c = \vartheta$, the fixed-probability level, i.e., the solution to equation* (2.3), *is*

$$u^{[\mathrm{dif}]}_{\alpha,t\,|\,\vartheta}(\vartheta) = \sigma\, \kappa_{\alpha/2}\sqrt{t}. \tag{2.15}$$

Proof. Using equality (2.8), equation (2.3) can be rewritten as

$$\Phi_{(0,1)}(u/(\sigma\sqrt{t}\,)) = 1 - \alpha/2,$$

which is easily solved w.r.t. u. This is an exceptional case, when a closed-form expression for $u^{[\mathrm{dif}]}_{\alpha,t\,|\,\vartheta}(\vartheta)$ exists for all $t > 0$. □

Although closed-form expressions for $u^{[\mathrm{dif}]}_{\alpha,t\,|\,\vartheta}(c)$ do not exist, when c differs from ϑ, the structure of this function, markedly different, when $0 \leqslant c < \vartheta$ and $c > \vartheta$, can be elucidated, as follows.

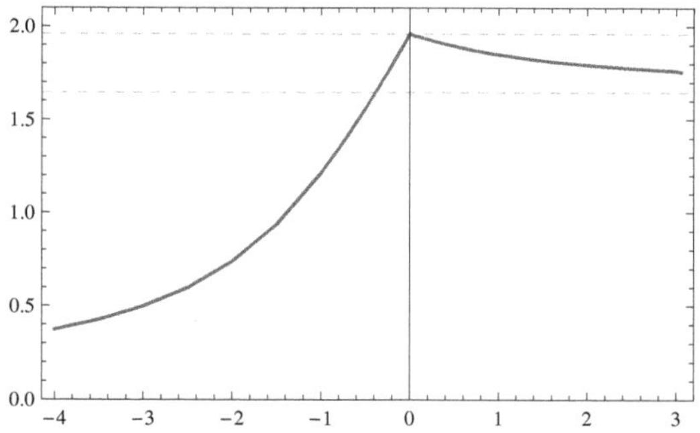

FIGURE 2.1: Graph (X-axis is y) of function $\mathsf{z}_\alpha(y)$, evaluated numerically, when $\alpha = 0.05$. Horizontal grid lines: $\kappa_\alpha = 1.65$ and $\kappa_{\alpha/2} = 1.96$.

Theorem 2.7 *For $0 < \alpha < 1/2$, the fixed-probability level, i.e., the solution to equation (2.3), is*

$$u^{[\mathrm{dif}]}_{\alpha,t\,|\,\vartheta}(c) = \begin{cases} (\vartheta - c)\,t + \sigma\,\mathsf{z}_\alpha\Big(\dfrac{\vartheta - c}{\sigma}\sqrt{t}\Big)\sqrt{t}, & 0 \leqslant c \leqslant \vartheta, \\ \sigma\,\mathsf{z}_\alpha\Big(\dfrac{\vartheta - c}{\sigma}\sqrt{t}\Big)\sqrt{t}, & c > \vartheta, \end{cases} \tag{2.16}$$

where the function $\mathsf{z}_\alpha(y)$, $y \in \mathsf{R}$, being, when $y > 0$, a solution to the equation

$$\mathsf{F}(\mathsf{z}_\alpha(y) + y, y \mid -\tfrac{1}{2}) = \alpha, \tag{2.17}$$

and, when $y < 0$, a solution to the equation

$$\mathsf{F}(\mathsf{z}_\alpha(y), y \mid -\tfrac{1}{2}) = \alpha, \tag{2.18}$$

is continuous, positive for all y, monotone increasing, as y increases from $-\infty$ to 0, monotone decreasing, as y increases from 0 to ∞, and such that

$$\lim_{y\to-\infty} \mathsf{z}_\alpha(y) = 0, \quad \mathsf{z}_\alpha(0) = \kappa_{\alpha/2}, \quad \lim_{y\to\infty} \mathsf{z}_\alpha(y) = \kappa_\alpha.$$

We recall (see (2.9)) that

$$\begin{aligned} \mathsf{F}(\mathsf{z}_\alpha(y) + y, y \mid -\tfrac{1}{2}) = {}& 1 - \Phi_{(0,1)}(\mathsf{z}_\alpha(y)) \\ & + \Phi_{(0,1)}(-2y - \mathsf{z}_\alpha(y)) \exp\{2\,(y + \mathsf{z}_\alpha(y))y\}, \end{aligned}$$

which is the left-hand side of (2.17), and

$$\begin{aligned} \mathsf{F}(\mathsf{z}_\alpha(y), y \mid -\tfrac{1}{2}) = {}& 1 - \Phi_{(0,1)}(\mathsf{z}_\alpha(y) - y) \\ & + \Phi_{(0,1)}(-y - \mathsf{z}_\alpha(y)) \exp\{2y\,\mathsf{z}_\alpha(y)\}, \end{aligned} \tag{2.19}$$

which is the left-hand side of (2.18).

Regarding Theorem 2.7, we note that although we came very close to finding a closed-form expression for $u^{[\mathrm{dif}]}_{\alpha,t\,|\,\vartheta}(c)$, $c \geqslant 0$, we still did not do it. To find the function $\mathsf{z}_\alpha(y)$, when $y > 0$, we need to solve the non-linear equation (2.17). To find the function $\mathsf{z}_\alpha(y)$, when $y < 0$, we need to solve the non-linear equation (2.18). These equations are easy to solve numerically, and the methods for this are well known (see, e.g., [10], [33]). The function $\mathsf{z}_\alpha(y)$, $y \in \mathsf{R}$, evaluated numerically for $\alpha = 0.05$, is shown in Fig. 2.1.

The following lemmas are auxiliary.

Lemma 2.1 *For $z + y > 0$, $y > 0$ and for*

$$\mathsf{F}(z+y, y \mid -\tfrac{1}{2}) = 1 - \Phi_{(0,1)}(z) + \exp\{2y\,(z+y)\}\,\Phi_{(0,1)}(-2y-z),$$

we have

$$\frac{d}{dz}\,\mathsf{F}(z+y, y \mid -\tfrac{1}{2}) < 0, \quad \frac{d}{dy}\,\mathsf{F}(z+y, y \mid -\tfrac{1}{2}) < 0.$$

Proof. The first inequality comes from (2.4) and

$$\begin{aligned}\frac{d}{dz}\,\mathsf{F}(z+y, y \mid -\tfrac{1}{2}) &= \mathsf{F}^{(1,0)}(v, y \mid -\tfrac{1}{2})\,\big|_{v=z+y}\\ &= 2\exp\{2y(z+y)\}\,\varphi_{(0,1)}(z+2y)(\,y\mathcal{M}(z+2y)-1) < 0.\end{aligned}$$

The second inequality comes from (2.5) and

$$\begin{aligned}\frac{d}{dy}\,\mathsf{F}(z+y, y \mid -\tfrac{1}{2}) &= \mathsf{F}^{(1,0)}(v, y \mid -\tfrac{1}{2})\,\big|_{v=z+y} + \mathsf{F}^{(0,1)}(v, y \mid -\tfrac{1}{2})\,\big|_{v=z+y}\\ &= 2\exp\{2y(z+y)\}\,\varphi_{(0,1)}(z+2y)\\ &\quad\times((z+2y)\,\mathcal{M}(z+2y)-1) < 0.\end{aligned}$$

The proof is complete. □

Lemma 2.2 *For $z, y > 0$, we have*

$$\mathsf{F}^{(1,0)}(z, y \mid -\tfrac{1}{2}) < 0, \quad \mathsf{F}^{(0,1)}(z, y \mid -\tfrac{1}{2}) > 0.$$

Proof. Bearing in mind (B.28), the first inequality comes from $y\,\mathcal{M}(z+y) - 1 = (v\,\mathcal{M}(v)-1)\,\big|_{v=z+y} - z\,\mathcal{M}(v)\,\big|_{v=z+y} < 0$, which is evident from (B.21). The second inequality is obvious. □

Lemma 2.3 *For $z, y > 0$, we have*

$$\mathsf{F}^{(1,0)}(z, y \mid -\tfrac{1}{2}) - 2\,y\,\mathsf{F}(z, y \mid -\tfrac{1}{2}) < 0, \quad \mathsf{F}^{(0,1)}(z, y \mid -\tfrac{1}{2}) - 2\,z\,\mathsf{F}(z, y \mid -\tfrac{1}{2}) < 0.$$

Proof. Bearing in mind (B.27) and (B.28), we have

$$\begin{aligned}&\mathsf{F}^{(1,0)}(z, y \mid -\tfrac{1}{2}) - 2y\,\mathsf{F}(z, y \mid -\tfrac{1}{2})\\ &\qquad = -2y\,\Phi_{(0,1)}(y-z) - 2\exp\{2zy\}\,\varphi_{(0,1)}(z+y) < 0,\\ &\mathsf{F}^{(0,1)}(z, y \mid -\tfrac{1}{2}) - 2z\,\mathsf{F}(z, y \mid -\tfrac{1}{2})\\ &\qquad = -2z\,\Phi_{(0,1)}(y-z) > 0,\end{aligned} \tag{2.20}$$

as required. □

Proof of Theorem 2.7. Using equality (2.7), equation (2.3) may be written as

$$F(t;\mu,\lambda,-\tfrac{1}{2})\,\big|_{\mu=\frac{u}{\vartheta-c},\lambda=\frac{u^2}{\sigma^2}}=\alpha \tag{2.21}$$

for $0\leqslant c<\vartheta$, and as

$$\big(e^{-\frac{2\lambda}{\hat{\mu}}}\,F(t;\hat{\mu},\lambda,-\tfrac{1}{2})\big)\big|_{\hat{\mu}=-\frac{u}{\vartheta-c},\lambda=\frac{u^2}{\sigma^2}}=\alpha, \tag{2.22}$$

when $c>\vartheta$. The proof is divided into two steps, one when $0\leqslant c<\vartheta$, another when $c>\vartheta$. In the first step, we analyze the solution to (2.21), and in the second step, we investigate the solution to (2.22). At each of these steps, we make a suitable change of variables. Regarding the function $\mathsf{z}_\alpha(y)$, $y\in\mathsf{R}$, in (2.16), we check its monotony by using the standard criterion based on the sign of its derivative calculated by means of (see Theorem A.4) the well-known theorem on the derivative of implicit function.

Step 1. In the case $0\leqslant c<\vartheta$, we switch from the variables u and c in the left-hand side of (2.21) to the variables

$$z=\frac{u}{\sigma\sqrt{t}}-\frac{(\vartheta-c)\sqrt{t}}{\sigma}\in\mathsf{R},\quad y=\frac{(\vartheta-c)\sqrt{t}}{\sigma}>0.$$

In this way, we transform (2.21) into

$$F(t;\mu,\lambda,-\tfrac{1}{2})\,\big|_{\mu=t\,(z+y)/y,\lambda=t\,(z+y)^2}=\alpha, \tag{2.23}$$

where both $\mu=t\,(z+y)/y$ and $\lambda=t(z+y)^2$ are positive. By (2.10), the left-hand side of (2.23) may be rewritten as

$$\begin{aligned}&F(t;\mu,\lambda,-\tfrac{1}{2})\,\big|_{\mu=t(z+y)/y,\lambda=t(z+y)^2}\\&\qquad=F(1;\mu,\lambda,-\tfrac{1}{2})\,\big|_{\mu=(z+y)/y,\lambda=(z+y)^2}=\mathsf{F}(\underbrace{z+y}_{>0},y\mid-\tfrac{1}{2}),\end{aligned}$$

which does not depend on t. Thus, equation (2.21) can be written as[4]

$$\mathsf{F}(z+y,y\mid-\tfrac{1}{2})=\alpha,$$

whose solution $z=\mathsf{z}_\alpha(y)$, $y>0$, obviously exists and is unique.

To prove that $\mathsf{z}_\alpha(y)$, $y>0$, is monotone decreasing, we use (see Theorem A.4) the implicit function derivative theorem and Lemma 2.1, having

$$\begin{aligned}\frac{d}{dy}\,\mathsf{z}_\alpha(y)&=-\left(\frac{\frac{\partial}{\partial y}\,F(t;\mu,\lambda,-\tfrac{1}{2})\,\big|_{\mu=t\,(z+y)/y,\lambda=t\,(z+y)^2}}{\frac{\partial}{\partial z}\,F(t;\mu,\lambda,-\tfrac{1}{2})\,\big|_{\mu=t\,(z+y)/y,\lambda=t\,(z+y)^2}}\right)\Bigg|_{z=\mathsf{z}_\alpha(y)}\\&=-\left(\frac{\frac{\partial}{\partial y}\,\mathsf{F}(z+y,y\mid-\tfrac{1}{2})}{\frac{d}{dz}\,\mathsf{F}(z+y,y\mid-\tfrac{1}{2})}\right)\Bigg|_{z=\mathsf{z}_\alpha(y)}\\&=-\left(\frac{(z+2\,y)\,\mathcal{M}(z+2\,y)-1}{y\,\mathcal{M}(z+2\,y)-1}\right)\Bigg|_{z=\mathsf{z}_\alpha(y)}<0,\end{aligned}$$

[4]Plainly, $\mathsf{F}(z+y,y\mid-\tfrac{1}{2})=1-\Phi_{(0,1)}(z)+\Phi_{(0,1)}(-2y-z)\exp\{2y(z+y)\}$.

whence $\mathsf{z}_\alpha(y)$, $y > 0$, monotone decreases, as y increases from 0 to $+\infty$, and is bounded:

$$\kappa_{\alpha/2} = \mathsf{z}_\alpha(0) \geqslant \mathsf{z}_\alpha(y) \geqslant \mathsf{z}_\alpha(+\infty) = \kappa_\alpha \geqslant 0.$$

Note also that for y fixed the function $\mathsf{z}_\alpha(y)$ is monotone decreasing, as α increases, so that $\infty = \mathsf{z}_0(y) \geqslant \mathsf{z}_\alpha(y) \geqslant \mathsf{z}_1(y) = 0$, and the function $y + \mathsf{z}_\alpha(y)$ is monotone increasing, as y increases from 0 to $+\infty$.

It is noteworthy that the function $y + \mathsf{z}_\alpha(y)$, $y > 0$, monotone increases, which follows from the inequality

$$\frac{d}{dy}\,(y + \mathsf{z}_\alpha(y)) = 1 + \frac{d}{dy}\,\mathsf{z}_\alpha(y) = -\left(\frac{(z+y)\,\mathcal{M}(z+2y)}{y\,\mathcal{M}(z+2y) - 1}\right)\Bigg|_{z=\mathsf{z}_\alpha(y)} > 0,$$

which is straightforward from (2.4).

Bearing in mind that for $0 \leqslant c < \vartheta$

$$\mathsf{z}_\alpha(y)\,\big|_{y=\frac{(\vartheta-c)\sqrt{t}}{\sigma}} = \frac{u^{[\mathrm{dif}]}_{\alpha,t\,|\,\vartheta}(c)}{\sigma\sqrt{t}} - \frac{(\vartheta-c)\sqrt{t}}{\sigma},$$

the proof completes by converting this equality to the form

$$u^{[\mathrm{dif}]}_{\alpha,t\,|\,\vartheta}(c) = t(\vartheta - c) + \sigma\sqrt{t}\,\mathsf{z}_\alpha(y)\,\big|_{y=\frac{(\vartheta-c)\sqrt{t}}{\sigma}}$$

with the function $\mathsf{z}_\alpha(y)$, $y > 0$, possessing the properties listed in the statement of theorem.

Step 2. In the case $c > \vartheta$, we switch from the variables u and c in the left-hand side of (2.22) to the variables

$$z = \frac{u}{\sigma\sqrt{t}} > 0, \quad y = \frac{(\vartheta-c)\sqrt{t}}{\sigma} < 0.$$

In this way, we transform (2.22) into

$$\exp\left\{-\frac{2\lambda}{\hat{\mu}}\right\} F(t; \hat{\mu}, \lambda, -\tfrac{1}{2})\,\big|_{\hat{\mu}=-t\frac{z}{y},\lambda=tz^2} = \alpha, \tag{2.24}$$

where both $\hat{\mu} = -tz/y$ and $\lambda = tz^2$ are positive. By (2.11), the left-hand side of (2.24) may be rewritten as

$$\exp\left\{-\frac{2\lambda}{\hat{\mu}}\right\} F(t; \hat{\mu}, \lambda, -\tfrac{1}{2})\,\big|_{\hat{\mu}=-t\frac{z}{y},\lambda=tz^2} = \exp\{2zy\}\,\mathsf{F}(z, \underbrace{-y}_{>0} \mid -\tfrac{1}{2}),$$

which does not depend on t. Thus, equation (2.22) can be written as

$$\exp\{2zy\}\,\mathsf{F}(z, -y \mid -\tfrac{1}{2}) = \alpha,$$

whose solution $z = \mathsf{z}_\alpha(y)$, $y < 0$, obviously exists and is unique.

To prove that $\mathsf{z}_\alpha(y)$, $y < 0$, is monotone, we use (see Theorem A.4) the theorem on the derivative of implicit function and Lemmas 2.2, 2.3, having

$$\frac{d}{dy}\,\mathsf{z}_\alpha(y) = -\left(\frac{\frac{\partial}{\partial y}\Big(\exp\big\{-\frac{2\lambda}{\hat\mu}\big\}\,F(t;\hat\mu,\lambda,-\tfrac{1}{2})\,\big|_{\hat\mu=-t\frac{z}{y},\lambda=tz^2}\Big)}{\frac{\partial}{\partial z}\Big(\exp\big\{-\frac{2\lambda}{\hat\mu}\big\}\,F(t;\hat\mu,\lambda,-\tfrac{1}{2})\,\big|_{\hat\mu=-t\frac{z}{y},\lambda=tz^2}\Big)}\right)\Bigg|_{z=\mathsf{z}_\alpha(y)}$$

$$= -\left(\frac{\frac{\partial}{\partial y}\,(\exp\{-2z|y|\}\,\mathsf{F}(z,|y|\mid-\tfrac{1}{2}))}{\frac{\partial}{\partial z}(\exp\{-2z|y|\}\,\mathsf{F}(z,|y|\mid-\tfrac{1}{2}))}\right)\Bigg|_{z=\mathsf{z}_\alpha(y)}$$

$$= -\left(\frac{z\,\mathcal{M}(z+|y|)}{|y|\,\mathcal{M}(z+|y|)-1}\right)\Bigg|_{z=\mathsf{z}_\alpha(y)} > 0.$$

Thereby, the function $\mathsf{z}_\alpha(y)$, $y < 0$, is monotone increasing, as y increases from $-\infty$ to 0, and is bounded:

$$0 = \mathsf{z}_\alpha(-\infty) \leqslant \mathsf{z}_\alpha(y) \leqslant \mathsf{z}_\alpha(0) = \kappa_{\alpha/2}.$$

Moreover, if y is fixed, then $\mathsf{z}_\alpha(y)$ is monotone decreasing, as α increases, and $\infty = \mathsf{z}_0(y) \geqslant \mathsf{z}_\alpha(y) \geqslant \mathsf{z}_1(y) = 0$.

Bearing in mind that, when $c > \vartheta$, we have

$$\mathsf{z}_\alpha(y)\Big|_{y=-\frac{(c-\vartheta)\sqrt{t}}{\sigma}} = \frac{1}{\sigma\sqrt{t}}\,u^{[\mathrm{dif}]}_{\alpha,t\,|\,\vartheta}(c),$$

the proof completes by converting this equality to the form

$$u^{[\mathrm{dif}]}_{\alpha,t\,|\,\vartheta}(c) = \sigma\sqrt{t}\,\mathsf{z}_\alpha(y)\,\Big|_{y=-\frac{(c-\vartheta)\sqrt{t}}{\sigma}},$$

with the function $\mathsf{z}_\alpha(y)$, $y > 0$, possessing the properties listed in the statement of theorem. □

2.3.2 Monotony of fixed-probability level

Monotony of the fixed-probability level $u^{[\mathrm{dif}]}_{\alpha,t\,|\,\vartheta}(c)$, $c \geqslant 0$, illustrated in Fig. 2.2, needs no proof: as c increases, the level that is crossed within time t with the probability α is obviously decreasing. However, to prepare the reader for the proofs in Section 2.3.3, we formulate the following monotony theorem and prove it by means of standard technique.

Theorem 2.8 (Monotony) *For all $t > 0$, the fixed-probability level $u^{[\mathrm{dif}]}_{\alpha,t\,|\,\vartheta}(c)$, $c \geqslant 0$, monotone decreases, as c increases.*

To prove Theorem 2.8, we apply the following standard criterion: a differentiable function, whose first-order derivative is negative on an interval, is monotone decreasing on this interval, whence Theorem 2.8 follows directly from the following Theorem 2.9.

Theorem 2.9 *For $0 \leqslant c < \vartheta$, we have*

$$\frac{d}{dc}\, u^{[\mathrm{dif}]}_{\alpha,t\,|\,\vartheta}(c) = t \left(\frac{z\,\mathcal{M}(z+y)\,\big|_{z=\frac{u}{\sigma\sqrt{t}},\, y=\frac{(\vartheta-c)\sqrt{t}}{\sigma}}}{\left(y\,\mathcal{M}(z+y)-1\right)\big|_{z=\frac{u}{\sigma\sqrt{t}},\, y=\frac{(\vartheta-c)\sqrt{t}}{\sigma}}} \right)\Bigg|_{u=u^{[\mathrm{dif}]}_{\alpha,t\,|\,\vartheta}(c)} < 0. \tag{2.25}$$

When $c > \vartheta$, we have

$$\frac{d}{dc}\, u^{[\mathrm{dif}]}_{\alpha,t\,|\,\vartheta}(c) = -t \left(\frac{z\,\mathcal{M}(z-y)\,\big|_{z=\frac{u}{\sigma\sqrt{t}},\, y=-\frac{(\vartheta-c)\sqrt{t}}{\sigma}}}{\left(y\,\mathcal{M}(z-y)+1\right)\big|_{z=\frac{u}{\sigma\sqrt{t}},\, y=-\frac{(\vartheta-c)\sqrt{t}}{\sigma}}} \right)\Bigg|_{u=u^{[\mathrm{dif}]}_{\alpha,t\,|\,\vartheta}(c)} < 0. \tag{2.26}$$

To prove Theorem 2.9, first let us find the derivatives (in both cases $0 \leqslant c < \vartheta$ and $c > \vartheta$) in terms of $\mathsf{F}(z, y \mid -\frac{1}{2})$, $z, y > 0$, and the derivatives $\mathsf{F}^{(i,j)}(z, y \mid -\frac{1}{2}) := \frac{\partial^{(i+j)}}{\partial z^i \partial y^j}\, \mathsf{F}(z, y \mid -\frac{1}{2})$, $z, y > 0$, $i, j = 0, 1, \ldots$. This is done in Theorems 2.10 and 2.11. Second, let us check inequalities in (2.25) and (2.26).

Theorem 2.10 *For $0 \leqslant c < \vartheta$, we have*

$$\frac{d}{dc}\, u^{[\mathrm{dif}]}_{\alpha,t\,|\,\vartheta}(c) = t \left(\frac{\mathsf{F}^{(0,1)}(z, y \mid -\frac{1}{2})\,\big|_{z=\frac{u}{\sigma\sqrt{t}},\, y=\frac{(\vartheta-c)\sqrt{t}}{\sigma}}}{\mathsf{F}^{(1,0)}(z, y \mid -\frac{1}{2})\,\big|_{z=\frac{u}{\sigma\sqrt{t}},\, y=\frac{(\vartheta-c)\sqrt{t}}{\sigma}}} \right)\Bigg|_{u=u^{[\mathrm{dif}]}_{\alpha,t\,|\,\vartheta}(c)}. \tag{2.27}$$

Proof. For $0 \leqslant c < \vartheta$, we start with equation (2.21). By (see Theorem A.4) the theorem on the derivative of implicit function, we have

$$\frac{d}{dc}\, u^{[\mathrm{dif}]}_{\alpha,t\,|\,\vartheta}(c) = -\left(\frac{\frac{\partial}{\partial c} F(t; \mu, \lambda, -\frac{1}{2})\,\big|_{\mu=\frac{u}{\vartheta-c},\, \lambda=\frac{u^2}{\sigma^2}}}{\frac{\partial}{\partial u} F(t; \mu, \lambda, -\frac{1}{2})\,\big|_{\mu=\frac{u}{\vartheta-c},\, \lambda=\frac{u^2}{\sigma^2}}} \right)\Bigg|_{u=u^{[\mathrm{dif}]}_{\alpha,t\,|\,\vartheta}(c)}. \tag{2.28}$$

By (2.10), in terms of the auxiliary function of the first kind, we have

$$F(t; \mu, \lambda, -\tfrac{1}{2})\,\big|_{\mu=\frac{u}{\vartheta-c},\, \lambda=\frac{u^2}{\sigma^2}} = \mathsf{F}(z, y \mid -\tfrac{1}{2})\,\big|_{z=\frac{u}{\sigma\sqrt{t}},\, y=\frac{(\vartheta-c)\sqrt{t}}{\sigma}}.$$

Applying (see (A.1)) chain rule for differentiation of a composite function, we have

$$\frac{\partial}{\partial c} F(t; \mu, \lambda, -\tfrac{1}{2})\,\big|_{\mu=\frac{u}{\vartheta-c},\, \lambda=\frac{u^2}{\sigma^2}} = -\frac{\sqrt{t}}{\sigma}\, \mathsf{F}^{(0,1)}(z, y \mid -\tfrac{1}{2})\,\big|_{z=\frac{u}{\sigma\sqrt{t}},\, y=\frac{(\vartheta-c)\sqrt{t}}{\sigma}},$$
$$\frac{\partial}{\partial u} F(t; \mu, \lambda, -\tfrac{1}{2})\,\big|_{\mu=\frac{u}{\vartheta-c},\, \lambda=\frac{u^2}{\sigma^2}} = \frac{1}{\sigma\sqrt{t}}\, \mathsf{F}^{(1,0)}(z, y \mid -\tfrac{1}{2})\,\big|_{z=\frac{u}{\sigma\sqrt{t}},\, y=\frac{(\vartheta-c)\sqrt{t}}{\sigma}}.$$

Put these equalities into equality (2.28), whence the result. □

Theorem 2.11 *When $c > \vartheta$, we have*

$$\frac{d}{dc}u^{[\mathrm{dif}]}_{\alpha,t\,|\,\vartheta}(c) = -t$$
$$\times \left(\frac{(\mathsf{F}^{(0,1)}(z,y\mid-\tfrac{1}{2}) - 2z\,\mathsf{F}(z,y\mid-\tfrac{1}{2}))\,\Big|_{z=\frac{u}{\sigma\sqrt{t}},y=-\frac{(\vartheta-c)\sqrt{t}}{\sigma}}}{(\mathsf{F}^{(1,0)}(z,y\mid-\tfrac{1}{2}) - 2y\,\mathsf{F}(z,y\mid-\tfrac{1}{2}))\,\Big|_{z=\frac{u}{\sigma\sqrt{t}},y=-\frac{(\vartheta-c)\sqrt{t}}{\sigma}}}\right)\Bigg|_{u=u^{[\mathrm{dif}]}_{\alpha,t\,|\,\vartheta}(c)}. \tag{2.29}$$

Proof. When $c > \vartheta$, we start with equation (2.22). By (see Theorem A.4) the theorem on the derivative of implicit function, we have

$$\frac{d}{dc}u^{[\mathrm{dif}]}_{\alpha,t\,|\,\vartheta}(c)$$
$$= -\left(\frac{\frac{\partial}{\partial c}\left(\exp\left\{-\frac{2\lambda}{\hat{\mu}}\right\}F(t;\hat{\mu},\lambda,\tfrac{1}{2})\,\Big|_{\hat{\mu}=-\frac{u}{\vartheta-c},\lambda=\frac{u^2}{\sigma^2}}\right)}{\frac{\partial}{\partial u}\left(\exp\left\{-\frac{2\lambda}{\hat{\mu}}\right\}F(t;\hat{\mu},\lambda,\tfrac{1}{2})\,\Big|_{\hat{\mu}=-\frac{u}{\vartheta-c},\lambda=\frac{u^2}{\sigma^2}}\right)}\right)\Bigg|_{u=u^{[\mathrm{dif}]}_{\alpha,t\,|\,\vartheta}(c)}. \tag{2.30}$$

By (2.11), in terms of the auxiliary function of the first kind, we have

$$\exp\left\{-\frac{2\lambda}{\hat{\mu}}\right\}F(t;\hat{\mu},\lambda,\tfrac{1}{2})\,\Big|_{\hat{\mu}=-\frac{u}{\vartheta-c},\lambda=\frac{u^2}{\sigma^2}}$$
$$= \exp\{-2zy\}\,\mathsf{F}(z,y\mid-\tfrac{1}{2})\,\Big|_{z=\frac{u}{\sigma\sqrt{t}},y=-\frac{(\vartheta-c)\sqrt{t}}{\sigma}}.$$

Applying (see (A.1)) chain rule for differentiation of a composite function, we have

$$\frac{\partial}{\partial c}\left(\left(\exp\left\{-\frac{2\lambda}{\hat{\mu}}\right\}F(t;\hat{\mu},\lambda,\tfrac{1}{2})\right)\Big|_{\hat{\mu}=-\frac{u}{\vartheta-c},\lambda=\frac{u^2}{\sigma^2}}\right) = \frac{\sqrt{t}}{\sigma}$$
$$\times\left(\exp\{-2zy\}\,(\mathsf{F}^{(0,1)}(z,y\mid-\tfrac{1}{2}) - 2z\,\mathsf{F}(z,y\mid-\tfrac{1}{2}))\right)\Big|_{z=\frac{u}{\sigma\sqrt{t}},y=-\frac{(\vartheta-c)\sqrt{t}}{\sigma}},$$
$$\frac{\partial}{\partial u}\left(\left(\exp\left\{-\frac{2\lambda}{\hat{\mu}}\right\}F(t;\hat{\mu},\lambda,\tfrac{1}{2})\right)\Big|_{\hat{\mu}=-\frac{u}{\vartheta-c},\lambda=\frac{u^2}{\sigma^2}}\right) = \frac{1}{\sigma\sqrt{t}}$$
$$\times\left(\exp\{-2zy\}\,(\mathsf{F}^{(1,0)}(z,y\mid-\tfrac{1}{2}) - 2y\,\mathsf{F}(z,y\mid-\tfrac{1}{2}))\right)\Big|_{z=\frac{u}{\sigma\sqrt{t}},y=-\frac{(\vartheta-c)\sqrt{t}}{\sigma}}.$$

Put these equalities into equality (2.30), whence the result. □

Proof of Theorem 2.9. Equality in (2.25) is straightforward from (B.28). Inequality in (2.25) is straightforward from Lemma 2.2. Equality in (2.26) is straightforward from (2.20) and (2.29). Inequality in (2.26) is straightforward from Lemma 2.2. □

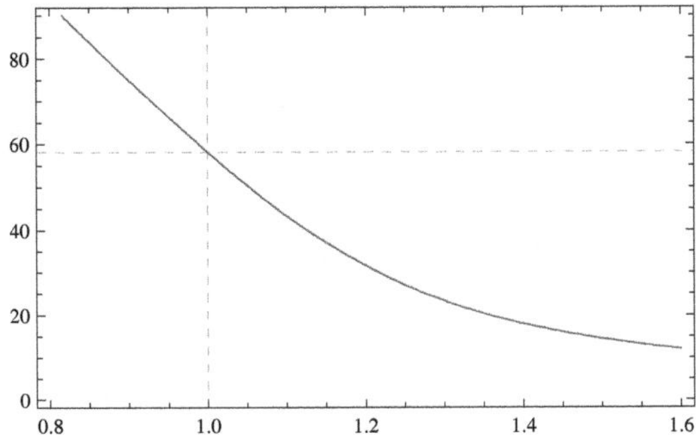

FIGURE 2.2: Graph (X-axis is c) of $u^{[\mathrm{dif}]}_{\alpha,t\,|\,\vartheta}(c)$, when $\alpha = 0.1$, $t = 200$, $\sigma = 2.5$, $\vartheta = 1$, and $\kappa_{\alpha/2} = 1.65$. Vertical grid line: ϑ, which equals 1. Horizontal grid line: $u^{[\mathrm{dif}]}_{\alpha,t\,|\,\vartheta}(\vartheta) = \sigma\kappa_{\alpha/2}\sqrt{t}$, which equals 58.15.

2.3.3 Convexity of fixed-probability level

Convexity[5] of the fixed-probability level $u^{[\mathrm{dif}]}_{\alpha,t\,|\,\vartheta}(c)$, $c \geqslant 0$, is illustrated in Fig. 2.2. Apparently, in contrast to monotony, convexity defies elementary explanation. An analytical proof of convexity, similar to the proof of monotony in Theorem 2.8, requires a straightforward, but rather cumbersome technique. It is based on the following well-known criterion: a twice-differentiable function, whose second derivative is positive on an interval, is convex on this interval.

Theorem 2.12 (Convexity) *For all $t > 0$, the fixed-probability level $u^{[\mathrm{dif}]}_{\alpha,t\,|\,\vartheta}(c)$, $c \geqslant 0$, is convex.*

The proof of Theorem 2.12, which immediately follows from Theorem 2.13 below, is given at the end of this section.

We need the following notation. For $z, y > 0$, we write

$$\boldsymbol{\Delta}(z,y) = 2y\,\mathcal{M}^3(z+y) - (2+z^2-y^2)\,\mathcal{M}^2(z+y) - 2y\,\mathcal{M}(z+y) + 1.$$
$$\nabla(z,y) = 2y\,\mathcal{M}^3(z-y) + (2+z^2-y^2)\,\mathcal{M}^2(z-y) - 2y\,\mathcal{M}(z-y) - 1.$$

The following lemmas are auxiliary.

Lemma 2.4 *For $z, y > 0$, we have $\boldsymbol{\Delta}(z,y) < 0$ and $(y\,\mathcal{M}(z+y)-1)^3 < 0$.*

Proof. Bearing in mind (B.21), note that

$$y\,\mathcal{M}(z+y) - 1 = \big(\underbrace{v\,\mathcal{M}(v) - 1}_{<0} - \underbrace{z\,\mathcal{M}(v)}_{>0}\big)\Big|_{v=z+y} < 0,$$

[5]A convex function is of the form $\smile$.

whence the second inequality. Note that $\boldsymbol{\Delta}(z, y)$ may be rewritten as

$$\begin{aligned}\boldsymbol{\Delta}(z, y) &= (2(v-z)\,\mathcal{M}^3(v) - (2+2zv-v^2)\,\mathcal{M}^2(v) - 2(v-z)\,\mathcal{M}(v) + 1)\,\big|_{v=z+y} \\ &= \boldsymbol{\Delta}_1(v)\,\big|_{v=z+y} + \boldsymbol{\Delta}_2(z,v)\,\big|_{v=z+y},\end{aligned}$$

where the first term $\boldsymbol{\Delta}_1(v)\,\big|_{v=z+y}$ is equal to $\boldsymbol{\Delta}(z, y)\,|_{z=0}$, and the second term $\boldsymbol{\Delta}_2(z, v)\,\big|_{v=z+y}$ is the rest. To prove the first inequality, bearing in mind (B.21), (B.23), we note that

$$\begin{aligned}\boldsymbol{\Delta}_1(v) &= 2v\,\mathcal{M}^3(v) - (2-v^2)\,\mathcal{M}^2(v) - 2v\,\mathcal{M}(v) + 1 \\ &= 2v\,\mathcal{M}^3(v) - 2\,\mathcal{M}^2(v) + v^2\,\mathcal{M}^2(v) - 2v\,\mathcal{M}(v) + 1 \\ &= -\underbrace{(1 - v\,\mathcal{M}(v))}_{>0}\,(\mathcal{M}^2(v) + \underbrace{\mathcal{M}^2(v) + v\,\mathcal{M}(v) - 1}_{>0}) < 0, \\ \boldsymbol{\Delta}_2(z,v) &= -2z\,\mathcal{M}^3(v) - 2zv\,\mathcal{M}^2(v) + 2z\,\mathcal{M}(v) \\ &= -2z\,\mathcal{M}(v)\,\underbrace{(\mathcal{M}^2(v) + v\,\mathcal{M}(v) - 1)}_{>0} < 0.\end{aligned}$$

The proof is complete. □

Lemma 2.5 *For $z, y > 0$, we have $\nabla(z, y) > 0$ and $(y\,\mathcal{M}(z-y) + 1)^3 > 0$.*

Proof. We note that

$$\begin{aligned}\nabla(z,y) &= 2y\,\mathcal{M}^3(z-y) + (2+z^2-y^2)\,\mathcal{M}^2(z-y) - 2y\,\mathcal{M}(z-y) - 1 \\ &= (2(z-v)\,\mathcal{M}^3(v) + (2+2zv-v^2)\,\mathcal{M}^2(v) \\ &\quad - 2(z-v)\,\mathcal{M}(v) - 1)\,\big|_{v=z-y\in\mathsf{R}} \\ &= \nabla_1(v)\,\big|_{v=z-y\in\mathsf{R}} + \nabla_2(z,v)\,\big|_{v=z-y\in\mathsf{R}},\end{aligned}$$

vhere, bearing in mind (B.21), (B.23),

$$\begin{aligned}\nabla_1(v) &= (-2v\,\mathcal{M}^3(v) + (2-v^2)\,\mathcal{M}^2(v) + 2v\,\mathcal{M}(v) - 1) \\ &= (1 - v\,\mathcal{M}(v))(2\,\mathcal{M}^2(v) - (1 - (v\,\mathcal{M}(v)))) \\ &= \underbrace{(1 - v\,\mathcal{M}(v))}_{>0}(\mathcal{M}^2(v) + \underbrace{\mathcal{M}^2(v) + v\,\mathcal{M}(v) - 1}_{>0}) > 0, \\ \nabla_2(z,v) &= (2z\,\mathcal{M}^3(v) + 2zv\,\mathcal{M}^2(v) - 2z\,\mathcal{M}(v)) \\ &= 2z\,\underbrace{(\mathcal{M}^2(v) + v\,\mathcal{M}(v) - 1)}_{>0}\,\mathcal{M}(v) > 0.\end{aligned}$$

The proof is complete. □

Theorem 2.12 is straightforward from the following Theorem 2.13, the proof of which is given at the end of this section.

Theorem 2.13 *For $0 \leqslant c < \vartheta$, we have*

$$\frac{d^2}{dc^2}\, u^{[\mathrm{dif}]}_{\alpha,t\,|\,\vartheta}(c) = \frac{t^{3/2}}{\sigma} \times \left(\frac{z\,\Delta(z,y)\,\big|_{z=\frac{u}{\sigma\sqrt{t}},\,y=\frac{(\vartheta-c)\sqrt{t}}{\sigma}}}{(y\,\mathcal{M}(z+y)-1)^3\big|_{z=\frac{u}{\sigma\sqrt{t}},\,y=\frac{(\vartheta-c)\sqrt{t}}{\sigma}}} \right)\Bigg|_{u=u^{[\mathrm{dif}]}_{\alpha,t\,|\,\vartheta}(c)} > 0. \tag{2.31}$$

When $c > \vartheta$, we have

$$\frac{d^2}{dc^2}\, u^{[\mathrm{dif}]}_{\alpha,t\,|\,\vartheta}(c) = \frac{t^{3/2}}{\sigma} \times \left(\frac{z\,\nabla(z,y)\,\big|_{z=\frac{u}{\sigma\sqrt{t}},\,y=-\frac{(\vartheta-c)\sqrt{t}}{\sigma}}}{(y\,\mathcal{M}(z-y)+1)^3\big|_{z=\frac{u}{\sigma\sqrt{t}},\,y=-\frac{(\vartheta-c)\sqrt{t}}{\sigma}}} \right)\Bigg|_{u=u^{[\mathrm{dif}]}_{\alpha,t\,|\,\vartheta}(c)} > 0. \tag{2.32}$$

To prove Theorem 2.13, we first find the derivatives (in both cases $0 \leqslant c < \vartheta$ and $c > \vartheta$) in terms of $\mathsf{F}^{(i,j)}(z, y \mid -\frac{1}{2})$, $z, y > 0$, $i, j = 0, 1, \ldots$.

Theorem 2.14 *For $0 \leqslant c < \vartheta$, we have*

$$\frac{d^2}{dc^2}\, u^{[\mathrm{dif}]}_{\alpha,t\,|\,\vartheta}(c) = -\frac{t^{3/2}}{\sigma} \left(\frac{\mathsf{F}^{(0,2)}(z,y\mid -\frac{1}{2})\,\big|_{z=\frac{u}{\sigma\sqrt{t}},\,y=\frac{(\vartheta-c)\sqrt{t}}{\sigma}}}{\mathsf{F}^{(1,0)}(z,y\mid -\frac{1}{2})\,\big|_{z=\frac{u}{\sigma\sqrt{t}},\,y=\frac{(\vartheta-c)\sqrt{t}}{\sigma}}} - 2\frac{\mathsf{F}^{(1,1)}(z,y\mid -\frac{1}{2})\,\mathsf{F}^{(0,1)}(z,y\mid -\frac{1}{2})\,\big|_{z=\frac{u}{\sigma\sqrt{t}},\,y=\frac{(\vartheta-c)\sqrt{t}}{\sigma}}}{(\mathsf{F}^{(1,0)}(z,y\mid -\frac{1}{2}))^2\,\big|_{z=\frac{u}{\sigma\sqrt{t}},\,y=\frac{(\vartheta-c)\sqrt{t}}{\sigma}}} + \frac{\mathsf{F}^{(2,0)}(z,y\mid -\frac{1}{2})\,(\mathsf{F}^{(0,1)}(z,y\mid -\frac{1}{2}))^2\,\big|_{z=\frac{u}{\sigma\sqrt{t}},\,y=\frac{(\vartheta-c)\sqrt{t}}{\sigma}}}{(\mathsf{F}^{(1,0)}(z,y\mid -\frac{1}{2}))^3\,\big|_{z=\frac{u}{\sigma\sqrt{t}},\,y=\frac{(\vartheta-c)\sqrt{t}}{\sigma}}} \right)\Bigg|_{u=u^{[\mathrm{dif}]}_{\alpha,t\,|\,\vartheta}(c)}. \tag{2.33}$$

Proof. For $0 \leqslant c < \vartheta$, we start with equation (2.21). By (see Theorem A.4) the theorem on the derivative of implicit function, we have

$$\frac{d^2}{dc^2}\, u^{[\mathrm{dif}]}_{\alpha,t\,|\,\vartheta}(c) = -\left(\frac{\frac{\partial^2}{\partial c^2} F(t;\mu,\lambda,-\frac{1}{2})\,\big|_{\mu=\frac{u}{\vartheta-c},\,\lambda=\frac{u^2}{\sigma^2}}}{\frac{\partial}{\partial u} F(t;\mu,\lambda,-\frac{1}{2})\,\big|_{\mu=\frac{u}{\vartheta-c},\,\lambda=\frac{u^2}{\sigma^2}}} - \frac{2\,\frac{\partial^2}{\partial c\partial u} F(t;\mu,\lambda,-\frac{1}{2})\,\frac{\partial}{\partial c} F(t;\mu,\lambda,-\frac{1}{2})\,\big|_{\mu=\frac{u}{\vartheta-c},\,\lambda=\frac{u^2}{\sigma^2}}}{(\frac{\partial}{\partial u} F(t;\mu,\lambda,-\frac{1}{2}))^2\,\big|_{\mu=\frac{u}{\vartheta-c},\,\lambda=\frac{u^2}{\sigma^2}}} + \frac{\frac{\partial^2}{\partial u^2} F(t;\mu,\lambda,-\frac{1}{2})\,(\frac{\partial}{\partial c} F(t;\mu,\lambda,-\frac{1}{2}))^2\,\big|_{\mu=\frac{u}{\vartheta-c},\,\lambda=\frac{u^2}{\sigma^2}}}{(\frac{\partial}{\partial u} F(t;\mu,\lambda,-\frac{1}{2}))^3\,\big|_{\mu=\frac{u}{\vartheta-c},\,\lambda=\frac{u^2}{\sigma^2}}} \right)\Bigg|_{u=u^{[\mathrm{dif}]}_{\alpha,t\,|\,\vartheta}(c)}. \tag{2.34}$$

By (2.10), in terms of the auxiliary function of the first kind, we have

$$F(t;\mu,\lambda,-\tfrac{1}{2})\,\big|_{\mu=\frac{u}{\vartheta-c},\lambda=\frac{u^2}{\sigma^2}} = \mathsf{F}(z,y\mid-\tfrac{1}{2})\,\big|_{z=\frac{u}{\sigma\sqrt{t}},y=\frac{(\vartheta-c)\sqrt{t}}{\sigma}}.$$

Applying (see (A.1)) chain rule for differentiation of a composite function, we have for the first-order derivatives

$$\frac{\partial}{\partial c}F(t;\mu,\lambda,-\tfrac{1}{2})\,\big|_{\mu=\frac{u}{\vartheta-c},\lambda=\frac{u^2}{\sigma^2}} = -\frac{\sqrt{t}}{\sigma}\,\mathsf{F}^{(0,1)}(z,y\mid-\tfrac{1}{2})\,\big|_{z=\frac{u}{\sigma\sqrt{t}},y=\frac{(\vartheta-c)\sqrt{t}}{\sigma}},$$
$$\frac{\partial}{\partial u}F(t;\mu,\lambda,-\tfrac{1}{2})\,\big|_{\mu=\frac{u}{\vartheta-c},\lambda=\frac{u^2}{\sigma^2}} = \frac{1}{\sigma\sqrt{t}}\,\mathsf{F}^{(1,0)}(z,y\mid-\tfrac{1}{2})\,\big|_{z=\frac{u}{\sigma\sqrt{t}},y=\frac{(\vartheta-c)\sqrt{t}}{\sigma}},$$

and for the second-order derivatives

$$\frac{\partial^2}{\partial c^2}F(t;\mu,\lambda,-\tfrac{1}{2})\,\big|_{\mu=\frac{u}{\vartheta-c},\lambda=\frac{u^2}{\sigma^2}} = \frac{t}{\sigma^2}\,\mathsf{F}^{(0,2)}(z,y\mid-\tfrac{1}{2})\,\big|_{z=\frac{u}{\sigma\sqrt{t}},y=\frac{(\vartheta-c)\sqrt{t}}{\sigma}},$$
$$\frac{\partial^2}{\partial u^2}F(t;\mu,\lambda,-\tfrac{1}{2})\,\big|_{\mu=\frac{u}{\vartheta-c},\lambda=\frac{u^2}{\sigma^2}} = \frac{1}{\sigma^2 t}\,\mathsf{F}^{(2,0)}(z,y\mid-\tfrac{1}{2})\,\big|_{z=\frac{u}{\sigma\sqrt{t}},y=\frac{(\vartheta-c)\sqrt{t}}{\sigma}},$$
$$\frac{\partial^2}{\partial c\,\partial u}F(t;\mu,\lambda,-\tfrac{1}{2})\,\big|_{\mu=\frac{u}{\vartheta-c},\lambda=\frac{u^2}{\sigma^2}} = -\frac{1}{\sigma^2}\,\mathsf{F}^{(1,1)}(z,y\mid-\tfrac{1}{2})\,\big|_{z=\frac{u}{\sigma\sqrt{t}},y=\frac{(\vartheta-c)\sqrt{t}}{\sigma}}.$$

Put these equalities into equality (2.34), whence equality (2.33). □

Bearing in mind (B.28) and (B.29), the following result needs only algebraic transformations. We leave its proof (which requires elementary but cumbersome calculations) to the reader.

Theorem 2.15 *We have*

$$\frac{\mathsf{F}^{(0,2)}(z,y\mid-\frac{1}{2})}{\mathsf{F}^{(1,0)}(z,y\mid-\frac{1}{2})} - 2\,\frac{\mathsf{F}^{(1,1)}(z,y\mid-\frac{1}{2})\,\mathsf{F}^{(0,1)}(z,y\mid-\frac{1}{2})}{(\mathsf{F}^{(1,0)}(z,y\mid-\frac{1}{2}))^2} + \frac{\mathsf{F}^{(2,0)}(z,y\mid-\frac{1}{2})\,(\mathsf{F}^{(0,1)}(z,y\mid-\frac{1}{2}))^2}{(\mathsf{F}^{(1,0)}(z,y\mid-\frac{1}{2}))^3} = -\frac{z\,\mathbf{\Delta}(z,y)}{(y\,\mathcal{M}(z+y)-1)^3}. \tag{2.35}$$

Theorem 2.16 *When $c>\vartheta$, we have*

$$\frac{d^2}{dc^2}u^{[\mathrm{dif}]}_{\alpha,t\,|\,\vartheta}(c) = -\frac{t^{3/2}}{\sigma} \times\Bigg(\frac{\mathsf{A}(z,y)\,\big|_{z=\frac{u}{\sigma\sqrt{t}},y=-\frac{(\vartheta-c)\sqrt{t}}{\sigma}}}{(\mathsf{F}^{(1,0)}(z,y\mid-\frac{1}{2})-2y\,\mathsf{F}(z,y\mid-\frac{1}{2}))\,\big|_{z=\frac{u}{\sigma\sqrt{t}},y=-\frac{(\vartheta-c)\sqrt{t}}{\sigma}}}$$
$$-\frac{2\,\mathsf{B}(z,y)\,(\mathsf{F}^{(0,1)}(z,y\mid-\frac{1}{2})-2z\,\mathsf{F}(z,y\mid-\frac{1}{2}))\,\big|_{z=\frac{u}{\sigma\sqrt{t}},y=-\frac{(\vartheta-c)\sqrt{t}}{\sigma}}}{(\mathsf{F}^{(1,0)}(z,y\mid-\frac{1}{2})-2y\,\mathsf{F}(z,y\mid-\frac{1}{2}))^2\,\big|_{z=\frac{u}{\sigma\sqrt{t}},y=-\frac{(\vartheta-c)\sqrt{t}}{\sigma}}}$$
$$+\frac{\mathsf{C}(z,y)\,(\mathsf{F}^{(0,1)}(z,y\mid-\frac{1}{2})-2z\,\mathsf{F}(z,y\mid-\frac{1}{2}))^2\,\big|_{z=\frac{u}{\sigma\sqrt{t}},y=-\frac{(\vartheta-c)\sqrt{t}}{\sigma}}}{(\mathsf{F}^{(1,0)}(z,y\mid-\frac{1}{2})-2y\,\mathsf{F}(z,y\mid-\frac{1}{2}))^3\,\big|_{z=\frac{u}{\sigma\sqrt{t}},y=-\frac{(\vartheta-c)\sqrt{t}}{\sigma}}}\Bigg)\Bigg|_{u=u^{[\mathrm{dif}]}_{\alpha,t\,|\,\vartheta}(c)}, \tag{2.36}$$

where

$$
\begin{aligned}
\mathsf{A}(z,y) &= \mathsf{F}^{(0,2)}(z,y\mid -\tfrac{1}{2}) - 4z\,\mathsf{F}^{(0,1)}(z,y\mid -\tfrac{1}{2}) + 4z^2\,\mathsf{F}(z,y\mid -\tfrac{1}{2}),\\
\mathsf{B}(z,y) &= \mathsf{F}^{(1,1)}(z,y\mid -\tfrac{1}{2}) - 2y\,\mathsf{F}^{(0,1)}(z,y\mid -\tfrac{1}{2})\\
&\quad - 2z\,\mathsf{F}^{(1,0)}(z,y\mid -\tfrac{1}{2}) + 2\,(2zy-1)\,\mathsf{F}(z,y\mid -\tfrac{1}{2}),\\
\mathsf{C}(z,y) &= \mathsf{F}^{(2,0)}(z,y\mid -\tfrac{1}{2}) - 4y\,\mathsf{F}^{(1,0)}(z,y\mid -\tfrac{1}{2}) + 4y^2\,\mathsf{F}(z,y\mid -\tfrac{1}{2}).
\end{aligned}
$$

Proof. When $c > \vartheta$, we start with equation (2.22). By (see Theorem A.4) the theorem on the derivative of implicit function, we have

$$
\begin{aligned}
&\frac{d^2}{dc^2}u^{[\mathrm{dif}]}_{\alpha,t\,|\,\vartheta}(c)\\
&= -\left(\frac{\frac{\partial^2}{\partial c^2}\Big(\exp\big\{-\frac{2\lambda}{\hat\mu}\big\}F(t;\hat\mu,\lambda,-\tfrac{1}{2})\,|_{\hat\mu=-\frac{u}{\vartheta-c},\lambda=\frac{u^2}{\sigma^2}}\Big)}{\frac{\partial}{\partial u}\Big(\exp\big\{-\frac{2\lambda}{\hat\mu}\big\}F(t;\hat\mu,\lambda,-\tfrac{1}{2})\,|_{\hat\mu=-\frac{u}{\vartheta-c},\lambda=\frac{u^2}{\sigma^2}}\Big)}\right.\\
&\quad - \frac{2\frac{\partial^2}{\partial c\partial u}\Big(\exp\big\{-\frac{2\lambda}{\hat\mu}\big\}F(t;\hat\mu,\lambda,-\tfrac{1}{2})\,|_{\hat\mu=-\frac{u}{\vartheta-c},\lambda=\frac{u^2}{\sigma^2}}\Big)}{\Big(\frac{\partial}{\partial u}\Big(\exp\big\{-\frac{2\lambda}{\hat\mu}\big\}F(t;\hat\mu,\lambda,-\tfrac{1}{2})\,|_{\hat\mu=-\frac{u}{\vartheta-c},\lambda=\frac{u^2}{\sigma^2}}\Big)\Big)^2}\\
&\quad \times \frac{\partial}{\partial c}\Big(\exp\Big\{-\frac{2\lambda}{\hat\mu}\Big\}F(t;\hat\mu,\lambda,-\tfrac{1}{2})\,|_{\hat\mu=-\frac{u}{\vartheta-c},\lambda=\frac{u^2}{\sigma^2}}\Big)\\
&\quad + \frac{\frac{\partial^2}{\partial u^2}\Big(\exp\big\{-\frac{2\lambda}{\hat\mu}\big\}F(t;\hat\mu,\lambda,-\tfrac{1}{2})\,|_{\hat\mu=-\frac{u}{\vartheta-c},\lambda=\frac{u^2}{\sigma^2}}\Big)}{\Big(\frac{\partial}{\partial u}\Big(\exp\big\{-\frac{2\lambda}{\hat\mu}\big\}F(t;\hat\mu,\lambda,-\tfrac{1}{2})\,|_{\hat\mu=-\frac{u}{\vartheta-c},\lambda=\frac{u^2}{\sigma^2}}\Big)\Big)^3}\\
&\quad \left.\times\Big(\frac{\partial}{\partial c}\Big(\exp\Big\{-\frac{2\lambda}{\hat\mu}\Big\}F(t;\hat\mu,\lambda,-\tfrac{1}{2})\,|_{\hat\mu=-\frac{u}{\vartheta-c},\lambda=\frac{u^2}{\sigma^2}}\Big)\Big)^2\right)\Bigg|_{u=u^{[\mathrm{dif}]}_{\alpha,t\,|\,\vartheta}(c)}.
\end{aligned}
\tag{2.37}
$$

By (2.11), in terms of the auxiliary function of the first kind, we have

$$
\begin{aligned}
&\exp\Big\{-\frac{2\lambda}{\hat\mu}\Big\}F(t;\hat\mu,\lambda,\tfrac{1}{2})\,|_{\hat\mu=-\frac{u}{\vartheta-c},\lambda=\frac{u^2}{\sigma^2}}\\
&\qquad = \exp\{-2zy\}\,\mathsf{F}(z,y\mid -\tfrac{1}{2})\,\Big|_{z=\frac{u}{\sigma\sqrt{t}},y=-\frac{(\vartheta-c)\sqrt{t}}{\sigma}}.
\end{aligned}
$$

Applying (see (A.1)) chain rule for differentiation of a composite function, we have

$$
\begin{aligned}
&\frac{\partial}{\partial c}\Big(\exp\Big\{-\frac{2\lambda}{\hat\mu}\Big\}F(t;\hat\mu,\lambda,\tfrac{1}{2})\,|_{\hat\mu=-\frac{u}{\vartheta-c},\lambda=\frac{u^2}{\sigma^2}}\Big)\\
&= \frac{\sqrt{t}}{\sigma}\big(\exp\{-2zy\}\,(\mathsf{F}^{(0,1)}(z,y\mid -\tfrac{1}{2}) - 2z\,\mathsf{F}(z,y\mid -\tfrac{1}{2}))\big)\Big|_{z=\frac{u}{\sigma\sqrt{t}},y=-\frac{(\vartheta-c)\sqrt{t}}{\sigma}},
\end{aligned}
$$

$$\frac{\partial}{\partial u}\Big(\exp\Big\{-\frac{2\lambda}{\hat\mu}\Big\}F(t;\hat\mu,\lambda,\tfrac12)\,\big|_{\hat\mu=-\frac{u}{\vartheta-c},\lambda=\frac{u^2}{\sigma^2}}\Big)$$
$$=\frac{1}{\sigma\sqrt t}\big(\exp\{-2zy\}\,(\mathsf F^{(1,0)}(z,y\mid-\tfrac12)-2y\,\mathsf F(z,y\mid-\tfrac12))\big)\big|_{z=\frac{u}{\sigma\sqrt t},y=-\frac{(\vartheta-c)\sqrt t}{\sigma}}$$

and

$$\frac{\partial^2}{\partial c^2}\Big(\exp\Big\{-\frac{2\lambda}{\hat\mu}\Big\}F(t;\hat\mu,\lambda,\tfrac12)\,\big|_{\hat\mu=-\frac{u}{\vartheta-c},\lambda=\frac{u^2}{\sigma^2}}\Big)$$
$$=\frac{\sqrt t}{\sigma}\frac{\partial}{\partial c}\big((\exp\{-2zy\}\,(\mathsf F^{(0,1)}(z,y\mid-\tfrac12)$$
$$-2z\,\mathsf F(z,y\mid-\tfrac12)))\big|_{z=\frac{u}{\sigma\sqrt t},y=-\frac{(\vartheta-c)\sqrt t}{\sigma}}\big)$$
$$=\frac{t}{\sigma^2}\,(\exp\{-2zy\}\,(\mathsf F^{(0,2)}(z,y\mid-\tfrac12)-4z\,\mathsf F^{(0,1)}(z,y\mid-\tfrac12)$$
$$+4z^2\,\mathsf F(z,y\mid-\tfrac12)))\,\big|_{z=\frac{u}{\sigma\sqrt t},y=-\frac{(\vartheta-c)\sqrt t}{\sigma}},$$

$$\frac{\partial^2}{\partial u^2}\Big(\exp\Big\{-\frac{2\lambda}{\hat\mu}\Big\}F(t;\hat\mu,\lambda,\tfrac12)\,\big|_{\hat\mu=-\frac{u}{\vartheta-c},\lambda=\frac{u^2}{\sigma^2}}\Big)$$
$$=\frac{1}{\sigma\sqrt t}\frac{\partial}{\partial u}\big((\exp\{-2zy\}\,(\mathsf F^{(1,0)}(z,y\mid-\tfrac12)$$
$$-2y\,\mathsf F(z,y\mid-\tfrac12)))\,\big|_{z=\frac{u}{\sigma\sqrt t},y=-\frac{(\vartheta-c)\sqrt t}{\sigma}}\big)$$
$$=\frac{1}{\sigma^2 t}\,(\exp\{-2zy\}\,(\mathsf F^{(2,0)}(z,y\mid-\tfrac12)-4y\,\mathsf F^{(1,0)}(z,y\mid-\tfrac12)$$
$$+4y^2\,\mathsf F(z,y\mid-\tfrac12)))\big|_{z=\frac{u}{\sigma\sqrt t},y=-\frac{(\vartheta-c)\sqrt t}{\sigma}},$$

$$\frac{\partial^2}{\partial c\,\partial u}\Big(\exp\Big\{-\frac{2\lambda}{\hat\mu}\Big\}F(t;\hat\mu,\lambda,\tfrac12)\,\big|_{\hat\mu=-\frac{u}{\vartheta-c},\lambda=\frac{u^2}{\sigma^2}}\Big)$$
$$=\frac{1}{\sigma\sqrt t}\frac{\partial}{\partial c}\big((\exp\{-2zy\}$$
$$\times(\mathsf F^{(1,0)}(z,y\mid-\tfrac12)-2y\,\mathsf F(z,y\mid-\tfrac12)))\,\big|_{z=\frac{u}{\sigma\sqrt t},y=-\frac{(\vartheta-c)\sqrt t}{\sigma}}\big)$$
$$=\frac{1}{\sigma^2}\,(\exp\{-2zy\}\,(\mathsf F^{(1,1)}(z,y\mid-\tfrac12)-2y\,\mathsf F^{(0,1)}(z,y\mid-\tfrac12)$$
$$-2z\,\mathsf F^{(1,0)}(z,y\mid-\tfrac12)+2(2zy-1)\,\mathsf F(z,y\mid-\tfrac12)))\big|_{z=\frac{u}{\sigma\sqrt t},y=-\frac{(\vartheta-c)\sqrt t}{\sigma}}.$$

Put these equalities into equality (2.37), whence equality (2.36). □

Bearing in mind (B.28) and (B.29) and the identity

$$\exp\{2zy\}\,\varphi_{(0,1)}(z+y)=\varphi_{(0,1)}(z-y),$$

the following result needs only algebraic transformations. We leave its proof (which requires elementary but cumbersome calculations) to the reader.

Theorem 2.17 *We have*

$$\begin{aligned} &\frac{\mathsf{A}(z,y)}{\mathsf{F}^{(1,0)}(z,y\mid -\frac{1}{2}) - 2y\,\mathsf{F}(z,y\mid -\frac{1}{2})} \\ &\quad - \frac{2\,\mathsf{B}(z,y)\,(\mathsf{F}^{(0,1)}(z,y\mid -\frac{1}{2}) - 2z\,\mathsf{F}(z,y\mid -\frac{1}{2}))}{(\mathsf{F}^{(1,0)}(z,y\mid -\frac{1}{2}) - 2y\,\mathsf{F}(z,y\mid -\frac{1}{2}))^2} \\ &\quad + \frac{\mathsf{C}(z,y)\,(\mathsf{F}^{(0,1)}(z,y\mid -\frac{1}{2}) - 2z\,\mathsf{F}(z,y\mid -\frac{1}{2}))^2}{(\mathsf{F}^{(1,0)}(z,y\mid -\frac{1}{2}) - 2y\,\mathsf{F}(z,y\mid -\frac{1}{2}))^3} \\ &= -\frac{z\,\nabla(z,y)}{(y\,\mathcal{M}(z-y)+1)^3}. \end{aligned} \tag{2.38}$$

Having Theorems 2.14–2.17 and Lemmas 2.4 and 2.5, we proceed to the proof of Theorem 2.13, whence Theorem 2.12 is straightforward.

Proof of Theorem 2.13. Equality in (2.31) is straightforward from (2.33) and (2.35). Inequality in (2.31) is straightforward from Lemma 2.4. Equality in (2.32) is straightforward from (2.36) and (2.38). Inequality in (2.32) is straightforward from Lemma 2.5. □

2.4 Asymptotic Behavior of Fixed-probability Level

Seeking for more explicit results, we can resort to the asymptotic analysis of $u^{[\mathrm{dif}]}_{\alpha,t\,|\,\vartheta}(c)$, $c \geqslant 0$, as $t \to \infty$, in certain specially selected areas. First, we will be focussed on $0 \leqslant c < K\vartheta$, $0 < K < 1$, then on the right and left $t^{-1/2}$-neighborhoods of ϑ, and finally on the case $c > K\vartheta$, where $K > 1$.

Theorem 2.18 *For* $0 \leqslant c < K\vartheta$, $0 < K < 1$, *we have*

$$u^{[\mathrm{dif}]}_{\alpha,t\,|\,\vartheta}(c) = (\vartheta - c)\,t + \sigma\,\kappa_\alpha\sqrt{t}\,(1 + o(1)), \quad t \to \infty.$$

Proof. Using equality (2.6), we rewrite equation (2.3) as

$$\begin{aligned} &1 - \varPhi_{(0,1)}\left(\frac{u - (\vartheta - c)\,t}{\sigma\sqrt{t}}\right) \\ &\qquad + \exp\left\{\frac{2(\vartheta - c)\,u}{\sigma^2}\right\}\varPhi_{(0,1)}\left(\frac{-u - (\vartheta - c)\,t}{\sigma\sqrt{t}}\right) = \alpha, \end{aligned} \tag{2.39}$$

and seek its solution's asymptotic (as $t \to \infty$) representation in the form[6] $u_t(c) = (\vartheta - c)\,t + \sigma\,z_t(c)\sqrt{t}$, where $z_t(c) = O(1)$, as $t \to \infty$.

[6]It is suggested by Theorem 2.5.

The left-hand side of equation (2.39), where u is substituted by $u_t(c)$, is

$$1-\Phi_{(0,1)}(z_t(c))+\exp\left\{2\sqrt{t}\,(\vartheta-c)\,\frac{(\vartheta-c)\sqrt{t}+\sigma\,z_t(c)}{\sigma^2}\right\}$$
$$\times\,\Phi_{(0,1)}\left(-\frac{2(\vartheta-c)\sqrt{t}+\sigma\,z_t(c)}{\sigma}\right)\sim 1-\Phi_{(0,1)}(z_t(c)),\quad t\to\infty.$$

Therefore, equation (2.39) may be rewritten as $1-\Phi_{(0,1)}(z_t(c))=\alpha\,(1+o(1))$, $t\to\infty$, whence $z_t(c)=\kappa_\alpha(1+o(1))$, $t\to\infty$. □

Theorem 2.19 *For* $c_{t,\epsilon}=\vartheta-\sigma\,\epsilon\,t^{-1/2}$, $0\leqslant\epsilon<K$, *we have*

$$u^{[\mathrm{dif}]}_{\alpha,t\,|\,\vartheta}(c)=\sigma\,x_\alpha(\epsilon)\sqrt{t}\,(1+o(1)),\quad t\to\infty,$$

where $x_\alpha(\epsilon)$ *is a solution to the equation*[7]

$$1-\Phi_{(0,1)}(-\epsilon+x)+\Phi_{(0,1)}(-\epsilon-x)\,\exp\{2\,\epsilon x\}=\alpha. \tag{2.40}$$

Proof. The left-hand side of (2.39), where c is substituted by $c_{t,\epsilon}=\vartheta-\sigma\,\epsilon\,t^{-1/2}$, $0\leqslant\epsilon<K$, and u is substituted by $u_t(c)=\sigma\,z_t(c)\sqrt{t}$, is $1-\Phi_{(0,1)}(-\epsilon+z_t(c))+\exp\{2\epsilon\,z_t(c)\}\,\Phi_{(0,1)}(-z_t(c)-\epsilon)$, whence the result. □

Theorem 2.20 *For* $c_{t,\epsilon}=\vartheta+\sigma\,\epsilon\,t^{-1/2}$, $0\leqslant\epsilon<K$, *we have*

$$u^{[\mathrm{dif}]}_{\alpha,t\,|\,\vartheta}(c)=\sigma\,x_\alpha(\epsilon)\sqrt{t}\,(1+o(1)),\quad t\to\infty,$$

where $x_\alpha(\epsilon)$ *is a solution to the equation*[8]

$$1-\Phi_{(0,1)}(\epsilon+x)+\Phi_{(0,1)}(\epsilon-x)\,\exp\{-2\,\epsilon x\}=\alpha. \tag{2.41}$$

Proof. The proof is analogous to the proof of Theorem 2.19 and is left to the reader. □

Theorem 2.21 *For* $c>K\vartheta$, $K>1$, *we have*

$$u^{[\mathrm{dif}]}_{\alpha,t\,|\,\vartheta}(c)=-\frac{\sigma^2\ln\alpha}{2(c-\vartheta)}\,(1+o(1)),\quad t\to\infty. \tag{2.42}$$

Proof. Plainly, $\vartheta-c<(1-K)\,\vartheta<0$. The left-hand side of (2.39), where u is substituted by $u_t(c)=\sigma\,z_t(c)$, with $z_t(c)=O(1)$, as $t\to\infty$, is

$$1-\Phi_{(0,1)}\left(\frac{\sigma\,z_t(c)-(\vartheta-c)\,t}{\sigma\sqrt{t}}\right)+\exp\left\{\frac{2(\vartheta-c)\,z_t(c)}{\sigma}\right\}$$
$$\times\,\Phi_{(0,1)}\left(\frac{-\sigma\,z_t(c)-(\vartheta-c)\,t}{\sigma\sqrt{t}}\right)\sim\exp\left\{\frac{2(\vartheta-c)\,z_t(c)}{\sigma}\right\},$$

as $t\to\infty$, whence the result. □

---

[7]Plainly, $x_\alpha(0)$ is a solution to the equation $1-\Phi_{(0,1)}(x)=\alpha/2$, i.e., is equal to $\kappa_{\alpha/2}$.
[8]One can easily see that $x_\alpha(0)=\kappa_{\alpha/2}$.

2.5 Primary Upper Bounds on Fixed-probability Level

By primary upper bounds on fixed-probability level, we mean upper bounds in the regions $0 \leqslant c \leqslant c^*$ and $c > c^*$, the former obtained from (2.16); the latter, which require further processing, follow from equation (2.44) below.

Bound on fixed-probability level, when $0 \leqslant c < \vartheta$. In this case, straightforwardly from Theorem 2.7, we have the two-sided bound

$$(\vartheta - c)\, t + \sigma\, \kappa_\alpha \sqrt{t} \leqslant u^{[\mathrm{dif}]}_{\alpha,t\,|\,\vartheta}(c) \leqslant (\vartheta - c)\, t + \sigma\, \kappa_{\alpha/2} \sqrt{t}, \tag{2.43}$$

valid for all $t > 0$. The asymptotic (as $t \to \infty$) behavior of $u^{[\mathrm{dif}]}_{\alpha,t\,|\,\vartheta}(c)$, when $0 \leqslant c < \vartheta$, is investigated in Theorems 2.18 and 2.19.

Bound on fixed-probability level, when $c > \vartheta$. The inequality

$$\mathsf{P}\{\, \Upsilon^{[\mathrm{dif}]}_{u,c\,|\,\vartheta} \leqslant t\} \leqslant \mathsf{P}\{\, \Upsilon^{[\mathrm{dif}]}_{u,c\,|\,\vartheta} < \infty\}$$

with the right-hand side

$$\mathsf{P}\{\, \Upsilon^{[\mathrm{dif}]}_{u,c\,|\,\vartheta} < \infty\} = \begin{cases} 1, & 0 \leqslant c < \vartheta, \\ \exp\Big\{ -\dfrac{2(c-\vartheta)\, u}{\sigma^2}\Big\}, & c > \vartheta, \end{cases}$$

straightforward from (2.7) and (2.8), holds for all c, u, t positive. The positive solution $u^{[\mathrm{dif}]}_{\alpha\,|\,\vartheta}(c)$ to the equation

$$\mathsf{P}\{\, \Upsilon^{[\mathrm{dif}]}_{u,c\,|\,\vartheta} < \infty\} = \alpha, \tag{2.44}$$

when it exists, is the upper bound for $u^{[\mathrm{dif}]}_{\alpha,t\,|\,\vartheta}(c)$.

Plainly, this solution does not exist for $0 \leqslant c < \vartheta$ because the left-hand side of (2.44) is identically equal to 1, and cannot be equal to $0 < \alpha < 1$. When $c > \vartheta$, the solution $u^{[\mathrm{dif}]}_{\alpha\,|\,\vartheta}(c)$ is a hyperbola easy to find, whence

$$u^{[\mathrm{dif}]}_{\alpha,t\,|\,\vartheta}(c) \leqslant u^{[\mathrm{dif}]}_{\alpha\,|\,\vartheta}(c) = -\frac{\sigma^2 \ln \alpha}{2\,(c - \vartheta)}. \tag{2.45}$$

Numerically calculated $u^{[\mathrm{dif}]}_{\alpha,t\,|\,\vartheta}(c)$ and its upper bound $u^{[\mathrm{dif}]}_{\alpha\,|\,\vartheta}(c)$, $c > \vartheta$, are shown in Fig. 2.3.

The bound (2.45), valid for all $t > 0$, is rather accurate, when c is far exceeding ϑ, but very poor, when c is equal to ϑ, or only a little larger than ϑ. In particular, whereas (see (2.15)) $u^{[\mathrm{dif}]}_{\alpha,t\,|\,\vartheta}(\vartheta) = \sigma\, \kappa_{\alpha/2}\sqrt{t}$ is finite for t finite, $u^{[\mathrm{dif}]}_{\alpha\,|\,\vartheta}(\vartheta)$ is infinite.

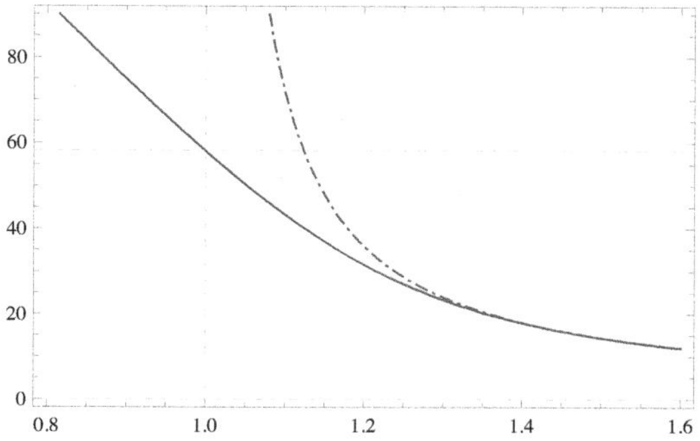

FIGURE 2.3: Graphs (X-axis is c) of $u^{[\mathrm{dif}]}_{\alpha,t\,|\,\vartheta}(c)$ (solid line) and $u^{[\mathrm{dif}]}_{\alpha\,|\,\vartheta}(c)$ (dash-dotted line), when $\alpha = 0.1$, $t = 200$, $\sigma = 2.5$, and $\vartheta = 1$. Vertical grid line: ϑ, which equals 1. Horizontal grid line: $u^{[\mathrm{dif}]}_{\alpha,t\,|\,\vartheta}(\vartheta) = \sigma\kappa_{\alpha/2}\sqrt{t}$, which equals 58.15.

Remark 2.2 Note that, despite similarity of the right-hand sides, the equalities in (2.45) and (2.42) are fundamentally different. The former yields an upper bound valid for all $t > 0$ and $c > \vartheta$, whereas the latter is an asymptotic equality valid for $t \to \infty$, when $c > K\vartheta$, $K > 1$.

2.6 Elaborated Upper Bounds on Fixed-probability Level

We strive to construct upper bounds on $u^{[\mathrm{dif}]}_{\alpha,t\,|\,\vartheta}(c)$, $c \geqslant 0$, which are

- computable, in contrast to the asymptotic equality (2.16), where the function $\mathsf{z}_\alpha(y)$, $y \in \mathsf{R}$, being a solution to an equation, is not expressed in a closed form,
- expressed in terms of elementary functions, simple or even elementary, in contrast to, e.g., sophisticated expressions like (2.12), presented in terms of special functions or integrals,
- accurate for all $c \geqslant 0$, in particular in the vicinity of ϑ.

While the bound (2.43) is quite satisfactory for all $0 \leqslant c < \vartheta$, the bound (2.45) is not satisfactory, when c is to the right of ϑ, and close to ϑ. In the same time, the bound (2.45) is very accurate, when $c > K\vartheta$, $K > 1$ (see illustration in Fig. 2.3): for such c, by Theorem 2.21, the fixed-probability level $u^{[\mathrm{dif}]}_{\alpha,t\,|\,\vartheta}(c)$ tends to $-\sigma^2 \ln \alpha/(2(c - \vartheta))$, as $t \to \infty$.

Further in this section, we will seek upper bounds for the fixed-probability level $u^{[\mathrm{dif}]}_{\alpha,t\,|\,\vartheta}(c)$, satisfactory over the entire range of $c \geqslant 0$.

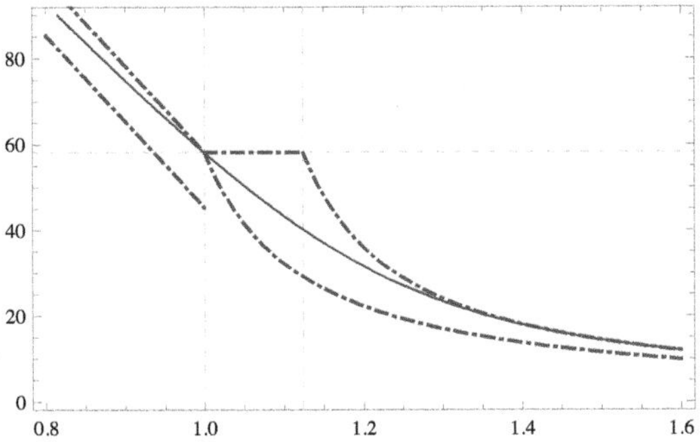

FIGURE 2.4: Graphs (X-axis is c) of $u^{[\text{dif}]}_{\alpha,t\,|\,\vartheta}(c)$ (solid line), when $\alpha = 0.1$, $t = 200$, $\sigma = 2.5$, $\vartheta = 1$, and $\kappa_{\alpha/2} = 1.65$, and of bounds of Theorem 2.22 (dash-dotted lines). Vertical grid line: $\vartheta = 1.0$ and $\hat{c} = 1.12$. Horizontal grid line: $u^{[\text{dif}]}_{\alpha,t\,|\,\vartheta}(\vartheta) = \sigma\kappa_{\alpha/2}\sqrt{t}$, which equals 58.15.

2.6.1 Bounds based on monotony

Let us construct elementary bounds on fixed-probability level $u^{[\text{dif}]}_{\alpha,t\,|\,\vartheta}(c)$ for $\vartheta < c < K\vartheta$, $K > 1$. We rely on the shape of this function: by Theorem 2.8, it monotone decreases, as c increases; by Theorem 2.13, it is convex.

Theorem 2.22 *For $0 \leqslant c < \vartheta$, we have*

$$(\vartheta - c)\,t + \sigma\,\kappa_\alpha\sqrt{t} \leqslant u^{[\text{dif}]}_{\alpha,t\,|\,\vartheta}(c) \leqslant (\vartheta - c)\,t + \sigma\,\kappa_{\alpha/2}\sqrt{t}, \tag{2.46}$$

and, when $c > \vartheta$, we have

$$u^{[\text{dif}]}_{\alpha,t\,|\,\vartheta}(c) \leqslant \begin{cases} \sigma\,\kappa_{\alpha/2}\sqrt{t}, & \vartheta < c \leqslant \hat{c} := \vartheta - \dfrac{\sigma\ln\alpha}{2\,\kappa_{\alpha/2}\sqrt{t}}, \\ -\dfrac{\sigma^2\ln\alpha}{2\,(c-\vartheta)}, & c > \hat{c}. \end{cases} \tag{2.47}$$

and

$$u^{[\text{dif}]}_{\alpha,t\,|\,\vartheta}(c) \geqslant -\frac{\sigma^2\ln\alpha}{2}\left(c - \vartheta - \frac{\sigma\ln\alpha}{2\sqrt{t}\,\kappa_{\alpha/2}}\right)^{-1}. \tag{2.48}$$

This bound, whose construction relies on monotony of $u^{[\text{dif}]}_{\alpha,t\,|\,\vartheta}(c)$, $c \geqslant 0$, is exceptionally simple; it is illustrated in Fig. 2.4.

Proof. Starting from (see (2.15)) the point in R^2 whose X-coordinate is ϑ and Y-coordinate is $u^{[\text{dif}]}_{\alpha,t\,|\,\vartheta}(\vartheta) = \sigma\,\kappa_{\alpha/2}\sqrt{t}$, we draw a horizontal straight line up to its intersection with the hyperbole $u^{[\text{dif}]}_{\alpha\,|\,\vartheta}(c) = -\sigma^2\ln\alpha/(2\,(c-\vartheta))$. Plainly,

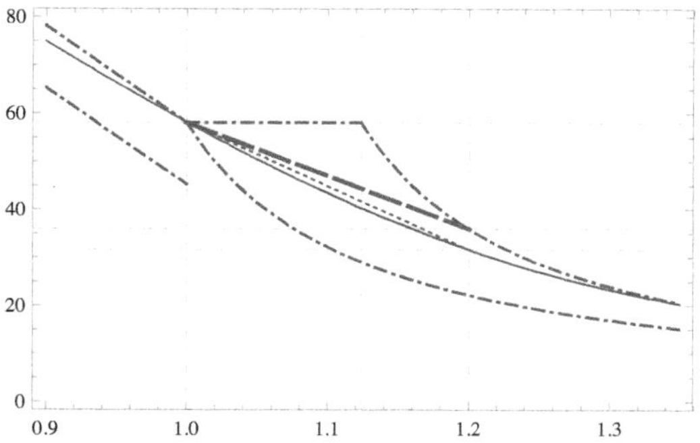

FIGURE 2.5: Graphs (X-axis is c) of $u^{[\text{dif}]}_{\alpha,t\,|\,\vartheta}(c)$ (solid line), where $\alpha = 0.1$, $t = 200$, $\sigma = 2.5$, $\vartheta = 1$, and $\kappa_{\alpha/2} = 1.65$, and of bounds of Theorem 2.23 (dash-dotted and dashed lines). Vertical grid lines: $\vartheta = 1$, $\hat{c} = 1.12$, $\tilde{c} = 1.2$. Horizontal grid lines: $u^{[\text{dif}]}_{\alpha,t\,|\,\vartheta}(\vartheta) = 58.15$, $u^{[\text{dif}]}_{\alpha\,|\,\vartheta}(\vartheta) = 35.98$, $u^{[\text{dif}]}_{\alpha,t\,|\,\vartheta}(\vartheta) = 31.60$.

the X-coordinate of the point to which we draw this horizontal line is $\hat{c}$, which is a unique solution to the equation

$$\sigma\,\kappa_{\alpha/2}\sqrt{t} = -\frac{\sigma^2 \ln\alpha}{2\,(c-\vartheta)}.$$

Since $u^{[\text{dif}]}_{\alpha,t\,|\,\vartheta}(c)$ monotone decreases, as c increases, the rest of the proof is elementary. The proof of (2.48) is left to the reader as Problem 2.7. □

2.6.2 Bounds based on convexity

The advantage of the bound (2.46)–(2.48) is its simplicity. The disadvantage is that the upper bound (2.47) is too rough not far to the right of ϑ; an easy method to cure it, which relies on convexity of $u^{[\text{dif}]}_{\alpha,t\,|\,\vartheta}(c)$, $c \geqslant 0$, is shown in Fig. 2.5. In the following theorem, we restrict ourselves to the upper bound on $u^{[\text{dif}]}_{\alpha,t\,|\,\vartheta}(c)$, when $c > \vartheta$. In other cases, the bounds of Theorem 2.22 hold.

Theorem 2.23 *When $c > \vartheta$, for any $\tilde{c} > \hat{c} := \vartheta - \sigma\ln\alpha/(2\,\kappa_{\alpha/2}\sqrt{t})$, we have*

$$u^{[\text{dif}]}_{\alpha,t\,|\,\vartheta}(c) \leqslant \begin{cases} \sigma\,\kappa_{\alpha/2}\sqrt{t} - \dfrac{\sigma^2\ln\alpha/(2\,(\tilde{c}-\vartheta)) + \sigma\,\kappa_{\alpha/2}\sqrt{t}}{\tilde{c}-\vartheta}\,(c-\vartheta), & \vartheta < c \leqslant \tilde{c}, \\ -\dfrac{\sigma^2\ln\alpha}{2\,(c-\vartheta)}, & c > \tilde{c}. \end{cases}$$

Proof. By Theorem 2.13, the fixed-probability level $u^{[\text{dif}]}_{\alpha,t\,|\,\vartheta}(c)$, $c \geqslant 0$, is convex, i.e., any line segment between any two points on the graph of this function lies above or on this graph.

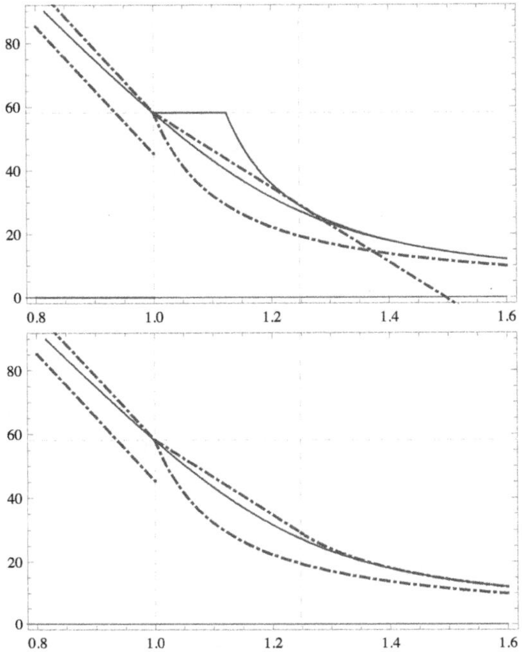

FIGURE 2.6: *Above*: graphs (X-axis is c) of the line segment $t\,\kappa^2_{\alpha/2}(c-\vartheta)/(2\ln\alpha)+\sigma\kappa_{\alpha/2}\sqrt{t}$ (dash-dotted line) released from the point $(\vartheta, u^{[\mathrm{dif}]}_{\alpha,t\,|\,\vartheta}(\vartheta))$ and tangent to $(-\sigma^2\ln\alpha)/(2(c-\vartheta))$ (solid line) at the point with abscissa $\vartheta-\sigma\ln\alpha/(\kappa_{\alpha/2}\sqrt{t})$, drawn above Fig. 2.4. *Below*: graphs of $u^{[\mathrm{dif}]}_{\alpha,t\,|\,\vartheta}(c)$ (solid line), upper bound (2.49), and lower bound (2.48) (dash-dotted lines), when $\alpha=0.1$, $t=200$, $\sigma=2.5$, and $\vartheta=1$. Vertical grid lines: $\vartheta=1$, and abscissa of the point of tangency $\vartheta-\sigma\ln\alpha/(\sqrt{t}\,\kappa_{\alpha/2})$, which equals 1.25. Horizontal grid line: $u^{[\mathrm{dif}]}_{\alpha,t\,|\,\vartheta}(\vartheta)=\sigma\kappa_{\alpha/2}\sqrt{t}$, which equals 58.15.

We focus on two points in R^2, whose coordinates are[9] $(\vartheta, u^{[\mathrm{dif}]}_{\alpha,t\,|\,\vartheta}(\vartheta))$ and $(\tilde{c}, u^{[\mathrm{dif}]}_{\alpha,t\,|\,\vartheta}(\vartheta))$. The line segment between these points lies above the graph of the fixed-probability level $u^{[\mathrm{dif}]}_{\alpha,t\,|\,\vartheta}(c)$. Second, because $u^{[\mathrm{dif}]}_{\alpha,t\,|\,\vartheta}(\tilde{c}) < u^{[\mathrm{dif}]}_{\alpha\,|\,\vartheta}(\tilde{c})$, it lies below the line segment between the points $(\vartheta, u^{[\mathrm{dif}]}_{\alpha,t\,|\,\vartheta}(\vartheta))$ and $(\tilde{c}, u^{[\mathrm{dif}]}_{\alpha\,|\,\vartheta}(\vartheta))$; according to (2.45), the latter is identical to $(\tilde{c}, -\sigma^2\ln\alpha/(2\,(\tilde{c}-\vartheta)))$. This gives the upper bound for $u^{[\mathrm{dif}]}_{\alpha,t\,|\,\vartheta}(c)$, $\vartheta<c\leqslant\tilde{c}$. When $c>\tilde{c}$, the upper bound on $u^{[\mathrm{dif}]}_{\alpha,t\,|\,\vartheta}(c)$ is given trivially by $u^{[\mathrm{dif}]}_{\alpha\,|\,\vartheta}(c)=-\sigma^2\ln\alpha/(2\,(c-\vartheta))$. □

[9]By (2.15), this may be rewritten as $(\vartheta, \sigma\,\kappa_{\alpha/2}\sqrt{t}\,)$.

In Theorem 2.23, the auxiliary point $\tilde{c} > \hat{c}$ can be arbitrarily selected. The upper bound of Theorem 2.23 has a singularity at $\tilde{c}$, where it is not differentiable[10], except when $\tilde{c}$ is the point of tangency of the line segment released from the point $(\vartheta, u^{[\text{dif}]}_{\alpha,t\,|\,\vartheta}(\vartheta))$ to the function $u^{[\text{dif}]}_{\alpha\,|\,\vartheta}(\vartheta)$. Let us consider this case separately.

Theorem 2.24 *For $c > \vartheta$, we have*

$$u^{[\text{dif}]}_{\alpha,t\,|\,\vartheta}(c) \leqslant \begin{cases} \dfrac{t\,\kappa_{\alpha/2}}{2\ln\alpha}\,(c-\vartheta) + \sigma\,\kappa_{\alpha/2}\sqrt{t}, & \vartheta < c \leqslant \vartheta - \dfrac{\sigma\ln\alpha}{\sqrt{t}\,\kappa_{\alpha/2}}, \\ -\dfrac{\sigma^2\ln\alpha}{2}\,(c-\vartheta)^{-1}, & c > \vartheta - \dfrac{\sigma\ln\alpha}{\sqrt{t}\,\kappa_{\alpha/2}}. \end{cases} \tag{2.49}$$

Proof. Let us apply Theorem A.4 with $A = u^{[\text{dif}]}_{\alpha,t\,|\,\vartheta}(\vartheta)$, $B = -(\sigma^2\ln\alpha)/2$, $C = \vartheta$, and sloping straight line

$$l(c) = -\frac{A^2}{4B}\,(c-C) + A = \frac{\kappa^2_{\alpha/2}}{2\ln\alpha}\,(c-\vartheta)\,t + \sigma\,\kappa_{\alpha/2}\sqrt{t}$$

tangent to the hyperbola

$$h(c) = \frac{B}{c-C}\,\bigg|_{B=-(\sigma^2\ln\alpha)/2,\,C=\vartheta} = -\frac{\sigma^2\ln\alpha}{2\,(c-\vartheta)}.$$

It is an upper bound for $u^{[\text{dif}]}_{\alpha,t\,|\,\vartheta}(c)$, $c > \vartheta$.

The abscissa and ordinate of the point of tangency are $\vartheta - \sigma\ln\alpha/(\sqrt{t}\,\kappa_{\alpha/2})$ and $\sigma\kappa_{\alpha/2}\sqrt{t}/2$, respectively. The composite bound is made up of the tangent line, when $\vartheta < c \leqslant \vartheta - \sigma\ln\alpha/(\sqrt{t}\,\kappa_{\alpha/2})$, and of hyperbola, when $c > \vartheta - \sigma\ln\alpha/(\sqrt{t}\,\kappa_{\alpha/2})$, as shown above, whence the result. □

2.7 Conclusions and Perspectives

The function $\underline{u}^{[\text{dif}]}_{\alpha,t\,|\,\vartheta}(c)$, $c \geqslant 0$, which is an implicit function defined by the equation $\mathsf{P}\{R_t < 0\} = \alpha$, or $\mathsf{P}\{u + (c-\vartheta)t - \sigma\,\mathsf{W}_t < 0\} = \alpha$, which may be rewritten as

$$\Phi_{(0,1)}\left(\frac{u + (c-\vartheta)t}{\sigma\sqrt{t}}\right) = 1 - \alpha,$$

can be expressed is a closed-form as follows:

$$\underline{u}^{[\text{dif}]}_{\alpha,t\,|\,\vartheta}(c) = \max\{0, (\vartheta - c)t + \sigma\sqrt{t}\,\kappa_\alpha\}.$$

[10]From where comes the term "broken-line bound" used in Section 2.6.1.

The presence of such a formula is an advantage. But it is nullified by the low accuracy of this lower bound for $u^{[\mathrm{dif}]}_{\alpha,t\,|\,\vartheta}(c)$, $c \geqslant 0$.

In particular, $\underline{u}^{[\mathrm{dif}]}_{\alpha,t\,|\,\vartheta}(\vartheta) = \sigma\sqrt{t}\,\kappa_\alpha$, whereas $u^{[\mathrm{dif}]}_{\alpha,t\,|\,\vartheta}(\vartheta) = \sigma\sqrt{t}\,\kappa_{\alpha/2}$. Recall that $0 < \kappa_\alpha < \kappa_{\alpha/2}$ for $\alpha < 1/2$. In particular, $\kappa_\alpha = 1.65$ and $\kappa_{\alpha/2} = 1.96$ for $\alpha = 0.05$. When $c > \vartheta$, the accuracy of $\underline{u}^{[\mathrm{dif}]}_{\alpha,t\,|\,\vartheta}(c)$ viewed as a lower bound for $u^{[\mathrm{dif}]}_{\alpha,t\,|\,\vartheta}(c)$, $c \geqslant 0$, is very poor.

Throughout this chapter, we found the following. For the left-hand side of equation (2.3) which defines the fixed-probability level as an implicit function, i.e., for $\mathsf{P}\{\varUpsilon^{[\mathrm{dif}]}_{u,c\,|\,\vartheta} \leqslant t\}$, we have closed-form expression, given in terms of c.d.f. of a standard Gaussian distribution[11]. This expression is simple enough, can be rewritten in several alternative forms, e.g., (2.12) or (2.7), and is fitted for calculating its partial derivatives of any order w.r.t. c and u.

This allows us to apply in full force the theory of implicit functions (see Section A.1.4). In particular, we can use Theorem A.4, which yields explicit expressions for $\frac{d}{dc}u^{[\mathrm{dif}]}_{\alpha,t\,|\,\vartheta}(c)$ and $\frac{d^2}{dc^2}u^{[\mathrm{dif}]}_{\alpha,t\,|\,\vartheta}(c)$, $c \geqslant 0$, and then apply the standard criteria of monotony and convexity (see Section A.1.1). The study of the sign of these derivatives is based on inequalities for Mills' ratio. This is the most ingenious, but still straightforward, part of the analysis in this chapter.

In conclusion, we say that the study of the fixed-probability level $u^{[\mathrm{dif}]}_{\alpha,t\,|\,\vartheta}(c)$, $c \geqslant 0$, which cannot be found explicitly[12], can still be carried out with great completeness. Our attention to the upper bounds in Section 2.6, ranging from simple (see Theorem 2.22) to more elaborated (see Theorems 2.23 and 2.24) ones, is due to a wish to have simple-looking, convenient for further applications, results.

Problems

Problem 2.1 Bearing in mind that R_t is normally distributed with the mean $\mathsf{E}R_t = u + (c - \vartheta)t$ and the variance $\mathsf{D}R_t = \sigma^2 t$, investigate the Value-at-Risk which is a positive solution to the equation $\mathsf{P}\{R_t < 0\} = \alpha$. Compare it to $u^{[\mathrm{dif}]}_{\alpha,t\,|\,\vartheta}(c)$, $c \geqslant 0$.

Problem 2.2 (Direct and inverse first-passage problems) Prove the following results for direct and inverse first-passage problems formulated in Remark 2.1. If necessary, see the proofs in [149]. If g is continuously differentiable

[11] We can also say, in terms of inverse Gaussian distribution.

[12] In Theorem 2.7, the function $\mathsf{z}_\alpha(y)$, $y \in \mathsf{R}$, which appears in (2.16), is a solution to equations (2.17) and (2.18), rather than a function given in a closed form.

on $(0,\infty)$, then Υ_g has a continuous p.d.f. f and

$$1-\Phi_{(0,1)}\left(\frac{g(t)}{\sqrt{t}}\right)=\int_0^t\left(1-\Phi_{(0,1)}\left(\frac{g(t)-g(s)}{\sqrt{t-s}}\right)\right)f(s)\,ds \qquad (2.50)$$

for all $t>0$.

[Hint: note that (2.50) is a linear Volterra integral equation of the first kind in f, if g is known; it is a non-linear equation in g, if f is known.]

Problem 2.3 (Constant boundary) If $g(t)\equiv d$ with $d\in\mathsf{R}$, then F, which denotes c.d.f. corresponding to p.d.f. f in (2.50), is

$$F(t)=2\left(1-\Phi_{(0,1)}\left(\frac{d}{\sqrt{t}}\right)\right),\quad t>0.$$

Equivalently, $\mathsf{P}\{\Upsilon_g\leqslant t\}=2\,\mathsf{P}\{\mathsf{W}_t\geqslant d\}$, which is the well-known reflection principle of André [4] (see also [11] and [112]).

Problem 2.4 (Linear boundary) If $g(t)=at+b$ with $a\in\mathsf{R}$ and $b>0$, then (2.50) yields

$$1-\Phi_{(0,1)}\left(\frac{at+b}{\sqrt{t}}\right)=\int_0^t(1-\Phi_{(0,1)}(a\sqrt{t-s}\,))f(s)\,ds,\quad t>0, \qquad (2.51)$$

where the right-hand side is a convolution.

Problem 2.5 By means of Laplace transform applied to (2.51), show that it yields the following explicit formula:

$$f(t)=\frac{b}{t^{3/2}}\,\varphi_{(0,1)}\left(\frac{at+b}{\sqrt{t}}\right),\quad t>0. \qquad (2.52)$$

Problem 2.6 Using the equality

$$\exp\{-2ab\}\,\varphi_{(0,1)}\left(\frac{at-b}{\sqrt{t}}\right)=\varphi_{(0,1)}\left(\frac{at+b}{\sqrt{t}}\right),\quad t>0,$$

show that the function $f(t)$, $t>0$, introduced in (2.52) writes as

$$f(t)=\begin{cases} f(t;\mu,\lambda,-\frac{1}{2})\,\big|_{\mu=-b/a,\lambda=b^2}, & a<0,\ b>0,\\[1ex] \exp\left\{-\frac{2\lambda}{\mu}\right\}f(t;\mu,\lambda,-\frac{1}{2})\,\big|_{\mu=b/a,\lambda=b^2}, & a>0,\ b>0,\end{cases} \qquad (2.53)$$

where

$$f(t;\mu,\lambda,-\tfrac{1}{2})=\lambda^{1/2}t^{-3/2}\,\varphi_{(0,1)}\left(\sqrt{\frac{\lambda}{t}}\left(\frac{t}{\mu}-1\right)\right),\quad t>0,$$

is p.d.f. of inverse Gaussian distribution with $\lambda>0$, $\mu>0$. Using (2.53), relate (2.52) and the material of Section 2.2.

Problem 2.7 Prove the lower bound (2.48).

Chapter 3

Fixed-probability Level in An Exceptional Renewal Model

In this chapter, we go along the road map of Chapter 2, dealing with the renewal model discussed in Section 1.3.4. In insurance risk theory, it is known as Lundberg's collective risk model with exponentially distributed inter-claim intervals and claim sizes. We focus on its mathematical essence, i.e., on the level-crossing problem for a compound renewal process with exponentially distributed jump sizes and inter-renewal intervals. The steps in this road map are the same as in Chapter 2, albeit significantly more analytically sophisticated.

3.1 Exponential Renewal Model: An Exceptional Case

When modeling the insurance business, it is often assumed that successive claim payouts, all positive, occur at discrete moments of time, rather than between them. Therefore, a Brownian motion with a trend (see (2.1)) is less adequate for modeling the risk reserve process than the compound renewal process, at which we will be focussed from this chapter onwards.

3.1.1 Model and equivalent terminology

At time $s \geqslant 0$, the renewal risk model (see Section 1.3.2) has the form

$$R_s := u + cs - V_s, \quad V_s := \sum_{i=1}^{N_s} Y_i, \tag{3.1}$$

where $V_s := 0$, if $T_1 > s$, u denotes the initial capital, c is the premium intensity called for simplicity price, and summation is taken up to the integer-valued random variable

$$N_s := \max\left\{n > 0 : \sum_{i=1}^{n} T_i \leqslant s\right\},$$

where $N_s := 0$, if $T_1 > s$.

TABLE 3.1: Equivalent terminology for $u_{\alpha,t\,|\,\delta,\rho}(c)$ and $\underline{u}_{\alpha,t\,|\,\delta,\rho}(c)$

	Value-at-Risk measure	Solvency benchmark	Solution to inverse level-crossing problem
$u_{\alpha,t\,\vert\,\delta,\rho}(c)$	Value-at-Risk based on sup-loss net of premium income, a solution to $\mathsf{P}\{\sup_{0\leqslant s\leqslant t}(V_s - cs) \leqslant u\} = A$	Non-ruin capital, a solution to $\psi_t(u, c \mid \delta, \rho) = \alpha$, i.e., $\mathsf{P}\{\inf_{0\leqslant s\leqslant t} R_s < 0\} = \alpha$	Fixed-probability level, a solution to $\mathsf{P}\{\varUpsilon_{u,c\,\vert\,\delta,\rho} \leqslant t\} = \alpha$, where $\varUpsilon_{u,c\,\vert\,\delta,\rho}$ is the time of the first level u crossing
$\underline{u}_{\alpha,t\,\vert\,\delta,\rho}(c)$	Value-at-Risk based on loss net of premium income, a solution to $\mathsf{P}\{V_t - ct \leqslant u\} = A$	Non-loss capital, a solution to $\mathsf{P}\{R_t < 0\} = \alpha$	A lower bound for $u_{\alpha,t\,\vert\,\delta,\rho}(c)$

When we focus on risk measures, insurance solvency, or mathematical level-crossing problem, we can switch to terminology (see Table 3.1) that is more appropriate for each of these fields. Since the mathematical aspects are the main challenge in the following presentation, we will adhere to the application-neutral terminology used in the level-crossing problem.

Using renewal terminology, we assume that the inter-renewal intervals

$$T_i \stackrel{d}{=} T, \quad i = 1, 2, \ldots,$$

are i.i.d. (including T_1) and sizes of jumps in the moments of renewals

$$Y_i \stackrel{d}{=} Y, \quad i = 1, 2, \ldots,$$

are i.i.d. Moreover, these sequences are assumed mutually independent. The trajectories of renewal process N_s, $s \geqslant 0$, and compound renewal process V_s, $s \geqslant 0$, are piecewise linear.

Throughout this chapter, the random variables T and Y are assumed exponentially distributed with parameters $\delta > 0$ and $\rho > 0$, respectively, whence N_s, $s \geqslant 0$, is a Poisson process with intensity δ. This allows us to express in a closed form most of the important results, as in the following theorem.

Theorem 3.1 *In the renewal model with T and Y exponentially distributed with parameters $\rho > 0$ and $\delta > 0$, respectively, we have for all $s \geqslant 0$*

$$\begin{aligned}\mathsf{P}\{V_s \leqslant x\} &= e^{-s\delta} + e^{-s\delta} \sum_{n=1}^{\infty} \frac{(s\delta)^n}{n!} \frac{\rho^n}{\Gamma(n)} \int_0^x e^{-\rho z}\, z^{n-1}\, dz \\ &= e^{-s\delta} + e^{-s\delta} (\delta\rho s)^{1/2} \\ &\quad \times \int_0^x z^{-1/2} I_1(2\sqrt{\delta\rho s z})\, e^{-\rho z}\, dz, \quad x > 0.\end{aligned} \tag{3.2}$$

Elementary calculation based on (3.2) yields (see [135], Theorem 4.2)

$$\begin{aligned} \mathsf{E}(V_s) &= \frac{s\delta}{\rho}, & \mathsf{E}({V_s}^2) &= \frac{s\delta\,(s\delta+2)}{\rho^2}, \\ \mathsf{D}V_s &= 2\,\frac{s\delta}{\rho^2}, & \mathsf{E}({V_s}^3) &= \frac{s\delta\,((s\delta)^2+6\,(s\delta+1))}{\rho^3}. \end{aligned} \tag{3.3}$$

To begin with, recall (see [135]) that the direct level-crossing problem is to explore the probability $\mathsf{P}\{\varUpsilon_{u,c\,|\,\delta,\rho} \leqslant t\}$, where

$$\begin{aligned} \varUpsilon_{u,c\,|\,\delta,\rho} &:= \inf\{s>0 : V_s - cs > u\} \\ &= \inf\{s>0 : R_s < 0\}, \end{aligned} \tag{3.4}$$

or $+\infty$, if $V_s - cs \leqslant u$ for all $s \geqslant 0$, is referred to as the time when the level u is crossed by the shifted compound renewal process $V_s - cs$, $s \geqslant 0$, for the first time. The inverse level-crossing problem is to study a solution (w.r.t. u) to the equation

$$\mathsf{P}\{\varUpsilon_{u,c\,|\,\delta,\rho} \leqslant t\} = \alpha. \tag{3.5}$$

This solution is denoted by $u_{\alpha,t\,|\,\delta,\rho}(c)$, $c \geqslant 0$, and is called the level which the shifted compound renewal process $V_s - cs$, $s \geqslant 0$, crosses before time t with the probability α, or fixed-probability level for short.

3.1.2 Outline of the road map

We largely follow the road map of Chapter 2. The first step is to investigate the analytical structure of the fixed-probability level $u_{\alpha,t\,|\,\delta,\rho}(c)$, $c \geqslant 0$. Being an implicit function defined by the equation (3.5), the left-hand side of which is specified in Theorems 3.2–3.4 below, it cannot be written in a closed form. But we can get a fairly complete insight into its global structure. The difference between this step and the similar step in Chapter 2 is that the problem becomes much more technically difficult to implement.

The second step is the study of monotony and convexity of the fixed-probability level. The first of these properties is obvious, whereas the second is not. We start by studying the former, focussing first on strong-form monotony, i.e., for all $t > 0$, and then on weak-form monotony, i.e., for t large, using analytical methods. This study shows that the strong-form monotony is much more difficult to prove than the weak-form monotony. Accordingly, we restrict ourselves to the study of weak-form convexity, focussing on $c > c^* := \mathsf{E}Y/\mathsf{E}T$, which is used to construct upper bounds for the fixed-probability level, as t is large. The strong-form convexity, which is a very plausible result, remains an open question which goes far beyond the scope of this book[1].

[1]In this book, convexity of the fixed-probability level has quite a narrow scope: it is only used to construct the upper bounds on $u_{\alpha,t\,|\,\delta,\rho}(c)$, $c \geqslant 0$, of a special type, similar to those constructed in Section 2.6.2.

The third step is investigation of the asymptotic behavior of $u_{\alpha,t\,|\,\delta,\rho}(c)$, $c \geqslant 0$, as $t \to \infty$, similar to what is done in Section 2.4. We show that, when c is less than a value slightly larger than c^*, it tends to infinity, as $t \to \infty$. When c exceeds such a value, it is bounded by a finite constant.

Finally, accepting the fact that no relatively simple closed-form expression for the fixed-probability level $u_{\alpha,t\,|\,\delta,\rho}(c)$, $c \geqslant 0$, may be found, we construct for it several bounds, some of them fairly accurate, which are represented in terms of elementary functions and are easy to use.

3.2 Direct Level-crossing Problem

The direct level-crossing problem focusses on the distribution of the first level-crossing time.

3.2.1 Closed-form expressions for the distribution of first level-crossing time

By $I_n(z)$ (see Section A.2.1) we denote the modified Bessel function of the first kind of order n. The formulas (3.6)–(3.8) for $\mathsf{P}\{\varUpsilon_{u,c\,|\,\delta,\rho} \leqslant t\}$, called Type I–Type III formulas (see [135], Section 5.2), are equivalent.

Theorem 3.2 *In the renewal model satisfying the standard assumptions, with T and Y exponentially distributed with positive parameters δ and ρ, respectively, we have*

$$\mathsf{P}\{\varUpsilon_{u,c\,|\,\delta,\rho} \leqslant t\} = e^{-\rho u}\delta \int_0^t e^{-(c\rho+\delta)x}\Big(I_0(2\sqrt{\delta\rho x\,(cx+u)}\,) - \frac{cx}{cx+u}\, I_2(2\sqrt{\delta\rho x\,(cx+u)}\,)\Big)\,dx. \tag{3.6}$$

Theorem 3.3 *In the renewal model satisfying the standard assumptions, with T and Y exponentially distributed with parameters δ and ρ, respectively, and with $c \geqslant 0$ we have*

$$\mathsf{P}\{\varUpsilon_{u,c\,|\,\delta,\rho} \leqslant t\} = e^{-\rho u}\frac{\sqrt{\delta}}{\sqrt{c\rho}} \int_0^{c\rho t} e^{-(1+\delta/(c\rho))x} \sum_{n=0}^{\infty} \frac{u^n}{n!}\left(\frac{\delta\rho}{c}\right)^{n/2} \times \frac{n+1}{x}\, I_{n+1}(2x\sqrt{\delta/(c\rho)}\,)\,dx. \tag{3.7}$$

Theorem 3.4 *In the renewal model satisfying the standard assumptions, with T and Y exponentially distributed with parameters δ and ρ, respectively, and with $c \geqslant 0$ we have*

$$\mathsf{P}\{\varUpsilon_{u,c\,|\,\delta,\rho} \leqslant t\} = \mathsf{P}\{\varUpsilon_{u,c\,|\,\delta,\rho} < \infty\} - \frac{1}{\pi}\int_0^{\pi} f(x)\,dx, \tag{3.8}$$

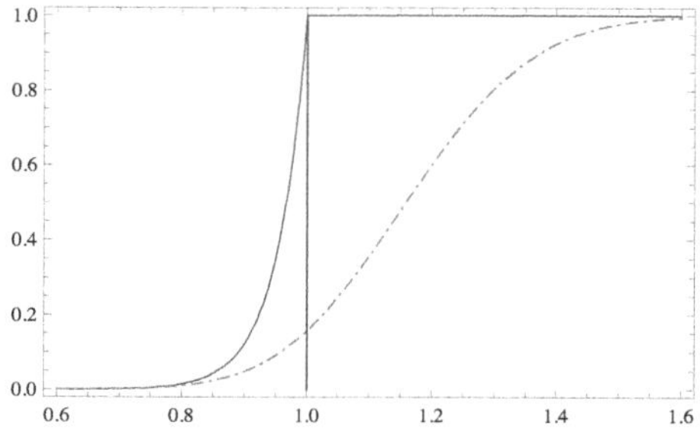

FIGURE 3.1: Graphs (X-axis is c) of $\mathsf{P}\{\varUpsilon_{u,c\,|\,\delta,\rho} \leqslant t\}$ and its upper bound $\mathsf{P}\{\varUpsilon_{u,c\,|\,\delta,\rho} < \infty\}$, when $\rho = \delta = 1$, $u = 20$, and $t = 100$.

where[2]

$$\mathsf{P}\{\varUpsilon_{u,c\,|\,\delta,\rho} < \infty\} = \begin{cases} 1, & \delta/(c\rho) \geqslant 1, \\ (\delta/(c\rho))\exp\{-u(c\rho - \delta)/c\}, & \delta/(c\rho) < 1, \end{cases} \tag{3.9}$$

and

$$\begin{aligned} f(x) &= (\delta/(c\rho))\big(1 + \delta/(c\rho) - 2\sqrt{\delta/(c\rho)}\cos x\big)^{-1} \\ &\quad \times \exp\big\{\rho u(\sqrt{\delta/(c\rho)}\cos x - 1) \\ &\quad - \delta t\,(c\rho/\delta)(1 + \delta/(c\rho) - 2\sqrt{\delta/(c\rho)}\cos x)\big\} \\ &\quad \times \big(\cos(\rho u\sqrt{\delta/(c\rho)}\sin x) - \cos(\rho u\sqrt{\delta/(c\rho)}\sin x + 2x)\big). \end{aligned}$$

The proofs of Theorems 3.2–3.4, which we do not present here, are given, using Kendall's identity, in great detail in [135]; see [135], Chapter 5, Theorems 5.6–5.8. Another variant of the proof of Theorem 3.4 is given in Chapter 5, Section 5.2.5.

3.2.2 A numerical comparison

Let us consider the difference between $\mathsf{P}\{\varUpsilon_{u,c\,|\,\delta,\rho} \leqslant t\}$, which stays in the left-hand side of (3.8), and $\mathsf{P}\{\varUpsilon_{u,c\,|\,\delta,\rho} < \infty\}$, which stays in the right-hand side of (3.8). Plainly (see graphical illustration in Fig. 3.1), for all positive u, c and t

$$\mathsf{P}\{\varUpsilon_{u,c\,|\,\delta,\rho} \leqslant t\} \leqslant \mathsf{P}\{\varUpsilon_{u,c\,|\,\delta,\rho} < \infty\}$$

and $\mathsf{P}\{\varUpsilon_{u,c\,|\,\delta,\rho} < \infty\}$, expressed in terms of elementary functions, is easy to calculate. On the contrary, to calculate $\mathsf{P}\{\varUpsilon_{u,c\,|\,\delta,\rho} \leqslant t\}$ is uneasy. To do this, we need to apply a numerical method, such as numerical integration.

[2]It is worth noting that $\delta/(c\rho)$ is Lundberg's constant, and $(c\rho - \delta)/c$ is Lundberg's exponent, also known as adjustment coefficient.

Another possibility is to find for $\mathsf{P}\{\varUpsilon_{u,c\,|\,\delta,\rho} \leqslant t\}$ an integro-differential equation, which may be used for numerical calculations, as follows.

We write $\phi_t(u,c) := \mathsf{P}\{\varUpsilon_{u,c\,|\,\delta,\rho} > t\}$ for brevity. If the first renewal occurs at time $z > t$, then the probability of non-crossing the level u within time t by the process $V_s - cs$, $s \geqslant 0$, is 1. Suppose that the first renewal occurs at time $z \leqslant t$ and the jump size is y with probability $dP_Y(y)$. Plainly, for $\phi_{t-z}(u+cz-y,c)$, which is the probability of non-crossing the level $u+cz-y$ within time $t-z$ by the process $V_s - cs$, $s \geqslant 0$, we have

$$\begin{aligned}\phi_t(u,c) &= \mathsf{E}(\phi_{t-T_1}(u+cT_1-Y_1,c)\mathbf{1}_{(-\infty,u]}(Y_1-cT_1)\mathbf{1}_{(-\infty,t]}(T_1)) \\ &\quad + \mathsf{P}\{T_1 > t\} \\ &= \int_0^t \int_0^{u+cz} \phi_{t-z}(u+cz-y,c)\,dP_T(z)\,dP_Y(y) + \mathsf{P}\{T_1 > t\}.\end{aligned}$$

Since $T_1 \stackrel{d}{=} T$ is exponentially distributed with parameter δ, we write this equation as

$$\phi_t(u,c) = \delta \int_0^t \int_0^{u+cz} \phi_{t-z}(u+cz-y,c)\,dF_Y(y)e^{-\delta z}\,dz + e^{-t\delta}.$$

The change of variable $x = u + cz$ leads to the equation

$$\begin{aligned}\phi_t(u,c) &= \frac{\delta}{c}\int_u^{u+ct} e^{-\delta(x-u)/c} \int_0^x \phi_{t-(x-u)/c}(x-y,c)\,dP_Y(y)\,dx \\ &\quad + e^{-t\delta}.\end{aligned} \tag{3.10}$$

Use the formula of differentiation of integrals containing a parameter[3]. The probability $\phi_t(u,c)$ is a solution to Arfwedson–Takåčs and Fokker–Planck integro-differential equation

$$\frac{\partial\phi_t(u,c)}{\partial t} = c\,\frac{\partial\phi_t(u,c)}{\partial u} - \delta\phi_t(u,c) + \delta\int_0^u \phi_t(u-y,c)\,dF_Y(y). \tag{3.11}$$

Assuming that Y is exponentially distributed with parameter ρ, the integral summand in equation (3.11) can be written in a simpler form.

Remark 3.1 Equation (3.11) was derived first in 1955 by L. Takåčs [183], under the assumption that δ is a function of t rather than a constant, and $c = 1$. This is equation (3) in [173], where, with reference to [162], it is called Takåčs integro-differential equation.

It is noteworthy that for $\delta = 1$ equation (3.11) is equation (8) in [5], derived even earlier, in 1950, by H. Arfwedson. We further note that equation (3.11) is a special case of the well-known Fokker–Planck equation (see, e.g., [78],

[3]See, e.g., [190], Section 4.2, Example 1 on p. 76.

TABLE 3.2: Probability $\mathsf{P}\{\Upsilon_{u,c\,|\,\delta,\rho} > t\}$, when $\delta = \rho = 1$ and $c = 1.1$

	Initial capital u						
t	0	2	4	6	8	9	10
1	0.53660	0.88029	0.97121	0.99342	0.99855	0.99933	0.99969
5	0.28040	0.64558	0.84164	0.93464	0.97474	0.98463	0.99077
10	0.21457	0.53087	0.73857	0.86312	0.93224	0.95323	0.96810
20	0.16816	0.43267	0.62889	0.76683	0.85904	0.89191	0.91785
30	0.14798	0.38578	0.57000	0.70760	0.80678	0.84458	0.87584
40	0.13621	0.35738	0.53247	0.66744	0.76871	0.80872	0.84269
50	0.12836	0.33804	0.50618	0.63827	0.73985	0.78090	0.81631
t	0	22	44	66	88	99	110
50	0.12836	0.98438	0.99996	1.0	1.0	1.0	1.0
100	0.11001	0.95621	0.99933	1.0	1.0	1.0	1.0
150	0.10282	0.93517	0.99786	0.99997	1.0	1.0	1.0
200	0.09902	0.92050	0.99602	0.99989	0.99999	1.0	1.0
400	0.09343	0.89287	0.98979	0.99927	0.99994	0.99998	0.99999
600	0.09191	0.88372	0.98652	0.99865	0.99986	0.99996	0.99998
∞	0.09091	0.87697	0.98335	0.99775	0.99970	0.99989	0.99996

Chapter X, Sections 1 and 2). With certain boundary conditions on $\phi_t(0, c)$ and on corresponding derivatives, this equation was used, as equation (21) in [172], for numerical calculations of the probability of ruin within finite time. Bearing in mind all these contributions, we call equation (3.11) Arfwedson–Takǎčs and Fokker–Planck equation[4].

In the early 1970s, at the beginning of the computer era, calculations were made by H. Seal in [172], [173] and presented in the form of Tables 3.2 and 3.3. This aimed to demonstrate (with perhaps too emotionally expressed conclusion) disadvantages of the probability of ultimate ruin in certain practical applications of risk theory.

In [172], a model is considered with Y exponentially distributed with parameter $\rho = 1$, i.e., when the mean value of a jump in the moment of renewal is 1, and with T exponentially distributed with parameter $\delta = 1$, i.e., with the intensity of Poisson renewal process (or with the average number of renewals per unit time) equal to 1. In [173], the jumps at the moments of renewal are just deterministic values, all equal exactly to 1. The first model is illustrated in Table 3.2. The second model is illustrated in Table 3.3.

Selecting first[5] $c = 1$, and then[6] $c = 1.1$, and solving the integro-differential equation (3.11) taken from the work by G. Arfwedson [5], H. Seal obtained $\mathsf{P}\{\Upsilon_{u,c\,|\,\delta,\rho} > t\}$ numerically. These results are shown in Tables 3.2 and 3.3. These Tables 3.2 and 3.3 are similar to Tables 2 and 3 in [172].

[4]In [171], the proof of this formula contains a technical error (cf. [171], equation (4.13) on p. 104, and equation (3.10)).

[5]In terms of risk theory, this means that the safety loading is $\tau = 0$.

[6]In terms of risk theory, this means that the safety loading is $\tau = 0.1$.

TABLE 3.3: Probability $\mathsf{P}\{\Upsilon_{u,c\,|\,\delta,\rho} > t\}$, when $\delta = \rho = 1$ and $c = c^* = 1$

	Initial capital u						
t	0	2	4	6	8	9	10
1	0.52378	0.87580	0.96993	0.99309	0.99848	0.99929	0.99967
5	0.24910	0.61280	0.82085	0.92399	0.96996	0.98154	0.98881
10	0.17729	0.47678	0.69263	0.83168	0.91338	0.93916	0.95782
20	0.12576	0.35614	0.54860	0.69804	0.80675	0.84783	0.88137
30	0.10279	0.29653	0.46767	0.61092	0.72505	0.77168	0.81191
40	0.08907	0.25939	0.41433	0.54942	0.66260	0.71093	0.75395
50	0.07969	0.23343	0.37584	0.50321	0.61341	0.66181	0.70578
t	0	22	44	66	88	99	110
50	0.07969	0.96330	0.99985	1.0	1.0	1.0	1.0
100	0.05638	0.87760	0.99617	0.99997	1.0	1.0	1.0
150	0.04605	0.80017	0.98492	0.99957	1.0	1.0	1.0
200	0.03988	0.73716	0.96746	0.99813	0.99995	0.99999	1.0
400	0.02821	0.57755	0.87868	0.97728	0.99721	0.99916	0.99977
600	0.02303	0.48941	0.79802	0.94037	0.98690	0.99450	0.99786
∞	Zero in all cases, if u is finite						

In his comment on these results, H. Seal noted (we almost quote his words) that with no risk loading at all (which, as is known, leads to ultimate ruin whatever finite value u was chosen) and with u equal to only ten times the mean unit claim, there is a 70.5% chance of not being ruined during an interval within which 50 claims are expected. Everyone sees, wrote Seal, how much 50 differs from infinity when the probability of ruin is considered! His final conclusion was that it strongly shows the poverty of asymptotic numerical approximations for a practical person. H. Seal concluded that the real value of risk theory is the early claims that worry the insurer just starting its business, rather than those that occur after a successful business was built.

This conclusion by H. Seal probably holds true regarding traditional risk theory. In the context of multi-year model that we are considering, the probability of ultimate ruin, of course, is not the main subject of our interest. Rather, it is a technical and very rough upper bound for the probability of ruin within one insurance year. This boundary in itself has a very limited practical value, especially since it gives a non-trivial result only when prices are higher than the marginal cost of insurance.

3.2.3 Links to a random walk with random displacements

For $0 < p < 1$, $q = 1 - p$, and $t > 0$, let us introduce

$$\mathsf{F}_t(x \mid p) = e^{-x} \sum_{n=0}^{\infty} \frac{x^n}{n!} \int_0^t \mathsf{v}_{n+1}(y \mid p)\, dy, \quad x > 0, \tag{3.12}$$

which is referred to as auxiliary function of the second kind, where

$$\mathsf{v}_{n+1}(y \mid p) = \left(\frac{p}{q}\right)^{(n+1)/2} \frac{n+1}{y}\, e^{-y/p} I_{n+1}(2y\sqrt{q/p}\,), \quad y > 0. \tag{3.13}$$

By the change of variable $y = x\delta/(c\rho)$ in the right-hand side of (3.7), this Type II formula may be rewritten as

$$\begin{aligned} \mathsf{P}\{\Upsilon_{u,c\,|\,\delta,\rho} \leqslant t\} &= e^{-\rho u} \sum_{n=0}^{\infty} \frac{(\rho u)^n}{n!} \int_0^{\delta t} \left(\frac{\delta}{c\rho}\right)^{(n+1)/2} \\ &\quad \times \frac{n+1}{y}\, e^{-y\,(c\rho+\delta)/\delta} I_{n+1}(2y\sqrt{(c\rho)/\delta}\,)\, dy \\ &= \mathcal{F}_{\delta t}(u\,\rho \mid \delta/(c\rho+\delta)), \end{aligned} \tag{3.14}$$

whence a clear probabilistic sense of the functions $\mathcal{F}_t(x \mid p)$ and $\mathsf{v}_{n+1}(y \mid p)$ introduced in (3.12) and (3.13).

To make this transparent, recall (see, e.g., [184], Chapter 4, § 22) the model of random walk with random displacements. Suppose that a particle performs a random walk on the X-axis. Starting at the origin, in each step the particle moves either a unit distance to the right with probability p or a unit distance to the left with probability q ($p + q = 1$, $0 < p < 1$). Suppose that the displacements of the particle occur at random times in the time interval $(0, \infty)$. Denote by $\nu(z)$ the number of steps taken in the interval $(0, z]$. We suppose that $\{\nu(z), 0 \leqslant z < \infty\}$ is a Poisson process of density $1/p$ and that the successive displacements are independent of each other and independent of the process $\{\nu(z), 0 \leqslant z < \infty\}$. Denote by $\xi_p(z)$ the position of the particle at time z. In this case $\{\xi_p(z), 0 \leqslant z < \infty\}$ is a stochastic process having stationary independent increments, $\mathsf{P}\{\xi_p(0) = 0\} = 1$ and almost all sample functions of $\{\xi_p(z), 0 \leqslant z < \infty\}$ are step functions having jumps of magnitude 1 and -1.

In this random walk model, for $y > 0$ and $k = 0, \pm 1, \pm 2, \ldots$, we have (see equality (3) in [184])

$$\mathsf{P}\{\xi_p(y) = k\} = e^{-y/p}(p/q)^{k/2} I_k(2y\sqrt{q/p}\,) = \frac{y}{k}\, \mathsf{v}_k(y \mid p). \tag{3.15}$$

Elementary calculations yield

$$\mathsf{E}\,\xi_p(y) = (1 - (q/p))y, \quad \mathsf{D}\,\xi_p(y) = y/p.$$

For $y > 0$ and $k \in \{1, 2, \ldots\}$, we have (see equalities (8) and (9) in [184])

$$\begin{aligned} \mathsf{P}\Big\{\sup_{0 \leqslant z \leqslant y} \xi_p(z) < k\Big\} &= \mathsf{P}\{\xi_p(y) < k\} - (p/q)^k\, \mathsf{P}\{\xi_p(y) < -k\} \\ &= 1 - k(p/q)^{k/2} \int_0^y e^{-z/p} I_k(2z\sqrt{q/p}\,)\, \frac{dz}{z} \\ &= 1 - k \int_0^y \mathsf{P}\{\xi_p(z) = k\}\, \frac{dz}{z} = 1 - \int_0^y \mathsf{v}_k(z \mid p)\, dz. \end{aligned} \tag{3.16}$$

Manipulating with (3.15) and (3.16), we have the equality

$$
\begin{aligned}
&k\,(p/q)^{k/2}\int_0^y e^{-z/p} I_k(2z\sqrt{q/p}\,)\,\frac{dz}{z}\\
&\quad = e^{-y/p}\sum_{i=k}^{\infty}(p/q)^{i/2} I_i(2y\sqrt{q/p}\,) + e^{-y/p}\sum_{i=k+1}^{\infty}(q/p)^{i/2-k} I_i(2y\sqrt{q/p}\,),
\end{aligned}
$$

the proof of which by means of the theory of Bessel functions is anything but simple.

Denote by $\varsigma_k(p)$ the first hitting time of the point k by the random walk with $p \in (0,1)$. Bearing in mind (3.16), we have

$$
\begin{aligned}
\mathsf{P}\{\varsigma_k(p) \leqslant y\} &= \mathsf{P}\Big\{\sup_{0\leqslant z\leqslant y} \xi_p(z) \geqslant k\Big\}\\
&= \int_0^y \mathsf{v}_k(z \mid p)\,dz.
\end{aligned} \tag{3.17}
$$

Thus, the function $\mathsf{v}_k(y \mid p)$ introduced in (3.13) has a clear probabilistic meaning. It is a probability density function of $\varsigma_k(p)$, i.e., of the first hitting time of the point k in the model of random walk with random displacements. It is not a surprise that the density $\mathsf{v}_k(y \mid p)$ is defective[7] for $p < 1/2$, i.e., when the random walk drifts to the left, and proper for $p \geqslant 1/2$, i.e., when the random walk has no drift, or drifts to the right. It was already established analytically in (A.35).

Going back to (3.14), i.e., to the equality

$$
\mathsf{P}\{\varUpsilon_{u,c\,|\,\delta,\rho} \leqslant t\} = \mathsf{F}_{\delta t}(\rho u \mid \delta/(c\rho+\delta)),
$$

whose right-hand side (see (3.12)) is

$$
\mathsf{F}_{\delta t}(\rho u \mid \delta/(c\rho+\delta)) = e^{-\rho u}\sum_{n=0}^{\infty}\frac{(\rho u)^n}{n\,!}\int_0^{\delta t} \mathsf{v}_{n+1}(y \mid p)\,\Big|_{p=\delta/(c\rho+\delta)}\,dy,
$$

where (see (3.17))

$$
\int_0^{\delta t} \mathsf{v}_{n+1}(y \mid p)\,\Big|_{p=\delta/(c\rho+\delta)}\,dy = \mathsf{P}\{\varsigma_{n+1}(p) \leqslant \delta t\}\,\Big|_{p=\delta/(c\rho+\delta)},
$$

we can rewrite (3.14) in the form

$$
\mathsf{P}\{\varUpsilon_{u,c\,|\,\delta,\rho} \leqslant t\} = e^{-\rho u}\sum_{n=0}^{\infty}\frac{(\rho u)^n}{n\,!}\,\mathsf{P}\{\varsigma_{n+1}(p) \leqslant \delta t\}\,\Big|_{p=\delta/(c\rho+\delta)}, \tag{3.18}
$$

which is a Poisson compound related to the first hitting time distribution.

---

[7]See [78], Chapter II, Section 7 and Chapter XIV, Section 6.

3.2.4 Pollaczek–Khinchin formula

In the compound Poisson model[8], a formula for $\mathsf{P}\{\Upsilon_{u,c} < \infty\}$, which is an upper bound for $\mathsf{P}\{\Upsilon_{u,c} \leqslant t\}$, is given in the form of an infinite series of convolutions, as follows[9]:

$$\mathsf{P}\{\Upsilon_{u,c} < \infty\} = \left(1 - \frac{\delta\,\mathsf{E}\,Y}{c}\right) \sum_{n=1}^{\infty} \left(\frac{\delta\,\mathsf{E}\,Y}{c}\right)^n (1 - F_{\hat{Y}}^{*n}(u)), \quad u \geqslant 0, \tag{3.19}$$

which us called Pollaczek–Khinchin formula[10], where $0 < \delta\,\mathsf{E}\,Y/c < 1$, and[11]

$$F_{\hat{Y}}(u) := \frac{1}{\mathsf{E}\,Y} \int_0^u (1 - F_Y(y))\,dy, \quad u \geqslant 0, \tag{3.20}$$

is referred to as integrated tail of the distribution F_Y.

When Y is exponentially distributed with parameter ρ, the random variable $\hat{Y}$, whose c.d.f. is given in (3.20), is also exponentially distributed with parameter ρ. Therefore, bearing in mind that $f_{\hat{Y}}^{*n}(x) = \rho\,\frac{(\rho x)^{n-1}}{\Gamma(n)}\,e^{-\rho x}$, and that $\sum_{n=1}^{\infty} x^n = x/(1-x)$, $\sum_{n=1}^{\infty} x^n/(n-1)! = x\,e^x$, $0 < x < 1$, we have for all $u \geqslant 0$

$$\begin{aligned}
\mathsf{P}\{\Upsilon_{u,c\,|\,\delta,\rho} < \infty\} &= \left(1 - \frac{\delta}{c\rho}\right) \sum_{n=1}^{\infty} \left(\frac{\delta}{c\rho}\right)^n (1 - F_{\hat{Y}}^{*n}(u)) \\
&= \left(1 - \frac{\delta}{c\rho}\right) \sum_{n=1}^{\infty} \left(\frac{\delta}{c\rho}\right)^n \left(1 - \int_0^u \rho\,\frac{(\rho x)^{n-1}}{(n-1)!}\,e^{-\rho x}\,dx\right) \\
&= \frac{\delta}{c\rho} - \left(1 - \frac{\delta}{c\rho}\right) \int_0^u \frac{1}{x} \underbrace{\left(\sum_{n=1}^{\infty} \left(\frac{\delta x}{c}\right)^n \frac{1}{(n-1)!}\right)}_{\frac{\delta x}{c}\exp\{\frac{\delta x}{c}\}} e^{-\rho x}\,dx \\
&= \frac{\delta}{c\rho} \exp\{-u(c\rho - \delta)/c\},
\end{aligned} \tag{3.21}$$

which is the same formula as in (3.9).

3.2.5 An upper bound undemanding to distribution

The Pollaczek–Khinchin formula allows to obtain the following simple-looking upper bounds for $\mathsf{P}\{\Upsilon_{u,c} < \infty\}$, which is undemanding to distribution.

---

[8]We use notation $\Upsilon_{u,c}$ instead of $\Upsilon_{u,c\,|\,\delta,\rho}$ because T is exponentially distributed with parameter $\delta > 0$, but the distribution of Y is not necessarily exponential.

[9]This well-known formula is a geometric (rather than Poisson) compound (see, e.g., [158], Section 4.5.1) with characteristics $(\delta\,\mathsf{E}\,Y/c, F_{\hat{Y}}(u))$. It is related to discrete distribution $\mathsf{P}\{\xi = k\} = (1-p)\,p^k$, $k = 0, 1, 2, \ldots$, where $0 < p < 1$.

[10]It is also called Beekman's convolution formula (see, e.g., Theorem 5.3.4 in [158]).

[11]Differentiating (3.20), note that $f_{\hat{Y}}(u) = \frac{1}{\mathsf{E}\,Y}(1 - F_Y(u))$, $u \geqslant 0$, and $\mathsf{E}(\hat{Y}) = \mathsf{E}(Y^2)/(2\,\mathsf{E}\,Y)$, $\mathsf{E}(\hat{Y}^2) = \mathsf{E}(Y^3)/(3\,\mathsf{E}\,Y)$, and so on.

Theorem 3.5 *Assume that* $\mathsf{E}(Y^2) < \infty$. *For* $0 < \delta\,\mathsf{E}\,Y/c < 1$, *we have*

$$\mathsf{P}\{\varUpsilon_{u,c} < \infty\} \leqslant \frac{\delta\,\mathsf{E}(Y^2)(c + \delta\,\mathsf{E}\,Y)}{2\,u\,(c - \delta\,\mathsf{E}\,Y)^2}, \quad u > 0. \tag{3.22}$$

Proof. With $\hat{Y}_i \stackrel{d}{=} \hat{Y}$, $i = 1, 2, \ldots$, we start with the trivial inequality

$$1 - F_{\hat{Y}}^{*n}(u) = \mathsf{P}\Big\{\sum_{i=1}^{n} \hat{Y}_i > u\Big\} \leqslant n\,\mathsf{P}\Big\{\hat{Y} > \frac{u}{n}\Big\}.$$

Bearing in mind that $\mathsf{E}\hat{Y} = \dfrac{\mathsf{E}(Y^2)}{2\,\mathsf{E}\,Y}$ and applying Markov's inequality, we have

$$1 - F_{\hat{Y}}^{*n}(u) = \mathsf{P}\Big\{\sum_{i=1}^{n} \hat{Y}_i > u\Big\} \leqslant n^2\,\frac{\mathsf{E}\hat{Y}}{u} = n^2\,\frac{\mathsf{E}(Y^2)}{2\,\mathsf{E}\,Y u}.$$

Bearing in mind that $\sum_{i=1}^{\infty} n^2 q^n = \dfrac{q(1+q)}{(1-q)^3}$, $0 < q < 1$, and applying this inequality to (3.19), we have

$$\begin{aligned}\mathsf{P}\{\varUpsilon_{u,c} < \infty\} &\leqslant \frac{\mathsf{E}(Y^2)}{2\,\mathsf{E}\,Y u}\Big((1-q)\sum_{n=1}^{\infty} n^2 q^n\Big)\Big|_{q=\frac{\delta\,\mathsf{E}\,Y}{c}} \\ &= \frac{\mathsf{E}(Y^2)}{2\,\mathsf{E}\,Y u}\Big(\frac{q\,(1+q)}{(1-q)^2}\Big)\Big|_{q=\frac{\delta\,\mathsf{E}\,Y}{c}},\end{aligned}$$

which may be easily rewritten as in (3.22). □

If power moments of a higher order are finite, then the upper bound (3.22) can be refined by using the corresponding Markov's inequality. Unfortunately, even more accurate upper bounds of this type are very imprecise.

3.3 Inverse Level-crossing Problem

The inverse level-crossing problem focusses on the analytical structure and shape of the fixed-probability level. Unfortunately, no explicit expression is available for it. Moreover, for the fixed-probability level, there are no results proven for all t. Therefore, we will focus on asymptotic results valid for $t \to \infty$.

3.3.1 Analytical structure of fixed-probability level

The following theorem, valid for large, rather than for all positive t, is analogous to Theorem 2.5. We will give two proofs. One, based on the explicit formula (3.6), links this chapter to Chapter 2. Another uses auxiliary function of the second kind (see Section A.2.5). The role of the second proof will be seen in the future, in Chapter 5, where the fixed-probability level is studied in the general renewal model.

Theorem 3.6 *When c is equal to zero, the solution to equation* (3.5) *is*

$$u_{\alpha,t\,|\,\delta,\rho}(0) = (\delta/\rho)\,t + \frac{\sqrt{2\,\delta}}{\rho}\,\kappa_\alpha\sqrt{t}\,(1+o(1)), \quad t\to\infty. \tag{3.23}$$

First proof of Theorem 3.6. The proof consists of two steps. The first step is to check that for $u_t := \frac{\delta}{\rho}\,t + \frac{\sqrt{2\,\delta}}{\rho}\,\kappa_\alpha\sqrt{t}$, we have

$$\mathsf{P}\{\varUpsilon_{u,0\,|\,\delta,\rho} \leqslant t\}\big|_{u=u_t} = \alpha\,(1+o(1)), \quad t\to\infty. \tag{3.24}$$

Bearing in mind that[12] $e^{-\rho u}\delta\int_0^\infty e^{-\delta x}\,I_0(2\sqrt{\delta\rho u x}\,)\,dx = 1$, we see that equality (3.6) yields[13]

$$\begin{aligned}\mathsf{P}\{\varUpsilon_{u,0\,|\,\delta,\rho} \leqslant t\}\big|_{u=u_t} &= 1 - e^{-\rho u_t}\,\delta\int_t^\infty e^{-\delta x}\,I_0(2\sqrt{\delta\rho u_t x}\,)\,dx\\ &\sim 1 - \frac{\delta}{\sqrt{2\,\pi}}\int_t^\infty \frac{e^{-\delta x}e^{-\rho u_t}e^{2\sqrt{\delta\rho u_t x}}}{(2\sqrt{\delta\rho u_t x}\,)^{1/2}}\,dx\\ &= 1 - \delta\int_t^\infty \frac{\varphi_{(0,1)}(\sqrt{2\,\delta x} - \sqrt{2\,\rho u_t}\,)}{(2\sqrt{\delta\rho u_t x}\,)^{1/2}}\,dx.\end{aligned} \tag{3.25}$$

Making the change of variables $\xi := \sqrt{2\delta x} - \sqrt{2\rho u_t}$ and bearing in mind that

$$x = \frac{(\xi + \sqrt{2\,\rho u_t}\,)^2}{2\,\delta}, \qquad dx = \frac{\xi + \sqrt{2\,\rho u_t}}{\delta}\,d\xi,$$

we obtain from (3.25)

$$\begin{aligned}&\mathsf{P}\{\varUpsilon_{u,0\,|\,\delta,\rho} \leqslant t\}\big|_{u=u_t}\\ &\quad\sim 1 - \int_{\sqrt{2\,\delta t}-\sqrt{2\,\rho u_t}}^\infty \Big(1 + \frac{\xi}{\sqrt{2\,\rho u_t}}\Big)^{1/2}\varphi_{(0,1)}(\xi)\,d\xi.\end{aligned} \tag{3.26}$$

Since[14]

$$\sqrt{2\,\delta t} - \sqrt{2\,\rho u_t} = \sqrt{2\,\delta t}\left(1 - \sqrt{1 + \frac{\sqrt{2}}{\sqrt{\delta t}}\,\kappa_\alpha}\right) \sim \sqrt{2\,\delta t}\,\Big(-\frac{\sqrt{2}}{2\sqrt{\delta t}}\,\kappa_\alpha\Big) = -\kappa_\alpha,$$

---

[12]Since (see [85], formula 6.643.2) $\int_0^\infty e^{-bz}\,I_0(a\sqrt{z}\,)\,dz = \frac{1}{b}\exp\left\{\frac{a^2}{4b}\right\}$, where $b, a > 0$.

[13]Recall (see (A.22)) $I_0(a\sqrt{x}\,) \sim \frac{e^{a\sqrt{x}}}{\sqrt{2\,\pi}\,(a\sqrt{x})^{1/2}}\Big(1 + \sum_{k=1}^\infty \frac{((2k-1)!!)^2}{(2a\sqrt{x})^k\,k!\,2^{2k}}\Big)$, $x\to\infty$.

[14]We use the relation $1 - \sqrt{1+x} \sim -x/2$, $x\to 0$.

we get $\mathsf{P}\{\varUpsilon_{u,0\,|\,\delta,\rho} \leqslant t\}\big|_{u=u_t} \sim \varPhi_{(0,1)}(\sqrt{2\,\delta t} - \sqrt{2\,\rho u_t}) \sim \varPhi_{(0,1)}(-\kappa_\alpha) = \alpha$, which is (3.24).

The second step is to prove that for $u_{\alpha,t\,|\,\delta,\rho}(0)$ given in (3.23)

$$\mathsf{P}\{\varUpsilon_{u,0\,|\,\delta,\rho} \leqslant t\}\big|_{u=u_{\alpha,t\,|\,\delta,\rho}(0)} = \alpha. \tag{3.27}$$

Let $F(u)$ be a shorthand for $\mathsf{P}\{\varUpsilon_{u,0\,|\,\delta,\rho} \leqslant t\}$. Since in the case[15] $c = 0$ the trajectories of compound Poisson process V_s, $s \geqslant 0$, are (a.s.) step functions with only jumps up, $\mathsf{P}\{\varUpsilon_{u,0\,|\,\delta,\rho} \leqslant t\}$ is identical to $\mathsf{P}\{V_t > u\}$, for which an explicit expression is given in (3.2).

In this notation, (3.24) writes as $F(u_t) = \alpha\,(1 + o(1))$, $t \to \infty$, and we need to prove (3.27), which writes as $F(u_{\alpha,t\,|\,\delta,\rho}(0)) = \alpha$, $t \to \infty$. In other words, bearing in mind that $u_{\alpha,t\,|\,\delta,\rho}(0) = u_t + o(t^{1/2})$, we need to prove that the solution $u_{\alpha,t}$ to the equation $F(u) = \alpha$ is $u_t + o(t^{1/2})$.

By Taylor's theorem, for $u_{\alpha,t} = F^{-1}(\alpha)$, $u_t = F^{-1}(\alpha\,(1 + o(1)))$ we have

$$|u_{\alpha,t} - u_t| = \big|\,F^{-1}(\alpha) - F^{-1}(\alpha\,(1 + o(1)))\big| \leqslant K\,\mathcal{U}_t\,o(1), \quad t \to \infty, \tag{3.28}$$

where $\mathcal{U}_t := \sup_{x\in\mathcal{O}(\alpha)} \big|\frac{d}{dx}\,(F^{-1})(x)\big|$. By $\mathcal{O}(\alpha)$ we denote an $o(1)$-neighborhood of α. In this way, the proof is reduced to the study of $\mathcal{U}_t$.

By Theorem A.3, we have

$$\mathcal{U}_t := \sup_{x\in\mathcal{O}(\alpha)} \big|(F'(F^{-1}(x)))^{-1}\big|.$$

By (3.2), we have $F'(x) = -(\delta\rho t)^{1/2} x^{-1/2} I_1(2\,\sqrt{\delta\rho t x}\,)\,e^{-t\delta-\rho x}$, $x > 0$, and

$$\begin{aligned}
F'(x)\,\Big|_{x=\frac{\delta}{\rho}\,t+\frac{\sqrt{2\,\delta}}{\rho}\,\kappa_\alpha\sqrt{t}} &= -(\delta t/\rho)^{1/2}(\delta\,t + \sqrt{2\,\delta}\,\kappa_\alpha\sqrt{t})^{-1/2} \\
&\quad \times I_1(2\,(\delta^2t^2 + \sqrt{2}\,\kappa_\alpha\delta^{3/2}t^{3/2})^{1/2}\,)\,e^{-2\,\delta\,t-\sqrt{2\,\delta}\,\kappa_\alpha\sqrt{t}} \\
&\sim -(\delta t/\rho)^{1/2}(\delta\,t + \sqrt{2\,\delta}\,\kappa_\alpha\sqrt{t}\,)^{-1/2} \\
&\quad \times \frac{e^{2\,(\delta^2t^2+\sqrt{2}\,\kappa_\alpha\delta^{3/2}t^{3/2})^{1/2}}}{2\,\sqrt{\pi}\,(\delta^2t^2 + \sqrt{2}\,\kappa_\alpha\delta^{3/2}t^{3/2})^{1/4}}\,e^{-2\,\delta\,t-\sqrt{2\,\delta}\,\kappa_\alpha\sqrt{t}}.
\end{aligned} \tag{3.29}$$

For the exponential terms in (3.29), we note that[16]

$$\begin{aligned}
&2\,(\delta^2t^2 + \sqrt{2}\,\kappa_\alpha\delta^{3/2}t^{3/2})^{1/2} - 2\,\delta\,t - \sqrt{2\,\delta}\,\kappa_\alpha\sqrt{t} \\
&\quad \sim 2\,\delta t\,(1 + \kappa_\alpha(2\,\delta t)^{-1/2} - \kappa_\alpha^2(4\delta t)^{-1} + \ldots) \\
&\quad - 2\,\delta\,t\,(1 + \kappa_\alpha(2\,\delta\,t)^{-1/2}) \sim -\kappa_\alpha^2/2,
\end{aligned}$$

---

[15]Plainly, from the standpoint of the level-crossing problem, the case $c = 0$ is simplistic, but its detailed consideration facilitates further exposition.

[16]We use the relation $(1 + x)^{1/2} = 1 + x/2 - x^2/8 + \ldots$, $x \to 0$.

whence

$$F'(x)\,\Big|_{x=\frac{\delta}{\rho}t+\frac{\sqrt{2\delta}}{\rho}\kappa_\alpha\sqrt{t}} \sim e^{-\kappa_\alpha^2/2}\frac{-(\delta t/\rho)^{1/2}(\delta t+\sqrt{2\delta}\,\kappa_\alpha\sqrt{t}\,)^{-1/2}}{2\sqrt{\pi}\,(\delta^2t^2+\sqrt{2}\,\kappa_\alpha\delta^{3/2}t^{3/2})^{1/4}}$$
$$\sim \frac{e^{-\kappa_\alpha^2/2}}{2\sqrt{\pi\rho\delta\, t}},$$

and $\mathcal{U}_t \sim t^{1/2}$. Put it in (3.28) to complete the proof. □

Second proof of Theorem 3.6. Using the shorthand notation $F(u)$ for[17] $\mathsf{P}\{\Upsilon_{u,0\,|\,\delta,\rho} \leqslant t\} = \mathsf{P}\{V_t > u\}$ introduced in the first proof of Theorem 3.6, central in this proof is an auxiliary function $G(u)$ which approximates the original function $F(u)$. More specifically, use CLT-type approximation for $F(u)$, which is well known (see, e.g., [135], Chapter 4). It is

$$\sup_u \big|F(u) - G(u)\big| = O(t^{-1/2}\,), \quad t \to \infty, \tag{3.30}$$

where $G(u) := 1 - \Phi_{(0,1)}((u - \mathsf{E}V_t)/\sqrt{\mathsf{D}V_t})$. Here (see (3.3)) $\mathsf{E}(V_t) = (\delta/\rho)\,t$, $\mathsf{D}V_t = (2\,\delta/\rho^2)\,t$. For $u_t := \frac{\delta}{\rho}\,t + \frac{\sqrt{2\,\delta}}{\rho}\,\kappa_\alpha\sqrt{t}$, elementary calculations yield

$$G(u_t) = 1 - \Phi_{(0,1)}\left(\frac{u_t - (\delta/\rho)\,t}{\sqrt{(2\,\delta/\rho^2)\,t}}\right) \sim \alpha,$$

whence (3.24). The rest of the proof is the same as in the first proof above. □

Remark 3.2 The main difference between the first proof of Theorem 3.6 and the second is the use of relation (3.26), which involves the Bessel function, rather than approximation (3.30), which is a standard result of probability theory. To the first proof, applicable is the following Feller's remark (see [78], Chapter II, Section 7): surprisingly many explicit solutions in diffusion theory, queuing theory, and in other applications involve the Bessel functions, and do not lend themselves to easy calculations because the analytical technique necessary for this is rather sophisticated; fortunately, this can be mitigated by using appropriate general results.

For the equilibrium price $c^* := \mathsf{E}Y/\mathsf{E}T$, which in our model writes as $c^* := \delta/\rho$, we have $\delta/(c^*\rho + \delta) = 1/2$, and equality (3.14) may be rewritten as $\mathsf{P}\{\Upsilon_{u,c^*\,|\,\delta,\rho} \leqslant t\} = \mathcal{F}_{\delta t}(\rho u \mid 1/2)$. Consequently, equation (3.5) may be rewritten as

$$\mathcal{F}_{\delta t}(\rho u \mid 1/2) = \alpha, \tag{3.31}$$

and for all $t > 0$ its solution cannot be expressed in closed form. Let us apply the asymptotic analysis, as $t \to \infty$. The following theorem, though valid for large t, rather than for all $t > 0$, is analogous to Theorem 2.6.

[17]Note that $\Upsilon_{u,0\,|\,\delta,\rho} := \inf\{s > 0 : V_s > u\}$ and V_s, $s \geqslant 0$, does not decrease over time.

Theorem 3.7 *When c is equal to the the equilibrium price $c^* := \delta/\rho$, the solution to equation* (3.5) *is*

$$u_{\alpha,t\,|\,\delta,\rho}(c^*) = \frac{\sqrt{2\,\delta}}{\rho}\,\kappa_{\alpha/2}\sqrt{t}\,(1+o(1)), \quad t\to\infty. \tag{3.32}$$

Proof. The main technical tool is the asymptotic expansion of the auxiliary function of the second kind $F_t(x \mid p)$. For $x > 0$, $q = 1-p$, and $p \in (0,1)$, it is (see Theorem A.13)

$$\begin{aligned} F_t(x \mid p) \sim F_\infty(x \mid p) - \frac{(p/q)^{1/4}}{2\sqrt{\pi}}\Bigg(& S_0(x \mid p) H_1(t \mid p) \\ &+ \sum_{k=1}^{\infty} (-1)^k \frac{(p/q)^{k/2}}{2^{2k} k!}\Big(S_{2k}(x \mid p) \\ &+ \sum_{j=1}^{k} \frac{A_{k,j}}{2^{2j}} S_{2(k-j)}(x \mid p)\Big) H_{k+1}(t \mid p)\Bigg), \quad t\to\infty. \end{aligned} \tag{3.33}$$

Recall (see (A.30), (A.27)) that in (3.33)

$$S_0(x \mid p) = \exp\{-x\,(1-\sqrt{p/q})\}\sqrt{p/q}\,(x\sqrt{p/q}+1),$$

and for $k = 1, 2, \ldots$

$$S_k(x \mid p) = \exp\{-x\,(1-\sqrt{p/q})\}\sqrt{p/q}\sum_{j=1}^{k+2} \mathcal{S}(k+2, j)\,(x\sqrt{p/q}\,)^{j-1},$$

$$\begin{aligned} H_k(t \mid p) = {} & \frac{2e^{-a_p\,t}}{(2k-1)!!}\,(\mathcal{P}_k(2a_p\,t) + (-1)^k (2a_p\,t)^{(2k-1)/2}\,\mathcal{M}((2a_p\,t)^{1/2})) \\ & \times t^{-k+1/2}, \end{aligned}$$

where $a_p = (1-\sqrt{q/p}\,)^2$, $\mathcal{P}_k(x)$, $k = 1, 2, \ldots$, are defined in (A.31), and $\mathcal{S}(k+2, j)$ are (see Section A.2.2) the Stirling numbers of the second kind.

Dealing with $F_t(x \mid 1/2)$, it is easily seen that $F_\infty(x \mid 1/2) = 1$, $S_0(x \mid 1/2) = 1 + x$, and that

$$S_{2k}(x \mid 1/2) = \sum_{j=1}^{2k+2} \mathcal{S}(2k+2, j)\,x^{j-1},$$

$$S_{2(k-j)}(x \mid 1/2) = \sum_{j=1}^{2(k-j)+2} \mathcal{S}(2(k-j)+2, j)\,x^{j-1},$$

and, by Corollary A.1,

$$H_{k+1}(t \mid 1/2) = \frac{2}{2k+1}\,t^{-(k+1/2)}.$$

Therefore, for $t \to \infty$ the left-hand side of equation (3.31) may be rewritten as

$$\begin{aligned} F_{\delta t}(\rho u \mid 1/2) \sim 1 - \frac{1}{\sqrt{\pi}} \Bigg((1+\rho u)\,(\delta t)^{-1/2} \\ + \sum_{k=1}^{\infty} \frac{(-1)^k}{2^{2k} k!} \Bigg(\sum_{j=1}^{2k+2} \mathcal{S}(2k+2, j)\,(\rho u)^{j-1} \\ + \sum_{j=1}^{k} \frac{A_{k,j}}{2^{2j}} \sum_{j=1}^{2(k-j)+2} \mathcal{S}(2(k-j)+2, j)\,(\rho u)^{j-1} \Bigg) \\ \times \frac{(\delta t)^{-(k+1/2)}}{2k+1} \Bigg), \end{aligned}$$

and equation (3.31) may be rewritten as

$$\begin{aligned} (1+\rho u)(\delta t)^{-1/2} + \sum_{k=1}^{\infty} \frac{(-1)^k}{2^{2k} k!} \Bigg(\sum_{j=1}^{2k+2} \mathcal{S}(2k+2, j)\,(\rho u)^{j-1} \\ + \sum_{j=1}^{k} \frac{A_{k,j}}{2^{2j}} \sum_{j=1}^{2(k-j)+2} \mathcal{S}(2(k-j)+2, j)\,(\rho u)^{j-1} \Bigg) \frac{(\delta t)^{-(k+1/2)}}{2k+1} \\ = \sqrt{\pi}\,(1-\alpha). \end{aligned} \tag{3.34}$$

The solution of (3.34) is an expression which depends on t in such a way that the left-hand side of (3.34), when this solution is put in it, does not tend neither to zero, nor to infinity, as $t \to \infty$. Consequently, this solution is $O(\sqrt{t}\,)$, as $t \to \infty$.

Let us extract the main term of this solution. We focus on the main term of the left-hand side in (3.34) and reject the terms of smaller orders. In this way, we have the equation

$$\begin{aligned} \sum_{k=0}^{\infty} \frac{(-1)^k}{k!\,(2k+1)} \underbrace{\mathcal{S}(2k+2, 2k+2)}_{1} \left(\frac{\rho u}{2\sqrt{\delta t}} \right)^{2k+1} (1+o(1)) \\ = \sqrt{\pi}\,(1-\alpha)/2, \end{aligned} \tag{3.35}$$

as $t \to \infty$. Bearing in mind (see (B.15)) that for any real x

$$\sum_{k=0}^{\infty} (-1)^k \frac{(x/2)^{2k+1}}{k!\,(2k+1)} = \sqrt{\pi}\,(\Phi_{(0,1)}(x/\sqrt{2}\,) - 1/2),$$

we rewrite (3.35) as

$$\sqrt{\pi}\,(\Phi_{(0,1)}(\rho u/\sqrt{2\delta t}\,) - 1/2)\,(1+o(1)) = \sqrt{\pi}\,(1-\alpha)/2, \quad t \to \infty.$$

It readily yields the required solution. The proof is complete. □

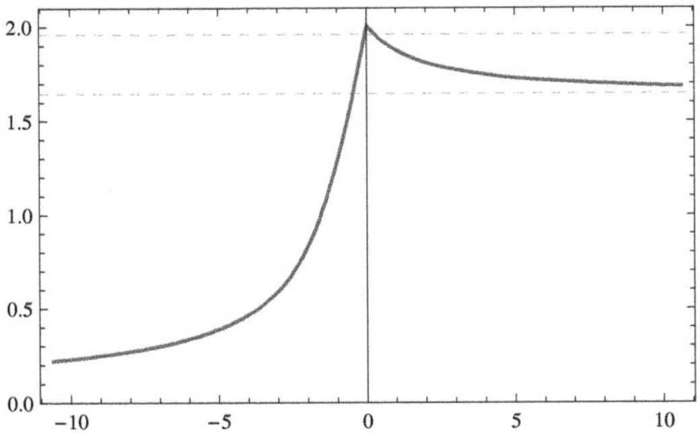

FIGURE 3.2: Graph (X-axis is y) of function $\mathsf{z}_{\alpha,t}(y)$, evaluated numerically, when $\rho = 1$, $\delta = 1$, $\alpha = 0.05$, and $t = 200$. Horizontal grid lines: $\kappa_\alpha = 1.65$ and $\kappa_{\alpha/2} = 1.96$.

Remark 3.3 Given that (see (3.3)) $\mathsf{D}V_t = (2\,\delta/\rho^2)\,t$, (3.32) is equivalent to

$$u_{\alpha,t\,|\,\delta,\rho}(c^*) = \sqrt{\mathsf{D}V_t}\,\kappa_{\alpha/2}\,(1 + o(1)), \quad t \to \infty.$$

Remark 3.4 The proof of Theorem 3.7 is based (see (3.14)) on the explicit expression $F_{\delta t}(\rho u \mid 1/2)$ in terms of Bessel functions for $\mathsf{P}\{\Upsilon_{u,c^*\,|\,\delta,\rho} \leqslant t\}$. In this sense, this proof is similar to the first proof of Theorem 3.6. For an alternative proof, similar to the second proof of Theorem 3.6, we need an approximation for $\mathsf{P}\{\Upsilon_{u,c^*\,|\,\delta,\rho} \leqslant t\}$, which differs significantly from that one used in the second proof of Theorem 3.6. The inverse Gaussian approximation described in [135] is suitable. We will return to this matter in Chapter 5.

The following theorem is analogous to Theorem 2.7.

Theorem 3.8 *For $0 < \alpha < 1/2$, the solution to equation* (3.5) *is*

$$u_{\alpha,t\,|\,\delta,\rho}(c) = \begin{cases} (\delta/\rho - c)\,t \\ \qquad + \dfrac{\sqrt{2\,\delta}}{\rho}\,\mathsf{z}_{\alpha,t}\!\left(\dfrac{\rho\,(\delta/\rho - c)}{\sqrt{2\,\delta}}\sqrt{t}\right)\sqrt{t}, & 0 \leqslant c \leqslant c^*, \\ \dfrac{\sqrt{2\,\delta}}{\rho}\,\mathsf{z}_{\alpha,t}\!\left(\dfrac{\rho\,(\delta/\rho - c)}{\sqrt{2\,\delta}}\sqrt{t}\right)\sqrt{t}, & c > c^*, \end{cases} \tag{3.36}$$

where the function $\mathsf{z}_{\alpha,t}(y)$, $y \in \mathsf{R}$, is continuous, positive for all y, and monotone increasing, as y increases from $-\infty$ to 0, monotone decreasing, as y increases from 0 to ∞, and such that

$$\lim_{y\to-\infty} \mathsf{z}_{\alpha,t}(y) = 0, \quad \lim_{y\to\infty} \mathsf{z}_{\alpha,t}(y) = \kappa_\alpha$$

and $\mathsf{z}_{\alpha,t}(0) = \kappa_{\alpha/2}\,(1 + o(1))$, as $t \to \infty$.

We recall that $0 < \kappa_\alpha < \kappa_{\alpha/2}$ for $0 < \alpha < \frac{1}{2}$. The function $\mathsf{z}_{\alpha,t}(y)$, $y \in \mathsf{R}$, evaluated numerically, when $t = 200$ and $\alpha = 0.05$, is shown in Fig. 3.2.

Remark 3.5 Comparing Theorems 3.6 and 3.8 to Theorems 2.6 and 2.7, we see that the structure of $u_{\alpha,t\,|\,\delta,\rho}(c)$ is similar to the structure of $u^{[\mathrm{dif}]}_{\alpha,t\,|\,\vartheta}(c)$, as t is sufficiently large. It is all the more remarkable because the expressions for $\mathsf{P}\{\Upsilon_{u,c\,|\,\delta,\rho} \leqslant t\}$ (see (3.6)–(3.8) and (3.18)) and for $\mathsf{P}\{\Upsilon^{[\mathrm{dif}]}_{u,c\,|\,\vartheta} \leqslant t\}$ (see equality (2.7)) are not alike at all.

Proof of Theorem 3.8. Bearing in mind (3.14), equation (3.5) may be rewritten as

$$F_{\delta t}(\rho u \mid \delta/(c\rho+\delta)) = \alpha. \tag{3.37}$$

This proof, as well as the proof of Theorem 2.7, is carried out in two stages. At each stage, we make a suitable change of variables. Our aim is to focus on the function $\mathsf{z}_{\alpha,t}(y)$, $y \in \mathsf{R}$, and to check its monotony using the standard criterion based on the sign of derivative. The derivative is calculated by means of (see Theorem A.4) the theorem on the derivative of implicit function.

Step 1. Let us consider the case $0 < c < c^* = \delta/\rho$. We switch from the variables u and c in (3.5) to the variables (since $c > 0$, we have $0 < y < \frac{\sqrt{\delta t}}{\sqrt{2}}$)

$$z = \frac{\rho u}{\sqrt{2\,\delta t}} - \frac{(\delta/\rho - c)\,\rho\sqrt{t}}{\sqrt{2\delta}} \in \mathsf{R}, \quad y = \frac{(\delta/\rho - c)\,\rho\sqrt{t}}{\sqrt{2\delta}} > 0, \tag{3.38}$$

note that $z + y > 0$ and write original equation (3.5) in the form

$$F_{\delta t}(\rho u \mid \delta/(c\rho+\delta))\,\Big|_{u=\frac{\sqrt{2\delta\,t}}{\rho}\,(z+y),\; c=\frac{\delta}{\rho}-\frac{\sqrt{2\delta}}{\rho\sqrt{t}}y} = \alpha,$$

or, which is completely equivalent, in the form

$$F_{\delta t}\Big(\sqrt{2\delta t}\,(z+y)\;\Big|\;\tfrac{\sqrt{\delta\,t}}{2\sqrt{\delta\,t}-\sqrt{2}y}\Big) = \alpha. \tag{3.39}$$

Note that $\frac{1}{2} < \frac{\sqrt{\delta\,t}}{2\sqrt{\delta\,t}-\sqrt{2}y} < 1$ since for $0 < c < \delta/\rho$ we have $0 < y < \frac{\sqrt{\delta t}}{\sqrt{2}}$.

We are ready to investigate $\mathsf{z}_{\alpha,t}(y)$, $y > 0$, i.e., the solution of (3.39), which obviously exists and is unique. To prove that $\mathsf{z}_{\alpha,t}(y)$, $y > 0$, is monotone decreasing, we have to prove that $\frac{d}{dy}\,\mathsf{z}_{\alpha,t}(y) < 0$, $y > 0$.

We apply (see Theorem A.4) the theorem on the derivative of implicit function and Theorem 2.1, which yield

$$\begin{aligned}
\frac{d}{dy}\,\mathsf{z}_{\alpha,t}(y) &= -\left(\frac{\frac{\partial}{\partial y}\Big(\mathsf{P}\{\Upsilon_{u,c\,|\,\delta,\rho} \leqslant t\}\,\big|_{u=\frac{\sqrt{2\delta\,t}}{\rho}\,(z+y),\; c=\frac{\delta}{\rho}-\frac{\sqrt{2\delta}}{\rho\sqrt{t}}y}\Big)}{\frac{\partial}{\partial z}\Big(\mathsf{P}\{\Upsilon_{u,c\,|\,\delta,\rho} \leqslant t\}\,\big|_{u=\frac{\sqrt{2\delta\,t}}{\rho}\,(z+y),\; c=\frac{\delta}{\rho}-\frac{\sqrt{2\delta}}{\rho\sqrt{t}}y}\Big)}\right)\Bigg|_{z=\mathsf{z}_{\alpha,t}(y)} \\
&= -\left(\frac{\frac{\partial}{\partial y}\,F_{\delta t}\Big(\sqrt{2\delta t}\,(z+y)\;\Big|\;\frac{\sqrt{\delta\,t}}{2\sqrt{\delta\,t}-\sqrt{2}y}\Big)}{\frac{\partial}{\partial z}\,F_{\delta t}\Big(\sqrt{2\delta t}\,(z+y)\;\Big|\;\frac{\sqrt{\delta\,t}}{2\sqrt{\delta\,t}-\sqrt{2}y}\Big)}\right)\Bigg|_{z=\mathsf{z}_{\alpha,t}(y)}.
\end{aligned} \tag{3.40}$$

First, let us show that the numerator in (3.40) is negative. By the chain rule for differentiation of a composite function, we have

$$\begin{aligned}
&\frac{\partial}{\partial y} F_{\delta t}\Big(\sqrt{2\delta t}\,(z+y)\,\Big|\,\tfrac{\sqrt{\delta\, t}}{2\sqrt{\delta\, t}-\sqrt{2}y}\Big)\\
&\quad = F_{\delta t}^{(1,0)}\Big(\sqrt{2\delta t}\,(z+y)\,\Big|\,\tfrac{\sqrt{\delta\, t}}{2\sqrt{\delta\, t}-\sqrt{2}y}\Big)\frac{\partial}{\partial y}(\sqrt{2\delta t}\,(z+y))\\
&\qquad + F_{\delta t}^{(0,1)}\Big(\sqrt{2\delta t}\,(z+y)\,\Big|\,\tfrac{\sqrt{\delta t}}{2\sqrt{\delta t}-\sqrt{2}y}\Big)\frac{\partial}{\partial y}\Big(\frac{\sqrt{\delta\, t}}{2\sqrt{\delta t}-\sqrt{2}y}\Big),
\end{aligned}$$

where $\frac{\partial}{\partial y}(\sqrt{2\delta t}\,(z+y)) = \sqrt{2\delta t}$, and $\frac{\partial}{\partial y}\Big(\frac{\sqrt{\delta t}}{2\sqrt{\delta t}-\sqrt{2}y}\Big) = \frac{\sqrt{2\delta t}}{(2\sqrt{\delta t}-\sqrt{2}y)^{2}}$. By Theorem A.14 (see (A.41)), we have

$$\begin{aligned}
&\frac{\partial}{\partial y} F_{\delta t}\Big(\sqrt{2\delta t}\,(z+y)\,\Big|\,\tfrac{\sqrt{\delta t}}{2\sqrt{\delta t}-\sqrt{2}y}\Big) = \sqrt{2\delta t}\\
&\quad \times \underbrace{\Big(F_{\delta t}^{(1,0)}(x\mid p) + \frac{p^{2}}{\delta t}F_{\delta t}^{(0,1)}(x\mid p)\Big)}_{<0}\Big|_{x=\sqrt{2\delta t}\,(z+y),\,p=\frac{\sqrt{\delta\, t}}{2\sqrt{\delta\, t}-\sqrt{2}y}} < 0,
\end{aligned}\tag{3.41}$$

with the inequality following from Theorem A.21.

Second, let us show that the denominator in (3.40) is negative. By the chain rule for differentiation of a composite function, we have

$$\begin{aligned}
&\frac{\partial}{\partial z} F_{\delta t}\Big(\sqrt{2\delta t}\,(z+y)\,\Big|\,\tfrac{\sqrt{\delta\, t}}{2\sqrt{\delta\, t}-\sqrt{2}y}\Big)\\
&\quad = F_{\delta t}^{(1,0)}\Big(\sqrt{2\delta t}\,(z+y)\,\Big|\,\tfrac{\sqrt{\delta\, t}}{2\sqrt{\delta\, t}-\sqrt{2}y}\Big)\frac{\partial}{\partial z}(\sqrt{2\delta t}\,(z+y))\\
&\qquad + F_{\delta t}^{(0,1)}\Big(\sqrt{2\delta t}\,(z+y)\,\Big|\,\tfrac{\sqrt{\delta\, t}}{2\sqrt{\delta\, t}-\sqrt{2}y}\Big)\frac{\partial}{\partial z}\Big(\tfrac{\sqrt{\delta\, t}}{2\sqrt{\delta t}-\sqrt{2}y}\Big),
\end{aligned}$$

where $\frac{\partial}{\partial z}(\sqrt{2\delta t}\,(z+y)) = \sqrt{2\delta t}$, and $\frac{\partial}{\partial z}\Big(\frac{\sqrt{\delta\, t}}{2\sqrt{\delta t}-\sqrt{2}y}\Big) = 0$. Consequently,

$$\begin{aligned}
&\frac{\partial}{\partial z} F_{\delta t}\Big(\sqrt{2\delta t}\,(z+y)\,\Big|\,\tfrac{\sqrt{\delta\, t}}{2\sqrt{\delta\, t}-\sqrt{2}y}\Big)\\
&\quad = F_{\delta t}^{(1,0)}\Big(\sqrt{2\delta t}\,(z+y)\,\Big|\,\tfrac{\sqrt{\delta\, t}}{2\sqrt{\delta\, t}-\sqrt{2}y}\Big)\sqrt{2\delta t} < 0,
\end{aligned}\tag{3.42}$$

with the inequality following from Theorem A.19. Apply (3.41) and (3.42) to (3.40), whence $\frac{d}{dy}\,\mathsf{z}_{\alpha,t}(y) < 0$, as required.

Step 2. Let us consider the case $c > c^{*} = \delta/\rho$. We switch from the variables u and c in (3.5) to the variables

$$z = \frac{\rho u}{\sqrt{2\delta t}} > 0, \quad y = \frac{(\delta/\rho - c)\rho\sqrt{t}}{\sqrt{2\delta}} < 0 \tag{3.43}$$

and write the original equation (3.5) in the form

$$F_{\delta t}(\rho u \mid \delta/(c\rho+\delta))\Big|_{u=\frac{\sqrt{2\delta\, t}}{\rho}\,z,\ c=\frac{\delta}{\rho}-\frac{\sqrt{2\delta}}{\rho\sqrt{t}}y} = \alpha,$$

or, which is completely equivalent, in the form

$$F_{\delta t}\left(\sqrt{2\delta t}\, z \,\middle|\, \frac{\sqrt{\delta\, t}}{2\sqrt{\delta\, t}-\sqrt{2}y}\right) = \alpha. \tag{3.44}$$

Note that $0 < \frac{\sqrt{\delta\, t}}{2\sqrt{\delta\, t}-\sqrt{2}y} < \frac{1}{2}$ since, when $c > c^* = \delta/\rho$, we have $-\infty < y < 0$.

We are ready to investigate the solution $\mathsf{z}_{\alpha,t}(y)$, $y < 0$, of (3.44) which obviously exists and is unique. To prove that $\mathsf{z}_{\alpha,t}(y)$, $y < 0$, is monotone increasing, we have to prove that $\frac{d}{dy}\, \mathsf{z}_{\alpha,t}(y) > 0$, $y < 0$.

We apply (see Theorem A.4) the theorem on the derivative of implicit function and Theorem 2.1, which yield

$$\begin{aligned}\frac{d}{dy}\,\mathsf{z}_{\alpha,t}(y) &= -\left.\left(\frac{\frac{\partial}{\partial y}\left(\mathsf{P}\{\Upsilon_{u,c\,|\,\delta,\rho} \leqslant t\}\big|_{u=\frac{\sqrt{2\delta\, t}}{\rho}\, z,\; c=\frac{\delta}{\rho}-\frac{\sqrt{2\delta}}{\rho\sqrt{t}}y}\right)}{\frac{\partial}{\partial z}\left(\mathsf{P}\{\Upsilon_{u,c\,|\,\delta,\rho} \leqslant t\}\Big|_{u=\frac{\sqrt{2\delta\, t}}{\rho}\, z,\; c=\frac{\delta}{\rho}-\frac{\sqrt{2\delta}}{\rho\sqrt{t}}y}\right)}\right)\right|_{z=\mathsf{z}_{\alpha,t}(y)} \\ &= -\left.\left(\frac{\frac{\partial}{\partial y}\, F_{\delta t}\left(\sqrt{2\delta t}\, z \,\middle|\, \frac{\sqrt{\delta\, t}}{2\sqrt{\delta\, t}-\sqrt{2}y}\right)}{\frac{\partial}{\partial z}\, F_{\delta t}\left(\sqrt{2\delta t}\, z \,\middle|\, \frac{\sqrt{\delta\, t}}{2\sqrt{\delta\, t}-\sqrt{2}y}\right)}\right)\right|_{z=\mathsf{z}_{\alpha,t}(y)}.\end{aligned} \tag{3.45}$$

The numerator in (3.45) is

$$\begin{aligned}&\frac{\partial}{\partial y}\, F_{\delta t}\left(\sqrt{2\delta t}\, z \,\middle|\, \frac{\sqrt{\delta t}}{2\sqrt{\delta\, t}-\sqrt{2}y}\right) \\ &\quad = \underbrace{F^{(0,1)}_{\delta t}\left(\sqrt{2\delta t}\, z \,\middle|\, \frac{\sqrt{\delta t}}{2\sqrt{\delta\, t}-\sqrt{2}y}\right)}_{>0} \frac{\partial}{\partial y}\left(\frac{\sqrt{\delta\, t}}{2\sqrt{\delta t}-\sqrt{2}y}\right),\end{aligned} \tag{3.46}$$

where $\frac{\partial}{\partial y}\left(\frac{\sqrt{\delta\, t}}{2\sqrt{\delta t}-\sqrt{2}y}\right) = \frac{\sqrt{2\delta\, t}}{(2\sqrt{\delta t}-\sqrt{2}y)^{\,2}}$. By Theorem A.20, this expression is positive.

The denominator in (3.45) is

$$\frac{\partial}{\partial z}\, F_{\delta t}\left(\sqrt{2\delta t}\, z \,\middle|\, \frac{\sqrt{\delta\, t}}{2\sqrt{\delta\, t}-\sqrt{2}y}\right) = F^{(1,0)}_{\delta t}\left(\sqrt{2\delta t}\, z \,\middle|\, \frac{\sqrt{\delta\, t}}{2\sqrt{\delta\, t}-\sqrt{2}y}\right)\sqrt{2\delta t}. \tag{3.47}$$

By Theorem A.19, this expression is negative. Inequalities (3.46) and (3.47) applied to (3.45) show that $\frac{d}{dy}\, \mathsf{z}_{\alpha,t}(y) > 0$, as required. □

Remark 3.6 In Theorem 3.8, we have proved that the function $\mathsf{z}_{\alpha,t}(y)$, $y \in \mathsf{R}$, is monotone increasing, as y increases from $-\infty$ to 0, and monotone decreasing, as y increases from 0 to ∞, for all $t > 0$. In what follows, we are only interested in the behavior of $u_{\alpha,t\,|\,\delta,\rho}(c)$ for t large. Therefore, it would be sufficient to carry out this monotony analysis only for t large.

3.3.2 Monotony of fixed-probability level

This section is similar to Section 2.3.2. The remarks made in Section 2.3.2 are applicable to monotony of the fixed-probability level in renewal model. In particular, just as in the diffusion model, the monotony[18] of $u_{\alpha,t\,|\,\delta,\rho}(c)$, $c \geqslant 0$, needs no proof: as c increases, the level that is crossed within time t with the (small) probability α is obviously decreasing. However, we formulate the following Theorems 3.9 and 3.10, the latter weaker than the former, and prove each of them to outline the analytical technique that will be used in Section 3.3.3.

Theorem 3.9 (Strong-form monotony) *For all $t > 0$, the fixed-probability level $u_{\alpha,t\,|\,\delta,\rho}(c)$, $c \geqslant 0$, monotone decreases, as c increases.*

Proof. To prove Theorem 3.9, just like Theorem 2.8, we apply the following standard criterion: a differentiable function, whose first-order derivative is negative on an interval, is monotone decreasing on this interval.

To calculate the derivative of $u_{\alpha,t\,|\,\delta,\rho}(c)$, $c \geqslant 0$, we apply (see Theorem A.4) the theorem on the derivative of implicit function. By (3.37), we have (cf. (2.28) and (2.30))

$$\begin{aligned}\frac{d}{dc}\, u_{\alpha,t\,|\,\delta,\rho}(c) &= -\left(\frac{\frac{\partial}{\partial c}\mathsf{P}\{\Upsilon_{u,c\,|\,\delta,\rho} \leqslant t\}}{\frac{\partial}{\partial u}\mathsf{P}\{\Upsilon_{u,c\,|\,\delta,\rho} \leqslant t\}}\right)\Bigg|_{u=u_{\alpha,t\,|\,\delta,\rho}(c)} \\ &= -\left(\frac{\frac{\partial}{\partial c}\big(F_{\delta t}(\rho u \mid p)\big|_{p=\delta/(c\rho+\delta)}\big)}{\frac{\partial}{\partial u}\big(F_{\delta t}(\rho u \mid p)\big|_{p=\delta/(c\rho+\delta)}\big)}\right)\Bigg|_{u=u_{\alpha,t\,|\,\delta,\rho}(c)}, \quad c \geqslant 0.\end{aligned} \tag{3.48}$$

Plainly, $\frac{d}{dc}\left(\delta/(c\rho+\delta)\right) = -\delta\rho/(c\rho+\delta)^{2}$ and by the chain rule for differentiation of a composite function, we have

$$\begin{aligned}\frac{\partial}{\partial u}\, F_{\delta t}(\rho u \mid \delta/(c\rho+\delta)) &= \rho\, F_{\delta t}^{(1,0)}(\rho u \mid \delta/(c\rho+\delta)), \\ \frac{\partial}{\partial c}\, F_{\delta t}(\rho u \mid \delta/(c\rho+\delta)) &= -\,\frac{\rho}{\delta}\,((\delta/(c\rho+\delta))^{2} \\ &\qquad \times F_{\delta t}^{(0,1)}(\rho u \mid \delta/(c\rho+\delta))).\end{aligned} \tag{3.49}$$

Equality (3.48) writes as

$$\frac{d}{dc}\, u_{\alpha,t\,|\,\delta,\rho}(c) = \left(\frac{\frac{\rho}{\delta}((\delta/(c\rho+\delta))^{2} F_{\delta t}^{(0,1)}(\rho u \mid \delta/(c\rho+\delta)))}{\rho F_{\delta t}^{(1,0)}(\rho u \mid \delta/(c\rho+\delta))}\right)\Bigg|_{u=u_{\alpha,t\,|\,\delta,\rho}(c)}, \quad c \geqslant 0.$$

By Theorem A.19, the denominator is negative. By Theorem A.20, the nominator is positive. It yields $\frac{d}{dc}\, u_{\alpha,t\,|\,\delta,\rho}(c) < 0$, $c \geqslant 0$, as required. □

[18] In both strong and weak forms.

Dealing with the approximations, as $t \to \infty$, rather than with the results which hold for all $t > 0$, we may be satisfied with the weak-form monotony, as below.

Theorem 3.10 (Weak-form monotony) *For $t > 0$ sufficiently large, the fixed-probability level $u_{\alpha,t\,|\,\delta,\rho}(c)$, $c \geqslant 0$, monotone decreases, as c increases.*

Proof. Just like the proof of Theorem 3.9, this proof is based on (see Theorem A.4) the theorem on the derivative of implicit function. But now it is sufficient to check that expression in (3.48) is negative for large t, rather than for all $t > 0$. We are focussed on the expression which is a limit for the right-hand side in (3.48), as $t \to \infty$.

By definition of the auxiliary function of the second kind (see (3.12)), we have

$$\mathsf{F}_\infty(x \mid p) = \lim_{t\to\infty} \mathsf{F}_t(x \mid p) = e^{-x} \sum_{n=0}^{\infty} \frac{x^n}{n!} \int_0^\infty \mathsf{v}_{n+1}(y \mid p)\, dy, \qquad x > 0,$$

where (see (A.35))

$$\int_0^\infty \mathsf{v}_{n+1}(y \mid p)\, dy = \begin{cases} 1, & p \geqslant 1/2, \\ (p/q)^{n+1}, & 0 < p < 1/2. \end{cases}$$

Therefore,

$$\begin{aligned} \mathsf{F}_\infty(x \mid p) &= \begin{cases} e^{-x} \displaystyle\sum_{n=0}^{\infty} \frac{x^n}{n!}, & p \geqslant 1/2, \\ e^{-x} \displaystyle\sum_{n=0}^{\infty} \frac{x^n}{n!} \left(\frac{p}{q}\right)^{n+1}, & 0 < p < 1/2, \end{cases} \\ &= \begin{cases} 1, & p \geqslant 1/2, \\ \dfrac{p}{q} \exp\left\{ -x\left(1 - \dfrac{p}{q}\right)\right\}, & 0 < p < 1/2. \end{cases} \end{aligned} \tag{3.50}$$

In the similar way, we can calculate both $\mathsf{F}_\infty^{(1,0)}(x \mid p)$ and $p^2 \mathsf{F}_\infty^{(0,1)}(x \mid p)$ in an explicit form. It completes the proof.

Note that for $x > 0$ and $0 < p < 1/2$ we have

$$\begin{aligned} \mathsf{F}_\infty^{(1,0)}(x \mid p) &= \lim_{t\to\infty} \mathsf{F}_t^{(1,0)}(x \mid p) \\ &= -\frac{p(q-p)}{q^2} \exp\left\{ -x\left(1 - \frac{p}{q}\right)\right\} < 0, \\ p^2 \mathsf{F}_\infty^{(0,1)}(x \mid p) &= \lim_{t\to\infty} p^2 \mathsf{F}_t^{(0,1)}(x \mid p) \\ &= \frac{p^2(q+px)}{q^3} \exp\left\{ -x\left(1 - \frac{p}{q}\right)\right\} > 0. \end{aligned}$$

For $p \geqslant 1/2$, calculations are similar, and we leave it to the reader. The proof is complete. □

Comparing the proofs of Theorems 3.9 and 3.10, we see that the former is more difficult than the latter: the proof of Theorem 3.9 is based on application of Theorems A.19 and A.20 which rely on identities (A.41) and are very strongly related to the properties of Bessel functions.

3.3.3 Convexity of fixed-probability level

Convexity[19] of the fixed-probability level $u_{\alpha,t\,|\,\delta,\rho}(c)$, $c \geqslant 0$, is readily seen from (see, e.g., Figs. 1.2 and 3.3) numerical illustrations. However, unlike monotony, it has no simple intuitive rationale. We put forth as a conjecture the statement (see Theorem 3.11) about strong-form convexity; this seems quite plausible, but difficult to prove, and it will not be needed in what follows since in the sequel we confine ourselves to asymptotic results, as $t \to \infty$. We formulate and prove by the same methods as in Section 3.3.2 the weak-form convexity theorem. It is based on the following well-known criterion: a twice-differentiable function, whose second derivative is positive on an interval, is convex on this interval.

Theorem 3.11 (Strong-form convexity) *For all $t > 0$, the fixed-probability level $u_{\alpha,t\,|\,\delta,\rho}(c)$, $c \geqslant 0$, is convex.*

Theorem 3.12 (Weak-form convexity) *For $t > 0$ sufficiently large, the fixed-probability level $u_{\alpha,t\,|\,\delta,\rho}(c)$, $c \geqslant 0$, is convex.*

Proof of Theorem 3.12. The beginning of the proof is like the beginning of the proof of convexity Theorem 2.13 for diffusion. By (see Theorem A.4) the theorem on the derivative of implicit function, we have

$$\frac{d^2}{dc^2}\, u_{\alpha,t\,|\,\delta,\rho}(c) = -\left(\frac{\frac{\partial^2}{\partial c^2}\mathsf{P}\{\Upsilon_{u,c\,|\,\delta,\rho} \leqslant t\}}{\frac{\partial}{\partial u}\mathsf{P}\{\Upsilon_{u,c\,|\,\delta,\rho} \leqslant t\}} - \frac{2\,\frac{\partial^2}{\partial u\,\partial c}\mathsf{P}\{\Upsilon_{u,c\,|\,\delta,\rho} \leqslant t\}\frac{\partial}{\partial c}\mathsf{P}\{\Upsilon_{u,c\,|\,\delta,\rho} \leqslant t\}}{\left(\frac{\partial}{\partial u}\mathsf{P}\{\Upsilon_{u,c\,|\,\delta,\rho} \leqslant t\}\right)^2} + \frac{\frac{\partial^2}{\partial u^2}\mathsf{P}\{\Upsilon_{u,c\,|\,\delta,\rho} \leqslant t\}\left(\frac{\partial}{\partial c}\mathsf{P}\{\Upsilon_{u,c\,|\,\delta,\rho} \leqslant t\}\right)^2}{\left(\frac{\partial}{\partial u}\mathsf{P}\{\Upsilon_{u,c\,|\,\delta,\rho} \leqslant t\}\right)^3} \right)\Bigg|_{u=u_{\alpha,t\,|\,\delta,\rho}(c)}. \tag{3.51}$$

In the same way as in (3.49) we find that[20]

$$\frac{\partial^2}{\partial u^2}\mathsf{P}\{\Upsilon_{u,c\,|\,\delta,\rho} \leqslant t\} = \rho^2 F^{(2,0)}_{\delta t}(\rho u \mid p)\,\big|_{p=\delta/(c\rho+\delta)},$$

[19]A convex function is of the form $\smile$.

[20]Plainly, $\frac{d^2}{dc^2}\,(\delta/(c\rho+\delta)) = (2\delta\rho^2)/(c\rho+\delta)^3$.

$$\frac{\partial^2}{\partial c^2}\mathsf{P}\{\varUpsilon_{u,c\,|\,\delta,\rho} \leqslant t\} = \frac{\rho^2}{\delta^2}\big(p^4 F_{\delta t}^{(0,2)}(\rho u \mid p) + 2p^3 F_{\delta t}^{(0,1)}(\rho u \mid p)\big)\big|_{p=\delta/(c\rho+\delta)},$$

$$\frac{\partial^2}{\partial u\,\partial c}\mathsf{P}\{\varUpsilon_{u,c\,|\,\delta,\rho} \leqslant t\} = -\frac{\rho^2}{\delta}(p^2 F_{\delta t}^{(1,1)}(\rho u \mid p))\big|_{p=\delta/(c\rho+\delta)}.$$

This allows us to write the right-hand side in (3.51) in terms of the auxiliary function of the second kind. Note that the investigation of the sign of $\frac{d^2}{dc^2}u_{\alpha,t\,|\,\delta,\rho}(c)$, $c \geqslant 0$, for all t (similar to what was done in the proof of strong-form monotony Theorem 3.9) is very laborious.

Let us show that $\frac{d^2}{dc^2}u_{\alpha,t\,|\,\delta,\rho}(c) > 0$, when $c > c^* = \delta/\rho$. For convenience of notation, we introduce

$$\begin{aligned}
\mathsf{H}_t^{(2,0)}(x \mid p) &= F_t^{(2,0)}(x \mid p),\\
\mathsf{H}_t^{(0,2)}(x \mid p) &= p^4 F_t^{(0,2)}(x \mid p) + 2p^3 F_t^{(0,1)}(x \mid p),\\
\mathsf{H}_t^{(1,1)}(x \mid p) &= p^2 F_t^{(1,1)}(x \mid p),
\end{aligned}$$

and note that

$$\begin{aligned}
\mathsf{H}_t^{(2,0)}(x \mid p) =& e^{-x}\sum_{n=0}^{\infty}\frac{x^n}{n!}\int_0^t (\mathsf{v}_{n+1}(y \mid p) - 2\,\mathsf{v}_{n+2}(y \mid p) + \mathsf{v}_{n+3}(y \mid p))\,dy,\\
\mathsf{H}_t^{(0,2)}(x \mid p) =& e^{-x}\sum_{n=0}^{\infty}\frac{x^n}{n!}\int_0^t y^2\Big(\mathsf{v}_{n+1}(y \mid p) - 2\,\frac{n+1}{n+2}\,\mathsf{v}_{n+2}(y \mid p)\\
&+ \frac{n+1}{n+3}\,\mathsf{v}_{n+3}(y \mid p)\Big)\,dy,\\
\mathsf{H}_t^{(1,1)}(x \mid p) =& -e^{-x}\sum_{n=0}^{\infty}\frac{x^n}{n!}\int_0^t y\,\Big(\Big(\mathsf{v}_{n+1}(y \mid p) - \frac{n+1}{n+2}\,\mathsf{v}_{n+2}(y \mid p)\Big)\\
&- \Big(\mathsf{v}_{n+2}(y \mid p) - \frac{n+2}{n+3}\,\mathsf{v}_{n+3}(y \mid p)\Big)\Big)\,dy.
\end{aligned}$$

Equality (3.51) transforms into

$$\frac{d^2}{dc^2}u_{\alpha,t\,|\,\delta,\rho}(c) = \big(\beth_{\delta t}(\rho u \mid p)\,\big|_{p=\delta/(c\rho+\delta)}\big)\big|_{u=u_{\alpha,t\,|\,\delta,\rho}(c)},$$

where

$$\begin{aligned}
\beth_t(x,p) =& -\frac{\rho}{\delta^2}\Bigg(\frac{\mathsf{H}_t^{(0,2)}(x \mid p)}{\mathsf{H}_t^{(1,0)}(x \mid p)} - 2\mathsf{H}_t^{(1,1)}(x \mid p)\frac{\mathsf{H}_t^{(0,1)}(x \mid p)}{(\mathsf{H}_t^{(1,0)}(x \mid p))^2}\\
&+ \mathsf{H}_t^{(2,0)}(x \mid p)\,\frac{(\mathsf{H}_t^{(0,1)}(x \mid p))^2}{(\mathsf{H}_t^{(1,0)}(x \mid p))^3}\Bigg).
\end{aligned}$$

Using equality (3.12), for $x > 0$ and $0 < p < \frac{1}{2}$ we have

$$\mathcal{F}_{\infty}^{(2,0)}(x \mid p) = \frac{p(q-p)^2}{q^3} \exp\left\{-x\left(1-\frac{p}{q}\right)\right\},$$
$$\mathcal{F}_{\infty}^{(1,1)}(x \mid p) = \frac{qp-(q-p)(q+px)}{q^4} \exp\left\{-x\left(1-\frac{p}{q}\right)\right\},$$
$$\mathcal{F}_{\infty}^{(0,2)}(x \mid p) = \frac{2q^2+2(1+p)qx+px^2}{q^5} \exp\left\{-x\left(1-\frac{p}{q}\right)\right\}$$

and consequently

$$\mathsf{H}_{\infty}^{(2,0)}(x \mid p) = \frac{p\,(p-q)^2}{q^3} \exp\left\{-x\left(1-\frac{p}{q}\right)\right\},$$
$$\mathsf{H}_{\infty}^{(1,1)}(x \mid p) = p^2\left(\frac{qp+(p-q)(q+px)}{q^4}\right) \exp\left\{-x\left(1-\frac{p}{q}\right)\right\},$$
$$\mathsf{H}_{\infty}^{(0,2)}(x \mid p) = p^3\left(\frac{q\,(q+2px)+(q+px)^2}{q^5}\right) \exp\left\{-x\left(1-\frac{p}{q}\right)\right\}.$$

Straightforward calculations finally yield

$$\begin{aligned}\beth_{\infty}(x,p) = &-\frac{\rho}{\delta^2}\left(\frac{\mathsf{H}_{\infty}^{(0,2)}(x \mid p)}{\mathsf{H}_{\infty}^{(1,0)}(x \mid p)} - 2\mathsf{H}_{\infty}^{(1,1)}(x \mid p)\frac{\mathsf{H}_{\infty}^{(0,1)}(x \mid p)}{(\mathsf{H}_{t}^{(1,0)}(x \mid p))^2}\right.\\ &\left.+\mathsf{H}_{\infty}^{(2,0)}(x \mid p)\,\frac{(\mathsf{H}_{t}^{(0,1)}(x \mid p))^2}{(\mathsf{H}_{\infty}^{(1,0)}(x \mid p))^3}\right) = \frac{\rho p^2(1+2px)}{\delta^2 q(q-p)^2} > 0,\end{aligned}$$

and $\beth_t(x,p) = \beth_{\infty}(x,p)\,(1+o(1))$, $t \to \infty$.

The proof in the case $0 \leqslant c < c^* = \delta/\rho$ is left to the reader. □

3.4 Asymptotic Behavior of Fixed-probability Level

Theorems 3.6–3.8 shed light on the structure of the fixed-probability level $u_{\alpha,t\,|\,\delta,\rho}(c)$, $c \geqslant 0$, which is a solution to the non-linear equation (see (3.37)) $\mathcal{F}_{\delta t}(\rho u \mid \delta/(c\rho+\delta)) = \alpha$. However, we still did not find a closed-form expression for $u_{\alpha,t\,|\,\delta,\rho}(c)$, $c \geqslant 0$, because $\mathsf{z}_{\alpha,t}(y)$, $y \in \mathsf{R}$, cannot be expressed in closed form. It seems that there is no such representation in a closed and relatively simple form.

Seeking for more explicit representation of $u_{\alpha,t\,|\,\delta,\rho}(c)$, we resort to its asymptotic analysis, as $t \to \infty$. First, we focus on $0 \leqslant c < Kc^*$, $0 < K < 1$, then on $c > Kc^*$, where $K > 1$, and finally on the $t^{-1/2}$-neighborhoods of the equilibrium price c^*.

Theorem 3.13 *For $0 \leqslant c < Kc^*$, $0 < K < 1$, the fixed-probability level has the following asymptotic representation:*

$$u_{\alpha,t\,|\,\delta,\rho}(c) = (\delta/\rho - c)\,t + \frac{\sqrt{2\,(\delta - c\rho)}}{\rho}\,\kappa_\alpha \sqrt{t}\,(1 + o(1)), \quad t \to \infty. \tag{3.52}$$

Proof. In the same way as in the first proof of Theorem 3.6, this proof consists of two steps. The first step is to check that for

$$\tilde{u}_{\alpha,t}(c) := (\delta/\rho - c)\,t + \frac{\sqrt{2\,(\delta - c\rho)}}{\rho}\,\kappa_\alpha \sqrt{t},$$

we have $\mathsf{P}\{\varUpsilon_{u,c\,|\,\delta,\rho} \leqslant t\}\,\big|_{u=\tilde{u}_{\alpha,t}(c)} = \alpha\,(1 + o(1))$, $t \to \infty$, or (see (3.14))

$$\mathcal{F}_{\delta t}(u\,\rho \mid \delta/(\delta + c\rho))\big|_{u=\tilde{u}_{\alpha,t}(c)} = \alpha\,(1 + o(1)), \quad t \to \infty. \tag{3.53}$$

Bearing in mind that $\mathcal{F}_\infty(u\,\rho \mid \delta/(\delta{+}c\rho)) = 1$, equality (3.53) may be rewritten as

$$\begin{aligned} \mathsf{P}\{\varUpsilon_{u,c\,|\,\delta,\rho} \leqslant t\}\big|_{u=\tilde{u}_{\alpha,t}(c)} &= 1 - e^{-\rho\tilde{u}_{\alpha,t}(c)}\delta \int_t^\infty e^{-(\delta+c\rho)x} \\ &\times \Big(I_0(2\sqrt{\delta\rho x\,(cx + \tilde{u}_{\alpha,t}(c))}\,) \\ &- \frac{cx}{cx + \tilde{u}_{\alpha,t}(c)}\,I_2(2\sqrt{\delta\rho x\,(cx + \tilde{u}_{\alpha,t}(c))}\,)\Big)\,dx, \end{aligned} \tag{3.54}$$

whence[21]

$$\begin{aligned} \mathsf{P}\{\varUpsilon_{u,c\,|\,\delta,\rho} \leqslant t\}\big|_{u=\tilde{u}_{\alpha,t}(c)} &\sim 1 - \frac{\delta}{\sqrt{2\pi}} \int_t^\infty \frac{\tilde{u}_{\alpha,t}(c)}{cx + \tilde{u}_{\alpha,t}(c)} \\ &\times \frac{e^{-(\delta+c\rho)x}e^{-\rho\tilde{u}_{\alpha,t}(c)}e^{2\sqrt{\delta\rho x\,(cx+\tilde{u}_{\alpha,t}(c))}}}{(2\sqrt{\delta\rho x\,(cx + \tilde{u}_{\alpha,t}(c))}\,)^{1/2}}\,dx. \end{aligned} \tag{3.55}$$

By elementary calculations, we have the identity

$$\begin{aligned} &\frac{1}{\sqrt{2\pi}}\,e^{-(\delta+c\rho)x}e^{-\rho\tilde{u}_{\alpha,t}(c)}e^{2\sqrt{\delta\rho x\,(cx+\tilde{u}_{\alpha,t}(c))}} \\ &\quad = \varphi_{(0,1)}\,(\sqrt{2\,(\delta - c\rho)\,x} - \sqrt{2\rho\,\tilde{u}_{\alpha,t}(c)}\,) \\ &\quad\quad \times \exp\{-2\sqrt{x\rho}\,(\sqrt{(\delta - c\rho)\,\tilde{u}_{\alpha,t}(c)} - \sqrt{\delta\,(cx + \tilde{u}_{\alpha,t}(c)) + c\sqrt{x\rho}}\,)\}, \end{aligned}$$

[21] Recall that $I_m(a\sqrt{x}\,) \sim \frac{e^{a\sqrt{x}}}{\sqrt{2\pi}\,(a\sqrt{x})^{1/2}}\left(1 + \sum_{k=1}^\infty \frac{(-1)^k}{(2a\sqrt{x})^k}\frac{1}{k!}\frac{\Gamma(m+k+1/2)}{\Gamma(m-k+1/2)}\right)$, $x \to \infty$.

and note that[22]

$$
\begin{aligned}
&\sqrt{2(\delta - c\rho)\,t} - \sqrt{2\rho\tilde{u}_{\alpha,t}(c)} \\
&\quad = \sqrt{2(\delta - c\rho)\,t} - \sqrt{2(\delta - c\rho)\,t + 2\sqrt{2\,(\delta - c\rho)}\,\kappa_\alpha\sqrt{t}} \\
&\quad = \sqrt{2(\delta - c\rho)\,t}\left(1 - \sqrt{1 + \frac{\sqrt{2\,(\delta - c\rho)}\,\kappa_\alpha\sqrt{t}}{(\delta - c\rho)t}}\right) \\
&\quad \sim -\sqrt{2(\delta - c\rho)\,t}\,\frac{\sqrt{2\,(\delta - c\rho)}\,\kappa_\alpha\sqrt{t}}{2(\delta - c\rho)\,t} = -\kappa_\alpha.
\end{aligned}
$$

Making the change of variables

$$
\xi := \sqrt{2(\delta - c\rho)x} - \sqrt{2\rho\tilde{u}_{\alpha,t}(c)}
$$

and bearing in mind that

$$
x = \frac{(\xi + \sqrt{2\rho\tilde{u}_{\alpha,t}(c)}\,)^2}{2\,(\delta - c\rho)}, \qquad dx = \frac{\xi + \sqrt{2\rho\tilde{u}_{\alpha,t}(c)}}{\delta - c\rho}\,d\xi,
$$

we obtain

$$
\begin{aligned}
&\mathsf{P}\{\Upsilon_{u,c\,|\,\delta,\rho} \leqslant t\}\,\Big|_{u=\tilde{u}_{\alpha,t}(c)} \\
&\quad \sim 1 - \frac{\delta}{(\delta - c\rho)^{1/2}(\delta\rho)^{1/4}} \int_{\sqrt{2(\delta-c\rho)t}-\sqrt{2\rho\tilde{u}_{\alpha,t}(c)}}^{\infty} \varphi_{(0,1)}(\xi) \\
&\quad \times \exp\left\{ - 2\sqrt{x\rho}\left(\sqrt{(\delta - c\rho)\tilde{u}_{\alpha,t}(c)}\right.\right. \\
&\qquad\qquad \left.\left. - \sqrt{\delta\,(cx + \tilde{u}_{\alpha,t}(c)) + c\sqrt{x\rho}}\right)\right\}\Bigg|_{x=\frac{(\xi+\sqrt{2\rho\tilde{u}_{\alpha,t}(c)}\,)^2}{2(\delta-c\rho)}} \\
&\quad \times \left.\frac{x^{1/4}\tilde{u}_{\alpha,t}(c)}{(cx + \tilde{u}_{\alpha,t}(c))^{5/4}}\right|_{x=\frac{(\xi+\sqrt{2\rho\tilde{u}_{\alpha,t}(c)}\,)^2}{2(\delta-c\rho)}} d\xi,
\end{aligned}
$$

where the exponent is

$$
\begin{aligned}
&\exp\left\{ - 2\sqrt{x\rho}\left(\sqrt{(\delta - c\rho)\,\tilde{u}_{\alpha,t}(c)}\right.\right. \\
&\qquad\qquad \left.\left. - \sqrt{\delta\,(cx + \tilde{u}_{\alpha,t}(c)) + c\sqrt{x\rho}}\right)\right\}\Bigg|_{x=\frac{(z+\sqrt{2\,\rho\tilde{u}_{\alpha,t}(c)}\,)^2}{2\,(\delta-c\rho)}} \\
&= \exp\left\{ - \frac{\sqrt{2\,\rho}}{\sqrt{\delta - c\rho}}\left(z + \sqrt{2\,\rho\tilde{u}_{\alpha,t}(c)}\right)\left(\sqrt{(\delta - c\rho)\tilde{u}_{\alpha,t}(c)}\right.\right. \\
&\left.\left. - \sqrt{\delta\left(c\,\frac{(z + \sqrt{2\,\rho\tilde{u}_{\alpha,t}(c)}\,)^2}{2\,(\delta - c\rho)} + \tilde{u}_{\alpha,t}(c)\right) + c\sqrt{\frac{(z + \sqrt{2\,\rho\tilde{u}_{\alpha,t}(c)}\,)^2}{2\,(\delta - c\rho)}\rho}}\right)\right\}
\end{aligned}
$$

[22]We use $1 - \sqrt{1 + x} \sim -x/2$, $x \to 0$.

$$\sim \exp\Bigg\{ -\frac{\sqrt{2\,\rho}}{\sqrt{\delta - c\rho}}\big(z + \sqrt{2\,(\delta - c\rho)\,t}\,\big)\Big((\delta - c\rho)\sqrt{\frac{t}{\rho}}$$

$$- \sqrt{\delta c}\sqrt{\frac{(z + \sqrt{2\,(\delta - c\rho)\,t}\,)^2}{2\,(\delta - c\rho)} + \frac{\delta - c\rho}{c\rho}\,t} + c\sqrt{\rho}\sqrt{\frac{(z + \sqrt{2\,(\delta - c\rho)\,t}\,)^2}{2\,(\delta - c\rho)}}\,\Big)\Bigg\}.$$

The proof is easy to complete. □

Theorem 3.14 *For $c > Kc^*$, $K > 1$, we have*

$$u_{\alpha,t\,|\,\delta,\rho}(c) = \max\left\{0, -\frac{\ln(\alpha c\rho/\delta)}{\rho - \delta/c}\right\}(1 + o(1)), \quad t \to \infty. \tag{3.56}$$

Proof. Using (3.7), the left-hand side of equation (3.37), where u is substituted by $u_{\alpha,t\,|\,\delta,\rho}(c)$, is

$$e^{-\rho u}\frac{\sqrt{\delta}}{\sqrt{c\rho}}\int_0^{c\rho t} e^{-(1+\delta/(c\rho))x}$$
$$\times \sum_{n=0}^{\infty}\frac{u^n}{n!}\left(\frac{\delta\rho}{c}\right)^{n/2}\frac{n+1}{x}\,I_{n+1}(2x\sqrt{\delta/(c\rho)}\,)\,dx\,\Big|_{u=u_{\alpha,t\,|\,\delta,\rho}(c)}$$
$$\sim e^{-\rho u}\frac{\sqrt{\delta}}{\sqrt{c\rho}}\int_0^{\infty} e^{-(1+\delta/(c\rho))x}$$
$$\times \sum_{n=0}^{\infty}\frac{u^n}{n!}\left(\frac{\delta\rho}{c}\right)^{n/2}\frac{n+1}{x}\,I_{n+1}(2x\sqrt{\delta/(c\rho)}\,)\,dx\,\Big|_{u=u_{\alpha,t\,|\,\delta,\rho}(c)}.$$

Changing the order of integration and summation, which is allowed, and using equality (A.17), the latter expression turns into $(\delta/(c\rho))\exp\{-u_{\alpha,t\,|\,\delta,\rho}(c)(\rho - \delta/c)\,\}$, whence the result. □

The investigation of $u_{\alpha,t\,|\,\delta,\rho}(c)$, when c lies in the right (left) $t^{-1/2}$-neighborhood of the equilibrium price c^*, which allows both approaches to the proof, is left to the reader. We will return to this matter in a more general setting, consistently using the inverse Gaussian approximation, in Chapter 5.

3.5 Primary Upper Bounds on Fixed-probability Level

We call primary upper bounds the bounds in the regions $0 \leqslant c \leqslant c^*$ and $c > c^*$, the former obtained from (3.36), the latter obtained by considering the equation $\mathsf{P}\{\varUpsilon_{u,c\,|\,\delta,\rho} < \infty\} = \alpha$. The bounds for $c > c^*$ require further processing, as they are unsatisfactory to the right near the point c^*. This will be done in Section 3.6.

Bound, when $0 \leqslant c \leqslant c^*$. For brevity, let us put (see (3.32)) $u^*_{\alpha,t} := u_{\alpha,t\,|\,\delta,\rho}(c^*) = \frac{\sqrt{2\delta}}{\rho}\,\kappa_{\alpha/2}\sqrt{t}\,(1+o(1))$, $t \to \infty$. Straightforwardly from Theorem 3.8, we have the two-sided asymptotic bound

$$(\delta/\rho - c)\,t + \frac{\kappa_\alpha}{\kappa_{\alpha/2}} u^*_{\alpha,t} \leqslant u_{\alpha,t\,|\,\delta,\rho}(c) \leqslant (\delta/\rho - c)\,t + u^*_{\alpha,t}, \tag{3.57}$$

valid for t sufficiently large. The asymptotic (as $t \to \infty$) behavior of $u_{\alpha,t\,|\,\delta,\rho}(c)$, $0 \leqslant c \leqslant c^*$, is investigated in Theorems 3.6, 3.7, and 3.13.

Bound, when $c > c^*$. The inequality $\mathsf{P}\{\varUpsilon_{u,c\,|\,\delta,\rho} \leqslant t\} \leqslant \mathsf{P}\{\varUpsilon_{u,c\,|\,\delta,\rho} < \infty\}$ with the right-hand side

$$\mathsf{P}\{\varUpsilon_{u,c\,|\,\delta,\rho} < \infty\} = \begin{cases} 1, & 0 \leqslant c \leqslant c^*, \\ (\delta/(c\rho))\,\exp\{-\rho\,(1 - \delta/(c\rho))\,u\}, & c > c^*, \end{cases} \tag{3.58}$$

straightforward from (3.9) (see also Section 3.2.4), holds for all c, u, and t positive, where $c^* := \delta/\rho$ is the equilibrium price. Therefore, the positive solution $u_{\alpha\,|\,\delta,\rho}(c)$ to the equation

$$\mathsf{P}\{\varUpsilon_{u,c\,|\,\delta,\rho} < \infty\} = \alpha, \tag{3.59}$$

when it exists, is the upper bound for $u_{\alpha,t\,|\,\delta,\rho}(c)$.

Plainly, this solution does not exist for $0 \leqslant c \leqslant c^*$ because the left-hand side of (3.59) is identically equal to 1, and cannot be equal to $0 < \alpha < 1$. When $c > c^*$, the solution to equation (3.59) is easy to find, but it is positive only for[23] $c < \delta/(\alpha\rho)$; setting it equal to zero, when $c \geqslant \delta/(\alpha\rho)$, we get

$$u_{\alpha,t\,|\,\delta,\rho}(c) \leqslant u_{\alpha\,|\,\delta,\rho}(c) = \max\left\{0, -\frac{\ln(\alpha c\rho/\delta)}{\rho - \delta/c}\right\}, \quad c > c^*. \tag{3.60}$$

Numerically calculated $u_{\alpha,t\,|\,\delta,\rho}(c)$ and its upper bound $u_{\alpha\,|\,\delta,\rho}(c)$, $c > c^*$, are shown in Fig. 3.3. The bound (3.60), valid for all $t > 0$, is rather accurate, when c far exceeds c^*, but very poor, when c is equal to c^*, or only a little larger than c^*. In particular, whereas (see (3.32)) $u_{\alpha,t\,|\,\delta,\rho}(c^*)$ is approximated by $\frac{\sqrt{2\delta}}{\rho}\,\kappa_{\alpha/2}\sqrt{t}$, as $t \to \infty$, $u_{\alpha\,|\,\delta,\rho}(c^*)$ is infinite.

Remark 3.7 Note that, despite similarity of the right-hand sides, the equalities in (3.60) and (3.56) are fundamentally different. The former yields an upper bound valid for all $t > 0$, when $c > c^*$, whereas the latter is an asymptotic equality valid for $t \to \infty$, when $c > Kc^*$, $K > 1$.

A coarser, but structurally simpler, is the upper bound $\bar{u}_{\alpha\,|\,\delta,\rho}(c)$ which comes in the same way from the inequality

$$\mathsf{P}\{\varUpsilon_{u,c\,|\,\delta,\rho} < \infty\} \leqslant \exp\{-u(c\rho - \delta)/c\}, \quad c > c^*, \tag{3.61}$$

[23] The value $\delta/(\alpha\rho)$ is a solution to the equation (w.r.t. c) $\mathsf{P}\{\varUpsilon_{0,c\,|\,\delta,\rho} < \infty\} = \alpha$.

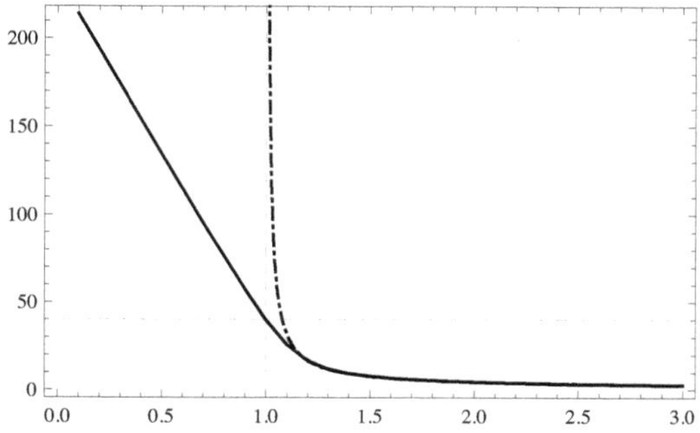

FIGURE 3.3: Graphs (X-axis is c) of $u_{\alpha,t\,|\,\delta,\rho}(c)$ (solid line) and $u_{\alpha\,|\,\delta,\rho}(c)$ (dash-dotted line), evaluated numerically, when $\delta = 1$, $\rho = 1$, $\alpha = 0.05$, and $t = 200$. Horizontal grid line: $u_{\alpha,t\,|\,\delta,\rho}(c^*) = 40.08$. Vertical grid line: $c^* = 1$.

which is straightforward from (3.58); it is noteworthy that this inequality is a special case of the celebrated Lundberg's inequality. The upper bound $\bar{u}_{\alpha\,|\,\delta,\rho}(c)$ is defined as a positive solution to the equation

$$\exp\{-u(c\rho - \delta)/c\} = \alpha.$$

Plainly,

$$u_{\alpha,t\,|\,\delta,\rho}(c) \leqslant u_{\alpha\,|\,\delta,\rho}(c) \leqslant \bar{u}_{\alpha\,|\,\delta,\rho}(c) = -\frac{\ln \alpha}{\rho - \delta/c}, \quad c > c^*. \tag{3.62}$$

Remark 3.8 The upper bound (3.60) and the coarser upper bound (3.62), evaluated numerically, are shown in Fig. 3.5. From the standpoint of mathematics, they are very different, and the latter can be seen too coarsened. However, from the standpoint of application to economics, this latter bound has significant advantages. First, the numerator in (3.62) is simpler, not including the variable c. Second, it monotone decreases to the value $-\ln \alpha/\rho > 0$, as c increases to infinity. Bearing in mind that $u_{\alpha,t\,|\,\delta,\rho}(c)$ models the non-ruin capital, or a solvency reserve, it is more natural to establish a nonzero flat lower bound for it, rather than to let it be null.

3.6 Elaborated Upper Bounds on Fixed-probability Level

We strive to find asymptotic bounds[24], valid for $t \to \infty$, on the fixed-probability level $u_{\alpha,t\,|\,\delta,\rho}(c)$, which are

[24]Because to find such bounds valid for all $t > 0$ seems impossible.

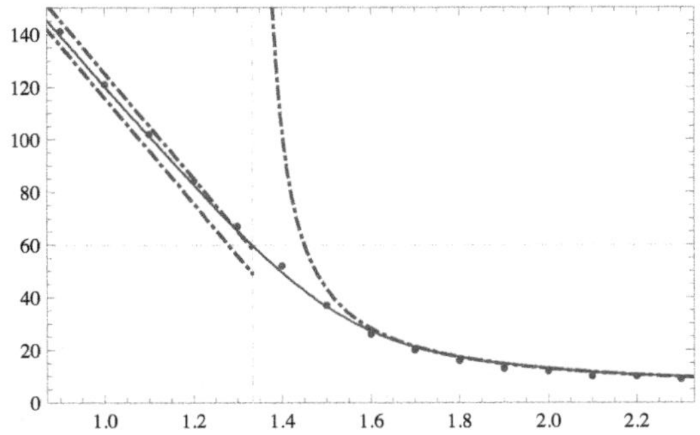

FIGURE 3.4: Graphs (X-axis is c) of two-sided bounds (3.57), when $0 < c < c^*$, upper bound (3.60), when $c > c^*$ (dash-dotted lines), exact values, evaluated numerically (solid line), and simulated values of $u_{\alpha,t\,|\,\delta,\rho}(c)$ (dots), when $\delta = 3/5$, $\rho = 4/5$, $\alpha = 0.05$, and $t = 200$. Vertical grid line: $c^* = 4/3$. Horizontal grid line: $u_{\alpha,t\,|\,\delta,\rho}(c^*) = 59.90$.

- computable, in contrast to the asymptotic equality (3.36), where the function $\mathsf{z}_{\alpha,t}(y)$, $y \in \mathsf{R}$, remains unwritten in a closed form,
- expressed in terms of elementary functions, in contrast to, e.g., sophisticated formulas (3.6)–(3.8) written in terms of Bessel functions or integrals,
- accurate over the entire range of $c \geqslant 0$, in particular in the vicinity of the equilibrium price $c^* := \delta/\rho$.

While the asymptotic bound (3.57) is quite satisfactory for all $0 \leqslant c \leqslant c^*$, the bounds (3.60) and (3.62), which hold for all $t > 0$, are not satisfactory, when c is to the right of c^*, close to c^*. In the same time, the bounds (3.60) and (3.62) are rather accurate[25], when $c > Kc^*$, $K > 1$ (see Figs. 3.3 and 3.5).

Further in this section, we will seek upper bounds for the fixed-probability level $u_{\alpha,t\,|\,\delta,\rho}(c)$, satisfactory over the entire range of $c \geqslant 0$.

3.6.1 Bounds based on monotony

The idea of bounds based on the monotony of $u_{\alpha,t\,|\,\delta,\rho}(c)$ is exactly the same as the idea used in Section 2.6.1. The gap, when c is to the right of c^* and close to c^*, is filled by a straight horizontal line drawn at the level (see (3.32)) $u_{\alpha,t\,|\,\delta,\rho}(c^*) = \frac{\sqrt{2\,\delta}}{\rho}\,\kappa_{\alpha/2}\sqrt{t}\,(1 + o(1))$, as t is large, up to the point of intersection with $u_{\alpha\,|\,\delta,\rho}(c)$ (see (3.60)), or with $\bar{u}_{\alpha\,|\,\delta,\rho}(c)$ (see (3.62)). Such a bound looks exactly the same as in Fig. 2.4, and we leave the details to the reader.

[25]This follows from Theorem 3.14: in this region $u_{\alpha,t\,|\,\delta,\rho}(c)$ tends to $u_{\alpha\,|\,\delta,\rho}(c)$, as $t \to \infty$.

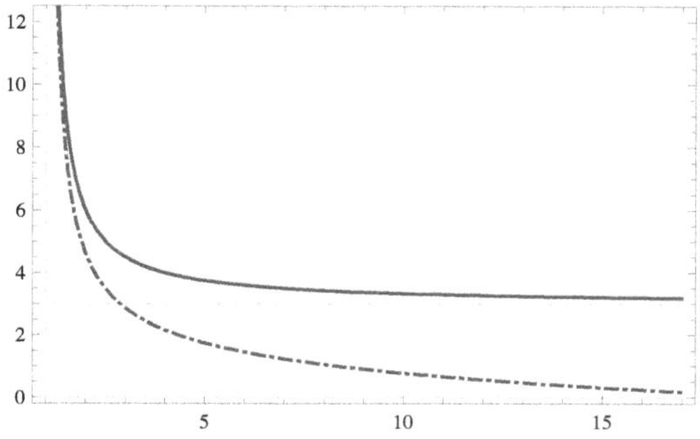

FIGURE 3.5: Graphs (X-axis is c) of upper bound $u_{\alpha\,|\,\delta,\rho}(c)$ (dash-dotted line) and coarse upper bound $\bar{u}_{\alpha\,|\,\delta,\rho}(c)$ (solid line), when $\delta = \rho = 1$, $\alpha = 0.05$. Vertical grid line: $c^* = 1$. Horizontal grid line: $-\ln\alpha/\rho = 3.00$

3.6.2 Bounds based on convexity

The idea of the bounds based on convexity of $u_{\alpha,t\,|\,\delta,\rho}(c)$ is largely the same as the idea used in Section 2.6.2. Note that while in Section 2.6.2 we relied on convexity of $u^{[\mathrm{dif}]}_{\alpha,t\,|\,\vartheta}(c)$ proved for all $t > 0$, in this section we can only use the weak-form convexity of $u_{\alpha,t\,|\,\delta,\rho}(c)$, proved in Theorem 3.12 for t large[26].

In conclusion, we give two examples of such bounds. First is a broken-line bound, second is a bound that uses tangency. The former is a coarse bound, whose construction requires significantly less effort than the construction of the latter one. The latter bound is more refined, and is similar to the bound of Section 2.6.2.

Broken-line bound. Let us construct elementary bounds on $u_{\alpha,t\,|\,\delta,\rho}(c)$ in the region $c > c^*$. In the same way as in Section 2.6.1, we will rely on the shape of this function; recall that by Theorem 3.10 the function $u_{\alpha,t\,|\,\delta,\rho}(c)$, $c \geqslant 0$, monotone decreases, as c increases, for $t > 0$ sufficiently large[27], and by Theorem 3.12 the function $u_{\alpha,t\,|\,\delta,\rho}(c)$, $c \geqslant 0$, is convex, for $t > 0$ sufficiently large.

Describing the adjustment procedure verbally, we start with the upper bounds (3.60) and (3.62) and chose some $\tilde{c} > c^*$, far enough to the right of the equilibrium price c^*, for which calculation of $u_{\alpha\,|\,\delta,\rho}(\tilde{c})$ is simple, and focus on the line segment between the points $(c^*, u_{\alpha,t\,|\,\delta,\rho}(c^*))$ and $(\tilde{c}, u_{\alpha,t\,|\,\delta,\rho}(\tilde{c}))$. Since $u_{\alpha,t\,|\,\delta,\rho}(c)$ is convex, its graph lies below this line segment for all $c^* < c < \tilde{c}$, and therefore (since $u_{\alpha,t\,|\,\delta,\rho}(\tilde{c}) < u_{\alpha\,|\,\delta,\rho}(\tilde{c})$) below the line segment between

---

[26]This is called "weak-form convexity". The "strong-form convexity", formulated as a conjecture in Theorem 3.11, has not been proven. Even if this is true, its proof is laborious and hardly justifies the effort.

[27]By Theorem 3.9, the function $u_{\alpha,t\,|\,\delta,\rho}(c)$, $c \geqslant 0$, monotone decreases, as c increases, for all $t > 0$.

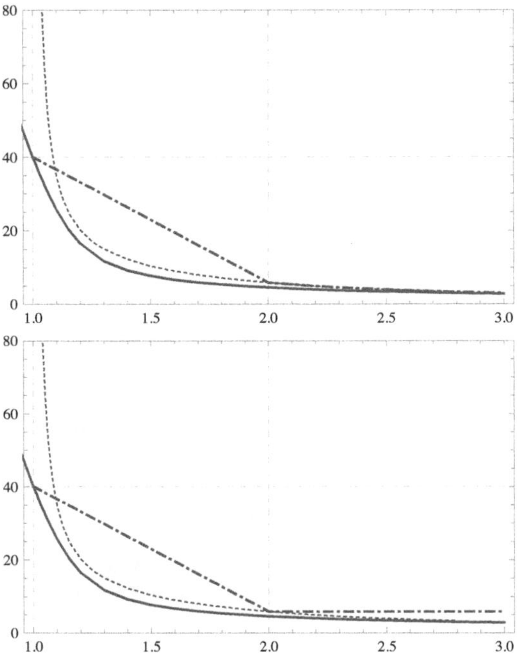

FIGURE 3.6: Graphs (X-axis is c) of $u_{\alpha,t\,|\,\delta,\rho}(c)$, evaluated numerically (solid line), infinite-time bound $u_{\alpha\,|\,\delta,\rho}(c)$ (dashed line), and broken-line bounds (dash-dotted lines) of Theorem 3.15 (above) and Theorem 3.16 (below), when $\delta = 1$, $\rho = 1$, $\alpha = 0.05$, $t = 200$. Vertical grid lines: $c^* = 1$, and $2c^* = 2$, which is break point. Horizontal grid line: $u^*_{\alpha,t} = 40.08$.

the points $(c^*, u_{\alpha,t\,|\,\delta,\rho}(c^*))$ and $(\tilde{c}, u_{\alpha\,|\,\delta,\rho}(\tilde{c}))$. When $c > \tilde{c}$, we extend this latter line segment either by the function $u_{\alpha\,|\,\delta,\rho}(c)$, $c > \hat{c}$, or by the constant $u_{\alpha\,|\,\delta,\rho}(\hat{c})$.

If we consider $\hat{c}$ as a solution to the equation

$$u^*_{\alpha,t} = -\frac{\ln(\alpha c\rho/\delta)}{\rho - \delta/c},$$

then there is no explicit expression for it.

To be specific, in the following Theorems 3.15 and 3.16 we choose the auxiliary point $\tilde{c}$ equal to $2c^*$. The bound of Theorem 3.15 is illustrated by the upper graph of Fig. 3.6.

Theorem 3.15 *For $t > 0$ sufficiently large, for $0 < c \leqslant c^* = \delta/\rho$ we have*

$$(\delta/\rho - c)\,t + \frac{\kappa_\alpha}{\kappa_{\alpha/2}} u^*_{\alpha,t} \leqslant u_{\alpha,t\,|\,\delta,\rho}(c) \leqslant (\delta/\rho - c)\,t + u^*_{\alpha,t},$$

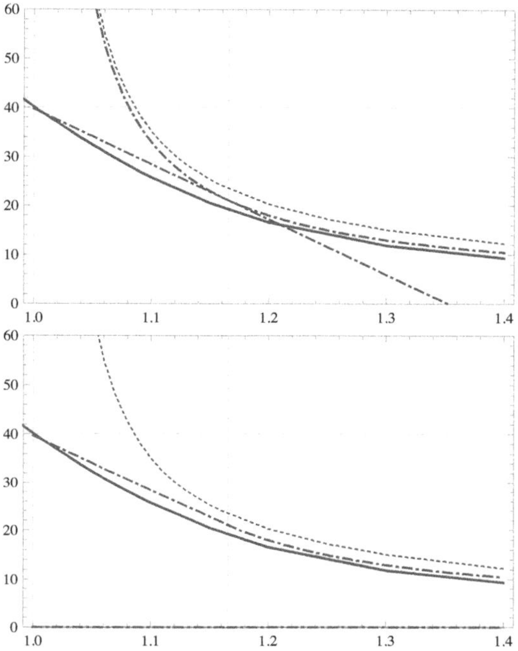

FIGURE 3.7: Graphs (X-axis is c) of $u_{\alpha,t\,|\,\delta,\rho}(c)$, evaluated numerically (solid line), coarse upper bound $\bar{u}_{\alpha\,|\,\delta,\rho}(c)$ (dashed line), and bound of Theorem 3.18 (dash-dotted line), when $\delta = 1$, $\rho = 1$, $\alpha = 0.05$, and $t = 200$. Vertical grid lines: $c^* = 1$, and 1.16, which is point of tangency. Horizontal grid line: $u_{\alpha,t\,|\,\delta,\rho}(c^*) = 40.08$.

and, when $c > c^*$, we have

$$u_{\alpha,t\,|\,\delta,\rho}(c) \leqslant \begin{cases} -\left(u^*_{\alpha,t} + \dfrac{\ln(2\,\alpha c^* \rho/\delta)}{\rho - \delta/(2\,c^*)}\right)c \\ \qquad + \left(2\,u^*_{\alpha,t} + \dfrac{\ln(2\,\alpha c^* \rho/\delta)}{\rho - \delta/(2\,c^*)}\right), & c^* < c < 2\,c^*, \\ \max\left\{0, -\dfrac{\ln(\alpha c \rho/\delta)}{\rho - \delta/c}\right\}, & c > 2\,c^*. \end{cases}$$

If we consider $\hat{c}$ as a solution to the equation

$$u^*_{\alpha,t} = -\frac{\ln\alpha}{\rho - \delta/c},$$

then the explicit expression for it is

$$\hat{c} = c^*\left(1 - \frac{\ln\alpha}{\rho u^*_{\alpha,t} + \ln\alpha}\right).$$

The bound of Theorem 3.16 is illustrated by the lower graph of Fig. 3.6. We say is again that the unique difference between the bounds in Theorem 3.15 and Theorem 3.16 is that, when $c > \tilde{c} := 2c^*$, the latter is horizontal.

Theorem 3.16 *For $t > 0$ sufficiently large, for $0 < c \leqslant c^*$ we have*

$$(\delta/\rho - c)\,t + \frac{\kappa_\alpha}{\kappa_{\alpha/2}} u^*_{\alpha,t} \leqslant u_{\alpha,t\,|\,\delta,\rho}(c) \leqslant (\delta/\rho - c)\,t + u^*_{\alpha,t},$$

and, when $c > c^*$, we have

$$u_{\alpha,t\,|\,\delta,\rho}(c) \leqslant \begin{cases} -\left(u^*_{\alpha,t} + \dfrac{\ln(2\,\alpha\, c^* \rho/\delta)}{\rho - \delta/(2\,c^*)}\right)c \\ \qquad\qquad +\left(2\,u^*_{\alpha,t} + \dfrac{\ln(2\,\alpha\, c^* \rho/\delta)}{\rho - \delta/(2\,c^*)}\right), & c^* < c < 2\,c^*, \\ -\dfrac{\ln(2\,\alpha\, c^* \rho/\delta)}{\rho - \delta/(2\,c^*)}, & c > 2\,c^*. \end{cases}$$

Proof of Theorems 3.15 and 3.16. The proof, when $c > c^*$, is straightforward from the obvious inequality $u_{\alpha,t\,|\,\delta,\rho}(c) \leqslant u_{\alpha\,|\,\delta,\rho}(c)$, from the weak-form (i.e., for t sufficiently large) convexity of the function $u_{\alpha,t\,|\,\delta,\rho}(c)$ proved in Theorem 3.12, and from convexity of the function $u_{\alpha\,|\,\delta,\rho}(c)$, which is straightforward. This proof is illustrated in Fig. 3.6.

On the X-axis, we take the point c^*, which is the equilibrium price, and (rather arbitrary) the point $2c^*$. On the Y-axis, we take respectively the values $u_{\alpha,t\,|\,\delta,\rho}(c^*)$ and $u_{\alpha\,|\,\delta,\rho}(2c^*)$. The segment of a slopped straight line passing through the points $(c^*, u_{\alpha,t\,|\,\delta,\rho}(c^*))$ and $(2c^*, u_{\alpha\,|\,\delta,\rho}(2c^*))$ obviously lies above the function $u_{\alpha,t\,|\,\delta,\rho}(c)$, $c \in [c^*, 2c^*]$.

To complete the proof of Theorem 3.15, we extend the bound, when $c > 2c^*$, by $u_{\alpha\,|\,\delta,\rho}(c) = -\ln(\alpha c \rho/\delta)/(\rho - \delta/c)$. To complete the proof of Theorem 3.16, we use instead the line $u_{\alpha\,|\,\delta,\rho}(2c^*) = -\ln(2\alpha c^* \rho/\delta)/(\rho - \delta/(2c^*))$, which is horizontal. □

Bound that uses tangency. The following bounds on $u_{\alpha,t\,|\,\delta,\rho}(c)$, $c \geqslant 0$, are based on the idea of Theorem 2.24, whence comes the name "bound that uses tangency".

Starting from the point with coordinates $(c^*, u_{\alpha,t\,|\,\delta,\rho}(c^*))$, we draw a line tangent to the graph of the function $u_{\alpha\,|\,\delta,\rho}(c)$, $c > c^*$, which is convex. Everywhere for $c^* < c < C$, where C is the point of tangency, this line lies above the graph of $u_{\alpha,t\,|\,\delta,\rho}(c)$, $c^* < c < C$. When $c > C$, we extend this straight line either by the function $u_{\alpha\,|\,\delta,\rho}(c)$, or by the constant $u_{\alpha\,|\,\delta,\rho}(C)$.

Theorem 3.17 *For $t > 0$ sufficiently large, we have*

$$(\delta/\rho - c)\,t + \frac{\kappa_\alpha}{\kappa_{\alpha/2}} u^*_{\alpha,t} \leqslant u_{\alpha,t\,|\,\delta,\rho}(c) \leqslant (\delta/\rho - c)\,t + u^*_{\alpha,t}, \quad 0 < c \leqslant c^*,$$

and

$$u_{\alpha,t\,|\,\delta,\rho}(c) \leqslant \begin{cases} \dfrac{\delta - \rho c^*_{\alpha,t} + \delta \ln(\alpha c^*_{\alpha,t}\rho/\delta)}{(\delta - \rho c^*_{\alpha,t})^2}(c - c^*_{\alpha,t}) \\ \qquad\qquad + \dfrac{c^*_{\alpha,t} \ln(\alpha c^*_{\alpha,t}\rho/\delta)}{\delta - \rho c^*_{\alpha,t}}, & c^* < c \leqslant c^*_{\alpha,t}, \\ \max\left\{0, -\dfrac{\ln(\alpha c\rho/\delta)}{\rho - \delta/c}\right\}, & c > c^*_{\alpha,t}, \end{cases}$$

where $c^*_{\alpha,t} = c^*_{\alpha,t}(\delta, \rho)$ *is a solution (w.r.t. c) to the non-linear equation*

$$\frac{\delta + c\rho}{\delta - c\rho} \ln\left(\alpha\,\frac{c\rho}{\delta}\right) = \rho u^*_{\alpha,t} - 1. \tag{3.63}$$

Proof. Recall that $c^* := \delta/\rho$. By Theorem A.1, the straight line passing through the point with abscissa (X-axis) c^* and ordinate (Y-axis) $u^*_{\alpha,t}$, and tangent to the function $f(c)$, $c > c^*$, is

$$l(c) = \frac{f(c^*_{\alpha,t}) - u^*_{\alpha,t}}{c^*_{\alpha,t} - c^*}(c - c^*) + u^*_{\alpha,t}, \quad c > c^*, \tag{3.64}$$

where $c^*_{\alpha,t}$ is a solution to the equation (w.r.t. x)

$$f(x) = f'(x)(x - c^*) + u^*_{\alpha,t}. \tag{3.65}$$

Let us apply this observation to the function

$$f(c) = -\frac{c \ln(\alpha c\rho/\delta)}{c\rho - \delta},$$

whose derivative is

$$f'(c) = \frac{\delta - c\rho + \delta \ln(\alpha c\rho/\delta)}{(\delta - c\rho)^2}.$$

Equation (3.65) immediately takes the form

$$\frac{x \ln(\alpha x\rho/\delta)}{\delta - x\rho} = \frac{\delta - \rho x + \delta \ln(\alpha x\rho/\delta)}{(\delta - x\rho)^2}(x - \delta/\rho) + u^*_{\alpha,t},$$

and is transformed into

$$\frac{\delta + x\rho}{\delta - x\rho} \ln\left(\alpha\,\frac{x\rho}{\delta}\right) = \rho u^*_{\alpha,t} - 1, \tag{3.66}$$

which is (3.63), by elementary calculations.

Bearing in mind (see definition of $c^*_{\alpha,t}$) that

$$u^*_{\alpha,t} = \frac{1}{\rho} + \frac{1}{\rho}\left(\frac{\delta + \rho c^*_{\alpha,t}}{\delta - \rho c^*_{\alpha,t}}\right) \ln\left(\alpha\,\frac{\rho c^*_{\alpha,t}}{\delta}\right), \tag{3.67}$$

let us transform equality (3.64), excluding from it the expression $u^*_{\alpha,t}$, as follows. Put (3.67) in the right-hand side of (3.64). By elementary calculations, it is reduced to

$$l(c) = \frac{\delta - \rho c^*_{\alpha,t} + \delta \ln(\alpha c^*_{\alpha,t}\rho/\delta)}{(\delta - \rho c^*_{\alpha,t})^2}(c - c^*_{\alpha,t}) + \frac{c^*_{\alpha,t}\ln(\alpha c^*_{\alpha,t}\rho/\delta)}{\delta - \rho c^*_{\alpha,t}},$$

whence the result. □

The following theorem gives less accurate, but explicit bounds. They are based on using an upper bound $\bar{u}_{\alpha\,|\,\delta,\rho}(c)$ which is coarser than $u_{\alpha\,|\,\delta,\rho}(c)$.

Theorem 3.18 *With $t > 0$ sufficiently large, for $0 < c \leqslant \delta/\rho$ we have*

$$(\delta/\rho - c)\,t + \frac{\kappa_\alpha}{\kappa_{\alpha/2}} u^*_{\alpha,t} \leqslant u_{\alpha,t\,|\,\delta,\rho}(c) \leqslant (\delta/\rho - c)\,t + u^*_{\alpha,t},$$

and, when $c > \delta/\rho$, we have

$$u_{\alpha,t\,|\,\delta,\rho}(c) \leqslant \begin{cases} \dfrac{(\rho u^*_{\alpha,t} + \ln\alpha)^2}{4\delta\ln\alpha}\,c \\ \qquad -\dfrac{(\rho u^*_{\alpha,t} - \ln\alpha)^2}{4\rho\ln\alpha}, & \dfrac{\delta}{\rho} < c \leqslant \dfrac{\delta}{\rho}\left(\dfrac{\rho u^*_{\alpha,t} - \ln\alpha}{\rho u^*_{\alpha,t} + \ln\alpha}\right), \\ -\dfrac{\ln\alpha}{\rho - \delta/c}, & c > \dfrac{\delta}{\rho}\left(\dfrac{\rho u^*_{\alpha,t} - \ln\alpha}{\rho u^*_{\alpha,t} + \ln\alpha}\right). \end{cases}$$

Proof of Theorem 3.18. For the function

$$f(c) = -\frac{c\ln\alpha}{c\rho - \delta},$$

whose derivative is

$$f'(c) = \frac{\delta\ln\alpha}{(\delta - c\rho)^2},$$

equation (3.65) takes the form

$$\frac{x\ln\alpha}{\delta - x\rho} = \frac{\delta\ln\alpha}{(\delta - x\rho)^2}(x - \delta/\rho) + u^*_{\alpha,t}.$$

Its solution is explicit:

$$c^*_{\alpha,t} = \frac{\delta}{\rho}\left(\frac{\rho u^*_{\alpha,t} - \ln\alpha}{\rho u^*_{\alpha,t} + \ln\alpha}\right). \tag{3.68}$$

To complete the proof, we need to simplify (3.64), i.e.,

$$\begin{aligned} l(c) &= \frac{f(c^*_{\alpha,t}) - u^*_{\alpha,t}}{c^*_{\alpha,t} - \delta/\rho}(c - \delta/\rho) + u^*_{\alpha,t} \\ &= \left(\frac{f(c^*_{\alpha,t}) - u^*_{\alpha,t}}{c^*_{\alpha,t} - \delta/\rho}\right)c - \left(\frac{f(c^*_{\alpha,t}) - u^*_{\alpha,t}}{c^*_{\alpha,t} - \delta/\rho}\,\delta/\rho - u^*_{\alpha,t}\right), \end{aligned} \tag{3.69}$$

substituting (3.68) in the right side of (3.69).

These calculations will be greatly simplified if we notice that

$$f(c^*_{\alpha,t}) - u^*_{\alpha,t} = f'(c^*_{\alpha,t})(c^*_{\alpha,t} - \delta/\rho) = \frac{\delta \ln \alpha}{\rho^2(c^*_{\alpha,t} - \delta/\rho)}$$

and that

$$c^*_{\alpha,t} - \delta/\rho = -\frac{\delta}{\rho}\left(\frac{2\ln\alpha}{\rho u^*_{\alpha,t} + \ln\alpha}\right).$$

The proof is complete. □

3.7 Conclusions

In the renewal model with T and Y exponentially distributed, we have closed-form expression for $\mathsf{P}\{\varUpsilon_{u,c\,|\,\delta,\rho} \leqslant t\}$, i.e., for the left-hand side of equation (3.5) which defines the fixed-probability level $u_{\alpha,t\,|\,\delta,\rho}(c)$, $c \geqslant 0$. Thus, we can go along the road map of Chapter 2. The expression for $\mathsf{P}\{\varUpsilon_{u,c\,|\,\delta,\rho} \leqslant t\}$ is much more sophisticated that the similar expression in diffusion model, but it is still fitted, e.g., for calculating the partial derivatives (w.r.t.) c and u.

This allows us to apply the theory of implicit functions (see Section A.1.4), in particular, Theorem A.4, which yields explicit expressions for $\frac{d}{dc}u_{\alpha,t\,|\,\delta,\rho}(c)$ and $\frac{d^2}{dc^2}u_{\alpha,t\,|\,\delta,\rho}(c)$, $c \geqslant 0$. However, it becomes extremely difficult to investigate the sign of these derivatives for all $t > 0$, as it require the standard criteria of monotony and convexity (see Section A.1.1). The study of the sign of these derivatives is easier to investigate asymptotically, that is, for $t \to \infty$.

The asymptotic results for the fixed-probability level $u_{\alpha,t\,|\,\delta,\rho}(c)$, $c \geqslant 0$, which cannot be found explicitly[28], can be obtained with great completeness. Our attention to the asymptotic upper bounds in Sections 3.5 and 3.6, ranging from simple to more elaborated (see Theorems 3.15–3.18) ones, is due to a wish to have simple-looking, convenient for further applications, results.

Studying the asymptotic behavior of the fixed-probability level $u_{\alpha,t\,|\,\delta,\rho}(c)$, as $t \to \infty$, we found that it is finite, when c exceeds a value slightly larger than $c^* := \delta/\rho$. Therefore, no approximation for $\mathsf{P}\{\varUpsilon_{u,c\,|\,\delta,\rho} \leqslant t\}$, as $u \to \infty$, is suitable (no matter what is its accuracy) to study $u_{\alpha,t\,|\,\delta,\rho}(c)$ for such c.

Problems

Problem 3.1 Prove Theorem 3.1.

[Hint: see the proof of Theorem 4.1 in [135].]

[28] In Theorem 3.8, the function $\mathsf{z}_{\alpha,t}(y)$, $y \in \mathsf{R}$, in (3.36) is not found in a closed form.

Problem 3.2 Prove equalities (3.3).
[Hint: see the proof of Theorem 4.2 in [135].]

Problem 3.3 Prove Theorems 3.2, 3.3, and 3.4.
[Hint: see [135], Theorems 5.6–5.8 (Types I–III formulas).]

Problem 3.4 Show an analogue of Theorem 3.5, when higher order moment conditions for Y are satisfied.

Problem 3.5 Compare *asymptotic* equalities (3.23) of Theorem 3.6 and (2.13) of Theorem 2.5. Then compare *asymptotic* equality (3.32) of Theorem 3.7 to *non-asymptotic* equality (2.15) of Theorem 2.6. Compare equality (3.36) of Theorem 3.8 to equality (2.16) of Theorem 2.7. Note the difference between $\mathsf{z}_\alpha(y)$, $y \in \mathsf{R}$, in Theorem 2.7 and $\mathsf{z}_{\alpha,t}(y)$, $y \in \mathsf{R}$, in Theorem 3.8.

Problem 3.6 Assuming that $c_{t,\delta} = c^* - \frac{\sqrt{2\delta}}{\rho}\,\epsilon t^{-1/2}$, $0 \leqslant \epsilon < K$, in the equality $u_{\alpha,t\,|\,\delta,\rho}(c) = \frac{\sqrt{2\delta}}{\rho}\,x_{\alpha,t}(\epsilon)\sqrt{t}$ investigate the factor $x_{\alpha,t}(\epsilon)$, as $t \to \infty$. Use the closed form expression for $F_{\delta t}(\rho u \mid \delta/(c\rho+\delta))$.

Problem 3.7 Assuming that $c_{t,\delta} = c^* + \frac{\sqrt{2\delta}}{\rho}\,\epsilon t^{-1/2}$, $0 \leqslant \epsilon < K$, in the equality $u_{\alpha,t\,|\,\delta,\rho}(c) = \frac{\sqrt{2\delta}}{\rho}\,x_{\alpha,t}(\epsilon)\sqrt{t}$ investigate the factor $x_{\alpha,t}(\epsilon)$, as $t \to \infty$. Use the closed form expression for $F_{\delta t}(\rho u \mid \delta/(c\rho+\delta))$.

Problem 3.8 Show a detailed study of the bounds based on monotony.

Problem 3.9 Construct the broken-line bounds with the break point different from $2c^*$.

Problem 3.10 Show detailed proof of Theorems 3.17 and 3.18.

Chapter 4

Implicit Function Defined by $\mathcal{M}$-Equation

This chapter links Chapter 3, devoted to exceptional renewal risk model, and Chapter 5, devoted to general renewal risk model. We focus on the implicit function defined by auxiliary $\mathcal{M}$-equation. This study is purely analytical, but is related to the inverse Gaussian approximation outlined in Section 1.3.5.

4.1 Analytical Properties of Core Integral Expression

In Section 1.3.6, we formulated a result (see Proposition 1.4) called inverse Gaussian approximation in the general renewal model. The approximating expression in it is denoted (see (1.40), (1.42)) by $\mathcal{M}_{u,c}(t)$. We will return to this matter in more detail in Section 5.2.

In Section 1.3.7, we noted that, when $0 \leqslant c \leqslant c^*$ (but not when $c > Kc^*$, $K > 1$) and t is sufficiently large, a numerical procedure for calculating a solution to the equation

$$\mathcal{M}_{u,c}(t) = \alpha, \tag{4.1}$$

denoted by $u_{\alpha,t}^{[\mathcal{M}]}(c)$ and called $\mathcal{M}$-level, at the same time may be viewed as a numerical procedure for calculating the non-ruin capital $u_{\alpha,t}(c)$. Since the left-hand side of equation (4.1) is written in closed form, this is similar to what we had in Chapters 2 and 3. In this chapter, we examine equation (4.1) and $\mathcal{M}$-level $u_{\alpha,t}^{[\mathcal{M}]}(c)$, $c \geqslant 0$, as a stand-alone object of analysis.

4.1.1 Equivalent expressions for $\mathcal{M}_{u,c}(t)$ and $\mathcal{M}_{u,c}$

For u, c, t, and M, D^2 positive, we start with a few results on the structure of the function[1]

$$\mathcal{M}_{u,c}(t) := \int_0^{\frac{ct}{u}} \frac{1}{x+1}\, \varphi_{\left(cM(x+1),\, \frac{c^2D^2}{u}(x+1)\right)}(x)\, dx, \tag{4.2}$$

[1] In [135], $\mathcal{M}_{u,c}(t)$ is called core integral expression. Note that M, D^2 in (4.2) are arbitrary positive values, rather than $M := \mathsf{E}\,T/\mathsf{E}\,Y$, $D^2 := ((\mathsf{E}\,T)^2\mathsf{D}\,Y + (\mathsf{E}\,Y)^2\mathsf{D}\,T)/(\mathsf{E}\,Y)^3)$, as it will be in Chapter 5.

and of its upper bound

$$\mathcal{M}_{u,c} := \lim_{t\to\infty} \mathcal{M}_{u,c}(t) = \int_0^\infty \frac{1}{x+1}\,\varphi_{\left(cM(x+1),\,\frac{c^2D^2}{u}(x+1)\right)}(x)\,dx,$$

Expressions for $\mathcal{M}_{u,c}(t)$. We start (see [135], Chapter 3) with several equivalent representations for $\mathcal{M}_{u,c}(t)$. In terms of (see (B.5)) p.d.f. of inverse Gaussian distribution, straightforwardly from (4.2), we have

$$\mathcal{M}_{u,c}(t) = \int_0^{\frac{ct}{u}} f(x+1;\mu,\lambda,-\tfrac{1}{2})\,dx\,\Big|_{\mu=\frac{1}{1-cM},\,\lambda=\frac{u}{c^2D^2}}. \tag{4.3}$$

In terms of (see (B.6)) c.d.f. of inverse Gaussian distribution, we have

$$\mathcal{M}_{u,c}(t) = \begin{cases} \left(F\left(\frac{ct}{u}+1;\mu,\lambda,-\frac{1}{2}\right) - F(1;\mu,\lambda,-\frac{1}{2})\right)\Big|_{\mu=\frac{1}{1-cM},\,\lambda=\frac{u}{c^2D^2}}, & 0<c<c^*,\\ \exp\left\{-\frac{2\lambda}{\hat{\mu}}\right\}\left(F\left(\frac{ct}{u}+1;\hat{\mu},\lambda,-\frac{1}{2}\right) - F(1;\hat{\mu},\lambda,-\frac{1}{2})\right)\Big|_{\hat{\mu}=\frac{1}{cM-1},\,\lambda=\frac{u}{c^2D^2}}, & c>c^*, \end{cases} \tag{4.4}$$

where $c^* := 1/M$ and, calculating the appropriate limits, $\mathcal{M}_{u,\infty}(t) = 0$ and

$$\begin{aligned} \mathcal{M}_{u,0}(t) &= \Phi_{(0,1)}\left(\frac{M\sqrt{u}}{D}\right) - \Phi_{(0,1)}\left(\frac{M\sqrt{u}}{D} - \frac{t}{D\sqrt{u}}\right),\\ \mathcal{M}_{u,c^*}(t) &= 2\left(\Phi_{(0,1)}\left(\frac{M\sqrt{u}}{D}\right) - \Phi_{(0,1)}\left(\frac{Mu}{D\sqrt{c^*t+u}}\right)\right). \end{aligned} \tag{4.5}$$

Remark 4.1 It is worth comparing (2.7), (2.8) to (4.4) (4.5): some similarity of these expressions is obvious. Much less obvious is similarity between (4.4) (4.5) and equivalent expressions (3.6)–(3.8), but it exists: under certain conditions, $\mathcal{M}_{u,c}(t)$ is (see Chapter 5) an approximation for $\mathsf{P}\{\Upsilon_{u,c\,|\,\delta,\rho} \leqslant t\}$.

Directly from (4.4), the upper bound

$$\mathcal{M}_{u,c}(t) \leqslant \begin{cases} 1, & c\leqslant c^*,\\ \exp\left\{-\frac{2\,(cM-1)}{c^2D^2}\,u\right\}, & c>c^*, \end{cases} \tag{4.6}$$

follows, whence, when $c > c^*$, the function $\mathcal{M}_{u,c}(t)$ tends to zero, as $u\to\infty$, exponentially fast.

Bearing in mind equality (B.6), an alternative expression in terms of c.d.f. of a standard Gaussian distribution is

$$\begin{aligned}\mathcal{M}_{u,c}(t) &= \Phi_{(0,1)}\Big(\frac{M}{D}\sqrt{u}\Big) - \Phi_{(0,1)}\Big(\frac{(cM-2)\sqrt{u}}{cD}\Big)\\ &\times \exp\Big\{-\frac{2\,(cM-1)\,u}{cD^2}\Big\} + \Phi_{(0,1)}\Big(\frac{(cM-1)\,ct+(cM-2)\,u}{cD\sqrt{u+ct}}\Big)\\ &\times \exp\Big\{-\frac{2\,(cM-1)\,u}{cD^2}\Big\} - \Phi_{(0,1)}\Big(\frac{(cM-1)\,t+M\,u}{D\sqrt{u+ct}}\Big),\end{aligned} \tag{4.7}$$

whereas an alternative expression in terms of Mills' ratio and p.d.f. of a standard Gaussian distribution is

$$\begin{aligned}\mathcal{M}_{u,c}(t) &= \Big(\mathcal{M}\Big(\frac{(cM-2)\sqrt{u}}{cD}\Big) - \mathcal{M}\Big(\frac{M\sqrt{u}}{D}\Big)\Big)\,\varphi_{(0,1)}\Big(\frac{M\sqrt{u}}{D}\Big)\\ &- \Big(\mathcal{M}\Big(\frac{c(cM-1)\,t+(cM-2)u}{cD\sqrt{u+ct}}\Big) - \mathcal{M}\Big(\frac{(cM-1)\,t+Mu}{D\sqrt{u+ct}}\Big)\Big)\\ &\times \varphi_{(0,1)}\Big(\frac{(cM-1)\,t+Mu}{D\sqrt{u+ct}}\Big).\end{aligned} \tag{4.8}$$

In terms of (see (2.9)) the auxiliary function of the first kind

$$\begin{aligned}\mathsf{F}(z,y\mid -\tfrac{1}{2}) := {}& 1-\Phi_{(0,1)}(z-y)\\ &+\Phi_{(0,1)}(-z-y)\exp\{2zy\}, \qquad z,y>0,\end{aligned}$$

an alternative expression is

$$\mathcal{M}_{u,c}(t) = \begin{cases} \mathsf{F}(z,y\mid -\tfrac{1}{2})\Big|_{z=\frac{u}{cD\sqrt{u+ct}},\,y=\frac{\sqrt{u+ct}\,(1-cM)}{cD}} \\ \quad -\mathsf{F}(z,y\mid -\tfrac{1}{2})\Big|_{z=\frac{\sqrt{u}}{cD},\,y=\frac{\sqrt{u}\,(1-cM)}{cD}}, & 0<c\leqslant c^*,\\ \exp\{-2zy\}\,\mathsf{F}(z,y\mid -\tfrac{1}{2})\Big|_{z=\frac{u}{cD\sqrt{u+ct}},\,y=\frac{\sqrt{u+ct}\,(cM-1)}{cD}} \\ \quad -\exp\{-2zy\}\,\mathsf{F}(z,y\mid -\tfrac{1}{2})\Big|_{z=\frac{\sqrt{u}}{cD},\,y=\frac{\sqrt{u}\,(cM-1)}{cD}}, & c>c^*.\end{cases} \tag{4.9}$$

The right-hand side of (4.9) is fit for calculating the derivatives of $\mathcal{M}_{u,c}(t)$ with respect to c and u, using a chain rule for differentiation of a composite function. Another representation of $\mathcal{M}_{u,c}(t)$ as a composite function, similar to (4.9), is as follows.

Theorem 4.1 *For positive u, c, t, and M, D^2, we have*

$$\mathcal{M}_{u,c}(t) = \boldsymbol{F}(v,\psi,\omega)\Big|_{v=\frac{M^2}{D^2}u,\,\psi=cM,\,\omega=\frac{M^2}{D^2}ct}, \tag{4.10}$$

where

$$
\begin{aligned}
&\boldsymbol{F}(\upsilon,\psi,\omega)\\
&\quad := \Phi_{(0,1)}(\sqrt{\upsilon}\,) - \Phi_{(0,1)}\Big(\frac{(\psi-2)\sqrt{\upsilon}}{\psi}\Big)\exp\Big\{-\frac{2\,(\psi-1)\,\upsilon}{\psi^2}\Big\}\\
&\qquad + \Phi_{(0,1)}\Big(\frac{(\psi-1)\,\omega+(\psi-2)\,\upsilon}{\psi\sqrt{\omega+\upsilon}}\Big)\exp\Big\{-\frac{2\,(\psi-1)\,\upsilon}{\psi^2}\Big\}\\
&\qquad - \Phi_{(0,1)}\Big(\frac{(\psi-1)\,\omega+\psi\,\upsilon}{\psi\sqrt{\omega+\upsilon}}\Big).
\end{aligned}
\tag{4.11}
$$

In terms of Mills' ratio, equality (4.11) may be rewritten as

$$
\begin{aligned}
\boldsymbol{F}(\upsilon,\psi,\omega) := &\Big(\mathcal{M}\Big(\frac{(\psi-2)\sqrt{\upsilon}}{\psi}\Big) - \mathcal{M}(\sqrt{\upsilon}\,)\Big)\,\varphi_{(0,1)}(\sqrt{\upsilon}\,)\\
&-\Big(\mathcal{M}\Big(\frac{(\psi-1)\,\omega+(\psi-2)\,\upsilon}{\psi\sqrt{\omega+\upsilon}}\Big) - \mathcal{M}\Big(\frac{(\psi-1)\,\omega+\psi\,\upsilon}{\psi\sqrt{\omega+\upsilon}}\Big)\Big)\\
&\times\varphi_{(0,1)}\Big(\frac{(\psi-1)\,\omega+\psi\,\upsilon}{\psi\sqrt{\omega+\upsilon}}\Big).
\end{aligned}
$$

We leave the proof of Theorem 4.1, which is straightforward from (4.7), to the reader.

Expressions for $\mathcal{M}_{u,c}$. It is easily seen (cf. (4.4)) that

$$
\mathcal{M}_{u,c} = \begin{cases}
(1-F(1;\mu,\lambda,-\tfrac{1}{2}))\,\big|_{\mu=\frac{1}{1-cM},\lambda=\frac{u}{c^2D^2}}, & 0<c\leqslant c^*,\\[2ex]
(e^{-\frac{2\lambda}{\hat{\mu}}}(1-F(1;\hat{\mu},\lambda,-\tfrac{1}{2})))\,\big|_{\hat{\mu}=\frac{1}{cM-1},\lambda=\frac{u}{c^2D^2}}, & c>c^*,
\end{cases}
$$

and the inequalities similar to (4.6) trivially hold for $\mathcal{M}_{u,c}$. The expression in terms of c.d.f. of a standard Gaussian distribution is

$$
\mathcal{M}_{u,c} = \begin{cases}
\Phi_{(0,1)}\Big(\dfrac{M\sqrt{u}}{D}\Big) - \exp\Big\{\dfrac{2\,(1-cM)}{c^2D^2}\,u\Big\}\\
\qquad\times\Phi_{(0,1)}\Big(\dfrac{cM-2}{cD}\sqrt{u}\Big), & 0<c\leqslant c^*,\\
\exp\Big\{-\dfrac{2\,(cM-1)}{c^2D^2}\,u\Big\}\,\Phi_{(0,1)}\Big(-\dfrac{cM-2}{cD}\sqrt{u}\Big)\\
\qquad-\Phi_{(0,1)}\Big(-\dfrac{M\sqrt{u}}{D}\Big), & c>c^*,
\end{cases}
$$

and, calculating the appropriate limits, $\mathcal{M}_{u,\infty}=0$,

$$
\mathcal{M}_{u,0} = \Phi_{(0,1)}\Big(\frac{M\sqrt{u}}{D}\Big),\quad \mathcal{M}_{u,c^*} = 2\,\Phi_{(0,1)}\Big(\frac{M\sqrt{u}}{D}\Big)-1. \tag{4.12}
$$

The alternative expression in terms of Mills' ratio and p.d.f. of a standard Gaussian distribution is

$$\mathcal{M}_{u,c} = \begin{cases} \left(\mathcal{M}\left(-\frac{M\sqrt{u}}{D}\right) - \mathcal{M}\left(\frac{(2-cM)\sqrt{u}}{cD}\right)\right) \\ \qquad \times\varphi_{(0,1)}\left(\frac{M\sqrt{u}}{D}\right), & 0 < c \leqslant c^*, \\ \left(\mathcal{M}\left(\frac{(cM-2)\sqrt{u}}{cD}\right) - \mathcal{M}\left(\frac{M\sqrt{u}}{D}\right)\right) \\ \qquad \times\varphi_{(0,1)}\left(\frac{M\sqrt{u}}{D}\right), & c > c^*. \end{cases} \tag{4.13}$$

Theorem 4.2 *For positive u, c, and M, D^2, we have*

$$\mathcal{M}_{u,c} = \boldsymbol{F}(\upsilon, \psi)\Big|_{\upsilon = \frac{M^2}{D^2}u,\ \psi = cM},$$

where

$$\boldsymbol{F}(\upsilon,\psi) := \begin{cases} \Phi_{(0,1)}\left(\sqrt{\upsilon}\right) - \left(1 - \Phi_{(0,1)}\left(\frac{(2-\psi)\sqrt{\upsilon}}{\psi}\right)\right) \\ \qquad \times \exp\left\{-\frac{2(\psi-1)\upsilon}{\psi^2}\right\}, & 0 < \psi \leqslant 1, \\ \left(1 - \Phi_{(0,1)}\left(\frac{(\psi-2)\sqrt{\upsilon}}{\psi}\right)\right) \\ \qquad \times \exp\left\{-\frac{2(\psi-1)\upsilon}{\psi^2}\right\} - \Phi_{(0,1)}\left(-\sqrt{\upsilon}\right), & \psi > 1. \end{cases}$$

The alternative expression in terms of Mills' ratio is[2]

$$\boldsymbol{F}(\upsilon,\psi) := \begin{cases} \left(\mathcal{M}\left(-\sqrt{\upsilon}\right) - \mathcal{M}\left(\frac{(2-\psi)\sqrt{\upsilon}}{\psi}\right)\right)\varphi_{(0,1)}\left(\sqrt{\upsilon}\right), & 0 < \psi \leqslant 1, \\ \left(\mathcal{M}\left(\frac{(\psi-2)\sqrt{\upsilon}}{\psi}\right) - \mathcal{M}\left(\sqrt{\upsilon}\right)\right)\varphi_{(0,1)}\left(\sqrt{\upsilon}\right), & \psi > 1. \end{cases}$$

We leave the proof of Theorem 4.2 to the reader.

4.1.2 Analytical structure of $\mathcal{M}_{u,c}(t)$ and $\mathcal{M}_{u,c}$

In this section, we seek to discover the shape of the expressions $\mathcal{M}_{u,c}(t)$ and $\mathcal{M}_{u,c}$ by elementary methods. Viewed as functions of c, they behave differently for $0 \leqslant c < 1/M$ and for $c > 1/M$. Bearing in mind that $\mathcal{M}_{u,c}$ is an upper bound for $\mathcal{M}_{u,c}(t)$, we are interested in the difference between them, in their behavior for large c, and on closed-form bounds on them written in terms of elementary functions.

[2]Recall (see (B.18)) that $\mathcal{M}(-x) + \mathcal{M}(x) = \varphi^{-1}_{(0,1)}(x)$.

Regarded as a function of t, with c and u fixed, the function $\mathcal{M}_{u,c}(t)$ is smooth and monotone increasing from zero to $\mathcal{M}_{u,c}$, as t increases from zero to infinity. This can be seen in many ways, one of which is straightforward from representation (4.4): in both cases $0 < c \leqslant c^*$ and $c > c^*$, the variable t enters only in the minuends. Since both $F(\frac{ct}{u}+1;\mu,\lambda,-\frac{1}{2})$ and $F(\frac{ct}{u}+1;\hat{\mu},\lambda,-\frac{1}{2})$ are c.d.f. of an absolutely continuous probability distribution, we readily get the desired result.

Approximation of $\mathcal{M}_{u,c}(t)$. Plainly, $\mathcal{M}_{u,c}(t)$ tends to $\mathcal{M}_{u,c}$, as $t \to \infty$. The following result (see [135], Theorem 3.9) refines this approximation. It is a corollary (see [135], Theorem 2.2) of expansion of Mills'-type ratio for inverse Gaussian distribution.

Theorem 4.3 *For $u \geqslant 0$, we have*

$$\begin{aligned}\mathcal{M}_{u,c}(t) = \mathcal{M}_{u,c} - \sqrt{\frac{2}{\pi}}\frac{cD}{(1-cM)^2}\,u\,(ct+u)^{-3/2}\exp\left\{\frac{1-cM}{c^2D^2}\,u\right\}\\ \times\exp\left\{-\frac{(1-cM)^2}{2c^2D^2}(ct+u)\right\}\\ \times\exp\left\{-\frac{1}{2c^2D^2}\frac{u^2}{ct+u}\right\}(1+o(1)),\quad t\to\infty.\end{aligned}$$

Inequalities for $\mathcal{M}_{u,c}(t)$. Besides the trivial inequality $\mathcal{M}_{u,c}(t) \leqslant \mathcal{M}_{u,c}$, many useful inequalities can be presented. The bounds in the following Theorems 4.4–4.6 stem from manipulations with the integrand in (4.2).

The following result improves the bounds (4.6).

Theorem 4.4 *For positive t, u, M, and D^2, we have*

$$\mathcal{M}_{u,c}(t) \leqslant \begin{cases} \frac{\sqrt{2u}}{\sqrt{\pi}\,cD}\left(1-\frac{\sqrt{u}}{\sqrt{u+ct}}\right), & cM \leqslant 1,\\ \frac{\sqrt{2u}}{\sqrt{\pi}\,cD}\left(1-\frac{\sqrt{u}}{\sqrt{u+ct}}\right)\exp\left\{-\frac{2\,(cM-1)}{c^2D^2}\,u\right\}, & 1 < cM \leqslant 2,\\ \frac{\sqrt{2u}}{\sqrt{\pi}\,cD}\left(1-\frac{\sqrt{u}}{\sqrt{u+ct}}\right)\exp\left\{-\frac{M^2}{2D^2}\,u\right\}, & cM > 2.\end{cases}$$

Proof of Theorem 4.4. The integrand in (4.2) is

$$\frac{\sqrt{u}}{\sqrt{2\pi}\,cD\,(x+1)^{3/2}}\exp\left\{-\frac{u}{2c^2D^2}\frac{(x-cM(x+1))^2}{x+1}\right\}.$$

The exponent in it takes the maximal value 1 at the point $x = \frac{cM}{1-cM}$ if $cM < 1$ (i.e., $c < c^*$), and the maximal value $\exp\{-\frac{2(cM-1)}{c^2D^2}u\}$ at the point $x = \frac{2-cM}{cM-1}$, if $1 < cM < 2$ (i.e., $c^* < c < 2c^*$). If $cM > 2$ (i.e., $c > 2c^*$), the maximal value is $\exp\{-\frac{M^2}{2D^2}u\}$ at the point $x = 0$. Finally,

$$\int_0^{\frac{ct}{u}}\frac{dx}{(x+1)^{3/2}} = 2\left(1-\frac{\sqrt{u}}{\sqrt{u+ct}}\right),$$

whence the result. □

Theorem 4.5 *For positive t, u, c, M, and D^2, we have*

$$\mathcal{M}_{u,c}(t) \leqslant 2\exp\left\{-\frac{c^2M^2-1}{2c^2D^2}u\right\} \times \left(\Phi_{(0,1)}\left(\frac{\sqrt{u}}{cD}\right)-\Phi_{(0,1)}\left(\frac{u}{cD\sqrt{u+ct}}\right)\right).$$

Proof of Theorem 4.5. Let us rewrite equality (4.3) as

$$\mathcal{M}_{u,c}(t) = \frac{\sqrt{u}}{\sqrt{2\pi}\,cD}\exp\{-2AH\} \times \int_1^{\frac{ct}{u}+1} x^{-3/2}\exp\left\{-A\left(x+\frac{H^2}{x}\right)\right\}dx, \tag{4.14}$$

where the shorthand notation $A := \frac{(cM-1)^2}{2c^2D^2}u$ and $H := \frac{1}{cM-1}$ is used. Bearing in mind that $A > 0$ for any $c > 0$, we have

$$0 < \exp\{-Az\} \leqslant \exp\{-A\}, \tag{4.15}$$

for any $z > 1$. If $c = c^*$, the second inequality in (4.15) becomes identity since $A = 0$. If $c \neq c^*$, the equality in (4.15) is achieved only when $z = 1$. Thus, we have from (4.14) the inequality

$$\mathcal{M}_{u,c}(t) \leqslant \frac{\sqrt{u}}{\sqrt{2\pi}cD}\exp\{-A(1+2H)\} \times \int_1^{\frac{ct}{u}+1} x^{-3/2}\exp\left\{-\frac{AH^2}{x}\right\}dx, \tag{4.16}$$

with the integral evaluated in Theorem B.4. The right-hand side in (4.16) is

$$\begin{aligned}&\frac{1}{\sqrt{2\pi}}\frac{\sqrt{u}}{cD}\exp\{-A(1+2H)\}\frac{2\sqrt{\pi}}{\sqrt{AH^2}}\left(\Phi_{(0,1)}(\sqrt{2AH^2})-\Phi_{(0,1)}\left(\frac{\sqrt{2AH^2}}{\sqrt{1+ct/u}}\right)\right)\\ &= 2\exp\left\{-\frac{c^2M^2-1}{2c^2D^2}u\right\}\left(\Phi_{(0,1)}\left(\frac{\sqrt{u}}{cD}\right)-\Phi_{(0,1)}\left(\frac{u}{cD\sqrt{u+ct}}\right)\right),\end{aligned}$$

whence the result. □

Theorem 4.6 *For positive t, u, c, M, and D^2, we have*

$$\exp\left\{-\frac{u}{2c^2D^2}\right\}\mathcal{B}_{u,c}(t) \leqslant \mathcal{M}_{u,c}(t) \leqslant \exp\left\{-\frac{u}{2c^2D^2(1+ct/u)}\right\}\mathcal{B}_{u,c}(t),$$

where

$$\mathcal{B}_{u,c}(t) = \frac{2\sqrt{u}}{cD}\varphi_{(0,1)}\Big(\frac{cM-1}{cD}\sqrt{u}\Big)\Big\{1 - \frac{\sqrt{u}}{\sqrt{u+ct}}\exp\Big\{-\frac{(cM-1)^2}{2cD^2}t\Big\}$$
$$- \frac{cM-1}{cD}\sqrt{u}\,\varphi^{-1}_{(0,1)}\Big(\frac{cM-1}{cD}\sqrt{u}\Big)$$
$$\times\Big(\Phi_{(0,1)}\Big(\frac{cM-1}{cD}\sqrt{u+ct}\Big) - \Phi_{(0,1)}\Big(\frac{cM-1}{cD}\sqrt{u}\Big)\Big)\Big\}.$$

Proof of Theorem 4.6. For $1 < x < \frac{ct}{u} + 1$, using shorthand notation $A := \frac{(cM-1)^2}{2c^2D^2}u$ and $H := \frac{1}{cM-1}$, whence $AH^2 = \frac{u}{2c^2D^2} > 0$, we have

$$0 < \exp\{-AH^2\} < \exp\Big\{-\frac{AH^2}{x}\Big\} < \exp\Big\{-\frac{AH^2}{1+\frac{ct}{u}}\Big\} < 1.$$

Thus, the upper and lower bounds for (see (4.14)) $\mathcal{M}_{u,c}(t)$ are respectively

$$\frac{\sqrt{u}}{\sqrt{2\pi}cD}\exp\Big\{-\frac{u}{2c^2D^2(1+\frac{ct}{u})}\Big\}\int_1^{\frac{ct}{u}+1} x^{-3/2}\exp\{-Ax\}\,dx,$$
$$\frac{\sqrt{u}}{\sqrt{2\pi}cD}\exp\Big\{-\frac{u}{2c^2D^2}\Big\}\int_1^{\frac{ct}{u}+1} x^{-3/2}\exp\{-Ax\}\,dx.$$

Apply Theorem B.5 to calculate the integral, whence the result. □

Analytical structure of $\mathcal{M}_{u,c}$. The following theorem yields closed-form bounds on $\mathcal{M}_{u,c}$ written in terms of elementary functions.

Theorem 4.7 *For positive u, c, M, and D^2, we have*

$$\underline{\mathcal{M}}_{u,c} \leqslant \mathcal{M}_{u,c} \leqslant \overline{\mathcal{M}}_{u,c}, \tag{4.17}$$

where for $0 < c \leqslant c^*$

$$\overline{\mathcal{M}}_{u,c} = 1 - \frac{\sqrt{2}}{\sqrt{\pi}}\exp\Big\{-\frac{M^2u}{2D^2}\Big\}\Big\{\Big(\Big(\frac{(2-cM)^2u}{c^2D^2}+4\Big)^{1/2} + \frac{(2-cM)\sqrt{u}}{cD}\Big)^{-1}$$
$$+ \Big(\Big(\frac{M^2u}{D^2}+4\Big)^{1/2} + \frac{M\sqrt{u}}{D}\Big)^{-1}\Big\},$$

$$\underline{\mathcal{M}}_{u,c} = 1 - \frac{\sqrt{2}}{\sqrt{\pi}}\exp\Big\{-\frac{M^2u}{2D^2}\Big\}\Big\{\Big(\Big(\frac{(2-cM)^2u}{c^2D^2}+2\Big)^{1/2} + \frac{(2-cM)\sqrt{u}}{cD}\Big)^{-1}$$
$$+ \Big(\Big(\frac{M^2u}{D^2}+2\Big)^{1/2} + \frac{M\sqrt{u}}{D}\Big)^{-1}\Big\},$$

for $c^* < c \leqslant 2c^*$

$$\overline{\mathcal{M}}_{u,c} = \exp\left\{ -\frac{2\,(cM-1)\,u}{c^2D^2}\right\} - \frac{\sqrt{2}}{\sqrt{\pi}}\exp\left\{ -\frac{M^2u}{2D^2}\right\} \times \left\{ \left(\left(\frac{(2-cM)^2u}{c^2D^2} + 4 \right)^{1/2} + \frac{(2-cM)\sqrt{u}}{cD} \right)^{-1} + \left(\left(\frac{M^2u}{D^2} + 4 \right)^{1/2} + \frac{M\sqrt{u}}{D} \right)^{-1} \right\},$$

$$\underline{\mathcal{M}}_{u,c} = \exp\left\{ -\frac{2\,(cM-1)\,u}{c^2D^2}\right\} - \frac{\sqrt{2}}{\sqrt{\pi}}\exp\left\{ -\frac{M^2u}{2D^2}\right\} \times \left\{ \left(\left(\frac{(2-cM)^2u}{c^2D^2} + 2 \right)^{1/2} + \frac{(2-cM)\sqrt{u}}{cD} \right)^{-1} + \left(\left(\frac{M^2u}{D^2} + 2 \right)^{1/2} + \frac{M\sqrt{u}}{D} \right)^{-1} \right\},$$

and, when $c > 2c^*$,

$$\overline{\mathcal{M}}_{u,c} = \frac{\sqrt{2}}{\sqrt{\pi}}\exp\left\{ -\frac{M^2u}{2D^2}\right\} \left\{ \left(\left(\frac{(cM-2)^2u}{c^2D^2} + 2 \right)^{1/2} + \frac{(cM-2)\sqrt{u}}{cD} \right)^{-1} - \left(\left(\frac{M^2u}{D^2} + 4 \right)^{1/2} + \frac{M\sqrt{u}}{D} \right)^{-1} \right\},$$

$$\underline{\mathcal{M}}_{u,c} = \frac{\sqrt{2}}{\sqrt{\pi}}\exp\left\{ -\frac{M^2u}{2D^2}\right\} \left\{ \left(\left(\frac{(cM-2)^2u}{c^2D^2} + 4 \right)^{1/2} + \frac{(cM-2)\sqrt{u}}{cD} \right)^{-1} - \left(\left(\frac{M^2u}{D^2} + 2 \right)^{1/2} + \frac{M\sqrt{u}}{D} \right)^{-1} \right\}.$$

Proof of Theorem 4.7. We rewrite equality (4.13) as

$$\mathcal{M}_{u,c} = \begin{cases} 1 - \varphi_{(0,1)}\left(\frac{M\sqrt{u}}{D}\right) \times \left(\mathfrak{M}\left(\frac{(2-cM)\sqrt{u}}{cD} \right) + \mathfrak{M}\left(\frac{M\sqrt{u}}{D} \right) \right), & 0 < c \leqslant c^*, \\ \exp\left\{ -\frac{2\,(cM-1)\,u}{c^2D^2}\right\} - \varphi_{(0,1)}\left(\frac{M\sqrt{u}}{D}\right) \times \left(\mathfrak{M}\left(\frac{(2-cM)\sqrt{u}}{cD} \right) + \mathfrak{M}\left(\frac{M\sqrt{u}}{D} \right) \right), & c^* < c \leqslant 2c^*, \\ \varphi_{(0,1)}\left(\frac{M\sqrt{u}}{D}\right) \times \left(\mathfrak{M}\left(\frac{(cM-2)\sqrt{u}}{cD} \right) - \mathfrak{M}\left(\frac{M\sqrt{u}}{D} \right) \right), & c > 2c^*, \end{cases}$$

when arguments of Mills' ratios are positive, and apply the upper and lower

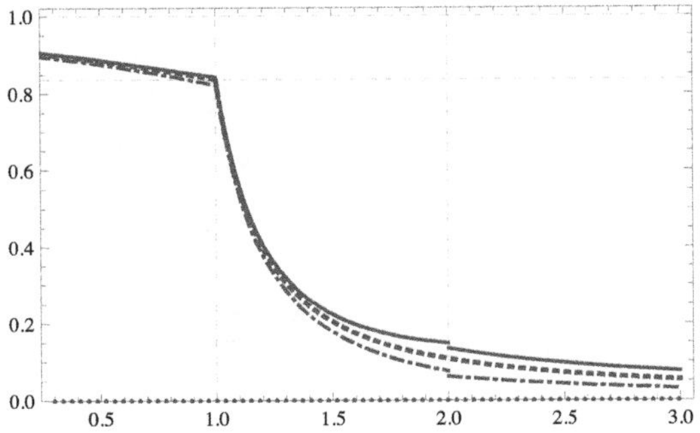

FIGURE 4.1: Graphs (X-axis is c) of $\underline{\mathcal{M}}_{u,c}$ (dash-dotted line), $\overline{\mathcal{M}}_{u,c}$ (solid line), and $\mathcal{M}_{u,c}$ (dashed line), where $M = 1$, $D = 6$, and $u = 70$. Horizontal grid line: $\mathcal{M}_{u,c^*} = 0.84$, vertical grid lines: $c^* = 1$, $2c^* = 2$.

bounds (see (B.24))

$$2\left((x^2+4)^{1/2}+x\right)^{-1} \leqslant \mathcal{M}(x) \leqslant 2\left((x^2+2)^{1/2}+x\right)^{-1}, \quad x > 0,$$

whence the result. □

The bound in Theorem 4.4 is fairly simple. The bound in Theorem 4.5 is accurate an the point c^*: at c^* it coincides with $\mathcal{M}_{u,c^*}(t)$ given in (4.5). The upper and lower bounds in Theorem 4.6 are accurate when $\frac{ct}{u}$ is sufficiently small. The upper and lower bounds (4.17) are illustrated in Fig. 4.1. The similar bounds on $\mathcal{M}_{u,c}(t)$ based on representation (4.8) are an easy development which is left to the reader.

The shape of $\mathcal{M}_{u,c}(t)$ and $\mathcal{M}_{u,c}$, as functions of c and u. The shape of $\mathcal{M}_{u,c}(t)$ and $\mathcal{M}_{u,c}$, considered as functions of c and u, is not obvious[3] from the analytic structure of these expressions and requires an analysis based on their derivatives.

Bearing in mind Theorem B.6, the representation (4.9) is convenient for calculating the derivatives

$$\mathcal{M}_{u,c}^{(i,j)}(t) := \frac{\partial^{i+j}}{\partial u^i \partial c^j}\mathcal{M}_{u,c}(t), \quad i,j = 0,1,\ldots.$$

Let us write

$$K_{u,c}^{(1)}(t) := \frac{u\,(2u+3ct)}{2c^2 D\,(u+ct)^{3/2}}, \quad K_{u,c}^{(2)}(t) := \frac{2u+ct+c^2Mt}{2c^2 D\sqrt{u+ct}}, \quad K_{u,c}^{(3)} := \frac{\sqrt{u}}{c^2 D},$$

$$\hat{K}_{u,c}^{(1)}(t) := \frac{u+2ct}{2cD\,(u+ct)^{3/2}}, \quad \hat{K}_{u,c}^{(2)}(t) := \frac{1-cM}{2cD\sqrt{u+ct}},$$

$$\hat{K}_{u,c}^{(3)} := \frac{1}{2cD\sqrt{u}}, \quad \hat{K}_{u,c}^{(4)} := \frac{1-cM}{2cD\sqrt{u}},$$

[3]Unlike as function of t for $\mathcal{M}_{u,c}(t)$.

$$
\begin{aligned}
\mathcal{S}_{u,c}^{[1]}(t) := & - \big(\varphi_{(0,1)}(z+y)\big(y\,\mathcal{M}(z+y)-1\big)\big)\Big|_{z=\frac{u}{cD\sqrt{u+ct}},\,y=\frac{\sqrt{u+ct}\,(1-cM)}{cD}} K_{u,c}^{(1)}(t) \\
& - \big(\varphi_{(0,1)}(z+y)z\,\mathcal{M}(z+y)\big)\Big|_{z=\frac{u}{cD\sqrt{u+ct}},\,y=\frac{\sqrt{u+ct}\,(1-cM)}{cD}} K_{u,c}^{(2)}(t), \\
\mathcal{S}_{u,c}^{[2]} := & \big(\varphi_{(0,1)}(z+y)(y\,\mathcal{M}(z+y)-1)\big)\Big|_{z=\frac{\sqrt{u}}{cD},\,y=\frac{\sqrt{u}\,(1-cM)}{cD}} K_{u,c}^{(3)} \\
& + \big(\varphi_{(0,1)}(z+y)z\,\mathcal{M}(z+y)\big)\Big|_{z=\frac{\sqrt{u}}{cD},\,y=\frac{\sqrt{u}\,(1-cM)}{cD}} K_{u,c}^{(3)},
\end{aligned}
$$

and

$$
\begin{aligned}
\hat{\mathcal{S}}_{u,c}^{[1]}(t) := & \big(\varphi_{(0,1)}(z+y)(y\,\mathcal{M}(z+y)-1)\big)\Big|_{z=\frac{u}{cD\sqrt{u+ct}},\,y=\frac{\sqrt{u+ct}\,(1-cM)}{cD}} \hat{K}_{u,c}^{(1)}(t), \\
& + \big(\varphi_{(0,1)}(z+y)z\,\mathcal{M}(z+y)\big)\Big|_{z=\frac{u}{cD\sqrt{u+ct}},\,y=\frac{\sqrt{u+ct}\,(1-cM)}{cD}} \hat{K}_{u,c}^{(2)}(t), \\
\hat{\mathcal{S}}_{u,c}^{[2]} := & - \big(\varphi_{(0,1)}(z+y)\big(y\,\mathcal{M}(z+y)-1\big)\big)\Big|_{z=\frac{\sqrt{u}}{cD},\,y=\frac{\sqrt{u}\,(1-cM)}{cD}} \hat{K}_{u,c}^{(3)}, \\
& - \big(\varphi_{(0,1)}(z+y)z\,\mathcal{M}(z+y)\big)\Big|_{z=\frac{\sqrt{u}}{cD},\,y=\frac{\sqrt{u}\,(1-cM)}{cD}} \hat{K}_{u,c}^{(4)}.
\end{aligned}
$$

The following result is Theorem 3.5 in [135]. It is proved by straightforward differentiation.

Theorem 4.8 *For u, t, c positive, we have*

$$
\begin{aligned}
\mathcal{M}_{u,c}^{(0,1)}(t) &= 2\exp\left\{\frac{2u\,(1-cM)}{c^2D^2}\right\}\big(\mathcal{S}_{u,c}^{[1]}(t)+\mathcal{S}_{u,c}^{[2]}\big), \\
\mathcal{M}_{u,c}^{(1,0)}(t) &= 2\exp\left\{\frac{2u\,(1-cM)}{c^2D^2}\right\}\big(\hat{\mathcal{S}}_{u,c}^{[1]}(t)+\hat{\mathcal{S}}_{u,c}^{[2]}\big).
\end{aligned}
$$

The following result is Theorem 3.6 in [135].

Theorem 4.9 *For any t, u finite and positive, we have*

$$\mathcal{M}_{u,c}^{(0,1)}(t) < 0, \quad c > 0,$$

and the function $\mathcal{M}_{u,c}(t)$ monotone decreases, as c increases.

This theorem establishes monotony of $\mathcal{M}_{u,c}(t)$, regarded as a function of c, with t and u fixed, yields a comprehensive idea about the structure of $\mathcal{M}_{u,c}(t)$ and $\mathcal{M}_{u,c}$. The function $\mathcal{M}_{u,c}(t)$ monotone decreases from (see (4.5))

$$\mathcal{M}_{u,0}(t) = \Phi_{(0,1)}\left(\frac{M\sqrt{u}}{D}\right) - \Phi_{(0,1)}\left(\frac{M\sqrt{u}}{D} - \frac{t}{D\sqrt{u}}\right)$$

to

$$\mathcal{M}_{u,c^*}(t) = 2\left(\Phi_{(0,1)}\left(\frac{M\sqrt{u}}{D}\right) - \Phi_{(0,1)}\left(\frac{Mu}{D\sqrt{c^*t+u}}\right)\right),$$

as c increases from zero to c^*, and then to zero, as c increases from c^* to infinity. The function $\mathcal{M}_{u,c}$ monotone decreases from (see (4.12))

$$\mathcal{M}_{u,0} = \Phi_{(0,1)}\left(\frac{M\sqrt{u}}{D}\right)$$

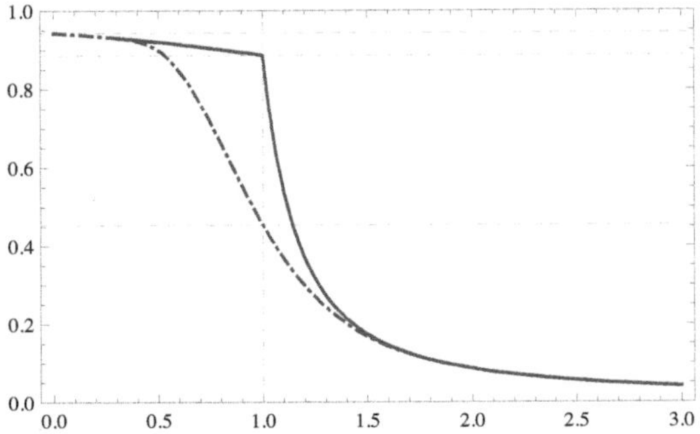

FIGURE 4.2: Graphs (X-axis is c) of $\mathcal{M}_{u,c}$ (solid line) and $\mathcal{M}_{u,c}(t)$ (dash-dotted line), when $M = 1$, $D^2 = 6$, $u = 15$, and $t = 100$. Horizontal grid lines: $\mathcal{M}_{u,0} = 0.94$, $\mathcal{M}_{u,c^*} = 0.89$, and $\mathcal{M}_{u,c^*}(t) = 0.45$.

to

$$\mathcal{M}_{u,c^*}(t) = 2\Phi_{(0,1)}\left(\frac{M\sqrt{u}}{D}\right) - 1,$$

as c increases from zero to c^*, and then to zero, as c increases from c^* to infinity.

Since $\mathcal{M}_{u,c}$ is monotone, we have the bounds

$$1 > \Phi_{(0,1)}\left(\frac{M\sqrt{u}}{D}\right) = \mathcal{M}_{u,0} > \mathcal{M}_{u,c} > \mathcal{M}_{u,c^*} = 2\Phi_{(0,1)}\left(\frac{M\sqrt{u}}{D}\right) - 1, \quad 0 < c \leqslant c^*,$$

whence for $0 < c \leqslant c^*$, the function $\mathcal{M}_{u,c}$ is sandwiched between $\mathcal{M}_{u,0}$ and $\mathcal{M}_{u,c^*}$, both tending to 1, as $u \to \infty$. The proximity of $\mathcal{M}_{u,c}$ to 1 uniformly in $c \in [0, c^*]$ is illustrated in Fig. 4.2.

The function $\mathcal{M}_{u,c}$ is continuous, but (unlike $\mathcal{M}_{u,c}(t)$) not differentiable at the point c^*:

$$\lim_{c \to c^*-} \mathcal{M}_{u,c}^{(0,1)} = \frac{2}{(c^*)^2 D}\left(\frac{u}{c^* D}\mathcal{M}\left(\frac{\sqrt{u}}{c^* D}\right) - \frac{\sqrt{u}}{2}\right)\varphi_{(0,1)}\left(\frac{\sqrt{u}}{c^* D}\right),$$

$$\lim_{c \to c^*+} \mathcal{M}_{u,c}^{(0,1)} = \frac{2}{(c^*)^2 D}\left(\frac{u}{c^* D}\mathcal{M}\left(\frac{\sqrt{u}}{c^* D}\right) - \frac{\sqrt{u}}{2}\right)\varphi_{(0,1)}\left(\frac{\sqrt{u}}{c^* D}\right) - \frac{u}{(c^*)^3 D^2}.$$

The following result is Theorem 3.7 in [135].

Theorem 4.10 *For any t, c finite and positive, there exists $u^*_{t,c} > 0$ such that*

$$\mathcal{M}_{u,c}^{(1,0)}(t) < 0, \quad u > u^*_{t,c},$$

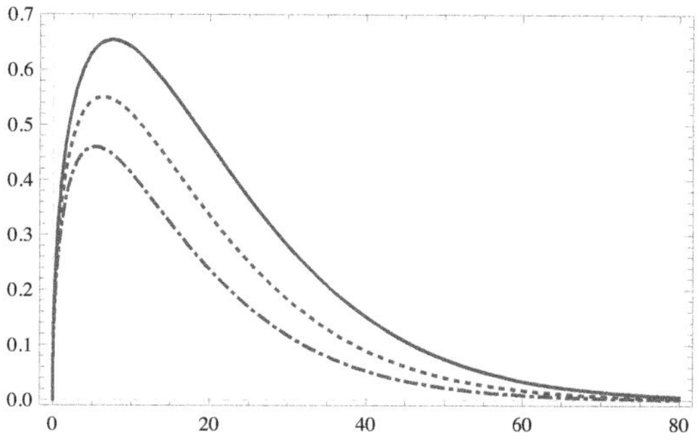

FIGURE 4.3: Graphs (X-axis is u) of $\mathcal{M}_{u,c}(t)$, when $t = 50$, $c = 1.8$ (solid line), $c = 2$ (dotted line), $c = 2.2$ (dash-dotted line). Here $M = 0.5$, $D^2 = 1$, and $c^* = 2$.

and the function $\mathcal{M}_{u,c}(t)$ monotone decreases, as $u > u^*_{t,c}$ increases.

This theorem yields a comprehensive idea about the structure of function $\mathcal{M}_{u,c}(t)$, regarded as a function of u, with t and c fixed, and $\mathcal{M}_{u,c}$, regarded as a function of u, with c fixed.

It is straightforward from (4.2) that the function $\mathcal{M}_{u,c}(t)$, $0 < u < \infty$, is strictly positive for all t and c positive. But (see illustration in Fig. 4.3) we have $\mathcal{M}_{0,c}(t) = 0$, $\mathcal{M}_{\infty,c}(t) = 0$, which easily follows from (4.4); to prove the first equality, note that $\lim_{\lambda\to 0} F(x; \mu, \lambda, -\frac{1}{2}) = 1$. Thereby, the function $\mathcal{M}_{u,c}(t)$ cannot be monotone decreasing for all $u \geqslant 0$. However, by Theorem 4.10, for any $t > 0$, $c > c^*$, there exists $u^*_{t,c} > 0$ such that $\mathcal{M}_{u,c}(t)$ monotone decreases, as $u > u^*_{t,c}$ increases. Moreover, it follows from (4.6) that for any $c > c^*$ and t fixed, the function $\mathcal{M}_{u,c}(t)$ decreases to zero exponentially fast, as $u \to \infty$. The similar conclusion holds for $\mathcal{M}_{u,c}$.

A deeper analysis of the functions $\mathcal{M}_{u,c}(t)$ and $\mathcal{M}_{u,c}$ when c, u, and t are finite can hardly be done. However, it is natural to address the asymptotic behavior of these functions, as $t \to \infty$.

4.1.3 Asymptotic behavior of $\mathcal{M}_{u,c}(t)$, as $t \to \infty$

We will consider the asymptotic behavior of $\mathcal{M}_{u,c}(t)$, as $t \to \infty$, on different ranges of the variable c. Firstly, we will be focussed on $0 \leqslant c < Kc^*$, where $0 < K < 1$, secondly, on $c > Kc^*$, where $K > 1$, and, thirdly, on the right-hand and left-hand $t^{-1/2}$-neighborhoods of the point c^*. In each of these four ranges, we will choose $u = u_t(c)$ in a special way. The reasons for this choice will be discussed in Section 5.5 below.

Theorem 4.11 *For $0 \leqslant c < Kc^*$, $0 < K < 1$, and*

$$u_t(c) := (c^* - c)\,t + \frac{D}{M^{3/2}}\, z_t(c)\sqrt{t}, \tag{4.18}$$

where $z_t(c) = O(1)$, *as* $t \to \infty$, *we have*

$$\mathcal{M}_{u,c}(t)\Big|_{u=u_t(c)} \sim 1 - \Phi_{(0,1)}(z_t(c)), \quad t \to \infty.$$

Proof of Theorem 4.11. Let us parameterize the variable c. We write $c := c^*\zeta$, $0 \leqslant \zeta < K < 1$, whence the functions $u_t(c)$ and $z_t(c)$ are re-parametrized accordingly. Plainly, (4.18) is rewritten as $u_{t,\zeta} = \frac{t}{M}(1-\zeta) + \frac{D}{M^{3/2}} z_{t,\zeta}\sqrt{t}$.

Let us note that for

$$v_t := \frac{M}{D^2}(1-\zeta)\,t + \frac{M^{1/2}}{D}\, z_{t,\zeta}\sqrt{t}, \quad \psi := \zeta, \quad \omega_t := \frac{M}{D^2}\,\zeta\, t$$

we have

$$\Phi_{(0,1)}(v_t^{1/2}) = \Phi_{(0,1)}\left(\left(\tfrac{M}{D^2}(1-\zeta)\,t + \tfrac{M^{1/2}}{D}\, z_{t,\zeta}\sqrt{t}\right)^{1/2}\right) \sim 1,$$

$$\Phi_{(0,1)}\left(\frac{(\psi-2)\,v_t^{1/2}}{\psi}\right) = \Phi_{(0,1)}\left(\tfrac{\zeta-2}{\zeta}\left(\tfrac{M}{D^2}(1-\zeta)\,t + \tfrac{M^{1/2}}{D}\, z_{t,\zeta}\sqrt{t}\right)^{1/2}\right)$$

$$\sim 0,$$

$$\exp\left\{-\frac{2\,(\psi-1)\,v_t}{\psi^2}\right\} = \exp\left\{2\,\tfrac{(\zeta-1)^2}{\zeta^2}\,\tfrac{M}{D^2}\,t - 2\,\tfrac{\zeta-1}{\zeta^2}\,\tfrac{M^{1/2}}{D}\, z_{t,\zeta}\sqrt{t}\right\} \to +\infty,$$

$$\Phi_{(0,1)}\left(\frac{(\psi-1)\,\omega_t + \psi\, v_t}{\psi\sqrt{\omega_t + v_t}}\right) = \Phi_{(0,1)}\left(\frac{\tfrac{M^{1/2}}{D}\, z_{t,\zeta}\sqrt{t}}{\sqrt{\tfrac{M}{D^2}\,t + \tfrac{M^{1/2}}{D}\, z_{t,\zeta}\sqrt{t}}}\right)$$

$$\sim \Phi_{(0,1)}\left(z_{t,\zeta}\right),$$

$$\Phi_{(0,1)}\left(\frac{(\psi-1)\,\omega_t + (\psi-2)\,v_t}{\psi\sqrt{\omega_t + v_t}}\right) = \Phi_{(0,1)}\left(\frac{2(\zeta-1)\,\tfrac{M}{D^2}\,t + (\zeta-2)\,\tfrac{M^{1/2}}{D}\, z_{t,\zeta}\sqrt{t}}{\zeta\sqrt{\tfrac{M}{D^2}\,t + \tfrac{M^{1/2}}{D}\, z_{t,\zeta}\sqrt{t}}}\right)$$

$$\sim 0,$$

as $t \to \infty$. Equality (4.10) rewrites as

$$\begin{aligned} &\mathcal{M}_{u,c}(t)\Big|_{u=u_{t,\zeta},\, c=c^*\zeta} \\ &\quad = \boldsymbol{F}(v_t, \psi, \omega_t)\Big|_{v_t=\frac{M}{D^2}(1-\zeta)\,t+\frac{M^{1/2}}{D}\, z_{t,\zeta}\sqrt{t},\ \psi=\zeta,\ \omega_t=\frac{M}{D^2}\,\zeta\, t}, \end{aligned} \tag{4.19}$$

where $\boldsymbol{F}(v_t, \psi, \omega_t)$ is written out in (4.11).

Let us consider the summands in the right-hand side of (4.19) one by one. The first summand is

$$\Phi_{(0,1)}\left(\left(\tfrac{M}{D^2}(1-\zeta)\,t + \tfrac{M^{1/2}}{D}\, z_{t,\zeta}\sqrt{t}\right)^{1/2}\right) \sim 1.$$

Using relation (B.26) and the identity

$$\begin{aligned} &\varphi_{(0,1)}\left(\tfrac{\zeta-2}{\zeta}\left(\tfrac{M}{D^2}(1-\zeta)\,t + \tfrac{M^{1/2}}{D}\, z_{t,\zeta}\sqrt{t}\right)^{1/2}\right) \\ &\qquad \times \exp\left\{2\,\tfrac{(\zeta-1)^2}{\zeta^2}\,\tfrac{M}{D^2}\,t - 2\,\tfrac{\zeta-1}{\zeta^2}\,\tfrac{M^{1/2}}{D}\, z_{t,\zeta}\sqrt{t}\right\} \\ &\quad = \frac{1}{\sqrt{2\pi}}\exp\left\{(\zeta-1)\tfrac{M}{2D^2}t - \tfrac{M^{1/2}}{2D}\, z_{t,\zeta}\sqrt{t}\right\}, \end{aligned}$$

which is checked directly, the second summand is

$$\begin{aligned}
&\Phi_{(0,1)}\big(\tfrac{\zeta-2}{\zeta}\big(\tfrac{M}{D^2}(1-\zeta)\,t+\tfrac{M^{1/2}}{D}\,z_{t,\zeta}\sqrt{t}\big)^{1/2}\big)\\
&\qquad\times\exp\big\{2\,\tfrac{(\zeta-1)^2}{\zeta^2}\,\tfrac{M}{D^2}\,t-2\,\tfrac{\zeta-1}{\zeta^2}\,\tfrac{M^{1/2}}{D}\,z_{t,\zeta}\sqrt{t}\,\big\}\\
&\sim\varphi_{(0,1)}\big(\tfrac{\zeta-2}{\zeta}\big(\tfrac{M}{D^2}(1-\zeta)\,t+\tfrac{M^{1/2}}{D}\,z_{t,\zeta}\sqrt{t}\big)^{1/2}\big)\\
&\qquad\times\exp\big\{2\,\tfrac{(\zeta-1)^2}{\zeta^2}\,\tfrac{M}{D^2}\,t-2\,\tfrac{\zeta-1}{\zeta^2}\,\tfrac{M^{1/2}}{D}\,z_{t,\zeta}\sqrt{t}\,\big\}\\
&\qquad\times\big(\tfrac{2-\zeta}{\zeta}\big(\tfrac{M}{D^2}(1-\zeta)\,t+\tfrac{M^{1/2}}{D}\,z_{t,\zeta}\sqrt{t}\big)^{1/2}\big)^{-1}\\
&=\tfrac{1}{\sqrt{2\pi}}\exp\big\{(\zeta-1)\tfrac{M}{2D^2}t-\tfrac{M^{1/2}}{2D}\,z_{t,\zeta}\sqrt{t}\,\big\}\\
&\qquad\times\big(\tfrac{2-\zeta}{\zeta}\big(\tfrac{M}{D^2}(1-\zeta)\,t+\tfrac{M^{1/2}}{D}\,z_{t,\zeta}\sqrt{t}\big)^{1/2}\big)^{-1}\sim 0.
\end{aligned}$$

The third summand is

$$\Phi_{(0,1)}\left(\frac{(\psi-1)\,\omega_t+(\psi-2)\,\upsilon_t}{\psi\sqrt{\omega_t+\upsilon_t}}\right)\sim\Phi_{(0,1)}(z_{t,\zeta}).$$

Using relation (B.26) and the identity

$$\begin{aligned}
&\varphi_{(0,1)}\left(\frac{2(\zeta-1)\,\frac{M}{D^2}\,t+(\zeta-2)\frac{M^{1/2}}{D}\,z_{t,\zeta}\sqrt{t}}{\zeta\sqrt{\frac{M}{D^2}\,t+\frac{M^{1/2}}{D}\,z_{t,\zeta}\sqrt{t}}}\right)\\
&\qquad\times\exp\left\{2\,\tfrac{(\zeta-1)^2}{\zeta^2}\,\tfrac{M}{D^2}\,t-2\,\tfrac{\zeta-1}{\zeta^2}\,\tfrac{M^{1/2}}{D}\,z_{t,\zeta}\sqrt{t}\right\}\\
&\qquad=\frac{1}{\sqrt{2\pi}}\exp\left\{-\frac{\frac{M^{1/2}}{D}\,z_{t,\zeta}^2\sqrt{t}}{2\frac{M^{1/2}}{D}\sqrt{t}+2z_{t,\zeta}}\right\},
\end{aligned}$$

which is checked directly, the fourth summand is

$$\begin{aligned}
&\Phi_{(0,1)}\left(\frac{2(\zeta-1)\,\frac{M}{D^2}\,t+(\zeta-2)\frac{M^{1/2}}{D}\,z_{t,\zeta}\sqrt{t}}{\zeta\sqrt{\frac{M}{D^2}\,t+\frac{M^{1/2}}{D}\,z_{t,\zeta}\sqrt{t}}}\right)\\
&\qquad\times\exp\left\{2\,\tfrac{(\zeta-1)^2}{\zeta^2}\,\tfrac{M}{D^2}\,t-2\,\tfrac{\zeta-1}{\zeta^2}\,\tfrac{M^{1/2}}{D}\,z_{t,\zeta}\sqrt{t}\right\}\\
&\sim\varphi_{(0,1)}\left(\frac{2(\zeta-1)\,\frac{M}{D^2}\,t+(\zeta-2)\frac{M^{1/2}}{D}\,z_{t,\zeta}\sqrt{t}}{\zeta\sqrt{\frac{M}{D^2}\,t+\frac{M^{1/2}}{D}\,z_{t,\zeta}\sqrt{t}}}\right)\\
&\qquad\times\exp\left\{2\,\tfrac{(\zeta-1)^2}{\zeta^2}\,\tfrac{M}{D^2}\,t-2\,\tfrac{\zeta-1}{\zeta^2}\,\tfrac{M^{1/2}}{D}\,z_{t,\zeta}\sqrt{t}\right\}\\
&\qquad\times\left(\frac{2(1-\zeta)\,\frac{M}{D^2}\,t+(2-\zeta)\frac{M^{1/2}}{D}\,z_{t,\zeta}\sqrt{t}}{\zeta\sqrt{\frac{M}{D^2}\,t+\frac{M^{1/2}}{D}\,z_{t,\zeta}\sqrt{t}}}\right)^{-1}
\end{aligned}$$

$$\sim \frac{1}{\sqrt{2\pi}} \exp\left\{ -\frac{\frac{M^{1/2}}{D} z_{t,\zeta}^2 \sqrt{t}}{2\frac{M^{1/2}}{D}\sqrt{t} + 2z_{t,\zeta}} \right\}$$

$$\times \left(\frac{2(1-\zeta)\frac{M}{D^2}t + (2-\zeta)\frac{M^{1/2}}{D} z_{t,\zeta}\sqrt{t}}{\zeta\sqrt{\frac{M}{D^2}t + \frac{M^{1/2}}{D} z_{t,\zeta}\sqrt{t}}} \right)^{-1} \sim 0.$$

After putting these four summands in the right-hand side of (4.19), we have $\mathcal{M}_{u_{t,\zeta},\, c^*\zeta}(t) \sim 1 - \Phi_{(0,1)}(z_{t,\zeta})$, as required. □

Theorem 4.12 *For* $c_{t,\delta} := c^* - \frac{D}{M^{3/2}}\,\delta\, t^{-1/2}$, $0 \leqslant \delta < K_1$, *and* $u_{t,\epsilon} := \frac{D}{M^{3/2}}\,\epsilon\sqrt{t}$, $0 < \epsilon < K_2$, *we have*

$$\mathcal{M}_{u,c}(t)\,\Big|_{u=u_{t,\epsilon},\, c=c_{t,\delta}} \sim 1 - \Phi_{(0,1)}(-\delta+\epsilon) + \Phi_{(0,1)}(-\delta-\epsilon)\exp\{2\,\delta\epsilon\}, \quad t\to\infty.$$

Proof of Theorem 4.12. Let us make the following preliminary observations: for

$$v_t := \frac{M^{1/2}}{D}\epsilon\sqrt{t}, \quad \psi_t := 1 - \delta\frac{D}{M^{1/2}}\,t^{-1/2}, \quad \omega_t := \frac{M}{D^2}\,t - \frac{M^{1/2}}{D}\,\delta\sqrt{t},$$

and $t\to\infty$, we have $\Phi_{(0,1)}(v_t^{1/2}) = \Phi_{(0,1)}\left(\frac{M^{1/4}}{D^{1/2}}\epsilon^{1/2}t^{1/4}\right) \sim 1$, and

$$\Phi_{(0,1)}\left(\frac{(\psi_t-2)\,v_t^{1/2}}{\psi_t}\right) = \Phi_{(0,1)}\left(-\frac{(1+\delta\frac{D}{M^{1/2}}\,t^{-1/2})\frac{M^{1/4}}{D^{1/2}}\,\epsilon^{1/2}\,t^{1/4}}{1-\delta\frac{D}{M^{1/2}}\,t^{-1/2}}\right)$$

$$\sim \Phi_{(0,1)}\left(-\frac{M^{1/4}}{D^{1/2}}\,\epsilon^{1/2}\,t^{1/4}\right) \sim 0,$$

$$\exp\left\{-\frac{2\,(\psi_t-1)\,v_t}{\psi_t^2}\right\} = \exp\left\{-\frac{-2\,\delta\frac{D}{M^{1/2}}\,t^{-1/2}\,\frac{M^{1/2}}{D}\epsilon\sqrt{t}}{(1-\delta\frac{D}{M^{1/2}}\,t^{-1/2})^2}\right\}$$

$$\sim \exp\{2\,\delta\epsilon\},$$

$$\Phi_{(0,1)}\left(\frac{(\psi_t-1)\,\omega_t + \psi_t\,v_t}{\psi_t\sqrt{\omega_t+v_t}}\right)$$

$$= \Phi_{(0,1)}\left(\frac{-(\delta-\epsilon)\frac{M^{1/2}}{D}\sqrt{t} + \delta^2 - \delta\epsilon}{(1-\delta\frac{D}{M^{1/2}}\,t^{-1/2})\sqrt{\frac{M}{D^2}\,t - \frac{M^{1/2}}{D}\,(\delta-\epsilon)\sqrt{t}}}\right)$$

$$\sim \Phi_{(0,1)}(-\delta+\epsilon),$$

$$\Phi_{(0,1)}\left(\frac{(\psi_t-1)\,\omega_t + (\psi_t-2)\,v_t}{\psi_t\sqrt{\omega_t+v_t}}\right)$$

$$= \Phi_{(0,1)}\left(\frac{-(\delta+\epsilon)\frac{M^{1/2}}{D}\sqrt{t} + \delta^2 - \delta\epsilon}{(1-\delta\frac{D}{M^{1/2}}\,t^{-1/2})\sqrt{\frac{M}{D^2}\,t - \frac{M^{1/2}}{D}\,(\delta-\epsilon)\sqrt{t}}}\right)$$

$$\sim \Phi_{(0,1)}(-\delta-\epsilon).$$

Equality (4.10) yields

$$\mathcal{M}_{u,c}(t)\,\Big|_{u=u_{t,\epsilon},\,c=c_{t,\delta}}$$

$$= \boldsymbol{F}(\upsilon_t,\psi_t,\omega_t)\,\Big|_{\upsilon_t=\frac{M^{1/2}}{D}\epsilon\sqrt{t},\ \psi_t=1-\delta\frac{D}{M^{1/2}}t^{-1/2},\ \omega_t=\frac{M}{D^2}t-\frac{M^{1/2}}{D}\delta\sqrt{t}},$$

where $\boldsymbol{F}(\upsilon_t,\psi_t,\omega_t)$ is given in (4.11). Considering the summands in the right-hand side of (4.19) one by one, using the above expressions, we get the result, as required. □

Theorem 4.13 *For $c_{t,\delta} := c^* + \frac{D}{M^{3/2}}\,\delta\, t^{-1/2}$, $0 \leqslant \delta < K_1$, and $u_{t,\epsilon} := \frac{D}{M^{3/2}}\,\epsilon\sqrt{t}$, $0<\epsilon<K_2$, we have*

$$\mathcal{M}_{u,c}(t)\,\Big|_{u=u_{t,\epsilon},\,c=c_{t,\delta}} \sim 1 - \Phi_{(0,1)}(\delta+\epsilon) + \Phi_{(0,1)}(\delta-\epsilon)\exp\{-2\,\delta\epsilon\},\quad t\to\infty.$$

Proof of Theorem 4.13. Let us make the following preliminary observations: for

$$\upsilon_t := \frac{M^{1/2}}{D}\,\epsilon\sqrt{t},\quad \psi_t := 1+\frac{D}{M^{1/2}}\,\delta\, t^{-1/2},\quad \omega_t := \frac{M}{D^2}\,t+\frac{M^{1/2}}{D}\,\delta\sqrt{t},$$

and $t\to\infty$, we have $\Phi_{(0,1)}(\upsilon_t^{1/2}) = \Phi_{(0,1)}\Big(\frac{M^{1/4}}{D^{1/2}}\epsilon^{1/2}t^{1/4}\Big) \sim 1$, and

$$\Phi_{(0,1)}\bigg(\frac{(\psi_t-2)\,\upsilon_t^{1/2}}{\psi_t}\bigg) = \Phi_{(0,1)}\left(\frac{(\delta\frac{D}{M^{1/2}}t^{-1/2}-1)\frac{M^{1/4}}{D^{1/2}}\,\epsilon^{1/2}\,t^{1/4}}{1+\delta\frac{D}{M^{1/2}}\,t^{-1/2}}\right)$$

$$\sim \Phi_{(0,1)}\Big(-\,\frac{M^{1/4}}{D^{1/2}}\,\epsilon^{1/2}\,t^{1/4}\Big) \sim 0,$$

$$\exp\bigg\{-\,\frac{2\,(\psi_t-1)\,\upsilon_t}{\psi_t^2}\bigg\} = \exp\left\{-\,\frac{2\,\delta\frac{D}{M^{1/2}}\,t^{-1/2}\,\frac{M^{1/2}}{D}\epsilon\sqrt{t}}{(1+\delta M t^{-1/2})^2}\right\}$$

$$\sim \exp\{-2\,\delta\epsilon\},$$

$$\Phi_{(0,1)}\bigg(\frac{(\psi_t-1)\,\omega_t+\psi_t\,\upsilon_t}{\psi_t\sqrt{\omega_t+\upsilon_t}}\bigg)$$

$$= \Phi_{(0,1)}\left(\frac{\frac{M^{1/2}}{D}\,(\delta+\epsilon)\sqrt{t}+\delta^2+\epsilon\delta}{(1+\delta\frac{D}{M^{1/2}}\,t^{-1/2})\sqrt{\frac{M}{D^2}\,t+\frac{M^{1/2}}{D}\,(\delta+\epsilon)\sqrt{t}}}\right)$$

$$\sim \Phi_{(0,1)}(\delta+\epsilon),$$

$$\Phi_{(0,1)}\bigg(\frac{(\psi_t-1)\,\omega_t+(\psi_t-2)\,\upsilon_t}{\psi_t\sqrt{\omega_t+\upsilon_t}}\bigg)$$

$$= \Phi_{(0,1)}\left(\frac{\frac{M^{1/2}}{D}\,(\delta-\epsilon)\sqrt{t}+\delta^2+\epsilon\delta}{(1+\delta\frac{D}{M^{1/2}}\,t^{-1/2})\sqrt{\frac{M}{D^2}\,t+\frac{M^{1/2}}{D}\,(\delta+\epsilon)\sqrt{t}}}\right)$$

$$\sim \Phi_{(0,1)}(\delta-\epsilon).$$

Equality (4.10) yields

$$\mathcal{M}_{u,c}(t)\Big|_{u=u_{t,\epsilon},\, c=c_{t,\delta}} = \boldsymbol{F}(v_t, \psi_t, \omega_t)\Big|_{v_t=\frac{M^{1/2}}{D}\epsilon\sqrt{t},\, \psi_t=1+\delta\frac{D}{M^{1/2}}t^{-1/2},\, \omega_t=\frac{M}{D^2}t+\frac{M^{1/2}}{D}\delta\sqrt{t}},$$

where $\boldsymbol{F}(v_t, \psi_t, \omega_t)$ is given in (4.11). Consider the summands in the right-hand side of (4.19) one by one, using the above expressions, whence the result.

□

Theorem 4.14 *For $c > Kc^*$, $K > 1$, and $u_t(c) := \frac{D^2}{M^2} z_t(c)$, where $z_t(c) = O(1)$, as $t \to \infty$, we have*

$$\mathcal{M}_{u,c}(t)\Big|_{u=u_t(c)} \sim \left(1 - \Phi_{(0,1)}\left(\frac{cM-2}{cM} z_t^{1/2}(c)\right)\right)\exp\left\{-2\frac{cM-1}{c^2M^2} z_t(c)\right\} - 1 + \Phi_{(0,1)}(z_t^{1/2}(c)), \quad t \to \infty.$$

Proof of Theorem 4.14. Let us go from variable c to variable ζ, writing $c = c^*\zeta$, $\zeta > K > 1$, and from $z_t(c)$ to $z_t(c^*\zeta) := z_{t,\zeta}$. Accordingly, the function $u_t(c)$ is written as $u_{t,\zeta} := \frac{D^2}{M^2} z_{t,\zeta}$. Let us focus on equality (4.10), i.e.,

$$\mathcal{M}_{u,c}(t)\Big|_{u=u_{t,\zeta},\, c=c^*\zeta} = \boldsymbol{F}(v_t, \psi, \omega_t)\Big|_{v_t=z_{t,\zeta}, \psi=\zeta, \omega_t=\frac{M}{D^2}\zeta t},$$

where $\boldsymbol{F}(v_t, \psi, \omega_t)$ is given in (4.11).

Let us note that for

$$v_t := \frac{M^2}{D^2} u_{t,\zeta} = z_{t,\zeta}, \quad \omega_t := \frac{M}{D^2}\zeta t, \quad \psi := \zeta,$$

we have

$$\Phi_{(0,1)}(v_t^{1/2}) = \Phi_{(0,1)}(z_{t,\zeta}^{1/2}), \quad \Phi_{(0,1)}\left(\frac{(\psi-2)\, v_t^{1/2}}{\psi}\right) = \Phi_{(0,1)}\left(\tfrac{\zeta-2}{\zeta} z_{t,\zeta}^{1/2}\right),$$

and

$$\exp\left\{-\frac{2(\psi-1)\,v_t}{\psi^2}\right\} = \exp\left\{-2\left((\zeta-1)/\zeta^2\right) z_{t,\zeta}\right\},$$

$$\Phi_{(0,1)}\left(\frac{(\psi-1)\,\omega_t + \psi\, v_t}{\psi\sqrt{\omega_t + v_t}}\right) = \Phi_{(0,1)}\left(\frac{(\zeta-1)\frac{M}{D^2}\zeta t + \zeta z_{t,\zeta}}{\zeta\sqrt{\frac{M}{D^2}\zeta t + z_{t,\zeta}}}\right) \sim 1,$$

$$\Phi_{(0,1)}\left(\frac{(\psi-1)\,\omega_t + (\psi-2)\, v_t}{\psi\sqrt{\omega_t + v_t}}\right) = \Phi_{(0,1)}\left(\frac{(\zeta-1)\frac{M}{D^2}\zeta t + (\zeta-2) z_{t,\zeta}}{\zeta\sqrt{\frac{M}{D^2}\zeta t + z_{t,\zeta}}}\right) \sim 1,$$

as $t \to \infty$. Consider the summands in the right-hand side of (4.19) one by one, using the above expressions. We get

$$\begin{aligned}\mathcal{M}_{u,c}(t)\,\big|_{u=u_{t,\zeta},c=c^*\zeta} \sim \Big(1 - \varPhi_{(0,1)}\Big(\tfrac{\zeta-2}{\zeta}\, z_{t,\zeta}^{1/2}\Big)\Big)\\ \times \exp\big\{-2\,((\zeta-1)/\zeta^2) z_{t,\zeta}\big\}\\ -1 + \varPhi_{(0,1)}(z_{t,\zeta}^{1/2}).\end{aligned}$$

Going back from the parametrization $c = c^*\zeta$, $\zeta > K > 1$, to the original notation, we get the result, as required. □

4.2 Proximity Between $\mathcal{M}_{u,c}(t)$ and $\mathcal{M}_{u,c}(t \mid v)$

For $t > v > 0$, $u > 0$, $c \geqslant 0$, and M, D^2 positive, we write

$$\begin{aligned}\mathcal{M}_{u,c}(t \mid v) &:= \mathcal{M}_{u+cv,\,c}(t-v)\\ &= \int_0^{\frac{c(t-v)}{u+cv}} \frac{1}{x+1}\, \varphi_{\left(cM(x+1),\, \frac{c^2D^2(x+1)}{u+cv}\right)}(x)\, dx.\end{aligned} \tag{4.20}$$

Plainly, we have $\mathcal{M}_{u,c}(t \mid 0) = \mathcal{M}_{u,c}(t)$, which was investigated in Section 4.1.

The proximity between $\mathcal{M}_{u,c}(t \mid v)$ and $\mathcal{M}_{u,c}(t)$, as u is sufficiently large[4], was examined in [135], Section 3.2.4, in two stages. The first stage is comparison of $\mathcal{M}_{u,c}(t \mid v)$ and $\mathcal{M}_{u,c}(t-v)$. It is based on the fact, clear from the definition (4.20), that $\mathcal{M}_{u,c}(t \mid v)$ viewed as a function of u coincides with $\mathcal{M}_{u,c}(t-v)$ shifted to the left by cv. The second stage is comparison of $\mathcal{M}_{u,c}(t-v)$ and $\mathcal{M}_{u,c}(t)$. It is based on the observation that $\mathcal{M}_{u,c}(t)$ viewed as a function of u is obtained from $\mathcal{M}_{u,c}(t-v)$ by stretching it up and to the right. Formal results are as follows.

Theorem 4.15 *When $c \geqslant 0$, we have*

$$\sup_{t>v} \big|\mathcal{M}_{u,c}(t \mid v) - \mathcal{M}_{u,c}(t-v)\big| \to 0, \quad u \to \infty,$$

where supremum is over $0 < v < t$ such that $t < t_u = o(u^\alpha)$, $u \to \infty$, where $0 < \alpha < 2$, and $v < v_u = o(u)$, $u \to \infty$,

Theorem 4.16 *When $c \geqslant 0$, we have*

$$\sup_{t>v} \Big|\mathcal{M}_{u,c}(t-v) - \mathcal{M}_{u,c}(t)\Big| \to 0, \quad u \to \infty,$$

where supremum is over $0 < v < t$ such that $t < t_u = o(u^\alpha)$, $u \to \infty$, where $0 < \alpha < 2$, and $v < v_u = o(u)$, as $u \to \infty$,

[4]Note that $\lim_{u\to 0} \mathcal{M}_{u,c}(t-v) = 0$, $\lim_{u\to 0} \mathcal{M}_{u,c}(t \mid v) > 0$, and for $u > 0$ small and moderate the discrepancy between $\mathcal{M}_{u,c}(t \mid v)$ and $\mathcal{M}_{u,c}(t-v)$ can be considerable.

Theorem 4.17 *For a function $f(x) > 0$, $x > 0$, such that $\int_0^\infty f(x)\,dx = 1$, $\int_0^\infty x f(x)\,dx < \infty$, we have*

$$\sup_{t>0} \left| \int_0^t \mathcal{M}_{u,c}(t \mid v)\, f(v)\, dv - \int_0^t \mathcal{M}_{u,c}(t - v)\, f(v)\, dv \right| \to 0, \quad u \to \infty.$$

Theorem 4.18 *For a function $f(x) > 0$, $x > 0$, such that $\int_0^\infty f(x)\,dx = 1$, $\int_0^\infty x f(x)\,dx < \infty$, we have*

$$\sup_{t>0} \left| \int_0^t \mathcal{M}_{u,c}(t \mid v)\, f(v)\, dv - \mathcal{M}_{u,c}(t) \right| \to 0, \quad t, u \to \infty. \tag{4.21}$$

4.3 Analytical Properties of $\mathcal{M}$-Level

For $\alpha > 0$, the equations (w.r.t. u)

$$\mathcal{M}_{u,c}(t) = \alpha \tag{4.22}$$

and $\mathcal{M}_{u,c} = \alpha$ are called $\mathcal{M}$-equation and infinite-time $\mathcal{M}$-equation, respectively. For brevity, we refer to the positive solution to $\mathcal{M}$-equation, denoted by $u_{\alpha,t}^{[\mathcal{M}]}(c)$, $c \geqslant 0$, as $\mathcal{M}$-level.

4.3.1 Analytical structure of $\mathcal{M}$-level

We start with the following result, the proof of which is elementary.

Theorem 4.19 *For $t \to \infty$, we have*

$$\begin{aligned} u_{\alpha,t}^{[\mathcal{M}]}(0) &= \frac{t}{M} + \frac{D}{M^{3/2}}\, \kappa_\alpha \sqrt{t}\, (1 + o(1)), \\ u_{\alpha,t}^{[\mathcal{M}]}(c^*) &= \frac{D}{M^{3/2}}\, \kappa_{\alpha/2} \sqrt{t}\, (1 + o(1)). \end{aligned} \tag{4.23}$$

Proof of Theorem 4.19. Bearing in mind the first equality in (4.5), the equation $\mathcal{M}_{u,0}(t) = \alpha$ may be rewritten as $\Phi_{(0,1)}\big(\frac{M\sqrt{u}}{D}\big) - \Phi_{(0,1)}\big(\frac{M\sqrt{u}}{D} - \frac{t}{D\sqrt{u}}\big) = \alpha$. We have

$$\begin{aligned} \Phi_{(0,1)}\left(\frac{M\sqrt{u}}{D}\right)\Big|_{u=\frac{t}{M}+\frac{D}{M^{3/2}}\sqrt{t}\,\kappa_\alpha\,(1+o(1))} &\sim 1, \\ \Phi_{(0,1)}\left(\frac{M\sqrt{u}}{D} - \frac{t}{D\sqrt{u}}\right)\Big|_{u=\frac{t}{M}+\frac{D}{M^{3/2}}\sqrt{t}\,\kappa_\alpha\,(1+o(1))} &\sim \Phi_{(0,1)}(\kappa_\alpha) \\ &= 1 - \alpha, \end{aligned}$$

as $t \to \infty$, whence the first equality in (4.23). Bearing in mind the second equality in (4.5), the equation $\mathcal{M}_{u,c^*}(t) = \alpha$ may be rewritten as $\Phi_{(0,1)}\left(\frac{M\sqrt{u}}{D}\right) - \Phi_{(0,1)}\left(\frac{Mu}{D\sqrt{c^*t+u}}\right) = \frac{\alpha}{2}$. We have

$$\begin{aligned}
\Phi_{(0,1)}\left(\frac{M\sqrt{u}}{D}\right)\Bigg|_{u=\frac{D}{M^{3/2}}\sqrt{t}\,\kappa_{\alpha/2}\,(1+o(1))} &\sim 1,\\
\Phi_{(0,1)}\left(\frac{Mu}{D\sqrt{c^*t+u}}\right)\Bigg|_{u=\frac{D}{M^{3/2}}\sqrt{t}\,\kappa_{\alpha/2}\,(1+o(1))} &\sim \Phi_{(0,1)}(\kappa_{\alpha/2})\\
&= 1-\alpha/2,
\end{aligned}$$

as $t \to \infty$, whence the second equality in (4.23). □

The following theorem is analogous to Theorems 2.7 and 3.8 and is proved by a similar method. When $c = 0$ and $c = c^*$, the equality (4.24) yields (4.23).

Theorem 4.20 *We have*

$$u_{\alpha,t}^{[\mathcal{M}]}(c) = \begin{cases} (c^*-c)\,t + \dfrac{D}{M^{3/2}}\,\hat{\mathsf{z}}_{\alpha,t}\left(\dfrac{M^{3/2}(c^*-c)}{D}\sqrt{t}\right)\sqrt{t}, & 0 \leqslant c < c^*,\\ \dfrac{D}{M^{3/2}}\,\hat{\mathsf{z}}_{\alpha,t}\left(\dfrac{M^{3/2}(c^*-c)}{D}\sqrt{t}\right)\sqrt{t}, & c \geqslant c^*, \end{cases} \tag{4.24}$$

where for t sufficiently large the function $\hat{\mathsf{z}}_{\alpha,t}(y)$, $y \in \mathsf{R}$, is continuous and monotone increasing, as y increases from $-\infty$ to 0, and monotone decreasing, as y increases from 0 to ∞, and such that[5]

$$\lim_{y\to-\infty} \hat{\mathsf{z}}_{\alpha,t}(y) = 0, \quad \lim_{y\to\infty} \hat{\mathsf{z}}_{\alpha,t}(y) = \kappa_\alpha$$

and $\hat{\mathsf{z}}_{\alpha,t}(0) = \kappa_{\alpha/2}\,(1+o(1))$, as $t \to \infty$.

Proof of Theorem 4.20. We note first that this proof is carried out along the same scheme as the proof of Theorem 2.7, in two stages — separately, when $0 < c \leqslant c^*$ and $c > c^*$. In both stages we make a suitable change of variables aimed to focus on the function $\hat{\mathsf{z}}_\alpha(y)$, $y \in \mathsf{R}$, and to check its monotony using the standard criterion applying the implicit function derivative theorem (see Theorem A.4) and focussed on the sign of the derivative.

Step 1. We focus on the case $0 < c \leqslant c^* := M^{-1}$ and switch from the variables u and c in the left-hand side of (4.22) to the variables

$$z := \frac{u}{DM^{-3/2}\sqrt{t}} - \frac{(M^{-1}-c)\sqrt{t}}{DM^{-3/2}} \in \mathsf{R}, \quad y := \frac{(M^{-1}-c)\sqrt{t}}{DM^{-3/2}} > 0, \tag{4.25}$$

[5]We recall that $0 < \kappa_\alpha < \kappa_{\alpha/2}$ for $0 < \alpha < \frac{1}{2}$.

noting that $z+y>0$. Vice versa, we have

$$u=\frac{D\sqrt{t}}{M^{3/2}}\,(z+y), \quad c=\frac{1}{M}-\frac{D}{M^{3/2}\sqrt{t}}\,y.$$

In this way, we rewrite equation (4.22) as

$$\mathcal{M}_{u,c}(t)\,\Big|_{u=\frac{D\sqrt{t}}{M^{3/2}}(z+y),\ c=\frac{1}{M}-\frac{D}{M^{3/2}\sqrt{t}}\,y}=\alpha. \tag{4.26}$$

It is worth noting that for T and Y exponentially distributed with parameters δ and ρ, equalities (4.25) become (3.38). Bearing in mind that in this case $M=\rho/\delta$, $D^2=2\rho/\delta^2$, it is easily checked by elementary calculations.

We are ready to investigate the solution $z=\hat{\mathbf{z}}_{\alpha,t}(y)$, $y>0$, to equation (4.26), which obviously exists and is unique. To prove that $\hat{\mathbf{z}}_{\alpha,t}(y)$, $y>0$, is monotone decreasing, we have to prove that $\frac{d}{dy}\,\hat{\mathbf{z}}_{\alpha,t}(y)<0$, $y>0$.

We apply the implicit function derivative theorem (see Theorem A.4), which yields

$$\frac{d}{dy}\,\hat{\mathbf{z}}_{\alpha,t}(y)=-\left.\left(\frac{\frac{\partial}{\partial y}\Big(\mathcal{M}_{u,c}(t)\,\Big|_{u=\frac{D\sqrt{t}}{M^{3/2}}(z+y),\ c=\frac{1}{M}-\frac{D}{M^{3/2}\sqrt{t}}\,y}\Big)}{\frac{\partial}{\partial z}\Big(\mathcal{M}_{u,c}(t)\,\Big|_{u=\frac{D\sqrt{t}}{M^{3/2}}(z+y),\ c=\frac{1}{M}-\frac{D}{M^{3/2}\sqrt{t}}\,y}\Big)}\right)\right|_{z=\hat{\mathbf{z}}_{\alpha,t}(y)}.$$

According to the chain rule for differentiation of a composite function (see (A.1)), we have

$$\begin{aligned}
&\frac{\partial}{\partial y}\Big(\mathcal{M}_{u,c}(t)\,\Big|_{u=\frac{D\sqrt{t}}{M^{3/2}}(z+y),\ c=\frac{1}{M}-\frac{D}{M^{3/2}\sqrt{t}}\,y}\Big)\\
&\qquad=\frac{D\sqrt{t}}{M^{3/2}}\Big(\mathcal{M}^{(1,0)}_{u,c}(t)\,\Big|_{u=\frac{D\sqrt{t}}{M^{3/2}}(z+y),\ c=\frac{1}{M}-\frac{D}{M^{3/2}\sqrt{t}}\,y}\\
&\qquad\quad-\frac{1}{t}\,\mathcal{M}^{(0,1)}_{u,c}(t)\,\Big|_{u=\frac{D\sqrt{t}}{M^{3/2}}(z+y),\ c=\frac{1}{M}-\frac{D}{M^{3/2}\sqrt{t}}\,y}\Big),\\
&\frac{\partial}{\partial z}\Big(\mathcal{M}_{u,c}(t)\,\Big|_{u=\frac{D\sqrt{t}}{M^{3/2}}(z+y),\ c=\frac{1}{M}-\frac{D}{M^{3/2}\sqrt{t}}\,y}\Big)\\
&\qquad=\frac{D\sqrt{t}}{M^{3/2}}\Big(\mathcal{M}^{(1,0)}_{u,c}(t)\,\Big|_{u=\frac{D\sqrt{t}}{M^{3/2}}(z+y),\ c=\frac{1}{M}-\frac{D}{M^{3/2}\sqrt{t}}\,y}\Big).
\end{aligned}$$

Step 2. Let us proceed with the case $c>c^*:=M^{-1}$. We switch from the variables u and c to the variables

$$z=\frac{u}{DM^{-3/2}\sqrt{t}}>0, \quad y=\frac{(M^{-1}-c)\sqrt{t}}{DM^{-3/2}}<0. \tag{4.27}$$

In the case when T, Y are exponentially distributed with parameters δ, ρ, equalities (4.27) become equalities (3.43). Since in this case $M=\rho/\delta$, $D^2=2\rho/\delta^2$, it is easily shown by elementary calculations.

Let us rewrite equation (4.22) as

$$\mathcal{M}_{u,c}(t)\,\Big|_{u=\frac{D\sqrt{t}}{M^{3/2}}z,\,c=\frac{1}{M}-\frac{D}{M^{3/2}\sqrt{t}}y} = \alpha.$$

We apply the implicit function derivative theorem, which yields

$$\frac{d}{dy}\,\hat{\mathbf{z}}_{\alpha,t}(y) = -\left(\frac{\frac{\partial}{\partial y}\Big(\mathcal{M}_{u,c}(t)\,\big|_{u=\frac{D\sqrt{t}}{M^{3/2}}z,\ c=\frac{1}{M}-\frac{D}{M^{3/2}\sqrt{t}}y}\Big)}{\frac{\partial}{\partial z}\Big(\mathcal{M}_{u,c}(t)\,\big|_{u=\frac{D\sqrt{t}}{M^{3/2}}z,\ c=\frac{1}{M}-\frac{D}{M^{3/2}\sqrt{t}}y}\Big)}\right)\Bigg|_{z=\hat{\mathbf{z}}_{\alpha,t}(y)}.$$

According to chain rule for differentiation of a composite function (see (A.1)), we have

$$\begin{aligned}
&\frac{\partial}{\partial y}\left(\mathcal{M}_{u,c}(t)\,\big|_{u=\frac{D\sqrt{t}}{M^{3/2}}z,\ c=\frac{1}{M}-\frac{D}{M^{3/2}\sqrt{t}}y}\right)\\
&\quad= -\left(\frac{D}{M^{3/2}\sqrt{t}}\right)\mathcal{M}^{(0,1)}_{u,c}(t)\,\big|_{u=\frac{D\sqrt{t}}{M^{3/2}}z,c=\frac{1}{M}-\frac{D}{M^{3/2}\sqrt{t}}y},\\
&\frac{\partial}{\partial z}\left(\mathcal{M}_{u,c}(t)\,\big|_{u=\frac{D\sqrt{t}}{M^{3/2}}z,\ c=\frac{1}{M}-\frac{D}{M^{3/2}\sqrt{t}}y}\right)\\
&\quad= \left(\frac{D\sqrt{t}}{M^{3/2}}\right)\mathcal{M}^{(1,0)}_{u,c}(t)\,\big|_{u=DM^{-3/2}\sqrt{t}z,c=M^{-1}-DM^{-3/2}v/\sqrt{t}}.
\end{aligned}$$

By Theorem 4.10, we have $\frac{d}{dy}\,\hat{\mathbf{z}}_{\alpha,t}(y) < 0$, $y < 0$, for u and t sufficiently large, as required. □

4.3.2 Monotony and convexity of $\mathcal{M}$-level

In Chapter 2, we have proved that for all $t > 0$ the fixed-probability level $u^{[\mathrm{dif}]}_{\alpha,t\,|\,\vartheta}(c)$, $c \geqslant 0$, is (which is obvious from its definition) monotone decreasing, as c increases, and (which is not obvious from its definition) convex. The analytic proof was based on standard criteria in terms of (first-order and second-order) derivatives of $u^{[\mathrm{dif}]}_{\alpha,t\,|\,\vartheta}(c)$, $c \geqslant 0$, i.e., Theorem A.4 on derivatives of implicit function.

In particular, we have found (see (2.28)) that, when $0 \leqslant c < \vartheta$,

$$\frac{d}{dc}u^{[\mathrm{dif}]}_{\alpha,t\,|\,\vartheta}(c) = -\left(\frac{\frac{\partial}{\partial c}\Big(F(t;\mu,\lambda,-\tfrac{1}{2})\,\big|_{\mu=\frac{u}{\vartheta-c},\lambda=\frac{u^2}{\sigma^2}}\Big)}{\frac{\partial}{\partial u}\Big(F(t;\mu,\lambda,-\tfrac{1}{2})\,\big|_{\mu=\frac{u}{\vartheta-c},\lambda=\frac{u^2}{\sigma^2}}\Big)}\right)\Bigg|_{u=u^{[\mathrm{dif}]}_{\alpha,t\,|\,\vartheta}(c)},$$

and (see (2.30)), when $c > \vartheta$,

$$\frac{d}{dc}u^{[\mathrm{dif}]}_{\alpha,t\,|\,\vartheta}(c) = -\left(\frac{\frac{\partial}{\partial c}\Big(\exp\Big\{-\frac{2\lambda}{\hat{\mu}}\Big\}F(t;\hat{\mu},\lambda,-\tfrac{1}{2})\,\Big|_{\substack{\hat{\mu}=-\frac{u}{\vartheta-c}\\ \lambda=\frac{u^2}{\sigma^2}}}\Big)}{\frac{\partial}{\partial u}\Big(\exp\Big\{-\frac{2\lambda}{\hat{\mu}}\Big\}F(t;\hat{\mu},\lambda,-\tfrac{1}{2})\Big|_{\substack{\hat{\mu}=-\frac{u}{\vartheta-c}\\ \lambda=\frac{u^2}{\sigma^2}}}\Big)}\right)\Bigg|_{u=u^{[\mathrm{dif}]}_{\alpha,t\,|\,\vartheta}(c)}.$$

Similar expression (see (2.34) and (2.37)) were found for the second-order derivatives.

Bearing in mind the similarity of the above expressions with the expressions written below, the same analysis is possible for $\mathcal{M}$-level. In particular, we have, when $0 < c \leqslant c^*$,

$$\frac{d}{dc}u_{\alpha,t}^{[\mathcal{M}]}(c) = -\left(\frac{\mathcal{M}_{u,c}^{(0,1)}(t)}{\mathcal{M}_{u,c}^{(1,0)}(t)}\right)\Bigg|_{u=u_{\alpha,t\,|\,\vartheta}^{[\mathrm{dif}]}(c)}$$

$$= -\left(\frac{\frac{\partial}{\partial c}\left(\left(F\left(\frac{ct}{u}+1;\mu,\lambda,-\frac{1}{2}\right) - F\left(1;\mu,\lambda,-\frac{1}{2}\right)\right)\Big|_{\substack{\mu=\frac{1}{1-cM}\\ \lambda=\frac{u}{c^2D^2}}}\right)}{\frac{\partial}{\partial u}\left(\left(F\left(\frac{ct}{u}+1;\mu,\lambda,-\frac{1}{2}\right) - F\left(1;\mu,\lambda,-\frac{1}{2}\right)\right)\Big|_{\substack{\mu=\frac{1}{1-cM}\\ \lambda=\frac{u}{c^2D^2}}}\right)}\right)\Bigg|_{u=u_{\alpha,t\,|\,\vartheta}^{[\mathrm{dif}]}(c)},$$

and, when $c > c^*$,

$$\frac{d}{dc}u_{\alpha,t}^{[\mathcal{M}]}(c) = -\left(\frac{\mathcal{M}_{u,c}^{(0,1)}(t)}{\mathcal{M}_{u,c}^{(1,0)}(t)}\right)\Bigg|_{u=u_{\alpha,t\,|\,\vartheta}^{[\mathrm{dif}]}(c)}$$

$$= -\left(\frac{\frac{\partial}{\partial c}\left(e^{-\frac{2\lambda}{\hat{\mu}}}\left(F\left(\frac{ct}{u}+1;\hat{\mu},\lambda,-\frac{1}{2}\right) - F\left(1;\hat{\mu},\lambda,-\frac{1}{2}\right)\right)\Big|_{\substack{\hat{\mu}=\frac{1}{cM-1}\\ \lambda=\frac{u}{c^2D^2}}}\right)}{\frac{\partial}{\partial u}\left(e^{-\frac{2\lambda}{\hat{\mu}}}\left(F\left(\frac{ct}{u}+1;\hat{\mu},\lambda,-\frac{1}{2}\right) - F\left(1;\hat{\mu},\lambda,-\frac{1}{2}\right)\right)\Big|_{\substack{\hat{\mu}=\frac{1}{cM-1}\\ \lambda=\frac{u}{c^2D^2}}}\right)}\right)\Bigg|_{u=u_{\alpha,t\,|\,\vartheta}^{[\mathrm{dif}]}(c)}.$$

We leave further analysis of monotony and convexity of $\mathcal{M}$-level to the reader by two reasons. Firstly, it is quite similar to the analysis carried out in Chapter 2. Second, this analysis stands aside from the main tend of research since constructing the upper bounds for $u_{\alpha,t\,|\,\vartheta}^{[\mathrm{dif}]}(c)$, $c \geqslant c^*$, for which convexity of $\mathcal{M}$-level would be useful, does not make clear sense in terms of this research.

4.3.3 Asymptotic behavior of $\mathcal{M}$-level, as $t \to \infty$

In Theorem 4.19, the asymptotic (as $t \to \infty$) expressions for $u_{\alpha,t}^{[\mathcal{M}]}(c)$ are found in two points, $c = 0$ and $c = c^*$. In Theorem 4.20, an asymptotic (as $t \to \infty$) representation for $u_{\alpha,t}^{[\mathcal{M}]}(c)$ is given for all $c \geqslant 0$, with the function $\hat{\mathsf{z}}_{\alpha,t}(y)$, $y \in \mathsf{R}$, described in terms of its properties, but for which an explicit expression, or a method of its finding, is not given yet.

We are going to give an asymptotic (as $t \to \infty$) representation for $u_{\alpha,t}^{[\mathcal{M}]}(c)$, $c \geqslant 0$. In the same way as in Theorems 4.11–4.14, we will be focussed first on the case when $0 \leqslant c < Kc^*$, $0 < K < 1$, then on the right and left $t^{-1/2}$-neighborhoods of c^*, and finally on the case $c > Kc^*$, where $K > 1$.

Theorem 4.21 *For* $0 \leqslant c < Kc^*$, $0 < K < 1$, *we have*[6]

$$u^{[\mathcal{M}]}_{\alpha,t}(c) = (c^* - c)\,t + \frac{D}{M^{3/2}}\,\kappa_\alpha\sqrt{t}\,(1 + o(1)), \quad t \to \infty.$$

Proof of Theorem 4.21. By Theorem 4.11, for $0 \leqslant c < Kc^*$, $0 < K < 1$, and $u_t(c) := (c^* - c)\,t + \frac{D}{M^{3/2}}\sqrt{t}\,z_t(c)$, where $z_t(c) = O(1)$, as $t \to \infty$, we have

$$\mathcal{M}_{u,c}(t)\,\Big|_{u=u_t(c)} \sim 1 - \varPhi_{(0,1)}(z_t(c)), \quad t \to \infty.$$

Therefore, the equation $\mathcal{M}_{u,c}(t)\,|_{u=u_t(c)} = \alpha$ may be rewritten as $1 - \varPhi_{(0,1)}(z_t(c)) = \alpha\,(1 + o(1))$, $t \to \infty$, whose solution is $z_t(c) = \kappa_\alpha\,(1 + o(1))$, $t \to \infty$. □

Theorem 4.22 *For* $c_{t,\delta} := c^* - \frac{D}{M^{3/2}}\,\delta\,t^{-1/2}$, $0 \leqslant \delta < K$, *we have*

$$u^{[\mathcal{M}]}_{\alpha,t}(c_{t,\delta}) = \frac{D}{M^{3/2}}\,x_\alpha(\delta)\sqrt{t}\,(1 + o(1)), \quad t \to \infty, \tag{4.28}$$

where $x_\alpha(\delta)$ *is a solution to the equation*

$$1 - \varPhi_{(0,1)}(-\delta + x\,) + \varPhi_{(0,1)}(-\delta - x\,)\exp\{\,2\,\delta x\,\} = \alpha. \tag{4.29}$$

Proof of Theorem 4.22. By Theorem 4.12, for $c_{t,\delta} := c^* - \frac{D}{M^{3/2}}\,\delta\,t^{-1/2}$, $0 \leqslant \delta < K$, and $u^{[\mathcal{M}]}_{\alpha,t}(c_{t,\delta})$ defined in (4.28), we have

$$\begin{aligned}\mathcal{M}_{u,c}(t)\,\Big|_{u=u^{[\mathcal{M}]}_{\alpha,t}(c_{t,\delta}),\,c=c_{t,\delta}} &\sim 1 - \varPhi_{(0,1)}(-\delta + x_\alpha(\delta)) \\ &\quad + \varPhi_{(0,1)}(-\delta - x_\alpha(\delta))\exp\{\,2\,\delta x_\alpha(\delta)\,\} \\ &= \alpha,\end{aligned}$$

as $t \to \infty$, whence the result. □

Theorem 4.23 *For* $c_{t,\delta} := c^* + \frac{D}{M^{3/2}}\,\delta\,t^{-1/2}$, $0 \leqslant \delta < K$, *we have*

$$u^{[\mathcal{M}]}_{\alpha,t}(c_{t,\delta}) = \frac{D}{M^{3/2}}\,x_\alpha(\delta)\sqrt{t}\,(1 + o(1)), \quad t \to \infty, \tag{4.30}$$

where $x_\alpha(\delta)$ *is a solution to the equation*

$$1 - \varPhi_{(0,1)}(\delta + x) + \varPhi_{(0,1)}(\delta - x)\exp\{-2\,\delta x\,\} = \alpha. \tag{4.31}$$

It is noteworthy that in both Theorems 4.22 and 4.23, the expression $x_\alpha(0)$ is a solution to the equation $1 - \varPhi_{(0,1)}(x) = \alpha/2$, i.e., is equal to $\kappa_{\alpha/2}$. It is also worthwhile to compare (4.29) to (2.40), and (4.31) to (2.41).

[6]When $c = 0$, it coincides with the first equality in (4.23).

Proof of Theorem 4.23. By Theorem 4.13, for $c_{t,\delta} := c^* + \frac{D}{M^{3/2}}\,\delta\, t^{-1/2}$, $0 \leqslant \delta < K$, and $u^{[\mathcal{M}]}_{\alpha,t}(c_{t,\delta})$ defined in (4.30), we have

$$\begin{aligned}\mathcal{M}_{u,c}(t)\,\Big|_{u=u^{[\mathcal{M}]}_{\alpha,t}(c_{t,\delta}),\, c=c_{t,\delta}} &\sim 1 - \Phi_{(0,1)}(\delta + x_\alpha(\delta)) \\ &\quad + \Phi_{(0,1)}(\delta - x_\alpha(\delta))\exp\{-2\,\delta x_\alpha(\delta)\} \\ &= \alpha,\end{aligned}$$

as $t \to \infty$, whence the result. □

Theorem 4.24 *For $c > Kc^*$, $K > 1$, we have*

$$u^{[\mathcal{M}]}_{\alpha,t}(c) = \frac{D^2}{M^2}\, x_\alpha(c)\,(1 + o(1)), \quad t \to \infty,$$

where $x_\alpha(c)$ is a positive solution to the equation

$$\begin{aligned}\left(1 - \Phi_{(0,1)}\left(\frac{cM-2}{cM}\, x^{1/2}\right)\right) \exp\left\{-2\,\frac{cM-1}{c^2M^2}\, x\right\} \\ + \Phi_{(0,1)}(x^{1/2}) = 1 + \alpha.\end{aligned} \tag{4.32}$$

Proof of Theorem 4.24. By Theorem 4.14, for $c > Kc^*$, $K > 1$, and $u_t(c) := \frac{D^2}{M^2}\, z_t(c)$, where $z_t(c)$ is a solution to (4.32), we have

$$\mathcal{M}_{u,c}(t)\,\Big|_{u=u_t(c)} \sim \alpha, \quad t \to \infty,$$

whence the result. □

Problems

Problem 4.1 Check that $F(x; \mu, \lambda, -\frac{1}{2}) = \int_0^x f(y; \mu, \lambda, -\frac{1}{2})\, dy$, where the expressions in the left-hand and right-hand sides are given in (B.6) and (B.5) respectively.

[Hint: see [135], Theorem 2.1.]

Problem 4.2 Show the equivalence of equalities (4.3) and (4.2).

Problem 4.3 Show the equivalence of equalities (4.4) and (4.7).

Problem 4.4 Calculating the corresponding limits, check equalities (4.5).

Problem 4.5 Using the properties of Mills' ratio (see Section B.2), check equality (4.8).

Problem 4.6 Check equality (4.9) by using the properties (see Section B.3) of the auxiliary function of the first kind $\mathsf{F}(z, y \mid -\frac{1}{2})$.

[Hint: see [135], equality (3.37).]

Problem 4.7 Prove Theorems 4.8, 4.9, and 4.10 independently, or use the proofs of Theorem 3.5, 3.6, and 3.7 in [135] as a hint.

Problem 4.8 Check that in the case when T and Y are exponentially distributed with parameters δ and ρ, equalities (4.25) turn into equalities (3.38).

Problem 4.9 In (4.25), z and y are expressed through u and c. Do the opposite, i.e., express u and c through z and y, showing that $u = \frac{D\sqrt{t}}{M^{3/2}}(z + y)$, $c = \frac{1}{M} - \frac{D}{M^{3/2}\sqrt{t}}y$, and check that $ct + u = \frac{t}{M} + \frac{D\sqrt{t}}{M^{3/2}}z$.

Chapter 5

Fixed-probability Level in General Renewal Model

In this chapter, which is the core of this book, we focus on compound renewal processes with generally distributed jump sizes and inter-renewal intervals, when the equation which defines the fixed-probability level as an implicit function can not be written out explicitly. In other words, the direct level crossing problem has no closed-form solution, as it had in Chapter 3, and we must modify the road map of Chapters 2 and 3 accordingly. However, using Kendall's identity, we can approximate $\mathsf{P}\{\varUpsilon_{u,c} \leqslant t\}$, as $t, u \to \infty$, as well as its derivatives w.r.t. u and c. This enables us to analyze the structure of the fixed-probability level $u_{\alpha,t}(c)$, when c is such that $u_{\alpha,t}(c)$ is growing to infinity, as $t \to \infty$, in particular, when $0 \leqslant c \leqslant c^* := \mathsf{E}\,Y/\mathsf{E}\,T$. For other c, when the fixed-probability level $u_{\alpha,t}(c)$ is not growing to infinity, as $t \to \infty$, it can be bounded from above, using non-asymptotic upper bounds for $\mathsf{P}\{\varUpsilon_{u,c} \leqslant t\}$; this requires case study, which is extended to Chapter 6.

5.1 General Renewal Model: Main Framework

5.1.1 Notations and terminology

The model we are addressing in this chapter differs from the model discussed in Chapter 3 only in that the mutually independent sequences of i.i.d. positive inter-renewal intervals[1] $T_i \overset{d}{=} T$, $i = 1, 2, \dots$, and i.i.d. positive sizes of jumps in the moments of renewals $Y_i \overset{d}{=} Y$, $i = 1, 2, \dots$, are not necessarily exponentially distributed. With this difference, we consider the renewal risk model (cf. (3.1)) defined by

$$R_s := u + cs - V_s, \quad V_s := \sum_{i=1}^{N_s} Y_i, \quad s \geqslant 0, \tag{5.1}$$

[1]For greater generality, it can be assumed that the distribution of T_1 differs from the distribution of T.

TABLE 5.1: Equivalent terminology for $u_{\alpha,t}(c)$ and $\underline{u}_{\alpha,t}(c)$

	Value-at-Risk measure	Solvency benchmark	Solution to inverse level-crossing problem
$u_{\alpha,t}(c)$	Value-at-Risk based on sup-loss net of premium income, a solution to $\mathsf{P}\{\sup_{0\leqslant s\leqslant t}(V_s - cs) \leqslant u\} = A$	Non-ruin capital, a solution to $\psi_t(u, c) = \alpha$, i.e., $\mathsf{P}\{\inf_{0\leqslant s\leqslant t} R_s < 0\} = \alpha$	Fixed-probability level, a solution to $\mathsf{P}\{\Upsilon_{u,c} \leqslant t\} = \alpha$, where $\Upsilon_{u,c}$ is the time of the first level u crossing
$\underline{u}_{\alpha,t}(c)$	Value-at-Risk based on loss net of premium income, a solution to $\mathsf{P}\{V_t - ct \leqslant u\} = A$	Non-loss capital, a solution to $\mathsf{P}\{R_t < 0\} = \alpha$	A lower bound for $u_{\alpha,t}(c)$

where $V_s := 0$, if $T_1 > s$, and

$$N_s := \max\left\{n > 0 : \sum_{i=1}^{n} T_i \leqslant s\right\},$$

where $N_s := 0$, if $T_1 > s$.

In this model, we can refer to [135], where the direct level-crossing problem, i.e., investigation of the probability $\mathsf{P}\{\Upsilon_{u,c} \leqslant t\}$, where (cf. (3.4))

$$\begin{aligned} \Upsilon_{u,c} &:= \inf\{s > 0 : V_s - cs > u\} \\ &= \inf\{s > 0 : R_s < 0\}, \end{aligned} \tag{5.2}$$

or $+\infty$, if $V_s - cs \leqslant u$ for all $s \geqslant 0$, was addressed. In [135], the study of a solution (w.r.t. u) to the equation (cf. (3.5))

$$\mathsf{P}\{\Upsilon_{u,c} \leqslant t\} = \alpha \tag{5.3}$$

was referred to as the inverse level-crossing problem. This solution is denoted by $u_{\alpha,t}(c)$, $c \geqslant 0$, and is called the level which the shifted compound renewal process $V_s - cs$, $s \geqslant 0$, crosses before time t with the probability α, or fixed-probability level for short. Mathematical aspects are the main issue in the next presentation, and we will stick to the application-neutral terminology used in the level-crossing problem. But if we focus on risk measures or insurance solvency, we can switch to the equivalent terminology shown in Table 5.3 (cf. Table 3.1).

5.1.2 Adjustment of the road map

We need to modify the road map of Chapters 2 and 3, which is caused by the following: unlike (see, e.g., (2.6) and (3.14)) in Chapters 2 and 3, in the general renewal model of this chapter, there are no closed-form expressions for $\mathsf{P}\{\varUpsilon_{u,c} \leqslant t\}$. In the model of this chapter, there are only approximations for this probability, as t and (mainly) u tend to infinity. Such approximations can be used for our purposes, but with some changes in reasoning. Let us take a closer look at this matter.

Firstly, we recall that the study of $\mathsf{P}\{\varUpsilon_{u,c} \leqslant t\}$ is the subject of the direct level crossing problem presented in [135]. We emphasize the inverse normal approximation, which looks like

$$\mathsf{P}\{\varUpsilon_{u,c} \leqslant t\} - \mathcal{M}_{u,c}(t) \to 0, \quad t, u \to \infty, \tag{5.4}$$

where $\mathcal{M}_{u,c}(t)$ is defined in (4.2); this is an alternative and a (stronger) contender for Cramér's (or normal) approximation, which also holds for $u \to \infty$.

The approximation (5.4) comes from Kendall's identity, which represents $\mathsf{P}\{\varUpsilon_{u,c} \leqslant t\}$ in terms of convolution powers of p.d.f. $f_T(x)$ and $f_Y(x)$, but can not be seen as a closed-form expression for this probability. For reader's convenience, an overview of these results is given in the next Section 5.2.

Secondly, it is noteworthy that the approximations in Chapters 2 and 3 are of another type than (5.4). They are used differently: the probabilities $\mathsf{P}\{\varUpsilon^{[\mathrm{dif}]}_{u,c\,|\,\vartheta} \leqslant t\}$ and $\mathsf{P}\{\varUpsilon_{u,c\,|\,\delta,\rho} \leqslant t\}$ in Chapters 2 and 3, respectively, were first written out explicitly (see, e.g., (2.6) and (3.6)–(3.8), (3.14)), and then expanded, as $t \to \infty$. This (see, e.g., (3.33)) was an element of standard asymptotic analysis valid for all positive u, rather than for u tending to infinity.

Thirdly, it may be also noted that in Chapter 3 we used the approximations like (see, e.g., [135], Chapter 4)

$$\mathsf{E}(N_t) - M_N t \to \frac{D_N^2 - M_N}{2\,M_N}, \quad t \to \infty,$$

and

$$\mathsf{P}\{\varUpsilon_{u,0} \leqslant t\} = \mathsf{P}\{V_t > u\} \approx \varPhi_{(0,1)}\left(\frac{u - M_V\,t}{D_V\sqrt{t}}\right), \quad t \to \infty,$$

where (see (1.31))

$$\begin{aligned} M_N &= 1/\mathsf{E}\,T, & M_V &= \mathsf{E}\,Y/\mathsf{E}\,T, \\ D_N^2 &= \mathsf{D}\,T/(\mathsf{E}\,T)^3, & D_V^2 &= \mathsf{E}(T\mathsf{E}\,Y - Y\mathsf{E}\,T)^2/(\mathsf{E}\,T)^3, \end{aligned}$$

standard in renewal theory and in central limit theory. Both of them are valid for all positive u, rather than for u tending to infinity.

The lack of closed-form expression for $\mathsf{P}\{\varUpsilon_{u,c} \leqslant t\}$ and the need to apply the approximations, such as the inverse normal approximation (5.4), cause the following major trouble in the inverse level-crossing problem (see Section 5.3) in the general renewal model of this chapter. We can no longer, as before, consider from a unified standpoint those c for which $u_{\alpha,t}(c)$ is tending to infinity, as $t \to \infty$, and those c for which $u_{\alpha,t}(c)$ is finite, as $t \to \infty$.

Accordingly, we must modify the road map of Chapters 2 and 3, as follows.

Firstly, for $0 \leqslant c < c^* := \mathsf{E}Y/\mathsf{E}T$, when $u_{\alpha,t}(c)$ is a value of the order not less than $O(\sqrt{t})$, as $t \to \infty$, we basically apply the same reasoning, as in Chapter 3, replacing the closed-form expression for $\mathsf{P}\{\varUpsilon_{u,c} \leqslant t\}$ with the approximation $\mathcal{M}_{u,c}(t)$.

Secondly, for $c > Kc^*$, $K > 1$, when $u_{\alpha,t}(c)$ is finite, as $t \to \infty$, we use non-asymptotic upper bounds on $\mathsf{P}\{\varUpsilon_{u,c} \leqslant t\}$, such as

$$\mathsf{P}\{\varUpsilon_{u,c} \leqslant t\} \leqslant \mathsf{P}\{\varUpsilon_{u,c} < \infty\},$$

and are looking for suitable upper bounds on $u_{\alpha,t}(c)$. For example, we are interested in the bound $u_{\alpha,t}(c) \leqslant \overline{u}_\alpha(c)$, where (see Definition 1.6) $\overline{u}_\alpha(c)$ is a positive solution (w.r.t. u) to the equation $\mathsf{P}\{\varUpsilon_{u,c} < \infty\} = \alpha$.

There are no universal non-asymptotic upper bounds or explicit expressions for $\mathsf{P}\{\varUpsilon_{u,c} < \infty\}$ that hold in the general model. But such results exist in special classes (see Section 6.1.2 for more detail), namely:

Model (A): compound Poisson model, when Y is exponentially distributed,

Model (B): compound Poisson model, when distribution of Y is light-tailed (but not exponential),

Model (C): compound Poisson model, when distribution of Y is fat-tailed,

Model (D): renewal (but not compound Poisson) model, when Y is exponentially distributed,

Model (E): renewal (but not compound Poisson) model, when distribution of Y is light-tailed (but not exponential),

Model (F): renewal (but not compound Poisson) model, when the distribution of Y is fat-tailed.

The two-sided bounds on $u_{\alpha,t}(c)$, when $0 \leqslant c < c^*$, analogous to (3.57), and the upper bounds on $u_{\alpha,t}(c)$, when $c > c^*$, are referred to as (see Section 3.5) primary bounds. The corresponding upper bounds are satisfactory for all $c \geqslant 0$, except for c in a right neighborhood of the point c^*. Striving for improvement, we construct various elaborated upper bounds (see Section 3.6) based on different ideas.

Firsts, we can use (strong-form and weak-form) convexity of $u_{\alpha,t}(c)$, when $0 \leqslant c < c^*$. Upper bounds on this basis are the most accurate and elegant. But the proof of convexity is very laborious. Second, we can use monotony of $u_{\alpha,t}(c)$, $c \geqslant 0$, which is obvious from the definition. But the corresponding elaborated upper bounds look rather rough. To improve them, we can focus on the right-hand $t^{-1/2}$-neighborhood of c^*, i.e., on $c = c^* + \xi t^{-1/2}$, $\xi > 0$. In this neighborhood $u_{\alpha,t}(c)$ is of order $O(\sqrt{t})$, as $t \to \infty$, and we can use $\mathcal{M}$-level $u_{\alpha,t}^{[\mathcal{M}]}(c)$, for which (see Theorem 4.23) an explicit asymptotic representation (4.30) is known. Moreover, $\mathcal{M}$-level is easy to calculate numerically. This and other issues related to numerical procedures are addressed in Chapter 6.

In Section 5.2, we outline the direct level-crossing problem.

In Section 5.2.4, we collect the information about the (non-asymptotic) upper bounds on $\mathsf{P}\{\varUpsilon_{u,c} \leqslant t\}$, when $c > c^*$.

In Section 5.3, we focus on (see Theorems 5.13–5.15) the structure theorems for the fixed-probability level $u_{\alpha,t}(c)$, $c \geqslant 0$, assuming t large. These theorems are analogous to Theorems 3.6–3.8, but differ due to the absence of a closed-form expression for $\mathsf{P}\{\varUpsilon_{u,c} \leqslant t\}$; we will comment on these differences.

In Section 5.4, we derive the asymptotic bounds for $u_{\alpha,t}(c)$, as $t \to \infty$, when $0 \leqslant c \leqslant c^*$, which follow from Theorem 5.15, and proceed with upper bounds for $u_{\alpha,t}(c)$, when $c > c^*$. We will comment on the elaborated bounds based on monotony and convexity. Since the results on convexity of $u_{\alpha,t}(c)$, when $c > c^*$, become technically very difficult, we comment on their practical necessity. We will delve much deeper into this matter in the next chapter devoted to numerical evaluation of fixed-probability level in Models (A)–(F).

In Section 5.6, some conclusions are given.

5.2 Direct Level-crossing Problem

In this section, we outline the direct level-crossing problem explored in detail in [135]. We start with Kendall's identity. It is a representation of the probability $\mathsf{P}\{\varUpsilon_{u,c} \leqslant t\}$ in terms of n-fold convolutions f_T^{*n} and f_Y^{*n}. On the one hand, in the model with T and Y exponentially distributed, this is the basis for getting closed-form expressions (3.6)–(3.9), (3.14). On the other hand, this is the basis for getting approximations. For derivatives, e.g., $\frac{\partial}{\partial c}\mathsf{P}\{\varUpsilon_{u,c} \leqslant t\}$, $\frac{\partial}{\partial u}\mathsf{P}\{\varUpsilon_{u,c} \leqslant t\}$, the same approach can be applied.

5.2.1 Kendall's identities: keystone results

Let us introduce[2]

$$M_x := \inf\Big\{k \geqslant 1 : \sum_{i=1}^{k} Y_i > x\Big\} - 1, \quad x > 0, \tag{5.5}$$

which is a renewal process generated by the random variables Y_i, $i = 1, 2, \ldots$. Fundamental identity in the level-crossing problem is the following.

The following result, which we refer to as Kendall's identity (see path-breaking paper [97], and then [24]–[25], [96], [157], [177], [198]), is paramount.

---

[2]The inf-definition for M_x, $x > 0$, in contrast to equivalent max-definition for N_s, $s \geqslant 0$, is used as a hint on the difference between these renewal processes.

Theorem 5.1 (Kendall's identity) *With* $0 < v < t$, *we have*

$$\begin{aligned} \mathsf{P}\{v < \varUpsilon_{u,c} \leqslant t \mid T_1 = v\} &= \int_v^t \frac{u+cv}{u+cz}\, \mathsf{p}_{\sum_{i=2}^{M_{u+cz}+1} T_i}(z-v)\, dz \\ &= \int_v^t \frac{u+cv}{u+cz} \sum_{n=1}^{\infty} \mathsf{P}\{M_{u+cz} = n\} \\ &\quad \times f_T^{*n}(z-v)\, dz. \end{aligned} \tag{5.6}$$

This Theorem 5.1 is Theorem 5.5 in [135]. The identity (5.6) may be rewritten exclusively in terms of n-fold convolutions. Indeed, bearing in mind that Y_i, $i = 1, 2, \ldots$, are i.i.d., we have

$$\begin{aligned} \mathsf{P}\{M_{u+cv+cy} = n\} &= \mathsf{P}\left\{ \sum_{i=1}^{n} Y_i \leqslant u + cv + cy < \sum_{i=1}^{n+1} Y_i \right\} \\ &= \int_0^{u+cv+cy} f_Y^{*n}(u+cv+cy-z)\, \mathsf{P}\{Y_{n+1} > z\}\, dz. \end{aligned}$$

Making the change of variables $y = z - v$ in (5.6), it may be rewritten as

$$\begin{aligned} \mathsf{P}\{v < \varUpsilon_{u,c} \leqslant t \mid T_1 = v\} &= \sum_{n=1}^{\infty} \int_0^{t-v} \frac{u+cv}{u+cv+cy} \int_0^{u+cv+cy} \mathsf{P}\{Y_{n+1} > z\} \\ &\quad \times f_Y^{*n}(u+cv+cy-z)\, f_T^{*n}(y)\, dy\, dz, \end{aligned} \tag{5.7}$$

where f_T^{*n} and f_Y^{*n} are n-fold convolutions of p.d.f. f_T and f_Y.

Proceeding from Theorem 5.1, we can easily go back to (unconditional) distribution of the level-crossing time, for

$$\begin{aligned} \mathsf{P}\{\varUpsilon_{u,c} \leqslant t\} &= \int_0^t \mathsf{P}\{u + cv - Y < 0\}\, f_{T_1}(v)\, dv \\ &\quad + \int_0^t \mathsf{P}\{v < \varUpsilon_{u,c} \leqslant t \mid T_1 = v\}\, f_{T_1}(v)\, dv. \end{aligned} \tag{5.8}$$

Equality (5.6), its copy (5.7), and straightforward equality (5.8) are fundamental in a series of approximations and closed-form results presented in [135]. In particular, the following corollary (see [135], Corollary 5.1) is a result from which follow all closed-form expressions (3.6)–(3.9), and (3.14).

Corollary 5.1 *For* Y *exponentially distributed with parameter* $\rho > 0$, *we have*

$$\begin{aligned} \mathsf{P}\{\varUpsilon_{u,c} \leqslant t\} &= \int_0^t e^{-\rho\,(u+cs)} \left(f_{T_1}(s) + \frac{1}{u+cs} \sum_{n=1}^{\infty} \frac{(\rho\,(u+cs))^n}{n!} \right. \\ &\quad \left. \times \int_0^s (u+cv) f_T^{*n}(s-v) f_{T_1}(v)\, dv \right) ds. \end{aligned} \tag{5.9}$$

Proof of Corollary 5.1. For $Y_i \overset{d}{=} Y$, $i = 1, 2, \ldots$, when Y is exponentially distributed with parameter ρ, we have $\mathsf{P}\{u + cv - Y < 0\} = e^{-\rho\,(u+cv)}$ and

$$\mathsf{P}\{M_{u+cs} = n\} = e^{-\rho\,(u+cs)}\,\frac{(\rho\,(u+cs))^n}{n!}, \qquad n = 1, 2, \ldots,$$

whence equality (5.8) may be rewritten as (5.9). □

Let us formulate Kendall's identity for first-order derivative w.r.t. c. We introduce the following expressions:

$$\begin{aligned}
\mathsf{C}^{[1]}_{u,c}(t \mid v) &= -\sum_{n=1}^{\infty} \int_0^{t-v} \frac{uy}{(u+cv+cy)^{\,2}} \\
&\quad \times \int_0^{u+cv+cy} \mathsf{P}\{Y_{n+1} > z\} f_Y^{*n}(u+cv+cy-z)\,dz\, f_T^{*n}(y)\,dy, \\
\mathsf{C}^{[2]}_{u,c}(t \mid v) &= \sum_{n=1}^{\infty} \int_0^{t-v} \frac{(u+cv)\,(v+y)}{u+cv+cy} \\
&\quad \times \int_0^{u+cv+cy} \mathsf{P}\{Y_{n+1} > z\} \Big\{ f_Y(0) f_Y^{*(n-1)}(u+cv+cy-z) \\
&\quad + \int_0^{u+cv+cy-z} f_Y'(\xi) f_Y^{*(n-1)}(u+cv+cy-z-\xi)\,d\xi \Big\}\,dz \\
&\quad \times f_T^{*n}(y)\,dy, \\
\mathsf{C}^{[3]}_{u,c}(t \mid v) &= \sum_{n=1}^{\infty} f_Y^{*n}(0) \int_0^{t-v} \frac{(u+cv)\,(v+y)}{u+cv+cy}\, \mathsf{P}\{Y_{n+1} > u+cv+cy\} \\
&\quad \times f_T^{*n}(y)\,dy.
\end{aligned} \tag{5.10}$$

Lemma 5.1 *For $c > 0$, $u > 0$, $t > v > 0$, we have*

$$\begin{aligned}
\frac{\partial}{\partial c}\mathsf{P}\{\Upsilon_{u,c} \leqslant t\} &= -\int_0^t f_Y(u+cv)\,v\,f_{T_1}(v)\,dv \\
&\quad + \int_0^t \frac{\partial}{\partial c}\mathsf{P}\{v < \Upsilon_{u,c} \leqslant t \mid T_1 = v\}\, f_{T_1}(v)\,dv,
\end{aligned} \tag{5.11}$$

where

$$\frac{\partial}{\partial c}\mathsf{P}\{v < \Upsilon_{u,c} \leqslant t \mid T_1 = v\} = \mathsf{C}^{[1]}_{u,c}(t \mid v) + \mathsf{C}^{[2]}_{u,c}(t \mid v) + \mathsf{C}^{[3]}_{u,c}(t \mid v). \tag{5.12}$$

Proof. The proof is based on identities (5.8) and (5.7), i.e.,

$$\begin{aligned}
\mathsf{P}\{\Upsilon_{u,c} \leqslant t\} &= \int_0^t \mathsf{P}\{u + cv - Y < 0\}\, f_{T_1}(v)\,dv \\
&\quad + \int_0^t \mathsf{P}\{v < \Upsilon_{u,c} \leqslant t \mid T_1 = v\}\, f_{T_1}(v)\,dv
\end{aligned} \tag{5.13}$$

and

$$\begin{aligned}\mathsf{P}\{v < \varUpsilon_{u,c} \leqslant t \mid T_1 = v\} \\ &= \sum_{n=1}^{\infty} \int_0^{t-v} \frac{u+cv}{u+cv+cy} \int_0^{u+cv+cy} \mathsf{P}\{Y_{n+1} > z\} \\ &\quad \times f_Y^{*n}(u+cv+cy-z)\, f_T^{*n}(y)\, dy\, dz.\end{aligned} \tag{5.14}$$

Differentiating (5.14), we have

$$\begin{aligned}\frac{\partial}{\partial c}\mathsf{P}\{v < \varUpsilon_{u,c} \leqslant t \mid T_1 = v\} \\ &= \sum_{n=1}^{\infty} \int_0^{t-v} \frac{\partial}{\partial c}\left(\frac{u+cv}{u+cv+cy} \int_0^{u+cv+cy} \mathsf{P}\{Y_{n+1} > z\}\right. \\ &\quad \left. \times f_Y^{*n}(u+cv+cy-z)\, dz\right) f_T^{*n}(y)\, dy.\end{aligned}$$

The integrand is

$$\begin{aligned}&\frac{\partial}{\partial c}\left(\frac{u+cv}{u+cv+cy} \int_0^{u+cv+cy} \mathsf{P}\{Y_{n+1} > z\}\, f_Y^{*n}(u+cv+cy-z)\, dz\right) \\ &= \frac{\partial}{\partial c}\left(\frac{u+cv}{u+cv+cy}\right) \int_0^{u+cv+cy} \mathsf{P}\{Y_{n+1} > z\}\, f_Y^{*n}(u+cv+cy-z)\, dz \\ &\quad + \frac{u+cv}{u+cv+cy}\frac{\partial}{\partial c}\left(\int_0^{u+cv+cy} \mathsf{P}\{Y_{n+1} > z\}\, f_Y^{*n}(u+cv+cy-z)\, dz\right),\end{aligned}$$

where

$$\frac{\partial}{\partial c}\left(\frac{u+cv}{u+cv+cy}\right) = -\frac{uy}{(u+cv+cy)^2}$$

and

$$\begin{aligned}&\frac{\partial}{\partial c}\left(\int_0^{u+cv+cy} \mathsf{P}\{Y_{n+1} > z\}\, f_Y^{*n}(u+cv+cy-z)\, dz\right) \\ &= \int_0^{u+cv+cy} \mathsf{P}\{Y_{n+1} > z\}\left(\frac{\partial}{\partial c} f_Y^{*n}(u+cv+cy-z)\right) dz \\ &\quad + (v+y)\,\mathsf{P}\{Y_{n+1} > u+cv+cy\}\, f_Y^{*n}(0).\end{aligned}$$

For $n \geqslant 2$, differentiation of n-fold convolutions yields

$$\begin{aligned}&\frac{\partial}{\partial c} f_Y^{*n}(u+cv+cy-z) \\ &= \frac{\partial}{\partial c}\int_0^{u+cv+cy-z} f_Y((u+cv+cy-z)-\zeta) f_Y^{*(n-1)}(\zeta)\, d\zeta \\ &= (v+y)\underbrace{\int_0^{u+cv+cy-z} f_Y'((u+cv+cy-z)-\zeta) f_Y^{*(n-1)}(\zeta)\, d\zeta}_{\int_0^{u+cv+cy-z} f_Y'(\xi) f_Y^{*(n-1)}((u+cv+cy-z)-\xi)\, d\xi} \\ &\quad + (v+y)\, f_Y(0) f_Y^{*(n-1)}(u+cv+cy-z),\end{aligned}$$

whence, by elementary calculations, the result. □

Let us formulate Kendall's identity for first-order derivative w.r.t. u. We introduce the following expressions:

$$\mathsf{U}^{[1]}_{u,c}(t \mid v) = \sum_{n=1}^{\infty} \int_0^{t-v} \frac{cy}{(u+cv+cy)^2} \times \int_0^{u+cv+cy} \mathsf{P}\{Y_{n+1} > z\}\, f_Y^{*n}(u+cv+cy-z)\, f_T^{*n}(y)\, dy\, dz,$$

$$\mathsf{U}^{[2]}_{u,c}(t \mid v) = \sum_{n=1}^{\infty} \int_0^{t-v} \frac{u+cv}{u+cv+cy} \times \int_0^{u+cv+cy} \mathsf{P}\{Y_{n+1} > z\} \Big\{ f_Y(0) f_Y^{*(n-1)}(u+cv+cy-z) + \int_0^{u+cv+cy-z} f_Y'(\xi) f_Y^{*(n-1)}((u+cv+cy-z)-\xi)\, d\xi \Big\} \times f_T^{*n}(y)\, dy\, dz,$$

$$\mathsf{U}^{[3]}_{u,c}(t \mid v) = \sum_{n=1}^{\infty} f_Y^{*n}(0) \int_0^{t-v} \frac{u+cv}{u+cv+cy} \mathsf{P}\{Y_{n+1} > u+cv+cy\} \times f_T^{*n}(y)\, dy.$$

Lemma 5.2 *For $c > 0$, $u > 0$, $t > v > 0$, we have*

$$\frac{\partial}{\partial u} \mathsf{P}\{\varUpsilon_{u,c} \leqslant t\} = -\int_0^t f_Y(u+cv)\, v\, f_{T_1}(v)\, dv + \int_0^t \frac{\partial}{\partial u} \mathsf{P}\{v < \varUpsilon_{u,c} \leqslant t \mid T_1 = v\}\, f_{T_1}(v)\, dv, \tag{5.15}$$

where

$$\frac{\partial}{\partial u} \mathsf{P}\{v < \varUpsilon_{u,c} \leqslant t \mid T_1 = v\} = \mathsf{U}^{[1]}_{u,c}(t \mid v) + \mathsf{U}^{[2]}_{u,c}(t \mid v) + \mathsf{U}^{[3]}_{u,c}(t \mid v). \tag{5.16}$$

Proof. Differentiating identity (5.14), we have

$$\frac{\partial}{\partial u} \mathsf{P}\{v < \varUpsilon_{u,c} \leqslant t \mid T_1 = v\} = \sum_{n=1}^{\infty} \int_0^{t-v} \frac{\partial}{\partial u} \left(\frac{u+cv}{u+cv+cy} \times \int_0^{u+cv+cy} \mathsf{P}\{Y_{n+1} > z\} f_Y^{*n}(u+cv+cy-z)\, dz \right) f_T^{*n}(y)\, dy.$$

The integrand is

$$
\begin{aligned}
&\frac{\partial}{\partial u}\left(\frac{u+cv}{u+cv+cy}\int_0^{u+cv+cy} \mathsf{P}\{Y_{n+1}>z\}\, f_Y^{*n}(u+cv+cy-z)\,dz\right) \\
&\quad = \frac{\partial}{\partial u}\left(\frac{u+cv}{u+cv+cy}\right)\int_0^{u+cv+cy} \mathsf{P}\{Y_{n+1}>z\}\, f_Y^{*n}(u+cv+cy-z)\,dz \\
&\quad + \frac{u+cv}{u+cv+cy}\frac{\partial}{\partial u}\left(\int_0^{u+cv+cy} \mathsf{P}\{Y_{n+1}>z\}\, f_Y^{*n}(u+cv+cy-z)\,dz\right),
\end{aligned}
$$

where $\dfrac{\partial}{\partial u}\left(\dfrac{u+cv}{u+cv+cy}\right) = \dfrac{cy}{(u+cv+cy)^2}$ and

$$
\begin{aligned}
&\frac{\partial}{\partial u}\left(\int_0^{u+cv+cy} \mathsf{P}\{Y_{n+1}>z\}\, f_Y^{*n}(u+cv+cy-z)\,dz\right) \\
&\quad = \int_0^{u+cv+cy} \mathsf{P}\{Y_{n+1}>z\}\left(\frac{\partial}{\partial u} f_Y^{*n}(u+cv+cy-z)\right) dz \\
&\quad + \mathsf{P}\{Y_{n+1}>u+cv+cy\}\, f_Y^{*n}(0),
\end{aligned}
$$

For $n \geqslant 2$, differentiation of n-fold convolutions yields

$$
\begin{aligned}
&\frac{\partial}{\partial u} f_Y^{*n}(u+cv+cy-z) \\
&\quad = \frac{\partial}{\partial u}\int_0^{u+cv+cy-z} f_Y((u+cv+cy-z)-\zeta) f_Y^{*(n-1)}(\zeta)\,d\zeta \\
&\quad = \underbrace{\int_0^{u+cv+cy-z} f_Y'((u+cv+cy-z)-\zeta) f_Y^{*(n-1)}(\zeta)\,d\zeta}_{\int_0^{u+cv+cy-z} f_Y'(\xi) f_Y^{*(n-1)}((u+cv+cy-z)-\xi)\,d\xi} \\
&\quad + f_Y(0) f_Y^{*(n-1)}(u+cv+cy-z).
\end{aligned}
$$

whence, by elementary calculations, the result. □

5.2.2 Inverse Gaussian approximation

The results of this section are detailed in [135], Chapter 6. We formulate them, but do not present the detailed proof. For $c \geqslant 0$, $u > 0$, $0 < v < t$, $c^* := \mathsf{E}\,Y/\mathsf{E}\,T$, and for

$$
M := \mathsf{E}\,T/\mathsf{E}\,Y, \quad D^2 := ((\mathsf{E}\,T)^2 \mathsf{D}\,Y + (\mathsf{E}\,Y)^2 \mathsf{D}\,T)/(\mathsf{E}\,Y)^3, \tag{5.17}
$$

we write (see (4.20))

$$
\mathcal{M}_{u,c}(t \mid v) := \int_0^{\frac{c(t-v)}{cv+u}} \frac{1}{x+1}\,\varphi_{\left(cM(x+1),\, \frac{c^2D^2}{cv+u}(x+1)\right)}(x)\,dx
$$

and (see (4.2))

$$\mathcal{M}_{u,c}(t) := \int_0^{\frac{ct}{u}} \frac{1}{x+1}\, \varphi_{\left(cM(x+1),\, \frac{c^2 D^2}{u}(x+1)\right)}(x)\, dx,$$

Plainly, $\mathcal{M}_{u,c}(t) = \mathcal{M}_{u,c}(t \mid 0)$.

Approximation, when only u tends to infinity. The following theorem for conditional distribution of $\Upsilon_{u,c}$, which is the left-hand side of identity (5.6), is fundamental. It is Theorem 6.1 in [135].

Theorem 5.2 *In the renewal model, let p.d.f. f_T and f_Y be bounded above by a finite constant, $D^2 > 0$, $\mathsf{E}(T^3) < \infty$, $\mathsf{E}(Y^3) < \infty$. Then for any fixed $c \geqslant 0$ and $0 < v < t$ we have*

$$\sup_{t>v} \left| \mathsf{P}\{v < \Upsilon_{u,c} \leqslant t \mid T_1 = v\} - \mathcal{M}_{u,c}(t \mid v) \right| = O\left(\frac{\ln(u+cv)}{u+cv}\right),$$

as $u + cv \to \infty$.

Note that with c and v fixed, $u + cv \to \infty$ is equivalent to $u \to \infty$. The following result for non-conditional distribution of $\Upsilon_{u,c}$ is an easy corollary of Theorem 5.2 and equality (5.8). It is Theorem 6.3 in [135].

Theorem 5.3 *Suppose that conditions of Theorem 5.2 are satisfied. Then*

$$\sup_{t>0} \left| \mathsf{P}\{\Upsilon_{u,c} \leqslant t\} - \int_0^t \mathcal{M}_{u,c}(t \mid v)\, f_{T_1}(v)\, dv \right| = O\left(\frac{\ln u}{u}\right), \quad u \to \infty.$$

The following result is Theorem 6.4 in [135]. It comes from Theorem 4.17.

Theorem 5.4 *Suppose that conditions of Theorem 5.2 are satisfied, and that $\mathsf{E}T_1 < \infty$. Then*

$$\sup_{t>0} \left| \mathsf{P}\{\Upsilon_{u,c} \leqslant t\} - \int_0^t \mathcal{M}_{u,c}(t-v)\, f_{T_1}(v)\, dv \right| = O\left(\frac{\ln u}{u}\right), \quad u \to \infty.$$

The approximating term $\int_0^t \mathcal{M}_{u,c}(t-v)\, f_{T_1}(v)\, dv$ in Theorem 5.4 is a convolution. This approximation structure agrees with the probabilistic intuition about the role which plays the first time interval T_1 in the event of crossing a high level within finite time t: given $T_1 = v$, the whole time length becomes $t - v$, with no other changes. This reduction of the whole time length is unnoticeable in the main-term approximation, if the level u is high.

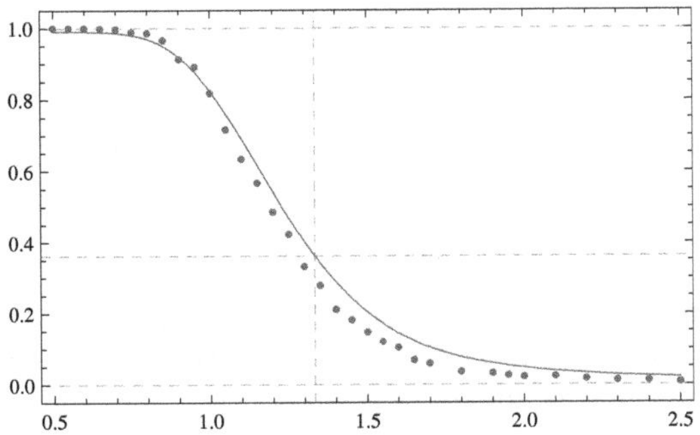

FIGURE 5.1: Graphs (X-axis is c) of $\mathcal{M}_{u,c}(t)$ and simulated values of $\mathsf{P}\{\Upsilon_{u,c} \leqslant t\}$, when T is exponentially distributed with parameter $\delta = 4/5$, Y is Pareto with parameters $a_Y = 3$, $b_Y = 0.3$, and $t = 200$, $u = 40$. Here $\mathsf{E}T = 1.25$, $\mathsf{D}T = 1.56$, $\mathsf{E}Y = 1.67$, $\mathsf{D}Y = 8.33$, $c^* = 1.33$, $\mathcal{M}_{40,c^*}(200) = 0.36$.

Approximation, when both u and t tend to infinity. Whereas the influence of T_1 in Theorem 5.4 can not be eliminated for t small and moderate, it becomes negligible for t large. Using asymptotic relation (4.21), we can replace, as $t \to \infty$, the integral $\int_0^t \mathcal{M}_{u,c}(t-v)\, f_{T_1}(v)\, dv$ by $\mathcal{M}_{u,c}(t)$.

Theorem 5.5 *Suppose that conditions of Theorem 5.2 are satisfied, and that* $\mathsf{E}T_1 < \infty$. *Then*

$$\sup_{t>0} \big| \mathsf{P}\{\Upsilon_{u,c} \leqslant t\} - \mathcal{M}_{u,c}(t) \big| = O\Big(\frac{\ln u}{u}\Big) + O\Big(\frac{1}{t^{1/2}}\Big), \qquad t, u \to \infty.$$

Remark 5.1 (Moment conditions) In Theorems 5.2–5.5, the moment conditions are quite satisfactory[3], but not minimal. Some numerical examples show that they can be weakened even further. For one thing, in Fig. 5.1 the simulated values[4] of $\mathsf{P}\{\Upsilon_{u,c} \leqslant t\}$ are shown by dots in Model (C), where T is exponentially distributed with parameter $\delta = 4/5$, Y is Pareto with parameters $a_Y = 3$, $b_Y = 0.3$, and $t = 200$, $u = 40$. Recall that p.d.f. of Pareto distribution is

$$f_Y(x) = \frac{a_Y b_Y}{(x b_Y + 1)^{a_Y+1}}, \quad x > 0,$$

whence the third moment $\mathsf{E}(Y^3)$ is infinite, when $a_Y = 3$, $b_Y = 0.3$. The function $\mathcal{M}_{u,c}(t)$ is shown by a solid line. Though conditions of Theorem 5.5 fail for $a_Y = 3$, $b_Y = 0.3$, and even though the value $u = 40$ is quite moderate,

[3] Being rather weak, they are balanced for T and Y.
[4] Algorithm of simulation is given in Chapter 6.

the approximation $\mathsf{P}\{\Upsilon_{u,c} \leqslant t\} \approx \mathcal{M}_{u,c}(t)$ looks satisfactory for all c. This suggests that the moment conditions in Theorems 5.2–5.5 can be relaxed[5].

5.2.3 Derivatives of the first level-crossing time distribution

This section can be skipped on first reading. Its goal is to show that, relying on Kendall's identity, one can also deal with approximations for the derivatives of $\mathsf{P}\{\Upsilon_{u,c} \leqslant t\}$.

Let us recall (see [135], Chapter 3) the elementary integral expressions

$$\mathcal{I}^{[k]}_{u,c}(t) := \int_0^{\frac{ct}{u}} \frac{1}{(x+1)^k}\, \varphi_{\left(cM(x+1),\, \frac{c^2D^2}{u}(x+1)\right)}(x)\, dx, \tag{5.18}$$

$k = 0, 1, 2, \ldots$, where $t > 0$, $u > 0$, $c > 0$, and M, D^2 are fixed positive constants, and modified elementary integral expressions

$$\mathcal{I}^{[k]}_{u,c}(t \mid v) := \mathcal{I}^{[k]}_{u+cv,\,c}(t-v), \quad k = 0, 1, 2, \ldots.$$

The results of this section are detailed in [135], Chapter 8. We will formulate them, but we will not prove them.

Approximation for derivative with respect to c. The following theorem is Theorem 8.1 in [135].

Theorem 5.6 *In the renewal model, let p.d.f. f_T and differentiable f_Y be bounded above by a finite constant, $D^2 > 0$, $\mathsf{E}(T^3) < \infty$, $\mathsf{E}(Y^3) < \infty$. Then for any fixed $c > 0$ and $0 < v < t$ we have*

$$\begin{aligned}\frac{\partial}{\partial c}\mathsf{P}\{\Upsilon_{u,c} \leqslant t\} = &-\int_0^t f_Y(u+cv)\, v\, f_{T_1}(v)\, dv \\ &+ \int_0^t \frac{\partial}{\partial c}\mathsf{P}\{v < \Upsilon_{u,c} \leqslant t \mid T_1 = v\}\, f_{T_1}(v)\, dv,\end{aligned} \tag{5.19}$$

where

$$\begin{aligned}\sup_{t>v} \Bigg| &\frac{\partial}{\partial c}\mathsf{P}\{v < \Upsilon_{u,c} \leqslant t \mid T_1 = v\} \\ &- \frac{M(u+cv)}{c^2D^2}\left((1-cM)\,\mathcal{I}^{[0]}_{u,c}(t \mid v) - \mathcal{I}^{[1]}_{u,c}(t \mid v)\right) \\ &+ \frac{Mu}{c^2D^2}\left((1-cM)\,\mathcal{I}^{[1]}_{u,c}(t \mid v) - \mathcal{I}^{[2]}_{u,c}(t \mid v)\right) + \frac{1}{c}\,\mathcal{I}^{[1]}_{u,c}(t \mid v) \\ &- \frac{1}{c}\,\mathcal{I}^{[2]}_{u,c}(t \mid v)\Bigg| = O\left(\frac{\ln(u+cv)}{u+cv}\right),\end{aligned} \tag{5.20}$$

as $u + cv \to \infty$.

[5]This remark does not apply to the rate of convergence in these theorems, but only to the approximation by $\mathcal{M}_{u,c}(t)$, as $t, u \to \infty$.

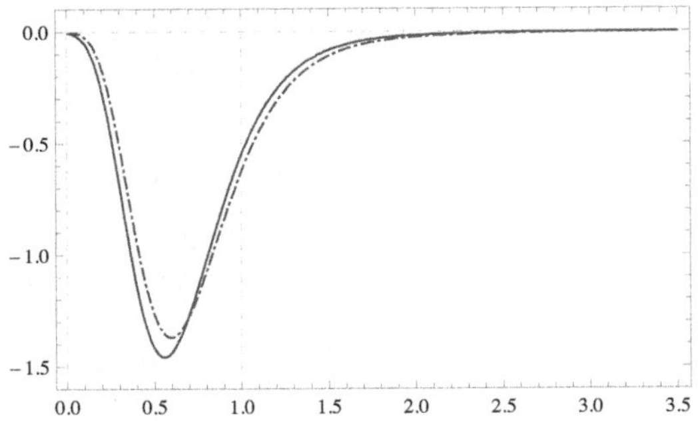

FIGURE 5.2: Graphs (X-axis is c) of $\mathcal{M}_{u,c}^{(0,1)}(t)$ (solid line) and $F_{u,c}(t)$ (dash-dotted line), when $t = 100$, $u = 40$, $M = 1$, and $D^2 = 6$.

In the same way as in Section 5.2.2, we can deduce from Theorem 5.6 that for $u, t \to \infty$ the derivative $\frac{\partial}{\partial c} \mathsf{P}\{\Upsilon_{u,c} \leqslant t\}$ is approximated by the expression

$$\begin{aligned} F_{u,c}(t) = {} & \frac{Mu}{c^2 D^2}\left((1-cM)\,\mathcal{I}_{u,c}^{[0]}(t) - \mathcal{I}_{u,c}^{[1]}(t)\right) \\ & - \frac{Mu}{c^2 D^2}\left((1-cM)\,\mathcal{I}_{u,c}^{[1]}(t) - \mathcal{I}_{u,c}^{[2]}(t)\right) - \frac{1}{c}\,\mathcal{I}_{u,c}^{[1]}(t) + \frac{1}{c}\,\mathcal{I}_{u,c}^{[2]}(t). \end{aligned} \tag{5.21}$$

Let us compare it with $\mathcal{M}_{u,c}^{(0,1)}(t)$, i.e., in other words, we compare the "approximation for derivative" with the "derivative of approximation".

For $u > 0$, $t > 0$, $c > 0$, we have by straightforward differentiation the equality

$$\begin{aligned} \mathcal{M}_{u,c}^{(0,1)}(t) = {} & \frac{u\,(1-cM)}{c^3 D^2}\,\mathcal{I}_{u,c}^{[0]}(t) - \frac{1}{c}\left(\frac{u\,(2-cM)}{c^2 D^2} + 1\right)\mathcal{I}_{u,c}^{[1]}(t) \\ & + \frac{u}{c^3 D^2}\,\mathcal{I}_{u,c}^{[2]}(t) + \frac{t}{u+ct}\,\varphi_{\left(cM(1+\frac{ct}{u}),\,\frac{c^2 D^2}{u}(1+\frac{ct}{u})\right)}\left(\frac{ct}{u}\right), \end{aligned}$$

Alternatively, this equality can be rewritten as

$$\begin{aligned} \mathcal{M}_{u,c}^{(0,1)}(t) = {} & \frac{u}{c^3 D^2}\left((1-cM)\,\mathcal{I}_{u,c}^{[0]}(t) - \mathcal{I}_{u,c}^{[1]}(t)\right) \\ & - \frac{u}{c^3 D^2}\left((1-cM)\,\mathcal{I}_{u,c}^{[1]}(t) - \mathcal{I}_{u,c}^{[2]}(t)\right) \\ & - \frac{1}{c}\,\mathcal{I}_{u,c}^{[1]}(t) + \frac{t}{u+ct}\,\varphi_{\left(cM(1+\frac{ct}{u}),\,\frac{c^2 D^2}{u}(1+\frac{ct}{u})\right)}\left(\frac{ct}{u}\right), \end{aligned} \tag{5.22}$$

which can be compared to equality (5.21). It is illustrated in Fig. 5.2.

Concerning the second summands in (5.21) and (5.22), it is worth recalling that

$$\begin{aligned} \mathcal{F}_{u,c}(t) &= (1-cM)\,\mathcal{I}_{u,c}^{[1]}(t) - \mathcal{I}_{u,c}^{[2]}(t) \\ &= O(u^{-1}), \quad u \to \infty. \end{aligned}$$

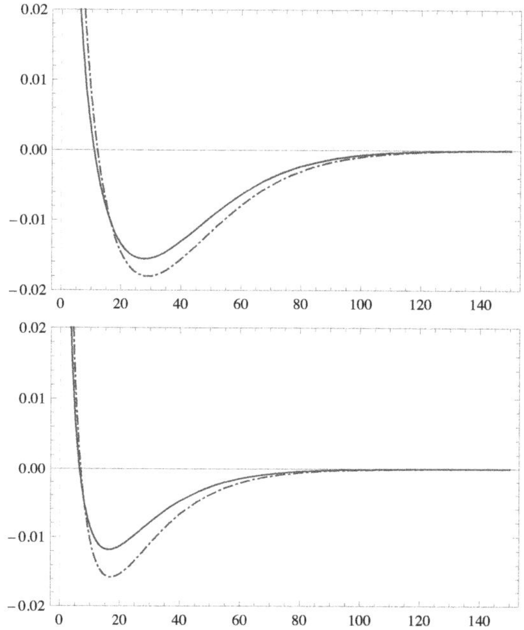

FIGURE 5.3: Graphs (X-axis is u) of $\mathcal{M}_{u,c}^{(1,0)}(t)$ (solid line) and $G_{u,c}(t)$ (dash-dotted line), when $t = 100$, $M = 1$, $D^2 = 6$, $c^* = 1$, $c = 0.8 < c^*$ (above), $c = 1.2 > c^*$ (below).

The similar remark holds for the first summand in (5.21) and (5.22), i.e.,

$$(1 - cM)\,\mathcal{I}_{u,c}^{[0]}(t) - \mathcal{I}_{u,c}^{[1]}(t) = O(u^{-1}), \quad u \to \infty.$$

We conclude this analysis with the following summary. Proximity between $F_{u,c}(t)$, i.e., the "approximation for derivative", and $\mathcal{M}_{u,c}^{(0,1)}(t)$, i.e., the "derivative of approximation", illustrated numerically in Fig. 5.2, can be substantiated by means of equalities (5.21) and (5.22) evaluated analytically. However, the "approximation for derivative" is one thing and the "derivative of approximation" another thing. Their investigation requires separate analysis; the naive belief that one may be a substitute for another is largely groundless.

Approximation for derivative with respect to u**.** The following theorem is Theorem 8.2 in [135].

Theorem 5.7 *In the renewal model, let p.d.f.* f_T *and differentiable* f_Y *be bounded above by a finite constant,* $D^2 > 0$, $\mathsf{E}(T^3) < \infty$, $\mathsf{E}(Y^3) < \infty$*. Then* *for any fixed* $c > 0$ *and* $0 < v < t$ *we have*

$$\begin{aligned}\frac{\partial}{\partial u}\mathsf{P}\{\Upsilon_{u,c} \leqslant t\} = &-\int_0^t f_Y(u+cv)\,v\,f_{T_1}(v)\,dv \\ &+\int_0^t \frac{\partial}{\partial u}\mathsf{P}\{v < \Upsilon_{u,c} \leqslant t \mid T_1 = v\}\,f_{T_1}(v)\,dv,\end{aligned} \tag{5.23}$$

where

$$\begin{aligned}\sup_{t>v}\Bigg| &\frac{\partial}{\partial u}\mathsf{P}\{v < \Upsilon_{u,c} \leqslant t \mid T_1 = v\} \\ &- \frac{M}{c\,D^2}((1-cM)\,\mathcal{I}^{[1]}_{u,c}(t \mid v) - \mathcal{I}^{[2]}_{u,c}(t \mid v)) \\ &- \frac{1}{u}(\mathcal{I}^{[1]}_{u,c}(t \mid v) - \mathcal{I}^{[2]}_{u,c}(t \mid v))\Bigg| = O\Big(\frac{\ln(u+cv)}{(u+cv)^2}\Big),\end{aligned} \tag{5.24}$$

as $u + cv \to \infty$.

In the same way as in Section 5.2.2, we can deduce from Theorem 5.7 that for $u, t \to \infty$ the derivative $\frac{\partial}{\partial u}\mathsf{P}\{\Upsilon_{u,c} \leqslant t\}$ is approximated by the expression

$$G_{u,c}(t) = \frac{M}{c\,D^2}((1-cM)\,\mathcal{I}^{[1]}_{u,c}(t) - \mathcal{I}^{[2]}_{u,c}(t)) + \frac{1}{u}(\mathcal{I}^{[1]}_{u,c}(t) - \mathcal{I}^{[2]}_{u,c}(t)). \tag{5.25}$$

Let us compare it with $\mathcal{M}^{(0,1)}_{u,c}(t)$, i.e., let us compare the "approximation for derivative" with the "derivative of approximation".

For $u > 0$, $t > 0$, $c > 0$, we have by straightforward differentiation the equality

$$\begin{aligned}\mathcal{M}^{(1,0)}_{u,c}(t) = &-\frac{(1-cM)^2}{2c^2D^2}\,\mathcal{I}^{[0]}_{u,c}(t) + \frac{1}{2u}\,\mathcal{I}^{[1]}_{u,c}(t) + \frac{(1-cM)}{c^2D^2}\,\mathcal{I}^{[1]}_{u,c}(t) \\ &- \frac{1}{2c^2D^2}\,\mathcal{I}^{[2]}_{u,c}(t) - \frac{ct}{u\,(u+ct)}\,\varphi_{\left(cM(1+\frac{ct}{u}),\,\frac{c^2D^2}{u}(1+\frac{ct}{u})\right)}\Big(\frac{ct}{u}\Big).\end{aligned}$$

Alternatively, this equality can be rewritten as

$$\begin{aligned}\mathcal{M}^{(1,0)}_{u,c}(t) = &\frac{1}{c^2D^2}((1-cM)\,\mathcal{I}^{[1]}_{u,c}(t) - \mathcal{I}^{[2]}_{u,c}(t \mid v)) \\ &- \frac{1}{2c^2D^2}((1-cM)^2\,\mathcal{I}^{[0]}_{u,c}(t) - \mathcal{I}^{[2]}_{u,c}(t)) \\ &+ \frac{1}{2u}\,\mathcal{I}^{[1]}_{u,c}(t) - \frac{ct}{u\,(u+ct)}\,\varphi_{\left(cM(1+\frac{ct}{u}),\,\frac{c^2D^2}{u}(1+\frac{ct}{u})\right)}\Big(\frac{ct}{u}\Big),\end{aligned} \tag{5.26}$$

which is illustrated in Fig. 5.3. It can be compared to equality (5.25).

Remark 5.2 We have already noticed as an obvious fact[6] that the derivative

[6]Because of monotone decrease of $\mathsf{P}\{\Upsilon_{u,c} \leqslant t\}$, as c increases, or as u increases.

$\frac{\partial}{\partial u}\mathsf{P}\{\varUpsilon_{u,c} \leqslant t\}$ is negative for all $u > 0$. But neither the approximation $G_{u,c}(t)$ obtained by rigorous methods, nor the heuristic expression $\mathcal{M}_{u,c}^{(1,0)}(t)$ are positive for all $u > 0$. The illustration in Fig. 5.3 shows that for small and moderate u these expressions assume positive values. This is not a flaw that contradicts the negativity of $\frac{\partial}{\partial u}\mathsf{P}\{\varUpsilon_{u,c} \leqslant t\}$ for all $u > 0$ because the approximation of Theorem 5.7 works only for u large.

5.2.4 Upper bounds on $\mathsf{P}\{\varUpsilon_{u,c} \leqslant t\}$, when $c > c^*$

When $c > c^*$, we focus on non-asymptotic results for $\mathsf{P}\{\varUpsilon_{u,c} \leqslant t\}$, in particular on the upper bounds for this probability that hold for all $u \geqslant 0$ (rather than for $u \to \infty$). Since

$$\mathsf{P}\{\varUpsilon_{u,c} \leqslant t\} \leqslant \mathsf{P}\{\varUpsilon_{u,c} < \infty\} \tag{5.27}$$

for all positive c, u, and t, the study of such upper bounds is closely related to the analysis of the probability[7] $\mathsf{P}\{\varUpsilon_{u,c} < \infty\}$.

We present, mainly without proofs, the corresponding well-known results that are readily available in the literature.

Model (A). This model is verbally described as compound Poisson[8] model, when Y is exponentially distributed. The attentive reader has already noticed that we return to the setting and notation of Chapter 3.

For[9] $c > c^* := \mathsf{E}\,Y/\mathsf{E}\,T = \delta/\rho$, an upper bound on $\mathsf{P}\{\varUpsilon_{u,c\,|\,\delta,\rho} \leqslant t\}$ is straightforward from inequality (5.27) and from the following closed-form expression (see, e.g., [158], Section 6.5.2): for $c > c^*$ and for all $u \geqslant 0$

$$\mathsf{P}\{\varUpsilon_{u,c\,|\,\delta,\rho} < \infty\} = (1 - \varkappa/\rho)\, e^{-\varkappa u} \leqslant e^{-\varkappa u}, \tag{5.28}$$

where[10] $\varkappa > 0$, dependent of c, is a unique positive root of Lundberg's equation

$$\mathsf{E}\exp\{\varkappa\,(Y - c\,T)\} = 1. \tag{5.29}$$

In this model, it may be rewritten as the quadratic equation $(\rho - \varkappa)\,(\delta + \varkappa c) - \delta\rho = 0$, whose positive solution is explicit: $\varkappa = \rho - \delta/c$. Plainly, $0 < 1 - \varkappa/\rho = c^*/c < 1$, when $c > c^*$, whence the inequality $\mathsf{P}\{\varUpsilon_{u,c\,|\,\delta,\rho} < \infty\} \leqslant e^{-\varkappa u}$.

Remark 5.3 In Chapter 3, equality (5.28) was obtained in two different ways. First, it was obtained in (3.9), as a part of Theorem 3.4. Second, when $c > c^*$, it was obtained in (3.21), by means (see (3.20)) of the Pollaczek–Khinchin formula; recall that for all $u \geqslant 0$ it represents $\mathsf{P}\{\varUpsilon_{u,c} < \infty\}$ as an infinite series of convolutions of the integrated tail $F_{\hat{Y}}$ of the distribution F_Y.

---

[7]In risk theory, this probability is known as the ultimate probability of ruin.
[8]In other words, when T is exponentially distributed with positive parameter δ.
[9]Note that condition $c > c^* := \mathsf{E}\,Y/\mathsf{E}\,T$ writes as $c > \delta/\rho$.
[10]In risk theory, this $\varkappa$ is called adjustment coefficient, or Lundberg's exponent.

Model (B). This model is verbally described as compound Poisson model, when Y is light-tail (but not exponentially distributed). In this case, it is difficult or even impossible to obtain a closed-form expression for $\mathsf{P}\{\Upsilon_{u,c} < \infty\}$. Instead, when $c > c^* := \mathsf{E}\,Y/\mathsf{E}\,T = \delta\,\mathsf{E}\,Y$, for all $u \geqslant 0$ the inequality

$$\mathsf{P}\{\Upsilon_{u,c} < \infty\} \leqslant e^{-\varkappa u}, \tag{5.30}$$

called Lundberg's inequality, holds. Here $\varkappa > 0$, dependent of c, is a unique positive root of Lundberg's equation $\mathsf{E}\exp\{\varkappa(Y - cT)\} = 1$. In this model, this equation may be rewritten as

$$\mathsf{E}\exp\{\varkappa Y\} = 1 + c\varkappa/\delta,$$

or as

$$\int_0^\infty e^{\varkappa y}\overline{F}_Y(y)\,dy = c/\delta,$$

where $\overline{F}_Y(y) := 1 - F_Y(y)$ is called tail function.

The inequality (5.30) can be refined; below is one such refinement (see, e.g., [158], Theorem 5.4.1).

Theorem 5.8 *Let in the model which we consider $c > c^*$ and a positive solution $\varkappa > 0$ to Lundberg's equation* (5.29) *exists. Then*

$$a_\ominus\, e^{-\varkappa u} \leqslant \mathsf{P}\{\Upsilon_{u,c} < \infty\} \leqslant a_\oplus\, e^{-\varkappa u} \tag{5.31}$$

for all $u \geqslant 0$, where $x_0 := \sup\{x : F_Y(x) < 1\}$,

$$a_\ominus := \inf_{x\in[0,x_0]} \frac{e^{\varkappa x}\int_x^\infty \overline{F}_Y(y)\,dy}{\int_x^\infty e^{\varkappa y}\,\overline{F}_Y(y)\,dy}, \qquad a_\oplus := \sup_{x\in[0,x_0]} \frac{e^{\varkappa x}\int_x^\infty \overline{F}_Y(y)\,dy}{\int_x^\infty e^{\varkappa y}\,\overline{F}_Y(y)\,dy}.$$

Moreover, $0 \leqslant a_\ominus \leqslant a_\oplus \leqslant 1$.

Plainly, an upper bound for $\mathsf{P}\{\Upsilon_{u,c} \leqslant t\}$, similar to (5.27)–(5.28), is straightforward from (5.27) and (5.30) or (5.31).

When Y is generally, rather than exponentially, distributed, much more laborious calculations are required to find the adjustment coefficient $\varkappa$. We illustrate this statement with the following examples.

Example (a). When T is exponentially distributed with parameter δ and Y is 2-mixture of exponential distributions[11], their p.d.f. are

$$f_T(x) = \delta\, e^{-\delta x}, \quad f_Y(x) = p\,\rho_1\, e^{-\rho_1 x} + q\,\rho_2\, e^{-\rho_2 x}, \quad x > 0,$$

[11] According to classification of Section 6.1.2, this model is (see Table 6.1) Model (B), Example (a).

where $0 < \rho_1 \leqslant \rho_2 < \infty$ and $0 \leqslant p, q \leqslant 1$, $p + q = 1$. Elementary calculations yield

$$\mathsf{E}\,T = 1/\delta, \qquad \mathsf{D}\,T = 1/\delta^2,$$
$$\mathsf{E}\,Y = p/\rho_1 + q/\rho_2, \quad \mathsf{D}\,Y = (q\rho_1^2 + p\rho_2^2 + pq(\rho_1 - \rho_2)^2)/(\rho_1^2\rho_2^2),$$

whence $c^* := \mathsf{E}\,Y/\mathsf{E}\,T$ is equal to $\delta(p/\rho_1 + q/\rho_2)$, and

$$\mathsf{E}\,e^{-\varkappa c T} = \int_0^\infty e^{-\varkappa c x}(\delta\, e^{-\delta x})\,dx = \frac{\delta}{\delta + c\varkappa},$$
$$\mathsf{E}\,e^{\varkappa Y} = \int_0^\infty e^{\varkappa x}(p\,\rho_1\, e^{-\rho_1 x} + q\,\rho_2\, e^{-\rho_2 x})\,dx = -\frac{p\,\rho_1}{\varkappa - \rho_1} - \frac{q\,\rho_2}{\varkappa - \rho_2}.$$

By elementary calculations, we get

$$\begin{aligned}\mathsf{E}\exp\{\varkappa(Y - cT)\} &= \mathsf{E}\exp\{\varkappa Y\}\,\mathsf{E}\exp\{-c\varkappa T\}\\ &= -\left(\frac{p\,\rho_1}{\varkappa - \rho_1} + \frac{q\,\rho_2}{\varkappa - \rho_2}\right)\frac{\delta}{\delta + c\varkappa}.\end{aligned}$$

Thereby, Lundberg's equation (5.29) may be rewritten as

$$-\left(\frac{p\,\rho_1}{\varkappa - \rho_1} + \frac{q\,\rho_2}{\varkappa - \rho_2}\right)\frac{\delta}{\delta + c\varkappa} = 1. \tag{5.32}$$

This equation, easily solved numerically, can be approached analytically in the following way. Assuming that $\varkappa < \rho_1 = \min\{\rho_1, \rho_2\}$, it may be rewritten as

$$(\delta + c\varkappa)(\varkappa - \rho_1)(\varkappa - \rho_2) + \delta(p\,\rho_1(\varkappa - \rho_2) + q\,\rho_2(\varkappa - \rho_1)) = 0,$$

which, since the term $\delta\rho_1\rho_2 - \delta p\rho_1\rho_2 - \delta q\rho_1\rho_2$ is zero, may be rewritten as

$$c\,\varkappa^3 + (\delta - c\rho_1 - c\rho_2)\,\varkappa^2 + (\delta p\rho_1 + \delta q\rho_2 + c\rho_1\rho_2 - \delta\rho_1 - \delta\rho_2)\,\varkappa = 0.$$

This equation, one of whose roots is zero, reduces to the quadratic equation[12]

$$c\,\varkappa^2 + (\delta - c\rho_1 - c\rho_2)\,\varkappa + (\delta p\rho_1 + \delta q\rho_2 + c\rho_1\rho_2 - \delta\rho_1 - \delta\rho_2) = 0. \tag{5.33}$$

We leave the reader to write down an explicit expression for the positive root, which is easy to find numerically. We will come back to this Model (B), Example (a) in Chapter 6.

---

[12]For $p = q = 1/2$ and $\rho_1 = \rho_1 = \rho$, equation (5.32) reduces to quadratic equation $(\delta + c\varkappa)(\varkappa - \rho) = -\delta\rho$, whose positive solution is $\varkappa = \rho - \delta/c$. Equation (5.33) reduces to $c\varkappa^2 + (\delta - 2c\rho)\,\varkappa + c\rho^2 - \delta\rho = 0$, whose solutions are ρ (which does not suit us) and $\rho - \delta/c$.

Example (b). When T is exponentially distributed with parameter δ and Y is Erlang, their p.d.f. are

$$f_T(x) = \delta e^{-\delta x}, \quad f_Y(x) = \frac{\rho^m x^{m-1}}{\Gamma(m)} e^{-\rho x}, \quad x > 0,$$

where $\rho > 0$ and m integer. Elementary calculations yield

$$\begin{aligned} \mathsf{E}\, T &= 1/\delta, \quad \mathsf{D}\, T = 1/\delta^2, \\ \mathsf{E}\, Y &= m/\rho, \quad \mathsf{D}\, Y = m/\rho^2, \end{aligned}$$

whence $c^* := \mathsf{E}\, Y/\mathsf{E}\, T$ is equal to $(m\delta)/\rho$, and

$$\begin{aligned} \mathsf{E}\, e^{-\varkappa c T} &= \delta \int_0^\infty e^{-(\varkappa c+\delta)x}\, dx = \frac{\delta}{\delta + c\varkappa}, \\ \mathsf{E}\, e^{\varkappa Y} &= \frac{\rho^m}{\Gamma(m)} \int_0^\infty e^{(\varkappa-\rho)x} x^{m-1}\, dx = \frac{\rho^m}{(\rho-\varkappa)^m}, \end{aligned}$$

whence for $c > (m\delta)/\rho$ Lundberg's equation $\mathsf{E} \exp\{\varkappa\,(Y - cT)\} = 1$ may be rewritten as

$$(\rho - \varkappa)^m\, (\delta + c\varkappa) - \delta\rho^m = 0.$$

Its unique positive solution is easy to find numerically[13]. We will come back to Model (B), Example (b) in Chapter 6.

Model (C). This model is verbally described as compound Poisson model, when Y is fat-tail. In this model, Lundberg's inequality (5.30) and its ramifications such as (5.31), provide an upper bound for $\mathsf{P}\{\Upsilon_{u,c} \leqslant t\}$, but can be applied only when the moment generating function of Y exists, i.e., when Y is light-tail.

Bounds for $\mathsf{P}\{\Upsilon_{u,c} < \infty\}$, when the moment generating function of Y does not exist[14], i.e., when Y is fat-tail, was obtained first in [60], and then in [35], using the following truncating in Lundberg's condition: for given $x > 0$, there exists a positive constant $\varkappa_x$ such that

$$\mathsf{E}(\exp\{\varkappa_x\,(Y - cT)\}\, \mathbf{1}_{\{Y \leqslant x\}}) = 1 \tag{5.34}$$

or, equivalently (see Problem 5.2 below),

$$\int_0^x e^{\varkappa_x y}(1 - F_Y(y))\, dy = \frac{c}{\delta}. \tag{5.35}$$

It is easily seen that $\varkappa_x$ always exists and is unique for every positive x. Regarded as a function of x, it decreases, as x increases, and

$$0 < \varkappa_x < \frac{\mathsf{E}\, Y(1 + \theta - \overline{F}_{\hat{Y}}(x))}{\int_0^x y(1 - F_Y(y))\, dy}, \tag{5.36}$$

---

[13]In the case $m = 2$, we have $\varkappa = (2c\rho - \delta - \sqrt{\delta\,(4c\rho + \delta)}\,)/(2c)$.

[14]Hence, there is no positive solution to Lundberg's equation (5.29).

where[15] $\theta = c/(\delta\,\mathsf{E}\,Y) - 1$, $\overline{F}_{\hat{Y}}(u) = 1 - F_{\hat{Y}}(u)$, and $F_{\hat{Y}}(u) := \frac{1}{\mathsf{E}\,Y}\int_0^u (1 - F_Y(y))\,dy$ is referred to as integrated tail of F_Y. If $\varkappa > 0$ exists, then $\varkappa \leqslant \varkappa_x$ and $\lim_{x\to\infty} \varkappa_x = \varkappa$.

The following result, from which an upper bound for $\mathsf{P}\{\varUpsilon_{u,c} \leqslant t\}$ follows, is Corollary 3 in [35].

Theorem 5.9 *When $c > c^*$, for all $u \geqslant 0$, we have*

$$\frac{\theta e^{-2\varkappa_u u} + \overline{F}_{\hat{Y}}(u)}{\theta + \overline{F}_{\hat{Y}}(u)} \leqslant \mathsf{P}\{\varUpsilon_{u,c} < \infty\} \leqslant \frac{\theta e^{-\varkappa_u u} + \overline{F}_{\hat{Y}}(u)}{\theta + \overline{F}_{\hat{Y}}(u)}. \tag{5.37}$$

This result refines the upper bound

$$\mathsf{P}\{\varUpsilon_{u,c} < \infty\} \leqslant e^{-\varkappa_u u} + \frac{\overline{F}_{\hat{Y}}(u)}{\theta + \overline{F}_{\hat{Y}}(u)}, \tag{5.38}$$

previously obtained in [60].

If F_Y is subexponential, i.e., $\overline{F}_{\hat{Y}}^{*2}(x)/\overline{F}_{\hat{Y}}(x) \to 2$, $x \to \infty$, then $\varkappa$ does not exist and (see [74]) $\mathsf{P}\{\varUpsilon_{u,c} < \infty\} \sim \overline{F}_{\hat{Y}}(u)/(\theta + \overline{F}_{\hat{Y}}(u))$, as $u \to \infty$.

The bound (5.38) is numerically compared with this asymptotics in [60]. It is shown there that either term in the bound (5.38) can be dominant term, so that although this bound looks like the bound given by Lundberg's inequality, it needs not behave like it.

When Y has only low-order power moments, i.e., is fat-tail, a rational intuitive conclusion about the structure of asymptotic upper bound on $\mathsf{P}\{\varUpsilon_{u,c} \leqslant t\}$ for c and t positive can be based also on the inverse Gaussian approximation. It stems from the following observation.

When the approximating term $\mathcal{M}_{u,c}(t)$ does not tend to zero, as $u \to \infty$, which happens, when $c \leqslant c^*$, or is a value tending to zero slower than the remainder term $\mathcal{R}_{u,c}(t)$, whose rate of decay to zero is always power, the bound is of the same order as $\mathcal{M}_{u,c}(t)$. When $\mathcal{M}_{u,c}(t)$ tends to zero, as $u \to \infty$, faster than the remainder term $\mathcal{R}_{u,c}(t)$, e.g., with the exponential rate (it happens, when c far exceeds c^*), the bound is of the same order as $\mathcal{R}_{u,c}(t)$, i.e., its rate of decay to zero is power.

We will come back to various examples within Model (C) in Chapter 6.

Model (D). This model is verbally described as renewal (but not compound Poisson) model, where Y is exponentially distributed with parameter ρ.

In this model, fundamental is the following observation (see, e.g., [158], Theorem 6.4.5): the distribution of descending ladder height is exponential with the same parameter ρ, and the following result (see [158], Corollary

[15] By the condition $c > c^* := \mathsf{E}\,Y/\mathsf{E}\,T$, which writes as $c > \delta\,\mathsf{E}\,Y$, we have $\theta = c/(\delta\,\mathsf{E}\,Y) - 1 > 0$. In risk theory, this θ is called relative safety loading.

6.5.2) holds: in the renewal model, where Y is exponentially distributed with parameter ρ, when $c > c^* := \mathsf{E}\,Y/\mathsf{E}\,T = 1/(\mathsf{E}\,T\rho)$,

$$\mathsf{P}\{\varUpsilon_{u,c} < \infty\} = (1 - \varkappa/\rho)\, e^{-\varkappa u}, \tag{5.39}$$

for all $u \geqslant 0$, where $\varkappa$, dependent of c, is a unique positive solution to Lundberg's equation (5.29).

Equality (5.39) is a straightforward generalization of (5.28). Plainly, by (5.27), the problem of constructing an upper bound for $\mathsf{P}\{\varUpsilon_{u,c} \leqslant t\}$ in the renewal model, when Y is exponentially distributed, reduces to finding a positive solution to Lundberg's equation (5.29).

Example (a). When T is 2-mixture of exponential distributions with parameters δ_1, δ_2, p, and Y is exponentially distributed with parameter $\rho > 0$, their p.d.f. are

$$f_T(x) = p\,\delta_1\, e^{-\delta_1 x} + q\,\delta_2\, e^{-\delta_2 x}, \quad f_Y(x) = \rho\, e^{-\rho x}, \quad x > 0,$$

where $0 < \delta_1 \leqslant \delta_2 < \infty$ and $0 \leqslant p, q \leqslant 1$, $p + q = 1$. Elementary calculations yield

$$\begin{aligned} \mathsf{E}\,T &= p/\delta_1 + q/\delta_2, & \mathsf{D}\,T &= (q\delta_1^2 + p\delta_2^2 + pq(\delta_1 - \delta_2)^2)/(\delta_1^2\delta_2^2), \\ \mathsf{E}\,Y &= 1/\rho, & \mathsf{D}\,Y &= 1/\rho^2, \end{aligned}$$

whence $c^* := \mathsf{E}\,Y/\mathsf{E}\,T$ is equal to $\delta_1\delta_2/(\rho(p\delta_2 + q\delta_1))$.

When $c > c^* = \delta_1\delta_2/(\rho(q\delta_1 + p\delta_2))$, investigation of Lundberg's equation (5.29) reduces to the quadratic equation

$$c^2\varkappa^2 - (\rho c^2 - (\delta_1 + \delta_2)c)\,\varkappa - (p\delta_2 + q\delta_1)\,\rho c + \delta_1\delta_2 = 0, \tag{5.40}$$

whence

$$\varkappa = \frac{\rho}{2} - \frac{\delta_1 + \delta_2}{2c} + \frac{1}{2c}\,(\rho^2c^2 + 2\,\rho c(\delta_1 - \delta_2)(q - p) + (\delta_1 - \delta_2)^2)^{1/2}. \tag{5.41}$$

We will come back to Model (D), Example (a) in Chapter 6.

Example (b). When T is Erlang and Y is exponentially distributed with parameter $\rho > 0$, their p.d.f. are

$$f_T(x) = \frac{\delta^k x^{k-1}}{\Gamma(k)}\, e^{-\delta x}, \quad f_Y(x) = \rho\, e^{-\rho x}, \quad x > 0.$$

Elementary calculations yield

$$\begin{aligned} \mathsf{E}\,T &= k/\delta, & \mathsf{D}\,T &= k/\delta^2, \\ \mathsf{E}\,Y &= 1/\rho, & \mathsf{D}\,Y &= 1/\rho^2 \end{aligned}$$

and

$$\mathsf{E}\, e^{-\varkappa c T} = \frac{\delta^k}{\Gamma(k)} \int_0^\infty e^{-(\varkappa c+\delta)x} x^{k-1}\, dx = \frac{\delta^k}{(\delta + c\varkappa)^k},$$

$$\mathsf{E}\, e^{\varkappa Y} = \rho \int_0^\infty e^{(\varkappa-\rho)x}\, dx = \frac{\rho}{\rho - \varkappa},$$

whence $c^* := \mathsf{E}\, Y / \mathsf{E}\, T$ is equal to $\delta/(k\rho)$.

When $c > \delta/(k\rho)$, Lundberg's equation $\mathsf{E} \exp\{\varkappa(Y - cT)\} = 1$ may be rewritten as

$$(\rho - \varkappa)\,(\delta + c\varkappa)^k - \delta^k \rho = 0.$$

Its unique positive solution is easy to find numerically. We will come back to Model (D), Example (b) in Chapter 6.

Model (E). This model is verbally described as renewal (but not compound Poisson) model, when Y is light-tail (but not exponentially distributed).

Recall that $X := Y - cT$ and that $\overline{F}_X(x) := 1 - F_X(x)$, called tail function. The following result is known as Lundberg's bound (see [158], Theorem 6.5.4).

Theorem 5.10 *Assume that $c > c^*$ and a positive solution $\varkappa$ to* (5.29) *exists. Then*

$$b_\ominus\, e^{-\varkappa u} \leqslant \mathsf{P}\{\varUpsilon_{u,c} < \infty\} \leqslant b_\oplus\, e^{-\varkappa u} \tag{5.42}$$

for all $u \geqslant 0$, where $x_0 := \sup\{x : F_X(x) < 1\}$,

$$b_\ominus = \inf_{x\in[0,x_0]} \frac{e^{\varkappa x}\overline{F}_X(x)}{\int_x^\infty e^{\varkappa y}\, dF_X(y)}, \qquad b_\oplus = \sup_{x\in[0,x_0]} \frac{e^{\varkappa x}\overline{F}_X(x)}{\int_x^\infty e^{\varkappa y}\, dF_X(y)}.$$

Moreover, $0 \leqslant b_\ominus \leqslant b_\oplus \leqslant 1$.

The following Lundberg's bound is a little less accurate, but given in terms of c.d.f. of Y, rather than c.d.f. of X (see [158], Theorem 6.5.5). As usual, $\overline{F}_Y(x) := 1 - F_Y(x)$.

Theorem 5.11 *For $x_0' := \sup\{x : F_Y(x) < 1\}$ and*

$$b_\ominus^* = \inf_{x\in[0,x_0']} \frac{e^{\varkappa x}\overline{F}_Y(x)}{\int_x^\infty e^{\varkappa y}\, dF_Y(y)}, \qquad b_\oplus^* = \sup_{x\in[0,x_0']} \frac{e^{\varkappa x}\overline{F}_Y(x)}{\int_x^\infty e^{\varkappa y}\, dF_Y(y)},$$

we have $0 \leqslant b_\ominus^* \leqslant b_\ominus \leqslant b_\oplus \leqslant b_\oplus^* \leqslant 1$, whence

$$b_\ominus^*\, e^{-\varkappa u} \leqslant \mathsf{P}\{\varUpsilon_{u,c} < \infty\} \leqslant b_\oplus^*\, e^{-\varkappa u}. \tag{5.43}$$

In conclusion, we say that, although analytic non-asymptotic bounds for $\mathsf{P}\{\varUpsilon_{u,c} < \infty\}$ thus exist, there are no simple closed-form analytic results for the analysis of fixed probability levels in Model (E). Even applying the above results, one inevitably has to move on to numerical calculations. We will return to Model (E) in Chapter 6.

Model (F). This model is verbally described as renewal (but not compound Poisson) model, when Y is fat-tail.

In this case, some upper bounds of our interest are constructed (see, e.g., [37], [38], [151]), the general idea of which is to apply ladder height distributions instead of the original ones. From an analytical point of view, these bounds are too complicated to be deemed acceptable (within the framework of our problems) closed-form results, whence it becomes necessary to turn to numerical calculations. We will come back to Model (F) in Chapter 6.

5.2.5 An approach based on Laplace transform

This section is optional and may be skipped on first reading. It outlines the numerical methods based on Laplace transforms. Such methods are used in a variety of applications, are highly accurate and error-controllable, and require less resources than the Monte Carlo simulation, which differs conceptually and will be discussed in Chapter 6. Usually, the numerical methods, like in Theorem 5.12 below, where Y is assumed exponentially distributed, work under rather rigid conditions.

Theorem 5.12 *Assume that Y is exponentially distributed with parameter $\rho > 0$. Denote by $\mathcal{L}_T(\alpha) := \mathsf{E}\, e^{-\alpha T}$ the Laplace transform of T. Then for $\alpha > 0$ we have*

$$\alpha \int_0^\infty e^{-\alpha t} \mathsf{P}\{\Upsilon_{u,c} \leqslant t\}\, dt = y(\alpha) \exp\{-u\rho(1 - y(\alpha))\}, \tag{5.44}$$

where $y(\alpha)$ is a solution[16] *to the equation*

$$y(\alpha) = \mathcal{L}_T(\alpha + c\rho(1 - y(\alpha))). \tag{5.45}$$

This result from [119] is given without proof. This is an example of analytical results which underly the numerical methods based on Laplace transforms. For curiosity, we will show that Theorem 3.4 follows from Theorem 5.12.

Proof of Theorem 3.4. The Laplace transform of exponentially distributed with parameter $\delta > 0$ random variable T is $\mathcal{L}_T(\alpha) = \delta/(\delta + \alpha)$. Therefore, the solution $y(\alpha)$ to Takáčs–Feller's equation (5.45) is

$$y(\alpha) = \sqrt{\delta/c\rho}(a - b)(\sqrt{a + \alpha} + \sqrt{b + \alpha}\,)^{-2},$$

where $a = (\sqrt{c\rho} + \sqrt{\delta}\,)^2$ and $b = (\sqrt{c\rho} - \sqrt{\delta}\,)^2$. Recall that the Laplace transform of

$$ne^{-(a+b)z/2} z^{-1} I_n((a - b)z/2)$$

is

$$((a - b)(\sqrt{a + \alpha} + \sqrt{b + \alpha})^{-2})^n.$$

[16] This equation is known as Takáčs–Feller's.

Expanding the exponent in (5.44), we have for $\alpha > 0$

$$\begin{aligned}\alpha \int_0^\infty & e^{-\alpha t} \mathsf{P}\{\Upsilon_{u,c} \leqslant t\}\, dt \\ &= y(\alpha)\exp\{-u\rho(1-y(\alpha))\} \\ &= e^{-u\rho} \sum_{n=0}^{\infty} \frac{(u\rho)^n}{n!} (y(\alpha))^{n+1} \\ &= e^{-u\rho} \sum_{n=0}^{\infty} \frac{(u\rho)^n}{n!} \frac{(a-b)^{n+1}}{(\sqrt{a+\alpha}+\sqrt{b+\alpha})^{2(n+1)}} \left(\frac{\delta}{c\rho}\right)^{(n+1)/2}.\end{aligned} \tag{5.46}$$

Let us write[17] $\mathsf{P}\{\Upsilon_{u,c\,|\,\delta,\rho} \leqslant t\} = \int_0^t f(x)\, dx$. We note that the right-hand side of equality (5.46) is the Laplace transform of the function

$$f(x) = e^{-u\rho} \frac{1}{x} \sqrt{\frac{\delta}{c\rho}}\, e^{-(c\rho+\delta)x} \sum_{n=0}^{\infty} \left(\frac{\rho\delta}{c}\right)^{n/2} \frac{u^n}{n!} (n+1)\, I_{n+1}(2\sqrt{c\delta\rho}\, x),$$

whence

$$\begin{aligned}\mathsf{P}\{\Upsilon_{u,c\,|\,\delta,\rho} \leqslant t\} = {}& e^{-u\rho} \sqrt{\frac{\delta}{c\rho}} \sum_{n=0}^{\infty} \left(\frac{\rho\delta}{c}\right)^{n/2} \frac{u^n}{n!} \int_0^{c\rho t} \frac{n+1}{x}\, e^{-(1+\delta/c\rho)x} \\ & \times I_{n+1}(2\sqrt{\delta/c\rho}\, x)\, dx.\end{aligned} \tag{5.47}$$

By Theorem A.8, equality (5.47) can be rewritten as

$$\mathsf{P}\{\Upsilon_{u,c\,|\,\delta,\rho} \leqslant t\} = \begin{cases} e^{-u\rho} \dfrac{\delta}{c\rho} \displaystyle\sum_{n=0}^{\infty} \left(\frac{\delta}{c}\right)^n \frac{u^n}{n!} (1 - v_n(c\rho t)), & c\rho/\delta > 1, \\ e^{-u\rho} \dfrac{\delta}{c\rho} \displaystyle\sum_{n=0}^{\infty} \left(\frac{\delta}{c}\right)^n \frac{u^n}{n!} & \\ \quad \times \left(\left(\dfrac{c\rho}{\delta}\right)^{n+1} - v_n(c\rho t)\right), & c\rho/\delta \leqslant 1, \end{cases} \tag{5.48}$$

where $v_n(c\rho t) = (2/\pi)(c\rho/\delta)^{n/2} \int_0^\pi \sin x \sin((n+1)\, x)\, e^{-c\rho A(x) t} A(x)^{-1}\, dx$ and $A(x) = 1 + \delta/c\rho - 2\sqrt{\delta/c\rho}\cos x$.

Regarding the right-hand side of (5.48), we note that

$$e^{-u\rho} \frac{\delta}{c\rho} \sum_{n=0}^{\infty} \left(\frac{\delta}{c}\right)^n \frac{u^n}{n!} = \frac{\delta}{c\rho} \exp\{-u(c\rho-\delta)/c\},$$

when $c\rho/\delta > 1$, and

$$e^{-u\rho} \frac{\delta}{c\rho} \sum_{n=0}^{\infty} \left(\frac{\delta}{c}\right)^n \frac{u^n}{n!} \left(\frac{c\rho}{\delta}\right)^{n+1} = 1,$$

[17]Thus the integrand is p.d.f. of the distribution of $\Upsilon_{u,c}$.

when $c\rho/\delta \leqslant 1$.

Proceeding with the summands

$$e^{-u\rho}\frac{\delta}{c\rho}\sum_{n=0}^{\infty}\left(\frac{\delta}{c}\right)^{n}\frac{u^{n}}{n\,!}\,v_{n}(c\rho t),$$

we note that $\sin((n+1)\,x) = (e^{i(n+1)x} - e^{-i(n+1)x})/(2i)$, that

$$\begin{aligned}\sum_{n=0}^{\infty}\frac{a^{n}}{n!}\sin((n+1)\,x) &= \frac{1}{2i}\sum_{n=0}^{\infty}\frac{a^{n}}{n!}\,(e^{i(n+1)x} - e^{-i(n+1)x})\\ &= \frac{1}{2i}\,(e^{ix}e^{ae^{ix}} - e^{-ix}e^{ae^{-ix}})\\ &= \frac{1}{2i}\,(e^{a\cos x+i(x+a\sin x)} - e^{a\cos x-i(x+a\sin x)})\\ &= e^{a\cos x}\sin(x+a\sin x),\end{aligned}$$

and that $\sin x\sin(x+a\sin x) = \frac{1}{2}(\cos(a\sin x) - \cos(a\sin x+2x))$. Finally, elementary calculations yield

$$\begin{aligned}&\sum_{n=0}^{\infty}\frac{(\delta\rho/c)^{n/2}u^{n}}{n!}(e^{i(n+1)x} - e^{-i(n+1)x})\\ &\qquad = 2\,i\exp\{u\sqrt{\delta\rho/c}\,\cos x\}\sin(x+u\sqrt{\delta\rho/c}\,\sin x).\end{aligned} \tag{5.49}$$

Applying the equality[18]

$$2\sin x\,\sin(x+u\sqrt{\delta\rho/c}\sin x) = \cos(u\sqrt{\delta\rho/c}\sin x) - \cos(u\sqrt{\delta\rho/c}\sin x+2x)$$

to the right-hand side of (5.49), we get (3.8), as required. □

Remark 5.4 Using equality (5.47) and equality

$$\int_{0}^{\infty}\frac{1}{x}\,e^{-(1+\delta/c\rho)x}I_{n+1}(2\sqrt{\delta/c\rho}\,x)\,dx = \frac{1}{n+1}\left(\frac{\delta}{c\rho}\right)^{(n+1)/2},$$

which follows from equality (A.17), we have

$$\begin{aligned}\mathsf{P}\{\Upsilon_{u,c\,|\,\delta,\rho} \leqslant t\} &\leqslant e^{-u\rho}\sqrt{\frac{\delta}{c\rho}}\sum_{n=0}^{\infty}\left(\frac{\rho\delta}{c}\right)^{n/2}\frac{u^{n}}{n\,!}\\ &\quad\times\int_{0}^{\infty}\frac{n+1}{x}\,e^{-(1+\delta/c\rho)x}I_{n+1}(2\sqrt{\delta/c\rho}\,x)\,dx\\ &= \frac{\delta}{c\rho}\exp\{-u(c\rho-\delta)/c\},\end{aligned}$$

as required: compare it to (3.9) and (3.21).

[18] See equality $\cos x - \cos y = 2\sin\{\frac{1}{2}(x+y)\}\sin\{\frac{1}{2}(y-x)\}$ in [85], p. 39.

5.3 Inverse Level-crossing Problem

This section is of paramount importance to this book. It will show to what extent the results of Section 3.3 can be extended to the general renewal model.

5.3.1 Analytical structure of fixed-probability level

The following theorem is a direct generalization of Theorem 3.6 since for T and Y exponentially distributed with parameters δ and ρ, respectively, elementary calculations yield $M = \rho/\delta$, $D^2 = 2\rho/\delta^2$. It is also instructive to compare (5.50) with the first equality (4.23) in Theorem 4.19.

Theorem 5.13 *Assume that $f_T(x)$ and $f_Y(x)$ are bounded above by a finite constant, $D^2 > 0$, $\mathsf{E}(T^3) < \infty$, and $\mathsf{E}(Y^3) < \infty$. Then for $t \to \infty$, we have*

$$u_{\alpha,t}(0) = \frac{t}{M} + \frac{D}{M^{3/2}}\,\kappa_\alpha \sqrt{t}\,(1 + o(1)). \tag{5.50}$$

Proof of Theorem 5.13. The proof is analogous to the second proof of Theorem 3.6. Note that $u_{\alpha,t}(0)$ is a solution to the equation $\mathsf{P}\{\varUpsilon_{u,0} \leqslant t\} = \alpha$, where $\varUpsilon_{u,0} := \inf\{s > 0 : V_s > u\}$. Since the trajectories of compound renewal process V_s, $s \geqslant 0$, are (a.s.) step functions with only jumps up, this equation may be rewritten as $\mathsf{P}\{V_t > u\} = \alpha$.

The normal approximation for the distribution of compound renewal process V_t is well known (see, e.g., [135], Chapter 4): we have

$$\begin{aligned} \mathsf{E}V_t &= (\mathsf{E}\,Y/\mathsf{E}\,T)\,t + \mathsf{E}\,Y(\mathsf{D}\,T - (\mathsf{E}\,T)^2)/(2(\mathsf{E}\,T)^2) + o(1), \\ \mathsf{D}V_t &= (((\mathsf{E}\,Y)^2\mathsf{D}\,T + (\mathsf{E}\,T)^2\mathsf{D}\,Y)/(\mathsf{E}\,Y)^3)\,t + o(t), \end{aligned} \tag{5.51}$$

as $t \to \infty$, and the probability $\mathsf{P}\{V_t > u\}$ is approximated by

$$1 - \varPhi_{(0,1)}\left(\frac{u - \mathsf{E}V_t}{\sqrt{\mathsf{D}V_t}}\right),$$

as $t \to \infty$, whence (5.50). □

The following theorem is a generalization of Theorem 3.7. It is also instructive to compare (5.52) with the second equality (4.23) in Theorem 4.19.

Theorem 5.14 *Assume that $f_T(x)$ and $f_Y(x)$ are bounded above by a finite constant, $D^2 > 0$, $\mathsf{E}(T^3) < \infty$, and $\mathsf{E}(Y^3) < \infty$. Then for $t \to \infty$, we have*

$$u_{\alpha,t}(c^*) = \frac{D}{M^{3/2}}\,\kappa_{\alpha/2}\sqrt{t}\,(1 + o(1)). \tag{5.52}$$

Proof of Theorem 5.14. The left-hand side of equation (5.3) is (see (5.8))

$$\begin{aligned}\mathsf{P}\{\Upsilon_{u,c} \leqslant t\} &= \int_0^t \mathsf{P}\{u + cv - Y < 0\}\, f_{T_1}(v)\, dv \\ &\quad + \int_0^t \mathsf{P}\{v < \Upsilon_{u,c} \leqslant t \mid T_1 = v\}\, f_{T_1}(v)\, dv,\end{aligned}$$

whence equation (5.3) with $c = c^*$ may be rewritten as

$$\begin{aligned}&\int_0^t \mathsf{P}\{u + c^* v < Y_1\} f_{T_1}(v)\, dv \\ &\qquad + \int_0^t \mathsf{P}\{v < \Upsilon_{u,c^*} \leqslant t \mid T_1 = v\} f_{T_1}(v)\, dy = \alpha.\end{aligned} \tag{5.53}$$

The integrand $\mathsf{P}\{v < \Upsilon_{u,c^*} \leqslant t \mid T_1 = v\}$ is approximated by $\mathcal{M}_{u,c^*}(t)$, which is (see (4.5))

$$2\left(\Phi_{(0,1)}\left(\sqrt{\frac{\mathsf{E}T(v\,\mathsf{E}Y + u\,\mathsf{E}T)}{(\mathsf{E}Y)^2 D^2}}\right) - \Phi_{(0,1)}\left(\sqrt{\frac{\mathsf{E}T}{(\mathsf{E}Y)^2 D^2}}\,\frac{u\,\mathsf{E}T + v\,\mathsf{E}Y}{\sqrt{u\,\mathsf{E}T + t\,\mathsf{E}Y}}\right)\right).$$

Let us show that $u_{\alpha,t}(c^*)$ in (5.52) is an asymptotic solution to equation (5.53). Firstly, bearing in mind that $\mathsf{E}(T^3) < \infty$, $\mathsf{E}(Y^3) < \infty$, it is easily seen that

$$\int_0^t \mathsf{P}\{u + c^* v - Y_1 < 0\} f_{T_1}(v)\, dv \to 0, \quad t \to \infty,\ u \to \infty.$$

Secondly, it is easily seen that

$$\Phi_{(0,1)}\left(\sqrt{\frac{\mathsf{E}T(v\,\mathsf{E}Y + u\,\mathsf{E}T)}{(\mathsf{E}Y)^2 D^2}}\right) \to 1, \quad u \to \infty.$$

Selecting in (5.52) u equal to $O(t^{1/2})$, we have

$$\frac{u\,\mathsf{E}T + v\,\mathsf{E}Y}{\sqrt{u\,\mathsf{E}T + t\,\mathsf{E}Y}} = \frac{u\,\mathsf{E}T}{\sqrt{t\,\mathsf{E}Y}}\,(1 + o(1)), \quad t \to \infty.$$

Therefore, (5.53) reduces to

$$2\left(1 - \Phi_{(0,1)}\left(\sqrt{\frac{\mathsf{E}T}{(\mathsf{E}Y)^2 D^2}}\,\frac{u\,\mathsf{E}T}{\sqrt{t\,\mathsf{E}Y}}\right)\right) = \alpha,$$

and the proof is easy to complete. □

The following result is formulated as a generalization of Theorem 3.8. It is instructive to compare it with Theorem 4.20.

Theorem 5.15 *Assume that $f_T(x)$ and $f_Y(x)$ are bounded above by a finite constant, and $D^2 > 0$, $\mathsf{E}(T^3) < \infty$, $\mathsf{E}(Y^3) < \infty$. Then for $c^* := M^{-1}$ we have*

$$u_{\alpha,t}(c) = \begin{cases} (c^* - c)\, t + \dfrac{D}{M^{3/2}}\, \mathsf{z}_{\alpha,t}\Big(\dfrac{M^{3/2}(c^* - c)}{D}\sqrt{t}\Big)\sqrt{t}, & 0 \leqslant c \leqslant c^*, \\ \dfrac{D}{M^{3/2}}\, \mathsf{z}_{\alpha,t}\Big(\dfrac{M^{3/2}(c^* - c)}{D}\sqrt{t}\Big)\sqrt{t}, & c > c^*, \end{cases}$$

where for t sufficiently large the function $\mathsf{z}_{\alpha,t}(y)$, $y \in \mathsf{R}$, is continuous and monotone increasing, as y increases from $-\infty$ to 0, and monotone decreasing, as y increases from 0 to ∞, and such that[19]

$$\lim_{y\to-\infty} \mathsf{z}_{\alpha,t}(y) = 0, \quad \lim_{y\to\infty} \mathsf{z}_{\alpha,t}(y) = \kappa_\alpha$$

and $\mathsf{z}_{\alpha,t}(0) = \kappa_{\alpha/2}\,(1 + o(1))$, as $t \to \infty$.

Proof of Theorem 5.15. The same way as the proof of Theorem 3.8, this proof is carried out in two stages. The proof in the case $0 < c < c^* := M^{-1}$ is analogous to the proof in Theorem 3.8. The proof in the case $c > c^*$ is different; we will comment on this.

Step 1. Let us consider the case $0 < c < c^* := M^{-1}$. Regarding equation (5.3), we switch from the variables u and c in its left-hand side to the variables

$$z = \frac{u}{DM^{-3/2}\sqrt{t}} - \frac{(M^{-1} - c)\sqrt{t}}{DM^{-3/2}} \in \mathsf{R}, \quad y = \frac{(M^{-1} - c)\sqrt{t}}{DM^{-3/2}} > 0. \tag{5.54}$$

For T and Y exponentially distributed with parameters δ and ρ, respectively, equalities (5.54) become equalities (3.38).

The original equation (5.3) may be rewritten as

$$\mathsf{P}\{\varUpsilon_{u,c} \leqslant t\}\,\Big|_{u=\frac{D\sqrt{t}}{M^{3/2}}(z+y),\, c=\frac{1}{M} - \frac{D}{M^{3/2}\sqrt{t}}y} = \alpha.$$

To prove that $\mathsf{z}_{\alpha,t}(y)$, $y > 0$, is monotone decreasing, we have to prove that $\frac{d}{dy}\,\mathsf{z}_{\alpha,t}(y) < 0$, $y > 0$. Referring to the implicit function derivative theorem (see Theorem A.4), we have (cf. (3.40))

$$\frac{d}{dy}\,\mathsf{z}_{\alpha,t}(y) = -\left.\left(\frac{\frac{\partial}{\partial y}\Big(\mathsf{P}\{\varUpsilon_{u,c} \leqslant t\}\,\Big|_{u=\frac{D\sqrt{t}}{M^{3/2}}(z+y),\, c=\frac{1}{M} - \frac{D}{M^{3/2}\sqrt{t}}y}\Big)}{\frac{\partial}{\partial z}\Big(\mathsf{P}\{\varUpsilon_{u,c} \leqslant t\}\,\Big|_{u=\frac{D\sqrt{t}}{M^{3/2}}(z+y),\, c=\frac{1}{M} - \frac{D}{M^{3/2}\sqrt{t}}y}\Big)}\right)\right|_{z=\mathsf{z}_{\alpha,t}(y)}. \tag{5.55}$$

[19]We recall that $0 < \kappa_\alpha < \kappa_{\alpha/2}$ for $0 < \alpha < \frac{1}{2}$.

The numerator is

$$\frac{\partial}{\partial y}\Big(\mathsf{P}\{\Upsilon_{u,c}\leqslant t\}\,\big|_{u=\frac{D\sqrt{t}}{M^{3/2}}(z+y),c=\frac{1}{M}-\frac{D}{M^{3/2}\sqrt{t}}y}\Big)$$
$$=\Big(\frac{\partial}{\partial u}\mathsf{P}\{\Upsilon_{u,c}\leqslant t\}\Big)\Big|_{u=\frac{D\sqrt{t}}{M^{3/2}}(z+y),c=\frac{1}{M}-\frac{D}{M^{3/2}\sqrt{t}}y}\underbrace{\frac{\partial}{\partial y}\Big(\frac{D\sqrt{t}}{M^{3/2}}(z+y)\Big)}_{\frac{D\sqrt{t}}{M^{3/2}}}$$
$$+\Big(\frac{\partial}{\partial c}\mathsf{P}\{\Upsilon_{u,c}\leqslant t\}\Big)\Big|_{u=\frac{D\sqrt{t}}{M^{3/2}}(z+y),c=\frac{1}{M}-\frac{D}{M^{3/2}\sqrt{t}}y}\underbrace{\frac{\partial}{\partial y}\Big(\frac{1}{M}-\frac{D}{M^{3/2}\sqrt{t}}y\Big)}_{-\frac{D}{M^{3/2}\sqrt{t}}},$$

and the denominator is

$$\begin{aligned}\frac{\partial}{\partial z}\Big(\mathsf{P}\{\Upsilon_{u,c}\leqslant t\}\,\big|_{u=\frac{D\sqrt{t}}{M^{3/2}}(z+y),c=\frac{1}{M}-\frac{D}{M^{3/2}\sqrt{t}}y}\Big)&\\=\Big(\frac{\partial}{\partial u}\mathsf{P}\{\Upsilon_{u,c}\leqslant t\}\Big)\Big|_{u=\frac{D\sqrt{t}}{M^{3/2}}(z+y),c=\frac{1}{M}-\frac{D}{M^{3/2}\sqrt{t}}y}&\\\times\underbrace{\frac{\partial}{\partial z}\Big(\frac{D\sqrt{t}}{M^{3/2}}(z+y)\Big)}_{\frac{D\sqrt{t}}{M^{3/2}}}.&\end{aligned}\tag{5.56}$$

The proof is completed by applying the results on the first-order derivatives of the first level-crossing time distribution from Section 5.2.3.

Step 2. Let us consider the case $c > c^* := M^{-1}$. As will be seen from what follows, no formal proof is required at this stage, but a detailed explanation is needed. It consists of several points. First of all, we note that, as such, the equality

$$u_{\alpha,t}(c)=\frac{D}{M^{3/2}}\,\mathsf{z}_{\alpha,t}\Big(\frac{M^{3/2}(c^*-c)}{D}\sqrt{t}\Big)\sqrt{t},\quad c>c^*,$$

is a trivial re-writing of the function $u_{\alpha,t}(c)$, $c > c^*$, in terms of $\mathsf{z}_{\alpha,t}(y)$, $y < 0$. Even the statement that the function $\mathsf{z}_{\alpha,t}(y)$, $y < 0$, monotone increases from 0 to a value close (as t is sufficiently large) to $\kappa_{\alpha/2}$, as y increases from $-\infty$ to 0, looks a trivial re-phrasing of the statement that the function $u_{\alpha,t}(c)$, $c > c^*$, is (by definition) monotone decreasing from $\frac{D}{M^{3/2}}\,\kappa_{\alpha/2}\sqrt{t}\,(1+o(1))$ to zero, as c increases from c^* to infinity; the latter comes from (5.52).

Thus, we claim that there is nothing to prove at Step 2. If so, then what have we done in diffusion and in exceptional renewal models, i.e., in Theorem 2.7, for $c > c^* := \vartheta$, and in Theorem 3.8, for $c > c^* := \delta/\rho$, respectively?

We have proven much more than was formally stated in each of the two cases. In Theorem 2.7, we displayed equation (2.18) with the left-hand side (2.19), whose solution is the function $\mathsf{z}_\alpha(y)$, $y < 0$. This makes it possible not only to calculate this function numerically, but to check its convexity. In our presentation, we did it later, in Theorem 2.12, which is a development of Theorem 2.7. Afterwards, we used convexity in Section 2.6.2, when constructing elaborated upper bounds in Theorems 2.23 and 2.24.

In Theorem 3.8, we were unable to write a closed-form equation for the function $\mathsf{z}_{\alpha,t}(y)$, $y < 0$, but we gave closed-form expressions for (see (3.46)) its first-order derivative $\frac{d}{dy}\,\mathsf{z}_{\alpha,t}(y)$ and (which follows from (3.51)) its second-order derivative $\frac{d^2}{dy^2}\,\mathsf{z}_{\alpha,t}(y)$. The latter paved the way for Theorem 3.12, where the weak-form[20] convexity was proved.

The major difference between the case $c > c^* := M^{-1}$ in the general renewal model, considered presently, and the similar case, considered in Theorems 3.8 and 3.12, in the model, when T and Y are exponentially distributed, is that in the latter case we possess (see (3.14)) explicit expression for $\mathsf{P}\{\Upsilon_{u,c\,|\,\delta,\rho} \leqslant t\}$, i.e., $\digamma_{\delta t}(u\,\rho \mid \delta/(c\rho+\delta))$, whereas in the former case we do not have such an explicit expression. To use in the general model, when $c > c^*$, the inverse Gaussian approximation, as we did when $0 \leqslant c \leqslant c^*$, is not allowed since it requires u tending to infinity, which does not hold (at least[21]) for $c > Kc^*$, $K > 1$.

Let us summarize. In the general renewal model, we cannot (at least by means of a direct analytical technique based on standard criteria) rigorously substantiate for $u_{\alpha,t}(c)$ such results as convexity, when $c > Kc^*$, $K > 1$. It follows, in particular, that we must be content with the upper bounds for $u_{\alpha,t}(c)$, $c > c^*$, based on monotony (like in Sections 2.6.1 and 3.6.1), rather than on convexity, like in Sections 2.6.2 and 3.6.2. □

For practical applications, a small (much less than would yield $\overline{u}_\alpha(c)$) overestimation of $u_{\alpha,t}(c)$ in a right-hand neighborhood of c^* is (see details in the next Section 5.5) not a big loss. This will be illustrated (see Fig. 6.13) in Chapter 6.

5.4 Primary Upper Bounds on Fixed-probability Level

Following Sections 2.5 and 3.5, let us turn to the primary upper bounds on the fixed-probability level $u_{\alpha,t}(c)$, $c \geqslant 0$.

[20]Recall that this is an asymptotic result, requiring t tending to infinity.

[21]Note that we have $u_{\alpha,t}(c)$ still tending to infinity, as $t \to \infty$, in the case, when c varies in some small, depending on t, right-hand neighborhood of the point c^*. This special case stands alone and will be considered on its own.

Bound, when $0 \leqslant c \leqslant c^*$**.** In this case, straightforwardly from Theorem 5.15, we have the two-sided asymptotic bound

$$\begin{aligned}(c^*-c)\,t + \frac{D}{M^{3/2}}\,\kappa_\alpha\sqrt{t}\,(1+o(1)) &\leqslant u_{\alpha,t}(c)\\ &\leqslant (c^*-c)\,t + \frac{D}{M^{3/2}}\,\kappa_{\alpha/2}\sqrt{t}\,(1+o(1)), \quad t\to\infty.\end{aligned} \tag{5.57}$$

Bound, when $c > c^*$**.** In this case, bearing in mind that

$$\mathsf{P}\{\varUpsilon_{u,c} \leqslant t\} \leqslant \mathsf{P}\{\varUpsilon_{u,c} < \infty\},$$

we have $u_{\alpha,t}(c) \leqslant \overline{u}_\alpha(c)$, where $\overline{u}_\alpha(c)$ is a solution to equation

$$\mathsf{P}\{\varUpsilon_{u,c} < \infty\} = \alpha.$$

In the same way, if we have another upper bound

$$\mathsf{P}\{\varUpsilon_{u,c} < \infty\} \leqslant B_{u,c},$$

then $\overline{u}_\alpha(c) \leqslant r(c)$, where $r(c)$ is a solution (w.r.t. u) to the equation $B_{u,c} = \alpha$.

The problem of finding $\overline{u}_\alpha(c)$, or $r(c)$, is tightly related to the problem of building an upper bound for the probability $\mathsf{P}\{\varUpsilon_{u,c} < \infty\}$, $c > c^*$, considered in Section 5.2.4, whence the same classification of models, as in Section 5.2.4:

- Model (A): compound Poisson model, when Y is exponentially distributed,
- Model (B): compound Poisson model, when distribution of Y is light-tailed (but not exponential),
- Model (C): compound Poisson model, when distribution of Y is fat-tailed,
- Model (D): renewal (but not compound Poisson) model, when Y is exponentially distributed,
- Model (E): renewal (but not compound Poisson) model, when distribution of Y is light-tailed (but not exponential),
- Model (F): renewal (but not compound Poisson) model, when the distribution of Y is fat-tailed.

We will merely browse these models here and return to them in detail in Chapter 6.

Model (A). In words, this is a compound Poisson model, when Y is exponentially distributed. It is explored in detail in Chapter 3. We recall that $c^* := \mathsf{E}Y/\mathsf{E}T$ is equal to δ/ρ, and (when $c > c^*$) a positive solution to Lundberg's equation (5.29) is $\varkappa = \rho - \delta/c$. Bearing in mind (see (5.28)) that $\mathsf{P}\{\varUpsilon_{u,c\,|\,\delta,\rho} < \infty\} = (1-\varkappa/\rho)\,e^{-\varkappa u}$, we have for $c > \delta/\rho$

$$\mathsf{P}\{\varUpsilon_{u,c\,|\,\delta,\rho} \leqslant t\} \leqslant \mathsf{P}\{\varUpsilon_{u,c\,|\,\delta,\rho} < \infty\} = (\delta/(c\rho))\,\exp\{-\rho\,(1-\delta/(c\rho))\,u\},$$

whence (cf. (3.60))

$$u_{\alpha,t\,|\,\delta,\rho}(c) \leqslant u_{\alpha\,|\,\delta,\rho}(c) = \max\left\{0, -\frac{\ln(\alpha c\rho/\delta)}{\rho-\delta/c}\right\}, \quad c > \delta/\rho. \tag{5.58}$$

This is (see (3.60)) a result of Section 3.6.

Model (B). In words, this is a compound Poisson model, when Y is light-tail (but not exponentially distributed). We proceed from Section 5.2.4 and use the bound (5.30). Thus, for $c^* := \mathsf{E}\,Y/\mathsf{E}\,T$, which equals $\delta\,\mathsf{E}\,Y$, we have

$$\mathsf{P}\{\varUpsilon_{u,c} < \infty\} \leqslant e^{-\varkappa u}, \quad c > c^*, \tag{5.59}$$

for all $u \geqslant 0$, where $\varkappa$ is a unique positive solution to Lundberg's equation (5.29), which may be rewritten as $\mathsf{E}\exp\{\varkappa Y\} = 1 + c\varkappa/\delta$.

From (5.59) follows $u_{\alpha,t}(c) \leqslant \overline{u}_\alpha(c) = -\ln\alpha/\varkappa$. To express this bound in closed form, we need to express in such form the adjustment coefficient $\varkappa$. As we have seen, this can be done in some cases, but in general it is not easy.

Model (C). In words, this is a compound Poisson model, when Y is fat-tail. An elementary upper bound on the fixed-probability level $u_{\alpha,t}(c)$, $c > c^* := \delta\,\mathsf{E}\,Y$, follows from (3.22): assuming that $\mathsf{E}(Y^2) < \infty$, we have

$$u_{\alpha,t}(c) \leqslant \frac{\delta\,\mathsf{E}(Y^2)(c+\delta\mathsf{E}\,Y)}{2\,\alpha\,(c-\delta\mathsf{E}\,Y)^2}, \quad c > \delta\,\mathsf{E}\,Y. \tag{5.60}$$

The hyperbola on the right-hand side of (5.60) decreases, as c increases.

The advantage of (5.60) is its simplicity. The disadvantage of (5.60) is its very low accuracy, even when c is large. To get more accurate (but less transparent) bounds, suitable for numerical calculations rather than for getting simple-looking analytical results, we can proceed from Section 5.2.4.

Model (D). In words, this is a renewal (but not compound Poisson) model, when Y is exponentially distributed. In renewal (called Sparre Andersen's in risk theory) model with Y exponentially distributed with parameter $\rho > 0$ and with $c^* := \mathsf{E}\,Y/\mathsf{E}\,T$ equal to $1/(\rho\,\mathsf{E}\,T)$, we have (see [158], Corollary 6.5.2)

$$\mathsf{P}\{\varUpsilon_{u,c} < \infty\} = (1-\varkappa/\rho)\,e^{-\varkappa u}, \quad c > c^*, \tag{5.61}$$

for all $u \geqslant 0$, where $\varkappa$ is a unique positive solution to Lundberg's equation (5.29), which may be rewritten as

$$\mathsf{E}\exp\{-\varkappa\,c\,T\} = 1 - \varkappa/\rho. \tag{5.62}$$

Model (E). In words, this is a renewal (but not compound Poisson) model, when Y is light-tail (but not exponentially distributed). Following [158], Theorem 6.5.4, for $x_0 = \sup\{x : F_X(x) < 1\}$, where $\overline{F}_X(x)$ is tail function for the random variable $X \stackrel{d}{=} Y - cT$, when $c > c^* := \mathsf{E}Y/\mathsf{E}T$, suppose that there exists the adjustment coefficient $\varkappa > 0$. Then

$$b_\ominus\, e^{-\varkappa u} \leqslant \mathsf{P}\{\varUpsilon_{u,c} < \infty\} \leqslant b_\oplus\, e^{-\varkappa u} \tag{5.63}$$

for all $u \geqslant 0$, where

$$b_\oplus = \inf_{x\in[0,x_0]} \frac{e^{\varkappa x}\overline{F}_X(x)}{\int_x^\infty e^{\varkappa y}\, dF_X(y)}, \quad b_\ominus = \sup_{x\in[0,x_0]} \frac{e^{\varkappa x}\overline{F}_X(x)}{\int_x^\infty e^{\varkappa y}\, dF_X(y)}.$$

For $x_0^* = \sup\{x : F_Y(x) < 1\}$, the upper and lower bounds like in (5.63) hold with

$$b_\oplus^* = \inf_{x\in[0,x_0]} \frac{e^{\varkappa x}\overline{F}_Y(x)}{\int_x^\infty e^{\varkappa y}\, dF_Y(y)}, \quad b_\ominus^* = \sup_{x\in[0,x_0]} \frac{e^{\varkappa x}\overline{F}_Y(x)}{\int_x^\infty e^{\varkappa y}\, dF_Y(y)}.$$

Moreover (see [158], Theorem 6.5.5),

$$0 \leqslant b_\ominus^* \leqslant b_\ominus \leqslant b_\oplus \leqslant b_\oplus^* \leqslant 1.$$

The simple-looking analytical upper bounds for $u_{\alpha,t}(c)$, $c > c^*$, is difficult to get from (5.63) and its analogues, but their numerical calculations are quite possible.

Model (F). In words, this is a renewal (but not compound Poisson) model, when Y is fat-tail. Although the situation in this case is clear (see, e.g., [37], [38], [151]), it is hard to expect simple-looking analytical bounds, even in specific examples. This does not interfere with the possibility of numerical calculations, particularly by means of simulation. These issues are addressed in Chapter 6.

To conclude, note that elaborated upper bounds on fixed-probability level, based on monotony, are also addressed in Chapter 6, mainly using simulation.

5.5 Proximity to $\mathcal{M}$-Level

Under certain conditions of regularity, Theorem A.5 from classical analysis asserts that (roughly speaking) if the left-hand sides of two equations, which define implicit functions, are close to each other, then these implicit functions are also close to each other.

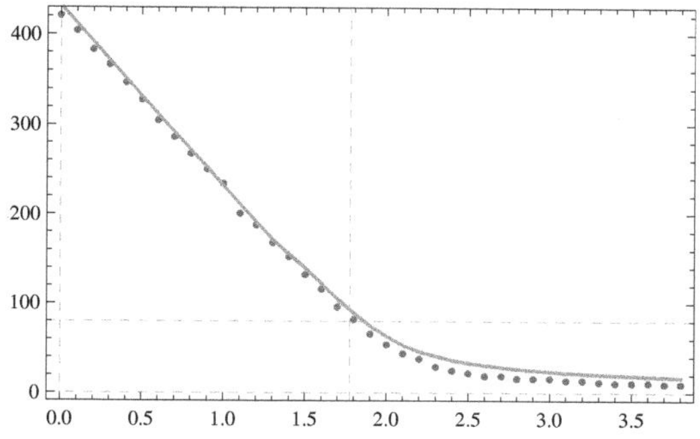

FIGURE 5.4: Graphs (X-axis is c) of simulated $u_{\alpha,t}(c)$ (dots) and $u_{\alpha,t}^{[\mathcal{M}]}(c)$, evaluated numerically (solid line), when T is exponentially distributed with parameter $\delta = 4/5$, Y is Pareto with parameters $a_Y = 10$, $b_Y = 0.05$, whence $\mathsf{E}\,Y = 2.22$, $\mathsf{D}\,Y = 6.17$, $\alpha = 0.05$, and $t = 200$. Vertical grid line: $\mathsf{E}\,Y/\mathsf{E}\,T = 1.78$. Horizontal grid line: simulated $u_{\alpha,t}(c^*) = 80$.

Recall that $\mathcal{M}$-level $u_{\alpha,t}^{[\mathcal{M}]}(c)$, $c \geqslant 0$, is a function defined by the equation (see (4.22))

$$\mathcal{M}_{u,c}(t) = \alpha,$$

called $\mathcal{M}$-equation, the fixed-probability level $u_{\alpha,t}(c)$, $c \geqslant 0$, is a function defined by the equation (see (5.3))

$$\mathsf{P}\{\varUpsilon_{u,c} \leqslant t\} = \alpha,$$

and (see Theorem 5.5) under certain regularity assumptions

$$\mathsf{P}\{\varUpsilon_{u,c} \leqslant t\} - \mathcal{M}_{u,c}(t) \to 0, \quad t, u \to \infty,$$

which is called inverse Gaussian approximation.

We know that for $0 \leqslant c \leqslant c^*$ (see (5.57) and Theorems 4.21 and 4.22) both $u_{\alpha,t}(c)$ and $u_{\alpha,t}^{[\mathcal{M}]}(c)$ are at least of order $O(t^{1/2})$, so $\mathsf{P}\{\varUpsilon_{u,c} \leqslant t\}$ is close[22] to $\mathcal{M}_{u,c}(t)$, as $t \to \infty$, whence it follows that the fixed-probability level is close to the $\mathcal{M}$-level for $0 \leqslant c \leqslant c^*$.

The same holds in the right-hand side $t^{1/2}$-neighborhood of c^*, where $u_{\alpha,t}^{[\mathcal{M}]}(c)$ is (see Theorem 4.23) a value of order $O(t^{1/2})$, as $t \to \infty$. However, in the $t^{1/2}$-neighborhood of c^* closeness of the fixed-probability level to the $\mathcal{M}$-level is obviously less than in the right-hand neighborhood of $c = 0$.

This observation has a number of useful applications. In particular, it yields the second proof of Theorem 5.15 for $0 \leqslant c \leqslant c^*$, when both $u_{\alpha,t}(c)$ and $u_{\alpha,t}^{[\mathcal{M}]}(c)$ are tending to infinity, as $t \to \infty$. It also yields a method of

[22]In points $(u_{\alpha,t}(c), c)$ and $(u_{\alpha,t}^{[\mathcal{M}]}(c), c)$, where $0 \leqslant c \leqslant c^*$.

numerical calculations based on the solution of the $\mathcal{M}$–equation, whose right-hand side is expressed in terms of elementary functions. The proximity of a fixed-probability level to $\mathcal{M}$-level, theoretically unfounded for $c > Kc^*$, $K > 1$, is illustrated in Fig. 5.4.

5.6 Conclusion

In the renewal model with a common (not obligatory exponential) distribution of T and Y, assuming that t is large, we obtain very general analytical results for $u_{\alpha,t}(c)$, $0 \leqslant c \leqslant c^*$. We do not have results of such generality for $u_{\alpha,t}(c)$, $c > Kc^*$, where $K > 1$, and we have to consider specific models, imposing different assumptions on the distributions of T and Y. Thus, we combine the analytical results in the former case and the results based on numerical calculations in the latter case.

It is worth noting that the accuracy of the analytical results for $u_{\alpha,t}(c)$, $0 \leqslant c \leqslant c^*$, is very satisfactory in comparison with the value of this fixed-probability level. What concerns $u_{\alpha,t}(c)$, $c > Kc^*$, where $K > 1$, these values are bounded by a constant, as $t \to \infty$, and the accuracy of evaluation in this case is much less critical than in the former case.

Problems

Problem 5.1 Show that in the compound Poisson model with intensity δ, when Y is exponentially distributed with parameter ρ, Lundberg's equation (5.29) may be rewritten as $\delta\rho = (c\varkappa + \delta)(\rho - \varkappa)$, whence $\varkappa = \rho - \delta/c$.

Problem 5.2 Show that in the compound Poisson model with intensity δ, when Y is generally distributed, Lundberg's equation (5.29) may be rewritten as $\mathsf{E}\exp\{\varkappa Y\} = 1 + c\varkappa/\delta$, or as $\int_0^\infty e^{\varkappa y}(1 - F_Y(y))\,dy = c/\delta$. Show that if, in addition, Y is exponentially distributed with parameter $\rho > 0$, then $\mathsf{E}\exp\{\varkappa Y\} = \rho/(\rho - \varkappa)$, whence $\varkappa = \rho - \delta/c$.

Problem 5.3 Show that in the renewal model, when Y is exponentially distributed with parameter $\rho > 0$, Lundberg's equation (5.29) may be rewritten as $\mathsf{E}\exp\{-\varkappa cT\} = 1 - \varkappa/\rho$. Show that if, in addition, T is exponentially distributed with parameter $\delta > 0$, then $\mathsf{E}\exp\{-\varkappa cT\} = \delta/(c\varkappa + \delta)$, whence $\varkappa = \rho - \delta/c$.

Problem 5.4 Bearing in mind that $e^x > 1 + x$ for all $x > 0$, prove (5.36).

Problem 5.5 In the compound Poisson model, with T exponentially distributed with parameter δ, assume that the distribution of Y is of Pareto type (cf. (B.8)), i.e., its p.d.f. is

$$f_Y(x) = \begin{cases} 0, & x < a, \\ r\, a^r x^{-(r+1)}, & x > a. \end{cases}$$

Show that $EY = ar/(r-1)$, whence the inequality $c > c^*$ may be rewritten as $c > ar\delta/(r-1)$. Show that, when $c > c^*$, we have

$$\mathsf{P}\{\Upsilon_{u,c} < \infty\} \sim \frac{\delta a}{c\,(r-1) - ar\,\delta}\,(a/u)^{r-1}, \quad u \to \infty.$$

[Hint: See [12].]

Problem 5.6 Show that the solution (5.41) to quadratic equation (5.40) is positive.

Problem 5.7 Show the proof of Theorem 5.12.
[Hint: See [119].]

Problem 5.8 Prove the following generalization of Theorem 5.12. Suppose that Y is the 2-mixture of exponential, with p.d.f.

$$f_Y(x) = \begin{cases} p\,\rho_1 e^{-\rho_1 x} + q\,\rho_2 e^{-\rho_2 x}, & x \geqslant 0, \\ 0, & x < 0, \end{cases}$$

where $0 < \rho_1 < \rho_2$, $p + q = 1$, $0 \leqslant p, q \leqslant 1$. Let the Laplace transform of T be denoted by $\mathcal{L}_T(\alpha) = \mathsf{E}\, e^{-\alpha T}$. For $\alpha > 0$, we have

$$\alpha \int_0^\infty e^{-\alpha t} \psi_t(u,c)\, dt = \frac{(\rho_1 - \rho_2)(y_1(\alpha)\beta_2(\alpha)e^{-\beta_1(\alpha)u} - y_2(\alpha)\beta_1(\alpha)e^{-\beta_2(\alpha)u})}{(\rho_1 - \beta_2(\alpha))(\rho_2 - \beta_1(\alpha)) - (\rho_1 - \beta_1(\alpha))(\rho_2 - \beta_2(\alpha))},$$

where

$$y_1(\alpha) = \left(1 - \frac{\beta_1(\alpha)}{\rho_1}\right)\left(1 - \frac{\beta_1(\alpha)}{\rho_2}\right), \quad y_2(\alpha) = \left(1 - \frac{\beta_2(\alpha)}{\rho_1}\right)\left(1 - \frac{\beta_2(\alpha)}{\rho_2}\right)$$

and $\beta_1(\alpha)$, $\beta_2(\alpha)$ are the unique solutions to

$$(\rho_1 - \beta)(\rho_2 - \beta) - (\rho_1\rho_2 - (p\rho_1 + q\rho_2)\beta)\,\mathcal{L}_T(\alpha + c\beta) = 0$$

which lie in the intervals $(0, \rho_1]$ and $[\beta_0, \rho_2]$ respectively. Here $\beta = \dfrac{\rho_1\rho_2}{p\rho_1 + q\rho_2}$.

[Hint: See [188].]

Problem 5.9 For the fixed-probability level, construct the upper bounds based on monotony in the models of Section 5.2.4.
[Hint: See Section 3.6.1. As a specimen, see Fig. 6.13.]

Chapter 6

Case Study: Numerical Evaluation of Fixed-probability Level

This chapter is devoted to numerical evaluation of the fixed-probability level for most typical distributions of inter-renewal intervals and jump sizes. We focus on Monte-Carlo simulation, which is a widespread area in computer science. This is a tool commonly used in practical insurance risk management.

6.1 Distributions of T and Y Selected for Numerical Calculations

Any numerical calculation, including the Monte Carlo simulation, starts with selecting the distributions of T and Y.

6.1.1 Rationales for the choice

In order to justify the choice made further in this chapter, we will follow the models classification of Section 5.4, i.e.,

- compound Poisson (i.e., when T is exponentially distributed) model, when Y is (a) light-tail, and (b) fat-tail,
- renewal model (i.e., when T is generally distributed), when Y is (a) light-tail, and (b) fat-tail.

Whereas the exponential distributions of Y and T is central, c.d.f. of the form

$$F_T(x) = 1 - \exp\left\{ - \int_0^x g(z)\, dz \right\}, \quad x > 0, \tag{6.1}$$

comes to the fore, when moving from compound Poisson to Andersen's renewal model (see, e.g., [180]). Here $g(z)$, $z > 0$, is called contagion rate[1]. When contagion is absent, $g(z) \equiv \delta > 0$, and the inter-claim times are exponential:

[1] Recall also the "lack of ageing" property of the exponential law: no matter which is the present age, the residual lifetime does not depend on the past and has the same distribution as the lifetime itself.

$F_T(x) = 1 - \exp\{-x\,\delta\}$, $x > 0$. The following result (see, e.g., [119]) is well-known.

Theorem 6.1 *Assume that c.d.f. $F_T(x)$ of the positive random variable T are absolutely continuous with respect to Lebesgue's measure. Then there exists a non-negative integrable function $g(z)$, $z > 0$, such that $\int_0^1 g(z)\,dz < \infty$, $\int_0^\infty g(z)\,dz = \infty$, and the equality (6.1) holds.*

The equality (6.1) allows us to move from p.d.f. $f_T(x)$, $x > 0$, corresponding to c.d.f. $F_T(x)$, $x > 0$, to contagion rate $g(z)$, $z > 0$, and vice versa:

$$f_T(x) = g(x) \exp\left\{ - \int_0^x g(z)\,dz \right\}, \quad x > 0, \tag{6.2}$$

and

$$g(z) = \frac{f_T(z)}{1 - \int_0^z f_T(x)\,dx}, \quad z > 0. \tag{6.3}$$

When T is a mixture of exponential p.d.f., with mixing function $f_\xi(z)$, i.e.,

$$f_T(x) = \int_0^\infty \exp\{-x\,z^{-1}\}\,z^{-1} f_\xi(z)\,dz, \quad x > 0, \tag{6.4}$$

then the equality (6.2) for $f_T(x)$ holds, with

$$g(z) = \frac{\int_0^\infty \exp\{-z\,x^{-1}\} x^{-1} f_\xi(x)\,dx}{\int_0^\infty \exp\{-z\,x^{-1}\} f_\xi(x)\,dx}. \tag{6.5}$$

The difference between fat-tail and light-tail distributions may be illustrated in terms of the contagion rate $g(z)$, $z > 0$. Note that

$$\mathsf{E}(T^k) = \int_0^\infty t^k \exp\left\{ - \int_0^t g(z)\,dz \right\} g(t)\,dt, \quad k = 1, 2, \ldots. \tag{6.6}$$

If $\int_0^t g(z)\,dz = O(t^s)$ for any $s > 0$, then the exponential factor in (6.6) decreases to zero and dominates the rest, whatever k may be selected: the exponential function grows faster than any power function. If $\int_0^t g(z)\,dz = O(\ln t)$, then the exponential factor reduces to a power. Therefore, it is possible to choose k so large that the integral (6.6) becomes divergent.

The rationale for choosing non-exponentially distributed Y are, on the one hand, obvious: claim sizes naturally have very diverse structure which depends on the context. On the other hand, they are deeply hidden in the mathematics developed for Lundberg's and Andersen's models: most of the known results are related to two different cases: claim sizes Y whose distribution is light-tail, and claim sizes Y whose distribution is fat-tail. To approach the former case, many ingenious methods were developed; to approach the latter case, the theory of regular variations is commonly used.

In the following presentation, we will be focussed on several light-tail distributions, in particular

- mixture of two exponential distributions (see Section B.1) called for brevity 2-mixture,
- Erlang distribution (see Section B.1),

and several fat-tail distributions, in particular

- Pareto distribution (see Section B.1),
- Kummer distribution (see Section B.1).

6.1.2 Models and examples selected for numerical calculations

According to the rationale for the choice of distributions of T and Y, stated in Section 6.1, and the classification in Section 3.5, we will focus on the following models and examples:

Model (A): compound Poisson model, when Y is exponentially distributed[2],

Model (B): compound Poisson model, when Y is light-tail (but not exponentially distributed),

Example (a): T is exponentially distributed and Y is 2-mixture,

Example (b): T is exponentially distributed and Y is Erlang,

Model (C): compound Poisson model, when Y is fat-tail,

Example (a): T is exponentially distributed and Y is Pareto,

Example (b): T is exponentially distributed and Y is Kummer,

Model (D): renewal model (but not Poisson), when Y is exponentially distributed,

Example (a): T is 2-mixture and Y is exponentially distributed,

Example (b): T is Erlang and Y is exponentially distributed,

Example (c): T is Pareto and Y is exponentially distributed,

Example (d): T is Kummer and Y is exponentially distributed,

Model (E): renewal model (but not Poisson), when Y is light-tail (but not exponentially distributed),

Example (a): T is Erlang and Y is Erlang,

Model (F): renewal model (but not Poisson), when Y is fat-tail,

Example (a): T is 2-mixture and Y is Pareto,

Example (b): T is Erlang and Y is Pareto,

Example (c): T is Pareto and Y is Pareto.

These models and examples are given for convenience in Table 6.1 and the basic information about them is given below.

[2]Plainly, this corresponds to one single case of T and Y exponentially distributed.

TABLE 6.1: Models selected for numerical calculations

Model (A):	*compound Poisson model, when Y is exponentially distributed*
	Example (a): T and Y are exponentially distributed
Model (B):	*compound Poisson model, when Y is light-tail (but not exponentially) distributed*
	Example (a): T exponentially distributed and Y 2-mixture
	Example (b): T exponentially distributed and Y Erlang
Model (C):	*compound Poisson model, when Y is fat-tail*
	Example (a): T exponentially distributed and Y Pareto
	Example (b): T exponentially distributed and Y Kummer
Model (D):	*renewal (but not Poisson) model, when Y is exponentially distributed*
	Example (a): T 2-mixture and Y exponentially distributed
	Example (b): T Erlang and Y exponentially distributed
	Example (c): T Pareto and Y exponentially distributed
	Example (d): T Kummer and Y exponentially distributed
Model (E):	*renewal (but not Poisson) model, when Y is light-tail (but not exponentially) distributed*
	Example (a): T Erlang and Y Erlang
Model (F):	*renewal (but not Poisson) model, when Y is fat-tail*
	Example (a): T 2-mixture and Y Pareto
	Example (b): T Erlang and Y Pareto
	Example (c): T Pareto and Y Pareto

Model (A). This model is verbally described as compound Poisson model, when Y is exponentially distributed. In other words, T is exponentially distributed with parameter $\delta > 0$ and Y is exponentially distributed with parameter $\rho > 0$, whose p.d.f. are

$$f_T(x) = \delta\, e^{-\delta x}, \quad f_Y(x) = \rho\, e^{-\rho x}, \quad x > 0.$$

Elementary calculations yield $\mathsf{E}(T^k) = k!/\delta^k$, $\mathsf{E}(Y^k) = k!/\rho^k$, $k = 1, 2, \ldots,$ whence

$$\mathsf{E}\,T = 1/\delta, \quad \mathsf{D}\,T = 1/\delta^2,$$
$$\mathsf{E}\,Y = 1/\rho, \quad \mathsf{D}\,Y = 1/\rho^2,$$

and

$$\mathsf{E}\,e^{-\varkappa c T} = \delta \int_0^\infty e^{-(\varkappa c+\delta)x}\,dx = \delta/(\delta + c\varkappa),$$
$$\mathsf{E}\,e^{\varkappa Y} = \rho \int_0^\infty e^{(\varkappa-\rho)x}\,dx = \rho/(\rho - \varkappa).$$

The following useful results are easy to check:

(1) $c^* := \mathsf{E}\,Y/\mathsf{E}\,T$ is equal to δ/ρ,

(2) the constants defined in (5.17) are

$$\begin{aligned} M &:= \mathsf{E}\,T/\mathsf{E}\,Y = \rho/\delta, \\ D^2 &:= ((\mathsf{E}\,T)^2\mathsf{D}\,Y + (\mathsf{E}\,Y)^2\mathsf{D}\,T)/(\mathsf{E}\,Y)^3 = 2\,\rho/\delta^2, \end{aligned} \tag{6.7}$$

(3) the adjustment coefficient, i.e., a unique positive solution to Lundberg's equation (1.34) which may be rewritten as quadratic equation

$$(\rho - \varkappa)\,(\delta + c\varkappa) - \delta\rho = 0,$$

given that $c > \delta/\rho$, is explicit: $\varkappa = \rho - \delta/c$.

Model (B), Example (a). This model is verbally described as compound Poisson model, i.e., T is exponentially distributed with parameter $\delta > 0$, when Y is 2-mixture of exponential distributions with parameters $0 < \rho_1 \leqslant \rho_2 < \infty$ and $0 \leqslant p, q \leqslant 1$, $p + q = 1$, whose p.d.f. are

$$f_T(x) = \delta\, e^{-\delta\, x}, \quad f_Y(x) = p\,\rho_1\, e^{-\rho_1\, x} + q\,\rho_2\, e^{-\rho_2\, x}, \quad x > 0.$$

Elementary calculations yield

$$\begin{aligned} &\mathsf{E}\,T = 1/\delta, && \mathsf{D}\,T = 1/\delta^2, \\ &\mathsf{E}\,Y = p/\rho_1 + q/\rho_2, && \mathsf{D}\,Y = (\,q\rho_1^2 + p\rho_2^2 + pq(\rho_1 - \rho_2)^2\,)/(\rho_1^2\rho_2^2) \end{aligned} \tag{6.8}$$

and

$$\begin{aligned} \mathsf{E}\,e^{-\varkappa\, c\, T} &= \int_0^\infty e^{-\varkappa c x}(\delta\, e^{-\delta\, x})\, dx = \delta/(\delta + c\varkappa), \\ \mathsf{E}\,e^{\varkappa\, Y} &= \int_0^\infty e^{\varkappa x}(p\,\rho_1\, e^{-\rho_1\, x} + q\,\rho_2\, e^{-\rho_2\, x})\, dx \\ &= p\,\rho_1/(\rho_1 - \varkappa) + q\,\rho_2/(\rho_2 - \varkappa). \end{aligned} \tag{6.9}$$

The following useful results are easy to check:

(1) $c^* := \mathsf{E}\,Y/\mathsf{E}\,T$ is equal to $\delta(p/\rho_1 + q/\rho_2)$,

(2) the constants defined in (5.17) are

$$\begin{aligned} M &:= \mathsf{E}\,T/\mathsf{E}\,Y = \frac{\rho_1\rho_2}{\delta(q\rho_1 + p\rho_2)}, \\ D^2 &:= ((\mathsf{E}\,T)^2\mathsf{D}\,Y + (\mathsf{E}\,Y)^2\mathsf{D}\,T)/(\mathsf{E}\,Y)^3 \\ &= \frac{\rho_1\rho_2(q^2\rho_1^2 + p(1+p)\rho_2^2 + q((1+p)\rho_1^2 + p\rho_2^2))}{\delta^2(q\rho_1 + p\rho_2)^3}. \end{aligned} \tag{6.10}$$

(3) given that $c > c^* = \delta(p/\rho_1 + q/\rho_2)$, the adjustment coefficient, i.e., a positive solution to Lundberg's equation $\mathsf{E}\exp\{\varkappa\,(Y - c\,T)\} = 1$, which (see

(6.9)) may be rewritten as[3]

$$\frac{\delta}{\delta + c\varkappa}\left(\frac{p\,\rho_1}{\rho_1 - \varkappa} + \frac{q\,\rho_2}{\rho_2 - \varkappa}\right) = 1,$$

whence

$$\begin{aligned}\varkappa = \frac{1}{2c}\,&(-\delta + c\,(\rho_1 + \rho_2)\\ &+ ((\delta - c\,(\rho_1 + \rho_2))^2 + 4c\,(\delta(q\rho_1 + p\rho_2) - c\rho_1\rho_2))^{1/2}).\end{aligned} \tag{6.11}$$

Model (B), Example (b). This model[4] is verbally described as compound Poisson model, i.e., T is exponentially distributed with parameter $\delta > 0$, when Y is Erlang with parameters $\rho > 0$ and m integer, whose p.d.f. are

$$f_T(x) = \delta e^{-\delta x}, \quad f_Y(x) = \frac{\rho^m x^{m-1}}{\Gamma(m)}\,e^{-\rho x}, \quad x > 0.$$

Elementary calculations yield

$$\begin{aligned}\mathsf{E}\,T &= 1/\delta, & \mathsf{D}\,T &= 1/\delta^2,\\ \mathsf{E}\,Y &= m/\rho, & \mathsf{D}\,Y &= m/\rho^2,\end{aligned}$$

and

$$\begin{aligned}\mathsf{E}\,e^{-\varkappa c T} &= \delta \int_0^\infty e^{-(\varkappa c + \delta)x}\,dx = \frac{\delta}{\delta + c\varkappa},\\ \mathsf{E}\,e^{\varkappa Y} &= \frac{\rho^m}{\Gamma(m)} \int_0^\infty e^{(\varkappa - \rho)x} x^{m-1}\,dx = \frac{\rho^m}{(\rho - \varkappa)^m}.\end{aligned}$$

The following useful results are easy to check:

(1) $c^* := \mathsf{E}\,Y/\mathsf{E}\,T$ is equal to $(m\delta)/\rho$,

(2) the constants defined in (5.17) are

$$\begin{aligned}M &:= \mathsf{E}\,T/\mathsf{E}\,Y = \rho/(m\delta),\\ D^2 &:= ((\mathsf{E}\,T)^2\mathsf{D}\,Y + (\mathsf{E}\,Y)^2\mathsf{D}\,T)/(\mathsf{E}\,Y)^3\\ &= (m+1)\,\rho/(m^2\delta^2),\end{aligned} \tag{6.12}$$

(3) the adjustment coefficient, i.e., a unique positive solution to Lundberg's equation $\mathsf{E}\exp\{\varkappa\,(Y - cT)\} = 1$ which may be rewritten as

$$(\rho - \varkappa)^m\,(\delta + c\varkappa) - \delta\rho^m = 0,$$

given that $c > (m\delta)/\rho$, is easy to find numerically but is not explicit[5].

[3]Plainly, when $p = q = 1/2$ and $\rho_1 = \rho_1 := \rho$, i.e., when Y is exponentially distributed with parameter ρ, this equation reduces to $(\delta + c\varkappa)(\varkappa - \rho) + \delta\rho = 0$, whose solution is $\varkappa = \rho - \delta/c$.

[4]For brevity, we optionally refer to this case as Model (B), Example (b). Its particular cases is Model (A).

[5]In the case $m = 2$, we have $\varkappa = (2c\rho - \delta - \sqrt{\delta\,(4c\rho + \delta)}\,)/(2c)$.

Model (C), Example (a). This model is verbally described as compound Poisson model, i.e., T is exponentially distributed with parameter $\delta > 0$, when Y is Pareto with parameters $a_Y > 0$, $b_Y > 0$, whose p.d.f. are

$$f_T(x) = \delta\, e^{-\delta\, x}, \quad f_Y(x) = \frac{a_Y b_Y}{(x\, b_Y + 1)^{a_Y+1}}, \quad x > 0.$$

Elementary calculations yield

$$\begin{aligned} \mathsf{E}\,T &= 1/\delta, & \mathsf{D}\,T &= 1/\delta^2, \\ \mathsf{E}\,Y &= 1/((a_Y - 1)\, b_Y), & \mathsf{D}\,Y &= a_Y/((a_Y-1)^2\,(a_Y-2)\, b_Y^2). \end{aligned}$$

The following useful results are easy to check:

(1) $c^* := \mathsf{E}\,Y/\mathsf{E}\,T$ is equal to $\delta/((a_Y - 1)\, b_Y)$,

(2) the constants defined in (5.17) are

$$\begin{aligned} M &:= \mathsf{E}\,T/\mathsf{E}\,Y = \frac{(a_Y-1)\, b_Y}{\delta}, \\ D^2 &:= ((\mathsf{E}\,T)^2 \mathsf{D}\,Y + (\mathsf{E}\,Y)^2 \mathsf{D}\,T)/(\mathsf{E}\,Y)^3 \\ &= \frac{2\,(a_Y-1)^2\, b_Y}{\delta^2\,(a_Y-2)}, \end{aligned} \tag{6.13}$$

(3) the adjustment coefficient does not exist.

Model (C), Example (b). This model[6] is verbally described as compound Poisson model, i.e., T is exponentially distributed with parameter $\delta > 0$, when Y is Kummer with parameters $k_Y > 0$, $l_Y > 0$, whose p.d.f. are[7]

$$f_T(x) = \delta\, e^{-\delta\, x}, \quad f_Y(x) = \frac{k_Y}{2} \frac{\Gamma\left(\frac{k_Y + l_Y}{2}\right)}{\Gamma\left(\frac{k_Y}{2}\right)}\, U\!\left(1 + \frac{l_Y}{2}, 2 - \frac{k_Y}{2}, \frac{k_Y}{l_Y}\, x\right), \quad x > 0.$$

Elementary calculations yield

$$\mathsf{E}(T^k) = k!/\delta^k, \quad \mathsf{E}(Y^k) = \frac{\Gamma\left(\frac{k_Y}{2} + k\right)\Gamma\left(\frac{l_Y}{2} - k\right)}{\Gamma\left(\frac{k_Y}{2}\right)\Gamma\left(\frac{l_Y}{2}\right)}\, l_Y^k\, k_Y^{-k}, \quad 2k < l_Y, \quad k = 1, 2, \ldots.$$

In particular,

$$\begin{aligned} \mathsf{E}\,T &= 1/\delta, & \mathsf{D}\,T &= 1/\delta^2, \\ \mathsf{E}\,Y &= \frac{l_Y}{l_Y - 2}, \quad l_Y > 2, & \mathsf{D}\,Y &= \frac{l_Y^2(4(l_Y-2) + k_Y l_Y)}{k_Y (l_Y - 2)^2 (l_Y - 4)}, \quad l_Y > 4. \end{aligned}$$

The following useful results are easy to check:

[6]For brevity, we optionally refer to this case as Model (C), Example (b).

[7]For other equivalent formulas for $f_Y(x)$ see (B.11).

(1) $c^* := \mathsf{E}\,Y/\mathsf{E}\,T$ is equal to $\delta\, l_Y/(l_Y-2)$, $l_Y > 2$,

(2) the constants defined in (5.17) are

$$\begin{aligned} M &:= \mathsf{E}\,T/\mathsf{E}\,Y = \frac{(l_Y-2)}{\delta\, l_Y}, \quad l_Y > 2, \\ D^2 &:= ((\mathsf{E}\,T)^2 \mathsf{D}\,Y + (\mathsf{E}\,Y)^2 \mathsf{D}\,T)/(\mathsf{E}\,Y)^3 \\ &= \frac{2\,(2+k_Y)(l_Y-2)^2}{\delta^2 k_Y (l_Y-4)\, l_Y}, \quad l_Y > 4, \end{aligned} \tag{6.14}$$

(3) the adjustment coefficient does not exist.

Model (D), Example (a). This model[8] is verbally described as renewal model, where the distribution of T is 2-mixture of exponential distributions with parameters $0 < \delta_1 < \delta_2 < \infty$ and $0 \leqslant p, q \leqslant 1$, $p+q=1$, and Y is exponentially distributed with parameter $\rho > 0$, whose p.d.f. are

$$f_T(x) = p\,\delta_1\, e^{-\delta_1 x} + q\,\delta_2\, e^{-\delta_2 x}, \quad f_Y(x) = \rho\, e^{-\rho\, x}, \quad x > 0.$$

Elementary calculations yield

$$\begin{aligned} \mathsf{E}\,T &= p/\delta_1 + q/\delta_2, & \mathsf{D}\,T &= (q\delta_1^2 + p\delta_2^2 + pq(\delta_1-\delta_2)^2)/(\delta_1^2\delta_2^2), \\ \mathsf{E}\,Y &= 1/\rho, & \mathsf{D}\,Y &= 1/\rho^2. \end{aligned}$$

The following useful results are easy to check:

(1) $c^* := \mathsf{E}\,Y/\mathsf{E}\,T$ is equal to $\delta_1\delta_2/(\rho(p\delta_2 + q\delta_1))$,

(2) the constants defined in (5.17) are

$$\begin{aligned} M &:= \mathsf{E}\,T/\mathsf{E}\,Y = \rho(p/\delta_1 + q/\delta_2), \\ D^2 &:= ((\mathsf{E}\,T)^2 \mathsf{D}\,Y + (\mathsf{E}\,Y)^2 \mathsf{D}\,T)/(\mathsf{E}\,Y)^3 \\ &= 2\rho\,(p/\delta_1^2 + q/\delta_2^2), \end{aligned} \tag{6.15}$$

(3) given that $c > \delta_1\delta_2/(\rho(p\delta_2 + q\delta_1))$, the adjustment coefficient, i.e., a positive solution to Lundberg's equation $\mathsf{E}\exp\{\varkappa\,(Y - cT)\} = 1$, is (see (5.41))

$$\varkappa = \frac{1}{2c}(c\rho - (\delta_1+\delta_2) + (\rho^2 c^2 + 2\,\rho c(\delta_1-\delta_2)(q-p) + (\delta_1-\delta_2)^2)^{1/2}). \tag{6.16}$$

Model (D), Example (b). This model[9] is verbally described as renewal model, where the distribution of T is Erlang with parameters $\delta > 0$ and k integer, and Y is exponentially distributed with parameter $\rho > 0$, whose p.d.f. are

$$f_T(x) = \frac{\delta^k x^{k-1}}{\Gamma(k)}\, e^{-\delta x}, \quad f_Y(x) = \rho\, e^{-\rho\, x}, \quad x > 0.$$

[8] For brevity, we optionally refer to this case as Model (D), Example (a).
[9] For brevity, we optionally refer to this case as Model (D), Example (b).

Elementary calculations yield

$$\mathsf{E}\,T = k/\delta, \quad \mathsf{D}\,T = k/\delta^2,$$
$$\mathsf{E}\,Y = 1/\rho, \quad \mathsf{D}\,Y = 1/\rho^2$$

and

$$\mathsf{E}\,e^{-\varkappa cT} = \frac{\delta^k}{\Gamma(k)}\int_0^\infty e^{-(\varkappa c+\delta)x}x^{k-1}\,dx = \frac{\delta^k}{(\delta+c\varkappa)^k},$$
$$\mathsf{E}\,e^{\varkappa Y} = \rho\int_0^\infty e^{(\varkappa-\rho)x}\,dx = \frac{\rho}{\rho-\varkappa}.$$

The following useful results are easy to check:

(1) $c^* := \mathsf{E}\,Y/\mathsf{E}\,T$ is equal to $\delta/(k\rho)$,

(2) the constants defined in (5.17) are

$$\begin{aligned} M &:= \mathsf{E}\,T/\mathsf{E}\,Y = k\rho/\delta, \\ D^2 &:= ((\mathsf{E}\,T)^2\mathsf{D}\,Y + (\mathsf{E}\,Y)^2\mathsf{D}\,T)/(\mathsf{E}\,Y)^3 \\ &= k\,(k+1)\,\rho/\delta^2, \end{aligned}$$

(3) the adjustment coefficient, i.e., a unique positive solution to Lundberg's equation $\mathsf{E}\exp\{\varkappa\,(Y-cT)\}=1$ which may be rewritten as

$$(\rho-\varkappa)\,(\delta+c\varkappa)^k - \delta^k\rho = 0,$$

given that $c > \delta/(k\rho)$, is not explicit but is easy to find numerically.

Model (D), Example (c). This model is verbally described as renewal model, where the distribution of T is Pareto with parameters $a_T>0$, $b_T>0$, and Y is exponentially distributed with parameter $\rho>0$, whose p.d.f. are

$$f_T(x) = \frac{a_T b_T}{(x\,b_T+1)^{a_T+1}}, \quad f_Y(x) = \rho\,e^{-\rho x}, \quad x>0.$$

Elementary calculations yield

$$\mathsf{E}\,T = 1/((a_T-1)\,b_T), \quad \mathsf{D}\,T = a_T/((a_T-1)^2\,(a_T-2)\,b_T^2),$$
$$\mathsf{E}\,Y = 1/\rho, \qquad \mathsf{D}\,Y = 1/\rho^2$$

and[10]

$$\begin{aligned} \mathsf{E}\,e^{-\varkappa cT} &= a_T b_T\int_0^\infty e^{-\varkappa cx}\frac{dx}{(x\,b_T+1)^{a_T+1}} \\ &= b_T^{-a_T}\,e^{c\varkappa/b_T}\,(c\varkappa)^{a_T-1}\,\Gamma(1-a_T, c\varkappa/b_T), \\ \mathsf{E}\,e^{\varkappa Y} &= \rho\int_0^\infty e^{(\varkappa-\rho)x}\,dx = \rho/(\rho-\varkappa). \end{aligned}$$

[10]Recall that $\Gamma(a,z) := \int_z^\infty t^{a-1}e^{-t}\,dt$ is (upper) incomplete gamma function.

The following useful results are easy to check:

(1) $c^* := \mathsf{E}\,Y/\mathsf{E}\,T$ is equal to $((a_T - 1)\,b_T)/\rho$,

(2) the constants defined in (5.17) are

$$\begin{aligned} M &:= \mathsf{E}\,T/\mathsf{E}\,Y = \rho/((a_T-1)\,b_T), \\ D^2 &:= ((\mathsf{E}\,T)^2 \mathsf{D}\,Y + (\mathsf{E}\,Y)^2 \mathsf{D}\,T)/(\mathsf{E}\,Y)^3 \\ &= 2\rho/((a_T-1)\,(a_T-2)\,b_T^2), \end{aligned} \tag{6.17}$$

(3) the adjustment coefficient, i.e., a unique positive solution to Lundberg's equation $\mathsf{E}\exp\{\varkappa\,(Y - c\,T)\} = 1$, given that $c > ((a_T-1)\,b_T)/\rho$, is not explicit but is easy to find numerically.

Model (D), Example (d). This model is verbally described as renewal model, where the distribution of T is Kummer with parameters $k_T > 0$, $l_T > 0$, and Y is exponentially distributed with parameter $\rho > 0$, whose p.d.f. are[11]

$$f_T(x) = \frac{k_T}{2}\frac{\Gamma\big(\frac{k_T+l_T}{2}\big)}{\Gamma\big(\frac{k_T}{2}\big)}\,U\Big(1+\frac{l_T}{2}, 2-\frac{k_T}{2}, \frac{k_T}{l_T}\,x\Big), \quad f_Y(x) = \rho\, e^{-\rho\, x}, \quad x > 0.$$

Elementary calculations yield

$$\mathsf{E}(T^k) = \frac{\Gamma\big(\frac{k_T}{2}+k\big)\Gamma\big(\frac{l_T}{2}-k\big)}{\Gamma\big(\frac{k_T}{2}\big)\Gamma\big(\frac{l_T}{2}\big)}\, l_T^k\, k_T^{-k}, \quad 2k < l_T, \quad \mathsf{E}(Y^k) = k!/\rho^k, \quad k = 1, 2, \ldots,$$

whence

$$\begin{aligned} \mathsf{E}\,T &= \frac{l_T}{l_T-2}, \quad l_T > 2, & \mathsf{D}\,T &= \frac{l_T^2(4(l_T-2)+k_T l_T)}{k_T(l_T-2)^2(l_T-4)}, \quad l_T > 4. \\ \mathsf{E}\,Y &= 1/\rho, & \mathsf{D}\,Y &= 1/\rho^2. \end{aligned}$$

The following useful results are easy to check:

(1) $c^* := \mathsf{E}\,Y/\mathsf{E}\,T$ is equal to $(l_T - 2)/(\rho\, l_T)$, $l_T > 2$,

(2) the constants defined in (5.17) are

$$\begin{aligned} M &:= \mathsf{E}\,T/\mathsf{E}\,Y = \rho\, l_T/(l_T-2), \\ D^2 &:= ((\mathsf{E}\,T)^2 \mathsf{D}\,Y + (\mathsf{E}\,Y)^2 \mathsf{D}\,T)/(\mathsf{E}\,Y)^3 \\ &= 2\rho\,(2+k_T)\,l_T^2/(k_T(8-6\,l_T+l_T^2)), \end{aligned}$$

(3) the adjustment coefficient, i.e., a unique positive solution to Lundberg's equation $\mathsf{E}\exp\{\varkappa\,(Y - c\,T)\} = 1$, given that $c > (l_T-2)/(\rho\, l_T)$ (this equation can be written out as a repeated integral with the integrand given in terms of elementary functions, see (B.11) and (B.12)), is not explicit but can be found numerically.

[11] For other equivalent formulas for $f_T(x)$ see (B.11).

Model (E), Example (a). This model[12] is verbally described as renewal model, where the distribution of T is Erlang with parameters $\delta > 0$ and k integer, and Y is Erlang with parameters $\rho > 0$ and m integer, whose p.d.f. are

$$f_T(x) = \frac{\delta^k x^{k-1}}{\Gamma(k)} e^{-\delta x}, \quad f_Y(x) = \frac{\rho^m x^{m-1}}{\Gamma(m)} e^{-\rho x}, \quad x > 0.$$

Elementary calculations yield

$$\mathsf{E}\,T = k/\delta, \quad \mathsf{D}\,T = k/\delta^2,$$
$$\mathsf{E}\,Y = m/\rho, \quad \mathsf{D}\,Y = m/\rho^2,$$

and

$$\mathsf{E}\,e^{-\varkappa c T} = \frac{\delta^k}{\Gamma(k)} \int_0^\infty e^{-(\varkappa c+\delta)x} x^{k-1}\,dx = \frac{\delta^k}{(\delta + c\varkappa)^k},$$
$$\mathsf{E}\,e^{\varkappa Y} = \frac{\rho^m}{\Gamma(m)} \int_0^\infty e^{(\varkappa-\rho)x} x^{m-1}\,dx = \frac{\rho^m}{(\rho - \varkappa)^m}.$$

The following useful results are easy to check:

(1) $c^* := \mathsf{E}\,Y/\mathsf{E}\,T$ is equal to $(m\delta)/(k\rho)$,

(2) the constants defined in (5.17) are

$$\begin{aligned} M &:= \mathsf{E}\,T/\mathsf{E}\,Y = k\rho/(m\delta), \\ D^2 &:= ((\mathsf{E}\,T)^2 \mathsf{D}\,Y + (\mathsf{E}\,Y)^2 \mathsf{D}\,T)/(\mathsf{E}\,Y)^3 \\ &= k\,(k+m)\,\rho/(m^2\delta^2). \end{aligned} \tag{6.18}$$

(3) the adjustment coefficient, i.e., a unique positive solution to Lundberg's equation $\mathsf{E}\exp\{\varkappa(Y - cT)\} = 1$ which may be rewritten as

$$(\rho - \varkappa)^m\,(\delta + c\varkappa)^k - \delta^k \rho^m = 0,$$

given that $c > (m\delta)/(k\rho)$, is not explicit but is easy to find numerically.

Model (F), Example (a). This model is verbally described as renewal model, where the distribution of T is 2-mixture of exponential distributions with parameters $0 < \delta_1 < \delta_2 < \infty$ and $0 \leqslant p, q \leqslant 1$, $p+q = 1$, and Y is Pareto with parameters $a_Y > 3$, $b_Y > 0$, whose p.d.f. are

$$f_T(x) = p\,\delta_1\,e^{-\delta_1 x} + q\,\delta_2\,e^{-\delta_2 x}, \quad f_Y(x) = \frac{a_Y b_Y}{(x\,b_Y + 1)^{a_Y+1}}, \quad x > 0.$$

Elementary calculations yield

$$\mathsf{E}\,T = p/\delta_1 + q/\delta_2, \qquad \mathsf{D}\,T = (q\delta_1^2 + p\delta_2^2 + pq(\delta_1 - \delta_2)^2)/(\delta_1^2\delta_2^2),$$
$$\mathsf{E}\,Y = 1/((a_Y - 1)\,b_Y), \quad \mathsf{D}\,Y = a_Y/((a_Y-1)^2\,(a_Y-2)\,b_Y^2).$$

[12]For brevity, we optionally refer to this case as Model (E), Example (a). Particular cases of this model are Model (A), Model (B), Example (b), and Model (D), Example (b).

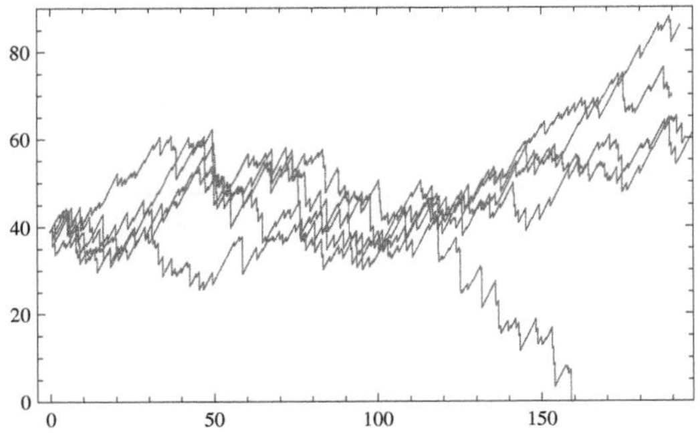

FIGURE 6.1: Graphs (X-axis is s) of five simulated trajectories of (see (1.8)) $R_s = u + cs - V_s$, $0 \leqslant s \leqslant 200$, when Y and T are exponentially distributed with parameters $\rho = 3/5$ and $\delta = 4/5$, respectively, $c = 3/2$, and $u = 39$. One of these five trajectories falls below zero.

The following useful results are easy to check.

(1) $c^* := \mathsf{E}\,Y/\mathsf{E}\,T$ is equal to $1/(\,(a_Y - 1)\,b_Y\,(p/\delta_1 + q/\delta_2)\,)$,

(2) the constants defined in (5.17) are

$$\begin{aligned} M &:= \mathsf{E}\,T/\mathsf{E}\,Y = (a_Y - 1)\,b_Y\,(p/\delta_1 + q/\delta_2), \\ D^2 &:= ((\mathsf{E}\,T)^2 \mathsf{D}\,Y + (\mathsf{E}\,Y)^2 \mathsf{D}\,T)/(\mathsf{E}\,Y)^3 \\ &= (a_Y - 1)\,b_Y \\ &\quad \times \left(\frac{a_Y}{a_Y - 2} \left(\frac{p}{\delta_1} + \frac{q}{\delta_2} \right)^2 + \frac{\delta_2^2 p + \delta_1^2 q + (\delta_1 - \delta_2)^2 pq}{\delta_1^2 \delta_2^2} \right), \end{aligned} \tag{6.19}$$

(3) the adjustment coefficient does not exist.

Model (F), Example (b). This model[13] is verbally described as renewal model, where the distribution of T is Erlang with parameters $\delta > 0$ and k integer, and Y is Pareto with parameters $a_Y > 3$, $b_Y > 0$, whose p.d.f. are

$$f_T(x) = \frac{\delta^k x^{k-1}}{\Gamma(k)} e^{-x\delta}, \quad f_Y(x) = \frac{a_Y b_Y}{(x\,b_Y + 1)^{a_Y + 1}}, \quad x > 0.$$

Elementary calculations yield

$$\begin{aligned} \mathsf{E}\,T &= k/\delta, & \mathsf{D}\,T &= k/\delta^2, \\ \mathsf{E}\,Y &= 1/((a_Y - 1)\,b_Y), & \mathsf{D}\,Y &= a_Y/((a_Y - 1)^2\,(a_Y - 2)\,b_Y^2). \end{aligned}$$

The following useful results are easy to check:

[13] For brevity, we optionally refer to this case as Model (F), Example (b).

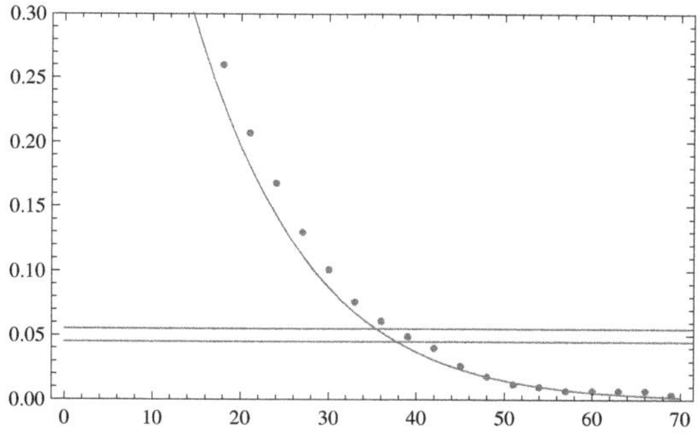

FIGURE 6.2: Graphs (X-axis is u) of $\mathsf{P}\{\varUpsilon_{u,c_i\,|\,\delta,\rho} \leqslant t\}$, when $t = 200$, $\delta = 4/5$, $\rho = 3/5$, $c_i = 3/2$, evaluated numerically by means of (3.8) (solid line), and simulated, with u_j in the lattice $\mathcal{U}$ (dots). Horizontal lines: $\alpha + \varepsilon = 0.055$, $\alpha - \varepsilon = 0.045$, when $\alpha = 0.05$ and $\varepsilon = 0.005$.

TABLE 6.2: An inventory of models in Figs. 6.3–6.7

	T	Y	M	D^2
Fig. 6.3:	Exponentially distributed; $\delta = 1$	Exponentially distributed; $\rho = 1$	1	2
Fig. 6.4:	Erlang; $k = 2$, $\delta = 1.2$	Erlang; $m = 2$, $\rho = 1$	0.83	1.39
Fig. 6.5:	2-mixture; $\delta_1 = 1$, $\delta_2 = 2$, $p = 2/3$	Pareto; $a_Y = 4.0$, $b_Y = 0.35$	0.88	2.30
Fig. 6.6:	Erlang; $\delta = 6.0$, $k = 4$	Pareto; $a_Y = 4.0$, $b_Y = 0.4$	0.8	1.2
Fig. 6.7:	Pareto; $a_T = 4.0$, $b_T = 0.4$	Pareto; $a_Y = 4.0$, $b_Y = 0.4$	1	1.33

(1) $c^* := \mathsf{E}\,Y/\mathsf{E}\,T$ is equal to $\delta/(k\,(a_Y - 1)\,b_Y)$,

(2) the constants defined in (5.17) are

$$
\begin{aligned}
M &:= \mathsf{E}\,T/\mathsf{E}\,Y = k\,(a_Y - 1)\,b_Y/\delta, \\
D^2 &:= ((\mathsf{E}\,T)^2\mathsf{D}\,Y + (\mathsf{E}\,Y)^2\mathsf{D}\,T)/(\mathsf{E}\,Y)^3 \\
&= \frac{k\,(a_Y - 1)\,b_Y}{\delta^2}\Big(1 + \frac{k\,a_Y}{a_Y - 2}\Big),
\end{aligned}
\tag{6.20}
$$

(3) the adjustment coefficient does not exist.

Model (F), Example (c). This model is verbally described as renewal model, where the distribution of T is Pareto with parameters $a_T > 3$, $b_T > 0$,

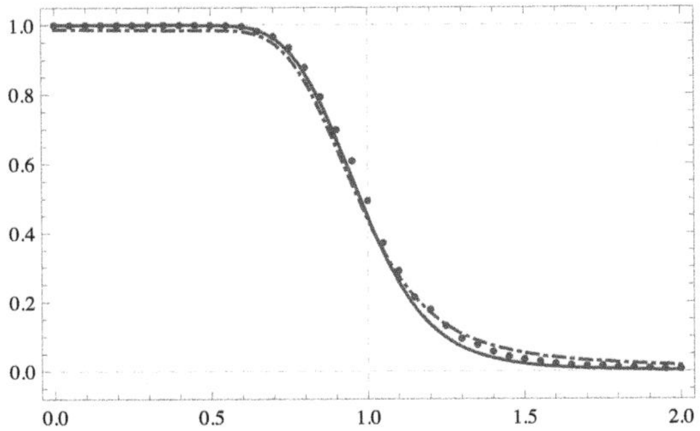

FIGURE 6.3: Graphs (X-axis is c) of $\mathsf{P}\{\varUpsilon_{u,c\,|\,\delta,\rho} \leqslant t\}$ evaluated numerically (solid line) and simulated with $\Delta c = 0.05$, $N = 1000$ (dots) and $\mathcal{M}_{u,c}(t)$ (dash-dotted line) in Model (A) (see details in Table 6.2), $t = 100$, $u = 10$.

TABLE 6.3: An inventory of models in Figs. 6.8–6.12

	T	Y	M	D^2
Fig. 6.8:	Exponentially distributed; $\delta = 4/5$	Exponentially distributed; $\rho = 3/5$	0.75	1.88
Fig. 6.9:	Erlang; $k = 2$, $\delta = 8/5$	Exponentially distributed; $\rho = 3/5$	0.75	1.41
Fig. 6.10:	Pareto; $a_T = 10$, $b_T = 4/45$	Exponentially distributed; $\rho = 3/5$	0.75	2.11
Fig. 6.11:	Exponentially distributed; $\delta = 4/5$	Pareto; $a_Y = 10$, $b_Y = 0.05$	0.56	1.58
Fig. 6.12:	Exponentially distributed; $\delta = 4/5$	Kummer; $k_Y = 200$, $l_Y = 200$	1.24	3.16

and Y is Pareto with parameters $a_Y > 3$, $b_Y > 0$, whose p.d.f. are

$$f_T(x) = \frac{a_T b_T}{(x\,b_T + 1)^{\,a_T+1}}, \quad f_Y(x) = \frac{a_Y b_Y}{(x\,b_Y + 1)^{\,a_Y+1}}, \quad x > 0.$$

Elementary calculations yield

$$\mathsf{E}\,T = 1/((a_T - 1)\,b_T), \quad \mathsf{D}\,T = a_T/((a_T - 1)^2\,(a_T - 2)\,b_T^2),$$
$$\mathsf{E}\,Y = 1/((a_Y - 1)\,b_Y), \quad \mathsf{D}\,Y = a_Y/((a_Y - 1)^2\,(a_Y - 2)\,b_Y^2).$$

The following useful results are easy to check:

(1) $c^* := \mathsf{E}\,Y/\mathsf{E}\,T$ is equal to $((a_T - 1)\,b_T)/((a_Y - 1)\,b_Y)$,

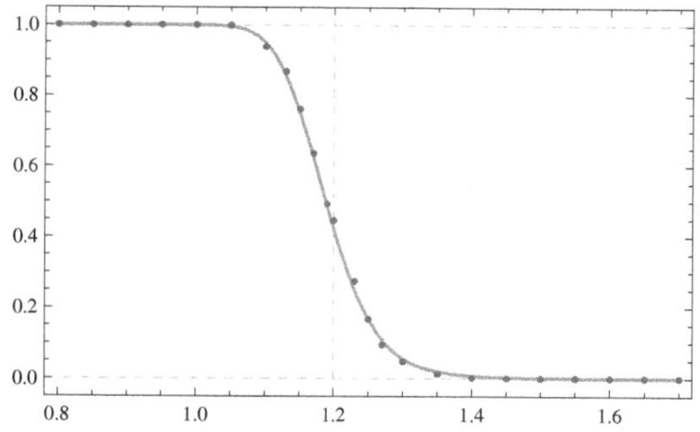

FIGURE 6.4: Graphs (X-axis is c) of simulated values of $\mathsf{P}\{\Upsilon_{u,c} \leqslant t\}$ with $\Delta c = 0.05$, $N = 1000$ (dots) and evaluated numerically $\mathcal{M}_{u,c}(t)$ (solid line) in Model (E), Example (a) (see details in Table 6.2), $t = 1000$, $u = 40$.

(2) the constants defined in (5.17) are

$$\begin{aligned} M &:= \mathsf{E}\,T/\mathsf{E}\,Y = ((a_Y - 1)\,b_Y)/((a_T - 1)\,b_T), \\ D^2 &:= ((\mathsf{E}\,T)^2\mathsf{D}\,Y + (\mathsf{E}\,Y)^2\mathsf{D}\,T)/(\mathsf{E}\,Y)^3 \\ &= \left(\frac{a_Y}{a_Y - 2} + \frac{a_T}{a_T - 2}\right)\frac{(a_Y - 1)\,b_Y}{(a_T - 1)^2\,b_T^2}, \end{aligned} \tag{6.21}$$

(3) the adjustment coefficient does not exist.

6.2 Simulation in Level-crossing Problems

With modern computing power, simulation is one of the most attractive methods of numerical computation. It can be applied in very general model conditions, in contrast to, e.g., methods based on the inversion of Laplace transforms.

In this chapter, we will focus on simulation used to obtain virtually exact values of $\mathsf{P}\{\Upsilon_{u,c} \leqslant t\}$ in the direct and $u_{\alpha,t}(c)$ in the inverse level-crossing problems. We compare them with $\mathcal{M}_{u,c}(t)$ in the former, and with $u^{[\mathcal{M}]}_{\alpha,t}(c)$ in the latter problems.

6.2.1 Algorithm of Monte Carlo simulation

The starting point for simulation in the direct level-crossing problem is the choice of the random number generator. It produces a sequence of real numbers, say pseudo-random numbers, in the interval $[0, 1]$. In other words, it

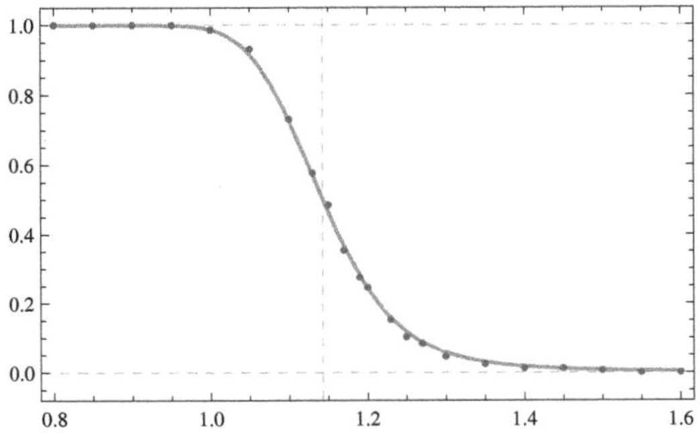

FIGURE 6.5: Graphs (X-axis is c) of simulated values of $\mathsf{P}\{\Upsilon_{u,c} \leqslant t\}$ with $\Delta c = 0.05$, $N = 1000$ (dots) and evaluated numerically $\mathcal{M}_{u,c}(t)$ (solid line) in Model (F), Example (a) (see details in Table 6.2), $t = 1000$, $u = 40$.

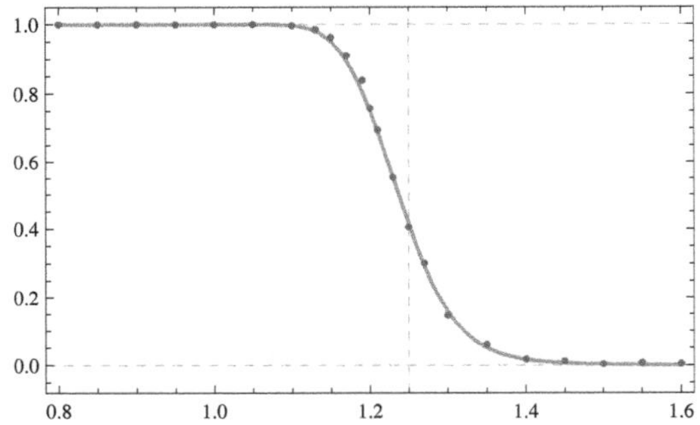

FIGURE 6.6: Graphs (X-axis is c) of simulated values of $\mathsf{P}\{\Upsilon_{u,c} \leqslant t\}$ with $\Delta c = 0.05$, $N = 1000$ (dots) and evaluated numerically $\mathcal{M}_{u,c}(t)$ (solid line) in Model (F), Example (b) (see details in Table 6.2), $t = 1000$, $u = 40$.

simulates a sequence of outcomes of a random variable uniformly distributed on $[0, 1]$.

For simplicity, we deal with rather elementary linear congruential method (see, e.g., [105], Section 3.2.1) based on the recurrent equation

$$x_{n+1} = (kx_n + a) \mod m, \quad n = 0, 1, \ldots,$$

where[14] $k = 23456789$ is the multiplier, $a = 22185$ is the increment, and $m = 2^{32}$ is the modulus. The initial seed x_0 is selected within the interval $[0, 1]$. By division by m, the sequence of real numbers x_n, $n = 0, 1, \ldots$, lying between 1 and $m - 1$, produces the desired pseudo-random numbers lying in the interval $[0, 1]$.

[14]It is known that the quality, i.e., the matching of the numbers thus produced to a sample from the uniform distribution, depends heavily on k and m.

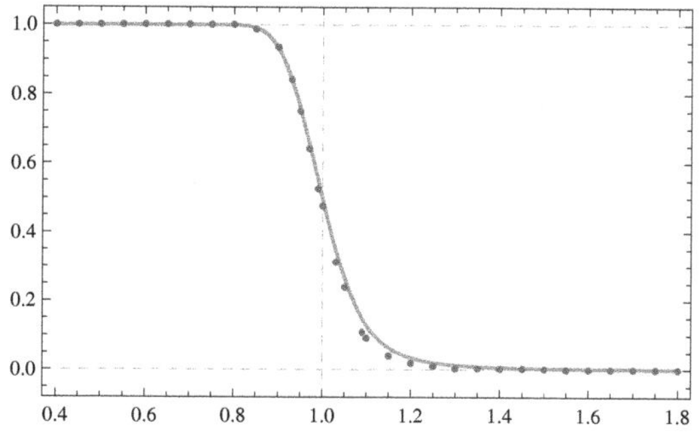

FIGURE 6.7: Graphs (X-axis is c) of simulated values of $\mathsf{P}\{\varUpsilon_{u,c} \leqslant t\}$ with $\Delta c = 0.05$, $N = 1000$ (dots) and evaluated numerically $\mathcal{M}_{u,c}(t)$ (solid line) in Model (F), Example (c) (see details in Table 6.2), $t = 1000$, $u = 40$.

Given this pseudo-random number generator, the pseudo-random variates from 2-mixture, Erlang[15], and Pareto distributions are all obtained by means of the inverse function method (see, e.g., [58], Chapter II, Section 2). For instance, pseudo-random variate from 2-mixture is $E = F_\xi^{-1}(U)$, where c.d.f. F_ξ is given in (B.2). For[16] $\theta_1 = 1$ and $\theta_2 = 2$,

$$E = -\ln\left(\frac{-p + \sqrt{p^2 + 4q(1-U)}}{2q}\right). \tag{6.22}$$

Pseudo-random variate from Pareto distribution is $P = F_\xi^{-1}(U)$, where c.d.f. F_ξ is given in (B.9). In the explicit form, it is

$$P = \frac{1}{b}\left(\frac{1}{(1-U)^{1/a}} - 1\right), \tag{6.23}$$

where U denotes a pseudo-random number from uniform distribution on $[0, 1]$.

To evaluate numerically the probability $\mathsf{P}\{\varUpsilon_{u,c} \leqslant t\}$ as a function of c, with u, t fixed, we proceed with an interval $[c_{\min}, c_{\max}]$ on the abscissa axis, where $c^* = 1/M \in [c_{\min}, c_{\max}]$. We introduce the lattice

$$\mathcal{C} = \{c_i,\ i = 0, 1, \ldots, n_{\mathcal{C}}\}$$

with the span $\Delta c > 0$, i.e., put $c_0 = 0$ and $c_i = c_{i-1} + \Delta c$, $i = 1, 2, \ldots, [c_{\max}/\Delta c] + 1$. Starting with c_0, we iterate through the nodes of $\mathcal{C}$.

To simulate the values of $\mathsf{P}\{\varUpsilon_{u,c} \leqslant t\}$ at the nodes c_i, $i = 0, 1, \ldots, n_{\mathcal{C}}$, we use definition of $\varUpsilon_{u,c}$. For each c_i we simulate the bundle of N trajectories of

[15]For Erlang with parameters $\theta > 0$ and integer k, simulation may be based on the fact that it is a sum of k i.i.d. exponentially distributed random variables with parameter $\theta > 0$.

[16]In the general case, for arbitrarily chosen $\theta_1 > 0$ and $\theta_2 > 0$, there is no explicit expression and one should solve numerically the equation $F_\xi(E) = U$ with respect to E.

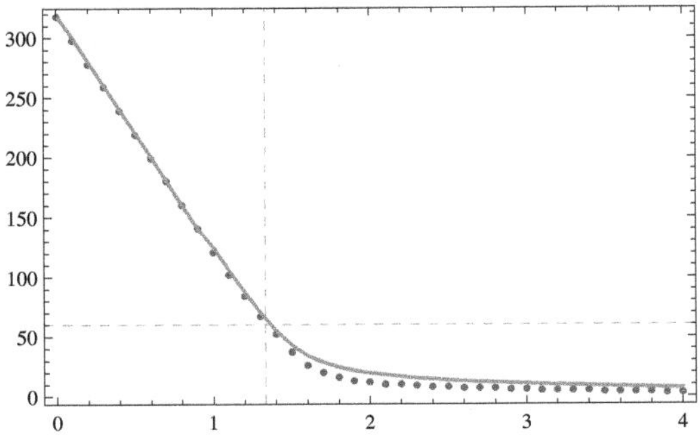

FIGURE 6.8: Graphs (X-axis is c) of simulated values of $u_{\alpha,t}(c)$ (dots) and evaluated numerically $u^{[\mathcal{M}]}_{\alpha,t}(c)$ (solid line) in Model (A) (see details in Table 6.3), with $\alpha = 0.05$, and $t = 200$. Vertical grid line: $c^* = 4/3$. Horizontal grid line: $u_{\alpha,t\,|\,\delta,\rho}(c^*) = 59.90$.

the process $V_s - c_i s$, $0 < s < t$. We calculate the number of trajectories that crossed the level u, divide it by the total number N, and take this ratio for the value of this probability in the node c_i.

To evaluate the ruin capital $u_{\alpha,t}(c)$ using numerical simulation, we address the interval $[0, c_{\max}]$ on the abscissa axis, where $c_{\max} > c^*$ is sufficiently large. We introduce the lattice

$$\mathcal{C} = \{c_i,\ i = 0, 1, \ldots, n_{\mathcal{C}}\}$$

with the span $\Delta c > 0$, i.e., put $c_0 = 0$ and $c_i = c_{i-1} + \Delta c$, $i = 1, 2, \ldots, [c_{\max}/\Delta c] + 1$. Second, we address the interval $[0, u_{\max}]$ on the ordinate axis, choosing $u_{\max}$ close to $u_{\alpha,t}(0)$ (see Theorem 5.13). We introduce the lattice

$$\mathcal{U} = \{u_j,\ j = 0, 1, \ldots, n_{\mathcal{U}}\}$$

with the span $\Delta u > 0$, i.e., put $u_0 = 0$ and $u_i = u_{i-1} + \Delta u$, $i = 1, 2, \ldots, [u_{\max}/\Delta u] + 1$.

Starting with c_0, we iterate through the nodes of $\mathcal{C}$. Dealing with the node c_i, we simulate the values

$$\mathsf{P}\{\varUpsilon_{u,c} \leqslant t\}|_{u=u_j, c=c_i}, \quad j = 0, 1, \ldots, n_{\mathcal{U}},$$

on the basis of the definition of this probability. Namely, for each j we simulate the bundle (see Fig. 6.1) consisting of N trajectories of the shifted compound renewal process $V_s - cs$, $s \geqslant 0$, with $c = c_i$ and with $u = u_j$. Then we pick up $\mathsf{P}\{\varUpsilon_{u,c} \leqslant t\}|_{u=u_{j_i}, c=c_i}$ closest to α and declare u_{j_i} a solution to $\mathsf{P}\{\varUpsilon_{u,c} \leqslant t\} = \alpha$ in the node c_i.

To control the accuracy of simulation, we always strive to ensure that this value lies inside the strip $[\alpha - \varepsilon, \alpha + \varepsilon]$. Here $\varepsilon > 0$ is a rather small

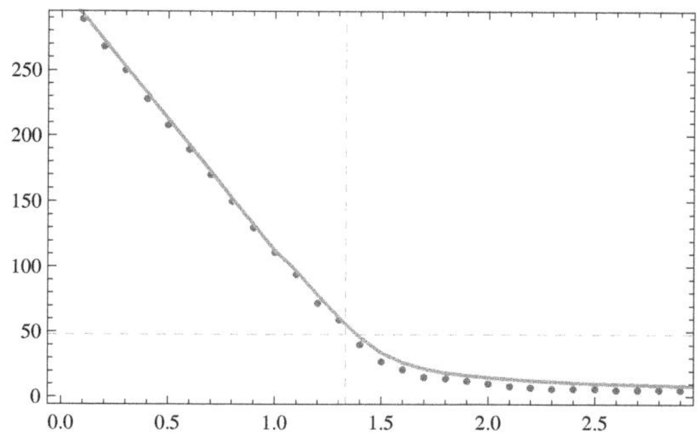

FIGURE 6.9: Graphs (X-axis is c) of simulated values of $u_{\alpha,t}(c)$ (dots) and evaluated numerically $u^{[\mathcal{M}]}_{\alpha,t}(c)$ (solid line) in Model (D), Example (b) (see details in Table 6.3), with $\alpha = 0.05$, and $t = 200$. Vertical grid line: $c^* = 4/3$. Horizontal grid line: $u_{\alpha,t}(c^*) = 48$.

pre-selected value, the same for the entire simulation process. Plainly, when $\mathsf{P}\{\Upsilon_{u,c} \leqslant t\}\,|_{u=u_j,c=c_i}$, $j = 0, 1, \ldots, n_{\mathcal{U}}$, are simulated, the values Δc, Δu and the number N used to achieve such accuracy are all dependent of ε. They must be such that at least one simulated point falls (see Fig. 6.2) within the strip $[\alpha - \varepsilon, \alpha + \varepsilon]$.

This algorithm, which starts from iterating through $c_i \in \mathcal{C}$, $i = 0, 1, \ldots, n_{\mathcal{C}}$, can be modified in order to avoid unnecessary calculations. It refers to the values $\mathsf{P}\{\Upsilon_{u,c} \leqslant t\}|_{u=u_j,c=c_i}$, with u_j in the lattice $\mathcal{U}$, such that it is immediately seen that the corresponding points do not fall into the target strip $[\alpha+\varepsilon, \alpha-\varepsilon]$. Sensible as well is to shift the bundle of trajectories corresponding to c_i by altering u in order to make the ratio of the number of trajectories fallen below zero to the total number of trajectories equal to α. This modification of the algorithm may yield a considerable gain in computation time. Being not focused in this paper on the optimality of the computational procedure, we leave it aside.

6.2.2 Simulated values versus inverse Gaussian approximation and solutions to $\mathcal{M}$-equation

In Chapter 4, we were focussed on non-linear $\mathcal{M}$-equation which defines the implicit function $u^{[\mathcal{M}]}_{\alpha,t}(c)$, $c \geqslant 0$. This issue was approached from a purely analytical standpoint; relations with direct and inverse level-crossing problems was not mentioned. But after the inverse Gaussian approximation for $\mathsf{P}\{\Upsilon_{u,c} \leqslant t\}$ was discussed in Chapter 5, it became obvious that (see Theorem 5.5) $\mathcal{M}_{u,c}(t)$ is the main term of such approximation (as $u \to \infty$) and the $\mathcal{M}$-equation follows from the original equation (see (5.3)) $\mathsf{P}\{\Upsilon_{u,c} \leqslant t\} = \alpha$ accordingly.

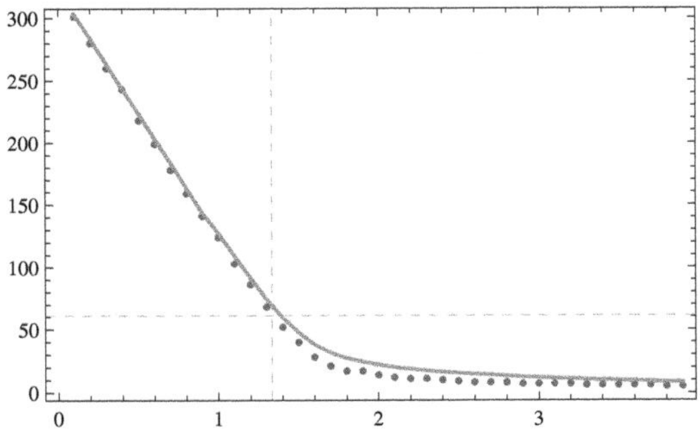

FIGURE 6.10: Graphs (X-axis is c) of simulated values of $u_{\alpha,t}(c)$ (dots) and evaluated numerically $u^{[\mathcal{M}]}_{\alpha,t}(c)$ (solid line) in Model (D), Example (c) (see details in Table 6.3), with $\alpha = 0.05$, and $t = 200$. Vertical grid line: $c^* = 4/3$. Horizontal grid line: $u_{\alpha,t}(c^*) = 61$.

TABLE 6.4: Numerically calculated $u^{[\mathcal{M}]}_{\alpha,t}(c)$ and simulated $u_{\alpha,t\,|\,\delta,\rho}(c)$ in Model (A) with parameters $\delta = 4/5$ and $\rho = 3/5$, $\alpha = 0.05$, and $t = 200$ (see Fig. 6.8)

c	$u_{\alpha,t\,\vert\,\delta,\rho}(c)$	$u^{[\mathcal{M}]}_{\alpha,t}(c)$	c	$u_{\alpha,t\,\vert\,\delta,\rho}(c)$	$u^{[\mathcal{M}]}_{\alpha,t}(c)$
0.1	298	300.42	1.1	102 (101.36)	105.58
0.2	278	280.42	1.2	84 (82.93)	87.49
0.3	259	260.42	1.3	67 (65.42)	70.48
0.4	239	240.42	1.4	52 (49.58)	55.37
0.5	219	220.42	1.5	37 (36.55)	43.17
0.6	199	200.42	1.6	26 (27.19)	34.39
0.7	180	180.42	1.7	20 (21.15)	28.50
0.8	160 (158.98)	160.42	1.8	16 (17.32)	24.54
0.9	141 (139.54)	140.42	1.9	13 (14.76)	21.78
1.0	121 (120.30)	125.42	2.0	12 (12.95)	19.65

The following remark concerns $\mathsf{P}\{\varUpsilon_{u,c} \leqslant t\}$ and $\mathcal{M}_{u,c}(t)$.

Remark 6.1 For u and t sufficiently large, $\mathsf{P}\{\varUpsilon_{u,c} \leqslant t\}$ and $\mathcal{M}_{u,c}(t)$ must be close to each other throughout the entire range of $c > 0$.

Referring to some models listed in Table 6.1, we graphically illustrate the proximity between $\mathsf{P}\{\varUpsilon_{u,c} \leqslant t\}$ and $\mathcal{M}_{u,c}(t)$. The exact values of $\mathsf{P}\{\varUpsilon_{u,c} \leqslant t\}$ are not available for all such models, except for Model (A) where closed-form expressions (3.6), (3.7), or (3.8) exist, and we choose the values obtained by simulation as reference values.

These illustrations are insightful and helpful: they demonstrate high accuracy (uniformly on c positive) of the inverse Gaussian approximation. A special attention deserve Fig. 6.5–6.7 for the models with fat-tail Y; for such

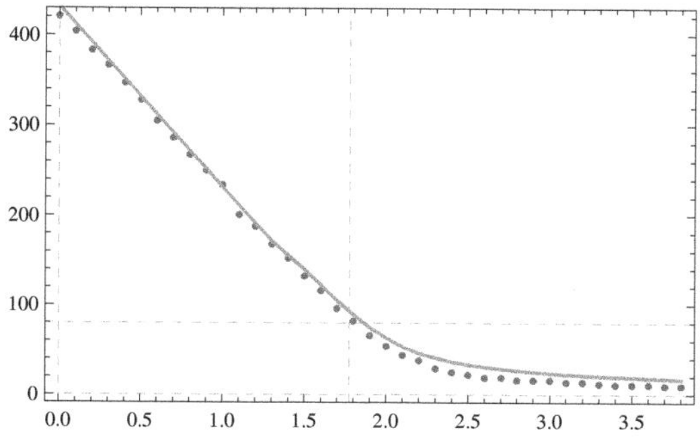

FIGURE 6.11: Graphs (X-axis is c) of $u_{\alpha,t}(c)$, simulated (dots), and $u^{[\mathcal{M}]}_{\alpha,t}(c)$, evaluated numerically (solid line) in Model (C), Example (a) (see details in Table 6.3), with $\alpha = 0.05$, and $t = 200$. Vertical grid line: $c^* = 1.78$. Horizontal grid line: $u_{\alpha,t}(c^*) = 80$.

Y both Cramér's (or normal) and diffusion approximations do not exist. An inventory of models studied in Figs. 6.3–6.7 is given for convenience in Table 6.2.

The following remark concerns comparison of numerical results for $u_{\alpha,t}(c)$ and $u^{[\mathcal{M}]}_{\alpha,t}(c)$.

Remark 6.2 Given asymptotic bounds (5.57), when t is sufficiently large, the functions $u_{\alpha,t}(c)$ and $u^{[\mathcal{M}]}_{\alpha,t}(c)$ must be close to each other, when $0 \leqslant c \leqslant c^*$. The proximity of these functions is not guaranteed, when c exceeds a value larger than c^*. It is awesome that $u_{\alpha,t}(c)$ and $u^{[\mathcal{M}]}_{\alpha,t}(c)$ are not far away from each other (see Figs. 6.8–6.12) even for such values of c.

The proximity of $u_{\alpha,t}(c)$ and $u^{[\mathcal{M}]}_{\alpha,t}(c)$, which are implicit functions defined by the original equation (5.3) and the modified $\mathcal{M}$-equation (4.22), was studied in Section 5.5. On the one hand, when $0 < c < c^*$, these implicit functions should be close to each other, as t is sufficiently large. On the other hand, generally speaking, when $c > Kc^*$, $K > 1$, there is no rational reason to deem these functions close to each other, even as t is sufficiently large.

Even more than what has already been said, in the models with fat-tail Y, when $c > Kc^*$, $K > 1$, there is substantial reason to expect a significant difference between $u_{\alpha,t}(c)$ and $u^{[\mathcal{M}]}_{\alpha,t}(c)$: whereas $\mathcal{M}_{u,c}(t)$, regarded as a function of the variable c, exponentially decreases to zero, as $c \to \infty$, the probability $\mathsf{P}\{\varUpsilon_{u,c} \leqslant t\}$, regarded as a function of the variable c, is decreasing to zero at a power rate.

To mitigate this, note that both $u_{\alpha,t}(c)$ and $u^{[\mathcal{M}]}_{\alpha,t}(c)$ are small, when $c > Kc^*$, $K > 1$; the discrepancy between them is insignificant from the standpoint of the capital which guarantees solvency.

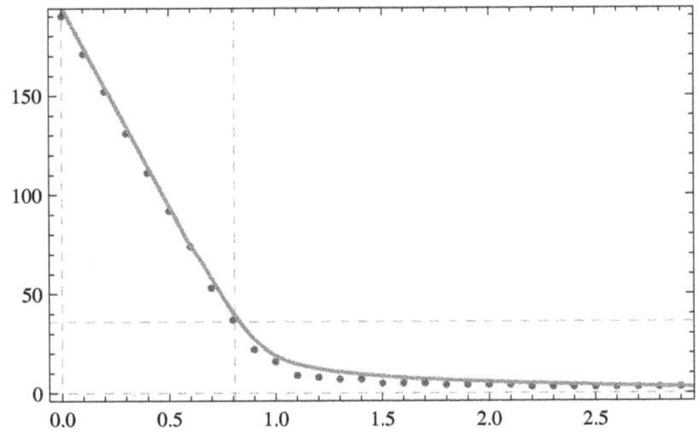

FIGURE 6.12: Graphs (X-axis is c) of $u_{\alpha,t}(c)$, simulated (dots), and $u_{\alpha,t}^{[\mathcal{M}]}(c)$, evaluated numerically (solid line) in Model (C), Example (b) (see details in Table 6.3), with $\alpha = 0.05$, and $t = 200$. Vertical grid line: $c^* = 0.81$. Horizontal grid line: $u_{\alpha,t}(c^*) = 36$.

Bearing in mind these general remarks, let us compare $u_{\alpha,t}(c)$, calculated by means of simulation, and $u_{\alpha,t}^{[\mathcal{M}]}(c)$, calculated as a numerical solution to the $\mathcal{M}$-equation (4.22), both regarded as the functions of the variable $c > 0$.

In Table 6.4, in the framework of exponential model defined by T with parameter $\delta = 4/5$ and Y with parameter $\rho = 3/5$, we represent some simulated values of $u_{\alpha,t\,|\,\delta,\rho}(c)$ and numerically evaluated values of $u_{\alpha,t}^{[\mathcal{M}]}(c)$, which are drawn in Fig. 6.8. Note that the simulated values are fairly accurate. For example, some values of $u_{\alpha,t\,|\,\delta,\rho}(c)$ calculated by numerical solution of equation (5.3) with the left-hand side given by the exact formula (3.8), are: 158.98 when $c = 0.8$, 139.54 when $c = 0.9$, and so on.

6.2.3 Simulated values in direct level-crossing problem

In Fig. 6.3, which refers to Model (A), i.e., T and Y exponentially distributed with parameters $\delta = 1$ and $\rho = 1$, whence $c^* = 1$ and (see (6.7)) $M = 1$, $D^2 = 2$, the graph of $\mathsf{P}\{\Upsilon_{u,c} \leqslant t\}$ (blue line) calculated by means of Type I formula (3.6) and the graph of $\mathcal{M}_{u,c}(t)$ (red line) calculated by means of numerical integration are drawn, when $t = 100$, $u = 10$. In this case, we do not need simulation since closed-form expressions are available. However, for completeness, the results of simulation according to the algorithm of Section 6.2.1 are shown by dots.

In Fig. 6.4, which refers to Model (E), Example (a), i.e., T Erlang with parameters $\delta = 1.2$, $k = 2$ and Y Erlang with parameters $\rho = 1$, $m = 2$, whence $c^* = 1.2$ and (see (6.18)) $M = 0.83$, $D^2 = 1.39$, the simulated values of $\mathsf{P}\{\Upsilon_{u,c} \leqslant t\}$ are shown by dots and the graph of $\mathcal{M}_{u,c}(t)$ calculated by means of numerical integration is drawn by red line; here $t = 1000$, $u = 40$.

In Fig. 6.5, which refers to Model (F), Example (a), i.e., T 2-mixture of

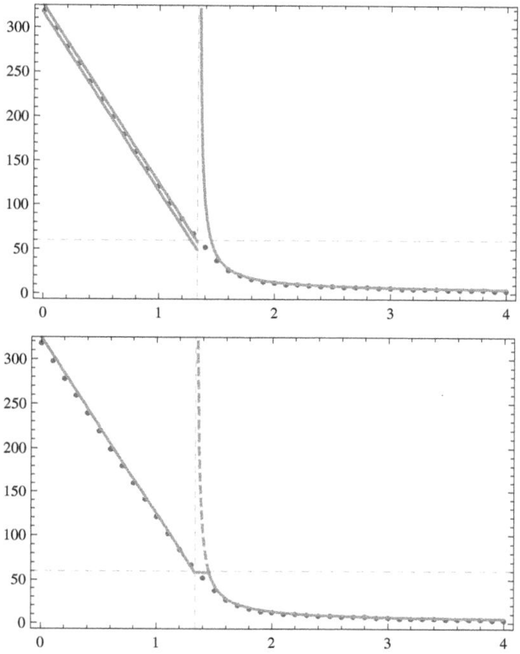

FIGURE 6.13: Above: graphs (X-axis is c) of two-sided bounds (6.26) when $0 < c < c^*$, upper bound (6.25), when $c > c^*$, and simulated values of $u_{\alpha,t\,|\,\delta,\rho}(c)$. Below: upper bound on $u_{\alpha,t\,|\,\delta,\rho}(c)$ and simulated values of $u_{\alpha,t\,|\,\delta,\rho}(c)$. In both cases T and Y are exponentially distributed with parameters $\delta = 3/5$, $\rho = 4/5$, respectively, $\alpha = 0.05$, and $t = 200$. Vertical grid line: $c^* = 4/3$. Horizontal grid line: $u_{\alpha,t\,|\,\delta,\rho}(c^*) = 59.90$.

exponential with parameters $\delta_1 = 1$, $\delta_2 = 2$, $p = 2/3$ and Y Pareto with parameters $a_Y = 4.0$, $b_Y = 0.35$, whence $c^* = 1.14$ and (see (6.19)) $M = 0.88$, $D^2 = 2.30$, the graph of $\mathcal{M}_{u,c}(t)$ calculated by means of numerical integration are drawn by red line and simulated values of $\mathsf{P}\{\Upsilon_{u,c} \leqslant t\}$ are shown by dots; here $t = 1000$, $u = 40$. When simulating, we take $\Delta c = 0.05$ (and even less in the vicinity of c^*, where flexure is strong), and $N = 1000$. We used equality (6.23) to create the random number generator for Pareto Y, and equality (6.22) to create the random number generator for 2-mixture T with $\delta_1 = 1$ and $\delta_2 = 2$.

In Fig. 6.6, which refers to Model (F), Example (b), i.e., T Erlang with parameters $\delta = 6.0$, $k = 4$ and Y Pareto with parameters $a_Y = 4.0$, $b_Y = 0.4$, whence $c^* = 1.25$ and (see (6.20)) $M = 0.8$, $D^2 = 1.2$, the graph of $\mathcal{M}_{u,c}(t)$ is drawn by red line and the simulated values of $\mathsf{P}\{\Upsilon_{u,c} \leqslant t\}$ are shown by dots; here $t = 1000$, $u = 40$. When simulating, we take $\Delta c = 0.05$ (and even less in the vicinity of c^*, where flexure is strong), and $N = 1000$. We used equality (6.23) to create the random number generator for Pareto Y. To simulate Erlang T with $k = 4$, we note that it is a sum of four independent random variables exponentially distributed with parameter equal to $\delta = 6.0$.

In Fig. 6.7, which refers to Model (F), Example (c), i.e., T Pareto with parameters $a_T = 4.0$, $b_T = 0.4$ and Y Pareto with parameters $a_Y = 4.0$, $b_Y = 0.4$, whence $c^* = 1$ and (see (6.21)) $M = 1$, $D^2 = 1.33$, the simulated values of $\mathsf{P}\{\varUpsilon_{u,c} \leqslant t\}$ are shown by dots and the graph of $\mathcal{M}_{u,c}(t)$ calculated by means of numerical integration is drawn by red line; here $t = 1000$, $u = 40$. When simulating, we take $\Delta c = 0.05$ (and even less in the vicinity of c^*, where flexure is strong), and $N = 1000$. We used equality (6.23) to create the random number generator for Pareto T and Y.

6.2.4 Simulated values in inverse level-crossing problem

In Fig. 6.8, which also refers to Model (A), i.e., in the framework of exponential model defined by T and Y exponentially distributed with parameters $\delta = 4/5$ and $\rho = 3/5$ respectively, whence $c^* = 1.33$ and (see (6.7)) $M = 0.75$, $D^2 = 1.88$, the values of $u^{[\mathcal{M}]}_{\alpha,t}(c)$ (red line) found as numerical solutions to the $\mathcal{M}$-equation (4.22) and the simulated values of $u_{\alpha,t\,|\,\delta,\rho}(c)$ (dots) are drawn, when $t = 200$, $\alpha = 0.05$.

It is noteworthy that to get the reference values for $u_{\alpha,t\,|\,\delta,\rho}(c)$ in this case, we can do without simulation. Indeed, for the probability $\mathsf{P}\{\varUpsilon_{u,c\,|\,\delta,\rho} \leqslant t\}$, which is the left-hand side of the fundamental equation (5.3), the closed-form expressions are available. Consequently, this equation can be solved numerically, as usual. But we prefer to resort to simulation, as to an alternative method of calculation, not tied to the explicit form of the equation, doing that according to the algorithm of Section 6.2.1.

In Fig. 6.9, which refers to Model (D), Example (b), i.e., where we set T Erlang with parameters $k = 2$ and $\delta = 8/5$, and Y exponentially distributed with parameter $\rho = 3/5$, whence $c^* = 1.33$ and (see (6.7)) $M = 0.75$, $D^2 = 1.41$, the values of $u^{[\mathcal{M}]}_{\alpha,t}(c)$ (red line) found as numerical solutions to $\mathcal{M}$-equation (4.22) and the simulated values of $u_{\alpha,t}(c)$ (dots) are drawn, when $t = 200$, $\alpha = 0.05$.

In Fig. 6.10, which refers to Model (D), Example (c), i.e., where we set T Pareto with parameters $a_T = 10$, $b_T = 4/45$, and Y exponentially distributed with parameter $\rho = 3/5$, whence $c^* = 1.33$ and (see (6.17)) $M = 0.75$, $D^2 = 2.11$, the values of $u^{[\mathcal{M}]}_{\alpha,t}(c)$ (red line) found as numerical solutions to $\mathcal{M}$-equation (4.22) and the simulated values of $u_{\alpha,t}(c)$ (dots) are drawn, when $t = 200$, $\alpha = 0.05$.

In Fig. 6.11, which refers to Model (C), Example (a), i.e., where T is set exponentially distributed with parameter $\delta = 4/5$ and Y Pareto with parameters $a_Y = 10$, $b_Y = 0.05$, whence $c^* = 1.78$ and (see (6.13)) $M = 0.56$, $D^2 = 1.58$, the values of $u^{[\mathcal{M}]}_{\alpha,t}(c)$ (red line) found as numerical solutions to

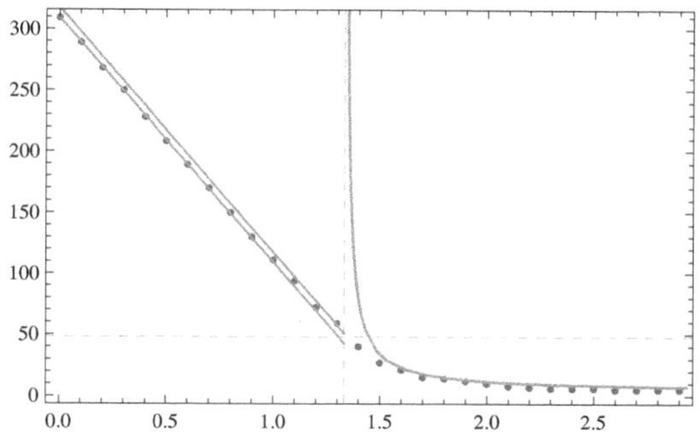

FIGURE 6.14: Graphs (X-axis is c) of simulated $u_{\alpha,t}(c)$ (dots), two-sided bounds (6.26), when $0 < c < c^*$, upper bound, when $c > c^*$, in Model (E), Example (a) (see details in Table 6.3), with $\alpha = 0.05$, and $t = 200$. Vertical grid line: $c^* = 4/3$. Horizontal grid line: simulated $u_{\alpha,t}(c^*) = 48$.

$\mathcal{M}$-equation (4.22) and the simulated values of $u_{\alpha,t}(c)$ (dots) are drawn, when $t = 200$, $\alpha = 0.05$.

In Fig. 6.12, which refers to Model (C), Example (b), i.e., where T is set exponentially distributed with parameter $\delta = 4/5$ and Y Kummer with parameters $k_Y = 200$, $l_Y = 200$, whence $c^* = 0.81$ and (see (6.14)) $M = 1.24$, $D^2 = 3.16$, the values of $u_{\alpha,t}^{[\mathcal{M}]}(c)$ (red line) found as numerical solutions to $\mathcal{M}$-equation (4.22) and the simulated values of $u_{\alpha,t}(c)$ (dots) are drawn, when $t = 200$, $\alpha = 0.05$.

6.3 Numerically Calculated Bounds on the Fixed-probability Level

6.3.1 Elementary upper bounds

Fig. 6.13, which refers to Model (A), i.e., when T and Y are exponentially distributed with parameters $\delta = 4/5$ and $\rho = 3/5$ respectively, whence $c^* = \delta/\rho = 1.33$, shows the simulated values[17] of $u_{\alpha,t\,|\,\delta,\rho}(c)$ (dots) for $t = 200$, $\alpha = 0.05$. This figure also shows the following.

For $0 < c < c^* = \delta/\rho$, it illustrates the asymptotic inequalities (3.57), i.e.,

$$(\delta/\rho - c)\,t + \frac{\kappa_\alpha}{\kappa_{\alpha/2}} u^*_{\alpha,t} \leqslant u_{\alpha,t\,|\,\delta,\rho}(c) \leqslant (\delta/\rho - c)\,t + u^*_{\alpha,t}, \tag{6.24}$$

[17]Generally speaking, to get the reference values for $u_{\alpha,t\,|\,\delta,\rho}(c)$, in this case we do not need simulation because closed-form expressions for $\mathsf{P}\{\Upsilon_{u,c\,|\,\delta,\rho} \leqslant t\}$, which is the left-hand side of the fundamental equation (5.3), are available.

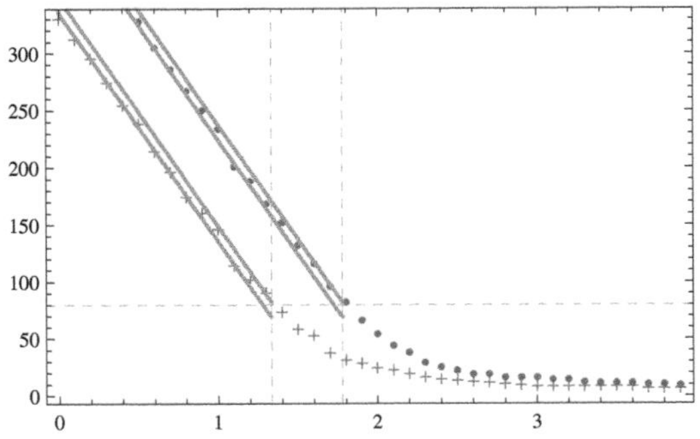

FIGURE 6.15: Graphs (X-axis is c) of simulated values of $u_{\alpha,t}(c)$ (dots), two-sided bounds (6.26), when $0 < c < c^*$, in Model (C), Example (a) (see details in Table 6.5), with $\alpha = 0.05$, and $t = 200$. Vertical grid line: $c^* = 1.78$ (dots) and $c^* = 1.33$ (crosses). Horizontal grid lines: simulated $u_{\alpha,t}(c^*) = 80$ (both for dots and crosses).

TABLE 6.5: Model (C), Example (a); cases in Fig. 6.15

	Exponentially distributed T	Pareto Y	M and D^2 (see (6.13))
(dots):	$\delta = 4/5$	$a_Y = 10$, $b_Y = 0.05$	$M = 0.56$, $D^2 = 1.58$
(crosses):	$\delta = 4/5$	$a_Y = 3$, $b_Y = 0.3$	$M = 0.75$ $D^2 = 3.75$

where[18] $u^*_{\alpha,t} := (\sqrt{2\delta}/\rho)\,\kappa_{\alpha/2}\sqrt{t}\,(1 + o(1))$, $t \to \infty$.

When $c > c^* = \delta/\rho$, it illustrates inequality (3.60), i.e.,

$$u_{\alpha,t\,|\,\delta,\rho}(c) \leqslant u_{\alpha\,|\,\delta,\rho}(c) = \max\left\{0, -\frac{\ln(\alpha c\rho/\delta)}{\rho - \delta/c}\right\}. \tag{6.25}$$

The lower graph on Fig. 6.13 shows an upper bound on $u_{\alpha,t}(c)$ constructed by the following elementary method. For $0 < c \leqslant c^*$, we take (assuming that t is large enough) the upper bound in (6.24). For $c^* < c \leqslant \hat{c}$, where $\hat{c} = 1.46$ is a solution to the equation

$$u^*_{\alpha,t} = -\frac{\ln(\alpha c\rho/\delta)}{\rho - \delta/c},$$

we set this bound equal to the constant value $u^*_{\alpha,t}$. When $c > \hat{c}$, we set it equal to the right-hand side of the inequality (6.25). Plainly, this elementary method is based only on monotone decreasing of $u_{\alpha,t}(c)$, as c increases, and does not need, e.g., convexity of this fixed-probability level considered in Section 3.3.3.

[18]Recall that for $\alpha = 0.05$, we have $\kappa_\alpha = 1.64$, $\kappa_{\alpha/2} = 1.96$.

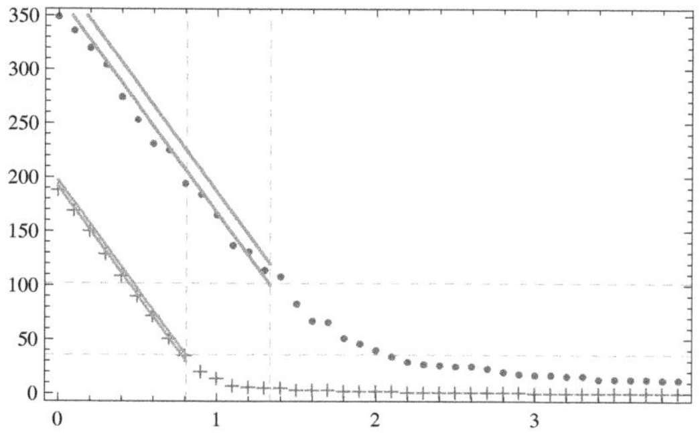

FIGURE 6.16: Graphs (X-axis is c) of simulated values of $u_{\alpha,t}(c)$ (dots), two-sided bounds (6.26), when $0 < c < c^*$, in Model (C), Example (b) (see details in Table 6.6), with $\alpha = 0.05$, and $t = 200$. Vertical grid line: $c^* = 1.33$ (dots) and $c^* = 0.81$ (crosses). Horizontal grid lines: simulated $u_{\alpha,t}(c^*) = 102$ (dots) and $u_{\alpha,t}(c^*) = 36$ (crosses).

TABLE 6.6: Model (C), Example (b); cases in Fig. 6.16

	Exponentially distributed T	Kummer Y	M and D^2 (see (6.14))
(dots):	$\delta = 4/5$	$k_Y = 5$, $l_Y = 5$	$M = 0.75$, $D^2 = 7.88$
(crosses):	$\delta = 4/5$	$k_Y = 200$, $l_Y = 200$	$M = 1.24$, $D^2 = 3.16$

Applying the results of Chapter 5, the bounds constructed for the simplest Model (A) can be extended to most models in Table 6.1. We will show this in the following examples.

In Fig. 6.14, which refers to Model (E), Example (a), when T is Erlang with parameters $\delta = 8/5$, $k = 2$ and Y is[19] exponentially distributed with parameter $\rho = 3/5$, whence $c^* = \mathsf{E}Y/\mathsf{E}T = 1.33$, (see (6.18)) $M = 0.75$, and $D^2 = 1.41$, the simulated values of $u_{\alpha,t}(c)$ (dots) are drawn for $t = 200$, $\alpha = 0.05$. This figure also shows the following.

For $0 < c \leqslant c^*$, it illustrates (see Theorem 5.15) the asymptotic inequalities[20]

$$(c^* - c)\,t + \frac{D}{M^{3/2}}\,\kappa_\alpha\sqrt{t} \leqslant u_{\alpha,t}(c) \leqslant (c^* - c)\,t + \frac{D}{M^{3/2}}\,\kappa_{\alpha/2}\sqrt{t}. \qquad (6.26)$$

[19]In other words, Y is Erlang with parameters $\rho = 3/5$, $m = 1$.

[20]For brevity, we write them in (6.26) as ordinary inequalities, but remember their asymptotic, as $t \to \infty$, nature.

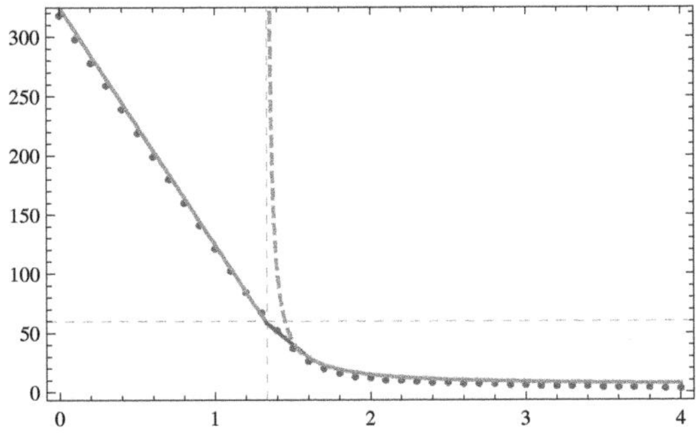

FIGURE 6.17: Graphs (X-axis is c) of simulated values of $u_{\alpha,t\,|\,\delta,\rho}(c)$ (dots) and refined upper bound (6.28), (6.29) in Model (A), i.e., for T and Y exponentially distributed with parameters $\delta = 3/5$, $\rho = 4/5$, respectively, $\alpha = 0.05$, $t = 200$. Vertical grid line: $c^* = 4/3$. Horizontal grid line: simulated $u_{\alpha,t\,|\,\delta,\rho}(c^*) = 59.90$.

When $c > c^*$, it illustrates the upper bound

$$u_{\alpha,t}(c) \leqslant -\frac{\ln\alpha}{\varkappa}. \tag{6.27}$$

which is straightforward from inequality (5.31) of Theorem 5.8, i.e.,

$$\mathsf{P}\{\varUpsilon_{u,c} < \infty\} \leqslant b_\oplus\, e^{-\varkappa\, u} \leqslant e^{-\varkappa\, u}.$$

Recall that in Model (E), Example (a) which we consider $\varkappa$ is a positive solution to the equation $(\rho - \varkappa)\,(\delta + c\varkappa)^k - \delta^k\rho = 0$, which is easy to find numerically. Note that $\varkappa$ is a function of c, and the upper bound in (6.27) is a function depending on c.

The procedure for building the upper bound similar to one shown in lower graph on Fig. 6.13 is now straightforward. To this end, for $c^* < c \leqslant \hat{c}$, where $\hat{c}$ is a solution to the equation

$$\frac{D}{M^{3/2}}\,\kappa_{\alpha/2}\sqrt{t} = -\frac{\ln\alpha}{\varkappa},$$

we set this bound equal to the constant value $\frac{D}{M^{3/2}}\,\kappa_{\alpha/2}\sqrt{t}$. For $0 < c \leqslant c^*$, we set it equal to $(c^* - c)\,t + \frac{D}{M^{3/2}}\,\kappa_{\alpha/2}\sqrt{t}$. When $c > \hat{c}$, we set it equal to $\max\{0, -\frac{\ln\alpha}{\varkappa}\}$. A graphical representation of this bound, as it is done in lower graph on Fig. 6.13, is left to the reader.

Model (C), Example (a) and Model (C), Example (b), to which Figs. 6.15 and 6.16 relate, are exceptional in the following sense: the adjustment coefficient does not exist, and, when $c > c^*$, the upper bound (5.37) on $\mathsf{P}\{\varUpsilon_{u,c} < \infty\}$, which holds for all $u \geqslant 0$, is given in Theorem 5.9. Therefore, the construction of an upper bound for $u_{\alpha,t}(c)$, $c > c^*$, is similar to the above, but requires more technical efforts.

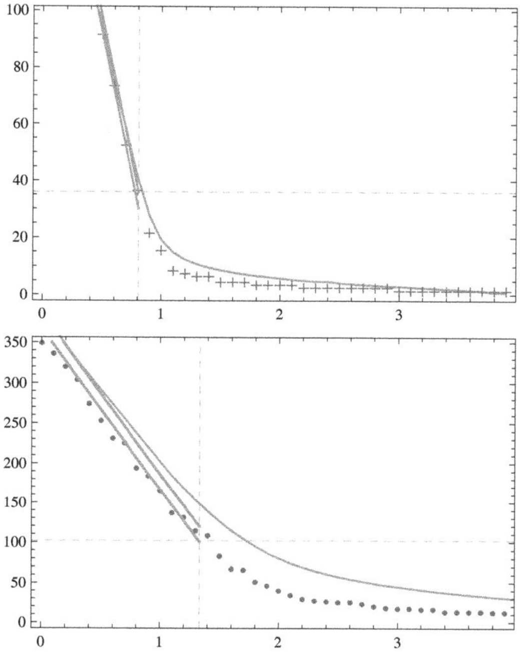

FIGURE 6.18: Above: graph (X-axis is c) of two-sided bounds (6.26) when $0 < c < c^*$, simulated values of $u_{\alpha,t}(c)$ (crosses, dots), and numerically evaluated $u_{\alpha,t}^{[\mathcal{M}]}(c)$ (solid lines) in Model (C), Example (b), i.e., T exponentially distributed with parameter $\delta = 4/5$ and Y Kummer with parameters $k_Y = 200$, $l_Y = 200$. Vertical and horizontal grid lines: $c^* = 0.81$, $u_{\alpha,t}(c^*) = 36$. Below: the same for $\delta = 4/5$, $k_Y = 5$, $l_Y = 5$. Vertical and horizontal grid lines: $c^* = 1.33$, $u_{\alpha,t}(c^*) = 102$. Here $\alpha = 0.05$, and $t = 200$.

At the same time, the construction of the bound for $u_{\alpha,t}(c)$, $0 < c \leqslant c^*$, shown in Figs. 6.15 and 6.16, does not get any harder. These bounds are given by (6.26), bearing in mind that in Model (C), Example (a) easy calculations yield (see Table 6.5) $c^* = 1.78$, $M = 0.56$, $D^2 = 1.58$ (dots), $c^* = 1.33$, $M = 0.75$, $D^2 = 3.75$ (crosses); in Model (C), Example (b) easy calculations yield (see Table 6.6) $c^* = 1.33$, $M = 0.75$, and $D^2 = 7.88$ (dots) and $c^* = 0.81$, $M = 1.24$, and $D^2 = 3.16$ (crosses).

Remark 6.3 (Continuation of Remark 5.1) In Fig. 6.15, which illustrates Model (C), Example (a), when $\delta = 4/5$, $a_Y = 3$, $b_Y = 0.3$, the third moment $\mathsf{E}(Y^3)$ is infinite. However, two-sided bounds (6.26) match very well the simulated values shown by crosses.

6.3.2 Refined upper bounds: price of elegance

A bound that uses tangency and convexity of $u_{\alpha,t}(c)$. In Fig. 6.17, which refers to Model (A), i.e., T and Y exponentially distributed with parameters $\delta = 4/5$ and $\rho = 3/5$ respectively, whence $c^* = 1.33$, the simulated values of $u_{\alpha,t\,|\,\delta,\rho}(c)$ (dots) and refined upper bound of Theorem 3.18 are drawn for $t = 200$, $\alpha = 0.05$.

Recall that this refined upper bound of Theorem 3.18 for $0 < c \leqslant \delta/\rho$ is

$$u_{\alpha,t\,|\,\delta,\rho}(c) \leqslant (\delta/\rho - c)\,t + u^*_{\alpha,t}, \tag{6.28}$$

and, when $c > \delta/\rho$, is

$$u_{\alpha,t\,|\,\delta,\rho}(c) \leqslant \begin{cases} \dfrac{(\rho u^*_{\alpha,t} + \ln\alpha)^2}{4\delta\ln\alpha}\,c \\ \qquad -\dfrac{(\rho u^*_{\alpha,t} - \ln\alpha)^2}{4\rho\ln\alpha}, & \dfrac{\delta}{\rho} < c \leqslant \dfrac{\delta}{\rho}\Big(\dfrac{\rho u^*_{\alpha,t} - \ln\alpha}{\rho u^*_{\alpha,t} + \ln\alpha}\Big), \\ -\dfrac{\ln\alpha}{\rho - \delta/c}, & c > \dfrac{\delta}{\rho}\Big(\dfrac{\rho u^*_{\alpha,t} - \ln\alpha}{\rho u^*_{\alpha,t} + \ln\alpha}\Big), \end{cases} \tag{6.29}$$

where $u^*_{\alpha,t} := (\sqrt{2\delta}/\rho)\,\kappa_{\alpha/2}\sqrt{t}\,(1 + o(1))$, $t \to \infty$.

A composite bound that uses $u^{[\mathcal{M}]}_{\alpha,t}(c)$. Pay attention to hight proximity of $u^{[\mathcal{M}]}_{\alpha,t}(c)$ to $u_{\alpha,t}(c)$ when $0 < c < c^*$, which is theoretically grounded, and to good proximity of $u^{[\mathcal{M}]}_{\alpha,t}(c)$ to $u_{\alpha,t}(c)$ when c is to the right of c^*, staying close enough to it, which is studied by asymptotical methods; in both these cases $u_{\alpha,t}(c) \to \infty$, as $t \to \infty$. Pay attention to the behavior of $u^{[\mathcal{M}]}_{\alpha,t}(c)$ to $u_{\alpha,t}(c)$, when c is to the right of c^*, and rather far from it; here $u_{\alpha,t}(c) \nrightarrow \infty$, as $t \to \infty$, and proximity of $u^{[\mathcal{M}]}_{\alpha,t}(c)$ to $u_{\alpha,t}(c)$ is not justified theoretically. Pay attention to the unequal accuracy of approximation in Figs. 6.18: in the vicinity of $c = 0$, the discrepancy between $u_{\alpha,t}(c)$ and $u^{[\mathcal{M}]}_{\alpha,t}(c)$ is much smaller than in the vicinity of $c = c^*$.

6.4 Conclusion

In the renewal model with T and Y generally distributed, we have no closed-form expression for $\mathsf{P}\{\varUpsilon_{u,c} \leqslant t\}$, i.e., for the left-hand side of equation (5.3) which defines the fixed-probability level $u_{\alpha,t}(c)$, $c \geqslant 0$. Thus, we can not go along the road map of Chapters 2 and 3 in full. However, combining analytical and numerical technique, we can investigate $u_{\alpha,t}(c)$, $c \geqslant 0$, with sufficient completeness, in particular for t large.

Problems

Problem 6.1 Check correctness of Figs. 6.3–6.7. Extend this analysis to other models listed in Table 6.1.

[Hint: Develop your own simulation program according to the algorithm presented in Section 6.2.1 for the analysis of $\mathsf{P}\{\varUpsilon_{u,c} \leqslant t\}$ in the models included in Table 6.2 and in the models listed in Table 6.1, but not included in Table 6.2. Do the same for numerical solution of $\mathcal{M}$-equation. When developing the simulation program, use different random number generators discussed in [105]; see also [27], [160], [197]. Pay attentions to the warning put into the title of [93] that "good random number generators are (not so) easy to find".]

Problem 6.2 Check correctness of Figs. 6.8–6.12. Extend this analysis to other models listed in Table 6.1.

[Hint: do largely the same, as in Problem 6.1.]

Problem 6.3 Check correctness of Figs. 6.13, 6.14. Extend the analysis like in Figs. 6.13, 6.14 to other models listed in Table 6.1, for which Lundberg's bound (5.59) exist.

[Hint: use the simulation program and the program for numerical solution of $\mathcal{M}$-equation developed in Problem 6.1. Focusing on the upper bound (6.27), when $c > c^*$, evaluate $\varkappa$ depending on c numerically.]

Problem 6.4 Check correctness of Figs. 6.15, 6.16. Note that the upper bounds like in (6.27), when $c > c^*$ fail because the adjustment coefficient $\varkappa$ does not exist. In Figs. 6.15 and 6.16, calculate the upper bounds on $u_{\alpha,t}(c)$, as $c > c^*$.

Problem 6.5 Compare the bound that uses tangency shown in Fig. 6.17 and the elementary upper bound shown in lower graph on Fig. 6.13; note the advantage of the former in elegance and of the latter in simplicity.

Problem 6.6 Check Fig. 6.18.

[Hint: use the simulation program and the program for numerical solution of $\mathcal{M}$-equation developed in Problem 6.1.]

Chapter 7

Probability Mechanism of Insurance with Migration and ERS-analysis

This chapter is closely related to the book [134] devoted to long-term insurance planning models for contending companies which operate in a regulated and non-monopolistic market. The main instrument of competition is usually price competition, which leads to migration of insureds and variable portfolio volumes. In this chapter, we go back to insurance terminology of Chapter 1 and focus on the expansion, revenue and solvency analysis, which is called ERS-analysis for short. We start with exponentially distributed claim size Y, and proceed with generally distributed claim size Y. Looking from the angle of level-crossing problem, we move from a homogeneous compound Poisson model to an inhomogeneous model.

7.1 Structural Model of Insurance Business: Origin and Purpose of ERS-analysis

Following the traditional practice, the structural multi-year model of a business process of an insurance company is a discrete-event model with continuous annual subsystems. It develops in time according to the diagram (see [134], Chapter 2)

$$\underbrace{\mathsf{w}^{[0]} \xrightarrow{\gamma^{[0]}} \mathsf{u}^{[0]}\Big(\overset{\mathfrak{F}^{[1]}}{\rightsquigarrow} \varPi^{[1]} \boxed{\downarrow\uparrow} \mathfrak{J}^{[1]}\Big) \xrightarrow{\pi^{[1]}} \mathsf{w}^{[1]}}_{\text{1-st year}} \cdots$$

$$\cdots \xrightarrow{\pi^{[k-1]}} \mathsf{w}^{[k-1]} \underbrace{\xrightarrow{\gamma^{[k-1]}} \mathsf{u}^{[k-1]}\Big(\overset{\mathfrak{F}^{[k]}}{\rightsquigarrow} \varPi^{[k]} \boxed{\downarrow\uparrow} \mathfrak{J}^{[k]}\Big) \xrightarrow{\pi^{[k]}} \mathsf{w}^{[k]}}_{k\text{-th year}} \cdots . \tag{7.1}$$

The multi-year business process looks like a chain ($k = 1, 2, \dots$) of state variables $\mathsf{w}^{[k]}$ and control variables $\mathsf{u}^{[k-1]}$; the latter are selected using the control rule $\gamma^{[k-1]}$. The main components of the diagram (7.1) are

- $\mathfrak{F}^{[k]}$, which is the mechanism that generates market price $\varPi^{[k]}$ on the basis of the entire set of prices of individual companies in the k-th year,

- $\pi^{[k]}$, which is the probability mechanism of insurance in the k-th year; its input is the control variable $\mathsf{u}^{[k-1]}$, and its output is the state variable $\mathsf{w}^{[k]}$,
- $\mathfrak{I}^{[k]}$, which is the mechanism of migration of insureds in the k-th year.

Regarding market price, note that it is an economic abstraction; it is formed from the individual prices of the companies. If it exceeds marginal cost of insurance, the market is called "hard", and otherwise, "soft". The definition of market price, and perception of participants about the outcome of the market price, as they make their pricing decisions, is an essential element of the insurance process.

In [134], the non-life insurer is seen as an agent in a complex reflexive system with at least two types of participants, i.e., competing businesses (which include individuals, such as shareholders, managers, underwriters, policyholders pursuing their own goals, which are different and change across time) and regulators (which are also humans and apt to err). This emphasizes the role of human error, and of incomplete understanding of the real market situation.

Many practitioners (see, e.g., [166]) and academics (see, e.g., [110]) claim that a quantitative analysis of a long-term insurance business requires multi-factorial approaches, and that all single-factorial approaches fail to reveal the real causes of long-term phenomena, such as underwriting cycles fraught with clustered insolvencies.

To develop rational long-term business strategies within the multi-year integral model (7.1), in each particular annual risk model at least three business aspects must be addressed: Expansion, Revenue, and Solvency. This synthetic approach, first proposed in [125] and called for brevity ERS-analysis, takes into account conflicting business aspects. For example, in certain circumstances, the desire to maximize profit can adversely affect financial stability, and vice versa. The main mistake of the agents of a complex reflective system, which leads to crises, is their inattentiveness to one of these three factors (most often to solvency) in a certain period of the business process.

In this chapter, looking at ERS-analysis from a fundamental point of view, we aim to extend the inverse level-crossing problem in the general risk model without migration, studied in Chapters 5 and 6, to the similar problem in the risk model with migration. We start by modeling the migration process by means of migration rate functions; they depend on the market price and individual prices. This formalizes the preferences of policyholders and is prompted by the case studies of the policyholders' behavior in real insurance markets.

7.2 Price Competition, Migration, and Market Price

Migration was not included in the risk models considered so far, and we studied — moving to the economic terms — the insurance process, when the portfolio volume was constant throughout the whole insurance year. Therefore, the claim arrival process was homogeneous; respective claim payout and risk reserve processes were homogeneous as well. Migration of policyholders caused by price competition of contending companies is paramount in ERS-analysis: this leads to changes in profitability and financial stability of the companies. In this section, we discuss price competition, migration, and market prices.

7.2.1 Migration and market price

By market price, we mean a reference value[1] related to the premium prices of all companies on the market; for some reasons (which may be different) the market price may be called fair for this particular market in the current insurance year. For one thing, if the latter is higher than the former, then the customer can decide[2] to find a company that provides services of the same quality at a lower price. Thus, price competition is the driving force behind the migration of policyholders.

Common sense tells us that if a company's price is higher than the market price, then this leads to emigration of customers. On the contrary, if a company's price is lower than the market price, then this leads to immigration of customers. Consequently, the portfolio's volume typically increases due to immigration and decreases due to emigration of customers. Incentives based on the difference in prices are not equally strong for different customers; therefore, they do not all behave the same. The mechanism for portfolio volume's increase or decrease due to migration of insureds is a result of complex interactions between many individual preferences, among which price considerations are of the most importance.

7.2.2 Ultimate migration rate function: M-function

The ultimate migration rate function models how a unit of portfolio's volume changes over infinite time. General requirements for such a function were formulated in [134], Chapter 4. We restrict ourselves to the following simple but sensible special model, called M-function; it is defined as

$$r_\infty(p \mid \varrho) := \begin{cases} \boldsymbol{C}, & 0 \leqslant p \leqslant \boldsymbol{p}, \\ 1 + (\boldsymbol{C} - 1)((\varrho - p)/(\varrho - \boldsymbol{p}))^{l}, & \boldsymbol{p} \leqslant p \leqslant \varrho, \\ 1 - (1 - \boldsymbol{c})((p - \varrho)/(\boldsymbol{P} - \varrho))^{l'}, & \varrho \leqslant p \leqslant \boldsymbol{P}, \\ \boldsymbol{c}, & p \geqslant \boldsymbol{P}, \end{cases} \tag{7.2}$$

---

[1] Such a reference value is a virtual value. This is not necessarily an average of the actual premium rates of individual companies. It can be produced by rating bureaus, which use complex algorithms to calculate it on the basis of loss information furnished by their member-insurers and approved by state regulation.

[2] Bearing in mind the Internet, it is typically assumed that any customer has a free and timely access to information about the prices of any individual company.

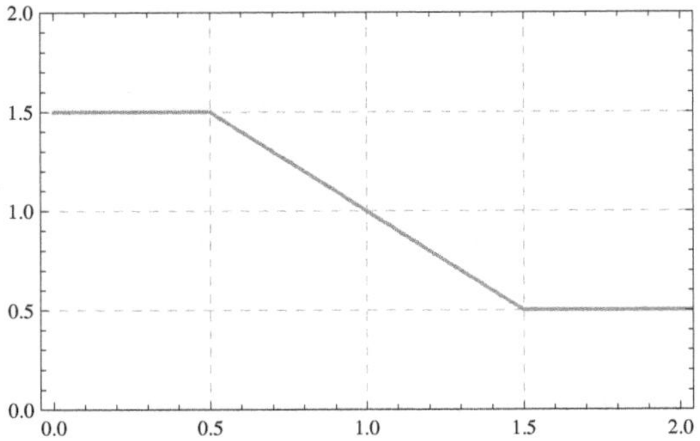

FIGURE 7.1: Ultimate migration rate function (see (7.2)) $r_\infty(p \mid \varrho)$, when $\boldsymbol{c} = 0.5$, $\boldsymbol{C} = 1.5$, $\boldsymbol{p} = 0.5$, $\boldsymbol{P} = 1.5$, $\varrho = 1$, $l = 1$, $l' = 1$.

where $\boldsymbol{c}$ is called insurer's lower capacity, $\boldsymbol{C}$ is called insurer's upper capacity, the values $\boldsymbol{p}$ and $\boldsymbol{P}$, such that $0 < \boldsymbol{p} < \varrho < \boldsymbol{P} < \infty$, are called left and right boundaries of the interval of insureds' sensitivity to price; when the company's price[3] p is equal to the market price ϱ, we naturally have $r_\infty(\varrho \mid \varrho) = 1$.

The main idea of this model is straightforward: the higher the company's price p within the interval $[\boldsymbol{p}, \boldsymbol{P}]$ of insureds' sensitivity to price, the larger the portfolio's volume. In what follows, we assume that $0 < \boldsymbol{c} < 1 < \boldsymbol{C} < \infty$ and that migration vanishes (and the portfolio volume assumes its limit values) when the price p lies outside the interval $[\boldsymbol{p}, \boldsymbol{P}]$.

Regarding the insurer's upper capacity, we assumed that $\boldsymbol{C}$, related to the company's ability to accept new customers, is finite; this assumption is quite natural. Regarding the insurer's lower capacity, we assumed that $\boldsymbol{c}$, related to the customers' loyalty[4] is strictly positive; this assumption requires comments.

As a rule, all policyholders seek to find the company that offers the lowest price for the same service. However, the portion of those who are guided only by this mercantile consideration and who move from company to company guided by this consideration alone, is not so large. This assessment is confirmed by many surveys of policyholders that confirm some stable reluctance to switch insurers. For example (see, e.g., [181], p. 39), a survey of 2462 policyholders is reported in [50], where 54% of respondents admitted that they never tried to understand the prices in auto insurance. To the question "what is the most significant factor for you when buying an insurance policy?", 40% of them answered that it was a company, 29% said that it was an insurance agent, and only 27% said that it was a policy price. In a similar survey of 2004 German insureds (see [168]), it was found that, while 67% of the respondents knew

[3] In this chapter, adjusting the risk model, by price p we mean the premium price per risk per unit time and per unit portfolio's volume. The concept of market price is discussed in [134], Chapter 3.

[4] Some customers remain with the company, although another company may offer a lower price.

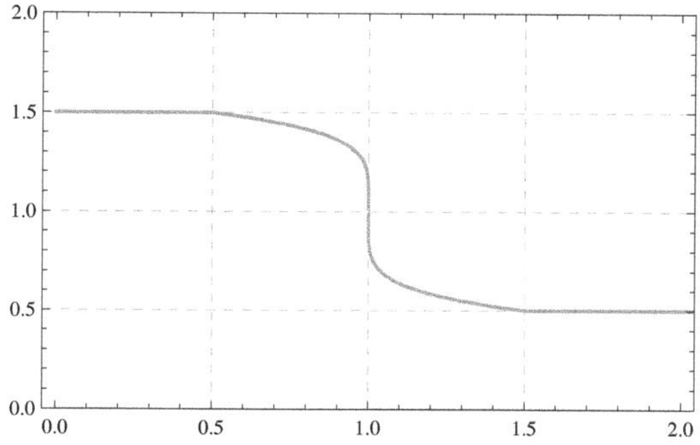

FIGURE 7.2: Ultimate migration rate function (see (7.2)) $r_\infty(p \mid \varrho)$, when $\boldsymbol{c} = 0.5$, $\boldsymbol{C} = 1.5$, $\boldsymbol{p} = 0.5$, $\boldsymbol{P} = 1.5$, $\varrho = 1$, $l = 0.2$, $l' = 0.2$.

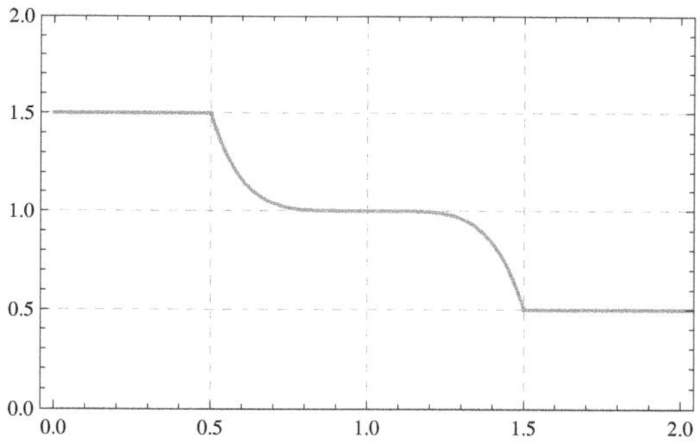

FIGURE 7.3: Ultimate migration rate function (see (7.2)) $r_\infty(p \mid \varrho)$, when $\boldsymbol{c} = 0.5$, $\boldsymbol{C} = 1.5$, $\boldsymbol{p} = 0.5$, $\boldsymbol{P} = 1.5$, $\varrho = 1$, $l = 5.0$, $l' = 5.0$.

about the significant difference in the prices of different automobile insurers, only 35% chose the company on the basis of their favorable premium. In [181], based on this actual state of affairs, it was assumed that if it was possible to go to a company offering lower prices, then only one third of the total number of policyholders would do so. Based on these considerations, we can argue that portfolio volume will never go to zero due to the outflow of policyholders looking for a lower price, i.e., that $\boldsymbol{c} > 0$.

The shape of M-functions can be very different within the interval $[\boldsymbol{p}, \boldsymbol{P}]$ of insureds' sensitivity to price. For example, M-function in Fig. 7.1 is linear. In contrast, for M-function drawn in Fig. 7.2, a significant portfolio's volume is acquired or lost by the insurer if p slightly deviates from the market price ϱ. For M-function drawn in Fig. 7.3, a very small portfolio's volume is acquired and lost when p slightly deviates from ϱ; large changes in the portfolio volume occur only if p significantly deviates from ϱ. The shape of M-function in (7.2) is regulated by choosing the exponents l and l'.

7.2.3 Migration rate function within finite time

Since we are always interested in the annual business process, we are focussed on finite time t. In particular, we deal with the probability of ruin within time t, the corresponding non-ruin capital depending on t, and migration rate functions within finite time t. We introduce migration rate function

$$r_s(p \mid \varrho) := r_\infty(p \mid \varrho) + (1 - r_\infty(p \mid \varrho))\, \varsigma_s, \quad s \geqslant 0, \tag{7.3}$$

where $r_\infty(p \mid \varrho)$ is M-function introduced in (7.2) and ς_s, $s \geqslant 0$, is a function decreasing to zero, as $s \to \infty$. It is called time-speed of migration.

Plainly, the time-speed of migration can be chosen rather arbitrary. For we do not strive for a formal generality, we restrict ourselves to (when time-speed of migration is high) $\varsigma_s := e^{-\epsilon s}$, $s \geqslant 0$, and (when time-speed of migration is low) $\varsigma_s := (1 + s)^{-\epsilon}$, $s \geqslant 0$, where $\epsilon > 0$ is a constant.

Proceeding from migration rate function within time t, which models the time-dynamics of a unit of portfolio volume, we are ready to introduce the process of changing the portfolio volume, taking into account that the initial portfolio volume consists of $\delta > 0$ such units. This process is

$$\mathcal{L}_s(p \mid \varrho) := \delta\, r_s(p \mid \varrho), \quad 0 < s \leqslant t, \tag{7.4}$$

where p denotes the company's price, t denotes the length of the year, δ stands for the initial portfolio's volume, i.e., the number of units, ϱ is the market price, and $r_s(p \mid \varrho)$, $0 < s \leqslant t$, is the migration rate function (7.3).

This formal definition requires informal comments. Firstly, when constructing a collective risk model, we switched from calendar time to operational time measured in monetary units. By measuring time in monetary units and calling t the length of the insurance year, we are dealing with an indicative company's annual turnover, or with an indicative amount of its annual financial transactions. Second, further in this chapter, referring to only one insurance year, the parameter δ is dummy[5]. But it is central in a multi-year model, since portfolio volume in each year is related to portfolio volume in the corresponding previous year, and since portfolio volume has a decisive influence on solvency in both years of hard and soft market (see [134]).

7.2.4 Cumulative migration rate functions

By cumulative (or integrated) migration rate function, which corresponds to the migration rate function $r_s(p \mid \varrho)$ introduced in (7.3), we call

$$\begin{aligned} \Upsilon_s(p \mid \varrho) &:= \int_0^s r_z(p \mid \varrho)\, dz \\ &= r_\infty(p \mid \varrho)\, s + (1 - r_\infty(p \mid \varrho)) \int_0^s \varsigma_z\, dz, \quad 0 < s \leqslant t. \end{aligned} \tag{7.5}$$

[5]Without loss of generality, we could calibrate the initial portfolio's volume to a unit volume.

Plainly, $\Upsilon_0(p \mid \varrho) \equiv 0$. When $p \geqslant \boldsymbol{p}$, we have $\Upsilon_s(p \mid \varrho) = \boldsymbol{C}s + (1 - \boldsymbol{C}) \int_0^s \varsigma_z \, dz$. Under natural assumptions on the time-speed of migration, this equals $\boldsymbol{C}s\,(1 + o(1))$, $s \to \infty$. When $0 \leqslant p \leqslant \boldsymbol{P}$, we have $\Upsilon_s(p \mid \varrho) = \boldsymbol{c}s + (1 - \boldsymbol{c}) \int_0^s \varsigma_z \, dz$. Under natural assumptions on the time-speed of migration, this equals $\boldsymbol{c}s\,(1 + o(1))$, $s \to \infty$.

Explosive migration. When $\varsigma_s = \begin{cases} 1, & s = 0, \\ 0, & s > 0, \end{cases}$ equality (7.3) yields

$$r_s(p \mid \varrho) = \begin{cases} 1, & s = 0, \\ r_\infty(p \mid \varrho), & s > 0, \end{cases}$$

whence

$$\mathcal{L}_s(p \mid \varrho) = \begin{cases} \delta, & s = 0, \\ \delta\, r_\infty(p \mid \varrho), & s > 0. \end{cases}$$

This corresponds to explosive migration: portfolio's volume reaches its value at infinity immediately after the start time.

Fast migration. When $\varsigma_s = e^{-\epsilon s}$, $s \geqslant 0$, where $\epsilon > 0$, we have

$$\int_0^s \varsigma_z \, dz = \int_0^s e^{-\epsilon z} \, dz = \frac{1 - e^{-\epsilon s}}{\epsilon},$$

and equality (7.5) yields

$$\Upsilon_s(p \mid \varrho) = r_\infty(p \mid \varrho)\, s + (1 - r_\infty(p \mid \varrho))\, \frac{1 - e^{-\epsilon s}}{\epsilon}. \tag{7.6}$$

This corresponds to exponentially fast migration: the portfolio's volume approaches its value at infinity very quickly over time.

Slow migration. When $\varsigma_s := (1 + s)^{-\epsilon}$, $s \geqslant 0$, where $\epsilon > 0$, we have

$$\int_0^s \varsigma_z \, dz = \int_0^s (1 + z)^{-\epsilon} \, dz = \begin{cases} \dfrac{(1 + s)^{-\epsilon}(1 + s - (1 + s)^{\epsilon})}{1 - \epsilon}, & \epsilon \neq 1, \\ \ln(1 + s), & \epsilon = 1, \end{cases}$$

and equality (7.5) yields

$$\Upsilon_s(p \mid \varrho) = \begin{cases} s - (1 - r_\infty(p \mid \varrho)) \\ \qquad \times (s - ((1 + s)^{1-\epsilon} - 1)/(1 - \epsilon)), & \epsilon \neq 1, \\ s - (1 - r_\infty(p \mid \varrho))\,(s - \ln(1 + s)), & \epsilon = 1. \end{cases} \tag{7.7}$$

This corresponds to power rate of migration: the portfolio's volume approaches its value at infinity rather slowly over time.

7.2.5 Stochastic migration rate functions

Migration rate function in (7.3) is deterministic. It does not account for the randomness that the migration process caused by price competition may be subject to. In this case, stochastic (see [134], Chapter 4) rather than deterministic migration rate functions are needed.

The change over time of a unit of portfolio's volume, when it occurs in a random, rather than deterministic, way is modeled by stochastic migration rate function corresponding to the ultimate migration rate function $r_\infty(p \mid \varrho)$ introduced in (7.2). This is a continuous-time random process $r_s(p \mid \varrho)$, $s \geqslant 0$, that takes positive values, starts at the unit point, and drifts to $r_\infty(p \mid \varrho)$ in some sense; for example, it may be

$$\lim_{s\to\infty} \mathsf{E}\, r_s(p \mid \varrho) = r_\infty(p \mid \varrho)$$

for all positive p and ϱ.

Effective models of the stochastic migration rate function are given by mean-reverting random processes, which tend to their own long-term mean. An example of such a process (see, e.g., [158], Section 13.1.2) is the Ornstein–Uhlenbeck process X_s, $s \geqslant 0$, that satisfies the stochastic differential equation

$$dX_s = \theta\,(\phi - X_s)\,ds + \sigma\, d\mathsf{W}_s,$$

where $\theta > 0$, ϕ and $\sigma > 0$ are real parameters and W_s, $s \geqslant 0$, is the standard Wiener process. This process is known (see, e.g., [78]) as the only Gaussian Markov process, which tends to its long-term mean $\lim_{s\to\infty} \mathsf{E}X_s$ the faster, the farther from this long-term mean this process is presently located.

7.3 Compound Poisson Risk Model with Migration

In order to avoid excessive complexity, we focus on inhomogeneous Poisson[6] claim arrival processes led by deterministic migration rate functions. With a certain stretching (or compressing) of time, such a process transforms into a homogeneous Poisson process. Thus, a new change of time, which compensates for changes in the portfolio's volume, brings us back to a homogeneous Poisson process over a modified time interval; its length depends on the structure of the migration rate function.

7.3.1 Basic inhomogeneous processes

Risk reserve process and its components. Starting from the cumulative migration rate function $\Upsilon_s(p \mid \varrho)$ defined in (7.5) for a unit of portfolio's

[6] Recall that when the portfolio's volume is large, it is natural to assume it Poisson.

volume and assuming that the initial portfolio's volume consists of δ such units, we define the claim arrival process in the model with migration as the inhomogeneous Poisson process $\mathcal{N}_s(p \mid \varrho)$, $0 \leqslant s \leqslant t$, whose integrated rate function is $\delta\,\Upsilon_s(p \mid \varrho)$, $0 \leqslant s \leqslant t$.

As usual, we assume that such claim arrival process is independent of i.i.d. claim sizes $Y_i \stackrel{d}{=} Y$, $i = 1, 2, \ldots$. Accordingly, the corresponding outflow of claim payments is modeled by the claim payout process

$$\mathcal{V}_s(p \mid \varrho) := \sum_{i=1}^{\mathcal{N}_s(p \mid \varrho)} Y_i, \quad 0 \leqslant s \leqslant t, \tag{7.8}$$

or 0, if $\mathcal{N}_s(p \mid \varrho) = 0$. The balance between the premiums inflow and claims outflow within a year of length t, when the initial capital is u, is modeled by the risk reserve process

$$\mathcal{R}_s(p \mid \varrho) := u + p\,(\delta\,\Upsilon_s(p \mid \varrho)) - \mathcal{V}_s(p \mid \varrho), \quad 0 \leqslant s \leqslant t. \tag{7.9}$$

Bearing in mind the first equality in (7.22), we have

$$\mathsf{E}\,\mathcal{R}_t(p \mid \varrho) = u + p\,(\delta\,\Upsilon_t(p \mid \varrho)) - \mathsf{E}\,Y\,\delta\,\Upsilon_t(p \mid \varrho),$$

whence $\mathsf{E}\,Y$ is a critical price value; this is a threshold between profitable and unprofitable business for the company in question.

Reduction to homogeneous processes. Since the cumulative migration rate function $\Upsilon_s(p \mid \varrho)$, regarded as a function of time $s \geqslant 0$, is positive-valued, continuous and non-decreasing, we have[7]

$$\mathcal{N}_s(p \mid \varrho) \stackrel{d}{=} N_{\Upsilon_s(p \mid \varrho)}, \quad 0 \leqslant s \leqslant t. \tag{7.10}$$

This reduces[8] the inhomogeneous Poisson process $\mathcal{N}_s(p \mid \varrho)$, whose integrated rate function is $\delta\,\Upsilon_s(p \mid \varrho)$, to the homogeneous Poisson process[9] N_s (see (1.10)), whose intensity is δ.

In the same way, we have

$$\mathcal{V}_s(p \mid \varrho) \stackrel{d}{=} V_{\Upsilon_s(p \mid \varrho)}, \quad \mathcal{R}_s(p \mid \varrho) \stackrel{d}{=} R_{\Upsilon_s(p \mid \varrho)}, \quad 0 \leqslant s \leqslant t, \tag{7.11}$$

---

[7]For transition from homogeneous to inhomogeneous process, we use the change of time $s \mapsto \Upsilon_s(p \mid \varrho)$. For transition from inhomogeneous to homogeneous process, we use the inverse change of time $s \mapsto \Upsilon_s^{-1}(p \mid \varrho)$. Since $\Upsilon_s(p \mid \varrho)$ is continuous and monotone function of time s, the inverse function $\Upsilon_s^{-1}(p \mid \varrho)$ always exists.

[8]This well-known fact can be found in many books. See, e.g., [31], pp. 38, 39 and Section 2.2.3, or [88], Section 2.1 on p. 33, or [8], Remark 1.6 on p. 60, or [51], Chapter 4, Section 7. Recall that $\mathsf{E}\,\mathcal{N}_s(p \mid \varrho) = \delta\,\Upsilon_s(p \mid \varrho)$, and the change of time leads to a homogeneous Poisson process with intensity δ. Although generally (see, e.g., [51], p. 96) the homogeneous Poisson process is set with unit rate, we take it δ which is not always equal to unit.

[9]In other words, to homogeneous renewal process whose inter-renewal interval T is exponentially distributed with parameter δ, or whose mean is $\mathsf{E}T = 1/\delta$.

and

$$\inf_{0 \leqslant s \leqslant t} \mathcal{R}_s(p \mid \varrho) \overset{d}{=} \inf_{0 \leqslant s \leqslant \Upsilon_t(p \mid \varrho)} R_s, \tag{7.12}$$

where (see (1.9)) $V_s := \sum_{i=1}^{N_s} Y_i$ or 0, if $N_s = 0$, is a homogeneous compound Poisson process with intensity δ, and $R_s := u + p\,\delta s - V_s$.

When $p \geqslant \boldsymbol{P}$, migration rate function $r_s(p \mid \varrho)$ is $\boldsymbol{c}+(1-\boldsymbol{c})\,\varsigma_s$, $s \geqslant 0$, which tends to $\boldsymbol{c}$, as s increases. Therefore, under natural assumptions on the time-speed of migration, we have $\Upsilon_s(p \mid \varrho) = \boldsymbol{c}s + (1-\boldsymbol{c}) \int_0^s \varsigma_z\,dz = \boldsymbol{c}s\,(1+o(1))$, whence[10]

$$\begin{aligned} \mathcal{R}_s(p \mid \varrho) &:= u + p\,(\delta\, \Upsilon_s(p \mid \varrho)) - \mathcal{V}_s(p \mid \varrho) \\ &\overset{d}{\approx} u + p\,(\delta \boldsymbol{c}s) - V_{\boldsymbol{c}s}, \quad 0 \leqslant s \leqslant t, \end{aligned}$$

for all $p \geqslant \boldsymbol{P}$. In the same way,

$$\begin{aligned} \mathcal{R}_s(p \mid \varrho) &:= u + p\,(\delta\, \Upsilon_s(p \mid \varrho)) - \mathcal{V}_s(p \mid \varrho) \\ &\overset{d}{\approx} u + p\,(\delta\, \boldsymbol{C}s) - V_{\boldsymbol{C}s}, \quad 0 \leqslant s \leqslant t, \end{aligned}$$

for all $0 \leqslant p \leqslant \boldsymbol{p}$.

Re-parametrization of premium intensity. This is clear that (when the definitions are given in a reasonable way) the model without migration should be a special case of the model with migration (7.8)–(7.9). One can argue like that: migration is absent if the company in question is the only one on the market and the market price ϱ always coincides with the price p of this company. This implies (see (7.5)) that the cumulative migration rate function $\Upsilon_s(p \mid \varrho)$ reduces to s and $\mathcal{N}_s(p \mid \varrho)$, $\mathcal{V}_s(p \mid \varrho)$ reduce to N_s and V_s respectively.

However (see (7.9)), $\mathcal{R}_s(p \mid \varrho)$ reduces to

$$R_s := u + p(\delta s) - V_s, \quad 0 \leqslant s \leqslant t,$$

which differs from

$$R_s := u + cs - V_s, \quad 0 \leqslant s \leqslant t, \tag{7.13}$$

where u is the initial capital and c is the premium intensity (or price).

This difference is minor and comes down to the fact that in the model with migration it is convenient to factor the premium intensity c into the product of premium intensity per unit portfolio's volume p and the number of units in this portfolio δ. The first factor p remains unchanged throughout the entire insurance year, for a company cannot change its tariff at will, and the second factor δ remains unchanged in the model without migration, but obviously changes throughout the year in the model with migration.

---

[10] Here $\overset{d}{\approx}$ is replaced with $\overset{d}{=}$ when migration is explosive.

Thus, we apply re-parametrization, moving from c in the model without migration to the product $p\,\delta$ of the annual premium rate p, or premium per unit time and per unit of portfolio's volume, which holds constant throughout the whole insurance year, and δ, which is the number of portfolio's volume units at the initial time. When migration is present and time goes on, this number δ changes due to migration. If migration is absent, δ remains unchanged all year long.

7.3.2 Technical instruments of ERS-analysis

Probability of ruin. The probability of ruin in finite time t for the model with migration is

$$\mathsf{P}\Big\{\inf_{0<s\leqslant t} \mathcal{R}_s(p \mid \varrho) < 0\Big\} = \mathsf{P}\Big\{\inf_{0\leqslant s\leqslant \Upsilon_t(p \mid \varrho)} R_s < 0\Big\}, \tag{7.14}$$

where $\mathcal{R}_s(p \mid \varrho)$ and R_s are defined in (7.9) and (5.1) respectively. This equality follows straightforwardly from equality (7.12).

Non-ruin capital. By $\boldsymbol{u}_{\alpha,t}(p \mid \varrho)$, $p \geqslant 0$, we denote a positive solution (with respect to u) to the equation (cf. (1.18) and (1.28))

$$\mathsf{P}\Big\{\inf_{0<s\leqslant t} \mathcal{R}_s(p \mid \varrho) < 0\Big\} = \alpha, \tag{7.15}$$

where $\alpha > 0$ is a small value. We call this solution fixed-probability level, or non-ruin capital of level α. By (7.14), this is rewritten as

$$\mathsf{P}\Big\{\inf_{0\leqslant s\leqslant \Upsilon_t(p \mid \varrho)} R_s < 0\Big\} = \alpha, \tag{7.16}$$

where R_s is defined in (5.1).

Based on the study in Chapter 3 for a model, when Y is exponentially distributed, and in Chapters 5 and 6, when Y is non-exponentially distributed, information that can be obtained about $\boldsymbol{u}_{\alpha,t}(p \mid \varrho)$ is contained in (asymptotic or non-asymptotic) lower and upper bounds on $\boldsymbol{u}_{\alpha,t}(p \mid \varrho)$. We will denote them $\underline{\boldsymbol{u}}_{\alpha,t}(p \mid \varrho)$ and $\overline{\boldsymbol{u}}_{\alpha,t}(p \mid \varrho)$, accordingly.

Intrinsic value. The annual intrinsic value of a company, when migration is modeled by $r_s(p \mid \varrho)$ (see (7.3)), is

$$\mathcal{E}_{\alpha,t}(p \mid \varrho) := \max\left\{0,\ \frac{\mathsf{E}\,\mathcal{R}_t(p \mid \varrho)\,|_{u=\boldsymbol{u}_{\alpha,t}(p \mid \varrho)}}{\boldsymbol{u}_{\alpha,t}(p \mid \varrho)}\right\}. \tag{7.17}$$

This is the ratio of the company's average earning to the non-ruin capital, both related to time t.

Commenting on this definition, we recall that managers must fight for investors' money. The main tool for attracting new and retaining old investors is making regular reports of earnings per share[11]. But the forecast for one year is a simplified indicator of a limited worth. A more informative indicator is the discounted amount of money that can be extracted from the company for the duration of its future life[12]. Therefore, the vital endeavor is to link the company's strategy with a sequence of annual intrinsic values in order to evaluate this indicator for a longer period of time, at least consisting of several insurance years.

We can rewrite (7.17) as

$$\mathcal{E}_{\alpha,t}(p \mid \varrho) = \max\left\{0,\ 1 + \frac{\delta(p - \mathsf{E}\,Y)\,\Upsilon_t(p \mid \varrho)}{\boldsymbol{u}_{\alpha,t}(p \mid \varrho)}\right\}. \tag{7.18}$$

Indeed, bearing in mind that (see first equality in (7.22))

$$\mathsf{E}\,\mathcal{V}_t(p \mid \varrho) = \delta\,\mathsf{E}\,Y\,\Upsilon_t(p \mid \varrho)$$

and (see (7.9)) that

$$\mathcal{R}_t(p \mid \varrho)\,|_{u=\boldsymbol{u}_{\alpha,t}(p \mid \varrho)} = \boldsymbol{u}_{\alpha,t}(p \mid \varrho) + (p\,\delta)\,\Upsilon_t(p \mid \varrho) - \mathcal{V}_t(p \mid \varrho),$$

we have

$$\mathsf{E}\,\mathcal{R}_t(p \mid \varrho)\,|_{u=\boldsymbol{u}_{\alpha,t}(p \mid \varrho)} = \boldsymbol{u}_{\alpha,t}(p \mid \varrho) + \delta(p - \mathsf{E}\,Y)\,\Upsilon_t(p \mid \varrho).$$

Put it in (7.17), whence (7.18).

From (7.18), it immediately follows that $\mathcal{E}_{\alpha,t}(\mathsf{E}\,Y \mid \varrho) = 1$, i.e., when the company's price p is equal to the critical price value $\mathsf{E}\,Y$, the entire annual income of the company is spent on maintaining its solvency.

Conservative intrinsic value. Let us write

$$\begin{aligned} \overline{\mathcal{E}}_{\alpha,t}(p \mid \varrho) &= \max\left\{0,\ 1 + \frac{(p - \mathsf{E}\,Y)\,\delta\,\Upsilon_t(p \mid \varrho)}{\underline{\boldsymbol{u}}_{\alpha,t}(p \mid \varrho)}\right\}, \quad 0 \leqslant p \leqslant \mathsf{E}\,Y, \\ \underline{\mathcal{E}}_{\alpha,t}(p \mid \varrho) &= \max\left\{0,\ 1 + \frac{(p - \mathsf{E}\,Y)\,\delta\,\Upsilon_t(p \mid \varrho)}{\overline{\boldsymbol{u}}_{\alpha,t}(p \mid \varrho)}\right\}, \quad p > \mathsf{E}\,Y, \end{aligned} \tag{7.19}$$

and call (7.19) conservative intrinsic values. This corresponds to the lower $\underline{\boldsymbol{u}}_{\alpha,t}(p \mid \varrho)$ and upper $\overline{\boldsymbol{u}}_{\alpha,t}(p \mid \varrho)$ (asymptotic) bounds on the non-ruin capital $\boldsymbol{u}_{\alpha,t}(p \mid \varrho)$. It is noteworthy that

$$\mathcal{E}_{\alpha,t}(\mathsf{E}\,Y \mid \varrho) = \overline{\mathcal{E}}_{\alpha,t}(\mathsf{E}\,Y \mid \varrho) = \underline{\mathcal{E}}_{\alpha,t}(\mathsf{E}\,Y \mid \varrho) = 1.$$

[11] W. Buffett said that when calculating intrinsic values, we regularly report our per-share book value which is an easily calculable number, though one of limited use.

[12] According to W. Buffett, intrinsic value is the most important concept that offers a single logical approach to assessing the relative attractiveness of investments and businesses. Intrinsic value can be defined simply: it is the discounted value of cash that can be taken out of a business during the remaining period of its life.

To clarify the reasons for choosing such a name, we note that

$$\begin{aligned} &\mathcal{E}_{\alpha,t\,|\,\delta,\rho}(p \mid \varrho) \leqslant \overline{\mathcal{E}}_{\alpha,t}(p \mid \varrho), \quad 0 \leqslant p \leqslant \mathsf{E}\,Y, \\ &\mathcal{E}_{\alpha,t\,|\,\delta,\rho}(p \mid \varrho) \geqslant \underline{\mathcal{E}}_{\alpha,t}(p \mid \varrho), \quad p > \mathsf{E}\,Y. \end{aligned} \tag{7.20}$$

When business is unprofitable, i.e., when $0 \leqslant p \leqslant \mathsf{E}\,Y$, the intrinsic value $\mathcal{E}_{\alpha,t}(p \mid \varrho)$ cannot rise above the conservative intrinsic value $\overline{\mathcal{E}}_{\alpha,t}(p \mid \varrho)$ obtained by replacing $\boldsymbol{u}_{\alpha,t}(p \mid \varrho)$ by $\underline{\boldsymbol{u}}_{\alpha,t}(p \mid \varrho)$. When business is profitable, i.e., when $p > \mathsf{E}\,Y$, the intrinsic value $\mathcal{E}_{\alpha,t}(p \mid \varrho)$ cannot fall below the conservative intrinsic value $\underline{\mathcal{E}}_{\alpha,t}(p \mid \varrho)$ obtained by replacing $\boldsymbol{u}_{\alpha,t}(p \mid \varrho)$ by $\overline{\boldsymbol{u}}_{\alpha,t}(p \mid \varrho)$.

Conclusion. Three major instruments of ERS-analysis are migration rate function $r_s(p \mid \varrho)$, non-ruin capital $\boldsymbol{u}_{\alpha,t}(p \mid \varrho)$, and annual intrinsic value $\mathcal{E}_{\alpha,t}(p \mid \varrho)$. For the reasons stated above, the latter can be replaced by the conservative intrinsic value $\underline{\mathcal{E}}_{\alpha,t}(p \mid \varrho)$. Keeping this triplet within certain limits is not easy. In particular, raising solvency and revenue can interfere with each other. Even if a satisfactory balance can be found between expansion, revenue, and solvency, this is usually not achieved in a single way.

From the angle of mathematical implementation of ERS-analysis, the main complexity is to find a suitable analytical expression for the non-ruin capital $\boldsymbol{u}_{\alpha,t}(p \mid \varrho)$, or to devise a numerical procedure for its numerical evaluation. In the model without migration, it was shown that we can find at best (asymptotic) bounds for $\boldsymbol{u}_{\alpha,t}(p \mid \varrho)$. Therefore, relying on Chapter 3, we will address such bounds in the risk model with migration, when Y is exponentially distributed. Then, relying on Chapters 5 and 6, we will consider the risk model with migration, when Y is non-exponentially, or generally, distributed.

7.4 ERS-analysis, when Y is Exponentially Distributed

In this section, we assume that Y is exponentially distributed with parameter ρ. Our goal is to extend the results of Chapter 3 to this model. Bearing in mind (7.10)–(7.12), to switch from a model without migration to a model with migration, we make the formal changes $c \rightarrowtail \delta p$ and $s \rightarrowtail \varUpsilon_s(p \mid \varrho)$, where $0 \leqslant s \leqslant t$.

7.4.1 Claim amount distribution

The following theorem concerning claim amount distribution at time s, is a direct corollary of Theorem 3.1 and of the first equality in (7.11).

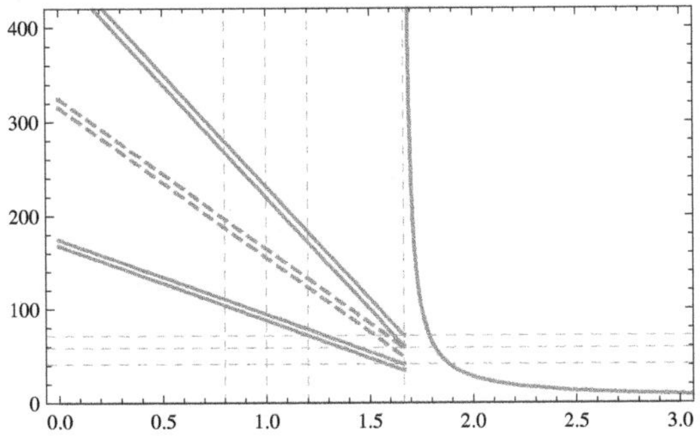

FIGURE 7.4: Graphs (X-axis is p) of two-sided bounds for $\boldsymbol{u}_{\alpha,t\,|\,\delta,\rho}(p \mid \varrho)$, $0 \leqslant p \leqslant \mathsf{E}\,Y$, and upper bound for $\boldsymbol{u}_{\alpha,t\,|\,\delta,\rho}(p \mid \varrho)$, $p > \mathsf{E}\,Y$; see Table 7.1.

Theorem 7.1 *In the risk model with migration, when* Y *is exponentially distributed with positive parameter* ρ, *we have for all positive* δ, ρ, p, ϱ, *and* s

$$\begin{aligned} \mathsf{P}\{\, \mathcal{V}_s(p \mid \varrho) \leqslant x\} &= e^{-\delta\,\Upsilon_s(p\,|\,\varrho)} + e^{-\delta\,\Upsilon_s(p\,|\,\varrho)} (\delta\rho\,\Upsilon_s(p \mid \varrho))^{1/2} \\ &\quad \times \int_0^x z^{-1/2} I_1(2\sqrt{\delta\rho\,\Upsilon_s(p \mid \varrho)\, z}\,)\, e^{-\rho z}\, dz, \qquad x > 0. \end{aligned} \tag{7.21}$$

Moreover (see (3.3)),

$$\begin{aligned} &\mathsf{E}\,\mathcal{V}_s(p \mid \varrho) = (\delta/\rho)\,\Upsilon_s(p \mid \varrho), \quad \mathsf{D}\,\mathcal{V}_s(p \mid \varrho) = 2\,(\delta/\rho^2)\,\Upsilon_s(p \mid \varrho), \\ &\mathsf{E}\,\mathcal{V}_s^2(p \mid \varrho) = (\delta/\rho^2)\,\Upsilon_s(p \mid \varrho)\,(\delta\,\Upsilon_s(p \mid \varrho) + 2), \\ &\mathsf{E}\,\mathcal{V}_s^3(p \mid \varrho) = (\delta/\rho^3)\,\Upsilon_s(p \mid \varrho)\,((\delta\,\Upsilon_s(p \mid \varrho))^2 + 6\,(\delta\,\Upsilon_s(p \mid \varrho) + 1)). \end{aligned} \tag{7.22}$$

7.4.2 Probability of ruin

The following theorem is a direct corollary of Theorem 3.4. Its proof is straightforward from equality (7.14).

Theorem 7.2 *In the classical risk model with migration, when claim sizes are exponentially distributed with parameter* $\rho > 0$, *we have*

$$\mathsf{P}\Big\{ \inf_{0<s\leqslant t} \mathcal{R}_s(p \mid \varrho) < 0 \Big\} = \mathsf{P}\Big\{ \inf_{s>0} \mathcal{R}_s(p \mid \varrho) < 0 \Big\} - \frac{1}{\pi} \int_0^{\pi} f(x)\, dx, \tag{7.23}$$

where, writing for brevity $g := \rho\, p$,

$$\mathsf{P}\Big\{ \inf_{s>0} \mathcal{R}_s(p \mid \varrho) < 0 \Big\} = \begin{cases} g^{-1} \exp\{-\rho u\,(1 - g^{-1})\}, & g > 1, \\ 1, & g \leqslant 1, \end{cases} \tag{7.24}$$

TABLE 7.1: An inventory of models in Figs. 7.4–7.7

	Model, when Y exponentially distributed, when $\varsigma_s \equiv 0$ (explosive migration at time zero), $r_\infty(p \mid \varrho)$ as in (7.2), with $\boldsymbol{c} = 0.5$, $\boldsymbol{C} = 1.5$, $\boldsymbol{p} = 0.8$, $\boldsymbol{\varrho} = 1.0$, $\boldsymbol{P} = 1.2$, $\mathsf{E}\,Y = 5/3$ (i.e., $\rho = 3/5$), $\delta = 4/5$, $\alpha = 0.05$, and $t = 200$.
Fig. 7.4:	Two-sided bounds for $\boldsymbol{u}_{\alpha,t\,\vert\,\delta,\rho}(p \mid \varrho)$, $0 \leqslant p \leqslant \mathsf{E}\,Y$, and upper bound for $\boldsymbol{u}_{\alpha,t\,\vert\,\delta,\rho}(p \mid \varrho)$, $p > \mathsf{E}\,Y$, when $l = l' = 1$. Horizontal grid lines: $\mathsf{E}\,Y\sqrt{2\,\delta}\,\kappa_{\alpha/2}\sqrt{\boldsymbol{C}t} = 71.57$, $\mathsf{E}\,Y\sqrt{2\,\delta}\,\kappa_{\alpha/2}\sqrt{t} = 58.44$, $\mathsf{E}\,Y\sqrt{2\,\delta}\,\kappa_{\alpha/2}\sqrt{\boldsymbol{c}t} = 41.32$.
Fig. 7.5:	Upper bound $\overline{\boldsymbol{u}}_{\alpha,t\,\vert\,\delta,\rho}(p \mid \varrho)$ for $\boldsymbol{u}_{\alpha,t\,\vert\,\delta,\rho}(p \mid \varrho)$, when $l = l' = 1$.
Fig. 7.6:	Upper bound $\overline{\boldsymbol{u}}_{\alpha,t\,\vert\,\delta,\rho}(p \mid \varrho)$ for $\boldsymbol{u}_{\alpha,t\,\vert\,\delta,\rho}(p \mid \varrho)$, when $l = l' = 0.2$.
Fig. 7.7:	Upper bound $\overline{\boldsymbol{u}}_{\alpha,t\,\vert\,\delta,\rho}(p \mid \varrho)$ for $\boldsymbol{u}_{\alpha,t\,\vert\,\delta,\rho}(p \mid \varrho)$, when $l = l' = 5.0$.

TABLE 7.2: An inventory of models in Figs. 7.8–7.10

	Model, when Y is exponentially distributed, when $\varsigma_s \equiv 0$ (explosive migration at time zero), $r_\infty(p \mid \varrho)$ as in (7.2), with $\boldsymbol{c} = 0.5$, $\boldsymbol{C} = 1.5$, $\boldsymbol{p} = 2.0$, $\boldsymbol{\varrho} = 2.2$, $\boldsymbol{P} = 2.4$, $\mathsf{E}\,Y = 5/3$ (i.e., $\rho = 3/5$), $\delta = 4/5$, $\alpha = 0.05$, and $t = 200$.
Fig. 7.8:	Conservative intrinsic value $\underline{\mathcal{E}}_{\alpha,t\,\vert\,\delta,\rho}(p \mid \varrho)$, when $l = l' = 1.0$.
Fig. 7.9:	Conservative intrinsic value $\underline{\mathcal{E}}_{\alpha,t\,\vert\,\delta,\rho}(p \mid \varrho)$, when $l = l' = 0.2$.
Fig. 7.10:	Conservative intrinsic value $\underline{\mathcal{E}}_{\alpha,t\,\vert\,\delta,\rho}(p \mid \varrho)$, when $l = l' = 5.0$.

and

$$\begin{aligned} f(x) &= g^{-1}(1 + g^{-1} - 2g^{-1/2}\cos x)^{-1} \\ &\quad \times \exp\{\rho u\,(g^{-1/2}\cos x - 1) - \Upsilon_t(p \mid \varrho)\,\delta g\,(1 + g^{-1} - 2g^{-1/2}\cos x)\} \\ &\quad \times (\cos(\rho u\, g^{-1/2}\sin x) - \cos(\rho u\, g^{-1/2}\sin x + 2x)). \end{aligned}$$

7.4.3 Non-ruin capital

The following theorem is a direct corollary of Theorem 3.6. To get (7.26) from (7.25), we note that (see (7.2)) $r_\infty(0 \mid \varrho) = \boldsymbol{C}$, whence (see (7.5))

$$\begin{aligned} \Upsilon_t(0 \mid \varrho) &= r_\infty(0 \mid \varrho)\,t + (1 - r_\infty(0 \mid \varrho)) \int_0^t \varsigma_z\,dz \\ &= \boldsymbol{C}\,t + (1 - \boldsymbol{C}) \int_0^t \varsigma_z\,dz. \end{aligned}$$

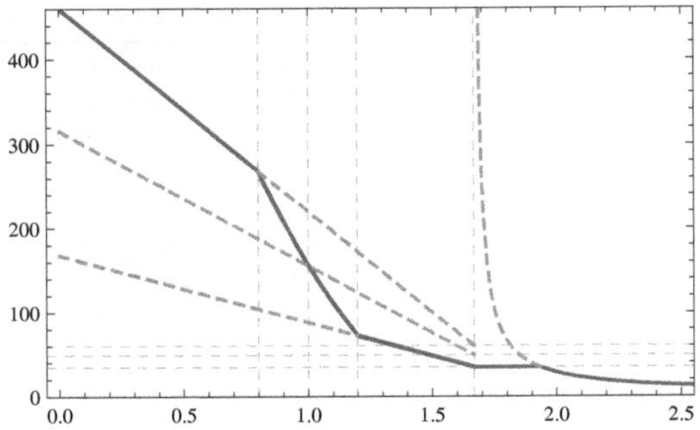

FIGURE 7.5: Graphs (X-axis is p) of $\overline{\boldsymbol{u}}_{\alpha,t\,|\,\delta,\rho}(p \mid \boldsymbol{\varrho})$ in Model (A) with migration; see Table 7.1.

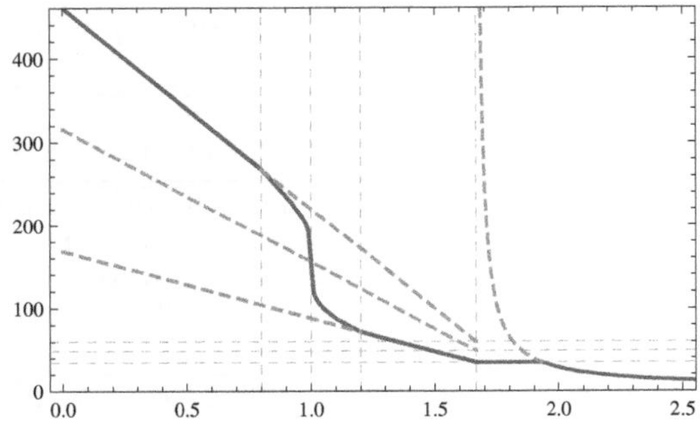

FIGURE 7.6: Graphs (X-axis is p) of $\overline{\boldsymbol{u}}_{\alpha,t\,|\,\delta,\rho}(p \mid \boldsymbol{\varrho})$ in Model (A) with migration; see Table 7.1.

Theorem 7.3 *In the risk model with migration, when Y is exponentially distributed with parameter ρ, we have*

$$\boldsymbol{u}_{\alpha,t\,|\,\delta,\rho}(0 \mid \boldsymbol{\varrho}) = \delta\, \mathsf{E}\, Y\, \varUpsilon_t(0 \mid \boldsymbol{\varrho}) + \sqrt{2\,\delta}\, \mathsf{E}\, Y\, \kappa_\alpha \sqrt{\varUpsilon_t(0 \mid \boldsymbol{\varrho})}\,(1 + o(1)), \quad t \to \infty. \quad (7.25)$$

Moreover, if $\int_0^t \varsigma_z\, dz = o(\sqrt{t})$, $t \to \infty$, then

$$\boldsymbol{u}_{\alpha,t\,|\,\delta,\rho}(0 \mid \boldsymbol{\varrho}) = \delta\, \mathsf{E}\, Y \boldsymbol{C}\, t + \sqrt{2\,\delta}\, \mathsf{E}\, Y\, \kappa_\alpha \sqrt{\boldsymbol{C}\, t}\,(1 + o(1)), \quad t \to \infty. \quad (7.26)$$

The following theorem is a direct corollary of Theorem 3.7.

Theorem 7.4 *In the risk model with migration, when Y is exponentially distributed with parameter ρ, we have*

$$\boldsymbol{u}_{\alpha,t\,|\,\delta,\rho}(\mathsf{E}\, Y \mid \boldsymbol{\varrho}) = \sqrt{2\,\delta}\, \mathsf{E}\, Y\, \kappa_{\alpha/2} \sqrt{\varUpsilon_t(\mathsf{E}\, Y \mid \boldsymbol{\varrho})}\,(1 + o(1)), \quad t \to \infty. \quad (7.27)$$

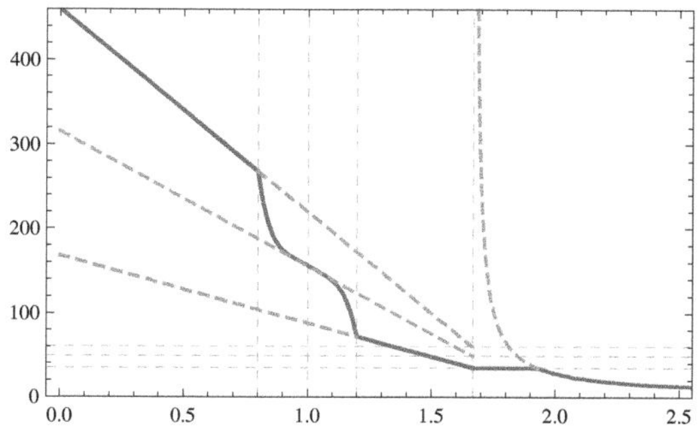

FIGURE 7.7: Graphs (X-axis is p) of $\overline{\boldsymbol{u}}_{\alpha,t\,|\,\delta,\rho}(p \mid \varrho)$ in Model (A) with migration; see Table 7.1.

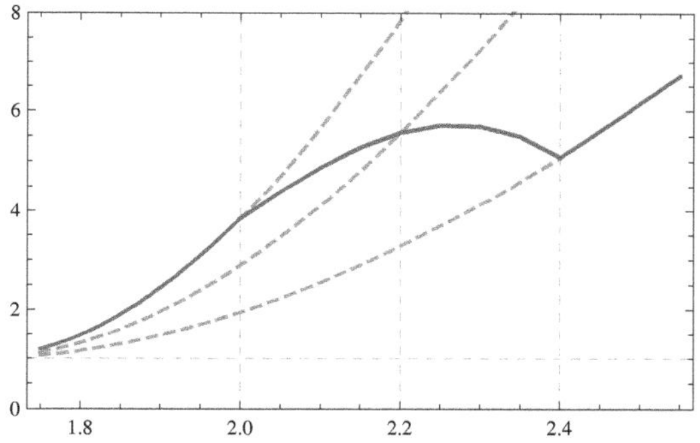

FIGURE 7.8: Graphs (X-axis is p) of $\underline{\mathcal{E}}_{\alpha,t\,|\,\delta,\rho}(p \mid \varrho)$; see Table 7.2.

The following theorem is a direct corollary of Theorem 3.8.

Theorem 7.5 *In the risk model with migration, when* Y *is exponentially distributed with parameter* ρ*, we have*

$$\boldsymbol{u}_{\alpha,t\,|\,\delta,\rho}(p \mid \varrho) = \begin{cases} \delta(\mathsf{E}\,Y - p)\,\Upsilon_t(p \mid \varrho) & \\ \qquad +\sqrt{2\,\delta}\,\mathsf{E}\,Y\,\mathsf{z}_{\alpha,t}(p \mid \varrho)\sqrt{\Upsilon_t(p \mid \varrho)}, & 0 \leqslant p \leqslant \mathsf{E}\,Y, \\ \sqrt{2\,\delta}\,\mathsf{E}\,Y\,\mathsf{z}_{\alpha,t}(p \mid \varrho)\sqrt{\Upsilon_t(p \mid \varrho)}, & p > \mathsf{E}\,Y, \end{cases}$$

where, for t *sufficiently large, the function* $\mathsf{z}_{\alpha,t}(p \mid \varrho)$ *is positive, continuous, and monotone increasing, as* p *increases from* 0 *to* $\mathsf{E}\,Y$*, monotone decreasing, as* p *increases from* $\mathsf{E}\,Y$ *to* ∞*, and such that*[13]*, when* $0 \leqslant p \leqslant \mathsf{E}\,Y$*,*

$$\lim_{t\to\infty} \mathsf{z}_{\alpha,t}(p \mid \varrho) = \kappa_\alpha,$$

[13]We recall that $0 < \kappa_\alpha < \kappa_{\alpha/2}$, when $0 < \alpha < 1/2$.

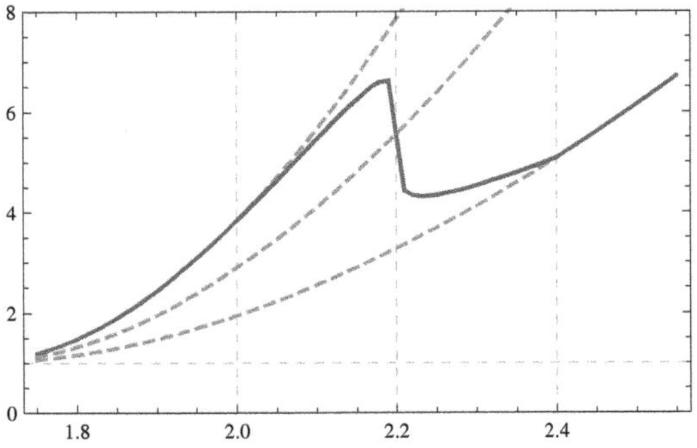

FIGURE 7.9: Graphs (X-axis is p) of $\underline{\mathcal{E}}_{\alpha,t\,|\,\delta,\rho}(p \mid \varrho)$; see Table 7.2.

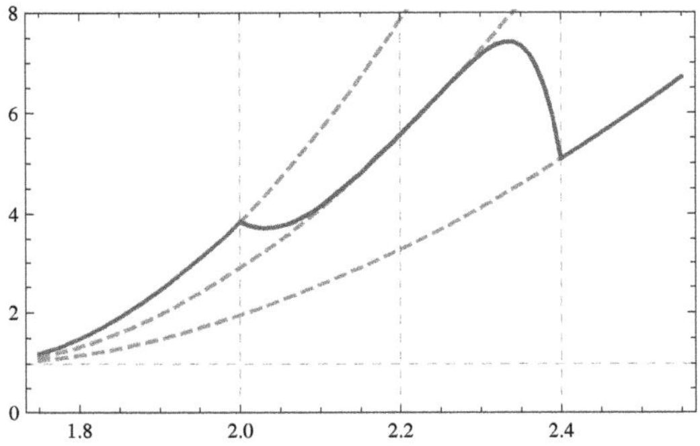

FIGURE 7.10: Graphs (X-axis is p) of $\underline{\mathcal{E}}_{\alpha,t\,|\,\delta,\rho}(p \mid \varrho)$; see Table 7.2.

when $p > \mathsf{E}\,Y$,

$$\lim_{t\to\infty} \mathsf{z}_{\alpha,t}(p \mid \varrho) = 0,$$

and $\lim_{t\to\infty} \mathsf{z}_{\alpha,t}(\mathsf{E}\,Y \mid \varrho) = \kappa_{\alpha/2}$.

In the same way as in the model without migration, the case $0 \leqslant p \leqslant \mathsf{E}\,Y$ is of primary interest. In this case, the non-ruin capital $\boldsymbol{u}_{\alpha,t\,|\,\delta,\rho}(p \mid \varrho)$ is a function of t, growing with t. In the case $p > \mathsf{E}\,Y$, when p is sufficiently larger than $\mathsf{E}\,Y$, the non-ruin capital is a function of t bounded by a constant.

First, when $0 \leqslant p \leqslant \mathsf{E}\,Y$, the non-ruin capital $\boldsymbol{u}_{\alpha,t\,|\,\delta,\rho}(p \mid \varrho)$ lies between $\boldsymbol{u}_{\alpha,\boldsymbol{C}t\,|\,\delta,\rho}(p \mid \varrho)$ and $\boldsymbol{u}_{\alpha,\boldsymbol{c}t\,|\,\delta,\rho}(p \mid \varrho)$. Note that the former (whose upper and lower bounds are shown in Fig. 7.4 by upper slanted lines) is the non-ruin capital in the model with the maximum possible portfolio's volume and without migration, whereas the latter (whose upper and lower bounds are shown in Fig. 7.4 by lower slanted lines) is the non-ruin capital in the model with minimum possible portfolio's volume and without migration. Moreover, $\boldsymbol{u}_{\alpha,t}(\mathsf{E}\,Y \mid \varrho)$ coincides with the non-ruin capital at the point $p = \mathsf{E}\,Y$ in the

TABLE 7.3: An inventory of models in Figs. 7.11–7.12

	Model, when Y is exponentially distributed, when $\varsigma_s \equiv 0$ (explosive migration at time zero), $r_\infty(p \mid \varrho)$ as in (7.2), with $\boldsymbol{c} = 0.15$, $\boldsymbol{C} = 2.5$, $\boldsymbol{p} = 2.28$, $\boldsymbol{\varrho} = 2.4$, $\boldsymbol{P} = 2.52$, $\mathsf{E}\,Y = 2.0$ (i.e., $\rho = 0.5$), $\delta = 4.0$, $\alpha = 0.12$, and $t = 300$.
Fig. 7.11:	$\mathcal{E}_{\alpha,t}(p \mid \varrho)$ (simulated values) and $\underline{\mathcal{E}}_{\alpha,t}(p \mid \varrho)$ calculated using (7.19), when $l = l' = 1$.
Fig. 7.12:	$\mathcal{E}_{\alpha,t}(p \mid \varrho)$ (simulated values) and $\underline{\mathcal{E}}_{\alpha,t}(p \mid \varrho)$ calculated using (7.19), when $l = l' = 0.3$.
Fig. 7.13:	$\mathcal{E}_{\alpha,t}(p \mid \varrho)$ (simulated values) and $\underline{\mathcal{E}}_{\alpha,t}(p \mid \varrho)$ calculated using (7.19), when $l = l' = 3.3$.

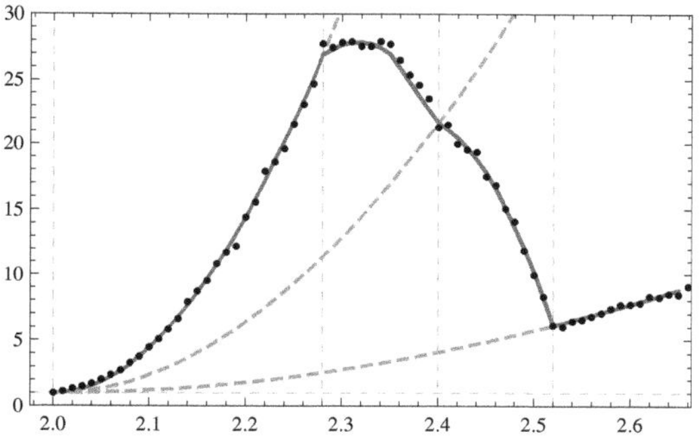

FIGURE 7.11: Graphs (X-axis is p) of $\mathcal{E}_{\alpha,t}(p \mid \varrho)$ (simulated values) and $\underline{\mathcal{E}}_{\alpha,t}(p \mid \varrho)$; see Table 7.3.

model without migration (whose upper and lower bounds are shown in Fig. 7.4 by dashed lines). Second, when $p > \mathsf{E}\,Y$, the upper bound on $\boldsymbol{u}_{\alpha,t\,|\,\delta,\rho}(p \mid \varrho)$, independent of t, is

$$-\frac{\ln(\alpha p\,\rho)}{\rho - 1/p}. \tag{7.28}$$

This is a solution (w.r.t. u) to the equation

$$(\rho p)^{-1} \exp\{-\rho u\,(1 - (\rho p)^{-1})\} = \alpha,$$

whose left-hand side is (see (7.24)) the probability of ultimate ruin.

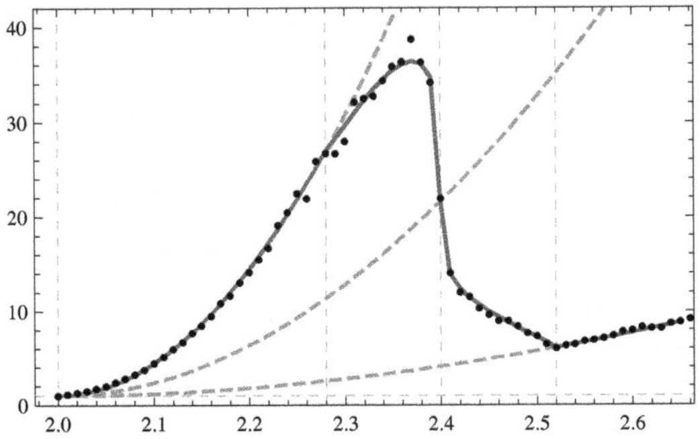

FIGURE 7.12: Graphs (X-axis is p) of $\boldsymbol{\mathcal{E}}_{\alpha,t}(p \mid \boldsymbol{\varrho})$ (simulated values) and $\underline{\mathcal{E}}_{\alpha,t}(p \mid \boldsymbol{\varrho})$; see Table 7.3.

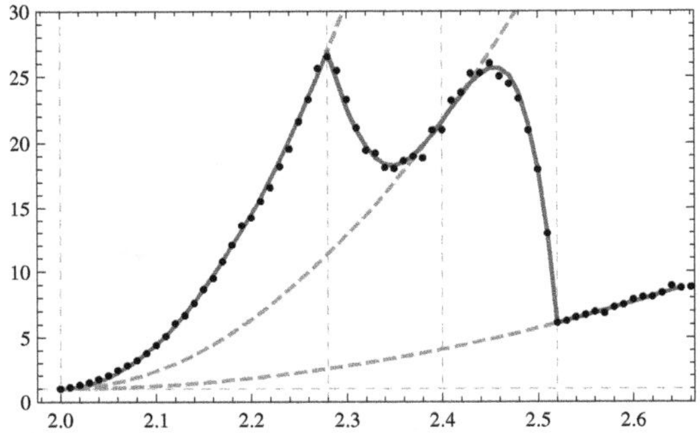

FIGURE 7.13: Graphs (X-axis is p) of $\boldsymbol{\mathcal{E}}_{\alpha,t}(p \mid \boldsymbol{\varrho})$ (simulated values) and $\underline{\mathcal{E}}_{\alpha,t}(p \mid \boldsymbol{\varrho})$; see Table 7.3.

Elementary bounds. In Fig. 7.4, when $0 \leqslant p \leqslant \mathsf{E}\,Y$, the graphs ($X$-axis is p) of the functions

$$\begin{aligned}
&\delta(\mathsf{E}\,Y - p)\,\boldsymbol{C}t + \sqrt{2\,\delta}\,\mathsf{E}\,Y\,\kappa_\alpha\sqrt{\boldsymbol{C}t}, && \delta(\mathsf{E}\,Y - p)\,\boldsymbol{C}t + \sqrt{2\,\delta}\,\mathsf{E}\,Y\,\kappa_{\alpha/2}\sqrt{\boldsymbol{C}t},\\
&\delta(\mathsf{E}\,Y - p)t + \sqrt{2\,\delta}\,\mathsf{E}\,Y\,\kappa_\alpha\sqrt{t}, && \delta(\mathsf{E}\,Y - p)t + \sqrt{2\,\delta}\,\mathsf{E}\,Y\,\kappa_{\alpha/2}\sqrt{t},\\
&\delta(\mathsf{E}\,Y - p)\,\boldsymbol{c}t + \sqrt{2\,\delta}\,\mathsf{E}\,Y\,\kappa_\alpha\sqrt{\boldsymbol{c}t}, && \delta(\mathsf{E}\,Y - p)\,\boldsymbol{c}t + \sqrt{2\,\delta}\,\mathsf{E}\,Y\,\kappa_{\alpha/2}\sqrt{\boldsymbol{c}t}.
\end{aligned} \tag{7.29}$$

and, when $p > \mathsf{E}\,Y$, of the function

$$-\frac{\ln(\alpha p\,\rho)}{\rho - 1/p}, \tag{7.30}$$

are drawn.

The functions in (7.29) are the upper and lower (asymptotic) bounds for the non-ruin capital, when migration is absent and the initial portfolio's volume is $\delta\boldsymbol{p}$, δ, and $\delta\boldsymbol{P}$ respectively. Plainly, the non-ruin capital $\boldsymbol{u}_{\alpha,t\,|\,\delta,\rho}(p \mid \boldsymbol{\varrho})$, when migration is present and is modeled by the migration rate function (7.3), where the ultimate migration rate function is the M-function (7.2), and were the time-speed of migration ς_t decreases to zero fast enough, as $t \to \infty$, when $0 \leqslant p \leqslant \boldsymbol{P}$, lies between the functions $\delta(\mathsf{E}\,Y - p)\,\boldsymbol{C}t + \sqrt{2\,\delta}\;\mathsf{E}\,Y\,\kappa_{\alpha}\sqrt{\boldsymbol{C}t}$, $\delta(\mathsf{E}\,Y - p)\,\boldsymbol{C}t + \sqrt{2\,\delta}\;\mathsf{E}\,Y\,\kappa_{\alpha/2}\sqrt{\boldsymbol{C}t}$, when $p > \boldsymbol{p}$, lies between the functions $\delta(\mathsf{E}\,Y - p)\,\boldsymbol{c}t + \sqrt{2\,\delta}\;\mathsf{E}\,Y\,\kappa_{\alpha}\sqrt{\boldsymbol{c}t}$ and $\delta(\mathsf{E}\,Y - p)\,\boldsymbol{c}t + \sqrt{2\,\delta}\;\mathsf{E}\,Y\,\kappa_{\alpha/2}\sqrt{\boldsymbol{c}t}$ and, as it is shown in Figs. 7.5–7.7, is descending in the interval $\boldsymbol{P} \leqslant p \leqslant \boldsymbol{p}$, passing, when p is equal to $\boldsymbol{\varrho}$, through a point which lies between the values $\delta(\mathsf{E}\,Y - \boldsymbol{\varrho})t + \sqrt{2\,\delta}\,\mathsf{E}\,Y\,\kappa_{\alpha}\sqrt{t}$ and $\delta(\mathsf{E}\,Y - \boldsymbol{\varrho})t + \sqrt{2\,\delta}\,\mathsf{E}\,Y\,\kappa_{\alpha/2}\sqrt{t}$.

The function (7.30), which does not depend on t, is the upper bound for all of the following non-ruin capitals: $\boldsymbol{u}_{\alpha,t\,|\,\delta,\rho}(p \mid \boldsymbol{\varrho})$, the non-ruin capital in the model without migration, where the initial portfolio's volume is either $\delta\boldsymbol{p}$, or δ, or $\delta\boldsymbol{P}$.

Bounds based on convexity. We proceed with refined bounds. Let us introduce the shorthand notation

$$u^{*}_{\alpha,t\,|\,\delta,\rho} := \sqrt{2\,\delta}\,\mathsf{E}\,Y\,\kappa_{\alpha/2}\sqrt{\varUpsilon_t(\mathsf{E}\,Y \mid \boldsymbol{\varrho})}\,(1+o(1)), \quad t \to \infty, \tag{7.31}$$

and

$$P^{*}_{\alpha,t\,|\,\delta,\rho} := \mathsf{E}\,Y\left(\frac{u^{*}_{\alpha,t\,|\,\delta,\rho} - \mathsf{E}\,Y\ln\alpha}{u^{*}_{\alpha,t\,|\,\delta,\rho} + \mathsf{E}\,Y\ln\alpha}\right). \tag{7.32}$$

Let us write

$$\underline{\boldsymbol{u}}_{\alpha,t\,|\,\delta,\rho}(p \mid \boldsymbol{\varrho}) = \delta\,(\mathsf{E}\,Y - p)\,\varUpsilon_t(p \mid \boldsymbol{\varrho}) + \frac{\kappa_{\alpha}}{\kappa_{\alpha/2}}u^{*}_{\alpha,t\,|\,\delta,\rho}, \quad 0 \leqslant p \leqslant \mathsf{E}\,Y, \tag{7.33}$$

and

$$\overline{\boldsymbol{u}}_{\alpha,t\,|\,\delta,\rho}(p \mid \boldsymbol{\varrho}) = \begin{cases} \delta(\mathsf{E}\,Y - p)\,\varUpsilon_t(p \mid \boldsymbol{\varrho}) + u^{*}_{\alpha,t\,|\,\delta,\rho}, & 0 \leqslant p \leqslant \mathsf{E}\,Y, \\ \dfrac{(u^{*}_{\alpha,t\,|\,\delta,\rho} + \mathsf{E}\,Y\ln\alpha)^2}{4\,(\mathsf{E}\,Y)^2\ln\alpha}\,p \\ \qquad - \dfrac{(u^{*}_{\alpha,t\,|\,\delta,\rho} - \mathsf{E}\,Y\ln\alpha)^2}{4\,\mathsf{E}\,Y\ln\alpha}, & \mathsf{E}\,Y < p \leqslant P^{*}_{\alpha,t\,|\,\delta,\rho}, \\ -\dfrac{p\,\mathsf{E}\,Y\ln\alpha}{p - \mathsf{E}\,Y}, & p > P^{*}_{\alpha,t\,|\,\delta,\rho}. \end{cases} \tag{7.34}$$

The following theorem is a direct corollary of Theorem 3.18.

Theorem 7.6 *For $t > 0$ sufficiently large, we have*

$$\underline{\boldsymbol{u}}_{\alpha,t\,|\,\delta,\rho}(p \mid \boldsymbol{\varrho}) \leqslant \boldsymbol{u}_{\alpha,t\,|\,\delta,\rho}(p \mid \boldsymbol{\varrho}) \leqslant \overline{\boldsymbol{u}}_{\alpha,t\,|\,\delta,\rho}(p \mid \boldsymbol{\varrho}),$$

when $0 \leqslant p \leqslant \mathsf{E}\,Y$, and

$$\boldsymbol{u}_{\alpha,t\,|\,\delta,\rho}(p \mid \boldsymbol{\varrho}) \leqslant \overline{\boldsymbol{u}}_{\alpha,t\,|\,\delta,\rho}(p \mid \boldsymbol{\varrho}),$$

when $p > \mathsf{E}\,Y$.

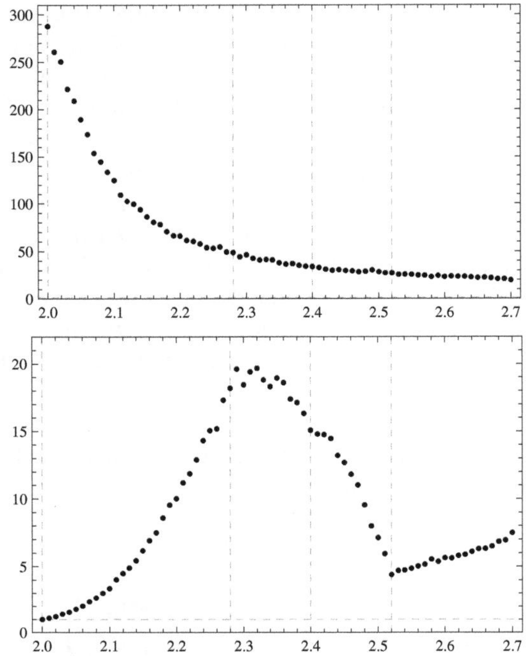

FIGURE 7.14: Graphs (X-axis is p) of simulated values of $\boldsymbol{u}_{\alpha,t}(p \mid \boldsymbol{\varrho})$ and $\mathcal{E}_{\alpha,t}(p \mid \boldsymbol{\varrho})$. Model with migration, when Y is 2-mixture of exponential with parameters $\rho_1 = 0.3$, $\rho_2 = 1.5$, $p = q = 0.5$, when $\varsigma_s \equiv 0$ (explosive migration at time zero), $r_\infty(p \mid \boldsymbol{\varrho})$ as in (7.2), with $\boldsymbol{c} = 0.15$, $\boldsymbol{C} = 2.5$, $\boldsymbol{p} = 2.28$, $\boldsymbol{\varrho} = 2.4$, $\boldsymbol{P} = 2.52$, $l = l' = 1$, $\mathsf{E}\,Y = 2.0$ (i.e., $\rho = 0.5$), $\delta = 4$, $\alpha = 0.12$, and $t = 300$.

When $0 \leqslant p \leqslant \mathsf{E}\,Y$, the shape of non-ruin capital $\boldsymbol{u}_{\alpha,t\,|\,\delta,\rho}(p \mid \boldsymbol{\varrho})$ strongly depends on the shape of migration rate function. On the contrary, when $p > \mathsf{E}\,Y$, with p sufficiently larger than $\mathsf{E}\,Y$, the shape of migration rate function has very little effect on the shape of non-ruin capital $\boldsymbol{u}_{\alpha,t\,|\,\delta,\rho}(p \mid \boldsymbol{\varrho})$. This is graphically illustrated in Figs. 7.5–7.7. When $0 \leqslant p \leqslant \mathsf{E}\,Y$, the non-ruin capital is evaluated numerically as a solution to equation (7.15), whose left-hand side is given in (7.23). When $p > \mathsf{E}\,Y$, we draw the upper bound (7.28) and use the fact that the non-ruin capital monotone decreases, as p increases; by our choice of migration rate function, portfolio's volume in this case drops to the minimum possible value.

In Fig. 7.5, the ultimate migration rate function is set similar to one drawn in Fig. 7.1: we put $l = 1$, $l' = 1$, and the shape of this migration rate function is linear. For simplicity[14], the time-speed of migration ς_s is set explosive at time

[14] Very little will change if we take $\varsigma_s := e^{-\epsilon s}$, $s \geqslant 0$, or even $\varsigma_s := (1+s)^{-\epsilon}$, $s \geqslant 0$, where $\epsilon > 0$ is a constant.

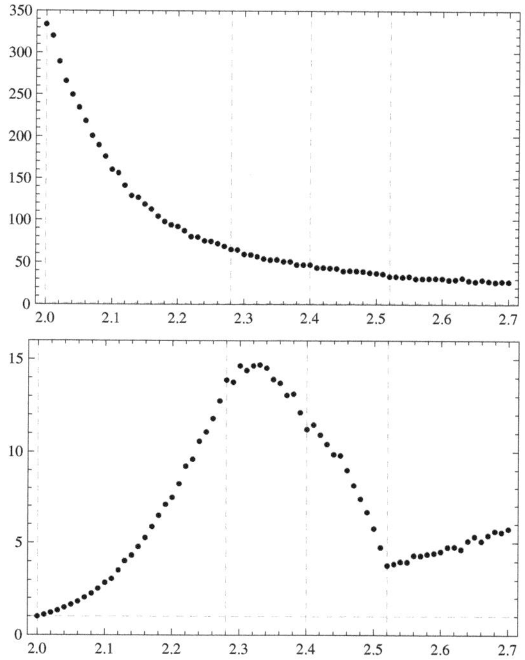

FIGURE 7.15: Graphs (X-axis is p) of simulated values of $\boldsymbol{u}_{\alpha,t}(p \mid \varrho)$ and $\mathcal{E}_{\alpha,t}(p \mid \varrho)$. Model with migration, when Y is Pareto with parameters $a = 3$, $b = 0.25$, when $\varsigma_s \equiv 0$ (explosive migration at time zero), $r_\infty(p \mid \varrho)$ as in (7.2), with $\boldsymbol{c} = 0.15$, $\boldsymbol{C} = 2.5$, $\boldsymbol{p} = 2.28$, $\varrho = 2.4$, $\boldsymbol{P} = 2.52$, $l = l' = 1$, $\mathsf{E}\,Y = 2.0$ (i.e., $\rho = 0.5$), $\delta = 4$, $\alpha = 0.12$, and $t = 300$.

zero, i.e., portfolio's volume reaches its value at infinity immediately after the initial time moment. In Fig. 7.6, the ultimate migration rate function is taken similar to one drawn in Fig. 7.2: we put $l = 0.2$, $l' = 0.2$, and the shape of this migration rate function is convex–concave. In Fig. 7.7, the ultimate migration rate function is taken similar to one drawn in Fig. 7.3: we put $l = 5.0$, $l' = 5.0$, and the shape of this migration rate function is concave–convex. Differences in Figs. 7.5–7.7 are especially noticeable in the vicinity of the point $\varrho = 1$.

7.4.4 Conservative intrinsic value

Let us put (7.33) and (7.34) in (7.19) and write[15]

$$\overline{\mathcal{E}}_{\alpha,t\,|\,\delta,\rho}(p \mid \varrho) = \frac{\sqrt{2}\,\mathsf{E}\,Y\,\kappa_\alpha}{\sqrt{\delta}(\mathsf{E}\,Y - p)\sqrt{\Upsilon_t(p \mid \varrho)} + \sqrt{2}\,\mathsf{E}\,Y\,\kappa_\alpha}, \quad 0 \leqslant p \leqslant \mathsf{E}\,Y,$$

[15]Note that $\overline{\mathcal{E}}_{\alpha,t\,|\,\delta,\rho}(p \mid \varrho) \leqslant 1$ and $\overline{\mathcal{E}}_{\alpha,t\,|\,\delta,\rho}(p \mid \varrho) \leqslant 1$, when $0 \leqslant p \leqslant \mathsf{E}\,Y$.

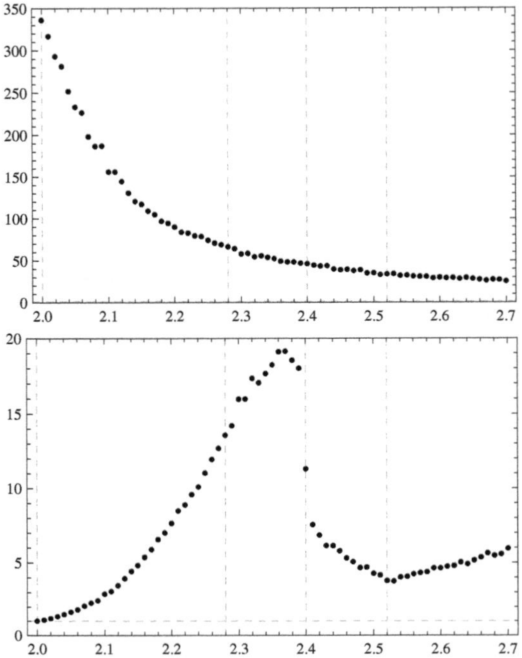

FIGURE 7.16: The same as in Fig. 7.15, but with $l = l' = 0.3$.

and

$$\underline{\mathcal{E}}_{\alpha,t\,|\,\delta,\rho}(p \mid \varrho) = \begin{cases} \dfrac{\sqrt{2}\,\mathsf{E}\,Y\,\kappa_{\alpha/2}}{\sqrt{\delta}(\mathsf{E}\,Y - p)\sqrt{\Upsilon_t(p \mid \varrho)} + \sqrt{2}\,\mathsf{E}\,Y\,\kappa_{\alpha/2}}, & 0 \leqslant p \leqslant \mathsf{E}\,Y, \\ 1 + \dfrac{\delta(p - \mathsf{E}\,Y)(\mathsf{E}\,Y)^2 4 \ln\alpha\,\Upsilon_t(p \mid \varrho)}{(u^*_{\alpha,t\,|\,\delta,\rho} + \mathsf{E}\,Y\ln\alpha)^2 p - (u^*_{\alpha,t\,|\,\delta,\rho} - \mathsf{E}\,Y\ln\alpha)^2\,\mathsf{E}\,Y}, & \mathsf{E}\,Y < p \leqslant P^*_{\alpha,t\,|\,\delta,\rho}, \\ 1 - \dfrac{\delta(p - \mathsf{E}\,Y)^2\,\Upsilon_t(p \mid \varrho)}{p\,\mathsf{E}\,Y\ln\alpha}, & p > P^*_{\alpha,t\,|\,\delta,\rho}, \end{cases}$$

where $u^*_{\alpha,t\,|\,\delta,\rho}$ and $P^*_{\alpha,t\,|\,\delta,\rho}$ are defined in (7.31) and (7.32). The following theorem is a direct corollary of equalities (7.19) and Theorem 7.6.

Theorem 7.7 *For $t > 0$ sufficiently large, we have*

$$\underline{\mathcal{E}}_{\alpha,t\,|\,\delta,\rho}(p \mid \varrho) \leqslant \boldsymbol{\mathcal{E}}_{\alpha,t\,|\,\delta,\rho}(p \mid \varrho) \leqslant \overline{\mathcal{E}}_{\alpha,t\,|\,\delta,\rho}(p \mid \varrho)$$

when $0 \leqslant p \leqslant \mathsf{E}\,Y$, *and*

$$\boldsymbol{\mathcal{E}}_{\alpha,t\,|\,\delta,\rho}(p \mid \varrho) \geqslant \underline{\mathcal{E}}_{\alpha,t\,|\,\delta,\rho}(p \mid \varrho)$$

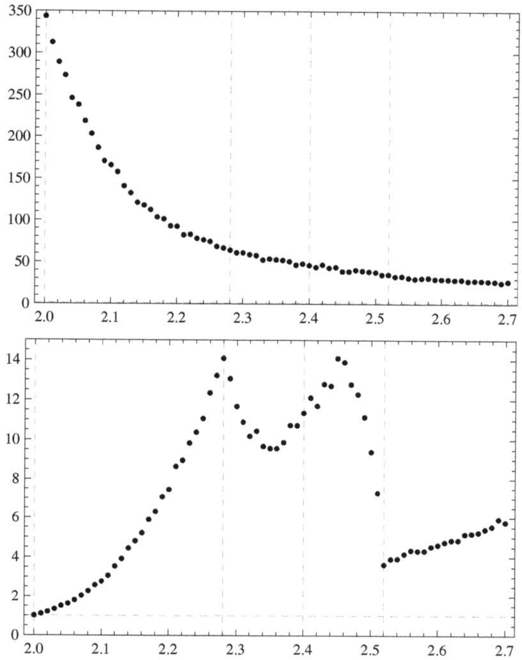

FIGURE 7.17: The same as in Fig. 7.15, but with $l = l' = 3.3$.

when $p > \mathsf{E}\,Y$.

When $p > \mathsf{E}\,Y$, with p sufficiently larger than $\mathsf{E}\,Y$, the shape of conservative intrinsic value $\underline{\mathcal{E}}_{\alpha,t\,|\,\delta,\rho}(p \mid \boldsymbol{\varrho})$ strongly depends on the shape of migration rate function. In this sense, the situation is exactly the opposite of what we have observed in the case of non-ruin capital $\boldsymbol{u}_{\alpha,t\,|\,\delta,\rho}(p \mid \boldsymbol{\varrho})$.

In Fig. 7.8, the ultimate migration rate function is set similar to one drawn in Fig. 7.1: we put $l = 1$, $l' = 1$, and the shape of this migration rate function is linear. In Fig. 7.9, the only difference is that $l = 0.2$, $l' = 0.2$. and the ultimate migration rate function $r_\infty(p \mid \boldsymbol{\varrho})$ is convex–concave (cf. Fig. 7.2). In Fig. 7.10, the only difference is that $l = 5.0$, $l' = 5.0$, and the ultimate migration rate function $r_\infty(p \mid \boldsymbol{\varrho})$ is concave–convex (cf. Fig. 7.3).

Conservative intrinsic value, which measures the attractiveness of an insurance business to investors, is only of interest when $p > \mathsf{E}\,Y$, i.e., when this business is profitable. When $0 \leqslant p \leqslant \mathsf{E}\,Y$, one can hardly talk about the attractiveness of a business that is unprofitable.

7.5 ERS-analysis, when Y is Generally Distributed

7.5.1 Non-ruin capital

The following theorem extends Theorem 7.3 to non-exponentially distributed Y. It is a direct corollary of Theorem 5.13.

Theorem 7.8 *In the risk model with migration, assume that $f_Y(x)$ is bounded above by a finite constant, $D^2 > 0$, $\mathsf{E}(Y^3) < \infty$, and $\boldsymbol{p} \geqslant 0$. We have*

$$\boldsymbol{u}_{\alpha,t}(0 \mid \varrho) = \frac{\Upsilon_t(0 \mid \varrho)}{M} + \frac{D}{M^{3/2}}\, \kappa_\alpha \sqrt{\Upsilon_t(0 \mid \varrho)}\, (1 + o(1)), \quad t \to \infty.$$

Moreover, if[16] $\int_0^t \varsigma_z \, dz = o(\sqrt{t})$, $t \to \infty$, *then*

$$\boldsymbol{u}_{\alpha,t}(0 \mid \varrho) = \frac{\boldsymbol{C}\, t}{M} + \frac{D}{M^{3/2}}\, \kappa_\alpha \sqrt{\boldsymbol{C}\, t}\, (1 + o(1)), \quad t \to \infty.$$

The following theorem extends Theorem 7.4 to non-exponentially distributed Y. It is a direct corollary of Theorem 5.14.

Theorem 7.9 *In the risk model with migration, assume that $f_Y(x)$ is bounded above by a finite constant, $D^2 > 0$, $\mathsf{E}(Y^3) < \infty$. We have*

$$\boldsymbol{u}_{\alpha,t}(\mathsf{E}\, Y \mid \varrho) = \frac{D}{M^{3/2}}\, \kappa_{\alpha/2} \sqrt{\Upsilon_t(\mathsf{E}\, Y \mid \varrho)}\, (1 + o(1)), \quad t \to \infty.$$

The following theorem extends Theorem 7.5 to non-exponentially distributed Y. It is a direct corollary of Theorem 5.15.

Theorem 7.10 *In the risk model with migration, assume that $f_Y(x)$ is bounded above by a finite constant, $D^2 > 0$, $\mathsf{E}(Y^3) < \infty$. We have*

$$\boldsymbol{u}_{\alpha,t}(p \mid \varrho) = \begin{cases} (\mathsf{E}\, Y - p)\, \delta\, \Upsilon_t(p \mid \varrho) & \\ \qquad + \dfrac{D}{M^{3/2}}\, \mathsf{z}_{\alpha,t}(p \mid \varrho) \sqrt{\Upsilon_t(p \mid \varrho)}, & 0 \leqslant p \leqslant \mathsf{E}\, Y, \\ \dfrac{D}{M^{3/2}}\, \mathsf{z}_{\alpha,t}(p \mid \varrho) \sqrt{\Upsilon_t(p \mid \varrho)}, & p > \mathsf{E}\, Y, \end{cases}$$

where, for t sufficiently large, the function $\mathsf{z}_{\alpha,t}(p \mid \varrho)$ is continuous and monotone increases from κ_α to $\kappa_{\alpha/2}$, as p increases from 0 to $\mathsf{E}\, Y$, and monotone decreases from $\kappa_{\alpha/2}$ to 0, as p increases from $\mathsf{E}\, Y$ to ∞. In particular, $\mathsf{z}_{\alpha,t}(\mathsf{E}\, Y \mid \varrho) = \kappa_{\alpha/2}\, (1 + o(1))$, as $t \to \infty$.

[16] In particular, if $\varsigma_t = e^{-\epsilon t}$, $t \to \infty$, where $\epsilon > 0$.

When $0 \leqslant p \leqslant \mathsf{E}\,Y$, the function $\boldsymbol{u}_{\alpha,t}(p \mid \varrho)$ lies between

$$(\mathsf{E}\,Y - p)\,\delta\,\Upsilon_t(p \mid \varrho) + \frac{D}{M^{3/2}}\,\kappa_\alpha\sqrt{\Upsilon_t(p \mid \varrho)}$$

and

$$(\mathsf{E}\,Y - p)\,\delta\,\Upsilon_t(p \mid \varrho) + \frac{D}{M^{3/2}}\,\kappa_{\alpha/2}\sqrt{\Upsilon_t(p \mid \varrho)}.$$

When $p > \mathsf{E}\,Y$, case study, like in Chapter 6, is required.

7.5.2 Conservative intrinsic value

The result for $u_{\alpha,t}(c)$ is sufficient as an upper bound that solves the solvency problem, but is poorly adapted to calculate the intrinsic value.

When $0 \leqslant p \leqslant \mathsf{E}\,Y$, we have

$$\underline{\mathcal{E}}_{\alpha,t}(p \mid \varrho)\,(1 + o(1)) \leqslant \boldsymbol{\mathcal{E}}_{\alpha,t}(p \mid \varrho) \leqslant \overline{\mathcal{E}}_{\alpha,t}(p \mid \varrho)\,(1 + o(1)),$$

as $t \to \infty$, where

$$\begin{aligned}\overline{\mathcal{E}}_{\alpha,t}(p \mid \varrho) &= \max\left\{0,\ 1 - \frac{(\mathsf{E}\,Y - p)\,\delta\,\Upsilon_t(p \mid \varrho)}{\underline{u}_{\alpha,t}(p \mid \varrho)}\right\}\\ &= \max\left\{0,\ \frac{D\,\kappa_\alpha}{(\mathsf{E}\,Y - p)\,\delta\,M^{3/2}\sqrt{\Upsilon_t(p \mid \varrho)} + D\,\kappa_\alpha}\right\}\end{aligned}$$

and

$$\begin{aligned}\underline{\mathcal{E}}_{\alpha,t}(p \mid \varrho) &= \max\left\{0,\ 1 - \frac{(\mathsf{E}\,Y - p)\,\delta\,\Upsilon_t(p \mid \varrho)}{\overline{u}_{\alpha,t}(p \mid \varrho)}\right\}\\ &= \max\left\{0,\ \frac{D\,\kappa_{\alpha/2}}{(\mathsf{E}\,Y - p)\,\delta\,M^{3/2}\sqrt{\Upsilon_t(p \mid \varrho)} + D\,\kappa_{\alpha/2}}\right\}.\end{aligned}$$

When $p > \mathsf{E}\,Y$, case study, like in Chapter 6, is required.

7.5.3 Algorithm of simulation and numerical illustrations

We re-visit (see [134], Chapter 11) the numerical illustrations of ERS-analysis, obtained by simulation.

Algorithm of simulation. The starting point for the entire simulation process is selection of the pseudo-random number generators. First, to get pseudo-random numbers from uniform distribution on the interval [0, 1], we apply Mersenne twister[17] (see [105]). Second, to have pseudo-random numbers

[17]The Mersenne twister is the default pseudo-random number generator in most standard packages. It is most widely used in applications. Note that in [136] we used instead the standard linear congruential random number generator.

selected from a non-uniform, but absolutely continuous distribution, we use the inverse function method (see, e.g., [58]).

For numerical evaluation of the ruin capital $\boldsymbol{u}_{\alpha,t}(p \mid \delta, \boldsymbol{\varrho}, l)$ which is a solution (w.r.t. u) of Eq. (7.15) (or (7.16)), we select the final interval $[p_{\min}, p_{\max}]$ as variation range of p. We choose $p_{\min} = \mathsf{E}\,Y$, where $\mathsf{E}\,Y$ is fixed and equal to 2 for all calculations which will be held in this paper, and $p_{\max} = 2.7$ which is markedly greater than $\boldsymbol{\varrho} = 2.4$. On $[p_{\min}, p_{\max}]$ we introduce the uniform lattice[18].

$$\mathcal{P} = \{p_i,\ i = 0, 1, \ldots, n_{\mathcal{P}}\}$$

with span $\Delta p = 0.01$, i.e., we put $p_0 = p_{\min}$, and $p_i = p_{i-1} + \Delta p$, $i = 1, 2, \ldots, n_{\mathcal{P}}$.

For each p_i from this lattice, we calculate[19] $\boldsymbol{u}_{\alpha,t}(p_i \mid \delta, \boldsymbol{\varrho}, l)$. To do it, we address the probability of ruin $\boldsymbol{\psi}_t(p_i \mid u, \delta, \boldsymbol{\varrho}, l)$ and consider it as a function of u. We wish to find $u > 0$ which makes $\boldsymbol{\psi}_t(p_i \mid u, \delta, \boldsymbol{\varrho}, l)$ different from α by less than 0.001. We do it in several iterations. We start with numerical evaluation of $\boldsymbol{\psi}_t(p_i \mid u, \delta, \boldsymbol{\varrho}, l)$ for u sufficiently large[20]. Bearing in mind the monotony of $\boldsymbol{\psi}_t(p_i \mid u, \delta, \boldsymbol{\varrho}, l)$ w.r.t. u, we localize the required value of u by bisection of successive intervals. In each step we choose that one which contains α.

This search method is based on successive numerical evaluations of the probability of ruin $\boldsymbol{\psi}_t(p_i \mid u, \delta, \boldsymbol{\varrho}, l)$ for selected u. We do it with standard simulation method. Namely, we simulate at first the bundle consisting of $N = 2000$ trajectories of the process $R_s(p_i \mid u, \delta, \boldsymbol{\varrho}, l)$, $0 \leqslant s \leqslant \tau(t)$, where $\tau(t) = \Upsilon_t(p_i \mid \boldsymbol{\varrho}, l)$. Then we form the fraction, the numerator of which is the number of trajectories which dropped below zero at least once within the time interval $[0, \Upsilon_t(p_i \mid \boldsymbol{\varrho}, l)]$, and the denominator of which is N. As the required value of the ruin probability, we choose this fraction.

To evaluate numerically the annual company's intrinsic values $\boldsymbol{\mathcal{E}}_{\alpha,t}(p \mid \delta, \boldsymbol{\varrho}, l)$ on the interval $[p_{\min}, p_{\max}]$, we address the same lattice $\mathcal{P}$ and apply the similar algorithm.

7.6 Conclusions

In the model with migration, when Y is non-exponentially distributed, it seems unrealistic to hope for a comprehensive analytical ERS-analysis. Firstly, in the case $0 < p \leqslant \mathsf{E}\,Y$, the approximation for $\boldsymbol{u}_{\alpha,t}(p \mid \boldsymbol{\varrho})$, as $t \to \infty$, as well as the expressions for the bounds $\overline{\boldsymbol{u}}_{\alpha,t\,|\,\delta,\rho}(p \mid \boldsymbol{\varrho})$ and $\underline{\boldsymbol{u}}_{\alpha,t\,|\,\delta,\rho}(p \mid \boldsymbol{\varrho})$, are

[18] Evidently, $n_{\mathcal{P}}$ is the integer part of $(p_{\max} - p_{\min})/\Delta p$.

[19] Compared with the algorithm in [136], our is an improvement. It allows us to avoid a large volume of unnecessary computations and to increase the speed of calculation. For not to complicate the presentation, we do not report certain easy technical details.

[20] In calculations presented below, we set it equal to 1000.

looking rather complicated. Second, in the case $p > \mathsf{E}\,Y$, there is no such approximation in most cases of fat-tail Y, e.g., Pareto, and the upper bound $\overline{\boldsymbol{u}}_{\alpha,t\,|\,\delta,\rho}(p \mid \varrho)$ strongly depends on the distribution of Y. The same remark applies to the annual intrinsic value and its simplified version, i.e., conservative intrinsic values.

Based on this observation about ERS-analysis, we conclude that the only way which seems realistic, is to rely on numerical methods. The simplest and most common approach to the numerical study, widely used in practice, is simulation. In Figs. 7.14–7.17, an example of such a simulation is given.

The analytical results correlate with simulation in two ways. First, they allow to set the agenda for simulation more accurately: in the design of the simulation process an understanding of the intrinsic nature of the model is paramount. Second, having an idea of the magnitude of the expected values, they allow to check the results after they are received: the correct results of numerical calculations should not deviate much from the expected.

Remark 7.1 To set an example, note that the value $\boldsymbol{u}_{\alpha,t}(\mathsf{E}\,Y \mid \varrho)$ is easy to predict, as t is sufficiently large. In Fig. 7.14, simulated values (X-axis is p) of $\boldsymbol{u}_{\alpha,t}(p \mid \varrho)$ and $\boldsymbol{\mathcal{E}}_{\alpha,t}(p \mid \varrho)$ are given, when $\varsigma_s \equiv 0$ (explosive migration at time zero), $r_\infty(p \mid \varrho)$ is as in (7.2), with $\boldsymbol{c} = 0.15$, $\boldsymbol{C} = 2.5$, $\boldsymbol{p} = 2.28$, $\boldsymbol{\varrho} = 2.4$, $\boldsymbol{P} = 2.52$, $l = l' = 1$, $\alpha = 0.12$, whence $\kappa_{\alpha/2} = 1.5548$, $t = 300$, $\delta = 4$, Y is 2-mixture of exponential distributions with parameters $\rho_1 = 0.3$, $\rho_2 = 1.5$, $p = q = 0.5$, whence (see (6.8))

$$\mathsf{E}\,Y = p/\rho_1 + q/\rho_2 = 2.0,$$
$$\mathsf{D}\,Y = (q\rho_1^2 + p\rho_2^2 + pq(\rho_1 - \rho_2)^2)/(\rho_1^2\rho_2^2) = 7.56,$$

and (see (6.10))

$$M := \mathsf{E}\,T/\mathsf{E}\,Y = \frac{\rho_1\rho_2}{\delta(q\rho_1 + p\rho_2)} = 0.125,$$
$$D^2 := ((\mathsf{E}\,T)^2\mathsf{D}\,Y + (\mathsf{E}\,Y)^2\mathsf{D}\,T)/(\mathsf{E}\,Y)^3$$
$$= \frac{\rho_1\rho_2(q^2\rho_1^2 + p(1+p)\rho_2^2 + q((1+p)\rho_1^2 + p\rho_2^2))}{\delta^2(q\rho_1 + p\rho_2)^3} = 0.0903.$$

The value $\boldsymbol{u}_{\alpha,t}(\mathsf{E}\,Y \mid \varrho)$ is approximated by

$$\frac{D}{M^{3/2}}\kappa_{\alpha/2}\sqrt{\boldsymbol{C}\,t} = 289.48.$$

The corresponding simulated value is 287.72, which demonstrates perfect accuracy of the analytical result.

In Figs. 7.15–7.17, simulated values (X-axis is p) of $\boldsymbol{u}_{\alpha,t}(p \mid \varrho)$ and $\boldsymbol{\mathcal{E}}_{\alpha,t}(p \mid \varrho)$ are given, when $\varsigma_s \equiv 0$ (explosive migration at time zero), $r_\infty(p \mid \varrho)$ is as in (7.2), with $\boldsymbol{c} = 0.15$, $\boldsymbol{C} = 2.5$, $\boldsymbol{p} = 2.28$, $\boldsymbol{\varrho} = 2.4$, $\boldsymbol{P} = 2.52$, $l = l' = 1$ in (7.15), $l = l' = 0.3$ in (7.16), $l = l' = 3.3$ in (7.17), $\alpha = 0.12$, whence

$\kappa_{\alpha/2} = 1.5548$, $t = 300$, $\delta = 4$, Y is Pareto with parameters $a = 3$, $b = 0.25$, whence

$$\mathsf{E}\,Y = 1/((a_Y - 1)\,b_Y) = 2,$$
$$\mathsf{D}\,Y = a_Y/((a_Y - 1)^2\,(a_Y - 2)\,b_Y^2) = 12,$$

and (see (6.13))

$$M := \mathsf{E}\,T/\mathsf{E}\,Y = \frac{(a_Y - 1)\,b_Y}{\delta} = 0.125,$$
$$D^2 := ((\mathsf{E}\,T)^2\mathsf{D}\,Y + (\mathsf{E}\,Y)^2\mathsf{D}\,T)/(\mathsf{E}\,Y)^3$$
$$= \frac{2\,(a_Y - 1)^2\,b_Y}{\delta^2\,(a_Y - 2)} = 0.125.$$

The value $\boldsymbol{u}_{\alpha,t}(\mathsf{E}\,Y \mid \boldsymbol{\varrho})$ is approximated by

$$\frac{D}{M^{3/2}}\kappa_{\alpha/2}\sqrt{\boldsymbol{C}\,t} = 340.63.$$

The corresponding simulated value is 336.18, which demonstrates perfect accuracy of the analytical result.

Remark 7.2 The simple-looking upper bound

$$\mathcal{E}_{\alpha,t}(p \mid \boldsymbol{\varrho}) \leqslant \frac{\mathsf{E}(Y^2)}{2\alpha}\,\frac{p + \mathsf{E}\,Y}{(p - \mathsf{E}\,Y)^2}, \quad p > \mathsf{E}\,Y,$$

which comes from (5.60) (see also (3.22)), is usually overly rough, even for c large.

Problems

Problem 7.1 Derive Theorem 7.1 from Theorem 3.1

Problem 7.2 Prove Theorem 7.2: replace c by δp and make the change of time $s \rightarrowtail \Upsilon_s(p \mid \boldsymbol{\varrho})$ in Theorem 3.4.

Problem 7.3 Extend the results of this chapter to the case when the claim arrival process is modeled by a general renewal, rather than Poisson, process.

Problem 7.4 Check equality (7.7) for $\varsigma_s := (1 + s)^{-\epsilon}$ and calculate $\Upsilon_t(p \mid \boldsymbol{\varrho})$ for $\varsigma_s := e^{-\epsilon s}$, where $\epsilon > 0$ is a constant.

Appendix A

Auxiliary Results from Analysis

This appendix, which refers to well-known textbooks such as [27], [30], [31], [105], [155], [160], [189], [190], [191], and [197], and reference books such as [1], [85], is a summary of standard results from basic and advanced analysis, and a set of less standard results, in particular, concerning simulation.

A.1 Elementary Concepts and Results

A.1.1 Criteria of monotony, convexity, and concavity

Criterion of monotony, based on differentiation (see, e.g., [191]), is as follows: for a differentiable function, if the derivative is positive, then the function monotone increases. If the derivative is negative, then the function monotone decreases.

Criterion of convexity and concavity, based on differentiation (see, e.g., [191]), is as follows: for a twice-differentiable function, if the second derivative is positive, then the function is convex. If the second derivative is negative, then the function is concave. The points at which the concavity changes for convexity, or vice versa, are called inflection points.

A.1.2 Chain rules of differentiation

The chain rule for differentiation of a composite function (see, e.g., [191]) is as follows:

$$\begin{aligned} \frac{d}{dx} F(u(x), v(x)) = {} & \frac{\partial}{\partial u} F(u, v) \Big|_{\substack{u=u(x) \\ v=v(x)}} u'(x) \\ & + \frac{\partial}{\partial v} F(u, v) \Big|_{\substack{u=u(x) \\ v=v(x)}} v'(x). \end{aligned} \tag{A.1}$$

The chain rule for differentiation of an integral containing a parameter, called Leibniz's rule (see, e.g., [190], Section 4.2), is as follows:

$$\frac{d}{dt}\left(\int_{a(t)}^{b(t)} f(x,t)\,dx\right) = \int_{a(t)}^{b(t)} \left(\frac{\partial}{\partial t} f(x,t)\right) dx + f(b(t),t)b'(t) - f(a(t),t)a'(t).$$

Application of Leibniz's rule yields the following equivalent formulas for derivative of a convolution of two probability density functions, $f(x)$ and $g(x)$ concentrated on R^+:

$$\begin{aligned}\frac{d}{dx}(f * g)(x) = \frac{d}{dx}\int_0^x f(x-z)g(z)\,dz &= \int_0^x f'(x-z)g(z)\,dz + f(0)g(x) \\ &= \int_0^x g(x-z)f'(z)\,dz + f(0)g(x) \\ = \frac{d}{dx}\int_0^x g(x-z)f(z)\,dz &= \int_0^x g'(x-z)f(z)\,dz + f(x)g(0) \\ &= \int_0^x f(x-z)g'(z)\,dz + f(x)g(0).\end{aligned}$$

It is noteworthy that subtracting integral $\int_0^x f(x-z)g'(z)\,dz + f(x)g(0)$ from integral $\int_0^x f'(x-z)g(z)\,dz - f(0)g(x)$ yields zero, as follows:

$$\begin{aligned}0 &= \int_0^x f(x-z)g'(z)\,dz + f(x)g(0) - \int_0^x f'(x-z)g(z)\,dz - f(0)g(x) \\ &= \int_0^x (f(x-z)g'(z) - f'(x-z)g(z))\,dz + f(x)g(0) - f(0)g(x) \\ &= \int_0^x \frac{d}{dz}(f(x-z)\,g(z))\,dz + f(x)g(0) - f(0)g(x) \\ &= f(x-z)\,g(z)\,\Big|_{z=0}^{x} - f(0)g(x) + f(x)g(0).\end{aligned}$$

A.1.3 Tangent line passing through a point

Theorem A.1 *For $A, C > 0$, let $f(x)$, $x > C$, be a positive differentiable function and $l(x)$, $x > C$, be a straight line tangent to $f(x)$ in a point (x_0, y_0) such that $l(C) = A$. Then*

$$l(x) = \frac{f(x_0) - A}{x_0 - C}(x - C) + A, \quad x > C,$$

where x_0 is a solution to equation $f(x_0) = f'(x_0)(x_0 - C) + A$.

Proof of Theorem A.1. The equation of a line passing through the point with abscissa (X-axis) C and ordinate (Y-axis) A and tangent to the function $f(x)$ at the point with abscissa (X-axis) $x_0 > C$ is $y = f'(x_0)(x - C) + A$, $x > C$. The ordinate (Y-axis) of the point of tangency is $y_0 = f'(x_0)(x_0 - C) + A$.

The value of the function f at the point of tangency is y_0: $f(x_0) = y_0$. This yields the equation $f(x_0) = f'(x_0)(x_0 - C) + A$ for the abscissa (X-axis) x_0 of the point of tangency. □

For the hyperbola $f(x) = B/(x-C)$, $x > C$, a unique solution to equation $f(x_0) = f'(x_0)(x_0 - C) + A$ is $x_0 = 2B/A + C$, and $y_0 = A/2$. This yields the following result.

Theorem A.2 *For $A, B, C > 0$ and for hyperbola $f(x) = B/(x-C)$, $x > C$, the straight line passing through the point with abscissa C and ordinate A and tangent to $f(x)$ is $l(x) = -(A^2/(4B))(x-C)+A$, $x > C$. The abscissa of the point of tangency is $2B/A+C$. The ordinate of the point of tangency is $A/2$.*

A.1.4 Inverse and implicit functions and their derivatives

The fixed-probability levels studied throughout the book are implicit functions. Theorem A.4 on the derivative of implicit functions formulated below appears in Chapters 2–5.

Derivative of inverse function. An inverse function (see, e.g., [190], [191]) is a function that "reverses" another function: if the function F applied to an input x gives a result of y, then applying its inverse function F^{-1} to y gives the result x, and vice versa, i.e., $F(x) = y$ if and only if $F^{-1}(y) = x$.

Theorem A.3 *Assuming that F has an inverse in a neighborhood of x and that its derivative at that point is non-zero, its inverse is guaranteed to be differentiable at x and have a derivative given by the formula*

$$\left(\frac{d}{dx}F^{-1}\right)(x) = \frac{1}{F'(F^{-1}(x))}.$$

Lagrange inversion theorem. The Lagrange inversion theorem gives a formal power series expansion of the implicit function determined by an implicit equation, which is a particular case of $F(w, z) = 0$, where w, z are complex. Namely, let the function $f(z)$ be analytic in some neighborhood of the point $z = 0$ of the complex plane. Assuming that $f(0) \neq 0$, we focus our attention on the equation $w = z/f(z)$, which is a particular case of $F(w, z) = 0$, and where z is the unknown. We seek to associate the variable w with z: $z = z(w)$.

The Lagrange inversion theorem claims that there exist positive numbers a and b such that for $|w| < a$ the equation has just one solution in the domain $|z| < b$, and this solution is an analytic function of w: $z(w) = \sum_{k=1}^{\infty} c_k w^k$, $|w| < a$, where the coefficients c_k are given by $c_k = \frac{1}{k!}\left\{(\frac{d}{dz})^{k-1}(f(z))^k\right\}\Big|_{z=0}$.

A generalization, usually called Lagrange inversion formula, gives the value of $g(z)$, where g is any function of z, analytic in the neighborhood of $z = 0$: $g(z) = g(0) + \sum_{k=1}^{\infty} d_k w^k$, where $d_k = \frac{1}{k!}\left\{(\frac{d}{dz})^{k-1}(g'(z)\,(f(z))^k)\right\}\Big|_{z=0}$.

Implicit functions and their derivatives. An implicit function (see, e.g., [30], Chapter 2, or [190], Section 7.32, or [191], Chapter 1, § 1.2) is a function that is determined by $F(x, y) = 0$, $x, y \in \mathsf{R}$, called implicit equation, by associating the variable x with y: $y = f(x)$ (or y with x: $x = g(y)$). If the equation $F(x, y) = 0$ has more than one root, it is decided, for each value of the argument, which one of the roots has to be chosen.

The most well-known and classical result is the implicit function theorem (see, e.g., [19], Chapter VII, § 8), which provides general conditions under which the implicit equation $F(w, z) = 0$, where w, z are complex, determines an implicit function. It is as follows. If $F(w, z)$ is an analytic function of both w and z, in some region $|z| < a_1$, $|w| < b_1$, if $F(0, 0) = 0$ and if $\frac{\partial}{\partial z} F(w, z)$ does not vanish at the point $z = w = 0$, then there are positive numbers a and b such that for each w in the domain $|w| < a$ the equation $F(w, z) = 0$ has just one solution z in the domain $|z| < b$, and this solution can be represented as a power series $z = \sum_{k=1}^{\infty} c_k w^k$.

A historical outline of the theory of implicit functions is presented, e.g., in [167]. It is argued that it starts with the algebraic geometry of Descartes (1637) and the infinitesimal calculus of Leibniz (circa 1677), Johann Bernoulli (1695) and Euler (1748), and Dini's contribution is emphasized: in the modern form, the implicit functions theory was settled by Ulisse Dini (1845–1918).

It focuses on finding the tangent to the curve given by the implicit relation, but not the implicit function itself, even if this relation is given explicitly. In general, the search for an implicit function is a hopeless problem, because we really want to express this function in a closed form, in terms of standard elementary functions or, at least, in terms of standard special functions. Even the problem of finding the asymptotic behavior of the implicit function $y = f(x)$, as $x \to \infty$, is rather vague. In some cases it can be approached by means of the following theorem.

Derivatives of implicit function. The derivatives of a function defined by the implicit equation $F(x, y) = 0$, $x, y \in \mathsf{R}$, can be obtained (see, e.g., [191], Chapter I, § 5.2 and § 5.3) without finding this implicit function in closed form.

Theorem A.4 *Assume that the function $F(x, y)$, $x, y \in \mathsf{R}$, possesses partial derivatives up to second order, which are continuous in some neighborhood of a solution (x_0, y_0) of the equation $F(x, y) = 0$. If $\frac{\partial}{\partial y} F(x_0, y_0) \neq 0$, then there exists an $\epsilon > 0$ and a unique continuously differentiable function f such that $f(x_0) = y_0$ and $F(x, f(x)) = 0$ for $|x - x_0| < \epsilon$. Moreover, for $|x - x_0| < \epsilon$ we have*

$$f'(x) = - \left. \frac{\frac{\partial}{\partial x} F(x, y)}{\frac{\partial}{\partial y} F(x, y)} \right|_{y = f(x)}, \tag{A.2}$$

and

$$f''(x) = -\left(\frac{\frac{\partial^2}{\partial x^2}F(x,y)}{\frac{\partial}{\partial y}F(x,y)} - \frac{2\,\frac{\partial^2}{\partial x\,\partial y}F(x,y)\,\frac{\partial}{\partial x}F(x,y)}{(\frac{\partial}{\partial y}F(x,y))^2} + \frac{\frac{\partial^2}{\partial y^2}F(x,y)(\frac{\partial}{\partial x}F(x,y))^2}{(\frac{\partial}{\partial y}F(x,y))^3}\right)\Bigg|_{y=f(x)}. \tag{A.3}$$

Proximity between two implicit functions. Let $F(x,y) = 0$ and $G(x,y) = 0$, $x, y \in \mathsf{R}$, be two implicit equations. For a neighborhood of (x_0, y_0) denoted by

$$\mathcal{O}(x_0, y_0) = \{(x,y) : |x - x_0| < a_1, |y - y_0| < b_1\},$$

we assume that

$$\sup_{x,y \in \mathcal{O}(x_0,y_0)} \big|F(x,y) - G(x,y)\big| < \delta. \tag{A.4}$$

We assume also that the conditions of the implicit function theorem are satisfied at the point (x_0, y_0) in both cases, i.e., both functions $F(x,y)$ and $G(x,y)$ are sufficiently smooth at $\mathcal{O}(x_0, y_0)$ and

$$\frac{\partial}{\partial y}F(x,y)\,|_{x_0,y_0} \neq 0, \qquad \frac{\partial}{\partial y}G(x,y)\,|_{x_0,y_0} \neq 0, \tag{A.5}$$

whence both implicit functions $y = f(x)$, $y = g(x)$ are well defined in $\mathcal{O}(x_0, y_0)$.

Theorem A.5 *Let $F(x,y)$ and $G(x,y)$, $x, y \in \mathsf{R}$, be the functions that possess partial derivatives continuous in a neighborhood $\mathcal{O}(x_0, y_0)$ of some solution, (x_0, y_0), of the equation $F(x,y) = 0$, for which* (A.4) *and* (A.5) *hold true. Then there are an $\epsilon > 0$, a unique continuously differentiable function f such that $f(x_0) = y_0$ and $F(x, f(x)) = 0$ for $|x - x_0| < \epsilon$, and a unique continuously differentiable function g such that $g(x_0) = y_1$ and $G(x, g(x)) = 0$ for $|x - x_0| < \epsilon$ such that*

$$\sup_{|x - x_0| < \epsilon} \big|f(x) - g(x)\big| < K\delta.$$

Proof of Theorem A.5. Let us introduce $y_0 = f(x_0)$ and $y_1 = g(x_0)$ such that $F(x_0, y_0) = 0$ and $G(x_0, y_1) = 0$, and consider $|f(x_0) - g(x_0)| = |y_0 - y_1|$. We expand the function $G(x_0, y)$, $y \in \mathsf{R}$, in a Taylor series as far as the $(y - y_0)^2$ term:

$$G(x_0, y) = G(x_0, y_0) + \underbrace{\tfrac{\partial}{\partial y}G(x_0, y)\,|_{y=y_0}}_{\neq 0}(y - y_0) + o((y - y_0)^2), \quad y \to y_0.$$

By (A.5), it yields

$$\begin{aligned} y - y_0 = {} & (\tfrac{\partial}{\partial y}G(x_0, y)\,|_{y=y_0})^{-1}(G(x_0, y) - G(x_0, y_0)) \\ & + o((y - y_0)^2), \quad y \to y_0, \end{aligned} \tag{A.6}$$

and since $(\frac{\partial}{\partial y}G(x_0,y)\,|_{y=y_0})^{-1}$ is finite, with $\left|(\frac{\partial}{\partial y}G(x_0,y)\,|_{y=y_0})^{-1}\right| < K_1 < \infty$, the estimate for $\left|G(x_0,y)-G(x_0,y_0)\right|$ can be applied to estimate $|y-y_0|$.

Note that for y_1 such that $G(x_0,y_1)=0$, by (A.4) we have

$$\begin{aligned}&\left|\,G(x_0,y_1)-G(x_0,y_0)\right|\\&\qquad\leqslant \left|\,\underbrace{G(x_0,y_1)-F(x_0,y_0)}_{0}\right| + \left|\,\underbrace{F(x_0,y_0)-G(x_0,y_0)}_{<\delta}\,\right| < \delta,\end{aligned}$$

and (A.6) yields $|y_1-y_0|<K\delta$, where $K_1<K<\infty$, as required.

Using the Taylor's expansions

$$f(x) = \underbrace{f(x_0)}_{y_0} + f'(x_0)(x-x_0) + o((x-x_0)^2), \quad x\to x_0,$$

$$g(x) = \underbrace{g(x_0)}_{y_1} + g'(x_0)(x-x_0) + o((x-x_0)^2), \quad x\to x_0,$$

we extend this estimate to x such that $|x-x_0|<\epsilon$, whence the result. □

A.1.5 Remarks on asymptotic methods

As a rule, in mathematics, asymptotic methods are a way of suppressing information when explicit formulas are unnecessarily cumbersome. Asymptotic methods can be used even if the original problem is so sophisticated that it does not allow getting explicit formulas. In probability theory, one of the most well-known problems of this type is the central limit theorem, in which the original expression, which is a convolution of the distributions of individual summands, is approximated by the normal distribution.

Regarded as an alternative to numerical methods, when the evaluation of a certain value involves a very large number of operations, the asymptotic analysis is used to seek information about this value on the basis of a subsidiary expression, which in a certain sense is close to the original. A distinctive feature of this approach is that its results are the better the more they are needed: as a rule, its accuracy increases with an increase in the number of operations needed to implement the direct numerical method. In particular, the central limit theorem works the better, the greater is the number of summands (or the degree of convolution); on the contrary, the direct calculation of the convolution power becomes more difficult with the growth of this power.

The Bachmann–Landau symbols. The Bachmann–Landau O-notation (see e.g., [30], Section 1.2, for more information of its use and misuse) is the following form to suppress information: the formula $f(x)=O(g(x))$, $x\to\infty$, means that there exist positive numbers a and A, not depending on x such that $|f(x)|\leqslant A\,|g(x)|$ whenever $a<x<\infty$.

The expression $f(x)=o(g(x))$, $x\to\infty$, means that $f(x)/g(x)$ tends to 0, as $x\to\infty$. This is a stronger assertion than the corresponding O-formula. The former implies the latter, as convergence implies boundedness from a certain point onwards. In o-notation, "$=$" is to be read as "is", and "o" is to be read as "something that tends to zero, multiplied by".

Asymptotic equivalence, asymptotic equalities and inequalities. In the asymptotic analysis, standard terminology and notation is developed (see, e.g., [190], [191]). The functions $f(x)$ and $g(x)$ are asymptotically equivalent, as $x \to \infty$, if the ratio $f(x)/g(x)$ tends to unity. We use notation[1]

$$f(x) \sim g(x), \quad x \to \infty. \tag{A.7}$$

The use of the symbol $\sim$ is only one option among many others, since $f(x) \sim g(x)$ is equivalent, e.g., to $f(x) = g(x)(1 + o(1))$, or to $f(x) = e^{o(1)}g(x)$.

We should pay attention to the difference between

$$f(x) = g(x)(1 + o(1)), \quad x \to \infty, \tag{A.8}$$

what is the twin of the formula (A.7), and[2]

$$f(x) = g(x) + o(1), \quad x \to \infty. \tag{A.9}$$

Strictly speaking, the asymptotic equality (A.9) means that (see, e.g., [191]) for each $\epsilon > 0$ there exists $\delta > 0$ such that for all $x > \delta$ we have $|f(x) - g(x)| < \epsilon$. The asymptotic equality (A.8) means that for each $\epsilon > 0$ there exists $\delta > 0$ such that for all $x > \delta$ we have $|f(x)/g(x) - 1| < \epsilon$.

When there exist positive numbers a and A, not depending on x such that $|g(x)| > A > 0$ whenever $a < x < \infty$, (A.8) and (A.9) are nearly the same, since (A.8) implies $f(x) = g(x) + g(x)\, o(1) = g(x) + o(1)$, $x \to \infty$, i.e., (A.9), and vice versa. But is $g(x) \to 0$, as $x \to \infty$, (A.8) is a much stronger statement than (A.9): it claims that $f(x) = g(x) + o(g(x))$, $x \to \infty$. In other words, the difference between (A.8), which is a stronger statement than (A.9), appears when comparing infinitesimals[3]: (A.8) means that $f(x)$ and $g(x)$ converge to zero at the same rate.

The remarks on asymptotic equalities (A.8) and (A.9) are true with respect to the asymptotic inequalities of the form

$$f(x) < g(x) + o(1), \quad x \to \infty, \tag{A.10}$$

---

[1]This notation holds for all other ways of passing to a limit (e.g., $x \to -\infty$, $x \to 0$, $x \downarrow 0$, $|z| \to 0$).

[2]In the List of abbreviations and symbols of [73] (see p. 647), it is said that $a(x) \sim b(x)$, as $x \to x_0$, means that $\lim_{x \to x_0} a(x)/b(x) = 1$, $a(x) \sim 0$ means $a(x) = o(1)$, $a(x) \approx b(x)$ as $x \to x_0$ means that $a(x)$ is approximately (roughly) of the same order as $b(x)$ as $x \to x_0$. This is only used in a heuristic sense.

[3]A function $f(x)$ is called infinitesimal as $x \to \infty$, if $\lim_{x \to \infty} f(x) = 0$. This means that for each $\epsilon > 0$ there exists $\delta > 0$ such that for all x satisfying the inequality $|x| > \delta$, we have $|f(x)| < \epsilon$.

which means that for each $\epsilon > 0$ there exists $\delta > 0$ such that for all $x > \delta$ we have $f(x) < g(x) + \epsilon$, and

$$f(x) < g(x)\,(1 + o(1)), \quad x \to \infty, \tag{A.11}$$

which means that for each $\epsilon > 0$ there exists $\delta > 0$ such that for all $x > \delta$ we have $f(x) < g(x)\,(1 + \epsilon)$. As stated above, (A.10) and (A.11) differ for infinitesimals.

In addition to (A.7), we introduce the shorthand notation for asymptotic equality (A.9) and asymptotic inequalities (A.10), (A.11):

$$f(x) \approx g(x), \quad f(x) \gtrapprox g(x), \quad f(x) \preccurlyeq g(x), \quad x \to \infty,$$

We omit, when it is obvious, the setting $x \to \infty$, or the verbal clause "for sufficiently large x". When signs of these inequalities are reversed, changes are obvious.

A.1.6 Remarks on analytical and numerical methods

Asymptotic results and numerical calculations. Asymptotic results, i.e., formulas in terms of O-symbols, or o-symbols, have, as they stand, little value for numerical purposes. First, these formulas cannot serve as a calculation plan for any specifically selected values of a parameter of this asymptotics[4]. Second, even being a hint for heuristic calculations, formulas in terms of O-symbols, or o-symbols, say nothing about which argument values are fit for it, i.e., which are large enough to expect from these heuristic result to be meaningfully close to the unknown value which is sought.

Nevertheless, in almost all cases when such formulas were obtained, the proof can be repeated by replacing all O-formulas, or o-formulas with closed-form estimates that include explicit numerical constants. That is, at each stage of the procedure it is possible to determine certain numbers or functions with certain properties, albeit in the asymptotic formulas only the existence of such numbers or functions was stated.

In most cases, the estimates obtained in this way are rather weak, with constants a thousand times, say, greater than they could be. The reason is, of course, that such estimates are obtained by means of a considerable number of steps, and in each step the accuracy is easily lost. Sometimes it is possible to increase the accuracy by a more careful examination. Usually, to bring this to an acceptable result, incredible efforts of many generations of researchers are being spent.

An example from the probability theory is the Berry-Esseen bound, first obtained in terms of O-symbol. Written as an inequality, with right-hand side given explicitly, this Berry-Esseen bound is

$$\sup_{x \in \mathsf{R}} \big|\, \mathsf{F}_n(x) - \Phi_{(0,1)}(x) \,\big| \leqslant A\, \frac{\mathsf{E}\,(|\xi\,|^3)}{\sigma^3\,\sqrt{n}}, \quad n \to \infty, \tag{A.12}$$

[4]Each asymptotic result is a statement about infinitely many values of this parameter.

where $\mathsf{F}_n(x)$ is c.d.f. of a sum of i.i.d. random variables $\xi_i \stackrel{d}{=} \xi$, $i = 1, 2, \dots, n$. Here $A > 0$ is an absolute constant. In [18], Theorem 12.4 (see inequality (12.16)), an upper bound 1.6 for A is given. The refinement of this upper bound is an exciting challenge. A series of works by various authors is devoted to it. In [174], it is refined to 0.47.

Analytical results suitable for numerical calculations. In most results obtained by analytical methods, accuracy is usually deemed the greatest advantage. Another thing that is usually sought, is the structural completeness, associated with the desire to obtain a result in the most general conditions. However, all these mathematically attractive properties (which make the analytical results complete and aesthetically beautiful) are usually achieved due to significant complications of both the results themselves and the technique of proving them.

Sometimes, e.g., for computational purposes, the results should be deliberately simplified. For example, exact asymptotics can be replaced by asymptotic inequalities. When a result is expressed by simple closed-form formulas, in a number of applications this simplicity compensates all losses in accuracy, or in mathematical elegance. To be specific, the bound

$$\mathsf{F}_n(x) \leqslant \Phi_{(0,1)}(x) + \frac{A\,\mathsf{E}(|\xi\,|^3)}{\sigma^3\sqrt{n}}, \quad n \to \infty,$$

is straightforward from (A.12). But simpler (albeit less accurate) bounds, especially for x large, can be obtained by simpler methods, e.g., using Chebyshev's inequality (see, e.g., [78], Chapter 5, § 7).

Plainly, calculations based on analytical results are typically faster, more reliable, and more convenient to perform than ones based on direct numerical method such as simulation. For example, calculating upper bounds on $\mathsf{F}_n(x)$, $x \in \mathsf{R}$, using the above formula, is much easier than calculating the n-th convolution power by means of simulation, especially if n is large.

Simulation: direct numerical method. Even if the asymptotic result is presented in its best possible form, like in (A.12), it needs not be satisfactory from the numerical point of view, in particular for small and moderate values of the variable which is the parameter of this asymptotics.

In the computers era[5], when price of elementary arithmetic operations is low, the implementation of direct algorithms[6] on a computer has become attractive. Detailed guides on the use of simulation methods, initially called Monte Carlo (after the gambling house) simulation, now simply simulation, are currently available (see, e.g., [27], [105], [160], and [197]).

[5]The random sampling of numbers for evaluating non-random values was used in the past, long before the development of the modern computers, e.g., by Buffon, Kelvin, Gosset (Student).

[6]The notion of an algorithm is basic to computer programming, but this concept itself is not new and goes back to the Middle Ages, as described in [105].

Simulation methods are understood by us in a narrow sense (since very complicated and consisting of many stages programs that simulate real processes in physics, economics, or technology are also meant by that), and are reduced to obtaining a sequence of pseudo-random numbers of different types and their use for calculating deterministic quantities, like the probabilities of ruin, which is mainly based on the law of large numbers.

Pseudo-random numbers generation. The primary input of a Monte Carlo simulation is pseudo-random numbers generated from the uniform distribution on $[0,1]$. They are so called (see, e.g., [27], Chapter 5) to emphasize their difference from pseudo-random variates[7], which are generated from other distributions.

In generating pseudo-random numbers, technical means, i.e., using a computer or performing mechanical or manual actions such as throwing dices or shuffling cards, are much less interesting than the appearance of these numbers as a sample from a uniform distribution on $[0,1]$. Since now computers are actually used for this, the groundwork of simulation is pseudo-random number generators, which are a special type of computer programs.

A standard (and currently outdated) method for generating a stream of pseudo-random numbers on $[0,1]$, actually implemented in a large part of commercial software, is the linear congruential generator. Actually, it generates a sequence of non-negative integer numbers, which are transformed into random numbers within $[0,1]$, as follows. The sequence of integer numbers starts from a user-selected seed Z_0; then, given the previous integer number Z_{i-1}, the next number in the sequence is generated as follows:

$$Z_i = (a\,Z_{i-1} + c) \mod m, \tag{A.13}$$

where the multiplier a, the shift c, and the modulus m are properly chosen integer numbers, and "mod" denotes the remainder of integer division. Finally, the integer number Z_i is transformed into[8] $U_i = Z_i/m$.

A discussion of desirable properties and flaws of pseudo-random number generators, including a folklore example of a lattice structure on a computer screen that a bad generator produces, can be found in many textbooks (see, e.g., [27], Chapter 5). We conclude with a trivial idea that each generator has its advantages and disadvantages. According to [93], they are similar to antibiotics. Each type of generator has its own undesirable side effects. There are no safe generators. Good generators are characterized by theoretical support, convincing empirical evidence, and positive practical aspects. They will give correct results in many, although not all situations. We leave aside the discussion of these issues, which is special.

---

[7]The difference between pseudo-random variate, that is a deterministic (in the sequence generated, e.g., by means of (A.13), there is nothing random) tool emulating randomness, and random variable, that embodies or models randomness, is obvious and paramount.

[8]Since Z_i ranges in the set $\{0,1,2,3,\ldots,m-1\}$, U_i ranges in the interval $[0,1)$, with 0 possible, whereas 1 not possible to get.

The inverse function method. The inverse function method of generating pseudo-random variate, given pseudo-random number, is based (see, e.g., [58]) on the following simple observation:

$$\begin{aligned}\mathsf{P}\{X < x\} &= \mathsf{P}\{F_X^{-1}(U) < x\}\\ &= \mathsf{P}\{U < F_X(x)\} = F_U(F_X(x)) = F_X(x),\end{aligned}$$

where F_X is a differentiable c.d.f.[9], U is a random variable distributed uniformly on the interval $[0, 1]$, whose c.d.f. is F_U, and $X \stackrel{d}{=} F_X^{-1}(U)$.

A compromise between simulation and analytical methods. The approaches based on simulation and on analytical results, being fundamentally different, complement each other. Simulation is an extensive source of relatively simple numerical illustrations for general analytical results, they are much less sensitive to technical limitations, and can serve as a tester in the search for analytical results that have not yet been obtained.

Analytical results have a much higher degree of generality than the results obtained by simulation, and can help to better understand the essence of the problem. But the ease of obtaining numerical illustrations contributes a lot to a better understanding and popularization of sophisticated analytical results.

With the right attitude to the balance between simulation and analytical methods, one reinforces the other. On the one hand (see [146], p. 45), analytical result, even in a very simplified situation, can lead to useful ideas for simulation analysis. For example, it helps to keep singularities of the model in check. They may be overlooked when simulation is performed, where many errors come from. In addition, a preliminary analytical study of the main variables included in the simulation model can improve the simulation plan by selecting the most appropriate distributions. In general, a preliminary acquaintance with the model by means of its analytical investigation can help to develop a reasonable simulation strategy, and may be useful for computational optimization.

A.2 Advanced Concepts and Results

A.2.1 Bessel functions

The Bessel functions of the first kind are used in Chapters 1, 3, 5, and 7. For $x > 0$ and n integer, the modified Bessel function of the first kind of

[9]This implies that the inverse function $F_X^{-1}(u)$, $u \in [0, 1]$, exists.

order n is defined by equality[10]

$$I_n(x) = \sum_{k=0}^{\infty} \frac{1}{k!\,(n+k)!} \left(\frac{x}{2}\right)^{n+2k}. \tag{A.14}$$

An integral representation for it is

$$I_n(x) = \frac{1}{\pi} \int_0^{\pi} e^{x \cos t} \cos nt \, dt. \tag{A.15}$$

Theorem A.6 *For $x > 0$ and n integer, we have*

$$|\, I_n(x) \,| \leqslant \frac{|\, x\,|^n}{2^n\, n!}\, e^{x^2/4}.$$

Proof of Theorem A.6. From inequalities

$$\begin{aligned} |\, I_n(x) \,| &\leqslant \frac{|\, x\,|^n}{2^n} \sum_{k=0}^{\infty} \frac{1}{k!(n+k)!} \frac{|\, x\,|^{2k}}{2^{2k}} \leqslant \frac{|\, x\,|^n}{2^n\, n!} \sum_{k=0}^{\infty} \frac{1}{k!(n+1)^k} \frac{|\, x\,|^{2k}}{2^{2k}} \\ &\leqslant \frac{|\, x\,|^n}{2^n\, n!} \exp\left\{\frac{x^2/4}{n+1}\right\} \leqslant \frac{|\, x\,|^n}{2^n\, n!}\, e^{x^2/4}, \end{aligned}$$

we have the result, as required. □

The following recurrent relations[11]

$$I_{n-1}(x) - I_{n+1}(x) = \frac{2n}{x} I_n(x), \quad I_{n-1}(x) + I_{n+1}(x) = 2\frac{d}{dx} I_n(x) \tag{A.16}$$

hold for $n = 1, 2, \ldots$. It is noteworthy that since $I_n(x) \geqslant 0$ for $x > 0$ and for any n integer, first equality in (A.16) yields

$$I_{n-1}(x) \geqslant I_{n+1}(x).$$

Theorem A.7 *For $b > a > 0$ and $n = 1, 2, \ldots$, we have*

$$\int_0^{\infty} \frac{e^{-bz}}{z}\, I_n(az)\, dz = \frac{a^n}{n\,(b + \sqrt{b^2 - a^2}\,)^n}, \tag{A.17}$$

$$\int_0^{\infty} e^{-bz}\, I_n(az)\, dz = \frac{a^n}{\sqrt{b^2 - a^2}\,(b + \sqrt{b^2 - a^2}\,)^n}. \tag{A.18}$$

Proof of Theorem A.7. Since $I_n(z) = \exp\{-n\pi i/2\} J_n(iz)$, equalities (A.17) and (A.18) follow from [85], formulas 6.611.4 and 6.623.3. One can also refer to [189], Chapter XIII, § 2, equalities (7) and (8). □

[10]See, e.g., [1], or [189], or [190], Chapter XVII, Section 17.7. The same formula yields $I_{-n}(x)$. Further in this book, we will be interested exclusively in $x > 0$ and n integer.

[11]See, e.g., [189], equalities 3.71 (1), (2).

A particular case of (A.18) yields Laplace transform of $I_n(x)$, which is

$$\int_0^\infty e^{-tz}\, I_n(z)\, dz = \frac{1}{\sqrt{t^2-1}\,(t+\sqrt{t^2-1}\,)^n}.$$

For $a, b > 0$, we have[12] the following results:

$$\begin{aligned} \int_0^\infty z^{1/2} e^{-bz}\, I_1(az^{1/2})\, dz &= \frac{a}{2b^2}\exp\left\{\frac{a^2}{4b}\right\}, \\ \int_0^\infty z^{3/2} e^{-bz}\, I_1(az^{1/2})\, dz &= \frac{a}{8b^4}(a^2+8b)\exp\left\{\frac{a^2}{4b}\right\}, \qquad \text{(A.19)} \\ \int_0^\infty z^{5/2} e^{-bz}\, I_1(az^{1/2})\, dz &= \frac{a}{32b^6}(a^4+24a^2b+96b^2)\exp\left\{\frac{a^2}{4b}\right\}. \end{aligned}$$

Theorem A.8 *For $\rho > 0$, we have*

$$\begin{aligned} &\rho^{-(n+1)/2} \int_0^t \frac{n+1}{z} e^{-(1+\rho)z}\, I_{n+1}(2\sqrt{\rho}\, z)\, dz \\ &\quad = \begin{cases} 1 - v_n(t), & \rho < 1, \\ \rho^{-(n+1)} - v_n(t), & \rho \geqslant 1, \end{cases} \end{aligned} \qquad \text{(A.20)}$$

where

$$v_n(t) = \frac{2}{\pi \rho^{n/2}} \int_0^\pi e^{-tA(\theta)}\, \frac{\sin((n+1)\theta)\sin\theta}{A(\theta)}\, d\theta,$$

$$A(\theta) = 1 + \rho - 2\sqrt{\rho}\cos\theta.$$

Proof of Theorem A.8. Using first equality in (A.16), we have

$$\begin{aligned} &\rho^{-(n+1)/2} \int_0^t \frac{n+1}{z} e^{-(1+\rho)z}\, I_{n+1}(2\sqrt{\rho}\, z)\, dz \\ &\quad = \rho^{-n/2} \int_0^t (I_n(2\sqrt{\rho}\, z) - I_{n+2}(2\sqrt{\rho}\, z)) e^{-(1+\rho)z}\, dz. \end{aligned}$$

Using equality (A.15) and changing the order of integration, we have

$$\begin{aligned} &\rho^{-n/2} \int_0^t (I_n(2\sqrt{\rho}\, z) - I_{n+2}(2\sqrt{\rho}\, z))\, e^{-(1+\rho)z}\, dz \\ &\quad = \frac{1}{\pi \rho^{n/2}} \int_0^\pi \int_0^t e^{-zA(\theta)}\, dz\, (\cos(n\theta) - \cos((n+2)\theta))\, d\theta. \end{aligned}$$

Since $\cos(n\theta) - \cos((n+2)\theta) = 2\sin((n+1)\theta)\sin\theta$ and

$$\int_0^t e^{-zA(\theta)}\, dz = (1 - e^{A(\theta)t})/A(\theta),$$

[12] See, e.g., [85], formula 6.643.2, which yields an even stronger assertion.

the right-hand side can be rewritten as

$$\frac{1}{\pi\rho^{n/2}}\int_0^\pi\int_0^t e^{-zA(\theta)}\,dz\,(\cos(n\theta)-\cos((n+2)\theta))\,d\theta$$
$$=\frac{2}{\pi\rho^{n/2}}\left(\int_0^\pi \frac{\sin((n+1)\theta)\sin\theta}{A(\theta)}\,d\theta-\int_0^\pi e^{-tA(\theta)}\frac{\sin((n+1)\theta)\sin\theta}{A(\theta)}\,d\theta\right).$$

Using the equality[13]

$$\int_0^\pi \frac{\sin(nz)\sin z}{1-2a\cos z+a^2}\,dz=\begin{cases}\dfrac{\pi}{2}\,a^{n-1}, & a^2<1,\\ \dfrac{\pi}{2a^{n+1}}, & a^2>1\end{cases}$$

we complete the proof. □

It is noteworthy that equality (A.20) when $\rho<1$ follows from equalities (5.73) and (5.73a) in [155], Section 5.7.

Theorem A.9 *For n natural, we have*

$$I_n(x)\sim\frac{e^x}{\sqrt{2\pi x}}\left(1+\sum_{k=1}^{\infty}\frac{(-1)^k}{(2x)^k}\frac{1}{k!}\frac{\Gamma(n+k+1/2)}{\Gamma(n-k+1/2)}\right),\quad x\to\infty,\tag{A.21}$$

where the absolute value of the remainder term does not exceed the absolute value of the first rejected term.

Proof of Theorem A.9. The expansion in (A.21) is [85], formula 8.451.5. The asymptotic expansion if $I_n(z)$ is also given in [190], Section 17.7, number (vi), and in [189], Section 7.23. □

Since (see [85], formulas 8.339.2 and 8.339.3) for k natural

$$\Gamma(k+1/2)=\frac{\sqrt{\pi}}{2^k}(2k-1)!!,\quad \Gamma(-k+1/2)=\frac{(-1)^k2^k\sqrt{\pi}}{(2k-1)!!},$$

for $n=0$ expansion (A.21) reduces to

$$I_0(x)\sim\frac{e^x}{\sqrt{2\pi x}}\left(1+\sum_{k=1}^{\infty}\frac{((2k-1)!!)^2}{(2x)^k k!2^{2k}}\right),\quad x\to\infty,\tag{A.22}$$

Regarding the right-hand side of (A.21), it is worth paying attention to equality (A.26) written above.

[13] See, e.g., [85], formula 3.613.3.

A.2.2 Stirling numbers of the second kind

The Stirling number of the second kind (see, e.g., [154], Chapter 2, § 7), denoted by $\mathcal{S}(n,k)$, or $\left\{ {n \atop k} \right\}$, is the number of ways to partition a set of n objects into k non-empty subsets. They are used in the analysis of the expressions $S_k(u \mid p)$, see equality (A.29) below.

For n integer, the Stirling numbers of the second kind satisfy the recurrence formula

$$\mathcal{S}(n,k) = \mathcal{S}(n-1,k-1) + k\,\mathcal{S}(n-1,k), \quad k = 1,2,\ldots,n, \tag{A.23}$$

with initial conditions $\mathcal{S}(0,0) = 0$ and $\mathcal{S}(n,0) = \mathcal{S}(0,n) = 0$. For $k < 0$ and $k > n$, the equality $\mathcal{S}(n,k) = 0$ holds. Some easily verified identities are

$$\mathcal{S}(n,n-1) = \binom{n}{2}, \quad \mathcal{S}(n,2) = 2^{n-1} - 1.$$

The first of them holds because dividing n elements into $n-1$ sets necessarily means dividing it into one set of size 2 and $n-2$ sets of size 1. Therefore, we need only pick those two elements. To verify the second identity, we note at first that there are 2^n ordered pairs of complementary subsets A and B. In one case, A is empty, and in another B is empty, so $2^n - 2$ ordered pairs of subsets remain. Since we want unordered pairs rather than ordered pairs, we divide this last number by 2, having the required identity.

An explicit expression for the Stirling numbers of the second kind is

$$\mathcal{S}(n,k) = \frac{1}{k!} \sum_{j=1}^{k} (-1)^{k-j} \binom{k}{j} j^n,$$

which yields $\mathcal{S}(n,1) = \mathcal{S}(n,n) = 1$ and

$$\mathcal{S}(n,2) = 2^{n-1} - 1,\ \mathcal{S}(n,3) = \frac{1}{6}(3^n - 3 \cdot 2^n + 3),\ \ldots,\ \mathcal{S}(n,n-1) = \binom{n}{2} = \frac{n(n-1)}{2}.$$

On the other hand, the recurrence formula (A.23) yields

$$\mathcal{S}(n,2) = \frac{\frac{1}{1}(2^{n-1} - 1^{n-1})}{0!},$$

$$\mathcal{S}(n,3) = \frac{\frac{1}{1}(3^{n-1} - 2^{n-1}) - \frac{1}{2}(3^{n-1} - 1^{n-1})}{1!},$$

$$\mathcal{S}(n,4) = \frac{\frac{1}{1}(4^{n-1} - 3^{n-1}) - \frac{2}{2}(4^{n-1} - 2^{n-1}) - \frac{1}{3}(4^{n-1} - 1^{n-1})}{2!},$$

$$\mathcal{S}(n,5) = \frac{\frac{1}{1}(5^{n-1} - 4^{n-1}) - \frac{3}{2}(5^{n-1} - 3^{n-1}) - \frac{3}{3}(5^{n-1} - 2^{n-1}) - \frac{1}{4}(5^{n-1} - 1^{n-1})}{3!},$$

and so on.

TABLE A.1: Stirling numbers of the second kind $\mathcal{S}(n,k)$ for integer $1 \leqslant n \leqslant 8$

	$k=1$	$=2$	$=3$	$=4$	$=5$	$=6$	$=7$	$=8$
$n=1$	1							
$=2$	1	1						
$=3$	1	3	1					
$=4$	1	7	6	1				
$=5$	1	15	25	10	1			
$=6$	1	31	90	65	15	1		
$=7$	1	63	301	350	140	21	1	
$=8$	1	127	966	1701	1050	266	28	1

For n large, the approximation $\mathcal{S}(n,k) \approx k^{n-1}$ holds. Indeed, for finite k we have

$$\frac{\mathcal{S}(n,k)}{k^n} = \frac{1}{k!}\sum_{j=1}^{k}(-1)^{k-j}\binom{k}{j}\left(\frac{j}{k}\right)^n \to \frac{1}{k}, \quad n \to \infty,$$

because each term in this sum, with the exception of the latter, tends to zero.

It is known that

$$\frac{m^n}{n!} = \sum_{k=1}^{n} \frac{\mathcal{S}(n,k)}{(m-k)!}$$

and that for $x > 0$

$$\sum_{m=1}^{\infty} \frac{m^n}{m!}\, x^m = \left(\sum_{k=1}^{n} \mathcal{S}(n,k)\, x^k\right)\left(\sum_{j=0}^{\infty} \frac{x^j}{j!}\right).$$

That yields

$$\sum_{k=1}^{n} \mathcal{S}(n,k)\, x^k = e^{-x} \sum_{m=1}^{\infty} \frac{x^m}{m!}\, m^n, \tag{A.24}$$

which is known as Dobinski's formula. It is noteworthy that the right hand side of equality (A.24) is the m-th power moment of a Poisson random variable with parameter 1.

A.2.3 A formula from combinatorics

This formula is used to proceed with the asymptotic expansion (A.21), see the proof of Theorem A.13 below.

Let us introduce $x_j = -(2j-1)^2$, $j = 1, 2, \ldots, k$, and set

$$A_{k,1} = \sum_{i=1}^{k} x_i, \quad A_{k,2} = \sum_{\substack{i,j=1 \\ i<j}}^{k} x_i\, x_j, \quad A_{k,3} = \sum_{\substack{i,j,\,l=1 \\ i<j<l}}^{k} x_i\, x_j\, x_l, \quad \ldots$$

$$A_{k,k} = x_1\, x_2 \cdots x_k,$$

or

$$A_{k,1} = \sum_{i=1}^{k} x_i = -\frac{1}{6}\,(2k-1)\,2k\,(2k+1),$$

$$A_{k,2} = \sum_{\substack{i,j=1\\ i<j}}^{k} x_i x_j = \frac{1}{90}\,(k-1)\,k\,(2k-3)\,(2k-1)\,(2k+1)\,(10k+7),$$

$$\vdots$$

$$A_{k,k} = x_1 x_2 \cdots x_k = (-1)^k\,((2k-1)!!)^2.$$

It is easily seen that $A_{1,1} = -1$,

$$\begin{aligned}
&A_{2,1} = -\frac{5}{2}\,2^2, \quad A_{2,2} = \frac{9}{16}\,2^4,\\
&A_{3,1} = -\frac{35}{4}\,2^2, \quad A_{3,2} = \frac{259}{16}\,2^4, \quad A_{3,3} = -\frac{225}{64}\,2^6,\\
&A_{4,1} = -21\,2^2, \quad A_{4,2} = \frac{987}{8}\,2^4, \quad A_{4,3} = -\frac{3229}{16}\,2^6, \quad A_{4,4} = \frac{11025}{256}\,2^8,\\
&A_{5,1} = -\frac{165}{4}\,2^2, \quad A_{5,2} = \frac{4389}{8}\,2^4, \quad \text{and so on.}
\end{aligned}$$

In these terms, we have the following identity.

Theorem A.10 *For $n, k = 1, 2, \ldots$, we have*

$$\frac{\Gamma(n+k+1/2)}{\Gamma(n-k+1/2)} = n^{2k} + \frac{A_{k,1}}{2^2}\,n^{2(k-1)} + \frac{A_{k,2}}{2^4}\,n^{2(k-2)} + \cdots + \frac{A_{k,k}}{2^{2k}}. \quad \text{(A.25)}$$

Proof of Theorem A.10. We start with the well-known equality[14]

$$\frac{\Gamma(n+k+1/2)}{\Gamma(n-k+1/2)} = (4n^2-1^2)\,(4n^2-3^2)\ldots(4n^2-(2k-1)^2)\,2^{-2k}. \quad \text{(A.26)}$$

In terms of $x_j = -(2j-1)^2$, $j = 1, 2, \ldots, k$, we rewrite it as

$$\frac{\Gamma(n+k+1/2)}{\Gamma(n-k+1/2)} = n^{2k}\,(1 + x_1(4n^2)^{-1})\,(1 + x_2(4n^2)^{-1})\cdots(1 + x_k(4n^2)^{-1}).$$

Straightforward transformation yields

$$\begin{aligned}
\frac{\Gamma(n+k+1/2)}{\Gamma(n-k+1/2)} = \frac{(4n^2)^k}{2^{2k}}\Bigg(&1 + (x_1 + \cdots + x_k)\,(4n^2)^{-1}\\
&+ \sum_{\substack{i,j=1\\ i<j}}^{k} x_i\,x_j\,(4n^2)^{-2} + \cdots + (x_1 \cdots x_k)\,(4n^2)^{-k}\Bigg),
\end{aligned}$$

as required. □

[14]See [85], formula 8.339.4, or [189], Section 7.2.

A.2.4 Series $S_k(u \mid p)$ and integrals $H_k(t \mid p)$

The results from this section are used to prove Theorem 3.7.

For $u > 0$, $p \in (0,1)$, $q = 1-p$, let us introduce the series

$$S_k(u \mid p) = e^{-u} \sum_{n=0}^{\infty} \frac{u^n}{n!} (p/q)^{(n+1)/2} (n+1)^{k+1}, \quad k = 0,1,2,\dots. \tag{A.27}$$

They appear in Section 3.3.1, in the asymptotic expansion (3.33) of the auxiliary function of the second kind $F_t(x \mid p)$.

Let us denote by $\Pi_{k+2}(u\sqrt{p/q}\,)$ the $(k+1)$-th power moment of a Poisson random variable with parameter $u\sqrt{p/q}$. It is easily seen that

$$S_k(u \mid p) = \exp\{-u\,(1-\sqrt{p/q}\,)\}\, u^{-1}\Pi_{k+2}(u\sqrt{p/q}\,). \tag{A.28}$$

In particular, we have

$$\begin{aligned}
S_0(u \mid p) &= \sqrt{p/q}\, \exp\{-u\,(1-\sqrt{p/q})\}\,(1+u\sqrt{p/q}\,),\\
S_1(u \mid p) &= \sqrt{p/q}\, \exp\{-u\,(1-\sqrt{p/q})\}\,(1+3\,u\sqrt{p/q}+(u\sqrt{p/q}\,)^2),\\
S_2(u \mid p) &= \sqrt{p/q}\, \exp\{-u\,(1-\sqrt{p/q})\}\,(1+7\,u\sqrt{p/q}+6(u\sqrt{p/q})^2\\
&\quad + (u\sqrt{p/q}\,)^3),\\
S_3(u \mid p) &= \sqrt{p/q}\, \exp\{-u\,(1-\sqrt{p/q})\}\,(1+15\,u\sqrt{p/q}+25(u\sqrt{p/q})^2\\
&\quad + 10(u\sqrt{p/q})^3 + (u\sqrt{p/q})^4),
\end{aligned}$$

which is easy to show using Table A.1 and the following theorem.

Theorem A.11 *The equalities*

$$S_k(u \mid p) = \exp\{-u\,(1-\sqrt{p/q}\,)\}\sqrt{p/q}\sum_{j=1}^{k+2} \mathcal{S}(k+2,j)\,(\sqrt{p/q}u\,)^{j-1} \tag{A.29}$$

are true for $u > 0$, $p \in (0,1)$, $q = 1-p$, *and* $k = 0,1,2,\dots$.

Proof of Theorem A.11. To prove equality (A.29), we recall that for $x > 0$ the recurrence relations

$$\Pi_{k+2}(x) = x \sum_{j=0}^{k+1} \binom{k+1}{j} \Pi_j(x), \quad k = 0,1,2,\dots,$$

with $\Pi_0(x) = 1$ and $\Pi_1(x) = x$, hold true. By Dobinski's formula (A.24), we have

$$\Pi_{k+2}(x) = \sum_{j=1}^{k+2} \mathcal{S}(k+2,j)\, x^j, \quad k = 0,1,2,\dots.$$

By putting in it $x = u\sqrt{p/q}$, we easily obtain (A.29) from (A.28). $\square$

For $t > 0$, $p \in (0,1)$, $q = 1-p$, and for $k = 1,2,\dots$, we set

$$H_k(t \mid p) = \int_t^\infty x^{-(2k+1)/2} \exp\{-a_p\, x\}\, dx, \tag{A.30}$$

where $a_p = (1-\sqrt{q/p}\,)^2$. The integrals $H_k(t \mid p)$, $k = 1,2,\dots$, appear in Section 3.3.1, in the asymptotic expansion (3.33) of the auxiliary function of the second kind $\digamma_t(x \mid p)$.

Let us introduce the polynomials

$$\mathcal{P}_k(x) = (-1)^{k-1} x^{k-1} \sum_{m=0}^{k-1} (-1)^m (2m-1)!!\, x^{-m}, \quad k = 1,2,\dots. \tag{A.31}$$

and recall that $(2k-1)!! = 1 \cdot 3 \cdot 5 \dots (2k-1)$, and that $(2k)!! = 2 \cdot 4 \cdot 6 \dots 2k$, with $-1!! = 1$, $0!! = 1$. In particular,

$$\begin{aligned}
&\mathcal{P}_1(x) = 1, \quad \mathcal{P}_2(x) = 1 - x, \quad \mathcal{P}_3(x) = 3!! - x + x^2, \\
&\mathcal{P}_4(x) = 5!! - 3!!\, x + x^2 - x^3, \quad \mathcal{P}_5(x) = 7!! - 5!!\, x + 3!!\, x^2 - x^3 + x^4.
\end{aligned}$$

These polynomials can be represented by means of the recurrence formula

$$\mathcal{P}_k(x) = (2k-3)!! - x\, \mathcal{P}_{k-1}(x), \quad k = 2,3,\dots,$$

with $\mathcal{P}_1(x) = 1$.

Theorem A.12 *For $t > 0$, $p \in (0,1)$, and $k = 1,2,\dots$, we have*

$$\begin{aligned}
H_k(t \mid p) = \frac{2e^{-a_p t}}{(2k-1)!!} \big(&\mathcal{P}_k(2a_p t) \\
&+ (-1)^k (2a_p t)^{(2k-1)/2} \mathcal{M}((2a_p t)^{1/2})\big)\, t^{-k+1/2}.
\end{aligned} \tag{A.32}$$

Proof of Theorem A.12. It is easy to show that

$$H_k(t \mid p) = 2^{k+1} \sqrt{\pi}\, a_p^{k-1/2} m_{2k}^{\ominus}((2a_p t)^{1/2}), \quad k = 1,2,\dots,$$

where $m_0^{\ominus}(x) = 1 - \Phi_{(0,1)}(x)$ and $m_k^{\ominus}(x) = \int_x^\infty z^{-k}\, \varphi_{(0,1)}(z)\, dz$, $k = 1,2,\dots$, are incomplete normal moments of negative order. The recurrence formula

$$m_{2k}^{\ominus}(x) = (x^{-2k+1}\, \varphi_{(0,1)}(x) - m_{2(k-1)}^{\ominus}(x))/(2k-1), \quad k = 1,2,\dots,$$

follows from (B.16) by simple transformations. In this way, we get the recurrence formula

$$\begin{aligned}
H_k(t \mid p) = (2k-1)^{-1} \big(&2\sqrt{2\pi}\, t^{-k+1/2}\, \varphi_{(0,1)}((2a_p t)^{1/2}) \\
&- 2a_p H_{k-1}(t \mid p)\big), \quad k = 2,3,\dots,
\end{aligned}$$

where $H_1(t \mid p) = 2\sqrt{2\pi}\, t^{-1/2}\, \varphi_{(0,1)}((2a_p t)^{1/2}) - 4\sqrt{\pi} a_p^{1/2} (1 - \Phi_{(0,1)}((2a_p t)^{1/2}))$. The equality (A.32) follows from it by elementary algebra. □

The following corollaries of Theorem A.12 are for $p = 1/2$ and for $p \neq 1/2$. It is easily seen that in the former case $a_p = 0$, while in the latter case $a_p > 0$.

Corollary A.1 *For t positive and for $k = 1, 2, \ldots$, we have*

$$H_k(t \mid \tfrac{1}{2}) = \frac{2}{(2k-1)!!}\, \mathcal{P}_k(0)\, t^{-k+1/2} = \frac{2}{2k-1}\, t^{-k+1/2}.$$

Proof of Corollary A.1. The result can be obtained either by integration, since

$$H_k(t \mid \tfrac{1}{2}) = \int_t^\infty x^{-(2k+1)/2}\, dx = \frac{2}{2k-1}\, t^{-k+1/2},$$

or by putting $p = 1/2$ in the equation of Theorem A.12. □

Corollary A.2 *For $t > 0$, $p \neq 1/2$, $k = 1, 2, \ldots$, and for any integer $n > k$, we have*

$$\begin{aligned} H_k(t \mid p) = {} & \frac{2e^{-a_p t}}{(2k-1)!!} \left(\sum_{m=k}^{n} (-1)^{k+m} (2m-1)!!\, (2a_p t)^{k-m-1} \right) t^{-k+1/2} \\ & + \frac{2e^{-a_p t}}{(2k-1)!!} (-1)^k (2a_p)^{k-1/2} R_n((2a_p t)^{1/2}), \end{aligned}$$

where $\left| R_n((2a_p t)^{1/2}) \right| < (2n+1)!!\, (2a_p t)^{-(n+3/2)}$.

Proof of Corollary A.2. The expansion (see Theorem B.3)

$$\mathcal{M}(x) = \sum_{k=0}^{n} (-1)^k (2k-1)!!\, x^{-2k-1} + R_n(x), \quad |R_n(x)| < (2n+1)!!\, x^{-(2n+3)}$$

and equality (A.31) yield the equality

$$\begin{aligned} & \mathcal{P}_k(x) + (-1)^k x^{(2k-1)/2}\, \mathcal{M}(x^{1/2}) \\ & \quad = \sum_{m=k}^{n} (-1)^{k+m} (2m-1)!!\, x^{k-m-1} + (-1)^k x^{k-1/2} R_n(x^{1/2}), \end{aligned}$$

where $|R_n(x^{1/2})| < (2n+1)!!\, x^{-(2n+3)/2}$. The required result follows from substituting this formula into formula (A.32). □

A.2.5 Auxiliary function of the second kind

The auxiliary function of the second kind and the related results are used in Chapter 3. In particular, Theorems A.19–A.21 are used in the proof of Theorem 3.8.

The auxiliary function of the second kind, defined (see (3.12)) as

$$\mathsf{F}_t(x \mid p) = e^{-x} \sum_{n=0}^{\infty} \frac{x^n}{n!} \int_0^t \mathsf{v}_{n+1}(y \mid p)\, dy, \quad x > 0, \tag{A.33}$$

where $t > 0$, $0 < p < 1$, $q = 1 - p$ and

$$\mathsf{v}_{n+1}(y \mid p) = \left(\frac{p}{q}\right)^{(n+1)/2} \frac{n+1}{y}\, e^{-y/p}\, I_{n+1}(2y\sqrt{q/p}), \quad y > 0, \tag{A.34}$$

is used in Chapter 3.

Some primary results. Some primary results for $\mathsf{F}_t(x \mid p)$ can be obtained by elementary calculations based on the Bessel functions theory. In particular, for k integer, $p \in (0,1)$, $q = 1 - p$, straightforwardly from Theorem A.7 we have

$$\int_0^\infty e^{-y/p} I_k(2y\sqrt{q/p})\, dy = \begin{cases} \left(\dfrac{q}{p}\right)^{k/2} \left(\dfrac{p}{p-q}\right), & p \geqslant 1/2, \\ \left(\dfrac{p}{q}\right)^{k/2} \left(\dfrac{p}{q-p}\right), & p < 1/2, \end{cases}$$

and

$$\int_0^\infty e^{-y/p} I_k(2y\sqrt{q/p})\, \frac{dy}{y} = \begin{cases} \dfrac{1}{k}\left(\dfrac{q}{p}\right)^{k/2}, & p \geqslant 1/2, \\ \dfrac{1}{k}\left(\dfrac{p}{q}\right)^{k/2}, & p < 1/2. \end{cases}$$

Bearing in mind (3.13), the latter equality yields

$$\int_0^\infty \mathsf{v}_{n+1}(y \mid p)\, dy = \begin{cases} 1, & p \geqslant 1/2, \\ (p/q)^{n+1}, & p < 1/2. \end{cases} \tag{A.35}$$

Bearing in mind (3.12) with t replaced by ∞, and the elementary equality

$$e^{-x} \sum_{n=0}^{\infty} \frac{x^n}{n!} (p/q)^{n+1} = (p/q) \exp\{-x\,(1 - (p/q))\},$$

we have (cf. (3.9))

$$\mathsf{F}_\infty(x \mid p) = \begin{cases} 1, & p \geqslant 1/2, \\ (p/q) \exp\{-x\,(1 - (p/q))\}, & p < 1/2. \end{cases} \tag{A.36}$$

Asymptotic expansions. The following theorem is devoted to asymptotic expansions of an auxiliary function of the second kind.

Theorem A.13 *For $t \to \infty$, we have*

$$\begin{aligned} &\mathsf{F}_\infty(x \mid p) - \mathsf{F}_t(x \mid p) \\ &\quad \sim \frac{(p/q)^{1/4}}{2\sqrt{\pi}} \Bigg(S_0(x \mid p) H_1(t \mid p) + \sum_{k=1}^{\infty} (-1)^k \frac{(p/q)^{k/2}}{2^{2k} k!} \\ &\quad \times \left(S_{2k}(x \mid p) + \sum_{j=1}^{k} \frac{A_{k,j}}{2^{2j}} S_{2(k-j)}(x \mid p) \right) H_{k+1}(t \mid p) \Bigg), \end{aligned} \tag{A.37}$$

where $H_k(t \mid p)$, $k = 1, 2, \ldots$, *are defined in* (A.30), *and* $S_k(x \mid p)$, $k = 0, 1, 2, \ldots$, *are defined in* (A.27).

Proof of Theorem A.13. For $p \in (0,1)$, $q = 1 - p$, bearing in mind (A.35), i.e.,

$$\int_0^\infty \mathsf{v}_{n+1}(y \mid p)\, dy = \begin{cases} 1, & p \geqslant 1/2, \\ (p/q)^{n+1}, & p < 1/2, \end{cases}$$

we have

$$\mathcal{F}_\infty(x \mid p) = e^{-x} \sum_{n=0}^{\infty} \frac{x^n}{n!} \int_0^\infty \mathsf{v}_{n+1}(y \mid p)\, dy. \tag{A.38}$$

Therefore,

$$\begin{aligned} \mathcal{F}_\infty(x \mid p) - \mathcal{F}_t(x \mid p) &= e^{-x} \sum_{n=0}^{\infty} \frac{x^n}{n!} \int_t^\infty \mathsf{v}_{n+1}(y \mid p)\, dy \\ &= e^{-x} \sum_{n=0}^{\infty} \frac{x^n}{n!} \left(\frac{p}{q}\right)^{(n+1)/2} \int_t^\infty \frac{n+1}{y} e^{-y/p} I_{n+1}(2y\sqrt{q/p}\,)\, dy. \end{aligned} \tag{A.39}$$

The lower limit of integration t in (A.39) is large. Therefore, for all $y > t$ we can expand the Bessel function $I_{n+1}(2y\sqrt{q/p})$. Applying Theorem A.9 and equality (A.25), we get

$$\begin{aligned} I_{n+1}(2y\sqrt{q/p}) \sim \frac{(p/q)^{1/4} e^{2y\sqrt{q/p}}}{2\sqrt{\pi y}} &\left(1 + \sum_{k=1}^{\infty} (-1)^k \frac{(p/q)^{k/2}}{(4y)^k k!}\right. \\ &\times \left.\left((n+1)^{2k} + \sum_{j=1}^{k} \frac{A_{k,j}}{2^{2j}} (n+1)^{2(k-j)}\right)\right). \end{aligned}$$

Since the series converges uniformly, integration term by term is allowed[15]. In this way, we transform (A.39) into

$$\begin{aligned} \mathcal{F}_\infty(x \mid p) - \mathcal{F}_t(x \mid p) &\sim e^{-x} \frac{(p/q)^{1/4}}{2\sqrt{\pi}} \sum_{n=0}^{\infty} \frac{x^n (n+1)}{n!} \\ &\times \left(\frac{p}{q}\right)^{(n+1)/2} \left(H_1(t \mid p) + \sum_{k=1}^{\infty} (-1)^k \frac{(p/q)^{k/2}}{4^k k!}\right. \\ &\times \left.\left((n+1)^{2k} + \sum_{j=1}^{k} \frac{A_{k,j}}{2^{2j}} (n+1)^{2(k-j)}\right) H_{k+1}(t \mid p)\right), \end{aligned} \tag{A.40}$$

and use (A.27). We change the order of summation in (A.40), which is allowed, whence (A.37). □

[15]See, e.g., [190], Chapter VIII, Section 8.31.

It is noteworthy that Theorem A.13 yields asymptotic expansions for the function $\mathsf{F}_\infty(x \mid p) - \mathsf{F}_t(x \mid p)$, as $t \to \infty$, in the usual sense[16]. Indeed, by Theorem A.12 and its corollaries, for $p \in (0,1)$ the functions $H_k(t \mid p)$, $k = 1, 2, \dots$, are positive and bounded by a power function of t.

Derivatives of the auxiliary function of the second kind. Let us consider the derivatives

$$\frac{\partial^{(i+j)}}{\partial x^i \partial p^j} \mathsf{F}_t(x \mid p), \quad i, j = 0, 1, \dots,$$

using for them the shorthand notation $\mathsf{F}_t^{(i,j)}(x \mid p)$. The proof of the following theorem is carried out by direct differentiation, with application of the formulas for derivative of the modified Bessel function of the first kind.

Theorem A.14 *For $x, t > 0$ and $0 < p < 1$, we have*

$$\begin{aligned} \mathsf{F}_t^{(1,0)}(x \mid p) &= -\, e^{-x} \sum_{n=0}^{\infty} \frac{x^n}{n!} \int_0^t (\mathsf{v}_{n+1}(y \mid p) - \mathsf{v}_{n+2}(y \mid p))\, dy, \\ \mathsf{F}_t^{(0,1)}(x \mid p) &= p^{-2} e^{-x} \sum_{n=0}^{\infty} \frac{x^n}{n!} \\ &\quad \times \int_0^t y \left(\mathsf{v}_{n+1}(y \mid p) - \frac{n+1}{n+2} \mathsf{v}_{n+2}(y \mid p) \right) dy, \end{aligned} \tag{A.41}$$

and

$$\begin{aligned} \mathsf{F}_t^{(2,0)}(x \mid p) &= e^{-x} \sum_{n=0}^{\infty} \frac{x^n}{n!} \int_0^t (\mathsf{v}_{n+1}(y \mid p) - 2\,\mathsf{v}_{n+2}(y \mid p) + \mathsf{v}_{n+3}(y \mid p))\, dy, \\ \mathsf{F}_t^{(0,2)}(x \mid p) &= p^{-4} e^{-x} \sum_{n=0}^{\infty} \frac{x^n}{n!} \int_0^t y^2 \Big(\mathsf{v}_{n+1}(y \mid p) - 2\,\frac{n+1}{n+2} \mathsf{v}_{n+2}(y \mid p) \\ &\quad + \frac{n+1}{n+3} \mathsf{v}_{n+3}(y \mid p) \Big)\, dy - 2p^{-1} \mathsf{F}_t^{(0,1)}(x \mid p), \\ \mathsf{F}_t^{(1,1)}(x \mid p) &= -\, p^{-2} e^{-x} \sum_{n=0}^{\infty} \frac{x^n}{n!} \int_0^t y \Big(\mathsf{v}_{n+1}(y \mid p) - \frac{n+1}{n+2} \mathsf{v}_{n+2}(y \mid p) \\ &\quad - \mathsf{v}_{n+2}(y \mid p) + \frac{n+2}{n+3} \mathsf{v}_{n+3}(y \mid p) \Big)\, dy. \end{aligned} \tag{A.42}$$

[16]See, for example, [190], Chapter VII.

Proof of Theorem A.14. To prove the first equality in (A.41), we note that

$$\begin{aligned} F_t^{(1,0)}(x \mid p) = & - e^{-x} \sum_{n=0}^{\infty} \frac{x^n}{n!} \int_0^t \mathsf{v}_{n+1}(y \mid p)\, dy \\ & + e^{-x} \sum_{n=1}^{\infty} \frac{x^{n-1}}{(n-1)!} \int_0^t \mathsf{v}_{n+1}(y \mid p)\, dy \\ = & e^{-x} \sum_{n=0}^{\infty} \frac{x^n}{n!} \int_0^t \big(\mathsf{v}_{n+2}(y \mid p) - \mathsf{v}_{n+1}(y \mid p)\big)\, dy. \end{aligned} \tag{A.43}$$

To prove the second equality in (A.41), we note that

$$\frac{\partial}{\partial p} \mathsf{v}_{n+1}(y \mid p) = \frac{y}{p^2} \Big(\mathsf{v}_{n+1}(y \mid p) - \frac{n+1}{n+2} \mathsf{v}_{n+2}(y \mid p) \Big),$$

which follows from the second equality (A.16) applied to $\mathsf{v}_{n+1}(y \mid p)$, and that

$$\begin{aligned} F_t^{(0,1)}(x \mid p) = & e^{-x} \sum_{n=0}^{\infty} \frac{x^n}{n!} \int_0^t \frac{\partial}{\partial p} \mathsf{v}_{n+1}(y \mid p)\, dy \\ = & e^{-x} \sum_{n=0}^{\infty} \frac{x^n}{n!} \\ & \times \int_0^t \frac{y}{p^2} \Big(\mathsf{v}_{n+1}(y \mid p) - \frac{n+1}{n+2} \mathsf{v}_{n+2}(y \mid p) \Big)\, dy. \end{aligned} \tag{A.44}$$

The proof of equalities in (A.42) is carried out in a similar way and is left to the reader as exercise. □

Auxiliary function of the second kind and random walk with random displacements. In Section 3.2.3, the functions (A.33) and (A.34) are endowed with a clear probabilistic meaning. In particular, the function $\mathsf{v}_k(y \mid p)$ expressed in terms of the modified Bessel function of the first kind is a p.d.f. of the distribution of a random variable $\varsigma_k(p)$, which is the first hitting time of the point k in the model of random walk with random displacements. This distribution is defective for $p < 1/2$, i.e., when the random walk drifts to the left, and proper for $p \geqslant 1/2$, i.e., when the random walk has no drift, or drifts to the right. In this section, we collect a number of results about these functions, mostly technical.

The auxiliary function of the second kind, being core element in the expression for the distribution of the first level-crossing time when jump sizes and inter-renewal intervals are exponentially distributed, is related to random walk with random displacements (see (3.14)–(3.18)). Using this observation, quoting [78], many relations lose their accidental character, and much hard analysis can be avoided. An illustration of this idea is the following result.

Theorem A.15 *For $p \in (0,1)$ and $n = 0, 1, \dots$, we have*

$$\int_0^y \mathsf{v}_{n+1}(z \mid p)\,dz - \int_0^y \mathsf{v}_{n+2}(z \mid p)\,dz > 0, \quad y > 0. \tag{A.45}$$

Proof of Theorem A.15. Straightforwardly from (3.17), we have

$$\begin{aligned}\int_0^y \mathsf{v}_{n+1}(z \mid p)\,dz &- \int_0^y \mathsf{v}_{n+2}(z \mid p)\,dz \\ &= \mathsf{P}\{\varsigma_{n+1}(p) \leqslant y\} - \mathsf{P}\{\varsigma_{n+2}(p) \leqslant y\} \\ &= \mathsf{P}\Big\{\sup_{0 \leqslant z \leqslant y} \xi_p(z) = n+1\Big\} > 0,\end{aligned} \tag{A.46}$$

and the proof is complete. □

Theorem A.15 can be strengthened as follows.

Theorem A.16 *For $p \in (0,1)$ and $n = 0, 1, \dots$, we have*

$$\int_0^y \mathsf{v}_{n+1}(z \mid p)\,dz - \int_0^y \mathsf{v}_{n+2}(z \mid p)\,dz > \frac{y}{n+2}\mathsf{v}_{n+2}(y \mid p), \quad y > 0. \tag{A.47}$$

Proof of Theorem A.16. Using equality (3.15) with $k = n+2$ and equality in (A.46), we rewrite inequality (A.47) in the form

$$\mathsf{P}\Big\{\sup_{0 \leqslant z \leqslant y} \xi_p(z) = n+1\Big\} - \mathsf{P}\{\xi_p(y) = n+2\} > 0.$$

Let us check this inequality. Denote by ω a sample path of the random process $\{\xi_p(z), 0 \leqslant z < \infty\}$. It is a point in the elementary state space. First, let us establish an one-to-one correspondence between the sets $A_1 = \{\omega : \xi_p(y) = n+2\}$ and

$$A_2 = \Big\{\omega : \sup_{0 \leqslant z \leqslant y} \xi_p(z) = n+1,\ \xi_p(y) = n\Big\}.$$

For each $\omega = \{\xi_p(z), 0 \leqslant z \leqslant y\} \in A_1$, we reflect (with respect to the level $n+1$) that part of ω that lies above the level $n+1$. In this way, for each $\omega \in A_1$ we obtain a unique $\omega' = \{\xi_p'(z), 0 \leqslant z \leqslant y\}$ such that $\sup_{0 \leqslant z \leqslant y} \xi_p'(z) \leqslant n+1$ and $\xi_p'(z) = n$.

Second, we note that the implication

$$A_2 = \Big\{\omega : \sup_{0 \leqslant z \leqslant y} \xi_p(z) = n+1,\ \xi_p(y) = n\Big\} \subset A_3 = \Big\{\omega : \sup_{0 \leqslant z \leqslant y} \xi_p(z) = n+1\Big\}$$

is strict. Indeed, the set A_3 contains, e.g., all trajectories of the random walk process which have only one hitting of the point $n+1$ within the interval $[0, y]$.

Such trajectories are not produced by the reflection described above: all the trajectories obtained by the reflection must hit the point $n+1$ at least twice. We have[17] $\mathsf{P}(A_1) = \mathsf{P}(A_2) < \mathsf{P}(A_3)$, and the proof is complete. □

[17]Note that the "infinitesimal probability masses" of the original sample path and of its twin obtained by reflection are the same.

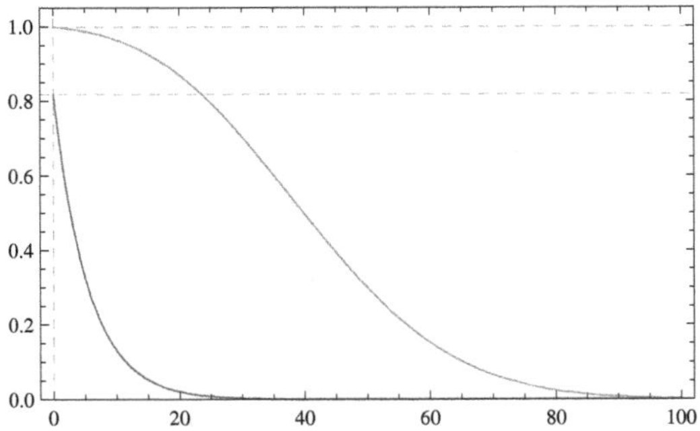

FIGURE A.1: Graphs (X-axis is x) of $F_t(x \mid p)$, $p = 0.45$ (below), $p = 0.55$ (above), and $t = 200$. Horizontal grid lines are 0.82 and 0.1.

Remark A.1 The proof of Theorems A.15 and A.16 by means of Bessel functions' theory is not easy[18]. In particular, to prove by these means positiveness of

$$\int_0^y \mathsf{v}_{n+1}(z \mid p)\,dz - \int_0^y \mathsf{v}_{n+2}(z \mid p)\,dz$$
$$= \left(\frac{p}{q}\right)^{(n+1)/2} \int_0^y \frac{n+1}{z}\, e^{-z/p} I_{n+1}(2z\sqrt{q/p})\,dz$$
$$- \left(\frac{p}{q}\right)^{(n+2)/2} \int_0^y \frac{n+2}{z}\, e^{-z/p} I_{n+2}(2z\sqrt{q/p})\,dz,$$

which is the left-hand side of (A.45), is an uneasy exercise.

The following result is illustrated in Fig. A.1. It is a corollary of Theorem A.15.

Theorem A.17 *For $p \in (0,1)$ and $t > 0$ fixed, the function $F_t(x \mid p)$ monotone decreases from $\int_0^t \mathsf{v}_1(y \mid p)\,dy$ to 0, as x increases from 0 to infinity.*

Proof of Theorem A.17. By the well-known criterion of monotony (see Section A.1.1), this proof follows from the inequality

$$\begin{aligned}\frac{\partial}{\partial x} F_t(x \mid p) &= \frac{\partial}{\partial x} e^{-x} \sum_{n=0}^{\infty} \frac{x^n}{n!} \int_0^t \mathsf{v}_{n+1}(y \mid p)\,dy \\ &= -e^{-x} \sum_{n=0}^{\infty} \frac{x^n}{n!} \int_0^t (\mathsf{v}_{n+1}(y \mid p) - \mathsf{v}_{n+2}(y \mid p))\,dy < 0,\end{aligned} \tag{A.48}$$

which is straightforward from inequality (A.45). □

The following result allows an elegant proof. Its illustration is Fig. A.2.

[18]Thought we do not claim that it seems like an insurmountable task.

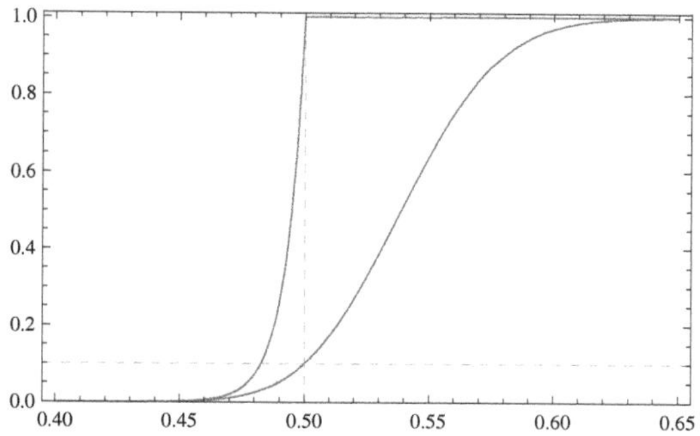

FIGURE A.2: Graphs (X-axis is p) of $F_\infty(x \mid p)$ (above) and $F_t(x \mid p)$ (below), with $x = 33.22$ and $t = 200$. Function $F_\infty(x \mid p)$ is 1 for $p \geqslant 1/2$. The value of the function $F_t(x \mid p)$ at the point $p = 0.5$ is 0.1.

Theorem A.18 *For positive x and t fixed, the function $F_t(x \mid p)$ monotone increases from 0 to 1, as p increases from 0 to 1.*

Proof of Theorem A.18. Recall that $\varsigma_k(p)$ is the first hitting time of the point k by the random walk with random displacements with parameter $p \in (0,1)$. By this definition, the random time $\varsigma_{n+2}(p)$ is stochastically larger than $\varsigma_{n+1}(p)$. About the distribution (see (3.17))

$$\mathsf{P}\{\varsigma_k(p) \leqslant t\} = \int_0^t \mathsf{v}_k(z \mid p)\, dz$$

with probability density function $\mathsf{v}_k(z \mid p)$, we know that it is defective for $p < 1/2$, and proper for $p \geqslant 1/2$. The first case corresponds to random walk with random displacements with a drift to the left, and the second case corresponds to this random walk with no drift, or with a drift to the right.

Evidently, for all $0 < p_1 < p_2 < 1$ the random time $\varsigma_{n+1}(p_1)$ is stochastically larger than $\varsigma_{n+1}(p_2)$. Therefore, we have

$$\int_0^t \mathsf{v}_{n+1}(z \mid p_1)\, dz = \mathsf{P}\{\varsigma_{n+1}(p_1) \leqslant t\} \leqslant \mathsf{P}\{\varsigma_{n+1}(p_2) \leqslant t\} = \int_0^t \mathsf{v}_{n+1}(z \mid p_2)\, dz.$$

Applying equation (3.18), for all $0 < p_1 < p_2 < 1$ we have

$$\begin{aligned} F_t(x \mid p_1) &= e^{-x} \sum_{n=0}^{\infty} \frac{x^n}{n!} \int_0^t \mathsf{v}_{n+1}(y \mid p_1)\, dy \\ &= e^{-x} \sum_{n=0}^{\infty} \frac{x^n}{n!} \mathsf{P}\{\varsigma_{n+1}(p_1) \leqslant t\} \leqslant e^{-x} \sum_{n=0}^{\infty} \frac{x^n}{n!} \int_0^t \mathsf{P}\{\varsigma_{n+1}(p_2) \leqslant t\} \\ &= e^{-x} \sum_{n=0}^{\infty} \frac{x^n}{n!} \int_0^t \mathsf{v}_{n+1}(y \mid p_2)\, dy = F_t(x \mid p_2), \end{aligned}$$

whence $\mathsf{F}_t(x \mid p)$ monotone increases. □

Remark A.2 The above probabilistic proof of Theorem A.18 looks elegant. If we wanted to use instead the standard criterion of monotony (see Section A.1.1), we would have to check first that

$$\frac{\partial}{\partial p}\mathsf{v}_{n+1}(y \mid p)\,dy = \frac{y}{p^2}\Big(\mathsf{v}_{n+1}(y \mid p) - \frac{n+1}{n+2}\mathsf{v}_{n+2}(y \mid p)\Big)\,dy.$$

This is obtained by differentiating both sides of equality (3.13) and by noting that

$$\frac{\partial}{\partial p}\mathsf{v}_{n+1}(y \mid p) = \Big(\frac{p}{q}\Big)^{(n+2)/2}\frac{n+1}{2p^2}e^{-y/p}\Big\{-I_n(2y\sqrt{q/p}) + \frac{(n+1)p+2yq}{y\sqrt{pq}}I_{n+1}(2y\sqrt{q/p}) - I_{n+2}(2y\sqrt{q/p})\Big\},$$

and that

$$I_n(2y\sqrt{q/p}) = I_{n+2}(2y\sqrt{q/p}) + \frac{n+1}{y\sqrt{q/p}}I_{n+1}(2y\sqrt{q/p}),$$

which follows from the first recurrent relation in (A.16) by direct algebra. Then we need the inequality

$$\frac{\partial}{\partial p}\mathsf{F}_t(x \mid p) = \frac{1}{p^2}e^{-x}\sum_{n=0}^{\infty}\frac{x^n}{n\,!}\int_0^t y \times\Big(\mathsf{v}_{n+1}(y \mid p) - \frac{n+1}{n+2}\mathsf{v}_{n+2}(y \mid p)\Big)\,dy > 0, \tag{A.49}$$

which straightforward analytical proof[19] is uneasy (see the second proof of Theorem 3.1 in [121]). This observation shows that certain deep analytical results can be obtained with surprising ease by means of probabilistic considerations.

The following result is a corollary of Theorems A.17 and A.18, or of inequalities (A.48) and (A.49).

Corollary A.3 *In the renewal model satisfying the standard assumptions, with T and Y exponentially distributed with positive parameters δ and ρ, we have*

$$\frac{\partial}{\partial u}\mathsf{P}\{\varUpsilon_{u,c\,|\,\delta,\rho} \leqslant t\} < 0, \qquad \frac{\partial}{\partial c}\mathsf{P}\{\varUpsilon_{u,c\,|\,\delta,\rho} \leqslant t\} > 0.$$

[19] If Theorem A.18 is proved by other means, this inequality follows from it.

Proof of Corollary A.3. Starting with equality (3.14) and applying the chain rule for differentiation of a composite function (see equality (A.1)), we have

$$\begin{aligned}\frac{\partial}{\partial u}\mathsf{P}\{\varUpsilon_{u,c\,|\,\delta,\rho} \leqslant t\} &= \frac{\partial}{\partial u}\mathcal{F}_{t\delta}(u\rho \mid \delta/(c\rho+\delta))\\ &= \rho\,\frac{\partial}{\partial x}\mathcal{F}_{t}(x \mid \delta/(c\rho+\delta))\Big|_{x=u\rho}\end{aligned}$$

The proof of the first inequality is straightforward from inequality (A.48).

For $\frac{d}{dc}(\delta/(c\rho+\delta) = c\rho/(\delta+c\rho)^2$, we have in the same way

$$\begin{aligned}\frac{\partial}{\partial c}\mathsf{P}\{\varUpsilon_{u,c\,|\,\delta,\rho} \leqslant t\} &= \frac{\partial}{\partial c}\mathcal{F}_{t\delta}(u\rho \mid \delta/(c\rho+\delta))\\ &= \frac{c\rho}{(\delta+c\rho)^2}\frac{\partial}{\partial p}\mathcal{F}_{t\delta}(u\rho \mid p)\Big|_{p=\delta/(c\rho+\delta)},\end{aligned}$$

and the proof of the second inequality is straightforward from inequality (A.49). The proof is complete. □

Inequalities related to auxiliary function of the second kind. The proofs of the following Theorems A.19–A.21 are based on the arguments of the theory of random walk with random displacements. If on the contrary we regard $\mathcal{F}_t(x \mid p)$ and its derivatives as merely expressions in terms of Bessel functions, and overlook the links with the theory of random walk with random displacements — which allows us using the probabilistic arguments — then the following results turn into difficult results within the Bessel functions theory.

Theorem A.19 *For any $t > 0$ and $p \in (0,1)$, we have*

$$\mathcal{F}_t^{(1,0)}(x \mid p) < 0, \quad x > 0. \tag{A.50}$$

Proof of Theorem A.19. Bearing in mind equality (A.43), the proof is straightforward from inequalities (A.45) of Theorem A.15. □

Theorem A.20 *For any $t > 0$ and $p \in (0,1)$, we have*

$$\mathcal{F}_t^{(0,1)}(x \mid p) > 0, \quad x > 0. \tag{A.51}$$

Proof of Theorem A.20. This theorem is equivalent to Theorem A.18, whose proof was based on the probabilistic arguments involving first hitting time of a point by the random walk with random displacements. □

Theorem A.21 *For any $t > 0$ and $p \in (0,1)$, we have*

$$\mathcal{F}_t^{(1,0)}(x \mid p) + \frac{p^2}{t}\mathcal{F}_t^{(0,1)}(x \mid p) < 0, \quad x > 0. \tag{A.52}$$

Proof of Theorem A.21. Using equalities (A.41), we easily have

$$\begin{aligned} \mathsf{F}_t^{(1,0)}(x \mid p) + \frac{p^2}{t} \mathsf{F}_t^{(0,1)}(x \mid p) \\ = \frac{e^{-x}}{t} \sum_{n=0}^{\infty} \frac{x^n}{n!} \int_0^t d_n(y \mid p)\, dy, \quad x > 0, \end{aligned} \tag{A.53}$$

where

$$\begin{aligned} d_n(y \mid p) = \frac{y}{n+2} \mathsf{v}_{n+2}(y \mid p) \\ - \left(\int_0^y \mathsf{v}_{n+1}(z \mid p)\, dz - \int_0^y \mathsf{v}_{n+2}(z \mid p)\, dz \right), \quad y > 0. \end{aligned}$$

By Theorem A.16, for $p \in (0,1)$ and $n = 0, 1, \ldots$, we have

$$\int_0^y \mathsf{v}_{n+1}(z \mid p)\, dz - \int_0^y \mathsf{v}_{n+2}(z \mid p)\, dz > \frac{y}{n+2} \mathsf{v}_{n+2}(y \mid p), \quad y > 0,$$

which is equivalent to

$$d_n(y \mid p) < 0, \quad y > 0.$$

Applying it to the right-hand side of (A.53), we complete the proof. □

Remark A.2 is quite applicable to Theorems A.19–A.21.

Appendix B

Auxiliary Results from Probability

In this appendix, we collect various results from probability.

B.1 Distributions on the Positive Half-line

The information about the distributions on the positive half-line, widely used to model loss or life distributions, can be found, e.g., in [94], [108], [103], [140], [145].

Exponential distribution. The random variable ξ is exponentially distributed if for $\theta > 0$ its probability density function (p.d.f.) is

$$f_\xi(x) = \theta\, e^{-x\,\theta}, \quad x > 0,$$

and zero for x non-positive[1]. By elementary calculations, it is easy to check that $\mathsf{E}(\xi^k) = k!/\theta^k$, $k = 1, 2, \ldots$. Consequently,

$$\mathsf{E}\,\xi = \frac{1}{\theta}, \quad \mathsf{D}\,\xi = \frac{1}{\theta^2}, \quad \mathsf{E}(\xi - \mathsf{E}\,\xi)^3 = \frac{2}{\theta^3}.$$

For $n > 0$ integer, we have

$$f_\xi^{*n}(x) = \theta\, \frac{(\theta x)^{n-1}}{\Gamma(n)}\, e^{-\theta x}, \quad x > 0. \tag{B.1}$$

Mixture of two exponential distributions. The random variable ξ is a mixture of two exponential distributions if for $0 < \theta_1 < \theta_2 < \infty$ and for $0 \leqslant p, q \leqslant 1$ such that $p + q = 1$, its p.d.f. is

$$f_\xi(x) = \theta_1 p\, e^{-\theta_1 x} + \theta_2\, q\, e^{-\theta_2 x}, \quad x > 0.$$

Plainly, the corresponding c.d.f. $F_\xi(x) = \int_0^x f_\xi(z)\, dz$ is

$$F_\xi(x) = 1 - (p\, e^{-\theta_1 x} + q\, e^{-\theta_2 x}), \quad x > 0. \tag{B.2}$$

[1]Further in Appendix B, even if it is not explicitly stated, we mean that the function considered on the positive half-line is set zero on the negative half-line.

For $g(z) = \dfrac{p\,\theta_1 e^{-\theta_1 z} + q\,\theta_2 e^{-\theta_2 z}}{p\,e^{-\theta_1 z} + q\,e^{-\theta_2 z}}$, called in [180] contagion rate,

$$F_\xi\,(x) = 1 - \exp\Big\{ - \int_0^x g(z)\,dz \Big\}.$$

Note that if $\theta_1 = \theta_2$, then there is no contagion, and the mixture of two exponential distributions degenerates into an exponential distribution. By elementary calculations, it is easy to check that

$$\mathsf{E}\,\xi = \frac{p}{\theta_1} + \frac{q}{\theta_2}, \quad \mathsf{D}\,\xi = \frac{q\,\theta_1^2 + p\,\theta_2^2 + p\,q\,(\theta_1 - \theta_2)^2}{\theta_1^2\theta_2^2}, \quad \mathsf{E}(\xi^3) = \frac{6p}{\theta_1^3} + \frac{6q}{\theta_2^3},$$

$$\mathsf{E}(\xi - \mathsf{E}\,\xi)^3 = -\frac{6pq^2}{\theta_1^2\theta_2} - \frac{6p^2q}{\theta_1\theta_2^2} + \frac{2p\,(3\,q + p^2)}{\theta_1^3} + \frac{2q\,(3p + q^2)}{\theta_2^3}.$$

Erlang distribution. The random variable ξ is Erlang if for $\theta > 0$ and integer k its p.d.f. is

$$f_\xi\,(x) = \frac{\theta^k x^{k-1}}{\Gamma(k)}\,e^{-x\,\theta}, \quad x > 0.$$

Plainly, Erlang p.d.f. is a particular case of the Gamma p.d.f.

By elementary calculations, it is easy to check that

$$\mathsf{E}\,\xi = \frac{k}{\theta}, \quad \mathsf{D}\,\xi = \frac{k}{\theta^2}, \quad \mathsf{E}(\xi - \mathsf{E}\,\xi)^3 = \frac{2k}{\theta^3}.$$

Gamma distribution. The random variable ξ is gamma with parameters $\alpha > 0$ and $\beta > 0$, if its p.d.f. is

$$f_\xi\,(x) = \frac{\beta^\alpha}{\Gamma(\alpha)}\,x^{\alpha-1}e^{-\beta x}, \quad x \geqslant 0, \tag{B.3}$$

and 0, if $x < 0$. The denominator is the gamma function $\Gamma(x) = \int_0^\infty z^{x-1}e^{-z}\,dz$, where $x > 0$. It is well-known that $\Gamma(n+1) = n!$, $n = 0, 1, \ldots$.

By elementary calculations, it is easy to check that

$$\mathsf{E}\,\xi = \frac{\alpha}{\beta}, \quad \mathsf{D}\,\xi = \frac{\alpha}{\beta^2}.$$

Beta distribution. The random variable ξ is beta with parameters $\alpha > 0$ and $\beta > 0$, if its p.d.f. is

$$f_\xi\,(x) = \frac{\Gamma(\alpha + \beta)}{\Gamma(\alpha)\,\Gamma(\beta)}\,(1 - x)^{\alpha-1}x^{\beta-1}, \quad 0 < x < 1, \tag{B.4}$$

and 0, if $x < 0$ or $x > 1$.

Inverse Gaussian distribution. The inverse Gaussian distribution is commonly defined (see, e.g., [94]) by its p.d.f.

$$\begin{aligned} f(x;\mu,\lambda,-\tfrac{1}{2}) &:= \frac{\lambda^{1/2}}{\sqrt{2\pi}}\, x^{-3/2} \exp\Big\{-\frac{\lambda(x-\mu)^2}{2\mu^2 x}\Big\} \\ &= \lambda^{1/2} x^{-3/2}\, \varphi_{(0,1)}\Big(\sqrt{\frac{\lambda}{x}}\Big(\frac{x}{\mu}-1\Big)\Big), \qquad x>0. \end{aligned} \tag{B.5}$$

Here $\mu > 0$ is referred to as mean parameter[2], and $\lambda > 0$ is called shape parameter. This distribution is skewed to the right, and its unique mode is

$$\mu\left(\sqrt{1+\frac{9\mu^2}{4\lambda^2}}-\frac{3\mu}{2\lambda}\right).$$

For μ fixed, this mode grows to μ, as $\lambda \to \infty$. For λ fixed, it grows to $\lambda/3$, as $\mu \to \infty$. The expression for the corresponding c.d.f., i.e.,

$$\begin{aligned} F(x;\mu,\lambda,-\tfrac{1}{2}) := & \int_0^x f(z;\mu,\lambda,-\tfrac{1}{2})\,dz \\ &= \Phi_{(0,1)}\Big(\sqrt{\frac{\lambda}{x}}\Big(\frac{x}{\mu}-1\Big)\Big) \\ &\quad + \exp\Big\{\frac{2\lambda}{\mu}\Big\}\,\Phi_{(0,1)}\Big(-\sqrt{\frac{\lambda}{x}}\Big(\frac{x}{\mu}+1\Big)\Big), \qquad x>0, \end{aligned} \tag{B.6}$$

can be derived (see [134], Chapter 2) by using Binet's integral; this is a result obtained in 1841. The reader will find this and many other facts in the book [134]. In particular, well-known (see, e.g., [94]) are the equalities

$$\int_0^\infty z\, f(z;\mu,\lambda,-\tfrac{1}{2})\,dz = \mu, \tag{B.7}$$

and

$$\begin{aligned} \int_0^\infty (z-\mu)^2 f(z;\mu,\lambda,-\tfrac{1}{2})\,dz &= \frac{\mu^3}{\lambda}, \\ \int_0^\infty (z-\mu)^3 f(z;\mu,\lambda,-\tfrac{1}{2})\,dz &= \frac{3\mu^5}{\lambda^2}. \end{aligned}$$

They follow from the equality[3]

$$\int_0^\infty e^{tz} f(z;\mu,\lambda,-\tfrac{1}{2})\,dz = \exp\left\{\frac{\lambda}{\mu}\left(1-\sqrt{1-\frac{2\mu^2 t}{\lambda}}\right)\right\}$$

for the moment generating function.

[2]Equality (B.7) below justifies this name.

[3]We recall that $\mathsf{E}(\xi^n) = M_\xi^{(n)}(0)$, where $M_\xi^{(n)}(t)$ is n-th derivative of the moment generating function.

Resorting to the auxiliary function of the first kind

$$\mathsf{F}(z,y \mid -\tfrac{1}{2}) := \Phi_{(0,1)}(y-z) + \exp\{2zy\}\,\Phi_{(0,1)}(-z-y), \quad z,y>0,$$

and using Theorem 2.3, i.e., that for $\mu>0$, $\lambda>0$

$$F(x;\mu,\lambda,-\tfrac{1}{2}) = \mathsf{F}(z,y \mid -\tfrac{1}{2})\Big|_{z=\frac{\sqrt{\lambda}}{\sqrt{x}},\,y=\frac{\sqrt{\lambda x}}{\mu}}, \quad x>0,$$

and for $\hat{\mu}>0$, $\lambda>0$

$$\exp\Big\{-\frac{2\lambda}{\hat{\mu}}\Big\}\,F(x;\hat{\mu},\lambda,-\tfrac{1}{2}) \\ = \big(\exp\{-2zy\}\,\mathsf{F}(z,y \mid -\tfrac{1}{2})\big)\Big|_{z=\frac{\sqrt{\lambda}}{\sqrt{x}},\,y=\frac{\sqrt{\lambda x}}{\hat{\mu}}}, \quad x>0,$$

we can (see [134], Chapter 2) get the derivatives of $F(x;\mu,\lambda,-\frac{1}{2})$ with respect to parameters by standard calculations based on using the chain rule for differentiation of a composite function.

Pareto distribution. The random variable ξ is Pareto if for $a>0$ and $b>0$ its p.d.f. is

$$f_\xi(x) = \frac{ab}{(x\,b+1)^{a+1}}, \quad x>0. \tag{B.8}$$

Plainly, the corresponding c.d.f. $F_\xi(x) = \int_0^x f_\xi(z)\,dz$ is

$$F_\xi(x) = 1-(x\,b+1)^{-a}, \quad x>0. \tag{B.9}$$

It is noteworthy (see e.g., [91]) that Pareto p.d.f. is a mixture of exponential p.d.f. with Gamma mixing distribution, i.e.,

$$f_\xi(x) = \int_0^\infty \exp\{-xz^{-1}\}\,z^{-1} f_{a,b}(z)\,dz, \quad x>0, \tag{B.10}$$

where $f_{a,b}(z) = (\Gamma(a)b^a)^{-1} z^{-(a+1)} e^{-z^{-b}}$, and that for $g_{a,b}(z) = ab(zb+1)^{-1}$, called in [180] contagion rate,

$$f_\xi(x) = g_{a,b}(x)\exp\Big\{-\int_0^x g_{a,b}(z)\,dz\Big\}.$$

By elementary calculations, it is easy to check that for $a>3$ we have

$$\mathsf{E}\,\xi = \frac{1}{(a-1)\,b}, \quad \mathsf{D}\,\xi = \frac{a}{(a-1)^2(a-2)\,b^2},$$

$$\mathsf{E}(\xi-\mathsf{E}\,\xi)^3 = \frac{2a\,(a+1)}{(a-1)^3(a-2)(a-3)\,b^3}.$$

Kummer distribution. The random variable ξ is Kummer if for $k > 0$, $l > 0$ its p.d.f. has one of the following equivalent representations:

$$f_\xi(x) = \frac{k}{2}\,\frac{\Gamma(\frac{k+l}{2})}{\Gamma(\frac{k}{2})}\,U\Big(1+\frac{l}{2}, 2-\frac{k}{2}, \frac{k}{l}\,x\Big), \quad x > 0,$$
$$f_\xi(x) = \int_0^\infty \exp\{-tz^{-1}\}z^{-1}\,f_{k,l}(z)\,dz, \quad x > 0, \qquad \text{(B.11)}$$
$$f_\xi(x) = g_{k,l}(z)\exp\Big\{-\int_0^x g_{k,l}(z)\,dz\Big\}, \quad x > 0.$$

Apparently, this distribution (or the distribution under this name) was first introduced in [119].

Here $U(a,b,z) = \Gamma(a)^{-1}\int_0^\infty e^{-zt}t^{a-1}(1+t)^{b-a-1}\,dt$, $a > 0$ (see e.g., equality (13.2.5) in [1]) is Kummer[4] confluent hypergeometric function,

$$f_{k,l}(z) = \frac{\Gamma(\frac{k+l}{2})}{\Gamma(\frac{k}{2})\Gamma(\frac{l}{2})}\,k^{\frac{k}{2}}l^{\frac{l}{2}}z^{\frac{k}{2}-1}(l+kz)^{-\frac{k+l}{2}}, \quad z > 0, \qquad \text{(B.12)}$$

where parameters $k > 0$, $l > 0$ are called degrees of freedom, if integers, is p.d.f. of Fisher–Snedecor distribution[5], and

$$g_{k,l}(z) = \frac{k}{2}\,\frac{U(1+\frac{l}{2}, 2-\frac{k}{2}, \frac{k}{l}z)}{U(\frac{l}{2}, 1-\frac{k}{2}, \frac{k}{l}z)}, \quad z > 0.$$

Recall that the Fisher–Snedecor density is unimodal if $k > 2$, with mode at $(k-2)l/((l+2)k)$. For $k = 1, 2, \ldots$, we have

$$\mathsf{E}(\xi^k) = \frac{\Gamma(\frac{k}{2}+k)\Gamma(\frac{l}{2}-k)}{\Gamma(\frac{k}{2})\Gamma(\frac{l}{2})}\,l^k k^{-k}, \quad \text{as} \quad 2k < l. \qquad \text{(B.13)}$$

In particular,

$$\mathsf{E}\xi = \frac{l}{l-2}, \quad \text{as} \quad l > 2,$$
$$\mathsf{D}\xi = \frac{l^2(4(l-2)+kl)}{k(l-2)^2(l-4)}, \quad \text{as} \quad l > 4. \qquad \text{(B.14)}$$

B.2 Gaussian Distribution and Related Issues

The information collected in this section can be found in [1], [23], [85], [145], and [103]. While Mills' ratio is used in Chapters 2–4, the Gaussian, or normal, distribution is used in most of them.

[4]From where comes the name of this distribution.

[5]Hence, Kummer c.d.f. is a mixture of exponential c.d.f. with Fisher–Snedecor mixing distribution.

Gaussian distribution. The random variable ξ has Gaussian, or normal distribution[6] with parameters $\mu \in \mathsf{R}$ and $\sigma^2 > 0$ if its probability density function (p.d.f.) is

$$\varphi_{(\mu,\sigma^2)}(x) = \frac{1}{\sqrt{2\pi}\,\sigma}\, e^{-\frac{(x-\mu)^2}{2\sigma^2}}, \quad x \in \mathsf{R}.$$

The corresponding cumulative distribution function (c.d.f.) is

$$\Phi_{(\mu,\sigma^2)}(x) = \int_{-\infty}^{x} \varphi_{(\mu,\sigma^2)}(z)\, dz,$$

where $x \in \mathsf{R}$. For $x > 0$, we have (see [85], formula 8.253.1)

$$\sum_{k=0}^{\infty} \frac{(-1)^k x^{2k}}{k!\,(2k+1)} = \frac{\sqrt{\pi}}{x}(\Phi_{(0,1)}(x\sqrt{2}\,) - 1/2). \tag{B.15}$$

The p.d.f. and c.d.f. of a Gaussian distribution with parameters $\mu \in \mathsf{R}$ and $\sigma^2 > 0$ are related to p.d.f. and c.d.f. of the Gaussian distribution with parameters 0 and 1 called standard Gaussian, or normal, as follows:

$$\varphi_{(\mu,\sigma^2)}(x) = \frac{1}{\sigma}\,\varphi_{(0,1)}\left(\frac{x-\mu}{\sigma}\right), \quad \Phi_{(\mu,\sigma^2)}(x) = \Phi_{(0,1)}\left(\frac{x-\mu}{\sigma}\right).$$

Repeated derivatives are:

$$\frac{d^m}{dx^m}\,\Phi_{(0,1)}(x) = \frac{d^{m-1}}{dx^{m-1}}\,\varphi_{(0,1)}(x) = (-1)^{m-1} H_{m-1}(x)\,\varphi_{(0,1)}(x), \quad m = 1, 2, \ldots,$$

where

$$\begin{aligned} H_m(x) &= (-1)^m e^{x^2/2}\, \frac{d^m}{dx^m}\, e^{-x^2/2} \\ &= m! \sum_{k=0}^{[m/2]} \frac{(-1)^k x^{m-2k}}{k!\,(m-2k)!\,2^k}, \quad m = 0, 1, \ldots, \end{aligned}$$

are Chebyshev–Hermite polynomials. In particular,

$$\begin{aligned} &H_0(x) = 1, && H_3(x) = x^3 - 3x, \\ &H_1(x) = x, && H_4(x) = x^4 - 6x^2 + 3, \\ &H_2(x) = x^2 - 1, && H_5(x) = x^5 - 10x^3 + 15x, \end{aligned}$$

and the recurrence relation $H_r(x) = xH_{r-1}(x) - (r-1)H_{r-2}(x)$, $r = 3, 4, \ldots,$ holds.

For $x > 0$, the incomplete moments of negative order[7] are

$$m_k^{\ominus}(x) = \int_x^{\infty} z^{-k}\,\varphi_{(0,1)}(z)\, dz, \quad k = 1, 2, \ldots,$$

[6] A collection of results related to this distribution see, e.g., in [145]. See also [94].

[7] In [145], the incomplete moments of negative orders are set equal to zero.

with $m_0^{\ominus}(x) = 1 - \Phi_{(0,1)}(x)$. The recurrence relation

$$m_k^{\ominus}(x) = x^{-(k+1)}\,\varphi_{(0,1)}(x) - (k+1)\,m_{k+2}^{\ominus}(x), \quad k = 0, 1, 2, \ldots. \tag{B.16}$$

is proved straightforwardly, via integration by parts.

Mills' ratio. The Mills' ratio is defined as

$$\begin{aligned} \mathcal{M}(x) &= e^{x^2/2} \int_x^{\infty} e^{-t^2/2}\,dt \\ &= \frac{1 - \Phi_{(0,1)}(x)}{\varphi_{(0,1)}(x)}, \quad x \in \mathsf{R}. \end{aligned} \tag{B.17}$$

It is easily seen that $\mathcal{M}(0) = \sqrt{\pi/2}$ and that

$$\mathcal{M}(-x) = \varphi_{(0,1)}^{-1}(x) - \mathcal{M}(x), \tag{B.18}$$

and that

$$\mathcal{M}'(x) = x\,\mathcal{M}(x) - 1, \quad \mathcal{M}''(x) = \mathcal{M}(x)(1 + x^2) - x. \tag{B.19}$$

The most well-known inequalities for Mills' ratio are

$$\mathcal{M}(x) > 0, \quad x \in \mathsf{R}, \tag{B.20}$$
$$\mathcal{M}'(x) < 0, \quad x \in \mathsf{R}, \tag{B.21}$$
$$\mathcal{M}''(x) > 0, \quad x \in \mathsf{R}. \tag{B.22}$$

It follows from them that the function $\mathcal{M}(x)$, $x \in \mathsf{R}$, is convex and decreasing from ∞ to 0, as x increases from $-\infty$ to $+\infty$.

It is worth noting the inequality

$$0 < 1 - x\,\mathcal{M}(x) < \mathcal{M}^2(x). \tag{B.23}$$

The lower bound in (B.23) is easy. Since $\frac{d}{dx}(x\,\mathcal{M}(x)) = \mathcal{M}''(x) > 0$ for x finite, the function $x\,\mathcal{M}(x)$ is increasing from $-\infty$ to 1, as x increases from $-\infty$ to $+\infty$. To prove the upper bound in (B.23), it has been observed in [163] that the function

$$e^{-t^2/2} \left(\int_x^{\infty} e^{-t^2/2}\,dt \right)^{-1}$$

is a p.d.f. over the range $x \leqslant t < \infty$, and its variance is $1 - \nu(x)(\nu(x) - x)$, where

$$\nu(x) = e^{-x^2/2} \left(\int_x^{\infty} e^{-t^2/2}\,dt \right)^{-1}$$

is the reciprocal of Mills' ratio. Since this must be positive for finite x, the inequality $\nu(x)(\nu(x) - x) < 1$ holds. We should only note that this is another form of writing the upper bound in (B.23).

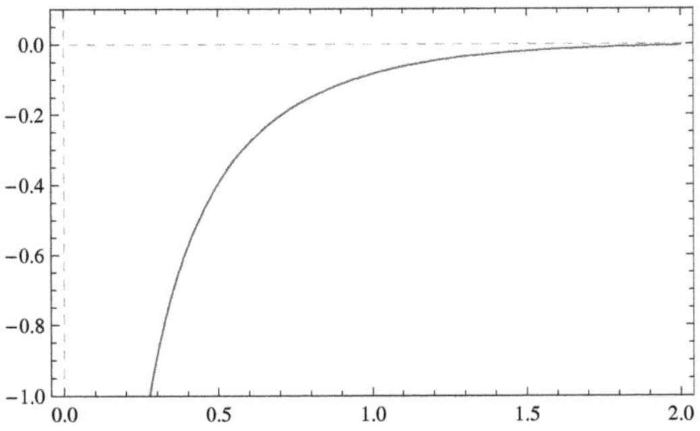

FIGURE B.1: Graph (X-axis is x) of $\mathbf{f}(x) = \varphi_{(0,1)}(x)(\mathcal{M}(x) - x^{-1})$.

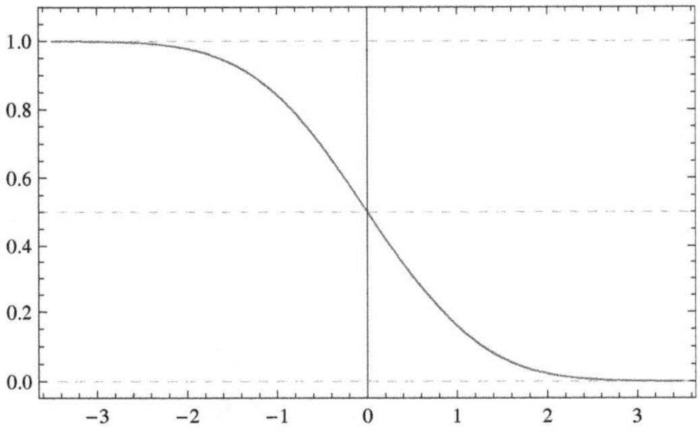

FIGURE B.2: Graph (X-axis is x) of $\mathbf{g}(x) = \varphi_{(0,1)}(x)\,\mathcal{M}(x)$.

There are many other useful inequalities for Mills' ratio. In particular, in [21] and [106] the inequalities

$$\frac{2}{\sqrt{x^2+4}+x} \leqslant \mathcal{M}(x) \leqslant \frac{2}{\sqrt{x^2+2}+x}, \quad x > 0, \tag{B.24}$$

are proved. Bearing in mind equality (B.18), it yields the upper and lower bounds for $\mathcal{M}(x)$, $x < 0$. A number of refined bounds of this type are presented in [196].

The following Theorems B.1 and B.2 are illustrated by Figs. B.1 and B.2.

Theorem B.1 *For $x > 0$, the function*

$$\mathbf{f}(x) = \varphi_{(0,1)}(x)\left(\mathcal{M}(x) - x^{-1}\right)$$

is negative and monotone increases from $-\infty$ to 0, as x increases from 0 to $+\infty$. For $x < 0$, this function exceeds 1 and monotone increases from 1 to $+\infty$, as x increases from $-\infty$ to 0.

Proof of Theorem B.1. Since $\mathbf{f}(x) = \varphi_{(0,1)}(x)x^{-1}(x\,\mathcal{M}(x) - 1)$ and $x\,\mathcal{M}(x) - 1 < 0$, $x \in \mathsf{R}$, by inequality (B.21), this function is negative for $x > 0$. Easy calculus yields $\mathbf{f}'(x) = x^{-2}\,\varphi_{(0,1)}(x) > 0$, which proves that for $x > 0$ the function $\mathbf{f}(x)$ monotone increases, as x increases. The proof in the case $x < 0$ is analogous. □

Theorem B.2 *The function* $\mathbf{g}(x) = \varphi_{(0,1)}(x)\,\mathcal{M}(x)$ *is positive for all* $x \in \mathsf{R}$, *and monotone decreases from* 1 *to* 0, *as* x *increases from* $-\infty$ *to* $+\infty$.

Proof of Theorem B.2. Bearing in mind that $\mathbf{g}(x) = 1 - \Phi_{(0,1)}(x)$, we have $\mathbf{g}'(x) = -\varphi_{(0,1)}(x) < 0$. By the criterion of monotony of a differentiable function, the function $\mathbf{g}(x)$ monotone decreases, as x increases. □

The following result (see, e.g., [178], p. 44; it follows directly from [85], formula 8.254) is the asymptotic expansion of $\mathcal{M}(x)$ at infinity, with the error term bounded by the first neglected term. Theorem B.3 yields Poincaré (see priority investigation [26]) asymptotic series: as $x \to \infty$ with n fixed, the value of the partial sum $x^{-1} - x^{-3} + 3!!x^{-5} - 5!!x^{-7} + \cdots + (-1)^n(2n-1)!!x^{-(2n+1)}$ approximates $\mathcal{M}(x)$ well. As $n \to \infty$, with x fixed, the series diverges.

Theorem B.3 *For* $x > 0$ *and* $n = 1, 2, \ldots$, *the expansion for Mills' ratio is*

$$\mathcal{M}(x) = \pi^{-1/2} \sum_{k=0}^{n-1} (-1)^k\, 2^k\, \Gamma(k + 1/2)\, x^{-(2k+1)} + R_n, \tag{B.25}$$

where $|R_n| < \pi^{-1/2}\,\Gamma(n + 1/2)\, 2^n x^{-(2n+1)}$.

From (B.25) follows the widely known relation

$$\mathcal{M}(x) \sim x^{-1} - x^{-3} + 3!!x^{-5} - 5!!x^{-7} + \cdots + (-1)^k\,(2k-1)!!x^{-(2k+1)} + \ldots, \quad x \to \infty,$$

which yields in particular

$$1 - \Phi_{(0,1)}(x) = x^{-1}\varphi_{(0,1)}(x)(1 + o(1)), \quad x \to \infty, \tag{B.26}$$

since (see [85], formula 8.254) $\Gamma(n + 1/2) = 2^{-n}\,(2n-1)!!\sqrt{\pi}$ for natural n. In particular, $\Gamma(1/2) = \sqrt{\pi}$, $\Gamma(3/2) = \frac{1}{2}\sqrt{\pi}$, $\Gamma(5/2) = \frac{3}{4}\sqrt{\pi}$, $\Gamma(7/2) = \frac{15}{8}\sqrt{\pi}$.

Integrals.

Theorem B.4 *For* $a > 0$, $x > 0$, *we have*

$$\int_0^x (1+y)^{-3/2} \exp\left\{-\frac{a}{1+y}\right\} dy = \frac{2\sqrt{\pi}}{\sqrt{a}} \left(\Phi_{(0,1)}(\sqrt{2a}\,) - \Phi_{(0,1)}\left(\frac{\sqrt{2a}}{\sqrt{1+x}}\right)\right).$$

Theorem B.5 *For $a > 0$, $b \geqslant 0$, and $x > 0$, we have*

$$\int_0^x (1+y)^{-3/2} \exp\{-a\,(b+y)\}\,dy = 2e^{-ab} \times \left\{1 - \frac{e^{-ax}}{\sqrt{1+x}} - 2\sqrt{a}\,e^a\sqrt{\pi}\,\bigl(\Phi_{(0,1)}(\sqrt{2a\,(1+x)}\,) - \Phi_{(0,1)}(\sqrt{2a}\,)\bigr)\right\}$$

and

$$\int_0^\infty (1+y)^{-3/2} \exp\{-a\,(b+y)\}\,dy = 2e^{-ab}\left\{1 - 2\sqrt{a}e^a\sqrt{\pi}\bigl(1-\Phi_{(0,1)}(\sqrt{2a}\,)\bigr)\right\}.$$

To prove Theorems B.4 and B.5, it is noteworthy that for $\varepsilon > 0$ and for any $k = 1, 2, \ldots$

$$\int_t^\infty y^{-(2k+1)/2} \exp\{-\varepsilon y\}\,dy = 2^{k+1}\sqrt{\pi}\varepsilon^{k-1/2} m_{2k}(\sqrt{2\varepsilon t}),$$

where $m_k(x) = \int_x^\infty y^{-k}\varphi_{(0,1)}(y)\,dy$ are incomplete moments of order $-k$ of a standard Gaussian distribution. It is easy to verify that

$$m_k(x) = (x^{-k+1}\varphi_{(0,1)}(x) - m_{k-2}(x))/(k-1), \quad k = 2, 3, \ldots,$$

where $m_0(x) = \int_x^\infty \varphi_{(0,1)}(z)\,dz = 1 - \Phi_{(0,1)}(x)$. In particular, for $\varepsilon > 0$ we have

$$\begin{aligned}\int_t^\infty x^{-3/2} \exp\{-\varepsilon x\}\,dx &= 4\sqrt{\pi}\varepsilon^{1/2} m_2(\sqrt{2\varepsilon t})\\ &= 4\sqrt{\pi}\varepsilon^{1/2}((\sqrt{2\varepsilon t})^{-1}\varphi_{(0,1)}(\sqrt{2\varepsilon t}) - m_0(\sqrt{2\varepsilon t}))\\ &= 2\sqrt{2\pi}\,t^{-1/2}\varphi_{(0,1)}(\sqrt{2\varepsilon t}) - 4\sqrt{\pi}\varepsilon^{1/2}\{1 - \Phi_{(0,1)}(\sqrt{2\varepsilon t})\}.\end{aligned}$$

B.3 Auxiliary Function of the First Kind

The auxiliary function of the first kind defined for $z, y > 0$, is

$$\begin{aligned}\mathsf{F}(z, y \mid -\tfrac{1}{2}) &:= 1 - \Phi_{(0,1)}(z-y) + \Phi_{(0,1)}(-z-y)\exp\{2zy\}\\ &= \Phi_{(0,1)}(y-z) + \exp\{2zy\}\,\Phi_{(0,1)}(-z-y)\\ &= \Phi_{(0,1)}(y-z) + \exp\{2zy\}\,\varphi_{(0,1)}(z+y)\,\mathcal{M}(z+y).\end{aligned} \tag{B.27}$$

Let us write $\mathsf{F}^{(i,j)}(z, y \mid -\frac{1}{2}) := \frac{\partial^{(i+j)}}{\partial z^i \partial y^j}\,\mathsf{F}(z, y \mid -\frac{1}{2})$, $i, j = 0, 1, \ldots$.

Theorem B.6 *For $z, y > 0$, we have*

$$\begin{aligned}\mathsf{F}^{(1,0)}(z, y \mid -\tfrac{1}{2}) &= 2\exp\{2zy\}\,\varphi_{(0,1)}(z+y)\,(y\,\mathcal{M}(z+y) - 1),\\ \mathsf{F}^{(0,1)}(z, y \mid -\tfrac{1}{2}) &= 2\exp\{2zy\}\,\varphi_{(0,1)}(z+y)\,z\,\mathcal{M}(z+y),\end{aligned} \tag{B.28}$$

and

$$\begin{aligned} \mathsf{F}^{(2,0)}(z,y \mid -\tfrac{1}{2}) &= 2\exp\{2zy\}\, \varphi_{(0,1)}(z+y)\, (2y^2\, \mathcal{M}(z+y) + z - 2y), \\ \mathsf{F}^{(0,2)}(z,y \mid -\tfrac{1}{2}) &= 2\exp\{2zy\}\, \varphi_{(0,1)}(z+y)\, z\, (2z\, \mathcal{M}(z+y) - 1), \\ \mathsf{F}^{(1,1)}(z,y \mid -\tfrac{1}{2}) &= 2\exp\{2zy\}\, \varphi_{(0,1)}(z+y) \\ &\quad \times (\mathcal{M}(z+y) + 2zy\, \mathcal{M}(z+y) - z). \end{aligned} \tag{B.29}$$

Proof of Theorem B.6. The use of equality

$$\varphi_{(0,1)}(z-y) = \exp\{2zy\}\, \varphi_{(0,1)}(y+z)$$

and straightforward differentiation yield

$$\begin{aligned} \mathsf{F}^{(0,1)}(z,y \mid -\tfrac{1}{2}) &= \varphi_{(0,1)}(z-y) + 2z\, \exp\{2zy\}\, \Phi_{(0,1)}(-z-y) \\ &\quad - \exp\{2zy\}\, \varphi_{(0,1)}(z+y) \\ &= 2z\, \exp\{2zy\}\, \Phi_{(0,1)}(-z-y) \\ &= 2\exp\{2zy\}\, \varphi_{(0,1)}(z+y)\, z\, \mathcal{M}(z+y), \\ \mathsf{F}^{(1,0)}(z,y \mid -\tfrac{1}{2}) &= -\varphi_{(0,1)}(z-y) + 2y \exp\{2zy\}\, \Phi_{(0,1)}(-z-y) \\ &\quad - \exp\{2zy\}\, \varphi_{(0,1)}(z+y) \\ &= -2\exp\{2zy\}\, (\varphi_{(0,1)}(y+z) - y\, \Phi_{(0,1)}(-z-y)) \\ &= 2\exp\{2zy\}\, \varphi_{(0,1)}(y+z)\, (y\, \mathcal{M}(z+y) - 1), \end{aligned}$$

as required. The equalities in (B.29) are obtained similarly. □

B.4 Random Walks and Ladder Random Variables

Let ξ_i, $i = 1, 2, \ldots$, be the sequence of independent and identically distributed[8] (i.i.d.) random variables. We consider the random walk $\zeta_n = \sum_{i=1}^{n} \xi_i$, $n = 1, 2, \ldots$, which starts at the origin (i.e., with $\zeta_0 = 0$). The following two theorems (see [78], Chapter XII, Section 2) classify the random walks according to their behavior, as $n \to \infty$.

Theorem B.7 *The random walk $\zeta_n = \sum_{i=1}^{n} \xi_i$, $n = 1, 2, \ldots$, which starts at the origin (i.e., $\zeta_0 = 0$), is only of two types:*

(a) oscillating, which means that the random walk ζ_n, $n = 1, 2, \ldots$, oscillates with probability one between $-\infty$ and $+\infty$.

[8]We emphasize it that $\xi_i \overset{d}{=} \xi \in \mathsf{R}$ takes both positive and negative values. The trivial case of ξ concentrated at zero is excluded, without further comment.

(b) drifting to $+\infty$ *(to* $-\infty$*), which means that with probability one the random walk* ζ_n*,* $n = 1, 2, \ldots$*, drifts to* $+\infty$ *(to* $-\infty$*) and reaches a finite minimum* $m = \min\{\zeta_0, \zeta_1, \ldots\} \leqslant 0$ *(maximum* $M = \max\{\zeta_0, \zeta_1, \ldots\} \geqslant 0$*).*

Theorem B.8 *For the random walk* $\zeta_n = \sum_{i=1}^{n} \xi_i$*,* $n = 1, 2, \ldots$*, which starts at the origin (i.e., with* $\zeta_0 = 0$*), the following alternatives exist:*

(a) If $\mathsf{E}\xi_1 = 0$*, then the random walk* ζ_n *is oscillating. Moreover, it is persistent.*

(b) If $0 < \mathsf{E}\xi_1 \leqslant +\infty$*, then the random walk* ζ_n *drifts to* $+\infty$*.*

(c) If $-\infty \leqslant \mathsf{E}\xi_1 < 0$*, then the random walk* ζ_n *drifts to* $-\infty$*.*

The following definitions are important for investigation of the random walk $\zeta_n = \sum_{i=1}^{n} \xi_i$, $n = 1, 2, \ldots$, which starts at the origin (i.e., with $\zeta_0 = 0$). Following [78], Chapter VI, Section 8, we call strong ascending ladder epochs[9], or ladder indices, the integer-valued random variables

$$\begin{aligned} \mathbb{E}_1 &= \inf\{n \geqslant 1 : \zeta_n > 0\}, \\ \mathbb{E}_k &= \inf\{n > \mathbb{E}_{k-1} : \zeta_n > \zeta_{\mathbb{E}_{k-1}}\}, \quad k = 2, 3, \ldots, \end{aligned}$$

i.e., the successive epochs when the previous record is exceeded. The corresponding ladder heights $\mathbb{H}_k = \zeta_{\mathbb{E}_k}$, $k = 1, 2, \ldots$, are the values of the random walk at the ladder epochs.

B.5 Wiener and Diffusion Processes

A random process with continuous time W_t, $t \geqslant 0$, is called Wiener process, or Brownian motion process, if it starts at zero, its trajectories are almost sure (a.s.) continuous, the distribution of the random variable W_t at any time moment $t > 0$ is normal with mean zero and variance t, and its increments are independent[10].

The following result for the Wiener process W_t, $t \geqslant 0$, is well-known (see, e.g., [23], Part II, Chapter 1, Equality 1.1.4).

Theorem B.9 *For* $x \geqslant 0$*, we have* $\mathsf{P}\big\{\sup_{0 \leqslant s \leqslant t} \mathsf{W}_s > x\big\} = 2\,\mathsf{P}\{\mathsf{W}_t > x\}$*.*

[9]Commenting on the selected terminology, Feller noted in [78], Chapter VI, Section 8, that when index n is deemed a time parameter, we shall speak of "epoch n".

[10]This means that for all time points $s, t > 0$ the random variables $\mathsf{W}_{t+s} - \mathsf{W}_t$ are independent of $\sigma\{\mathsf{W}_u, 0 \leqslant u \leqslant t\}$, which denotes the σ-field that contains all information about the process up to the time moment t; the random variable $\mathsf{W}_{t+s} - \mathsf{W}_t$ is normally distributed with mean zero and variance s.

For diffusion process with linear drift $\theta t + \sigma \mathsf{W}_t$, $t > 0$, where $\theta \in \mathsf{R}$ is drift and $\sigma > 0$ diffusion coefficients, the following result is also well-known (see, e.g., [23], Part II, Chapter 2, Equality 1.1.4, or [111], Example 1 on p. 27).

Theorem B.10 *For $x \geqslant 0$, $\theta \in \mathsf{R}$ and $\sigma > 0$, we have*

$$\mathsf{P}\Big\{ \sup_{0 \leqslant s \leqslant t} (\theta s + \sigma \mathsf{W}_s) \leqslant x \Big\} = \Phi_{(0,1)}\Big(\frac{x - \theta t}{\sigma \sqrt{t}} \Big) - \exp\Big\{ \frac{2\theta x}{\sigma^2} \Big\} \Phi_{(0,1)}\Big(\frac{-x - \theta t}{\sigma \sqrt{t}} \Big).$$

The following result is a generalization of the previous one; see [23], Part II, Chapter 2, Equalities 1.0.6 and 1.1.8.

Theorem B.11 *For $x \geqslant 0$, $\theta \in \mathsf{R}$ and $\sigma > 0$, we have*

$$\begin{aligned} \mathsf{P}\Big\{ \theta t + \sigma \mathsf{W}_t \in dy, \sup_{0 \leqslant s \leqslant t} (\theta s + \sigma \mathsf{W}_s) \leqslant x \Big\} &= \mathsf{P}\{ \theta t + \sigma \mathsf{W}_t \in dy \} \\ &- \mathsf{P}\Big\{ \theta t + \sigma \mathsf{W}_t \in dy, \sup_{0 \leqslant s \leqslant t} (\theta s + \sigma \mathsf{W}_s) \geqslant x \Big\}, \end{aligned}$$

where

$$\mathsf{P}\big\{ \theta t + \sigma \mathsf{W}_t \in dy \big\} = \frac{1}{\sigma \sqrt{2\pi\, t}} \exp\big\{ -(y - \theta t)^2 / (2\sigma^2 t) \big\}\, dy$$

and

$$\begin{aligned} &\mathsf{P}\Big\{ \theta t + \sigma \mathsf{W}_t \in dy, \sup_{0 \leqslant s \leqslant t} (\theta s + \sigma \mathsf{W}_s) \geqslant x \Big\} \\ &\quad = \frac{1}{\sigma \sqrt{2\pi\, t}} \exp\big\{ (2\theta y t - \theta^2 t^2 - (|y - x| + x)^2) / (2\sigma^2 t) \big\}\, dy. \end{aligned}$$

List of Notations

This is intended to aid cross-referencing. Some symbols are used locally, without ambiguity, in senses other than those given here.

$f(x;\theta)\,\vert_{\theta=a}$	$f(x;a)$
$f(x)\,\vert_{x=a}^{b}$	$f(b)-f(a)$
R	real line
R^+, R^-	positive half-line, negative half-line
$\mathbf{1}_A(x)$	indicator function of the set A
$\Phi_{(0,1)}(x)$	standard Gaussian (or normal) c.d.f.
$\varphi_{(0,1)}(x)$	standard Gaussian (or normal) p.d.f.
$\mathcal{M}(x)$	Mills' ratio
κ_γ	γ-quantile of a standard Gaussian distribution
δ	parameter of exponentially distributed T
ρ	parameter of exponentially distributed Y
μ	mean parameter of inverse Gaussian distribution
λ	shape parameter of inverse Gaussian distribution
$I_n(x)$	modified Bessel function of the first kind of order n
W_s	Brownian motion, or standard Wiener process
ϑ	drift parameter of diffusion process $\vartheta s+\sigma\mathsf{W}_s$
σ	volatility parameter of diffusion process $\vartheta s+\sigma\mathsf{W}_s$
$\Upsilon_{u,c}$	time of the first crossing of the level u by a general shifted compound renewal process
$\Upsilon_{u,c\,\vert\,\delta,\rho}$	time of the first crossing of the level u by a shifted compound renewal process with exponentially distributed T and Y
$\Upsilon^{[\mathrm{dif}]}_{u,c\,\vert\,\vartheta}$	time of the first crossing of the level u by a shifted diffusion process
$\psi_t(u,c)$	probability of ruin within time t
$\psi_\infty(u,c)$	probability of ultimate ruin
$\phi_t(u,c)$	probability of survival, or non-ruin within time t
$\phi_\infty(u,c)$	probability of ultimate survival, or ultimate non-ruin
$\varphi_t(u,c)$	probability of ultimate ruin after, but not before time t
$F(x;\mu,\lambda,p)$	c.d.f. of a generalized inverse Gaussian distribution
$f(x;\mu,\lambda,p)$	p.d.f. of a generalized inverse Gaussian distribution

$\mathsf{F}(z, v \mid p)$	auxiliary function of the first kind
$\mathsf{F}^{(i,j)}(z, v \mid p)$	$\frac{\partial^{(i+j)}}{\partial z^i \partial v^j} \mathsf{F}(z, v \mid p)$
$\mathcal{I}^{[k]}_{u,c}(t \mid v)$	integral expression $\int_0^{\frac{c(t-v)}{cv+u}} \frac{1}{(1+x)^k} \varphi_{\left(cM(1+x), \frac{c^2D^2(1+x)}{cv+u}\right)}(x)\, dx$
$\mathcal{M}_{u,c}(t \mid v)$	core integral expression $\int_0^{\frac{c(t-v)}{cv+u}} \frac{1}{1+x} \varphi_{\left(cM(1+x), \frac{c^2D^2}{cv+u}(1+x)\right)}(x)\, dx$
$\mathcal{M}^{(i,j)}_{u,c}(t \mid v)$	$\frac{\partial(i+j)}{\partial u^i\, \partial c^j} \mathcal{M}_{u,c}(t \mid v)$
$\mathcal{M}_{u,c}(\infty \mid v)$	$\lim_{t\to\infty} \mathcal{M}_{u,c}(t \mid v)$
$\mathcal{M}_{u,c}(t)$	$\mathcal{M}_{u,c}(t \mid 0)$
$\mathcal{M}^{(i,j)}_{u,c}(t)$	$\frac{\partial(i+j)}{\partial u^i\, \partial c^j} \mathcal{M}_{u,c}(t)$
$\mathcal{M}_{u,c}$	$\lim_{t\to\infty} \mathcal{M}_{u,c}(t)$
$m_{u,c}(v)$	summand independent of t in the equality $\mathcal{M}_{u,c}(t \mid v) = m_{u,c}(v) + m_{u,c}(t \mid v)$
$m_{u,c}(t \mid v)$	summand dependent of t in the equality $\mathcal{M}_{u,c}(t \mid v) = m_{u,c}(v) + m_{u,c}(t \mid v)$
$\mathcal{F}_{u,c}(t \mid v)$	expression involved in the correction term of inverse Gaussian approximation
$f_{u,c}(v)$	summand independent of t in the equality $\mathcal{F}_{u,c}(t \mid v) = f_{u,c}(v) + f_{u,c}(t \mid v)$
$f_{u,c}(t \mid v)$	summand dependent of t in the equality $\mathcal{F}_{u,c}(t \mid v) = f_{u,c}(v) + f_{u,c}(t \mid v)$
$\mathcal{S}_{u,c}(t \mid v)$	expression involved in the correction term of inverse Gaussian approximation
$s_{u,c}(v)$	summand independent of t in the equality $\mathcal{S}_{u,c}(t \mid v) = s_{u,c}(v) + s_{u,c}(t \mid v)$
$s_{u,c}(t \mid v)$	summand dependent of t in the equality $\mathcal{S}_{u,c}(t \mid v) = s_{u,c}(v) + s_{u,c}(t \mid v)$
N_s	notation for $\max\{n > 0 : \sum_{i=1}^n T_i \leqslant s\}$
M_s	notation for $\inf\{k \geqslant 1 : \sum_{i=1}^k Y_i > s\} - 1$
$\eta(u)$	notation for $\min\{n \geqslant 1 : S_n > u\}$, or 0, if the random walk $S_n = \sum_{i=1}^n X_i$, $n = 1, 2, \ldots,$ never crosses the level $u > 0$
$\bar{\eta}(u)$	notation for $\min\{n \geqslant 1 : \bar{S}_n > u\}$, or 0, if the random walk $\bar{S}_n = \sum_{i=1}^n \bar{X}_i$, $n = 1, 2, \ldots,$ never crosses the level $u > 0$
$\phi_t(u, c)$	shorthand notation for $\mathsf{P}\{\Upsilon_{u,c} > t\}$
$\psi_t(u, c)$	shorthand notation for $\mathsf{P}\{\Upsilon_{u,c} \leqslant t\}$
$\mathcal{L}_f(\alpha)$, $\mathcal{L}_T(\alpha)$	Laplace transform of function f, of random variable T
$F_t(v \mid p)$	auxiliary function of the second kind

$F_t^{(i,j)}(v \mid p)$	$\frac{\partial^{(i+j)}}{\partial v^i \partial p^j} F_t(v \mid p)$
$\xi_p(z)$	position at time z of a particle subject to a random walk with random displacements; it moves either a unit distance to the right with probability p or a unit distance to the left with probability q, and displacements of this particle occur at random times
$\varsigma_k(p)$	first hitting time of the point k by the random walk with random displacements, when $p \in (0,1)$
$r^{(j)}$	Pochhammer's (rising) symbol
T_i	i-th inter–renewal time
Y_i	jump size, with jump at the moment of i-th renewal
$\tilde{T}_i$	normalized random variable $(T_i - \mathsf{E}\,T)/\sqrt{\mathsf{D}\,T}$
$\tilde{Y}_i$	normalized random variable $(Y_i - \mathsf{E}\,Y)/\sqrt{\mathsf{D}\,Y}$
μ_ξ	mean of ξ
σ_ξ	standard deviation of r.v. ξ
$\varkappa_{\xi\,\zeta}$	covariance of r.v. ξ and ζ
$\varkappa_{YT}^{(i,j)}$	$\mathsf{E}((T - \mathsf{E}\,T)^i (Y - \mathsf{E}\,Y)^j)$
$\varkappa_{\tilde{Y}\tilde{T}}^{(i,j)}$	$\varkappa_{YT}^{(i,j)} (\mathsf{D}\,Y)^{-i/2} (\mathsf{D}\,T)^{-j/2}$
$\mathcal{Y}_n(x)$	$(x - n\mathsf{E}\,Y)/\sqrt{n\mathsf{D}\,Y}$
$\mathcal{T}_n(t)$	$(t - n\mathsf{E}\,T)/\sqrt{n\mathsf{D}\,T}$
M_N	$1/\mathsf{E}\,T$
M_V	$\mathsf{E}\,Y/\mathsf{E}\,T$
R_{VN}	$(\mathsf{E}\,Y\mathsf{D}\,T - \mathsf{E}\,T\varkappa_{TY})/(\mathsf{E}\,T)^3$
D_N^2	$\mathsf{D}\,T/(\mathsf{E}\,T)^3$
D_V^2	$((\mathsf{E}\,Y)^2\mathsf{D}\,T - 2\mathsf{E}\,Y\mathsf{E}\,T\varkappa_{TY} + (\mathsf{E}\,T)^2\mathsf{D}\,Y)/(\mathsf{E}\,T)^3$
M	$\mathsf{E}\,T/\mathsf{E}\,Y$
D^2	$((\mathsf{E}\,T)^2\mathsf{D}\,Y + (\mathsf{E}\,Y)^2\mathsf{D}\,T)/(\mathsf{E}\,Y)^3$
$m_\triangledown$	$\mathsf{E}\,T/\mathsf{E}X$
$D_\triangledown^2$	$\mathsf{E}(X\,\mathsf{E}\,T - T\,\mathsf{E}X)^2/(\mathsf{E}X)^3$
$m_\vartriangle$	$\mathsf{E}\bar{T}/\mathsf{E}\bar{X}$
$D_\vartriangle^2$	$\mathsf{E}(\bar{X}\mathsf{E}\bar{T} - \bar{T}\mathsf{E}\bar{X})^2/(\mathsf{E}\bar{X})^3$
S_n	$\sum_{i=1}^n X_i$
$\mathcal{Z}_n$	$\sum_{i=1}^n T_i$
$U(t)$	$\sum_{n=0}^\infty F_T^{*n}(t)$
$\bar{\mathbb{N}}_k$	ladder epoch for associated random walk
$\bar{\mathbb{T}}_k$	random variable $\bar{Z}_{\bar{\mathbb{N}}_k} - \bar{Z}_{\bar{\mathbb{N}}_{k-1}}$ generated by ladder times
$\bar{\mathbb{X}}_k$	random variable $\bar{S}_{\bar{\mathbb{N}}_k} - \bar{S}_{\bar{\mathbb{N}}_{k-1}}$ generated by ladder heights
$\mathcal{B}_k$	Bernoulli number
$\mathcal{B}_n(x)$	Bernoulli polynomial
$\Gamma(a)$	Euler's gamma function
$\mathrm{B}(a,b)$	beta function

$I_p(a,b)$	incomplete beta function
$\psi(x)$	psi, or digamma function
$\psi^{(m)}(x)$	polygamma function of order m
$m_k^{\oplus}(x)$	incomplete normal moment of positive order
$m_k^{\ominus}(x)$	incomplete normal moment of negative order
$\mathsf{F}_n(x)$	shorthand notation for $\mathsf{P}\{S_n \leqslant x\}$

Notes and Comments

Chapter 1 The emergence and development of the Value-at-Risk as a generally accepted methodology for quantifying market risk and its widespread acceptance by bank regulators marks a recent evolution of risk management. The Value-at-Risk technique for measuring financial risks, first used in [13] to select the Markowitz portfolio, was then applied by J.P. Morgan in [142], [143], extended to commercial banks and corporations, and became widely used since the 1996 Basel amendment [14]. It is often referred to (see, e.g., [92]) as a principle when various regulatory systems are constructed.

The Tail Value-at-Risk is defined as the expected loss given that a loss beyond some critical value, typically set equal to Value-at-Risk, has occurred. This measure of risk has a variety of variants, including Expected shortfall (the difference is up to a factor), expected tail loss, tail conditional expectation. There exist a number of expressions used for evaluating the Expected shortfall, although they generally reduce to the same formula.

From the standpoint of the theory of distributions, finding the Value-at-Risk and Tail Value-at-Risk is the same as finding a distribution's quantile and a conditional average, respectively. The expressions for them are given in several papers for a number of underlying distributions. For example, for exponential distribution it is done in [57], [144], for log-normal distribution it is done in [57], for Student's distribution it is done in [118], [144]. For a general skewed distribution concentrated on the positive half-line, the Cornish–Fisher expansion can be used (see, e.g., [165], Chapter 14).

The Solvency II (see Directives [63], [64], monographs and research papers [7], [65]–[67], [72], [80]. [92], [139], [141], [150], [159] [165], and a historical overview [164]) is a system of regulating a competitive insurance market, which applies to Europe and came into effect on January 1, 2016. This is a system of governance focussed on the strategy development process and on the financial planning process. An integral part of the latter is an internal control effected by a risk management system. An alternative to the Solvency II system is the risk-based capital system (see, e.g., [49], [66] and references therein) went into effect in the U.S. property-liability insurance industry in 1994. Both systems mandate intervention by the regulator when capital reserve is deemed deficient.

The solvency capital requirements formulated in Directives [63], [64] are based on the risk approach to insurance management (see, e.g., [65]–[67], [152], [187]). It took decades of research; see, e.g., [15], [56], [148], [159], and overview in [164], [165]. Theoretical treatment of different measures of risk, including insight into advantages and disadvantages of the Value-at-Risk measure, may be found, e.g., in [6], [48], [56]. An alternative to Solvency II system, which went into effect in the U.S. property-liability insurance industry in 1994, is the risk-based capital system (see, e.g., [49], [66] and references therein). A critical analysis of the Solvency II regulatory framework is contained in many papers, e.g., [66], [71], [72], [80]. [92], [139], [141], [150]. Disadvantages arising from use of the Value-at-Risk measure are examined in [80], [141], [150]. Shortcomings of the former Directive [62] related to the multi-year dynamics are discussed in [134].

A huge number of articles have been written over the last century about the collective risk model, which is based on the probabilistic laws of large-scale phenomena; pioneering papers in this field are [113]–[116] and [43]–[45]. Recently, there has been a spate of books on the current state of the art, mainly with respect to the analysis of surplus and ruin-theoretic analysis, for the class of Sparre Andersen, or renewal, insurance risk models. Some of the claims, such as (see, e.g., [194]) that "the analysis of this class of models seems to have reached a plateau", i.e., the collective risk theory reached its completeness, have been greatly exaggerated: the inverse Gaussian approximation is an innovative result, as well as the results for the non-ruin capital.

An analytical study of the non-ruin capital $u_{\alpha,t}(c)$, $c > 0$, in the classical Lundberg's model with exponential claim sizes Y was first done in [128]. The analytical results for the non-ruin capital $u^{[\mathrm{dif}]}_{\alpha,t\,|\,\vartheta}(c)$, $c > 0$, in the diffusion risk model was done in [127].

A simulation study of $u_{\alpha,t}(c)$, $c > 0$, was carried out for the first time in [136]. This study, with T and Y being a mixture of a finite number of exponential distributions, Erlang, Pareto (i.e., a gamma mixture of exponential distributions) and Kummer (i.e., a Fisher–Snedecor mixture of exponential distributions) gave very encouraging results. It is noteworthy that, although a mixture of a finite number of exponential distributions and Erlang are light-tail, Pareto and Kummer are fat-tail distributions. The simulation analysis focused on the question of whether the form of $u_{\alpha,t}(c)$, $c > 0$, observed in the classical Lundberg's risk model with exponential claim sizes, in the general risk model remains similar.

The Monte Carlo simulation (see, e.g., [27], [161], [109], [105], [160], [197]) is a well-known technique of numerical analysis, especially popular in computer science. The problem of selecting adequate random number generators (see, e.g., [93]) was addressed in a great number of papers. In insurance applications, this method has come to the fore in [15], [56], [103]. Simulation analysis of probabilities of ruin and non-ruin capital was done in [136], [137].

Chapter 2 The results of this chapter were published in [127]. Despite their relative mathematical simplicity, they have a considerable background.

The reflection principle for standard Brownian motion is well-known for a long time (see [4], [11], [112]). The first passage time distribution of Brownian motion with a drift, presently known as the inverse Gaussian distribution, was first obtained (in order to correct a flaw in [79] uncritically repeated in [107]) by Schrödinger [169] and Smoluchowski [179]. The presentation with an emphasis on Chapman-Kolmogorov equation (associated with many names, e.g., of Kolmogorov, Chapman, Smoluchowski, Fokker, Planck) see in [81], [82], [55]; see also [69], [111], [138], [175]. The results on first-passage problems for Brownian motion are collected in handbooks, see, e.g., [23]. For a general boundary, see, e.g., [53], [70], and [149]. In [149], both direct and inverse first-passage problems for Brownian motion are re-visited by means of a strong Markov processes technique and efficient methods for numerical computations were discussed. The numerical technique is further developed in a number of papers (see, e.g., [153], [199] and references therein).

The results of Section 2.2 directly follow from the results on the crossing a horizontal boundary, or a linear slopped boundary, by a standard Brownian motion; see Problem 2.2. The results of Section 2.3.1 were first published in [127] and then included in Appendix C of [134]. The results of Section 2.3 are central. Theorem 2.6 is Theorem 2.1 in [120]. Theorem 2.7 is Theorem 4.4 in [123]. Theorem 2.10 proved analytically is evident from the definition of $\mathsf{P}\{\Upsilon^{[\mathrm{dif}]}_{u,c\,|\,\vartheta} \leqslant t\}$: for each fixed u positive, this function is monotone decreasing, as the variable $c \geqslant 0$ monotone increases; for each fixed c positive, this function is monotone decreasing, as the variable $u \geqslant 0$ monotone increases. However, we pay attention to a detail study of these derivatives. First, we want to have expressions for them that will allow us to draw conclusions about their magnitude. Secondly, we want to develop a technique that will allow us to investigate higher-order derivatives. Theorem 2.13 on convexity of the fixed-probability level was first proved in [127]. This result is central in the proof of Theorem 2.24.

Chapter 3 Renewal theory, which is an important component of the probabilistic theory, goes back to [76], [77], [68], [100], [101], [102], and [46]. Its detailed presentation is contained in the books [40], [41], [42]. An overview of the level-crossing problem which goes beyond risk theory is, e.g., [22]. Some famous results were first obtained in the risk theory, when the renewal theory was not yet created. Then, in the late 1950s, the renewal theory influenced back (see [180]) the risk theory models.

The main results for compound renewal process at a fixed time point in this exceptional risk model were outlined in [135], Chapter 4. Theorem 3.1 is Theorem 4.1 in [135]. Equalities (3.3) are Theorem 4.2 in [135]. Random walk with random displacements (see, e.g., [184], Chapter 4, § 22) was linked to the level-crossing problem in [135], Section 5.4. Concerning auxiliary functions of the second kind considered in Section A.2.5, note that Theorem A.19 is Theorem 5.4 in [124], Theorem A.20 is Theorem 5.5 in [124], Theorem A.21 is Theorem 5.6 in [124].

The direct level-crossing problems in this exceptional risk model was investigated in [135], Chapter 5. Theorem 3.2, yielding Type I formula (3.6), is Theorem 5.6 in [135]. Theorem 3.3, yielding Type II formula (3.7), is Theorem 5.7 in [135]. Theorem 3.4, yielding Type III formula (3.8)–(3.9), is Theorem 5.8 in [135].

The inverse level-crossing problems in this exceptional risk model was investigated in [124], [128]. Theorem 3.6 is straightforward; see, e.g., (2.4) in [136]. Theorem 3.7 is Theorem 3.1 in [124], or Theorem C.19 in [134]. Theorem 3.8 is Theorem 3.2 in [124], or Theorem C.20 in [134]. Theorem 3.17 is Theorems 2.4 and 3.3 in [128], or Theorem C.21 in [134]. Theorem 3.18 is Theorem 3.4 in [128], or Theorem C.22 in [134].

Chapter 4 Equivalent representations of $\mathcal{M}_{u,c}(t)$ and $\mathcal{M}_{u,c}$ were first given in [135]. Analytical investigation of $\mathcal{M}_{u,c}(t)$ and $\mathcal{M}_{u,c}$ is a continuation of research started in [135]. Analytical investigation of solution to $\mathcal{M}$-equation is new, but it is a rather standard piece of asymptotic analysis.

Chapter 5 The results of this chapter, which are of primary interest to this book, are new. The direct level-crossing problem in general renewal risk model is a classic setting of the probability theory. Kendall's identity (see [97], and [24]–[25], [96], [157], [177], [198]) is well known. The representation for the first level-crossing time's distribution (called "second-type representation" in [135], Chapter 5) is fundamental in the proof of the inverse Gaussian approximation and in the proofs of a number of related results (see [135], Chapters 6–8). This representation is also a keystone result in realization of the road map outlined in Chapter 2. The closeness of the approaches used in [135] and in this book, including the analytical technique developed to analyze expressions obtained after applying Kendall's identity, links these two books together.

Section 5.2 is a summary of most important results in the direct level-crossing problem. In particular, Theorem 5.1 is Theorem 5.5 in [135]. Corollary 5.1 is Corollary 5.1 in [135]. It was first proved in [25]. Theorem 5.2 is Theorem 6.1 in [135]. Theorem 5.3 is Theorem 6.3 in [135]. Theorem 5.4 is Theorem 6.4 in [135].

Bounds on $\mathsf{P}\{\varUpsilon_{u,c} \leqslant t\}$, when $c > c^*$, valid for all $u \geqslant 0$, are closely related to the asymptotic results for $\mathsf{P}\{\varUpsilon_{u,c} \leqslant t\}$, as $u \to \infty$, but obviously differ from them. The results of both of these types were fundamental in the early stages of risk theory, and both were associated with the names of Lundberg (see [113]–[117]) and Cramér ([43], [44], [45], [47]). The current state of this problem may be seen, e.g., in [158], [194]. In the compound Poisson risk model with general light-tail and fat-tail Y, such bounds were derived, e.g., in [59], [60], [193], and [35]. In the general renewal risk model with light-tail and fat-tail Y, such bounds were derived, e.g., in [37], [38], [151], [95]. Theorem 5.12 was proved in [119]. Its generalization to Y whose distribution is a finite mixture of exponential distributions was proved in [188].

Chapter 6 This chapter is a supplement and extension of Chapter 5, were some illustrative examples deserved to be given in full are considered. For a range of particular models used for numerical illustrations, we outline the simulation analysis and present several numerical results obtained by using the analytical results of Chapter 5. It demonstrates the advantages of combining analytical and numerical procedures. The simulation analysis of the probability $\mathsf{P}\{\varUpsilon_{u,c} \leqslant t\}$, i.e., the simulation analysis in the direct level-crossing problem, was reported in [137], and simulation of $u_{\alpha,t}(c)$, i.e., simulation analysis in the inverse level-crossing problem, was reported in [136].

Chapter 7 This chapter is closely related to [134], Chapters 5–11. The main innovation is Section 7.5, where ERS-analysis is extended to generally, rather than exponentially, distributed claim size Y.

Bibliography

[1] Abramowitz, M., and Stegun, I.A. (1972) Handbook of Mathematical Functions. 10-th ed., Dover, New York.

[2] Acerbi, C., and Tasche, D. (2002) On the coherence of expected shortfall. Journal of Banking and Finance, Vol. 26, No. 7, 1487–1503.

[3] Andersen, E.S. (1957) On the collective theory of risk in case of contagion between the claims. In book: Transactions of the 15-th International Congress of Actuaries, New York, Vol. 2, 219–229.

[4] André, D. (1887) Solution directe du problème résolu par M. Bertrand, C. R. Acad. Sci. Paris, Vol. 105, 436–437.

[5] Arfwedson, G. (1950) Some problems in the collective theory of risk, Skandinavisk Aktuarietidskrift, 1–38.

[6] Artzner, P., Delbaen, F., Eber, J.M., and Heath, D. (1999) Coherent measures of risk. Mathematical Finance, Vol. 9, No. 3 203–228.

[7] Ashby, S. (2011) Risk management and the global banking crisis: lessons for insurance solvency regulation, The Geneva Papers on Risk and Insurance – Issues and Practice, Vol. 36, No. 3, 330–347.

[8] Asmussen, S. (2000) Ruin Probabilities. World Scientific Publishers, Singapore.

[9] Asmussen, S., and Albrecher, H. (2010) Ruin Probabilities. World Scientific Publishers, Singapore.

[10] Atkinson, K.E. An Introduction to Numerical Analysis. 2-nd ed., John Wiley & Sons.

[11] Bachelier, L. (1900) Théorie de la Spéculation. Annales Scientifiques de l'École Normale Supérieure, 3 (17): 21–86. English translation: Theory of Speculation. In: The Random Character of Stock Market Prices, MIT Press, Cambridge, Mass. 1964 (ed. P.H. Cootner), 17–78.

[12] von Bahr, B. (1975) Asymptotic ruin probability when exponential moments do not exist, Scandinavian Actuarial Journal, 6–10.

[13] Baumol, W.J. (1963) An expected gain-confidence limit criterion for portfolio selection, Management Science, Vol. 10, No. 1, 174–182.

[14] Basel Committee on Banking Supervision (1996) Amendment to the Capital Accord to Incorporate Market Risks. Bank for International Settlements. Basel, Switzerland; http://www.bis.org/publ/bcbs24.pdf.

[15] Beard, R.E., Pentikäinen, T., and Pesonen, E. (1984) Risk Theory. The Stochastic Basis of Insurance. 3-rd ed., Chapman and Hall, London, etc.

[16] Bernstein, P.L. (2007) Capital Ideas Evolving. John Wiley & Sons, Hoboken, NJ.

[17] Besson, J.-L., Dacorogna, M., and Trainar, P. (2010). Adapting the solvency regulations to times of crisis, accepting the riskiness of the situation, SCOR Paper No. 6; http://www.scor.com/en/sgrc/scor-publications/scor-papers.html.

[18] Bhattacharya, R.N., and Ranga Rao, R. (1976) Normal Approximation and Asymptotic Expansions. John Wiley & Sons, New York.

[19] Bieberbach, L. (1930) Lehrbuch der Funktionentheorie. Teubner, Leipzig, Berlin.

[20] Billingsley, P. (1999) Convergence of Probability Measures. 2-nd ed., John Wiley & Sons, New York.

[21] Birnbaum, Z.W. An inequality for Mills' ratio, Ann. Math. Statist., Vol. 13, No. 2, 245–246.

[22] Blake, I., and Lindsey, W. (1973) Level-crossing problems for random processes, IEEE Transactions on Information Theory, Vol. 19, No. 3, 295–315.

[23] Borodin, A.N., and Salminen, P. (1996) Handbook of Brownian Motion. Facts and Formulæ. Birkhäuser, Basel.

[24] Borovkov, A.A. (1965) On the first passage time for one class of processes with independent increments, Theory Probab. Appl., Vol. 10, 331–334.

[25] Borovkov, K.A., and Dickson, D.C.M. (2008) On the ruin time distribution for a Sparre Andersen process with exponential claim sizes, Insurance: Mathematics and Economics, Vol. 42, 1104–1108.

[26] van Boven, H., Wesselink, R., and Wepster, S. (2012) Asymptotic series of Poincaré and Stieltjes, Nieuw archief voor wiskunde., Serie 5, Vol. 13, No. 3, 187–190.

[27] Brandimarte, P. (2014) Handbook in Monte Carlo Simulation. John Wiley & Sons, Hoboken, New Jersey.

[28] Briys, E., and de Varenne, F. (2001) Insurance: From Underwriting to Derivatives. Asset Liability Management in Insurance Companies. John Wiley & Sons, Chichester.

[29] Brockwell, P.J., and Davis, R.A. (2016) Time Series: Theory and Methods. 3-rd ed., Springer, New York.

[30] de Bruijn, N.G. (1958) Asymptotic Methods in Analysis. North-Holland.

[31] Bühlmann, H. (1970) Mathematical Methods in Risk Theory. Springer-Verlag, New York.

[32] Bühlmann, H. (1985) Premium calculation from top down, ASTIN Bulletin, Vol. 15, No. 2, 89–101.

[33] Burden, R.L., and Faires, J.D. (2010) Numerical Analysis. 9-th ed., Brooks / Cole, Cengage Learning, Boston.

[34] Bürgi, R., Dacorogna, M., and Iles, R. (2008) Risk aggregation, dependence structure and diversification benefit. In: Stress Testing for Financial Institutions. Applications, Regulations and Techniques. Edited by D. Rösch and H. Scheule, No. 12, 265–306. Risk Books, London.

[35] Cai, J., and Garrido, J. (1999) Two-sided bounds for ruin probabilities when the adjustment coefficient does not exist, Scandinavian Actuarial Journal, 80–92.

[36] Carter, R.L. (1983) Reinsurance. Springer Science and Business Media, Dordrecht.

[37] Chadjiconstantinidis, S, and Politis, K. (1996) Non-exponential bounds for stop-loss premiums and ruin probabilities, Scandinavian Actuarial Journal, Vol 2: 124-147.

[38] Chadjiconstantinidis, S, and Politis, K. Two-sided bounds for the distribution of the deficit at ruin in the renewal risk model, Insurance: Mathematics and Economics, Vol. 41, 41–52.

[39] Choudhry, M. (2006) An Introduction to Value-at-Risk. 4-th ed., John Wiley & Sons, Chichester.

[40] Cox, D.R. (1970) Renewal Theory. Methuen & Co., London.

[41] Cox, D.R., and Miller, H.D. (2001) The Theory of Stochastic Processes. Chapman and Hall / CRC, Boca Raton, etc.

[42] Cox, D.R., and Smith, W.L. (1967) Queues. Methuen, London.

[43] Cramér, H. (1930) On the mathematical theory of risk. In book: Skandia Jubilee Volume, Stockholm Centraltryckeriet. Reprinted in: Harald Cramér Collective works, Vol. 1, 601–678, ed. by A. Martin-Löf, Springer-Verlag, Berlin (1994).

[44] Cramér, H. (1955) Collective risk theory: a survey of the theory from the point of view of the theory of stochastic process, 7-th Jubilee Volume of Skandia Insurance Company, Stockholm, 5–92; also in: Harald Cramér: Collected Works, Vol. II, 1028–1116.

[45] Cramér, H. (1969) Historical review of Filip Lundberg's works on risk theory, Skandinavisk Aktuarietidskrift, 52 (Suppl. 3–4), 6–12; also in: Harald Cramér: Collected Works, Vol. II, 1288–1294.

[46] Cramér, H. (1969) On streams of random events, Skandinavisk Aktuarietidskrift, Suppl., 13–23.

[47] Cramér, H. (1976) Half a century with probability theory: some personal recollections, Annals of Probability, Vol. 4, 509–546.

[48] Culp, C.L., Miller, M.H., and Neves, A.M.P. (1997) Value-at-Risk: uses and abuses, Journal of Applied Corporate Finance, Vol. 10, 26–38.

[49] Cummins, D., Harrington, S., and Niehaus, G. (1994) An economic overview of risk-based capital requirements for the property-liability industry, Journal of Insurance Regulation, Vol. 11, 427–447.

[50] Cummins, D., McGill, D., Winklevoss, H., and Zelten, H. (1974) Consumer Attitudes Toward Auto and Homeowners Insurance. Philadelphia, Pa.; Department of Insurance, Wharton School.

[51] Çinlar, E. (1975) Introduction to Stochastic Processes. Prentice-Hall, New Jersey.

[52] Dacorogna, M. (2018) A change of paradigm for the insurance industry, Annals of Actuarial Science, Vol. 12, Part 2, 211–232.

[53] Daniels, H.E. (1969) The minimum of a stationary Markov process superimposed on a U-shaped trend, J. Appl. Probability, Vol. 6, 399–408.

[54] Danielsson, J., and Zhou, C. (2015) Why risk is so hard to measure. Systemic Risk Centre, The London School of Economics and Political Science. Discussion Paper No 36, April 2015.

[55] Darling, D, and Siegert, A. (1953) The first passage time problem for a continuous Markov process, Ann. Math. Statist., Vol. 24, 624–639.

[56] Daykin, C.D., Pentikäinen, T., and Pesonen, M. (1996) Practical Risk Theory for Actuaries. Chapman and Hall, London.

[57] Denuit, M., Dhaene, J,, Goovaerts, M., and Kaas, R. (2005) Actuarial Theory for Dependent Risks: Measures, Orders and Models. John Wiley & Sons, Chichester.

[58] Devroye, L. (1986) Non-uniform Random Variate Generation. Springer-Verlag, New York.

[59] De Vylder, F., and Goovaerts, M. (1984) Bounds for classical ruin probabilities, Insurance: Mathematics and Economics, Vol. 3, 121–131.

[60] Dickson, D.C.M. (1994) An upper bound for the probability of ultimate ruin, Scandinavian Actuarial Journal, Vol 2: 161-174.

[61] Directive 2002/12/EC of the European Parliament and of the Council of 5 March 2002, Brussels, 5 March 2002.

[62] Directive 2002/13/EC of the European Parliament and of the Council of 5 March 2002, Brussels, 5 March 2002.

[63] Directive 2009/138/EC of the European Parliament and of the Council of 25 November 2009 on the taking-up and pursuit of the business of Insurance and Reinsurance (Solvency II), Brussels, 25 November 2009.

[64] Directive 2014/51/EU of the European Parliament and of the Council of 16 April 2014 amending Directives 2003/71/EC and 2009/138/EC and Regulations (EC) No 1060/2009, (EU) No 1094/2010 and (EU) No 1095/2010 in respect of the powers of the European Supervisory Authority (European Insurance and Occupational Pensions Authority) and the European Supervisory Authority (European Securities and Markets Authority), Brussels, 16 April 2016.

[65] Doff, R.R. (2006) Risk Management for Insurance Firms: A Framework for Fair Value and Economic Capital. Twente University.

[66] Doff, R.R. (2008) A critical analysis of the Solvency II proposals, The Geneva Papers on Risk and Insurance – Issues and Practice, Vol. 33, No. 2, 193–206.

[67] Doff, R.R. (2011) Risk Management for Insurers: Risk Control, Economic Capital and Solvency II. 2-nd ed., Risk Books, London.

[68] Doob, J.L. (1948) Renewal theory from the point of view of the theory of probability, Trans. Amer. Math. Soc., Vol. 63, No. 3, 422–438.

[69] Doob, J.L. (1949) Heuristic approach to the Kolmogorov-Smirnov theorems, Ann. Math. Statist., Vol. 20, 393–403.

[70] Durbin, J. (1985) The first-passage density of a continuous Gaussian process to a general boundary, J. Appl. Probability, Vol. 22, 99–122.

[71] Eling, M., and Schmeiser, H. (2010) Insurance and the credit crisis: impact and ten consequences for risk management and supervision, The Geneva Papers on Risk and Insurance – Issues and Practice, Vol. 35, No. 1, 9–34.

[72] Eling, M., Schmeiser, H., and Schmit, J. (2007) The Solvency II process: overview and critical analysis, Risk Management and Insurance Review, Vol. 10, 69–85.

[73] Embrechts, P., Klüppelberg, C., and Mikosch, T. (1997) Modelling Extremal Events for Insurance and Finance. Springer, Berlin.

[74] Embrechts, P., and Veraverbeke, N. (1982) Estimates for the probability of ruin with special emphasis on the possibility of large claims, Insurance: Mathematics and Economics, Vol. 1, No. 1, 55–72.

[75] Emmer, S., Kratz, M., and Tasche, D. (2015) What is the best risk measure in practice? A comparison of standard measures, Journal of Risk, Vol. 18, No. 2, 31–60.

[76] Feller, W. (1941) On the integral equation of renewal theory, Ann. Math. Statist., Vol. 12, 243–267.

[77] Feller, W. (1949) Fluctuation theory of recurrent events, Trans. Amer. Math. Soc., Vol. 67, 98–119.

[78] Feller, W. (1971) An Introduction to Probability Theory and its Applications. Vol. II. 2-nd ed., John Wiley & Sons, New York.

[79] Fletcher, H. (1911) A verification of the theory of Brownian movements and a direct determination of the value of NE for gaseous ionization, Phys. Rev., Vol. 33, 81–110.

[80] Floreani, A. (2013) Risk measures and capital requirements: a critique of the Solvency II approach, The Geneva Papers on Risk and Insurance – Issues and Practice, Vol. 38, 189–212.

[81] Fortet, R. (1943) Les fonctions aléatoires du type Markoff associées à certaines équations linéaires aux dérivées partielles du type parabolique, J. Math. Pures Appl., Vol. 9, No. 22, 177–243.

[82] Fortet, R. (1949) Quelques travaux récents sur le mouvement brownien, Ann. Inst. H. Poincare, Vol. 11, No. 4, 175–226.

[83] Gatto, R., and Baumgartner, B. (2014) Value at ruin and tail value at ruin of the compound Poisson process with diffusion and efficient computational methods, Methodology and Computing in Applied Probability, Vol. 16, No. 3, 561–582.

[84] Gerber, H.U., and Shiu, E.S.W. (1998) On the time value of ruin, North American Actuarial Journal, Vol. 2, 48–78.

[85] Gradshtein, I.S., and Ryzhik, I.M. (1980) Table of Integrals, Series, and Products. Academic Press, New York.

[86] Grandell, J. (1977) A class of approximations of ruin probabilities, Scandinavian Actuarial Journal, Suppl., 1977, 37–52.

[87] Grandell, J. (1978) A remark on "A class of approximations of ruin probabilities", Scandinavian Actuarial Journal, 1978, 77–78.

[88] Grandell, J. (1991) Aspects of Risk Theory. Springer-Verlag, New York, etc.

[89] Habart-Corlosquet, M., Janssen, J., and Manca, R. (2013) VaR Methodology for Non-Gaussian Finance. Wiley–ISTE.

[90] Hamilton, J.D. (1994) Time Series Analysis. Princeton University Press, Princeton, New Jersey.

[91] Harris, C.M. (1968) The Pareto distribution as a queue service discipline, Operat. Res., Vol. 16, 307–313.

[92] Heep-Altiner, M., Mullins, M., and Rohlfs, T., Eds. (2018) Solvency II in the Insurance Industry. Application of a Non-Life Data Model. Springer.

[93] Hellekalek, P. (1998) Good random number generators are (not so) easy to find, Mathematics and Computers in Simulation, Vol. 46, 485–505.

[94] Johnson, N.L., Kotz, S., and Balakrishnan, N. (1994) Continuous Univariate Distributions. Vol. 1. 2-nd ed., John Wiley & Sons.

[95] Kalashnikov, V. (1997) Geometric Sums: Bounds for Rare Events with Applications. Kluwer Academic Publishers, Dordrecht.

[96] Keilson, J. (1963) The first passage time density for homogeneous skip-free walks on the continuum, Ann. Math. Statist., Vol. 34, 1003–1011.

[97] Kendall, D.G. (1957) Some problems in the theory of dams, Journal of the Royal Statist. Soc., Ser. B, Vol. 19, 207–212.

[98] Kendall, M.G., and Stuart, A. (1958) The Advanced Theory of Statistics. Volume 1: Distribution Theory. Griffin. London.

[99] Kendall, M.G., and Stuart, A. (1961) The Advanced Theory of Statistics. Volume 2: Inference and relationship. Griffin. London.

[100] Khintchine, A.Ya. (1956) Sequences of chance events without aftereffect, Theory Probab. Appl., Vol. 1, 3–18.

[101] Khintchine, A.Ya. (1956) On Poisson sequences of chance events, Theory Probab. Appl., Vol. 1, 291–297.

[102] Khintchine, A.Ya. (1960) Mathematical Methods in the Theory of Queueing. Griffin, London.

[103] Klugman, S.A., Panjer, H.H., and Willmot, G.E. (1998) Loss Models: From Data to Decisions. Wiley, New York.

[104] Klugman, S.A., Panjer, H.H., and Willmot, G.E. (2013) Loss Models: Further Topics. John Wiley & Sons, Hoboken, NJ.

[105] Knuth, D.E. (1981) The Art of Computer Programming. Vol. 2, Seminumerical Algorithms, 2-nd ed., Addison Wesley.

[106] Komatu, Y. (1955) Elementary inequalities for Mills' ratio, Rep. Statist. Appl. Res. Un. Jap. Sci. Engrs., Vol. 4, 69–70.

[107] Konstantinowsky, D. (1914) Elektrische Ladungen und Brown'sche Bewegung sehr kleiner Metallteilchen in Gasen. Sitzungsberichte der Kaiserlichen Akademie der Wissenschaften, Vol. 123, 1697–1752.

[108] Kotz, S., Read, C.B., and Banks, D.L. Encyclopedia of Statistical Sciences. John Wiley & Sons, New York.

[109] Kroese, D.P., Taimre, T., Botev, Z.I., and Rubinstein, R.Y. (2008) Solutions Manual to Accompany Simulation and the Monte Carlo Method. 2-nd ed., John Wiley & Sons, Hoboken.

[110] Lai, G.C., Witt, R.C., Hung-Gay Fung, MacMinn, R.D., and Brockett, P.L. (2000) Great (and not so great) expectations: an endogenous economic explication of insurance cycles and liability crises, Journal of Risk and Insurance, Vol. 67, No. 4, 617–652.

[111] Lerche, H.R. (1986) Boundary Crossing of Brownian Motion. Lecture Notes in Statistics, 40, Springer, Berlin.

[112] Lévy, P. (1939) Sur certains processus stochastiques homogènes. Compositio Math., Vol. 7, 283–339.

[113] Lundberg, F. (1903) I. Approximerad Framställning av Sannolikhetsfunktionen. II. Återförsäkring av Kollektivrisker. Almqvist & Wiksell, Uppsala.

[114] Lundberg, F. (1909) Zür Theorie der Rückversicherung, In book: Transactions of the 6-th International Congress of Actuaries, Wien, Vol. 1, 877–955.

[115] Lundberg, F. (1919) Theori för riskmassor. Försäkringsinspektionen, Stockholm.

[116] Lundberg, F. (1926) Försäkringsteknisk Riskutjämning. F. Englunds boktryckeri A.B., Stockholm.

[117] Lundberg, F. (1934) On the Numerical Application of the Collective Risk Theory. De Förenade Jubilee Volume, Stockholm.

[118] McNeil, A., Frey, R., and Embrechts, P. (2015) Quantitative Risk Management: Concepts, Techniques and Tools. Revised edition. Princeton University Press. Princeton series in Finance, Princeton.

[119] Malinovskii, V.K. (1998) Non-Poissonian claims arrivals and calculation of the probability of ruin. Insurance: Mathematics and Economics, Vol. 22, 123–138.

[120] Malinovskii, V.K. (2007) Zone-adaptive control strategy for a multiperiodic model of risk, Annals of Actuarial Science, Vol. 2, 391–409.

[121] Malinovskii, V.K. (2008) Adaptive control strategies and dependence of finite time ruin on the premium loading, Insurance: Mathematics and Economics, Vol. 42, 81–94.

[122] Malinovskii, V.K. (2008) Risk theory insight into a zone-adaptive control strategy, Insurance: Mathematics and Economics, Vol. 42, 656–667.

[123] Malinovskii, V.K. (2009) Scenario analysis for a multi-period diffusion model of risk, ASTIN Bulletin, Vol. 39, 649–676.

[124] Malinovskii, V.K. (2012) Equitable solvent controls in a multi-period game model of risk, Insurance: Mathematics and Economics, Vol. 51, 599–616.

[125] Malinovskii, V.K. (2013) Reflexivity in competition-originated underwriting cycles, Journal of Risk and Insurance, Vol. 81, No. 4, 883–905.

[126] Malinovskii, V.K. (2013) Level premium rates as a function of initial capital, Insurance: Mathematics and Economics, Vol. 52, 370–380.

[127] Malinovskii, V.K. (2014) Elementary bounds on the ruin capital in a diffusion model of risk, Risks, Vol. 2, 249–259; DOI information: 10.3390/risks2020249.

[128] Malinovskii, V.K. (2014) Improved asymptotic upper bounds on ruin capital in Lundberg model of risk, Insurance: Mathematics and Economics, Vol. 55, 301–309.

[129] Malinovskii, V.K. (2016) How an aggressively expanding insurance company becomes insolvent, Scandinavian Actuarial Journal, Vol. 2016, No. 8, 1–19.

[130] Malinovskii, V.K. (2017) On the time of first level crossing and inverse Gaussian distribution; https://arxiv.org/pdf/1708.08665.pdf

[131] Malinovskii, V.K. (2017) Generalized inverse Gaussian distributions and the time of first level crossing; https://arxiv.org/pdf/1708.08671.pdf

[132] Malinovskii, V.K. (2018) Approximations in the problem of level crossing by a compound renewal process, Doklady Akademii Nauk, Vol. 483, No. 5, 622–625.

[133] Malinovskii, V.K. (2020) Value-at-Risk substitute for non-ruin capital is fallacious and redundant; https://arxiv.org/pdf/2005.05428.pdf

[134] Malinovskii, V.K. (2021) Insurance Planning Models. Price Competition and Regulation of Financial Stability. World Scientific Publishers, Singapore.

[135] Malinovskii, V.K. (2021) Level-Crossing Problems and Inverse Gaussian Distributions. Closed-Form Results and Approximations. Chapman and Hall/CRC Monographs and Research Notes in Mathematics.

[136] Malinovskii, V.K., and Kosova, K.O. (2014) Simulation analysis of ruin capital in Sparre Andersen's model of risk, Insurance: Mathematics and Economics, Vol. 59, 184–193.

[137] Malinovskii, V.K., and Malinovskii, K.V. (2017) On approximations for the distribution of first level crossing time; https://arxiv.org/pdf/1708.08678.pdf.

[138] Malmquist, V.K. (1954) On certain confidence contours for distribution functions, Ann. Math. Statist., Vol. 25, 523–533.

[139] Marano, P., and Siri, M., Eds. (2017) Insurance Regulation in the European Union. Solvency II and Beyond. Palgrave Macmillan.

[140] Marshall, A.W., and Olkin, I. (2007) Life Distributions. Structure of Nonparametric, Semiparametric, and Parametric Families. Springer, New York.

[141] Mittnik, S. (2011) Solvency II calibrations: where curiosity meets spuriosity, Working Paper Number 04, 2011 Center for Quantitative Risk Analysis (CEQURA) Department of Statistics University of Munich.

[142] J.P. Morgan (1996) RiskMetrics — Technical Document.

[143] J.P. Morgan (1997) Introduction to CreditMetrics.

[144] Panjer, H. (2006) Operational Risk: Modeling Analytics. John Wiley & Sons, Hoboken.

[145] Patel, J.K., and Read, C.B. (1982) Handbook of the Normal Distribution. Marcel Dekker, New York.

[146] Pentikäinen, T. (1975) A model of stochastic-dynamic prognosis. An application of risk theory to business planning, Scandinavian Actuarial Journal, 29–53.

[147] Pentikäinen, T. (1988) On the solvency of insurers. In book: Classical Insurance Solvency Theory, ed. by D. Cummins and R. Derring, Kluwer, Boston, etc.

[148] Pentikäinen, T., Bonsdorff, H., Pesonen, M., Rantala, J., and Ruohonen, M. (1989) Insurance Solvency and Financial Strength. Finnish Insurance Training and Publishing Co., Helsinki.

[149] Peskir, G. (2002) On integral equations arising in the first-passage problem for Brownian motion, J. Integral Equations Appl., Vol. 14, No. 4, 397–423.

[150] Pfeifer, D., and Straßburger, D. (2008) Solvency II: stability problems with the SCR aggregation formula, Scandinavian Actuarial Journal, Vol. 1, 61–77.

[151] Politis, K. Bounds for the probability and severity of ruin in the Sparre Andersen model, Insurance: Mathematics and Economics, Vol. 36, 165–177.

[152] Rejda, G.E., and McNamara, M.J. (2014) Principles of Risk Management and Insurance. 12-th ed., Pearson.

[153] Ricciardi, L.M., Sacerdote, L., and Sato, S. (1984) On an integral equation for first-passage-time probability densities, J. Appl. Probability, Vol. 21, 302–314.

[154] Riordan, J. (1958) An Introduction To Combinatorial Analysis. Chapman & Hall, New York etc.

[155] Riordan, J. (1962) Stochastic Service Systems. John Wiley & Sons, New York.

[156] Rootzén, H., and Klüppelberg, C. (1999) A single number can't hedge against economic catastrophes. Ambio, Vol. 28, No. 6, 550–555.

[157] Rogozin, B.A. (1966) Distribution of certain functionals related to boundary value problems for processes with independent increments, Theory Probab. Appl., Vol. 11, 656–670.

[158] Rolski, T., Schmidli, H., Schmidt, V., and Teugels, J. (1999) Stochastic Processes for Insurance and Finance. John Wiley & Sons, Chichester.

[159] Ronkainen, V., Koskinen, L., and Berglund, R. (2007) Topical modelling issues in Solvency II, Scandinavian Actuarial Journal, Vol. 2007, No. 2, 135–146.

[160] Ross, S.M. (2013) Simulation. 5-th ed., Elsevier, Boston.

[161] Rubinstein, R.Y., and Kroese, D.P. (2017) Simulation and the Monte Carlo Method. 3-rd ed., John Wiley & Sons, Hoboken, etc.

[162] Saaty, T.L. (1961) Elements of Queueing Theory. McGraw–Hill, New York.

[163] Sampford, M.R. (1953) Some inequalities on Mill's ratio and related functions, Ann. Math. Statist., Vol. 24, 130–132.

[164] Sandström, A. (2006) Solvency. Models, Assessment and Regulation. Chapman & Hall / CRC, Taylor & Francis Group. Boca Raton, etc.

[165] Sandström, A. (2011) Handbook of Solvency for Actuaries and Risk Managers: Theory and Practice. Chapman & Hall / CRC, Taylor & Francis Group. Boca Raton.

[166] Savelli, N. (2002) Risk analysis of a non-life insurer and traditional reinsurance effects on the solvency profile. Presented at 6-th International Congress of Insurance: Mathematics and Economics, Lisbon.

[167] Scarpello, G.M., and Ritelli, D. (2002) A historical outline of the theorem of implicit functions, Divulgaciones Matemáticas, Vol. 10, No. 2, 171–180.

[168] Schlesinger, H., and Schulenburg, J.M.v.d. (1993) Consumer information and decisions to switch insurers, Journal of Risk and Insurance, Vol. 55, No. 4, 591–615.

[169] Schrödinger, E. (1915) Zür Theorie der Fall- und Steigversuche an Teilchen mit Brownscher Bewegung, Physikalische Zeitschrift, Vol. 16, 289–295.

[170] Schweizer, M. (2001) From actuarial to financial valuation principles, Insurance: Mathematics and Economics, Vol. 28, 31–47.

[171] Seal, H.L. (1969) Stochastic Theory of a Risk Business. John Wiley & Sons, New York, etc.

[172] Seal, H.L. (1972) Numerical calculation of the probability of ruin in the Poisson/Exponential case, Mitt. Verein. Schweiz. Versich. Math., Vol. 72, 77–100.

[173] Seal, H.L. (1974) The numerical calculation of $U(w, t)$, the probability of non-ruin in an interval $(0, t)$, Scandinavian Actuarial Journal, 121–139.

[174] Shevtsova, I.G. (2011) On the absolute constants in the Berry Esseen type inequalities for identically distributed summands; https://arxiv.org/abs/1111.6554.

[175] Siegert, A.J.F. On the first passage time probability problem, Phys. Rev., Vol. 81, 617–623.

[176] Siegmund, D. (1979) Corrected diffusion approximations in certain random walk problems, Adv. in Appl. Probab., Vol. 11, 701–719.

[177] Skorohod, A.V. (1991) Random Processes with Independent Increments. Kluwer.

[178] Small, C.G. (2010) Expansions and Asymptotics for Statistics. Chapman and Hall / CRC Press, Boca Raton.

[179] Smoluchowski, M.v. (1915) Notiz über die Berechning der Brownschen Molkularbewegung bei des Ehrenhaft–millikanchen Versuchsanordnung. Physikalische Zeitschrift, Physikalische Zeitschrift Vol. 16, 318–321.

[180] Sparre-Andersen, E. (1957) On the collective theory of risk in case of contagion between the claims. In book: Transactions of the XV-th International Congress of Actuaries, Vol. 2, 219–229.

[181] Subramanian, K. (1998) Bonus-Malus systems in a competitive environment, North American Actuarial Journal, Vol. 2, 38–44.

[182] Sweeting, P. (2011) Financial Enterprise Risk Management. Cambridge University Press, Cambridge, etc.

[183] Takács, L. (1955) Investigation of waiting time problems by reduction to Markov processes, Acta Math. Acad. Sci. Hungar., Vol. 6, 101–129.

[184] Takács, L. (1967) Combinatorial Methods in the Theory of Stochastic Processes. John Wiley & Sons, New York.

[185] Trufin, J., Albrecher, H., and Denuit, M.M. (2011). Properties of a risk measure derived from ruin theory, The Geneva Risk and Insurance Review, Vol. 36, No. 2, 174–188.

[186] Tsay, R.S. (2010) Analysis of Financial Time Series., 3-rd ed., John Wiley & Sons, Hoboken, New Jersey.

[187] Vaughan, E.J., and Vaughan, T.M. (2014) Fundamentals of Risk and Insurance. 11-th ed., Wiley.

[188] Wang, R., and Liu, H. (2002) On the ruin probability under a class of risk processes, ASTIN Bulletin, Vol. 32, No. 1, 81–90.

[189] Watson, G.N. (1945) A Treatise on the Theory of Bessel Functions. Cambridge University Press, Cambridge.

[190] Whittaker, E.T., and Watson, G.N. (1963) A Course of Modern Analysis. 4-th ed., Cambridge University Press, Cambridge.

[191] Widder, D.V. (1947) Advanced Calculus. Prentice-Hall, New York.

[192] Wiener, N. (1949) Extrapolation, Interpolation, and Smoothing of Stationary Time Series: With Engineering Applications. MIT Press, Cambridge, MA.

[193] Willmot, G.E. (1994) Refinements and distributional generalizations of Lundberg's inequality, Insurance: Mathematics and Economics, Vol. 15, 49–63.

[194] Willmot, G.E., and Lin, X.S. (2001) Lundberg Approximations for Compound Distributions with Insurance Applications. Springer, New York.

[195] Willmot, G.E., and Jae-Kyung Woo (2017) Surplus Analysis of Sparre Andersen Insurance Risk Processes. Springer.

[196] Yang, Z-H., and Chu, Y-M. (2015) On approximating Mills' ratio, Journal of Inequalities and Applications, 2015:273. DOI: 10.1186/s13660-015-0792-3.

[197] Zio, E. (2013) The Monte Carlo Simulation Method for System Reliability and Risk Analysis. Springer, London.

[198] Zolotarev, V.M. (1964) The first passage time of a level and the behaviour at infinity of a class of processes with independent increments, Theory Probab. Appl., Vol. 9, 653–662.

[199] Zucca, C., and Sacerdote, L. (2009) On the inverse first-passage-time problem for a Wiener process, Annals of Applied Probability, Vol. 19, 1319–1346.

Index

For Product Safety Concerns and Information please contact our EU representative GPSR@taylorandfrancis.com
Taylor & Francis Verlag GmbH, Kaufingerstraße 24, 80331 München, Germany

www.ingramcontent.com/pod-product-compliance
Ingram Content Group UK Ltd.
Pitfield, Milton Keynes, MK11 3LW, UK
UKHW021622240425
457818UK00018B/684
9780367744021